Family Maps
of
Morgan County, Illinois
Deluxe Edition

With Homesteads, Roads, Waterways, Towns, Cemeteries, Railroads, and More

Family Maps
of
Morgan County, Illinois
Deluxe Edition

With Homesteads, Roads, Waterways, Towns, Cemeteries, Railroads, and More

by Gregory A. Boyd, J.D.

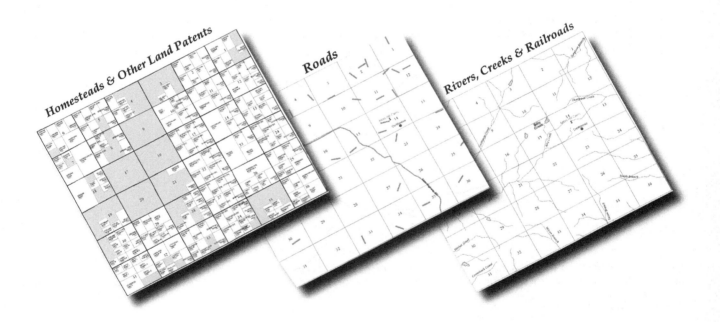

Featuring 3 *Maps Per Township ...*

Arphax Publishing Co.
www.arphax.com

Family Maps of Morgan County, Illinois, Deluxe Edition: With Homesteads, Roads, Waterways, Towns, Cemeteries, Railroads, and More.
by Gregory A. Boyd, J.D.

ISBN 1-4203-1325-8

Published by Arphax Publishing Co., 2210 Research Park Blvd., Norman, Oklahoma, USA 73069
www.arphax.com

First Edition

ATTENTION HISTORICAL & GENEALOGICAL SOCIETIES, UNIVERSITIES, COLLEGES, CORPORATIONS, FAMILY REUNION COORDINATORS, AND PROFESSIONAL ORGANIZATIONS: Quantity discounts are available on bulk purchases of this book. For information, please contact Arphax Publishing Co., at the address listed above, or at (405) 366-6181, or visit our web-site at www.arphax.com and contact us through the "Bulk Sales" link.

—LEGAL—

The contents of this book rely on data published by the United States Government and its various agencies and departments, including but not limited to the General Land Office–Bureau of Land Management, the Department of the Interior, and the U.S. Census Bureau. The author has relied on said government agencies or re-sellers of its data, but makes no guarantee of the data's accuracy or of its representation herein, neither in its text nor maps. Said maps have been proportioned and scaled in a manner reflecting the author's primary goal—to make patentee names readable. This book will assist in the discovery of possible relationships between people, places, locales, rivers, streams, cemeteries, etc., but "proving" those relationships or exact geographic locations of any of the elements contained in the maps will require the use of other source material, which could include, but not be limited to: land patents, surveys, the patentees' applications, professionally drawn road-maps, etc.

Neither the author nor publisher makes any claim that the contents herein represent a complete or accurate record of the data it presents and disclaims any liability for reader's use of the book's contents. Many circumstances exist where human, computer, or data delivery errors could cause records to have been missed or to be inaccurately represented herein. Neither the author nor publisher shall assume any liability whatsoever for errors, inaccuracies, omissions or other inconsistencies herein.

This book is dedicated to my wonderful family:

Vicki, Jordan, & Amy Boyd

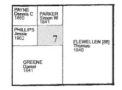

Contents

- Part I -

The Big Picture

- Part II -

Township Map Groups

(each Map Group contains a Patent Index, Patent Map, Road Map, & Historical Map)

Appendices

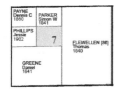

Preface

The quest for the discovery of my ancestors' origins, migrations, beliefs, and life-ways has brought me rewards that I could never have imagined. The *Family Maps* series of books is my first effort to share with historical and genealogical researchers, some of the tools that I have developed to achieve my research goals. I firmly believe that this effort will allow many people to reap the same sorts of treasures that I have.

The Illinois State Archives (much like the Federal Government's Bureau of Land Management) has given genealogists and historians an incredible gift by virtue of its enormous database housed on its web-site at www.cyberdriveillinois.com. There, you can search for and find over half-a-million descriptions of original land-purchases in Illinois.

This Illinois Archives site is in a small class of truly unique web-sites that present such a vast collection of records for FREE. But, the site is not for the faint of heart, nor is it for those unwilling or unable to to sift through and analyze the thousands of records that exist for most counties.

My immediate goal with this series is to spare you the hundreds of hours of work that it would take you to map the Land Patents for this county. Every Morgan County homestead or land patent that I have gleaned from the Illinos State Archives database is mapped here (at least ones that can be). Consequently, I can usually show you in an instant, where your ancestor's land is located, as well as the names of nearby land-owners.

Originally, that was my primary goal. But after speaking to other genealogists, it became clear that there was much more that they wanted. Taking their advice set me back almost a full year, but I think you will agree it was worth the wait. Because now, you can learn so much more.

Now, this book answers these sorts of questions:

- Are there any variant spellings for surnames that I have missed in searching Illinois land-records?
- Where is my family's traditional home-place?
- What cemeteries are near Grandma's house?
- My Granddad used to swim in such-and-such-Creek—where is that?
- How close is this little community to that one?
- Are there any other people with the same surname who bought land in the county?
- How about cousins and in-laws—did they buy land in the area?

And these are just for starters!

The rules for using the *Family Maps* books are simple, but the strategies for success are many. Some techniques are apparent on first use, but many are gained with time and experience. Please take the time to notice the roads, cemeteries, creek-names, family names, and unique first-names throughout the whole county. You cannot imagine what YOU might be the first to discover.

I hope to learn that many of you have answered age-old research questions within these pages or that you have discovered relationships previously not even considered. When these sorts of things happen to you, will you please let me hear about it? I would like nothing better. My contact information can always be found at www.arphax.com.

One more thing: please read the "How To Use This Book" chapter; it starts on the next page. This will give you the very best chance to find the treasures that lie within these pages.

My family and I wish you the very best of luck, both in life, and in your research.   Greg Boyd

How to Use This Book - A Graphical Summary

Part I
"The Big Picture"

Map A ▸ *Counties in the State*

Map B ▸ *Surrounding Counties*

Map C ▸ *Congressional Townships (Map Groups) in the County*

Map D ▸ *Cities & Towns in the County*

Map E ▸ *Cemeteries in the County*

Surnames in the County ▸ *Number of Land-Parcels for Each Surname*

Surname/Township Index ▸ Directs you to Township Map Groups in Part II

The <u>Surname/Township Index</u> can direct you to any number of **Township Map Groups**

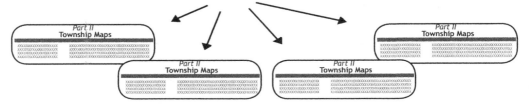

Part II
Township Map Groups
(1 for each Township in the County)

Each Township Map Group contains all four of of the following tools . . .

Land Patent Index ▸ *Every-name Index of Patents Mapped in this Township*

Land Patent Map ▸ *Map of Patents as listed in above Index*

Road Map ▸ *Map of Roads, City-centers, and Cemeteries in the Township*

Historical Map ▸ *Map of Railroads, Lakes, Rivers, Creeks, City-Centers, and Cemeteries*

Appendices

Appendix A ▸ *Illinois State Archives Abbreviations*

Appendix B ▸ *Section-Parts / Aliquot Parts (a comprehensive list)*

Appendix C ▸ *Multi-patentee Groups (Individuals within Buying Groups)*

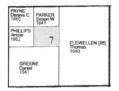

How to Use This Book

The two "Parts" of this *Family Maps* volume seek to answer two different types of questions. Part I deals with broad questions like: what counties surround Morgan County, are there any ASHCRAFTs in Morgan County, and if so, in which Townships or Maps can I find them? Ultimately, though, Part I should point you to a particular Township Map Group in Part II.

Part II concerns itself with details like: where exactly is this family's land, who else bought land in the area, and what roads and streams run through the land, or are located nearby. The Chart on the opposite page, and the remainder of this chapter attempt to convey to you the particulars of these two "parts", as well as how best to use them to achieve your research goals.

Part I
"The Big Picture"

Within Part I, you will find five "Big Picture" maps and two county-wide surname tools.

These include:

- Map A - Where Morgan County lies within the state
- Map B - Counties that surround Morgan County
- Map C - Congressional Townships of Morgan County (+ Map Group Numbers)
- Map D - Cities & Towns of Morgan County (with Index)
- Map E - Cemeteries of Morgan County (with Index)
- Surnames in Morgan County Patents (with Parcel-counts for each surname)
- Surname/Township Index (with Parcel-counts for each surname by Township)

The five "Big-Picture" Maps are fairly self-explanatory, yet should not be overlooked. This is particularly true of Maps "C", "D", and "E", all of which show Morgan County and its Congressional Townships (and their assigned Map Group Numbers).

Let me briefly explain this concept of Map Group Numbers. These are a device completely of our own invention. They were created to help you quickly locate maps without having to remember the full legal name of the various Congressional Townships. It is simply easier to remember "Map Group 1" than a legal name like: "Township 9-North Range 6-West, 5th Principal Meridian." But the fact is that the TRUE legal name for these Townships IS terribly important. These are the designations that others will be familiar with and you will need to accurately record them in your notes. This is why both Map Group numbers AND legal descriptions of Townships are almost always displayed together.

Map "C" will be your first intoduction to "Map Group Numbers", and that is all it contains: legal Township descriptions and their assigned Map Group Numbers. Once you get further into your research, and more immersed in the details, you will likely want to refer back to Map "C" from time to time, in order to regain your bearings on just where in the county you are researching.

Remember, township boundaries are a completely artificial device, created to standardize land descriptions. But do not let them become a boundary in your mind when choosing which townships to research. Your relative's in-laws, children, cousins, siblings, and mamas and papas, might just as easily have lived in the township next to the one your grandfather lived in—rather than in the one where he actually lived. So Map "C" can be your guide to which other Townships/Map Groups you likewise ought to analyze.

Of course, the same holds true for County lines; this is the purpose behind Map "B". It shows you surrounding counties that you may want to consider for further reserarch.

Map "D", the Cities and Towns map, is the first map with an index. Map "E" is the second (Cemeteries). Both, Maps "D" and "E" give you broad views of City (or Cemetery) locations in the County. But they go much further by pointing you toward pertinent Township Map Groups so you can locate the patents, roads, and waterways located near a particular city or cemetery.

Once you are familiar with these *Family Maps* volumes and the county you are researching, the "Surnames In Morgan County" chapter (or its sister chapter in other volumes) is where you'll likely start your future research sessions. Here, you can quickly scan its few pages and see if anyone in the county possesses the surnames you are researching. The "Surnames in Morgan County" list shows only two things: surnames and the number of parcels of land we have located for that surname in Morgan County. But whether or not you immediately locate the surnames you are researching, please do not go any further without taking a few moments to scan ALL the surnames in these very few pages.

You cannot imagine how many lost ancestors are waiting to be found by someone willing to take just a little longer to scan the "Surnames In Morgan County" list. Misspellings and typographical errors abound in most any index of this sort. Don't miss out on finding your Kinard that was written Rynard or Cox that was written Lox. If it looks funny or wrong, it very often is. And one of those little errors may well be your relative.

Now, armed with a surname and the knowledge that it has one or more entries in this book, you are ready for the "Surname/Township Index." Unlike the "Surnames In Morgan County", which has only one line per Surname, the "Surname/Township Index" contains one line-item for each Township Map Group in which each surname is found. In other words, each line represents a different Township Map Group that you will need to review.

Specifically, each line of the Surname/Township

Index contains the following four columns of information:

1. Surname
2. Township Map Group Number (these Map Groups are found in Part II)
3. Parcels of Land (number of them with the given Surname within the Township)
4. Meridian/Township/Range (the legal description for this Township Map Group)

The key column here is that of the Township Map Group Number. While you should definitely record the Meridian, Township, and Range, you can do that later. Right now, you need to dig a little deeper. That Map Group Number tells you where in Part II that you need to start digging.

But before you leave the "Surname/Township Index", do the same thing that you did with the "Surnames in Morgan County" list: take a moment to scan the pages of the Index and see if there are similarly spelled or misspelled surnames that deserve your attention. Here again, is an easy opportunity to discover grossly misspelled family names with very little effort. Now you are ready to turn to . . .

Part II
"Township Map Groups"

You will normally arrive here in Part II after being directed to do so by one or more "Map Group Numbers" in the Surname/Township Index of Part I.

Each Map Group represents a set of four tools dedicated to a single Congressional Township that is either wholly or partially within the county. If you are trying to learn all that you can about a particular family or their land, then these tools should usually be viewed in the order they are presented.

These four tools include:

1. a Land Patent Index
2. a Land Patent Map
3. a Road Map, and
4. an Historical Map

As I mentioned earlier, each grouping of this sort is assigned a Map Group Number. So, let's now move on to a discussion of the four tools that make up one of these Township Map Groups.

Land Patent Index

Each Township Map Group's Index begins with a title, something along these lines:

MAP GROUP 1: Index to Land Patents
Township 16-North Range 5-West (2nd PM)

The Index contains eight (8) columns. They are:

1. ID (a unique ID number for this Individual and a corresponding Parcel of land in this Township)
2. Individual in Patent (name)
3. Sec. (Section), and
4. Sec. Part (Section Part, or Aliquot Part)
5. Purchase Date (Patent)
6. Sale Type (IL Archives Abbreviation).
7. IL Aliquot Part (more on this, below).
8. For More Info: varying information which often requires you to turn to Appendices A or C for clarification..

While most of these eight columns are self-explanatory, I will take a few moments to explain the "Sec. Part." "Purchase Date," "Sale Type, "IL Aliquot Part," and "For More Info" columns.

The "Sec. Part" column refers to what surveryors and other land professionals refer to as an Aliquot Part. The origins and use of such a term mean little to a non-surveyor, and I have chosen to simply call these sub-sections of land what they are: a "Section Part". No matter what we call them, what we are referring to are things like a quarter-section or half-section or quarter-quarter-section. See Appendix "B" for most of the "Section Parts" you will come across (and many you will not) and what size land-parcel they represent.

In the volumes in this series which rely on Illinois Archives data rather than on that of the Bureau of Land Management, this value is our translation of that Aliquot Part as recorded by the Illinois Archives. Because the Archives chose to add much additional information to that value (more on this, below), sometimes the underlying Section Part is not ascertainable with complete certainty.

In short, the Sec. Part column will tell you where we mapped the parcel, whether or not that is where it actually lies. In the vast majority of cases, we feel like we will hit the spot.

The "Purchase Date" column displays just that: the date on which the patentee signed the necessary documents in the relevant Land Office, in order to seek his or her land-claim. This value differs from that stored in the BLM databases (and in our books based on them) where the "Issue date" is given---the "issue-date" is a later date on which the Federal Government effectively finalized the transaction.

The "Sale Type" column offers an abbreviation which you can locate in Appendix A. The vast majority of the patents here will be noted as an "FD" (Federal) sale-type.

The "IL Aliquot Part" column is one which we include as a response to the problem we identified above: sometimes we cannot ascertain the true location of the land based on the the Illinois Archive's stated "Aliquot Part." We do not state this as any sort of criticism: I challenge anyone to read a few hundred of these patents (particularly in urban areas or along rivers or canals) and try to come up with a standard way to describe the legal descriptions they contain---frankly, such a chore is beyond that which most of us would choose to entertain.

The Archives had a hard-time decyphering these legal descriptions, as did we. And because of this confession, we repeat, verbatim, the "IL Aliquot Part" in each Patent-Index so you may see what source information we used in our decision-making. We acknowledge that you may come to a different conclusion as to where some of these parcels actually lie.

A couple of final points need be made with regard to this "IL Aliquot Part" column.

First, if the meaning of its contents are not readily apparent, then it is likely you have come across one of the numerous examples wherein the Archives tacked on information not technically belonging to a standard legal description (and yet existed in the underlying patent). For instance, you may find a value like "NWNANDWRR." I hate to tell you, but this could mean several things: the northwest-quarter section, north and west of Rock River, being one reasonable intepretation, but there could be others. See Appendix "A" for the numerous abbreviations used in these descriptions.

Next, if the "IL Aliquot Part" entry contains the words "Lot" or "Block" or begins with either "L" or "B" and is then followed by a number (and sometimes an alphabetic character), then this is a lot. Its whereabouts within a section cannot be ascertained with the legal description alone, and so we cannot map them with the resources we possess. This does not thwart the uses for which we contemplate this series will be used, but we want you to be aware that you will need to locate plat-maps from the individual counties if you need to more precisely locate land within lots. We do list the lots out for you in the map, so you can know which section they fall within.

The "For More Info" column of the Index is variable in its content from one patent to another, as is the case with the underlying data provided by the Illinois Archives. There are three primary possible items you may find here, as evinced by looking at a sample of the Legend which accompanies each Patent-Map Index:

LEGEND
```
         "For More Info . . . " column
─────────────────────────────────────────────────
G = Group (Multi-Patentee Patent, see Appendix "C")
R = Residence
S = Social Status
```

Below, I will explain what each of these items means to you as a researcher.

G = Group

(Multi-Patentee Patent, see Appendix "C")
A "G" designation means that the Patent was issued to a GROUP of people (Multi-patentees). The "G" will always be followed by a number. Some such groups were quite large and it was impractical if not impossible to display each individual in our maps without unduly affecting readability. EACH person in the group is named in the Index, but they won't all be found on the Map. You will find the name of only person listed in such a Group on the map with the Group number next to it, enclosed in [square brackets]. That square bracket [ ] is your key to locating patents on the patent map.

To find all the members of the Group you can either scan the Index for all people with the same Group Number or you can simply refer to Appendix "C" where all members of the Group are listed next to their number.

R = Residence

Though only a fraction of the patents here contain this wonderful bit of data, those which do, offer up a nice windfall to many researchers. This value comes from the language in patents which often includes words like "John Smith of Franklin County" or some similiar verbiage. There are people identified as having been "from" numerous states. If the location is within Illinois, usually we are given simply the county name.

S = Social Status

Again, most patents are not accompanied by this information, but those which do, will contain a value that can be looked-up in the Abbreviations found in Appendix "C."

Land Patent Map

On the first two-page spread following each Township's Index to Land Patents, you'll find the corresponding Land Patent Map. And here lies the real heart of our work. For the first time anywhere, researchers will be able to observe and analyze, on a grand scale, most of the original land-owners for an area AND see them mapped in proximity to each one another.

We encourage you to make vigorous use of the accompanying Index described above, but then later, to abandon it, and just stare at these maps for a while. This is a great way to catch misspellings or to find collateral kin you'd not known were in the area.

Each Land Patent Map represents one Congressional Township containing approximately 36-square miles. Each of these square miles is labeled by an accompanying Section Number (1 through 36, in most cases). Keep in mind, that this book concerns itself solely with Morgan County's patents. Townships which creep into one or more other counties will not be shown in their entirety in any one book. You will need to consult other books, as they become available, in order to view other countys' patents, cities, cemeteries, etc.

But getting back to Morgan County: each Land Patent Map contains a Statistical Chart that looks like the following:

Township Statistics

Parcels Mapped	:	173
Number of Patents	:	163
Number of Individuals	:	152
Patentees Identified	:	151
Number of Surnames	:	137
Multi-Patentee Parcels	:	4
Oldest Patent Date	:	11/27/1820
Most Recent Patent	:	9/28/1917
Block/Lot Parcels	:	0
Cities and Towns	:	6
Cemeteries	:	6

This information may be of more use to a social statistician or historian than a genealogist, but I think all three will find it interesting.

Most of the statistics are self-explanatory, and what is not, was described in the above discussion of the Index's Legend, but I do want to mention a few of them that may affect your understanding of the Land Patent Maps.

First of all, Patents often contain more than one Parcel of land, so it is common for there to be more Parcels than Patents. Also, the Number of Individuals will more often than not, not match the number of Patentees. A Patentee is literally the person or PERSONS named in a patent. So, a Patent may have a multi-person Patentee or a single-person patentee. Nonetheless, we account for all these individuals in our indexes.

On the lower-righthand side of the Patent Map is a Legend which describes various features in the map, including Section Boundaries, Patent (land) Boundaries, Lots (numbered), and Multi-Patentee Group Numbers. You'll also find a "Helpful Hints" Box that will assist you.

One important note: though the vast majority of Patents mapped in this series will prove to be reasonably accurate representations of their actual locations, we cannot claim this for patents lying along state and county lines, or waterways, or that have been platted (lots). Shifting boundaries and sparse legal descriptions in the Illinois Archives data make this a reality that we have nonetheless tried to overcome by estimating these patents' locations the best that we can.

Road Map

On the two-page spread following each Patent Map you will find a Road Map covering the exact same area (the same Congressional Township).

For me, fully exploring the past means that every once in a while I must leave the library and travel to the actual locations where my ancestors once walked and worked the land. Our Township Road Maps are a great place to begin such a quest.

Keep in mind that the scaling and proportion of these maps was chosen in order to squeeze hundreds of people-names, road-names, and place-names into tinier spaces than you would traditionally see. These are not professional road-maps, and like any secondary genealogical source, should be looked upon as an entry-way to original sources—in this case, original patents and applications, professionally produced maps and surveys, etc.

Both our Road Maps and Historical Maps contain cemeteries and city-centers, along with a listing of these on the left-hand side of the map. I should note that I am showing you city center-points, rather than city-limit boundaries, because in many instances, this will represent a place where settlement began. This may be a good time to mention that many cemeteries are located on private property, Always check with a local historical or genealogical society to see if a particular cemetery is publicly accessible (if it is not obviously so). As a final point, look for your surnames among the road-names. You will often be surprised by what you find.

Historical Map

The third and final map in each Map Group is our attempt to display what each Township might have looked like before the advent of modern roads. In frontier times, people were usually more determined to settle near rivers and creeks than they were near roads, which were often few and far between. As was the case with the Road Map, we've included the same cemeteries and city-centers. We've also included railroads, many of which came along before most roads.

While some may claim "Historical Map" to be a bit of a misnomer for this tool, we settled for this label simply because it was almost as accurate as saying "Railroads, Lakes, Rivers, Cities, and Cemeteries," and it is much easier to remember.

In Closing . . .

By way of example, here is *A Really Good Way to Use a Township Map Group.* First, find the person you are researching in the Township's Index to Land Patents, which will direct you to the proper Section and parcel on the Patent Map. But before leaving the Index, scan all the patents within it, looking for other names of interest. Now, turn to the Patent Map and locate your parcels of land. Pay special attention to the names of patent-holders who own land surrounding your person of interest. Next, turn the page and look at the same Section(s) on the Road Map. Note which roads are closest to your parcels and also the names of nearby towns

and cemeteries. Using other resources, you may be able to learn of kin who have been buried here, plus, you may choose to visit these cemeteries the next time you are in the area.

Finally, turn to the Historical Map. Look once more at the same Sections where you found your research subject's land. Note the nearby streams, creeks, and other geographical features. You may be surprised to find family names were used to name them, or you may see a name you haven't heard mentioned in years and years—and a new research possibility is born.

Many more techniques for using these *Family Maps* volumes will no doubt be discovered. If from time to time, you will navigate to Morgan County's web-page at www.arphax.com (use the "Research" link), you can learn new tricks as they become known (or you can share ones you have employed). But for now, you are ready to get started. So, go, and good luck.

Postscript: these "Illinois Archives" editions, though substantially similar to their "GLO" (General Land Office) counterparts, do have a few important differences. First, Illinois has indexed far more patents (for Illinois, of course) than has the GLO and second, the Illinois data contains the residences for numerous patentees. In order to make room for this latter benefit, we have, by necessity, had to remove some features that are present in the GLO indexes: for example the noting of cancellations, overlaps, re-issues, and the like. We think the trade-off is a minor one and that on balance, the increased research value is enormous.

– Part I –

The Big Picture

Map A - Where Morgan County, Illinois Lies Within the State

Legend

State Boundary
County Boundaries
Morgan County, Illinois

Helpful Hints

1 We start with Map "A" which simply shows us where within the State this county lies.

2 Map "B" zooms in further to help us more easily identify surrounding Counties.

3 Map "C" zooms in even further to reveal the Congressional Townships that either lie within or intersect Morgan County.

Map B - Morgan County, Illinois and Surrounding Counties

——— Legend ———

——— State Boundaries (when applicable)

——— County Boundary

——— Helpful Hints ———

1 Many Patent-holders and their families settled across county lines. It is always a good idea to check nearby counties for your families.

2 Refer to Map "A" to see a broader view of where this County lies within the State, and Map "C" to see which Congressional Townships lie within Morgan County.

Map C - Congressional Townships of Morgan County, Illinois

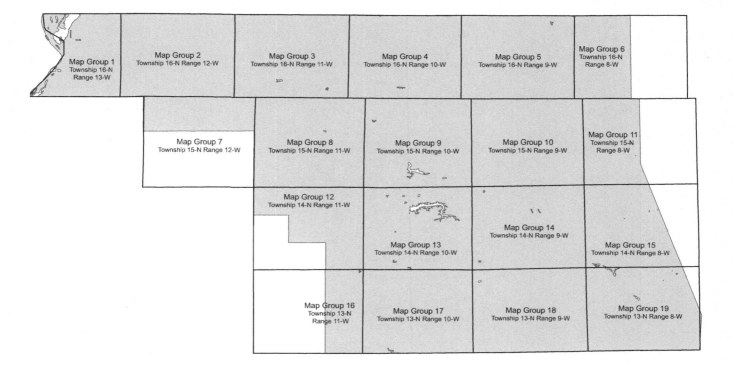

—— Legend ——

Morgan County, Illinois

Congressional Townships

—— Helpful Hints ——

1 Many Patent-holders and their families settled across county lines. It is always a good idea to check nearby counties for your families (See Map "B").

2 Refer to Map "A" to see a broader view of where this county lies within the State, and Map "B" for a view of the counties surrounding Morgan County.

Map D Index: Cities & Towns of Morgan County, Illinois

The following represents the Cities and Towns of Morgan County, along with the corresponding Map Group in which each is found. Cities and Towns are displayed in both the Road and Historical maps in the Group.

City/Town	Map Group No.
Alexander	11
Appalokia (historical)	19
Arcadia	4
Arnold	10
Bethel	7
Brownton (historical)	9
Centerville	19
Chapin	7
Clements	14
Concord	3
Davis (historical)	13
Franklin	14
Jacksonville	9
Jordanville (historical)	5
Joy Prairie	8
Literberry	4
Lynnville	12
Markham	8
Meredosia	1
Morgan City (historical)	7
Murrayville	17
Nortonville	18
Orleans	10
Pisgah	14
Portuguese Hill	9
Prentice	6
Rees	14
Rohrer	19
Savage (historical)	9
Shady Acres	1
Sinclair	5
South Jacksonville	9
Strawns Crossing	5
Waverly	19
Woodson	13
Yatesville	5
Yeomans	14

Map D - Cities & Towns of Morgan County, Illinois

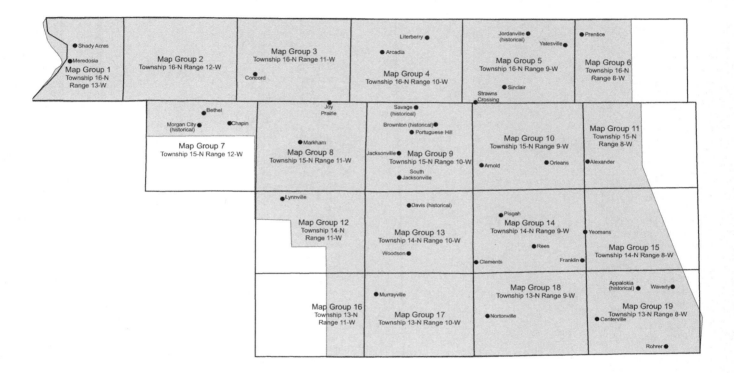

--- Legend ---

Morgan County, Illinois

Congressional Townships

--- Helpful Hints ---

1 Cities and towns are marked only at their center-points as published by the USGS and/or NationalAtlas.gov. This often enables us to more closely approximate where these might have existed when first settled.

2 To see more specifically where these Cities & Towns are located within the county, refer to both the Road and Historical maps in the Map-Group referred to above. See also, the Map "D" Index on the opposite page.

Map E Index: Cemeteries of Morgan County, Illinois

The following represents many of the Cemeteries of Morgan County, along with the corresponding Township Map Group in which each is found. Cemeteries are displayed in both the Road and Historical maps in the Map Groups referred to below.

Cemetery	Map Group No.	Cemetery	Map Group No.
Allis Cem.	19	New Salem Cem.	1
Allison Cem.	8	Newman Cem.	2
Angel Cem.	3	Oak Ridge Cem.	5
Antioch Cem.	10	Oakland Cem.	1
Arcadia Cem.	4	Phillips Cem.	4
Asbury Cem.	13	Pisgah Cem.	14
Augustine Cem.	1	Providence Cem.	18
Berea Cem.	6	Reed Cem.	18
Bethel Cem.	16	Richardson Cem.	8
Bull Cem.	18	Robert Cem.	18
Burrus Cem.	2	Roberts Cem.	17
Caldwell Cem.	8	Rogers Cem.	19
Calvary Cem.	9	Rucker Cem.	4
Campbell Cem.	8	Sacred Heart Cem.	15
Chapin Cem.	8	Saint Bartholomew Cem.	17
Charles Schlickers Cem.	2	Saint Sebastians Cem.	19
Concord Cem.	3	Sample Cem.	9
Conlee Cem.	19	Scott Cem.	9
Craig-Burrows Cem.	13	Seymour Bird Cem.	18
Criswell George Cem.	18	Sheppard Cem.	13
Crum Cem.	3	Sibert Cem.	2
Davis Cem.	14	Smith Cem.	3
Diamond Grove Cem.	9	Sooy Cem.	17
East Cem.	9	South Fork Mauvaise Terre Cem.	9
East Cem.	19	Sulphur Springs Cem.	14
Ebenezer Cem.	9	Tholen Cem.	2
Fanning Ollie Cem.	18	Tippet William Cem.	2
Flinn Cem.	6	Turner Cem.	19
Franklin Cem.	14	Union Cem.	14
Grace Cem.	2	Walnut Grove Cem.	3
Graham Cem.	2	Weeks Cem.	2
Harts Prairie Cem.	18	Whitlock Cem.	17
Hazel Green Cem.	9	Wood Cem.	8
Hebron Cem.	5	Woodward Cem.	8
Heffner Cem.	2	Yatesville Cem.	5
Hemminghaus Cem.	2	Youngblood Cem.	18
Henderson-McFadden Cem.	4	Zion Cem.	17
Henry Cem.	17	Zion Number One Cem.	17
Hoag Cem.	13		
Hodges Cem.	1		
Holmes Daniel D Cem.	13		
Houston Cem.	2		
Jones Cem.	19		
Kiel Cem.	1		
Lewis Cem.	13		
Liberty Cem.	8		
Liter Cem.	4		
Little York Cem.	15		
Luken Cem.	15		
Lynnville Cem.	12		
Memorial Lawn Cem.	13		
Morgan City Cem.	7		
Morgan County Farm Cem.	8		
Morgan County Poor Farm Cem.	8		
Mount Vernon Cem.	3		
Mount Zion Lutheran Cem.	8		
Murrayville Cem.	17		
Nergenah Cem.	2		
New Hope Cem.	19		

Map E - Cemeteries of Morgan County, Illinois

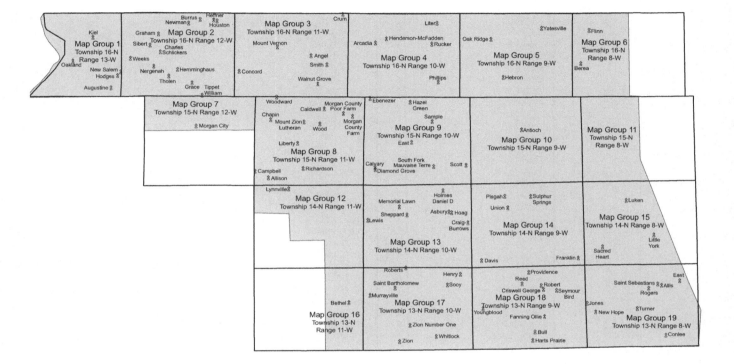

---- Legend ----

Morgan County, Illinois

Congressional Townships

---- Helpful Hints ----

1 Cemeteries are marked at locations as published by the USGS and/or NationalAtlas.gov.

2 To see more specifically where these Cemeteries are located, refer to the Road & Historical maps in the Map-Group referred to above. See also, the Map "E" Index on the opposite page to make sure you don't miss any of the Cemeteries located within this Congressional township.

Surnames in Morgan County, Illinois Patents

The following list represents the surnames that we have located in Morgan County, Illinois Patents and the number of parcels that we have mapped for each one. Here is a quick way to determine the existence (or not) of Patents to be found in the subsequent indexes and maps of this volume.

Surname	# of Land Parcels	Surname	# of Land Parcels	Surname	# of Land Parcels	Surname	# of Land Parcels
ABBEY	2	BARD	1	BOYCE	2	CAMPBELL	4
ABBOTT	2	BARKER	2	BOYD	3	CAMREN	2
ABBY	1	BARLAND	4	BOYER	5	CANDLE	1
ABRAM	1	BARNET	1	BOZARTH	3	CANNON	2
ABRAMS	2	BARNETT	2	BRACKENRIDGE	2	CARLOCK	4
ADALMAN	1	BARNS	4	BRADBURY	4	CARNES	1
ADAMS	20	BARRET	6	BRADLEY	1	CARNEY	2
ADDINGTON	1	BARRETT	3	BRADSHAW	4	CARNS	2
AKERS	2	BARRICKLOW	1	BRANER	3	CARR	1
AKIRS	1	BARROW	6	BRATTAIN	1	CARRATHER	1
ALBIN	4	BARROWS	14	BRATTON	1	CARRICK	1
ALDERSON	1	BARTLETT	3	BRAUR	1	CARRUTHERS	1
ALEXANDER	6	BARTON	8	BRAYHAW	1	CARSELL	1
ALFKIN	2	BATEMAN	1	BRENENK	1	CARTER	21
ALLEN	8	BATES	7	BRIAN	8	CARUTHERS	3
ALLINSON	35	BATTY	2	BRICH	2	CARY	2
ALLIS	1	BEACRAFT	1	BRIDGEMAN	6	CASSEL	2
ALLYN	1	BEAGLE	1	BRIEDEN	1	CASSELL	5
ALTMANN	1	BEARCRAFT	1	BRISBIN	6	CASTLE	1
ANDERSON	18	BEASLEY	4	BRISBY	1	CASTLEBERRY	1
ANGDANO	1	BEAUCHAMP	1	BRISTOE	2	CATLIN	4
ANGEL	5	BEAVERS	2	BRISTOW	9	CAUBY	1
ANGELO	5	BEFON	1	BROADHEAD	3	CAUDEL	2
ANGELON	1	BEGGS	4	BROADWELL	7	CAUDLE	1
ANGELOW	10	BELL	1	BROCKENBROUGH	12	CAULKINS	1
ANTLE	1	BELLAMMY	1	BROCKHOUSE	2	CAVE	2
APLER	1	BELLOWS	2	BROCKMAN	2	CAWOOD	4
ARCHER	1	BENFER	1	BROKENBOUGH	1	CHADWICK	3
ARENZ	3	BENNET	1	BROKENBROUGH	2	CHALLEN	4
ARMSTRONG	5	BENNETT	5	BROKHAUS	1	CHAMBER	1
ARNETT	15	BENNINGER	1	BROMLY	2	CHAMBERLAIN	1
ARNOLD	4	BENTLEY	2	BROTHERS	1	CHAMBERLIN	2
ARNZ	2	BENTON	1	BROWN	93	CHAMBERS	1
ASH	2	BERDAN	1	BRUCE	1	CHANCE	1
ASHBAUGH	2	BERGEN	6	BRUNING	1	CHAPMAN	3
ASHBRAUGH	1	BERGHAUS	2	BRUTON	2	CHASTAIN	1
ASHER	3	BERNARD	1	BRYAMT	1	CHERRY	1
ATER	2	BERRY	18	BRYANT	2	CHESNUTT	1
ATTEBERY	1	BIBB	3	BUCHANAN	10	CHILTON	2
ATTICK	1	BIDWELL	1	BUCHANNON	1	CHRISMAN	1
AUGUSTINE	1	BILLINGS	4	BUCKHANAN	1	CHRISTMAN	1
AUSEMNS	1	BINGMAN	1	BUCKINGHAM	2	CHURCH	4
AUSEMUS	5	BIRDSELL	4	BUCKMASTER	1	CLACK	2
AUSMUS	5	BIRKBY	2	BUCKSTON	1	CLACKE	1
AUSTIN	10	BIRKLEY	1	BUCY	1	CLARK	14
AUTLE	1	BLACK	7	BUGBY	2	CLARKE	10
AVERITT	3	BLAIR	4	BULL	1	CLARY	1
AYERS	2	BLANEY	8	BULLARD	3	CLAY	1
AYLESWORTH	5	BLEVINS	1	BURBAGE	1	CLAYTON	6
AYRES	3	BLISH	1	BURBANK	2	CLOPTON	1
BABB	2	BLODGETT	1	BURCH	5	CLOTFETTER	4
BADGER	3	BOGART	1	BURK	1	CLOUD	3
BAILEY	2	BONDURANT	3	BURNETT	7	COBB	11
BAIRD	3	BOOKES	1	BURNS	1	CODDINGTON	4
BAKER	4	BOSWELL	1	BURROWS	1	COEN	3
BALDWIN	6	BOTTS	4	BURTON	2	COFFIN	27
BALEY	2	BOULWARD	1	BUSH	1	COFFMAN	6
BALL	2	BOULWARE	2	BUTLER	8	COGBURN	2
BALLARD	9	BOURLAND	1	CADWELL	3	COGER	1
BANCROFT	3	BOWEN	1	CAINEY	1	COKER	6
BANNING	2	BOWYER	3	CALDWELL	12	COLE	5
BARBER	6	BOX	2	CAMP	1	COLLINS	19

Surname	# of Land Parcels	Surname	# of Land Parcels	Surname	# of Land Parcels	Surname	# of Land Parcels
COMBS	1	DEWITT	1	FARMING	3	GREENE	4
COMER	1	DIAL	4	FARNUN	1	GREENUP	1
CONLEE	1	DICK	2	FARRIS	1	GREGORY	7
CONN	8	DICKERSON	3	FARTHING	1	GRIDER	1
CONNAWAY	1	DICUS	2	FATHERKILE	4	GRIFFITTS	1
COOK	1	DIEUS	2	FEATHERKILE	1	GRIGG	68
COOKE	5	DIKES	5	FERIS	4	GRIGGS	12
COONRAD	1	DILLER	4	FERNING	1	GRIMSLEY	4
COONS	3	DINWIDDIE	1	FIKE	2	GROUT	2
COOPER	7	DIXON	1	FILEY	3	GROVES	3
COREY	1	DOAK	1	FILSON	1	GUM	2
CORRINGTON	3	DOBSON	1	FINCH	1	GUNN	9
COUCHMAN	4	DODD	9	FINDLEY	2	GUNNELS	1
COULEE	1	DODSON	1	FISK	3	GWENS	1
COULTER	1	DODSWORTH	4	FITZHUGH	2	HACKETT	3
COUNTY	1	DOOD	1	FLETCHER	3	HAEFFNER	1
COURTIS	1	DOSGOOD	1	FLIN	3	HAGGARD	6
COWAN	2	DOUGHTY	3	FLINN	12	HAHN	2
COWARD	1	DOWLING	1	FOLDEN	1	HALL	19
COWEN	1	DOWNER	1	FOLDON	1	HAM	9
COWNOVER	13	DOWNS	1	FORSYTHE	1	HAMAKER	1
COX	25	DOYAL	1	FOSTER	4	HAMBROUGH	1
CRABTREE	1	DRAKE	1	FOX	6	HAMILTON	19
CRAGGS	1	DRENNAN	1	FRASER	3	HAMMER	1
CRAIG	13	DRURY	2	FRASIN	1	HAMPTON	1
CRAWFORD	7	DRYER	1	FREEMAN	1	HANDY	2
CREED	1	DUDHOPE	5	FRENCH	11	HANES	5
CRISMAN	4	DUFF	1	FRISBIE	1	HANEY	3
CRISWELL	4	DUFFIELD	1	FRY	13	HARDIN	16
CROMWELL	1	DUNCAN	40	FULLER	4	HARDING	2
CROSS	4	DUNLAP	4	FUNK	5	HARGROVE	1
CROUCH	1	DUNN	1	GADDES	1	HARLAN	1
CROW	6	DUNSMORE	1	GADDIS	6	HARNAKER	1
CRUM	1	DURANT	5	GAINES	2	HARNEY	6
CUMMING	1	DURYEE	1	GAINS	1	HARP	10
CUMMINGS	2	DUVAL	1	GALBRAITH	1	HARRIS	9
CUNNINGHAM	4	DYE	1	GALLAHER	1	HARRISON	2
CUREE	1	DYER	2	GAMBLE	1	HARRISS	1
CURLL	1	DYERS	1	GARMAN	1	HART	27
CURTIS	1	EADS	3	GASAWAY	3	HARTMORE	1
CURTS	1	EARLL	1	GEAR	1	HARTWELL	1
CUTLER	1	EASTHAM	2	GEERS	3	HARVEY	2
CYRUS	7	EASTMAN	5	GENTRY	2	HARVY	1
DALTON	5	EDGELL	2	GESFORD	2	HATCH	2
DANIEL	2	EDMONDSON	1	GEST	3	HATCHER	3
DANIELS	6	EDMONSON	1	GIBBON	2	HATFIELD	1
DAUGHERTY	3	EDMUNDSON	1	GIBBONS	2	HAWN	1
DAVENPORT	2	EDWARDS	20	GIBSON	15	HAYES	2
DAVIDSON	1	ELDER	2	GIDEON	1	HAYNES	7
DAVIS	6	ELDRIDGE	4	GILBERT	2	HAYWARD	1
DAWSON	1	ELLISTON	1	GILLELAND	2	HEADINGTON	2
DEAN	1	ELMER	1	GILLETT	1	HEDENBERG	3
DEANE	2	ELMORE	1	GILLHAM	1	HEDENBURG	1
DEATHERAGE	20	EMMERSON	7	GILLIAM	1	HEDINBERG	1
DEATON	8	EMRICK	2	GILLILAND	6	HEMBROUGH	3
DECK	1	ENGLAND	3	GILMORE	1	HEMMINGHAUS	1
DEEDS	2	ENGLEBACK	1	GILTNER	1	HEMSTED	1
DEITRICK	2	ENGLISH	4	GINTHER	1	HENDERSHOT	3
DELAHAY	3	ENNOS	1	GISH	1	HENDERSON	21
DELANEY	1	ENYART	3	GIVENS	3	HENDRICK	1
DELANY	2	EONIGER	1	GLESENER	2	HENRY	29
DELPH	1	EPLER	1	GODDARD	1	HENSON	1
DENNIS	5	ERLER	1	GOFF	3	HEREN	1
DEVANPORT	1	ETHEL	5	GOODPASTURE	10	HERRIN	1
DEVENPORT	1	EVANS	8	GORE	1	HERRING	2
DEVOLT	2	EVENS	2	GORHAM	5	HEUY	1
DEVORE	5	FAHNESTOCK	1	GRAHAM	5	HEWETT	5
DEW	2	FAIRFIELD	1	GRAVES	8	HEWITT	2
DEWEESE	11	FANCIL	1	GRAY	6	HIBARD	1
DEWIT	1	FANNING	55	GREEN	27	HICKENBOTTOM	1

Surname	# of Land Parcels	Surname	# of Land Parcels	Surname	# of Land Parcels	Surname	# of Land Parcels
HICKEY	1	JOUETT	1	LOVE	5	MCELFRESH	1
HICKMAN	1	JOURDAN	1	LOWRANCE	4	MCFADDEN	2
HICKS	1	JOURDON	1	LOWRENCE	1	MCFALL	2
HILHOUSE	1	JOY	3	LOWRIE	1	MCFALLS	1
HILL	7	KEATH	1	LOYD	1	MCFILLON	3
HILLARD	1	KELLEY	2	LUCAS	1	MCGEE	3
HILLS	1	KELLOGG	1	LUDWICK	4	MCGINNIS	4
HINDES	1	KELTNER	1	LUMSDEN	1	MCKEAND	1
HOAG	2	KENDALL	2	LUND	1	MCKEE	12
HOAGLAND	6	KENNEDY	1	LUNDAY	1	MCKINNEY	2
HOBBS	2	KENNETT	3	LURTON	2	MCKNIGHT	1
HOBIN	1	KENNEY	1	LUSK	2	MCLAIN	2
HODGE	1	KEPLINGER	3	LUTRELL	1	MCLAUGHLIN	2
HODGEN	1	KER	1	LUTTRELL	8	MCMURRAY	1
HODGES	9	KERR	6	LUTTRILL	1	MCMURRY	4
HOFFMAN	1	KERSHAW	1	LYNCH	2	MCNEELY	1
HOGAN	1	KETTNER	1	MACAIN	3	MCPERSON	1
HOGIN	1	KEYES	1	MACKEY	1	MCPHEETERS	3
HOGLIN	2	KIBLINGER	1	MADDOX	3	MCPHERSON	7
HOLIDAY	6	KILLAM	5	MADISON	3	MCRACKIN	1
HOLLIDAY	2	KILPATRICK	1	MAGILL	16	MCWAIN	1
HOLME	7	KIMBALL	8	MAJORS	3	MCWILLIAM	1
HOLMES	20	KING	15	MALONE	1	MEADOWS	1
HOMES	1	KINGSTON	1	MALONEY	1	MEARS	3
HOPPER	3	KINNEY	2	MANARY	2	MEDCALF	3
HORRELL	1	KIPLINGER	1	MANCHESTER	5	MEEK	1
HORTON	1	KIRKMAN	4	MANDAIN	1	MEEKS	1
HOSKINS	2	KIRKPATRICK	7	MANNING	4	MEISENHEIMER	1
HOUGHAN	8	KLEIN	6	MANSFIELD	3	METCALF	2
HOUSTON	10	KROSA	1	MARA	2	MICKEY	3
HOVEY	1	KROZA	1	MARCH	2	MILLAM	1
HOWARD	14	KRUSE	1	MARKHAM	1	MILLEN	11
HOWELL	1	LAKE	1	MARSHALL	6	MILLER	10
HUDDLESTON	7	LAMB	5	MARTIN	4	MILLION	4
HUDELSON	6	LAMM	1	MARVIN	1	MILLS	2
HUDELSTON	2	LAMME	1	MASON	4	MILNOR	1
HUDSON	2	LANDRETH	1	MASSES	1	MILSTEAD	1
HUDSPETH	7	LANDRUM	1	MASSEY	2	MINER	9
HUEY	19	LANHAM	2	MASTERS	7	MISENHEIMER	1
HUFFAKER	17	LARIMORE	7	MASTERSON	5	MITCHELL	4
HUGHES	9	LATIMER	1	MATHERS	2	MLODZIANOWSKI	1
HUGHS	1	LAUGHERY	1	MATHEUS	1	MOBLEY	5
HULL	2	LAURIE	1	MATHEWS	17	MONDON	1
HUMMER	2	LAW	1	MATHIS	2	MONTGOMERY	2
HUMPHREY	1	LAYCOCK	1	MATHUS	2	MOODY	1
HUNTER	6	LAYTON	3	MATTHEWS	5	MOORE	16
HUNTLY	1	LAZEMBY	1	MATTINGLY	1	MORGAN	5
HURST	3	LEACH	1	MAUPIN	3	MORLAN	1
HURTS	1	LEE	2	MAXFIELD	1	MORRELL	1
HUSSEY	1	LEEPER	6	MAY	3	MORRIS	2
HUSTON	4	LEFFLER	12	MAYFIELD	6	MORRISON	7
HUTCHESON	2	LEICH	2	MCALISTER	3	MORRISS	1
IDE	5	LEIGHTON	2	MCALLISTER	1	MORSE	1
INGALES	1	LEMON	2	MCAVOY	2	MORTEN	1
INGALLS	2	LENARD	1	MCCAMMON	1	MORTON	11
ISRAEL	1	LEONARD	4	MCCAULEY	2	MOSELY	2
JACKSON	11	LESLIE	14	MCCEARLEY	2	MOSES	1
JAMES	6	LEWIS	12	MCCEARLY	2	MOSS	12
JANUARY	11	LINDSEY	7	MCCLEARLY	1	MULLEN	2
JARMAN	1	LITTON	5	MCCLURE	4	MUNDAY	1
JARRED	2	LOAR	3	MCCLURR	1	MURPHEY	2
JAY	5	LOCKWOOD	2	MCCOMB	1	MURPHY	6
JAYNE	3	LODWICK	1	MCCONNEL	17	MURRAY	4
JENKINS	3	LOGAN	1	MCCONNELL	15	MURRY	2
JOETT	1	LOGSDON	2	MCCORMAC	2	MUSIC	1
JOHNSON	21	LOHR	2	MCCORMICK	13	MUSICK	1
JOHNSTON	1	LOLLARS	1	MCCOY	2	NALL	3
JOLLY	1	LONDON	2	MCCRACKEN	1	NASH	2
JONES	35	LONG	28	MCCULLEY	1	NAULTY	1
JORDEN	3	LOOSE	2	MCDONALD	19	NEILL	2

Surname	# of Land Parcels	Surname	# of Land Parcels	Surname	# of Land Parcels	Surname	# of Land Parcels
NELSON	8	PLANTE	4	ROBESON	3	SHELTON	2
NEVINS	1	POCKLINGTON	1	ROBESSON	1	SHEPARD	2
NEW	2	POINDEXTER	2	ROBINSON	26	SHEPHERD	12
NEWLON	1	POINTER	9	ROBISON	3	SHEPLER	1
NEWMAN	46	POLAND	3	ROBLEY	3	SHEPPARD	3
NICHOLLS	4	POND	6	ROCKWELL	4	SHEUMAKER	1
NICHOLS	6	POOL	1	ROGERS	6	SHEWSBERRY	2
NICKOL	1	PORTER	3	ROGES	2	SHIBE	2
NILES	1	POSEY	2	ROHER	1	SHIPLAR	1
NILSON	1	POST	9	ROHRER	14	SHIPLER	1
NISBIT	1	POWELL	1	ROLAND	2	SHIRTCLIFF	1
NIX	1	POWERS	1	ROLL	1	SHOEMAKER	1
NOLL	1	PRATHER	1	ROLLINS	1	SHORES	5
NORISS	1	PRATT	1	RONSEY	1	SHORT	4
NORTHCUT	2	PRENTICE	5	ROSE	1	SHREWBURY	1
NOWLAN	1	PREVOST	6	ROSS	6	SHREWSBERRY	1
NOWLIN	1	PREWITT	1	ROSSON	3	SHUFF	1
NOYES	1	PRICE	7	ROUNDS	3	SHUMAKER	1
NUNNS	1	PRIEST	1	ROUSEY	8	SHURTLEFF	4
OBANION	2	PROCTOR	2	ROUTT	4	SHURTLIFF	1
OGG	1	PROSSEE	2	RUARK	1	SIBERT	4
OGLE	5	PROVOST	2	RUBART	6	SILES	1
OKEAR	1	PUCKETT	1	RUBLE	8	SIMMONS	4
OKEEFFE	2	PURKITT	4	RUCKER	2	SIMMS	6
OLMSTEAD	1	PURVIANCE	12	RUDE	1	SIMPLOT	1
ONEAL	4	PURVINE	7	RUDISELL	1	SIMS	16
OREAR	14	PYLE	1	RULON	1	SINCLAIR	12
ORR	3	RAFFERTY	1	RUSK	5	SLAT	1
ORTZ	1	RANNELLS	3	RUSSEL	21	SLATTEN	5
OSBORN	1	RANSDELL	8	RUSSELL	14	SLATTER	1
OSBORNE	1	RANSON	5	RUTHERFORD	2	SLATTIN	4
OSBOURN	1	RATLIFF	4	RUYLE	4	SMADLEY	1
OSBURN	1	RATLIFFE	1	RUYNKLE	1	SMART	7
OSCAR	1	RAUGH	1	RYNDERS	1	SMEDLEY	6
PACK	1	RAWLIN	1	SACKETT	3	SMIDLEY	4
PACKER	6	RAWNELLS	1	SADDLER	1	SMITH	92
PALMER	1	RAY	1	SAGE	1	SNOW	2
PARK	8	RAYBON	1	SAIGHMAN	2	SOLOMON	1
PARKASON	1	REAKER	1	SALLEE	1	SOOY	1
PARKER	11	REAM	4	SALTER	20	SOWRY	1
PARKINSON	9	REAUGH	18	SAMMONS	1	SPAINHOWER	1
PARKISON	1	REDDING	4	SAMPLE	12	SPARKS	3
PARKS	2	REDING	2	SAMPLES	4	SPATES	1
PARR	1	REDMAN	2	SANNDERSON	3	SPAULDING	1
PARROTT	2	REDMON	1	SAPPINGTON	2	SPEANHOWER	1
PATRICK	1	REED	19	SARGEANT	5	SPEARMAN	2
PATTEN	1	REES	2	SARGENT	2	SPEARS	1
PATTERSON	10	REEVE	4	SAUNDERSON	4	SPENCER	18
PATTON	2	REEVES	1	SAVAGE	3	SPERRY	1
PEARCY	1	REEVIS	1	SAXTON	3	SPIRES	7
PEARSON	2	REID	21	SCARTH	2	SPOTSWOOD	10
PEMBERTON	8	REOUSEY	1	SCOGGINS	1	SPOTWOOD	2
PENNOYER	5	REXROOT	1	SCOTT	21	SPRAGUE	1
PENSON	2	REXROTE	2	SCROGGIN	3	SPRINGER	2
PERKINS	1	REXROUT	2	SCROGGINS	1	ST LEWIS	2
PERVIANCE	2	REYNOLDS	9	SEAMORE	3	STACY	3
PERVINE	1	RHEA	3	SEARTH	1	STAGNER	1
PETER	1	RHODES	3	SEDGWICK	1	STAMPS	1
PETERS	1	RHORER	1	SEMOORE	1	STANDLEY	2
PETREE	3	RICE	3	SERALES	2	STANLEY	2
PETTYJOHN	1	RICHARDS	5	SEVIDE	1	STANLY	1
PEXTON	3	RICHARDSON	18	SEWALL	1	STAPLETON	2
PFEIL	2	RIDGLEY	5	SEYMORE	13	STARMER	7
PHEASANT	1	RIEMAN	2	SEYMOUR	1	STARR	2
PHIEL	1	RIGGIN	2	SHALDON	1	STAUDLEY	1
PHILIPPI	4	RIMBEY	8	SHARP	3	STEBBINS	2
PHILIPS	2	ROACH	4	SHARTZER	2	STEEL	1
PHILLIPS	1	ROBB	1	SHEARER	2	STEELE	1
PIPER	1	ROBERTS	11	SHEETS	1	STEIR	1
PITNER	3	ROBERTSON	8	SHEFLER	1	STEPHENSON	6

Surname	# of Land Parcels	Surname	# of Land Parcels	Surname	# of Land Parcels
STETTINIUS	3	VANWINKLE	16	WISWALL	3
STEWART	10	VARNER	4	WISWELL	3
STICE	1	VARY	1	WOLCOTT	41
STILLWELL	1	VEACH	1	WOLF	6
STITES	6	VENABLE	1	WOLFE	1
STITINIUS	1	VERERS	1	WOOD	14
STOCKTON	2	VERRY	2	WOODS	6
STODDARD	1	VERTREES	1	WOODWARD	4
STONE	2	VINSON	1	WOOLCOTT	3
STORY	18	VOYLES	3	WOOLLOMES	3
STOUT	13	WACKERLE	1	WOOLMES	1
STRAWN	51	WADDELL	1	WOOLMS	1
STRIBLING	1	WADE	1	WOOSTER	1
STRODE	2	WAFSON	1	WORKMAN	1
STRONER	1	WALDO	12	WORTH	1
STULL	1	WALKER	8	WRIGHT	35
STURGIS	12	WALLER	2	WYATT	32
SUMMERS	1	WALSH	1	WYETH	1
SUMMONS	1	WALTON	1	YACK	3
SUSK	1	WARD	2	YAPLE	5
SUTER	1	WARE	6	YATES	14
SWALES	11	WARREN	8	YORK	5
SWAN	4	WARRENS	1	YOUNG	1
SWEET	7	WASHBURN	1	YOUNGBLOOD	2
SWIGERT	3	WASSON	2		
SWINNERTON	1	WATERS	5		
TAGGART	1	WATKINS	1		
TAINTON	1	WATSON	3		
TALKINGTON	1	WAY	1		
TANNEHILL	1	WEATHERFORD	9		
TANNER	9	WEATHERS	2		
TATNALL	1	WEBB	2		
TAUMHILL	1	WEEKS	10		
TAYLOR	22	WELCH	1		
TEAS	1	WELTY	1		
TENNISON	2	WESSON	1		
THOMAS	4	WEST	4		
THOMPSON	41	WESTFALL	2		
THOMSON	1	WESTHROPE	1		
THORNBY	1	WESTROPE	9		
THORNLEY	5	WETHERFIELD	1		
THORNTON	9	WETHERFORD	2		
TICKNOR	3	WHEELER	3		
TIFFT	1	WHIPP	1		
TILTON	1	WHITE	8		
TINGLE	4	WHITEAKER	2		
TINSLEY	1	WHITEHEAD	3		
TITUS	2	WHITLEY	6		
TODD	7	WHITLOCK	13		
TOLKINTON	3	WHITWORTH	1		
TOLLY	1	WHORTON	1		
TROTTER	1	WIENSCHE	2		
TROY	12	WILCOX	3		
TUCKER	5	WILHELM	1		
TUNNELL	10	WILKERSON	1		
TURLEY	2	WILKINSON	7		
TURNBULL	5	WILLARD	8		
TURNER	22	WILLETT	3		
TURNEY	2	WILLHITE	1		
TURNHAM	2	WILLIAM	1		
TYLER	2	WILLIAMS	5		
ULLERY	1	WILLSON	5		
URBEAN	1	WILSON	9		
VALLENTINE	1	WINEGAR	2		
VANCE	6	WING	3		
VANCIL	3	WINNINGHAM	1		
VANDEGRIFT	2	WINSLOW	1		
VANEATON	1	WINTERS	1		
VANNEST	3	WISE	3		
VANOATE	1	WISNELL	1		

Surname/Township Index

This Index allows you to determine which *Township Map Group(s)* contain individuals with the following surnames. Each *Map Group* has a corresponding full-name index of all individuals who obtained patents for land within its Congressional township's borders. After each index you will find the Patent Map to which it refers, and just thereafter, you can view the township's Road Map and Historical Map, with the latter map displaying streams, railroads, and more.

So, once you find your Surname here, proceed to the Index at the beginning of the **Map Group** indicated below.

Surname	Map Group	Parcels of Land	Meridian/Township/Range
ABBEY	**7**	1	3rd PM 15-N 12-W
" "	**2**	1	3rd PM 16-N 12-W
ABBOTT	**16**	1	3rd PM 13-N 11-W
" "	**7**	1	3rd PM 15-N 12-W
ABBY	**1**	1	3rd PM 16-N 13-W
ABRAM	**9**	1	3rd PM 15-N 10-W
ABRAMS	**9**	1	3rd PM 15-N 10-W
" "	**2**	1	3rd PM 16-N 12-W
ADALMAN	**3**	1	3rd PM 16-N 11-W
ADAMS	**5**	8	3rd PM 16-N 9-W
" "	**13**	5	3rd PM 14-N 10-W
" "	**8**	3	3rd PM 15-N 11-W
" "	**17**	1	3rd PM 13-N 10-W
" "	**18**	1	3rd PM 13-N 9-W
" "	**12**	1	3rd PM 14-N 11-W
" "	**11**	1	3rd PM 15-N 8-W
ADDINGTON	**3**	1	3rd PM 16-N 11-W
AKERS	**4**	2	3rd PM 16-N 10-W
AKIRS	**4**	1	3rd PM 16-N 10-W
ALBIN	**2**	4	3rd PM 16-N 12-W
ALDERSON	**2**	1	3rd PM 16-N 12-W
ALEXANDER	**11**	6	3rd PM 15-N 8-W
ALFKIN	**3**	2	3rd PM 16-N 11-W
ALLEN	**12**	4	3rd PM 14-N 11-W
" "	**5**	2	3rd PM 16-N 9-W
" "	**18**	1	3rd PM 13-N 9-W
" "	**6**	1	3rd PM 16-N 8-W
ALLINSON	**8**	14	3rd PM 15-N 11-W
" "	**9**	13	3rd PM 15-N 10-W
" "	**12**	4	3rd PM 14-N 11-W
" "	**4**	2	3rd PM 16-N 10-W
" "	**7**	1	3rd PM 15-N 12-W
" "	**3**	1	3rd PM 16-N 11-W
ALLIS	**19**	1	3rd PM 13-N 8-W
ALLYN	**9**	1	3rd PM 15-N 10-W
ALTMANN	**3**	1	3rd PM 16-N 11-W
ANDERSON	**17**	6	3rd PM 13-N 10-W
" "	**10**	5	3rd PM 15-N 9-W
" "	**5**	3	3rd PM 16-N 9-W
" "	**13**	2	3rd PM 14-N 10-W
" "	**15**	1	3rd PM 14-N 8-W
" "	**14**	1	3rd PM 14-N 9-W
ANGDANO	**13**	1	3rd PM 14-N 10-W
ANGEL	**3**	4	3rd PM 16-N 11-W

Surname	Map Group	Parcels of Land	Meridian/Township/Range
ANGEL (Cont'd)	**4**	1	3rd PM 16-N 10-W
ANGELO	**12**	3	3rd PM 14-N 11-W
" "	**13**	2	3rd PM 14-N 10-W
ANGELON	**12**	1	3rd PM 14-N 11-W
ANGELOW	**12**	8	3rd PM 14-N 11-W
" "	**13**	2	3rd PM 14-N 10-W
ANTLE	**14**	1	3rd PM 14-N 9-W
APLER	**5**	1	3rd PM 16-N 9-W
ARCHER	**4**	1	3rd PM 16-N 10-W
ARENZ	**3**	3	3rd PM 16-N 11-W
ARMSTRONG	**19**	3	3rd PM 13-N 8-W
" "	**5**	2	3rd PM 16-N 9-W
ARNETT	**9**	8	3rd PM 15-N 10-W
" "	**13**	3	3rd PM 14-N 10-W
" "	**19**	2	3rd PM 13-N 8-W
" "	**12**	2	3rd PM 14-N 11-W
ARNOLD	**15**	4	3rd PM 14-N 8-W
ARNZ	**3**	2	3rd PM 16-N 11-W
ASH	**16**	2	3rd PM 13-N 11-W
ASHBAUGH	**19**	2	3rd PM 13-N 8-W
ASHBRAUGH	**19**	1	3rd PM 13-N 8-W
ASHER	**11**	2	3rd PM 15-N 8-W
" "	**16**	1	3rd PM 13-N 11-W
ATER	**3**	2	3rd PM 16-N 11-W
ATTEBERY	**18**	1	3rd PM 13-N 9-W
ATTICK	**1**	1	3rd PM 16-N 13-W
AUGUSTINE	**1**	1	3rd PM 16-N 13-W
AUSEMNS	**8**	1	3rd PM 15-N 11-W
AUSEMUS	**3**	5	3rd PM 16-N 11-W
AUSMUS	**3**	3	3rd PM 16-N 11-W
" "	**1**	2	3rd PM 16-N 13-W
AUSTIN	**8**	6	3rd PM 15-N 11-W
" "	**18**	2	3rd PM 13-N 9-W
" "	**19**	1	3rd PM 13-N 8-W
" "	**12**	1	3rd PM 14-N 11-W
AUTLE	**14**	1	3rd PM 14-N 9-W
AVERITT	**2**	2	3rd PM 16-N 12-W
" "	**3**	1	3rd PM 16-N 11-W
AYERS	**16**	1	3rd PM 13-N 11-W
" "	**15**	1	3rd PM 14-N 8-W
AYLESWORTH	**2**	2	3rd PM 16-N 12-W
" "	**1**	2	3rd PM 16-N 13-W
" "	**8**	1	3rd PM 15-N 11-W
AYRES	**15**	3	3rd PM 14-N 8-W
BABB	**4**	2	3rd PM 16-N 10-W
BADGER	**4**	3	3rd PM 16-N 10-W
BAILEY	**13**	2	3rd PM 14-N 10-W
BAIRD	**17**	3	3rd PM 13-N 10-W
BAKER	**2**	2	3rd PM 16-N 12-W
" "	**3**	1	3rd PM 16-N 11-W
" "	**5**	1	3rd PM 16-N 9-W
BALDWIN	**19**	3	3rd PM 13-N 8-W
" "	**18**	2	3rd PM 13-N 9-W
" "	**5**	1	3rd PM 16-N 9-W
BALEY	**2**	2	3rd PM 16-N 12-W
BALL	**18**	1	3rd PM 13-N 9-W
" "	**5**	1	3rd PM 16-N 9-W
BALLARD	**3**	7	3rd PM 16-N 11-W
" "	**9**	1	3rd PM 15-N 10-W
" "	**10**	1	3rd PM 15-N 9-W

Surname	Map Group	Parcels of Land	Meridian/Township/Range		
BANCROFT	**12**	2	3rd PM	14-N	11-W
" "	**3**	1	3rd PM	16-N	11-W
BANNING	**1**	2	3rd PM	16-N	13-W
BARBER	**4**	4	3rd PM	16-N	10-W
" "	**3**	1	3rd PM	16-N	11-W
" "	**2**	1	3rd PM	16-N	12-W
BARD	**17**	1	3rd PM	13-N	10-W
BARKER	**19**	1	3rd PM	13-N	8-W
" "	**4**	1	3rd PM	16-N	10-W
BARLAND	**4**	4	3rd PM	16-N	10-W
BARNET	**5**	1	3rd PM	16-N	9-W
BARNETT	**18**	1	3rd PM	13-N	9-W
" "	**3**	1	3rd PM	16-N	11-W
BARNS	**17**	4	3rd PM	13-N	10-W
BARRET	**2**	3	3rd PM	16-N	12-W
" "	**15**	2	3rd PM	14-N	8-W
" "	**11**	1	3rd PM	15-N	8-W
BARRETT	**11**	3	3rd PM	15-N	8-W
BARRICKLOW	**2**	1	3rd PM	16-N	12-W
BARROW	**17**	6	3rd PM	13-N	10-W
BARROWS	**13**	6	3rd PM	14-N	10-W
" "	**14**	5	3rd PM	14-N	9-W
" "	**18**	3	3rd PM	13-N	9-W
BARTLETT	**9**	3	3rd PM	15-N	10-W
BARTON	**7**	5	3rd PM	15-N	12-W
" "	**9**	2	3rd PM	15-N	10-W
" "	**8**	1	3rd PM	15-N	11-W
BATEMAN	**4**	1	3rd PM	16-N	10-W
BATES	**3**	5	3rd PM	16-N	11-W
" "	**2**	2	3rd PM	16-N	12-W
BATTY	**12**	2	3rd PM	14-N	11-W
BEACRAFT	**15**	1	3rd PM	14-N	8-W
BEAGLE	**1**	1	3rd PM	16-N	13-W
BEARCRAFT	**15**	1	3rd PM	14-N	8-W
BEASLEY	**19**	2	3rd PM	13-N	8-W
" "	**12**	2	3rd PM	14-N	11-W
BEAUCHAMP	**2**	1	3rd PM	16-N	12-W
BEAVERS	**12**	1	3rd PM	14-N	11-W
" "	**5**	1	3rd PM	16-N	9-W
BEFON	**19**	1	3rd PM	13-N	8-W
BEGGS	**4**	4	3rd PM	16-N	10-W
BELL	**9**	1	3rd PM	15-N	10-W
BELLAMMY	**8**	1	3rd PM	15-N	11-W
BELLOWS	**17**	2	3rd PM	13-N	10-W
BENFER	**1**	1	3rd PM	16-N	13-W
BENNET	**5**	1	3rd PM	16-N	9-W
BENNETT	**5**	2	3rd PM	16-N	9-W
" "	**19**	1	3rd PM	13-N	8-W
" "	**9**	1	3rd PM	15-N	10-W
" "	**6**	1	3rd PM	16-N	8-W
BENNINGER	**1**	1	3rd PM	16-N	13-W
BENTLEY	**13**	1	3rd PM	14-N	10-W
" "	**9**	1	3rd PM	15-N	10-W
BENTON	**8**	1	3rd PM	15-N	11-W
BERDAN	**18**	1	3rd PM	13-N	9-W
BERGEN	**5**	3	3rd PM	16-N	9-W
" "	**4**	2	3rd PM	16-N	10-W
" "	**3**	1	3rd PM	16-N	11-W
BERGHAUS	**2**	2	3rd PM	16-N	12-W
BERNARD	**1**	1	3rd PM	16-N	13-W

Surname	Map Group	Parcels of Land	Meridian/Township/Range
BERRY	**12**	6	3rd PM 14-N 11-W
" "	**10**	5	3rd PM 15-N 9-W
" "	**4**	4	3rd PM 16-N 10-W
" "	**14**	2	3rd PM 14-N 9-W
" "	**13**	1	3rd PM 14-N 10-W
BIBB	**4**	3	3rd PM 16-N 10-W
BIDWELL	**9**	1	3rd PM 15-N 10-W
BILLINGS	**16**	4	3rd PM 13-N 11-W
BINGMAN	**5**	1	3rd PM 16-N 9-W
BIRDSELL	**16**	4	3rd PM 13-N 11-W
BIRKBY	**9**	1	3rd PM 15-N 10-W
" "	**5**	1	3rd PM 16-N 9-W
BIRKLEY	**9**	1	3rd PM 15-N 10-W
BLACK	**4**	5	3rd PM 16-N 10-W
" "	**17**	1	3rd PM 13-N 10-W
" "	**3**	1	3rd PM 16-N 11-W
BLAIR	**16**	2	3rd PM 13-N 11-W
" "	**17**	1	3rd PM 13-N 10-W
" "	**9**	1	3rd PM 15-N 10-W
BLANEY	**19**	4	3rd PM 13-N 8-W
" "	**10**	4	3rd PM 15-N 9-W
BLEVINS	**19**	1	3rd PM 13-N 8-W
BLISH	**16**	1	3rd PM 13-N 11-W
BLODGETT	**2**	1	3rd PM 16-N 12-W
BOGART	**8**	1	3rd PM 15-N 11-W
BONDURANT	**2**	3	3rd PM 16-N 12-W
BOOKES	**18**	1	3rd PM 13-N 9-W
BOSWELL	**1**	1	3rd PM 16-N 13-W
BOTTS	**13**	4	3rd PM 14-N 10-W
BOULWARD	**15**	1	3rd PM 14-N 8-W
BOULWARE	**19**	1	3rd PM 13-N 8-W
" "	**15**	1	3rd PM 14-N 8-W
BOURLAND	**14**	1	3rd PM 14-N 9-W
BOWEN	**5**	1	3rd PM 16-N 9-W
BOWYER	**19**	2	3rd PM 13-N 8-W
" "	**15**	1	3rd PM 14-N 8-W
BOX	**4**	1	3rd PM 16-N 10-W
" "	**3**	1	3rd PM 16-N 11-W
BOYCE	**5**	2	3rd PM 16-N 9-W
BOYD	**17**	3	3rd PM 13-N 10-W
BOYER	**14**	3	3rd PM 14-N 9-W
" "	**5**	2	3rd PM 16-N 9-W
BOZARTH	**3**	2	3rd PM 16-N 11-W
" "	**7**	1	3rd PM 15-N 12-W
BRACKENRIDGE	**3**	2	3rd PM 16-N 11-W
BRADBURY	**7**	2	3rd PM 15-N 12-W
" "	**2**	2	3rd PM 16-N 12-W
BRADLEY	**5**	1	3rd PM 16-N 9-W
BRADSHAW	**9**	3	3rd PM 15-N 10-W
" "	**3**	1	3rd PM 16-N 11-W
BRANER	**3**	3	3rd PM 16-N 11-W
BRATTAIN	**3**	1	3rd PM 16-N 11-W
BRATTON	**3**	1	3rd PM 16-N 11-W
BRAUR	**3**	1	3rd PM 16-N 11-W
BRAYHAW	**2**	1	3rd PM 16-N 12-W
BRENENK	**2**	1	3rd PM 16-N 12-W
BRIAN	**19**	6	3rd PM 13-N 8-W
" "	**18**	2	3rd PM 13-N 9-W
BRICH	**9**	2	3rd PM 15-N 10-W
BRIDGEMAN	**3**	6	3rd PM 16-N 11-W

Surname	Map Group	Parcels of Land	Meridian/Township/Range		
BRIEDEN	**12**	1	3rd PM	14-N	11-W
BRISBIN	**13**	2	3rd PM	14-N	10-W
" "	**14**	2	3rd PM	14-N	9-W
" "	**12**	1	3rd PM	14-N	11-W
" "	**7**	1	3rd PM	15-N	12-W
BRISBY	**5**	1	3rd PM	16-N	9-W
BRISTOE	**4**	2	3rd PM	16-N	10-W
BRISTOW	**4**	6	3rd PM	16-N	10-W
" "	**18**	2	3rd PM	13-N	9-W
" "	**9**	1	3rd PM	15-N	10-W
BROADHEAD	**4**	2	3rd PM	16-N	10-W
" "	**9**	1	3rd PM	15-N	10-W
BROADWELL	**7**	6	3rd PM	15-N	12-W
" "	**8**	1	3rd PM	15-N	11-W
BROCKENBROUGH	**3**	8	3rd PM	16-N	11-W
" "	**2**	3	3rd PM	16-N	12-W
" "	**10**	1	3rd PM	15-N	9-W
BROCKHOUSE	**2**	2	3rd PM	16-N	12-W
BROCKMAN	**18**	2	3rd PM	13-N	9-W
BROKENBOUGH	**19**	1	3rd PM	13-N	8-W
BROKENBROUGH	**19**	1	3rd PM	13-N	8-W
" "	**3**	1	3rd PM	16-N	11-W
BROKHAUS	**2**	1	3rd PM	16-N	12-W
BROMLY	**2**	1	3rd PM	16-N	12-W
" "	**1**	1	3rd PM	16-N	13-W
BROTHERS	**2**	1	3rd PM	16-N	12-W
BROWN	**11**	32	3rd PM	15-N	8-W
" "	**13**	17	3rd PM	14-N	10-W
" "	**10**	8	3rd PM	15-N	9-W
" "	**17**	7	3rd PM	13-N	10-W
" "	**15**	7	3rd PM	14-N	8-W
" "	**18**	5	3rd PM	13-N	9-W
" "	**14**	4	3rd PM	14-N	9-W
" "	**5**	4	3rd PM	16-N	9-W
" "	**19**	3	3rd PM	13-N	8-W
" "	**4**	2	3rd PM	16-N	10-W
" "	**2**	2	3rd PM	16-N	12-W
" "	**12**	1	3rd PM	14-N	11-W
" "	**9**	1	3rd PM	15-N	10-W
BRUCE	**17**	1	3rd PM	13-N	10-W
BRUNING	**2**	1	3rd PM	16-N	12-W
BRUTON	**14**	1	3rd PM	14-N	9-W
" "	**10**	1	3rd PM	15-N	9-W
BRYAMT	**5**	1	3rd PM	16-N	9-W
BRYANT	**13**	1	3rd PM	14-N	10-W
" "	**5**	1	3rd PM	16-N	9-W
BUCHANAN	**14**	8	3rd PM	14-N	9-W
" "	**10**	2	3rd PM	15-N	9-W
BUCHANNON	**14**	1	3rd PM	14-N	9-W
BUCKHANAN	**14**	1	3rd PM	14-N	9-W
BUCKINGHAM	**4**	2	3rd PM	16-N	10-W
BUCKMASTER	**18**	1	3rd PM	13-N	9-W
BUCKSTON	**4**	1	3rd PM	16-N	10-W
BUCY	**9**	1	3rd PM	15-N	10-W
BUGBY	**17**	2	3rd PM	13-N	10-W
BULL	**18**	1	3rd PM	13-N	9-W
BULLARD	**14**	2	3rd PM	14-N	9-W
" "	**18**	1	3rd PM	13-N	9-W
BURBAGE	**3**	1	3rd PM	16-N	11-W
BURBANK	**3**	1	3rd PM	16-N	11-W

Surname	Map Group	Parcels of Land	Meridian/Township/Range
BURBANK (Cont'd)	**1**	1	3rd PM 16-N 13-W
BURCH	**14**	3	3rd PM 14-N 9-W
" "	**19**	1	3rd PM 13-N 8-W
" "	**15**	1	3rd PM 14-N 8-W
BURK	**2**	1	3rd PM 16-N 12-W
BURNETT	**15**	7	3rd PM 14-N 8-W
BURNS	**19**	1	3rd PM 13-N 8-W
BURROWS	**13**	1	3rd PM 14-N 10-W
BURTON	**3**	2	3rd PM 16-N 11-W
BUSH	**2**	1	3rd PM 16-N 12-W
BUTLER	**15**	3	3rd PM 14-N 8-W
" "	**10**	3	3rd PM 15-N 9-W
" "	**3**	2	3rd PM 16-N 11-W
CADWELL	**8**	3	3rd PM 15-N 11-W
CAINEY	**16**	1	3rd PM 13-N 11-W
CALDWELL	**19**	7	3rd PM 13-N 8-W
" "	**16**	3	3rd PM 13-N 11-W
" "	**18**	2	3rd PM 13-N 9-W
CAMP	**9**	1	3rd PM 15-N 10-W
CAMPBELL	**19**	2	3rd PM 13-N 8-W
" "	**17**	1	3rd PM 13-N 10-W
" "	**18**	1	3rd PM 13-N 9-W
CAMREN	**5**	2	3rd PM 16-N 9-W
CANDLE	**9**	1	3rd PM 15-N 10-W
CANNON	**5**	2	3rd PM 16-N 9-W
CARLOCK	**8**	3	3rd PM 15-N 11-W
" "	**18**	1	3rd PM 13-N 9-W
CARNES	**14**	1	3rd PM 14-N 9-W
CARNEY	**16**	2	3rd PM 13-N 11-W
CARNS	**14**	2	3rd PM 14-N 9-W
CARR	**5**	1	3rd PM 16-N 9-W
CARRATHER	**19**	1	3rd PM 13-N 8-W
CARRICK	**2**	1	3rd PM 16-N 12-W
CARRUTHERS	**19**	1	3rd PM 13-N 8-W
CARSELL	**14**	1	3rd PM 14-N 9-W
CARTER	**12**	6	3rd PM 14-N 11-W
" "	**2**	5	3rd PM 16-N 12-W
" "	**1**	4	3rd PM 16-N 13-W
" "	**3**	3	3rd PM 16-N 11-W
" "	**13**	2	3rd PM 14-N 10-W
" "	**8**	1	3rd PM 15-N 11-W
CARUTHERS	**19**	3	3rd PM 13-N 8-W
CARY	**19**	2	3rd PM 13-N 8-W
CASSEL	**17**	1	3rd PM 13-N 10-W
" "	**10**	1	3rd PM 15-N 9-W
CASSELL	**10**	4	3rd PM 15-N 9-W
" "	**9**	1	3rd PM 15-N 10-W
CASTLE	**10**	1	3rd PM 15-N 9-W
CASTLEBERRY	**3**	1	3rd PM 16-N 11-W
CATLIN	**18**	2	3rd PM 13-N 9-W
" "	**19**	1	3rd PM 13-N 8-W
" "	**6**	1	3rd PM 16-N 8-W
CAUBY	**6**	1	3rd PM 16-N 8-W
CAUDEL	**18**	2	3rd PM 13-N 9-W
CAUDLE	**8**	1	3rd PM 15-N 11-W
CAULKINS	**9**	1	3rd PM 15-N 10-W
CAVE	**10**	2	3rd PM 15-N 9-W
CAWOOD	**19**	3	3rd PM 13-N 8-W
" "	**2**	1	3rd PM 16-N 12-W
CHADWICK	**17**	3	3rd PM 13-N 10-W

Surname	Map Group	Parcels of Land	Meridian/Township/Range
CHALLEN	14	3	3rd PM 14-N 9-W
" "	5	1	3rd PM 16-N 9-W
CHAMBER	2	1	3rd PM 16-N 12-W
CHAMBERLAIN	2	1	3rd PM 16-N 12-W
CHAMBERLIN	7	1	3rd PM 15-N 12-W
" "	2	1	3rd PM 16-N 12-W
CHAMBERS	1	1	3rd PM 16-N 13-W
CHANCE	18	1	3rd PM 13-N 9-W
CHAPMAN	19	1	3rd PM 13-N 8-W
" "	9	1	3rd PM 15-N 10-W
" "	5	1	3rd PM 16-N 9-W
CHASTAIN	19	1	3rd PM 13-N 8-W
CHERRY	18	1	3rd PM 13-N 9-W
CHESNUTT	19	1	3rd PM 13-N 8-W
CHILTON	16	1	3rd PM 13-N 11-W
" "	14	1	3rd PM 14-N 9-W
CHRISMAN	8	1	3rd PM 15-N 11-W
CHRISTMAN	8	1	3rd PM 15-N 11-W
CHURCH	9	4	3rd PM 15-N 10-W
CLACK	19	2	3rd PM 13-N 8-W
CLACKE	19	1	3rd PM 13-N 8-W
CLARK	14	3	3rd PM 14-N 9-W
" "	4	3	3rd PM 16-N 10-W
" "	17	2	3rd PM 13-N 10-W
" "	13	2	3rd PM 14-N 10-W
" "	19	1	3rd PM 13-N 8-W
" "	12	1	3rd PM 14-N 11-W
" "	11	1	3rd PM 15-N 8-W
" "	5	1	3rd PM 16-N 9-W
CLARKE	10	4	3rd PM 15-N 9-W
" "	17	3	3rd PM 13-N 10-W
" "	4	2	3rd PM 16-N 10-W
" "	14	1	3rd PM 14-N 9-W
CLARY	9	1	3rd PM 15-N 10-W
CLAY	3	1	3rd PM 16-N 11-W
CLAYTON	14	3	3rd PM 14-N 9-W
" "	3	3	3rd PM 16-N 11-W
CLOPTON	5	1	3rd PM 16-N 9-W
CLOTFETTER	1	3	3rd PM 16-N 13-W
" "	2	1	3rd PM 16-N 12-W
CLOUD	19	3	3rd PM 13-N 8-W
COBB	7	4	3rd PM 15-N 12-W
" "	1	3	3rd PM 16-N 13-W
" "	12	2	3rd PM 14-N 11-W
" "	8	2	3rd PM 15-N 11-W
CODDINGTON	9	2	3rd PM 15-N 10-W
" "	12	1	3rd PM 14-N 11-W
" "	8	1	3rd PM 15-N 11-W
COEN	4	3	3rd PM 16-N 10-W
COFFIN	16	9	3rd PM 13-N 11-W
" "	12	8	3rd PM 14-N 11-W
" "	13	7	3rd PM 14-N 10-W
" "	2	3	3rd PM 16-N 12-W
COFFMAN	10	4	3rd PM 15-N 9-W
" "	9	1	3rd PM 15-N 10-W
" "	2	1	3rd PM 16-N 12-W
COGBURN	2	2	3rd PM 16-N 12-W
COGER	9	1	3rd PM 15-N 10-W
COKER	5	3	3rd PM 16-N 9-W
" "	10	2	3rd PM 15-N 9-W

Surname	Map Group	Parcels of Land	Meridian/Township/Range
COKER (Cont'd)	**14**	1	3rd PM 14-N 9-W
COLE	**4**	2	3rd PM 16-N 10-W
" "	**16**	1	3rd PM 13-N 11-W
" "	**9**	1	3rd PM 15-N 10-W
" "	**10**	1	3rd PM 15-N 9-W
COLLINS	**8**	13	3rd PM 15-N 11-W
" "	**7**	4	3rd PM 15-N 12-W
" "	**16**	2	3rd PM 13-N 11-W
COMBS	**3**	1	3rd PM 16-N 11-W
COMER	**2**	1	3rd PM 16-N 12-W
CONLEE	**19**	1	3rd PM 13-N 8-W
CONN	**1**	8	3rd PM 16-N 13-W
CONNAWAY	**10**	1	3rd PM 15-N 9-W
COOK	**18**	1	3rd PM 13-N 9-W
COOKE	**19**	5	3rd PM 13-N 8-W
COONRAD	**7**	1	3rd PM 15-N 12-W
COONS	**4**	2	3rd PM 16-N 10-W
" "	**16**	1	3rd PM 13-N 11-W
COOPER	**3**	4	3rd PM 16-N 11-W
" "	**5**	3	3rd PM 16-N 9-W
COREY	**15**	1	3rd PM 14-N 8-W
CORRINGTON	**6**	2	3rd PM 16-N 8-W
" "	**4**	1	3rd PM 16-N 10-W
COUCHMAN	**4**	3	3rd PM 16-N 10-W
" "	**9**	1	3rd PM 15-N 10-W
COULEE	**19**	1	3rd PM 13-N 8-W
COULTER	**3**	1	3rd PM 16-N 11-W
COUNTY	**14**	1	3rd PM 14-N 9-W
COURTIS	**14**	1	3rd PM 14-N 9-W
COWAN	**19**	1	3rd PM 13-N 8-W
" "	**15**	1	3rd PM 14-N 8-W
COWARD	**8**	1	3rd PM 15-N 11-W
COWEN	**15**	1	3rd PM 14-N 8-W
COWNOVER	**5**	5	3rd PM 16-N 9-W
" "	**9**	4	3rd PM 15-N 10-W
" "	**4**	2	3rd PM 16-N 10-W
" "	**14**	1	3rd PM 14-N 9-W
" "	**10**	1	3rd PM 15-N 9-W
COX	**14**	5	3rd PM 14-N 9-W
" "	**2**	5	3rd PM 16-N 12-W
" "	**6**	4	3rd PM 16-N 8-W
" "	**4**	3	3rd PM 16-N 10-W
" "	**1**	3	3rd PM 16-N 13-W
" "	**18**	2	3rd PM 13-N 9-W
" "	**10**	2	3rd PM 15-N 9-W
" "	**3**	1	3rd PM 16-N 11-W
CRABTREE	**4**	1	3rd PM 16-N 10-W
CRAGGS	**12**	1	3rd PM 14-N 11-W
CRAIG	**14**	6	3rd PM 14-N 9-W
" "	**13**	4	3rd PM 14-N 10-W
" "	**17**	1	3rd PM 13-N 10-W
" "	**18**	1	3rd PM 13-N 9-W
" "	**4**	1	3rd PM 16-N 10-W
CRAWFORD	**2**	6	3rd PM 16-N 12-W
" "	**1**	1	3rd PM 16-N 13-W
CREED	**5**	1	3rd PM 16-N 9-W
CRISMAN	**2**	4	3rd PM 16-N 12-W
CRISWELL	**18**	4	3rd PM 13-N 9-W
CROMWELL	**1**	1	3rd PM 16-N 13-W
CROSS	**10**	3	3rd PM 15-N 9-W

Surname	Map Group	Parcels of Land	Meridian/Township/Range		
CROSS (Cont'd)	**15**	1	3rd PM	14-N	8-W
CROUCH	**17**	1	3rd PM	13-N	10-W
CROW	**6**	3	3rd PM	16-N	8-W
" "	**5**	2	3rd PM	16-N	9-W
" "	**9**	1	3rd PM	15-N	10-W
CRUM	**4**	1	3rd PM	16-N	10-W
CUMMING	**19**	1	3rd PM	13-N	8-W
CUMMINGS	**19**	2	3rd PM	13-N	8-W
CUNNINGHAM	**15**	3	3rd PM	14-N	8-W
" "	**14**	1	3rd PM	14-N	9-W
CUREE	**2**	1	3rd PM	16-N	12-W
CURLL	**2**	1	3rd PM	16-N	12-W
CURTIS	**19**	1	3rd PM	13-N	8-W
CURTS	**10**	1	3rd PM	15-N	9-W
CUTLER	**2**	1	3rd PM	16-N	12-W
CYRUS	**14**	5	3rd PM	14-N	9-W
" "	**18**	1	3rd PM	13-N	9-W
" "	**10**	1	3rd PM	15-N	9-W
DALTON	**18**	4	3rd PM	13-N	9-W
" "	**3**	1	3rd PM	16-N	11-W
DANIEL	**12**	1	3rd PM	14-N	11-W
" "	**5**	1	3rd PM	16-N	9-W
DANIELS	**7**	3	3rd PM	15-N	12-W
" "	**8**	2	3rd PM	15-N	11-W
" "	**4**	1	3rd PM	16-N	10-W
DAUGHERTY	**18**	3	3rd PM	13-N	9-W
DAVENPORT	**18**	1	3rd PM	13-N	9-W
" "	**14**	1	3rd PM	14-N	9-W
DAVIDSON	**17**	1	3rd PM	13-N	10-W
DAVIS	**3**	4	3rd PM	16-N	11-W
" "	**15**	1	3rd PM	14-N	8-W
" "	**1**	1	3rd PM	16-N	13-W
DAWSON	**4**	1	3rd PM	16-N	10-W
DEAN	**3**	1	3rd PM	16-N	11-W
DEANE	**3**	2	3rd PM	16-N	11-W
DEATHERAGE	**19**	19	3rd PM	13-N	8-W
" "	**18**	1	3rd PM	13-N	9-W
DEATON	**8**	7	3rd PM	15-N	11-W
" "	**3**	1	3rd PM	16-N	11-W
DECK	**5**	1	3rd PM	16-N	9-W
DEEDS	**13**	1	3rd PM	14-N	10-W
" "	**9**	1	3rd PM	15-N	10-W
DEITRICK	**3**	1	3rd PM	16-N	11-W
" "	**2**	1	3rd PM	16-N	12-W
DELAHAY	**1**	3	3rd PM	16-N	13-W
DELANEY	**18**	1	3rd PM	13-N	9-W
DELANY	**13**	2	3rd PM	14-N	10-W
DELPH	**18**	1	3rd PM	13-N	9-W
DENNIS	**18**	2	3rd PM	13-N	9-W
" "	**19**	1	3rd PM	13-N	8-W
" "	**8**	1	3rd PM	15-N	11-W
" "	**5**	1	3rd PM	16-N	9-W
DEVANPORT	**14**	1	3rd PM	14-N	9-W
DEVENPORT	**14**	1	3rd PM	14-N	9-W
DEVOLT	**17**	1	3rd PM	13-N	10-W
" "	**16**	1	3rd PM	13-N	11-W
DEVORE	**14**	3	3rd PM	14-N	9-W
" "	**18**	2	3rd PM	13-N	9-W
DEW	**13**	1	3rd PM	14-N	10-W
" "	**1**	1	3rd PM	16-N	13-W

Surname	Map Group	Parcels of Land	Meridian/Township/Range		
DEWEESE	**3**	7	3rd PM	16-N	11-W
" "	**8**	3	3rd PM	15-N	11-W
" "	**17**	1	3rd PM	13-N	10-W
DEWIT	**9**	1	3rd PM	15-N	10-W
DEWITT	**9**	1	3rd PM	15-N	10-W
DIAL	**8**	3	3rd PM	15-N	11-W
" "	**9**	1	3rd PM	15-N	10-W
DICK	**17**	1	3rd PM	13-N	10-W
" "	**18**	1	3rd PM	13-N	9-W
DICKERSON	**1**	2	3rd PM	16-N	13-W
" "	**17**	1	3rd PM	13-N	10-W
DICUS	**17**	2	3rd PM	13-N	10-W
DIEUS	**17**	2	3rd PM	13-N	10-W
DIKES	**17**	4	3rd PM	13-N	10-W
" "	**18**	1	3rd PM	13-N	9-W
DILLER	**15**	4	3rd PM	14-N	8-W
DINWIDDIE	**4**	1	3rd PM	16-N	10-W
DIXON	**9**	1	3rd PM	15-N	10-W
DOAK	**12**	1	3rd PM	14-N	11-W
DOBSON	**4**	1	3rd PM	16-N	10-W
DODD	**14**	5	3rd PM	14-N	9-W
" "	**19**	2	3rd PM	13-N	8-W
" "	**10**	2	3rd PM	15-N	9-W
DODSON	**18**	1	3rd PM	13-N	9-W
DODSWORTH	**10**	2	3rd PM	15-N	9-W
" "	**5**	2	3rd PM	16-N	9-W
DOOD	**10**	1	3rd PM	15-N	9-W
DOSGOOD	**19**	1	3rd PM	13-N	8-W
DOUGHTY	**19**	3	3rd PM	13-N	8-W
DOWLING	**13**	1	3rd PM	14-N	10-W
DOWNER	**8**	1	3rd PM	15-N	11-W
DOWNS	**17**	1	3rd PM	13-N	10-W
DOYAL	**8**	1	3rd PM	15-N	11-W
DRAKE	**4**	1	3rd PM	16-N	10-W
DRENNAN	**14**	1	3rd PM	14-N	9-W
DRURY	**10**	2	3rd PM	15-N	9-W
DRYER	**2**	1	3rd PM	16-N	12-W
DUDHOPE	**13**	2	3rd PM	14-N	10-W
" "	**14**	2	3rd PM	14-N	9-W
" "	**18**	1	3rd PM	13-N	9-W
DUFF	**8**	1	3rd PM	15-N	11-W
DUFFIELD	**17**	1	3rd PM	13-N	10-W
DUNCAN	**8**	13	3rd PM	15-N	11-W
" "	**3**	9	3rd PM	16-N	11-W
" "	**17**	7	3rd PM	13-N	10-W
" "	**10**	4	3rd PM	15-N	9-W
" "	**7**	3	3rd PM	15-N	12-W
" "	**14**	2	3rd PM	14-N	9-W
" "	**11**	1	3rd PM	15-N	8-W
" "	**5**	1	3rd PM	16-N	9-W
DUNLAP	**7**	2	3rd PM	15-N	12-W
" "	**14**	1	3rd PM	14-N	9-W
" "	**10**	1	3rd PM	15-N	9-W
DUNN	**19**	1	3rd PM	13-N	8-W
DUNSMORE	**8**	1	3rd PM	15-N	11-W
DURANT	**3**	5	3rd PM	16-N	11-W
DURYEE	**19**	1	3rd PM	13-N	8-W
DUVAL	**5**	1	3rd PM	16-N	9-W
DYE	**18**	1	3rd PM	13-N	9-W
DYER	**19**	1	3rd PM	13-N	8-W

Surname	Map Group	Parcels of Land	Meridian/Township/Range		
DYER (Cont'd)	**3**	1	3rd PM	16-N	11-W
DYERS	**15**	1	3rd PM	14-N	8-W
EADS	**13**	1	3rd PM	14-N	10-W
" "	**14**	1	3rd PM	14-N	9-W
" "	**5**	1	3rd PM	16-N	9-W
EARLL	**8**	1	3rd PM	15-N	11-W
EASTHAM	**10**	1	3rd PM	15-N	9-W
" "	**1**	1	3rd PM	16-N	13-W
EASTMAN	**19**	4	3rd PM	13-N	8-W
" "	**15**	1	3rd PM	14-N	8-W
EDGELL	**19**	1	3rd PM	13-N	8-W
" "	**18**	1	3rd PM	13-N	9-W
EDMONDSON	**8**	1	3rd PM	15-N	11-W
EDMONSON	**7**	1	3rd PM	15-N	12-W
EDMUNDSON	**2**	1	3rd PM	16-N	12-W
EDWARDS	**10**	7	3rd PM	15-N	9-W
" "	**8**	4	3rd PM	15-N	11-W
" "	**16**	2	3rd PM	13-N	11-W
" "	**18**	2	3rd PM	13-N	9-W
" "	**17**	1	3rd PM	13-N	10-W
" "	**19**	1	3rd PM	13-N	8-W
" "	**12**	1	3rd PM	14-N	11-W
" "	**14**	1	3rd PM	14-N	9-W
" "	**5**	1	3rd PM	16-N	9-W
ELDER	**5**	2	3rd PM	16-N	9-W
ELDRIDGE	**1**	2	3rd PM	16-N	13-W
" "	**5**	2	3rd PM	16-N	9-W
ELLISTON	**4**	1	3rd PM	16-N	10-W
ELMER	**4**	1	3rd PM	16-N	10-W
ELMORE	**4**	1	3rd PM	16-N	10-W
EMMERSON	**5**	7	3rd PM	16-N	9-W
EMRICK	**4**	2	3rd PM	16-N	10-W
ENGLAND	**19**	2	3rd PM	13-N	8-W
" "	**18**	1	3rd PM	13-N	9-W
ENGLEBACK	**2**	1	3rd PM	16-N	12-W
ENGLISH	**15**	4	3rd PM	14-N	8-W
ENNOS	**13**	1	3rd PM	14-N	10-W
ENYART	**5**	3	3rd PM	16-N	9-W
EONIGER	**12**	1	3rd PM	14-N	11-W
EPLER	**4**	1	3rd PM	16-N	10-W
ERLER	**2**	1	3rd PM	16-N	12-W
ETHEL	**7**	4	3rd PM	15-N	12-W
" "	**2**	1	3rd PM	16-N	12-W
EVANS	**3**	5	3rd PM	16-N	11-W
" "	**18**	1	3rd PM	13-N	9-W
" "	**15**	1	3rd PM	14-N	8-W
" "	**9**	1	3rd PM	15-N	10-W
EVENS	**9**	1	3rd PM	15-N	10-W
" "	**3**	1	3rd PM	16-N	11-W
FAHNESTOCK	**13**	1	3rd PM	14-N	10-W
FAIRFIELD	**9**	1	3rd PM	15-N	10-W
FANCIL	**19**	1	3rd PM	13-N	8-W
FANNING	**18**	20	3rd PM	13-N	9-W
" "	**17**	19	3rd PM	13-N	10-W
" "	**14**	14	3rd PM	14-N	9-W
" "	**13**	2	3rd PM	14-N	10-W
FARMING	**14**	2	3rd PM	14-N	9-W
" "	**18**	1	3rd PM	13-N	9-W
FARNUN	**5**	1	3rd PM	16-N	9-W
FARRIS	**9**	1	3rd PM	15-N	10-W

Surname	Map Group	Parcels of Land	Meridian/Township/Range
FARTHING	**7**	1	3rd PM 15-N 12-W
FATHERKILE	**17**	2	3rd PM 13-N 10-W
" "	**13**	2	3rd PM 14-N 10-W
FEATHERKILE	**17**	1	3rd PM 13-N 10-W
FERIS	**10**	4	3rd PM 15-N 9-W
FERNING	**17**	1	3rd PM 13-N 10-W
FIKE	**7**	1	3rd PM 15-N 12-W
" "	**2**	1	3rd PM 16-N 12-W
FILEY	**2**	3	3rd PM 16-N 12-W
FILSON	**10**	1	3rd PM 15-N 9-W
FINCH	**18**	1	3rd PM 13-N 9-W
FINDLEY	**9**	1	3rd PM 15-N 10-W
" "	**10**	1	3rd PM 15-N 9-W
FISK	**7**	2	3rd PM 15-N 12-W
" "	**8**	1	3rd PM 15-N 11-W
FITZHUGH	**10**	1	3rd PM 15-N 9-W
" "	**5**	1	3rd PM 16-N 9-W
FLETCHER	**3**	3	3rd PM 16-N 11-W
FLIN	**5**	2	3rd PM 16-N 9-W
" "	**6**	1	3rd PM 16-N 8-W
FLINN	**6**	8	3rd PM 16-N 8-W
" "	**5**	3	3rd PM 16-N 9-W
" "	**15**	1	3rd PM 14-N 8-W
FOLDEN	**17**	1	3rd PM 13-N 10-W
FOLDON	**13**	1	3rd PM 14-N 10-W
FORSYTHE	**4**	1	3rd PM 16-N 10-W
FOSTER	**14**	4	3rd PM 14-N 9-W
FOX	**5**	3	3rd PM 16-N 9-W
" "	**7**	2	3rd PM 15-N 12-W
" "	**1**	1	3rd PM 16-N 13-W
FRASER	**10**	3	3rd PM 15-N 9-W
FRASIN	**18**	1	3rd PM 13-N 9-W
FREEMAN	**16**	1	3rd PM 13-N 11-W
FRENCH	**13**	7	3rd PM 14-N 10-W
" "	**7**	2	3rd PM 15-N 12-W
" "	**5**	2	3rd PM 16-N 9-W
FRISBIE	**18**	1	3rd PM 13-N 9-W
FRY	**14**	9	3rd PM 14-N 9-W
" "	**13**	3	3rd PM 14-N 10-W
" "	**18**	1	3rd PM 13-N 9-W
FULLER	**17**	2	3rd PM 13-N 10-W
" "	**18**	2	3rd PM 13-N 9-W
FUNK	**12**	3	3rd PM 14-N 11-W
" "	**8**	1	3rd PM 15-N 11-W
" "	**2**	1	3rd PM 16-N 12-W
GADDES	**8**	1	3rd PM 15-N 11-W
GADDIS	**3**	5	3rd PM 16-N 11-W
" "	**8**	1	3rd PM 15-N 11-W
GAINES	**4**	2	3rd PM 16-N 10-W
GAINS	**4**	1	3rd PM 16-N 10-W
GALBRAITH	**16**	1	3rd PM 13-N 11-W
GALLAHER	**18**	1	3rd PM 13-N 9-W
GAMBLE	**16**	1	3rd PM 13-N 11-W
GARMAN	**12**	1	3rd PM 14-N 11-W
GASAWAY	**1**	3	3rd PM 16-N 13-W
GEAR	**9**	1	3rd PM 15-N 10-W
GEERS	**4**	2	3rd PM 16-N 10-W
" "	**13**	1	3rd PM 14-N 10-W
GENTRY	**13**	1	3rd PM 14-N 10-W
" "	**4**	1	3rd PM 16-N 10-W

Surname	Map Group	Parcels of Land	Meridian/Township/Range		
GESFORD	**5**	2	3rd PM	16-N	9-W
GEST	**9**	3	3rd PM	15-N	10-W
GIBBON	**9**	2	3rd PM	15-N	10-W
GIBBONS	**9**	2	3rd PM	15-N	10-W
GIBSON	**18**	15	3rd PM	13-N	9-W
GIDEON	**18**	1	3rd PM	13-N	9-W
GILBERT	**2**	2	3rd PM	16-N	12-W
GILLELAND	**15**	2	3rd PM	14-N	8-W
GILLETT	**9**	1	3rd PM	15-N	10-W
GILLHAM	**3**	1	3rd PM	16-N	11-W
GILLIAM	**4**	1	3rd PM	16-N	10-W
GILLILAND	**17**	4	3rd PM	13-N	10-W
" "	**13**	2	3rd PM	14-N	10-W
GILMORE	**13**	1	3rd PM	14-N	10-W
GILTNER	**6**	1	3rd PM	16-N	8-W
GINTHER	**3**	1	3rd PM	16-N	11-W
GISH	**3**	1	3rd PM	16-N	11-W
GIVENS	**19**	1	3rd PM	13-N	8-W
" "	**18**	1	3rd PM	13-N	9-W
" "	**15**	1	3rd PM	14-N	8-W
GLESENER	**19**	2	3rd PM	13-N	8-W
GODDARD	**10**	1	3rd PM	15-N	9-W
GOFF	**19**	3	3rd PM	13-N	8-W
GOODPASTURE	**8**	4	3rd PM	15-N	11-W
" "	**9**	2	3rd PM	15-N	10-W
" "	**7**	2	3rd PM	15-N	12-W
" "	**3**	2	3rd PM	16-N	11-W
GORE	**5**	1	3rd PM	16-N	9-W
GORHAM	**8**	4	3rd PM	15-N	11-W
" "	**11**	1	3rd PM	15-N	8-W
GRAHAM	**9**	2	3rd PM	15-N	10-W
" "	**2**	2	3rd PM	16-N	12-W
" "	**8**	1	3rd PM	15-N	11-W
GRAVES	**9**	3	3rd PM	15-N	10-W
" "	**4**	3	3rd PM	16-N	10-W
" "	**8**	2	3rd PM	15-N	11-W
GRAY	**11**	5	3rd PM	15-N	8-W
" "	**5**	1	3rd PM	16-N	9-W
GREEN	**9**	7	3rd PM	15-N	10-W
" "	**13**	6	3rd PM	14-N	10-W
" "	**14**	6	3rd PM	14-N	9-W
" "	**2**	2	3rd PM	16-N	12-W
" "	**18**	1	3rd PM	13-N	9-W
" "	**10**	1	3rd PM	15-N	9-W
" "	**4**	1	3rd PM	16-N	10-W
" "	**3**	1	3rd PM	16-N	11-W
" "	**1**	1	3rd PM	16-N	13-W
" "	**6**	1	3rd PM	16-N	8-W
GREENE	**9**	2	3rd PM	15-N	10-W
" "	**2**	1	3rd PM	16-N	12-W
" "	**1**	1	3rd PM	16-N	13-W
GREENUP	**17**	1	3rd PM	13-N	10-W
GREGORY	**10**	6	3rd PM	15-N	9-W
" "	**13**	1	3rd PM	14-N	10-W
GRIDER	**14**	1	3rd PM	14-N	9-W
GRIFFITTS	**2**	1	3rd PM	16-N	12-W
GRIGG	**11**	14	3rd PM	15-N	8-W
" "	**13**	10	3rd PM	14-N	10-W
" "	**2**	8	3rd PM	16-N	12-W
" "	**6**	8	3rd PM	16-N	8-W

Surname	Map Group	Parcels of Land	Meridian/Township/Range
GRIGG (Cont'd)	**18**	6	3rd PM 13-N 9-W
" "	**15**	6	3rd PM 14-N 8-W
" "	**19**	5	3rd PM 13-N 8-W
" "	**4**	3	3rd PM 16-N 10-W
" "	**17**	2	3rd PM 13-N 10-W
" "	**16**	2	3rd PM 13-N 11-W
" "	**12**	2	3rd PM 14-N 11-W
" "	**8**	1	3rd PM 15-N 11-W
" "	**7**	1	3rd PM 15-N 12-W
GRIGGS	**6**	11	3rd PM 16-N 8-W
" "	**17**	1	3rd PM 13-N 10-W
GRIMSLEY	**13**	2	3rd PM 14-N 10-W
" "	**18**	1	3rd PM 13-N 9-W
" "	**9**	1	3rd PM 15-N 10-W
GROUT	**3**	2	3rd PM 16-N 11-W
GROVES	**19**	3	3rd PM 13-N 8-W
GUM	**17**	1	3rd PM 13-N 10-W
" "	**13**	1	3rd PM 14-N 10-W
GUNN	**17**	7	3rd PM 13-N 10-W
" "	**13**	2	3rd PM 14-N 10-W
GUNNELS	**18**	1	3rd PM 13-N 9-W
GWENS	**19**	1	3rd PM 13-N 8-W
HACKETT	**9**	2	3rd PM 15-N 10-W
" "	**16**	1	3rd PM 13-N 11-W
HAEFFNER	**1**	1	3rd PM 16-N 13-W
HAGGARD	**15**	3	3rd PM 14-N 8-W
" "	**3**	2	3rd PM 16-N 11-W
" "	**19**	1	3rd PM 13-N 8-W
HAHN	**16**	2	3rd PM 13-N 11-W
HALL	**6**	8	3rd PM 16-N 8-W
" "	**15**	3	3rd PM 14-N 8-W
" "	**18**	2	3rd PM 13-N 9-W
" "	**5**	2	3rd PM 16-N 9-W
" "	**8**	1	3rd PM 15-N 11-W
" "	**4**	1	3rd PM 16-N 10-W
" "	**3**	1	3rd PM 16-N 11-W
" "	**2**	1	3rd PM 16-N 12-W
HAM	**2**	4	3rd PM 16-N 12-W
" "	**15**	2	3rd PM 14-N 8-W
" "	**3**	2	3rd PM 16-N 11-W
" "	**18**	1	3rd PM 13-N 9-W
HAMAKER	**4**	1	3rd PM 16-N 10-W
HAMBROUGH	**8**	1	3rd PM 15-N 11-W
HAMILTON	**14**	5	3rd PM 14-N 9-W
" "	**9**	5	3rd PM 15-N 10-W
" "	**17**	2	3rd PM 13-N 10-W
" "	**18**	2	3rd PM 13-N 9-W
" "	**7**	2	3rd PM 15-N 12-W
" "	**13**	1	3rd PM 14-N 10-W
" "	**8**	1	3rd PM 15-N 11-W
" "	**1**	1	3rd PM 16-N 13-W
HAMMER	**19**	1	3rd PM 13-N 8-W
HAMPTON	**19**	1	3rd PM 13-N 8-W
HANDY	**9**	2	3rd PM 15-N 10-W
HANES	**16**	5	3rd PM 13-N 11-W
HANEY	**12**	3	3rd PM 14-N 11-W
HARDIN	**5**	8	3rd PM 16-N 9-W
" "	**10**	6	3rd PM 15-N 9-W
" "	**17**	1	3rd PM 13-N 10-W
" "	**4**	1	3rd PM 16-N 10-W

Surname	Map Group	Parcels of Land	Meridian/Township/Range		
HARDING	5	2	3rd PM	16-N	9-W
HARGROVE	4	1	3rd PM	16-N	10-W
HARLAN	18	1	3rd PM	13-N	9-W
HARNAKER	3	1	3rd PM	16-N	11-W
HARNEY	13	5	3rd PM	14-N	10-W
" "	18	1	3rd PM	13-N	9-W
HARP	14	8	3rd PM	14-N	9-W
" "	16	1	3rd PM	13-N	11-W
" "	18	1	3rd PM	13-N	9-W
HARRIS	3	4	3rd PM	16-N	11-W
" "	15	2	3rd PM	14-N	8-W
" "	19	1	3rd PM	13-N	8-W
" "	18	1	3rd PM	13-N	9-W
" "	2	1	3rd PM	16-N	12-W
HARRISON	4	1	3rd PM	16-N	10-W
" "	5	1	3rd PM	16-N	9-W
HARRISS	19	1	3rd PM	13-N	8-W
HART	18	23	3rd PM	13-N	9-W
" "	19	4	3rd PM	13-N	8-W
HARTMORE	9	1	3rd PM	15-N	10-W
HARTWELL	1	1	3rd PM	16-N	13-W
HARVEY	13	2	3rd PM	14-N	10-W
HARVY	8	1	3rd PM	15-N	11-W
HATCH	2	2	3rd PM	16-N	12-W
HATCHER	12	3	3rd PM	14-N	11-W
HATFIELD	2	1	3rd PM	16-N	12-W
HAWN	1	1	3rd PM	16-N	13-W
HAYES	9	1	3rd PM	15-N	10-W
" "	1	1	3rd PM	16-N	13-W
HAYNES	18	5	3rd PM	13-N	9-W
" "	5	2	3rd PM	16-N	9-W
HAYWARD	2	1	3rd PM	16-N	12-W
HEADINGTON	18	2	3rd PM	13-N	9-W
HEDENBERG	13	1	3rd PM	14-N	10-W
" "	14	1	3rd PM	14-N	9-W
" "	9	1	3rd PM	15-N	10-W
HEDENBURG	14	1	3rd PM	14-N	9-W
HEDINBERG	14	1	3rd PM	14-N	9-W
HEMBROUGH	8	3	3rd PM	15-N	11-W
HEMMINGHAUS	2	1	3rd PM	16-N	12-W
HEMSTED	4	1	3rd PM	16-N	10-W
HENDERSHOT	4	3	3rd PM	16-N	10-W
HENDERSON	4	9	3rd PM	16-N	10-W
" "	3	8	3rd PM	16-N	11-W
" "	12	2	3rd PM	14-N	11-W
" "	10	2	3rd PM	15-N	9-W
HENDRICK	5	1	3rd PM	16-N	9-W
HENRY	17	13	3rd PM	13-N	10-W
" "	13	6	3rd PM	14-N	10-W
" "	6	5	3rd PM	16-N	8-W
" "	18	3	3rd PM	13-N	9-W
" "	8	2	3rd PM	15-N	11-W
HENSON	8	1	3rd PM	15-N	11-W
HEREN	16	1	3rd PM	13-N	11-W
HERRIN	16	1	3rd PM	13-N	11-W
HERRING	17	1	3rd PM	13-N	10-W
" "	16	1	3rd PM	13-N	11-W
HEUY	17	1	3rd PM	13-N	10-W
HEWETT	10	5	3rd PM	15-N	9-W
HEWITT	10	2	3rd PM	15-N	9-W

Surname	Map Group	Parcels of Land	Meridian/Township/Range
HIBARD	**8**	1	3rd PM 15-N 11-W
HICKENBOTTOM	**10**	1	3rd PM 15-N 9-W
HICKEY	**1**	1	3rd PM 16-N 13-W
HICKMAN	**17**	1	3rd PM 13-N 10-W
HICKS	**17**	1	3rd PM 13-N 10-W
HILHOUSE	**1**	1	3rd PM 16-N 13-W
HILL	**1**	3	3rd PM 16-N 13-W
\\ //	**2**	2	3rd PM 16-N 12-W
\\ //	**12**	1	3rd PM 14-N 11-W
\\ //	**10**	1	3rd PM 15-N 9-W
HILLARD	**7**	1	3rd PM 15-N 12-W
HILLS	**12**	1	3rd PM 14-N 11-W
HINDES	**18**	1	3rd PM 13-N 9-W
HOAG	**13**	2	3rd PM 14-N 10-W
HOAGLAND	**5**	6	3rd PM 16-N 9-W
HOBBS	**14**	2	3rd PM 14-N 9-W
HOBIN	**5**	1	3rd PM 16-N 9-W
HODGE	**3**	1	3rd PM 16-N 11-W
HODGEN	**10**	1	3rd PM 15-N 9-W
HODGES	**2**	6	3rd PM 16-N 12-W
\\ //	**1**	3	3rd PM 16-N 13-W
HOFFMAN	**9**	1	3rd PM 15-N 10-W
HOGAN	**6**	1	3rd PM 16-N 8-W
HOGIN	**6**	1	3rd PM 16-N 8-W
HOGLIN	**5**	2	3rd PM 16-N 9-W
HOLIDAY	**8**	6	3rd PM 15-N 11-W
HOLLIDAY	**17**	1	3rd PM 13-N 10-W
\\ //	**16**	1	3rd PM 13-N 11-W
HOLME	**8**	4	3rd PM 15-N 11-W
\\ //	**12**	3	3rd PM 14-N 11-W
HOLMES	**5**	9	3rd PM 16-N 9-W
\\ //	**13**	7	3rd PM 14-N 10-W
\\ //	**17**	2	3rd PM 13-N 10-W
\\ //	**10**	2	3rd PM 15-N 9-W
HOMES	**17**	1	3rd PM 13-N 10-W
HOPPER	**17**	2	3rd PM 13-N 10-W
\\ //	**3**	1	3rd PM 16-N 11-W
HORRELL	**12**	1	3rd PM 14-N 11-W
HORTON	**12**	1	3rd PM 14-N 11-W
HOSKINS	**7**	2	3rd PM 15-N 12-W
HOUGHAN	**14**	4	3rd PM 14-N 9-W
\\ //	**15**	2	3rd PM 14-N 8-W
\\ //	**13**	1	3rd PM 14-N 10-W
\\ //	**2**	1	3rd PM 16-N 12-W
HOUSTON	**2**	5	3rd PM 16-N 12-W
\\ //	**3**	3	3rd PM 16-N 11-W
\\ //	**1**	2	3rd PM 16-N 13-W
HOVEY	**1**	1	3rd PM 16-N 13-W
HOWARD	**13**	9	3rd PM 14-N 10-W
\\ //	**18**	4	3rd PM 13-N 9-W
\\ //	**12**	1	3rd PM 14-N 11-W
HOWELL	**1**	1	3rd PM 16-N 13-W
HUDDLESTON	**3**	4	3rd PM 16-N 11-W
\\ //	**4**	3	3rd PM 16-N 10-W
HUDELSON	**2**	5	3rd PM 16-N 12-W
\\ //	**1**	1	3rd PM 16-N 13-W
HUDELSTON	**2**	2	3rd PM 16-N 12-W
HUDSON	**4**	2	3rd PM 16-N 10-W
HUDSPETH	**6**	6	3rd PM 16-N 8-W
\\ //	**5**	1	3rd PM 16-N 9-W

Surname	Map Group	Parcels of Land	Meridian/Township/Range		
HUEY	**15**	12	3rd PM	14-N	8-W
" "	**19**	3	3rd PM	13-N	8-W
" "	**14**	3	3rd PM	14-N	9-W
" "	**18**	1	3rd PM	13-N	9-W
HUFFAKER	**10**	12	3rd PM	15-N	9-W
" "	**15**	5	3rd PM	14-N	8-W
HUGHES	**5**	5	3rd PM	16-N	9-W
" "	**17**	4	3rd PM	13-N	10-W
HUGHS	**5**	1	3rd PM	16-N	9-W
HULL	**17**	2	3rd PM	13-N	10-W
HUMMER	**2**	2	3rd PM	16-N	12-W
HUMPHREY	**3**	1	3rd PM	16-N	11-W
HUNTER	**5**	3	3rd PM	16-N	9-W
" "	**13**	2	3rd PM	14-N	10-W
" "	**14**	1	3rd PM	14-N	9-W
HUNTLY	**19**	1	3rd PM	13-N	8-W
HURST	**18**	1	3rd PM	13-N	9-W
" "	**13**	1	3rd PM	14-N	10-W
" "	**9**	1	3rd PM	15-N	10-W
HURTS	**18**	1	3rd PM	13-N	9-W
HUSSEY	**3**	1	3rd PM	16-N	11-W
HUSTON	**16**	3	3rd PM	13-N	11-W
" "	**3**	1	3rd PM	16-N	11-W
HUTCHESON	**19**	2	3rd PM	13-N	8-W
IDE	**1**	3	3rd PM	16-N	13-W
" "	**2**	2	3rd PM	16-N	12-W
INGALES	**9**	1	3rd PM	15-N	10-W
INGALLS	**9**	2	3rd PM	15-N	10-W
ISRAEL	**9**	1	3rd PM	15-N	10-W
JACKSON	**19**	3	3rd PM	13-N	8-W
" "	**9**	3	3rd PM	15-N	10-W
" "	**15**	2	3rd PM	14-N	8-W
" "	**5**	2	3rd PM	16-N	9-W
" "	**1**	1	3rd PM	16-N	13-W
JAMES	**8**	3	3rd PM	15-N	11-W
" "	**5**	2	3rd PM	16-N	9-W
" "	**12**	1	3rd PM	14-N	11-W
JANUARY	**13**	5	3rd PM	14-N	10-W
" "	**2**	4	3rd PM	16-N	12-W
" "	**18**	1	3rd PM	13-N	9-W
" "	**5**	1	3rd PM	16-N	9-W
JARMAN	**18**	1	3rd PM	13-N	9-W
JARRED	**8**	2	3rd PM	15-N	11-W
JAY	**1**	3	3rd PM	16-N	13-W
" "	**3**	2	3rd PM	16-N	11-W
JAYNE	**12**	1	3rd PM	14-N	11-W
" "	**9**	1	3rd PM	15-N	10-W
" "	**4**	1	3rd PM	16-N	10-W
JENKINS	**13**	1	3rd PM	14-N	10-W
" "	**9**	1	3rd PM	15-N	10-W
" "	**4**	1	3rd PM	16-N	10-W
JOETT	**8**	1	3rd PM	15-N	11-W
JOHNSON	**3**	6	3rd PM	16-N	11-W
" "	**13**	4	3rd PM	14-N	10-W
" "	**8**	3	3rd PM	15-N	11-W
" "	**12**	2	3rd PM	14-N	11-W
" "	**4**	2	3rd PM	16-N	10-W
" "	**14**	1	3rd PM	14-N	9-W
" "	**9**	1	3rd PM	15-N	10-W
" "	**10**	1	3rd PM	15-N	9-W

Surname	Map Group	Parcels of Land	Meridian/Township/Range
JOHNSON (Cont'd)	**2**	1	3rd PM 16-N 12-W
JOHNSTON	**15**	1	3rd PM 14-N 8-W
JOLLY	**14**	1	3rd PM 14-N 9-W
JONES	**8**	13	3rd PM 15-N 11-W
" "	**10**	8	3rd PM 15-N 9-W
" "	**19**	4	3rd PM 13-N 8-W
" "	**18**	4	3rd PM 13-N 9-W
" "	**15**	3	3rd PM 14-N 8-W
" "	**9**	1	3rd PM 15-N 10-W
" "	**4**	1	3rd PM 16-N 10-W
" "	**5**	1	3rd PM 16-N 9-W
JORDEN	**9**	3	3rd PM 15-N 10-W
JOUETT	**8**	1	3rd PM 15-N 11-W
JOURDAN	**9**	1	3rd PM 15-N 10-W
JOURDON	**9**	1	3rd PM 15-N 10-W
JOY	**3**	3	3rd PM 16-N 11-W
KEATH	**13**	1	3rd PM 14-N 10-W
KELLEY	**17**	2	3rd PM 13-N 10-W
KELLOGG	**14**	1	3rd PM 14-N 9-W
KELTNER	**5**	1	3rd PM 16-N 9-W
KENDALL	**16**	2	3rd PM 13-N 11-W
KENNEDY	**17**	1	3rd PM 13-N 10-W
KENNETT	**2**	3	3rd PM 16-N 12-W
KENNEY	**2**	1	3rd PM 16-N 12-W
KEPLINGER	**15**	1	3rd PM 14-N 8-W
" "	**4**	1	3rd PM 16-N 10-W
" "	**5**	1	3rd PM 16-N 9-W
KER	**19**	1	3rd PM 13-N 8-W
KERR	**9**	4	3rd PM 15-N 10-W
" "	**15**	2	3rd PM 14-N 8-W
KERSHAW	**3**	1	3rd PM 16-N 11-W
KETTNER	**5**	1	3rd PM 16-N 9-W
KEYES	**1**	1	3rd PM 16-N 13-W
KIBLINGER	**19**	1	3rd PM 13-N 8-W
KILLAM	**8**	5	3rd PM 15-N 11-W
KILPATRICK	**19**	1	3rd PM 13-N 8-W
KIMBALL	**2**	7	3rd PM 16-N 12-W
" "	**1**	1	3rd PM 16-N 13-W
KING	**14**	8	3rd PM 14-N 9-W
" "	**8**	4	3rd PM 15-N 11-W
" "	**12**	2	3rd PM 14-N 11-W
" "	**3**	1	3rd PM 16-N 11-W
KINGSTON	**17**	1	3rd PM 13-N 10-W
KINNEY	**2**	2	3rd PM 16-N 12-W
KIPLINGER	**18**	1	3rd PM 13-N 9-W
KIRKMAN	**9**	2	3rd PM 15-N 10-W
" "	**17**	1	3rd PM 13-N 10-W
" "	**8**	1	3rd PM 15-N 11-W
KIRKPATRICK	**7**	5	3rd PM 15-N 12-W
" "	**3**	2	3rd PM 16-N 11-W
KLEIN	**13**	2	3rd PM 14-N 10-W
" "	**9**	2	3rd PM 15-N 10-W
" "	**12**	1	3rd PM 14-N 11-W
" "	**3**	1	3rd PM 16-N 11-W
KROSA	**1**	1	3rd PM 16-N 13-W
KROZA	**1**	1	3rd PM 16-N 13-W
KRUSE	**1**	1	3rd PM 16-N 13-W
LAKE	**1**	1	3rd PM 16-N 13-W
LAMB	**15**	5	3rd PM 14-N 8-W
LAMM	**17**	1	3rd PM 13-N 10-W

Surname	Map Group	Parcels of Land	Meridian/Township/Range		
LAMME	**17**	1	3rd PM	13-N	10-W
LANDRETH	**19**	1	3rd PM	13-N	8-W
LANDRUM	**12**	1	3rd PM	14-N	11-W
LANHAM	**19**	1	3rd PM	13-N	8-W
" "	**5**	1	3rd PM	16-N	9-W
LARIMORE	**4**	4	3rd PM	16-N	10-W
" "	**9**	3	3rd PM	15-N	10-W
LATIMER	**10**	1	3rd PM	15-N	9-W
LAUGHERY	**3**	1	3rd PM	16-N	11-W
LAURIE	**4**	1	3rd PM	16-N	10-W
LAW	**8**	1	3rd PM	15-N	11-W
LAYCOCK	**3**	1	3rd PM	16-N	11-W
LAYTON	**3**	3	3rd PM	16-N	11-W
LAZEMBY	**8**	1	3rd PM	15-N	11-W
LEACH	**12**	1	3rd PM	14-N	11-W
LEE	**8**	1	3rd PM	15-N	11-W
" "	**2**	1	3rd PM	16-N	12-W
LEEPER	**9**	4	3rd PM	15-N	10-W
" "	**14**	2	3rd PM	14-N	9-W
LEFFLER	**3**	8	3rd PM	16-N	11-W
" "	**13**	4	3rd PM	14-N	10-W
LEICH	**8**	2	3rd PM	15-N	11-W
LEIGHTON	**17**	2	3rd PM	13-N	10-W
LEMON	**16**	2	3rd PM	13-N	11-W
LENARD	**2**	1	3rd PM	16-N	12-W
LEONARD	**2**	2	3rd PM	16-N	12-W
" "	**17**	1	3rd PM	13-N	10-W
" "	**3**	1	3rd PM	16-N	11-W
LESLIE	**19**	4	3rd PM	13-N	8-W
" "	**18**	3	3rd PM	13-N	9-W
" "	**15**	3	3rd PM	14-N	8-W
" "	**14**	2	3rd PM	14-N	9-W
" "	**8**	1	3rd PM	15-N	11-W
" "	**2**	1	3rd PM	16-N	12-W
LEWIS	**19**	4	3rd PM	13-N	8-W
" "	**12**	2	3rd PM	14-N	11-W
" "	**5**	2	3rd PM	16-N	9-W
" "	**8**	1	3rd PM	15-N	11-W
" "	**7**	1	3rd PM	15-N	12-W
" "	**4**	1	3rd PM	16-N	10-W
" "	**6**	1	3rd PM	16-N	8-W
LINDSEY	**10**	3	3rd PM	15-N	9-W
" "	**4**	2	3rd PM	16-N	10-W
" "	**5**	2	3rd PM	16-N	9-W
LITTON	**5**	3	3rd PM	16-N	9-W
" "	**13**	1	3rd PM	14-N	10-W
" "	**14**	1	3rd PM	14-N	9-W
LOAR	**3**	2	3rd PM	16-N	11-W
" "	**2**	1	3rd PM	16-N	12-W
LOCKWOOD	**9**	1	3rd PM	15-N	10-W
" "	**3**	1	3rd PM	16-N	11-W
LODWICK	**8**	1	3rd PM	15-N	11-W
LOGAN	**10**	1	3rd PM	15-N	9-W
LOGSDON	**19**	1	3rd PM	13-N	8-W
" "	**1**	1	3rd PM	16-N	13-W
LOHR	**3**	2	3rd PM	16-N	11-W
LOLLARS	**19**	1	3rd PM	13-N	8-W
LONDON	**19**	2	3rd PM	13-N	8-W
LONG	**2**	20	3rd PM	16-N	12-W
" "	**1**	7	3rd PM	16-N	13-W

Surname	Map Group	Parcels of Land	Meridian/Township/Range
LONG (Cont'd)	**17**	1	3rd PM 13-N 10-W
LOOSE	**1**	2	3rd PM 16-N 13-W
LOVE	**19**	5	3rd PM 13-N 8-W
LOWRANCE	**16**	2	3rd PM 13-N 11-W
" "	**3**	2	3rd PM 16-N 11-W
LOWRENCE	**3**	1	3rd PM 16-N 11-W
LOWRIE	**9**	1	3rd PM 15-N 10-W
LOYD	**1**	1	3rd PM 16-N 13-W
LUCAS	**1**	1	3rd PM 16-N 13-W
LUDWICK	**7**	4	3rd PM 15-N 12-W
LUMSDEN	**17**	1	3rd PM 13-N 10-W
LUND	**2**	1	3rd PM 16-N 12-W
LUNDAY	**12**	1	3rd PM 14-N 11-W
LURTON	**4**	2	3rd PM 16-N 10-W
LUSK	**14**	1	3rd PM 14-N 9-W
" "	**1**	1	3rd PM 16-N 13-W
LUTRELL	**14**	1	3rd PM 14-N 9-W
LUTTRELL	**18**	6	3rd PM 13-N 9-W
" "	**14**	2	3rd PM 14-N 9-W
LUTTRILL	**18**	1	3rd PM 13-N 9-W
LYNCH	**14**	2	3rd PM 14-N 9-W
MACAIN	**14**	3	3rd PM 14-N 9-W
MACKEY	**3**	1	3rd PM 16-N 11-W
MADDOX	**5**	2	3rd PM 16-N 9-W
" "	**2**	1	3rd PM 16-N 12-W
MADISON	**4**	3	3rd PM 16-N 10-W
MAGILL	**9**	10	3rd PM 15-N 10-W
" "	**10**	3	3rd PM 15-N 9-W
" "	**14**	2	3rd PM 14-N 9-W
" "	**13**	1	3rd PM 14-N 10-W
MAJORS	**9**	2	3rd PM 15-N 10-W
" "	**10**	1	3rd PM 15-N 9-W
MALONE	**5**	1	3rd PM 16-N 9-W
MALONEY	**1**	1	3rd PM 16-N 13-W
MANARY	**2**	1	3rd PM 16-N 12-W
" "	**1**	1	3rd PM 16-N 13-W
MANCHESTER	**7**	4	3rd PM 15-N 12-W
" "	**5**	1	3rd PM 16-N 9-W
MANDAIN	**6**	1	3rd PM 16-N 8-W
MANNING	**2**	2	3rd PM 16-N 12-W
" "	**7**	1	3rd PM 15-N 12-W
" "	**1**	1	3rd PM 16-N 13-W
MANSFIELD	**18**	3	3rd PM 13-N 9-W
MARA	**2**	2	3rd PM 16-N 12-W
MARCH	**10**	2	3rd PM 15-N 9-W
MARKHAM	**8**	1	3rd PM 15-N 11-W
MARSHALL	**8**	3	3rd PM 15-N 11-W
" "	**12**	2	3rd PM 14-N 11-W
" "	**3**	1	3rd PM 16-N 11-W
MARTIN	**3**	3	3rd PM 16-N 11-W
" "	**4**	1	3rd PM 16-N 10-W
MARVIN	**1**	1	3rd PM 16-N 13-W
MASON	**13**	2	3rd PM 14-N 10-W
" "	**2**	2	3rd PM 16-N 12-W
MASSES	**9**	1	3rd PM 15-N 10-W
MASSEY	**12**	1	3rd PM 14-N 11-W
" "	**8**	1	3rd PM 15-N 11-W
MASTERS	**16**	6	3rd PM 13-N 11-W
" "	**8**	1	3rd PM 15-N 11-W
MASTERSON	**2**	5	3rd PM 16-N 12-W

Surname	Map Group	Parcels of Land	Meridian/Township/Range		
MATHERS	**17**	1	3rd PM	13-N	10-W
" "	**5**	1	3rd PM	16-N	9-W
MATHEUS	**2**	1	3rd PM	16-N	12-W
MATHEWS	**10**	9	3rd PM	15-N	9-W
" "	**5**	6	3rd PM	16-N	9-W
" "	**3**	2	3rd PM	16-N	11-W
MATHIS	**1**	2	3rd PM	16-N	13-W
MATHUS	**17**	2	3rd PM	13-N	10-W
MATTHEWS	**10**	3	3rd PM	15-N	9-W
" "	**2**	1	3rd PM	16-N	12-W
" "	**1**	1	3rd PM	16-N	13-W
MATTINGLY	**4**	1	3rd PM	16-N	10-W
MAUPIN	**19**	3	3rd PM	13-N	8-W
MAXFIELD	**12**	1	3rd PM	14-N	11-W
MAY	**1**	3	3rd PM	16-N	13-W
MAYFIELD	**15**	5	3rd PM	14-N	8-W
" "	**14**	1	3rd PM	14-N	9-W
MCALISTER	**13**	3	3rd PM	14-N	10-W
MCALLISTER	**13**	1	3rd PM	14-N	10-W
MCAVOY	**17**	1	3rd PM	13-N	10-W
" "	**13**	1	3rd PM	14-N	10-W
MCCAMMON	**5**	1	3rd PM	16-N	9-W
MCCAULEY	**19**	2	3rd PM	13-N	8-W
MCCEARLEY	**18**	2	3rd PM	13-N	9-W
MCCEARLY	**17**	1	3rd PM	13-N	10-W
" "	**18**	1	3rd PM	13-N	9-W
MCCLEARLY	**18**	1	3rd PM	13-N	9-W
MCCLURE	**4**	4	3rd PM	16-N	10-W
MCCLURR	**5**	1	3rd PM	16-N	9-W
MCCOMB	**3**	1	3rd PM	16-N	11-W
MCCONNEL	**2**	10	3rd PM	16-N	12-W
" "	**3**	5	3rd PM	16-N	11-W
" "	**9**	1	3rd PM	15-N	10-W
" "	**4**	1	3rd PM	16-N	10-W
MCCONNELL	**2**	8	3rd PM	16-N	12-W
" "	**3**	3	3rd PM	16-N	11-W
" "	**9**	2	3rd PM	15-N	10-W
" "	**12**	1	3rd PM	14-N	11-W
" "	**4**	1	3rd PM	16-N	10-W
MCCORMAC	**13**	2	3rd PM	14-N	10-W
MCCORMICK	**14**	5	3rd PM	14-N	9-W
" "	**18**	3	3rd PM	13-N	9-W
" "	**13**	3	3rd PM	14-N	10-W
" "	**15**	2	3rd PM	14-N	8-W
MCCOY	**13**	1	3rd PM	14-N	10-W
" "	**4**	1	3rd PM	16-N	10-W
MCCRACKEN	**16**	1	3rd PM	13-N	11-W
MCCULLEY	**18**	1	3rd PM	13-N	9-W
MCDONALD	**17**	10	3rd PM	13-N	10-W
" "	**16**	5	3rd PM	13-N	11-W
" "	**9**	2	3rd PM	15-N	10-W
" "	**13**	1	3rd PM	14-N	10-W
" "	**4**	1	3rd PM	16-N	10-W
MCELFRESH	**4**	1	3rd PM	16-N	10-W
MCFADDEN	**3**	2	3rd PM	16-N	11-W
MCFALL	**18**	2	3rd PM	13-N	9-W
MCFALLS	**16**	1	3rd PM	13-N	11-W
MCFILLON	**4**	3	3rd PM	16-N	10-W
MCGEE	**3**	3	3rd PM	16-N	11-W
MCGINNIS	**8**	4	3rd PM	15-N	11-W

Surname	Map Group	Parcels of Land	Meridian/Township/Range		
MCKEAND	**13**	1	3rd PM	14-N	10-W
MCKEE	**8**	4	3rd PM	15-N	11-W
" "	**7**	4	3rd PM	15-N	12-W
" "	**17**	2	3rd PM	13-N	10-W
" "	**14**	2	3rd PM	14-N	9-W
MCKINNEY	**8**	2	3rd PM	15-N	11-W
MCKNIGHT	**4**	1	3rd PM	16-N	10-W
MCLAIN	**19**	2	3rd PM	13-N	8-W
MCLAUGHLIN	**17**	1	3rd PM	13-N	10-W
" "	**4**	1	3rd PM	16-N	10-W
MCMURRAY	**10**	1	3rd PM	15-N	9-W
MCMURRY	**10**	4	3rd PM	15-N	9-W
MCNEELY	**18**	1	3rd PM	13-N	9-W
MCPERSON	**2**	1	3rd PM	16-N	12-W
MCPHEETERS	**16**	3	3rd PM	13-N	11-W
MCPHERSON	**2**	5	3rd PM	16-N	12-W
" "	**16**	1	3rd PM	13-N	11-W
" "	**7**	1	3rd PM	15-N	12-W
MCRACKIN	**16**	1	3rd PM	13-N	11-W
MCWAIN	**13**	1	3rd PM	14-N	10-W
MCWILLIAM	**16**	1	3rd PM	13-N	11-W
MEADOWS	**19**	1	3rd PM	13-N	8-W
MEARS	**9**	3	3rd PM	15-N	10-W
MEDCALF	**9**	3	3rd PM	15-N	10-W
MEEK	**1**	1	3rd PM	16-N	13-W
MEEKS	**3**	1	3rd PM	16-N	11-W
MEISENHEIMER	**16**	1	3rd PM	13-N	11-W
METCALF	**9**	1	3rd PM	15-N	10-W
" "	**4**	1	3rd PM	16-N	10-W
MICKEY	**5**	3	3rd PM	16-N	9-W
MILLAM	**1**	1	3rd PM	16-N	13-W
MILLEN	**3**	6	3rd PM	16-N	11-W
" "	**13**	2	3rd PM	14-N	10-W
" "	**8**	2	3rd PM	15-N	11-W
" "	**9**	1	3rd PM	15-N	10-W
MILLER	**8**	3	3rd PM	15-N	11-W
" "	**5**	2	3rd PM	16-N	9-W
" "	**13**	1	3rd PM	14-N	10-W
" "	**12**	1	3rd PM	14-N	11-W
" "	**14**	1	3rd PM	14-N	9-W
" "	**9**	1	3rd PM	15-N	10-W
" "	**2**	1	3rd PM	16-N	12-W
MILLION	**17**	2	3rd PM	13-N	10-W
" "	**13**	2	3rd PM	14-N	10-W
MILLS	**16**	1	3rd PM	13-N	11-W
" "	**8**	1	3rd PM	15-N	11-W
MILNOR	**7**	1	3rd PM	15-N	12-W
MILSTEAD	**7**	1	3rd PM	15-N	12-W
MINER	**15**	9	3rd PM	14-N	8-W
MISENHEIMER	**16**	1	3rd PM	13-N	11-W
MITCHELL	**18**	2	3rd PM	13-N	9-W
" "	**4**	1	3rd PM	16-N	10-W
" "	**2**	1	3rd PM	16-N	12-W
MLODZIANOWSKI	**1**	1	3rd PM	16-N	13-W
MOBLEY	**14**	4	3rd PM	14-N	9-W
" "	**13**	1	3rd PM	14-N	10-W
MONDON	**9**	1	3rd PM	15-N	10-W
MONTGOMERY	**19**	1	3rd PM	13-N	8-W
" "	**12**	1	3rd PM	14-N	11-W
MOODY	**14**	1	3rd PM	14-N	9-W

Surname	Map Group	Parcels of Land	Meridian/Township/Range		
MOORE	**2**	7	3rd PM	16-N	12-W
" "	**10**	3	3rd PM	15-N	9-W
" "	**1**	3	3rd PM	16-N	13-W
" "	**14**	2	3rd PM	14-N	9-W
" "	**12**	1	3rd PM	14-N	11-W
MORGAN	**17**	3	3rd PM	13-N	10-W
" "	**7**	1	3rd PM	15-N	12-W
" "	**5**	1	3rd PM	16-N	9-W
MORLAN	**18**	1	3rd PM	13-N	9-W
MORRELL	**7**	1	3rd PM	15-N	12-W
MORRIS	**8**	1	3rd PM	15-N	11-W
" "	**6**	1	3rd PM	16-N	8-W
MORRISON	**3**	4	3rd PM	16-N	11-W
" "	**4**	1	3rd PM	16-N	10-W
" "	**2**	1	3rd PM	16-N	12-W
" "	**6**	1	3rd PM	16-N	8-W
MORRISS	**6**	1	3rd PM	16-N	8-W
MORSE	**12**	1	3rd PM	14-N	11-W
MORTEN	**13**	1	3rd PM	14-N	10-W
MORTON	**14**	6	3rd PM	14-N	9-W
" "	**9**	2	3rd PM	15-N	10-W
" "	**17**	1	3rd PM	13-N	10-W
" "	**18**	1	3rd PM	13-N	9-W
" "	**10**	1	3rd PM	15-N	9-W
MOSELY	**4**	1	3rd PM	16-N	10-W
" "	**5**	1	3rd PM	16-N	9-W
MOSES	**3**	1	3rd PM	16-N	11-W
MOSS	**3**	7	3rd PM	16-N	11-W
" "	**8**	2	3rd PM	15-N	11-W
" "	**12**	1	3rd PM	14-N	11-W
" "	**4**	1	3rd PM	16-N	10-W
" "	**2**	1	3rd PM	16-N	12-W
MULLEN	**17**	2	3rd PM	13-N	10-W
MUNDAY	**5**	1	3rd PM	16-N	9-W
MURPHEY	**8**	1	3rd PM	15-N	11-W
" "	**7**	1	3rd PM	15-N	12-W
MURPHY	**5**	2	3rd PM	16-N	9-W
" "	**18**	1	3rd PM	13-N	9-W
" "	**8**	1	3rd PM	15-N	11-W
" "	**7**	1	3rd PM	15-N	12-W
" "	**10**	1	3rd PM	15-N	9-W
MURRAY	**16**	2	3rd PM	13-N	11-W
" "	**13**	1	3rd PM	14-N	10-W
" "	**4**	1	3rd PM	16-N	10-W
MURRY	**17**	1	3rd PM	13-N	10-W
" "	**12**	1	3rd PM	14-N	11-W
MUSIC	**1**	1	3rd PM	16-N	13-W
MUSICK	**1**	1	3rd PM	16-N	13-W
NALL	**18**	3	3rd PM	13-N	9-W
NASH	**9**	2	3rd PM	15-N	10-W
NAULTY	**5**	1	3rd PM	16-N	9-W
NEILL	**16**	2	3rd PM	13-N	11-W
NELSON	**17**	4	3rd PM	13-N	10-W
" "	**18**	3	3rd PM	13-N	9-W
" "	**13**	1	3rd PM	14-N	10-W
NEVINS	**19**	1	3rd PM	13-N	8-W
NEW	**7**	2	3rd PM	15-N	12-W
NEWLON	**9**	1	3rd PM	15-N	10-W
NEWMAN	**2**	35	3rd PM	16-N	12-W
" "	**8**	6	3rd PM	15-N	11-W

Surname	Map Group	Parcels of Land	Meridian/Township/Range
NEWMAN (Cont'd)	**9**	3	3rd PM 15-N 10-W
" "	**1**	2	3rd PM 16-N 13-W
NICHOLLS	**18**	3	3rd PM 13-N 9-W
" "	**17**	1	3rd PM 13-N 10-W
NICHOLS	**17**	5	3rd PM 13-N 10-W
" "	**18**	1	3rd PM 13-N 9-W
NICKOL	**18**	1	3rd PM 13-N 9-W
NILES	**5**	1	3rd PM 16-N 9-W
NILSON	**3**	1	3rd PM 16-N 11-W
NISBIT	**4**	1	3rd PM 16-N 10-W
NIX	**15**	1	3rd PM 14-N 8-W
NOLL	**18**	1	3rd PM 13-N 9-W
NORISS	**8**	1	3rd PM 15-N 11-W
NORTHCUT	**13**	1	3rd PM 14-N 10-W
" "	**5**	1	3rd PM 16-N 9-W
NOWLAN	**19**	1	3rd PM 13-N 8-W
NOWLIN	**19**	1	3rd PM 13-N 8-W
NOYES	**19**	1	3rd PM 13-N 8-W
NUNNS	**4**	1	3rd PM 16-N 10-W
OBANION	**6**	1	3rd PM 16-N 8-W
" "	**5**	1	3rd PM 16-N 9-W
OGG	**1**	1	3rd PM 16-N 13-W
OGLE	**4**	4	3rd PM 16-N 10-W
" "	**3**	1	3rd PM 16-N 11-W
OKEAR	**5**	1	3rd PM 16-N 9-W
OKEEFFE	**5**	2	3rd PM 16-N 9-W
OLMSTEAD	**8**	1	3rd PM 15-N 11-W
ONEAL	**11**	2	3rd PM 15-N 8-W
" "	**10**	2	3rd PM 15-N 9-W
OREAR	**5**	11	3rd PM 16-N 9-W
" "	**6**	3	3rd PM 16-N 8-W
ORR	**17**	2	3rd PM 13-N 10-W
" "	**16**	1	3rd PM 13-N 11-W
ORTZ	**2**	1	3rd PM 16-N 12-W
OSBORN	**3**	1	3rd PM 16-N 11-W
OSBORNE	**10**	1	3rd PM 15-N 9-W
OSBOURN	**7**	1	3rd PM 15-N 12-W
OSBURN	**7**	1	3rd PM 15-N 12-W
OSCAR	**5**	1	3rd PM 16-N 9-W
PACK	**18**	1	3rd PM 13-N 9-W
PACKER	**15**	6	3rd PM 14-N 8-W
PALMER	**8**	1	3rd PM 15-N 11-W
PARK	**3**	5	3rd PM 16-N 11-W
" "	**8**	1	3rd PM 15-N 11-W
" "	**4**	1	3rd PM 16-N 10-W
" "	**1**	1	3rd PM 16-N 13-W
PARKASON	**8**	1	3rd PM 15-N 11-W
PARKER	**17**	6	3rd PM 13-N 10-W
" "	**2**	2	3rd PM 16-N 12-W
" "	**16**	1	3rd PM 13-N 11-W
" "	**4**	1	3rd PM 16-N 10-W
" "	**1**	1	3rd PM 16-N 13-W
PARKINSON	**14**	6	3rd PM 14-N 9-W
" "	**18**	1	3rd PM 13-N 9-W
" "	**9**	1	3rd PM 15-N 10-W
" "	**8**	1	3rd PM 15-N 11-W
PARKISON	**14**	1	3rd PM 14-N 9-W
PARKS	**3**	1	3rd PM 16-N 11-W
" "	**1**	1	3rd PM 16-N 13-W
PARR	**5**	1	3rd PM 16-N 9-W

Surname	Map Group	Parcels of Land	Meridian/Township/Range		
PARROTT	6	1	3rd PM	16-N	8-W
" "	5	1	3rd PM	16-N	9-W
PATRICK	4	1	3rd PM	16-N	10-W
PATTEN	8	1	3rd PM	15-N	11-W
PATTERSON	4	5	3rd PM	16-N	10-W
" "	18	2	3rd PM	13-N	9-W
" "	13	2	3rd PM	14-N	10-W
" "	1	1	3rd PM	16-N	13-W
PATTON	4	2	3rd PM	16-N	10-W
PEARCY	19	1	3rd PM	13-N	8-W
PEARSON	18	1	3rd PM	13-N	9-W
" "	5	1	3rd PM	16-N	9-W
PEMBERTON	10	5	3rd PM	15-N	9-W
" "	14	2	3rd PM	14-N	9-W
" "	15	1	3rd PM	14-N	8-W
PENNOYER	16	5	3rd PM	13-N	11-W
PENSON	4	2	3rd PM	16-N	10-W
PERKINS	4	1	3rd PM	16-N	10-W
PERVIANCE	2	1	3rd PM	16-N	12-W
" "	5	1	3rd PM	16-N	9-W
PERVINE	3	1	3rd PM	16-N	11-W
PETER	14	1	3rd PM	14-N	9-W
PETERS	3	1	3rd PM	16-N	11-W
PETREE	14	3	3rd PM	14-N	9-W
PETTYJOHN	18	1	3rd PM	13-N	9-W
PEXTON	14	2	3rd PM	14-N	9-W
" "	18	1	3rd PM	13-N	9-W
PFEIL	3	2	3rd PM	16-N	11-W
PHEASANT	3	1	3rd PM	16-N	11-W
PHIEL	3	1	3rd PM	16-N	11-W
PHILIPPI	3	4	3rd PM	16-N	11-W
PHILIPS	5	2	3rd PM	16-N	9-W
PHILLIPS	17	1	3rd PM	13-N	10-W
PIPER	18	1	3rd PM	13-N	9-W
PITNER	9	3	3rd PM	15-N	10-W
PLANTE	1	4	3rd PM	16-N	13-W
POCKLINGTON	8	1	3rd PM	15-N	11-W
POINDEXTER	5	2	3rd PM	16-N	9-W
POINTER	2	5	3rd PM	16-N	12-W
" "	1	4	3rd PM	16-N	13-W
POLAND	17	3	3rd PM	13-N	10-W
POND	2	6	3rd PM	16-N	12-W
POOL	15	1	3rd PM	14-N	8-W
PORTER	14	1	3rd PM	14-N	9-W
" "	10	1	3rd PM	15-N	9-W
" "	4	1	3rd PM	16-N	10-W
POSEY	9	2	3rd PM	15-N	10-W
POST	2	9	3rd PM	16-N	12-W
POWELL	8	1	3rd PM	15-N	11-W
POWERS	9	1	3rd PM	15-N	10-W
PRATHER	4	1	3rd PM	16-N	10-W
PRATT	1	1	3rd PM	16-N	13-W
PRENTICE	12	5	3rd PM	14-N	11-W
PREVOST	3	4	3rd PM	16-N	11-W
" "	2	2	3rd PM	16-N	12-W
PREWITT	7	1	3rd PM	15-N	12-W
PRICE	3	2	3rd PM	16-N	11-W
" "	2	2	3rd PM	16-N	12-W
" "	9	1	3rd PM	15-N	10-W
" "	4	1	3rd PM	16-N	10-W

Surname	Map Group	Parcels of Land	Meridian/Township/Range
PRICE (Cont'd)	**5**	1	3rd PM 16-N 9-W
PRIEST	**2**	1	3rd PM 16-N 12-W
PROCTOR	**4**	2	3rd PM 16-N 10-W
PROSSEE	**15**	1	3rd PM 14-N 8-W
" "	**14**	1	3rd PM 14-N 9-W
PROVOST	**2**	2	3rd PM 16-N 12-W
PUCKETT	**2**	1	3rd PM 16-N 12-W
PURKITT	**3**	4	3rd PM 16-N 11-W
PURVIANCE	**5**	6	3rd PM 16-N 9-W
" "	**4**	5	3rd PM 16-N 10-W
" "	**2**	1	3rd PM 16-N 12-W
PURVINE	**3**	3	3rd PM 16-N 11-W
" "	**2**	3	3rd PM 16-N 12-W
" "	**1**	1	3rd PM 16-N 13-W
PYLE	**4**	1	3rd PM 16-N 10-W
RAFFERTY	**12**	1	3rd PM 14-N 11-W
RANNELLS	**17**	2	3rd PM 13-N 10-W
" "	**14**	1	3rd PM 14-N 9-W
RANSDELL	**14**	6	3rd PM 14-N 9-W
" "	**18**	2	3rd PM 13-N 9-W
RANSON	**2**	3	3rd PM 16-N 12-W
" "	**12**	1	3rd PM 14-N 11-W
" "	**3**	1	3rd PM 16-N 11-W
RATLIFF	**3**	4	3rd PM 16-N 11-W
RATLIFFE	**3**	1	3rd PM 16-N 11-W
RAUGH	**12**	1	3rd PM 14-N 11-W
RAWLIN	**14**	1	3rd PM 14-N 9-W
RAWNELLS	**14**	1	3rd PM 14-N 9-W
RAY	**5**	1	3rd PM 16-N 9-W
RAYBON	**2**	1	3rd PM 16-N 12-W
REAKER	**2**	1	3rd PM 16-N 12-W
REAM	**4**	4	3rd PM 16-N 10-W
REAUGH	**17**	15	3rd PM 13-N 10-W
" "	**12**	2	3rd PM 14-N 11-W
" "	**13**	1	3rd PM 14-N 10-W
REDDING	**9**	3	3rd PM 15-N 10-W
" "	**2**	1	3rd PM 16-N 12-W
REDING	**4**	2	3rd PM 16-N 10-W
REDMAN	**5**	2	3rd PM 16-N 9-W
REDMON	**5**	1	3rd PM 16-N 9-W
REED	**19**	7	3rd PM 13-N 8-W
" "	**18**	3	3rd PM 13-N 9-W
" "	**8**	3	3rd PM 15-N 11-W
" "	**1**	3	3rd PM 16-N 13-W
" "	**7**	2	3rd PM 15-N 12-W
" "	**4**	1	3rd PM 16-N 10-W
REES	**18**	2	3rd PM 13-N 9-W
REEVE	**9**	2	3rd PM 15-N 10-W
" "	**13**	1	3rd PM 14-N 10-W
" "	**10**	1	3rd PM 15-N 9-W
REEVES	**5**	1	3rd PM 16-N 9-W
REEVIS	**5**	1	3rd PM 16-N 9-W
REID	**9**	11	3rd PM 15-N 10-W
" "	**4**	5	3rd PM 16-N 10-W
" "	**16**	2	3rd PM 13-N 11-W
" "	**8**	1	3rd PM 15-N 11-W
" "	**7**	1	3rd PM 15-N 12-W
" "	**3**	1	3rd PM 16-N 11-W
REOUSEY	**17**	1	3rd PM 13-N 10-W
REXROOT	**4**	1	3rd PM 16-N 10-W

Surname	Map Group	Parcels of Land	Meridian/Township/Range
REXROTE	4	1	3rd PM 16-N 10-W
" "	3	1	3rd PM 16-N 11-W
REXROUT	4	2	3rd PM 16-N 10-W
REYNOLDS	14	5	3rd PM 14-N 9-W
" "	18	3	3rd PM 13-N 9-W
" "	19	1	3rd PM 13-N 8-W
RHEA	19	2	3rd PM 13-N 8-W
" "	11	1	3rd PM 15-N 8-W
RHODES	18	2	3rd PM 13-N 9-W
" "	12	1	3rd PM 14-N 11-W
RHORER	19	1	3rd PM 13-N 8-W
RICE	19	2	3rd PM 13-N 8-W
" "	10	1	3rd PM 15-N 9-W
RICHARDS	8	3	3rd PM 15-N 11-W
" "	4	2	3rd PM 16-N 10-W
RICHARDSON	14	6	3rd PM 14-N 9-W
" "	18	4	3rd PM 13-N 9-W
" "	8	4	3rd PM 15-N 11-W
" "	3	3	3rd PM 16-N 11-W
" "	19	1	3rd PM 13-N 8-W
RIDGLEY	14	4	3rd PM 14-N 9-W
" "	13	1	3rd PM 14-N 10-W
RIEMAN	1	2	3rd PM 16-N 13-W
RIGGIN	14	1	3rd PM 14-N 9-W
" "	10	1	3rd PM 15-N 9-W
RIMBEY	17	8	3rd PM 13-N 10-W
ROACH	10	3	3rd PM 15-N 9-W
" "	4	1	3rd PM 16-N 10-W
ROBB	16	1	3rd PM 13-N 11-W
ROBERTS	18	5	3rd PM 13-N 9-W
" "	4	5	3rd PM 16-N 10-W
" "	19	1	3rd PM 13-N 8-W
ROBERTSON	10	4	3rd PM 15-N 9-W
" "	4	2	3rd PM 16-N 10-W
" "	3	1	3rd PM 16-N 11-W
" "	5	1	3rd PM 16-N 9-W
ROBESON	6	3	3rd PM 16-N 8-W
ROBESSON	4	1	3rd PM 16-N 10-W
ROBINSON	6	8	3rd PM 16-N 8-W
" "	13	4	3rd PM 14-N 10-W
" "	5	4	3rd PM 16-N 9-W
" "	18	3	3rd PM 13-N 9-W
" "	17	2	3rd PM 13-N 10-W
" "	9	2	3rd PM 15-N 10-W
" "	4	2	3rd PM 16-N 10-W
" "	2	1	3rd PM 16-N 12-W
ROBISON	6	2	3rd PM 16-N 8-W
" "	10	1	3rd PM 15-N 9-W
ROBLEY	13	2	3rd PM 14-N 10-W
" "	9	1	3rd PM 15-N 10-W
ROCKWELL	13	2	3rd PM 14-N 10-W
" "	8	2	3rd PM 15-N 11-W
ROGERS	19	3	3rd PM 13-N 8-W
" "	10	3	3rd PM 15-N 9-W
ROGES	10	2	3rd PM 15-N 9-W
ROHER	19	1	3rd PM 13-N 8-W
ROHRER	19	14	3rd PM 13-N 8-W
ROLAND	18	2	3rd PM 13-N 9-W
ROLL	4	1	3rd PM 16-N 10-W
ROLLINS	9	1	3rd PM 15-N 10-W

Surname	Map Group	Parcels of Land	Meridian/Township/Range
RONSEY	**17**	1	3rd PM 13-N 10-W
ROSE	**17**	1	3rd PM 13-N 10-W
ROSS	**19**	3	3rd PM 13-N 8-W
" "	**4**	3	3rd PM 16-N 10-W
ROSSON	**19**	3	3rd PM 13-N 8-W
ROUNDS	**1**	2	3rd PM 16-N 13-W
" "	**7**	1	3rd PM 15-N 12-W
ROUSEY	**17**	8	3rd PM 13-N 10-W
ROUTT	**13**	4	3rd PM 14-N 10-W
RUARK	**9**	1	3rd PM 15-N 10-W
RUBART	**3**	4	3rd PM 16-N 11-W
" "	**10**	2	3rd PM 15-N 9-W
RUBLE	**9**	4	3rd PM 15-N 10-W
" "	**4**	2	3rd PM 16-N 10-W
" "	**11**	1	3rd PM 15-N 8-W
" "	**5**	1	3rd PM 16-N 9-W
RUCKER	**17**	1	3rd PM 13-N 10-W
" "	**4**	1	3rd PM 16-N 10-W
RUDE	**5**	1	3rd PM 16-N 9-W
RUDISELL	**4**	1	3rd PM 16-N 10-W
RULON	**1**	1	3rd PM 16-N 13-W
RUSK	**10**	2	3rd PM 15-N 9-W
" "	**5**	2	3rd PM 16-N 9-W
" "	**9**	1	3rd PM 15-N 10-W
RUSSEL	**17**	19	3rd PM 13-N 10-W
" "	**15**	1	3rd PM 14-N 8-W
" "	**14**	1	3rd PM 14-N 9-W
RUSSELL	**17**	11	3rd PM 13-N 10-W
" "	**13**	2	3rd PM 14-N 10-W
" "	**19**	1	3rd PM 13-N 8-W
RUTHERFORD	**10**	1	3rd PM 15-N 9-W
" "	**5**	1	3rd PM 16-N 9-W
RUYLE	**14**	2	3rd PM 14-N 9-W
" "	**10**	2	3rd PM 15-N 9-W
RUYNKLE	**5**	1	3rd PM 16-N 9-W
RYNDERS	**19**	1	3rd PM 13-N 8-W
SACKETT	**4**	2	3rd PM 16-N 10-W
" "	**5**	1	3rd PM 16-N 9-W
SADDLER	**9**	1	3rd PM 15-N 10-W
SAGE	**5**	1	3rd PM 16-N 9-W
SAIGHMAN	**7**	2	3rd PM 15-N 12-W
SALLEE	**4**	1	3rd PM 16-N 10-W
SALTER	**19**	18	3rd PM 13-N 8-W
" "	**18**	2	3rd PM 13-N 9-W
SAMMONS	**3**	1	3rd PM 16-N 11-W
SAMPLE	**19**	7	3rd PM 13-N 8-W
" "	**9**	3	3rd PM 15-N 10-W
" "	**14**	1	3rd PM 14-N 9-W
" "	**5**	1	3rd PM 16-N 9-W
SAMPLES	**9**	2	3rd PM 15-N 10-W
" "	**15**	1	3rd PM 14-N 8-W
" "	**14**	1	3rd PM 14-N 9-W
SANNDERSON	**19**	3	3rd PM 13-N 8-W
SAPPINGTON	**14**	2	3rd PM 14-N 9-W
SARGEANT	**8**	5	3rd PM 15-N 11-W
SARGENT	**8**	2	3rd PM 15-N 11-W
SAUNDERSON	**14**	4	3rd PM 14-N 9-W
SAVAGE	**8**	3	3rd PM 15-N 11-W
SAXTON	**2**	2	3rd PM 16-N 12-W
" "	**9**	1	3rd PM 15-N 10-W

Surname	Map Group	Parcels of Land	Meridian/Township/Range
SCARTH	**18**	1	3rd PM 13-N 9-W
" "	**14**	1	3rd PM 14-N 9-W
SCOGGINS	**4**	1	3rd PM 16-N 10-W
SCOTT	**10**	7	3rd PM 15-N 9-W
" "	**19**	3	3rd PM 13-N 8-W
" "	**4**	3	3rd PM 16-N 10-W
" "	**15**	2	3rd PM 14-N 8-W
" "	**14**	2	3rd PM 14-N 9-W
" "	**16**	1	3rd PM 13-N 11-W
" "	**18**	1	3rd PM 13-N 9-W
" "	**9**	1	3rd PM 15-N 10-W
" "	**5**	1	3rd PM 16-N 9-W
SCROGGIN	**9**	2	3rd PM 15-N 10-W
" "	**14**	1	3rd PM 14-N 9-W
SCROGGINS	**4**	1	3rd PM 16-N 10-W
SEAMORE	**18**	3	3rd PM 13-N 9-W
SEARTH	**15**	1	3rd PM 14-N 8-W
SEDGWICK	**4**	1	3rd PM 16-N 10-W
SEMOORE	**18**	1	3rd PM 13-N 9-W
SERALES	**8**	2	3rd PM 15-N 11-W
SEVIDE	**19**	1	3rd PM 13-N 8-W
SEWALL	**5**	1	3rd PM 16-N 9-W
SEYMORE	**18**	13	3rd PM 13-N 9-W
SEYMOUR	**18**	1	3rd PM 13-N 9-W
SHALDON	**2**	1	3rd PM 16-N 12-W
SHARP	**3**	2	3rd PM 16-N 11-W
" "	**4**	1	3rd PM 16-N 10-W
SHARTZER	**8**	2	3rd PM 15-N 11-W
SHEARER	**15**	2	3rd PM 14-N 8-W
SHEETS	**3**	1	3rd PM 16-N 11-W
SHEFLER	**17**	1	3rd PM 13-N 10-W
SHELTON	**14**	2	3rd PM 14-N 9-W
SHEPARD	**13**	1	3rd PM 14-N 10-W
" "	**12**	1	3rd PM 14-N 11-W
SHEPHERD	**13**	6	3rd PM 14-N 10-W
" "	**4**	3	3rd PM 16-N 10-W
" "	**18**	1	3rd PM 13-N 9-W
" "	**3**	1	3rd PM 16-N 11-W
" "	**5**	1	3rd PM 16-N 9-W
SHEPLER	**17**	1	3rd PM 13-N 10-W
SHEPPARD	**18**	2	3rd PM 13-N 9-W
" "	**13**	1	3rd PM 14-N 10-W
SHEUMAKER	**17**	1	3rd PM 13-N 10-W
SHEWSBERRY	**3**	2	3rd PM 16-N 11-W
SHIBE	**10**	2	3rd PM 15-N 9-W
SHIPLAR	**17**	1	3rd PM 13-N 10-W
SHIPLER	**17**	1	3rd PM 13-N 10-W
SHIRTCLIFF	**12**	1	3rd PM 14-N 11-W
SHOEMAKER	**2**	1	3rd PM 16-N 12-W
SHORES	**18**	5	3rd PM 13-N 9-W
SHORT	**5**	2	3rd PM 16-N 9-W
" "	**3**	1	3rd PM 16-N 11-W
" "	**6**	1	3rd PM 16-N 8-W
SHREWBURY	**4**	1	3rd PM 16-N 10-W
SHREWSBERRY	**3**	1	3rd PM 16-N 11-W
SHUFF	**10**	1	3rd PM 15-N 9-W
SHUMAKER	**12**	1	3rd PM 14-N 11-W
SHURTLEFF	**19**	4	3rd PM 13-N 8-W
SHURTLIFF	**19**	1	3rd PM 13-N 8-W
SIBERT	**2**	4	3rd PM 16-N 12-W

Surname	Map Group	Parcels of Land	Meridian/Township/Range		
SILES	**3**	1	3rd PM	16-N	11-W
SIMMONS	**8**	3	3rd PM	15-N	11-W
" "	**7**	1	3rd PM	15-N	12-W
SIMMS	**14**	2	3rd PM	14-N	9-W
" "	**8**	2	3rd PM	15-N	11-W
" "	**13**	1	3rd PM	14-N	10-W
" "	**9**	1	3rd PM	15-N	10-W
SIMPLOT	**7**	1	3rd PM	15-N	12-W
SIMS	**19**	7	3rd PM	13-N	8-W
" "	**4**	4	3rd PM	16-N	10-W
" "	**6**	3	3rd PM	16-N	8-W
" "	**17**	1	3rd PM	13-N	10-W
" "	**5**	1	3rd PM	16-N	9-W
SINCLAIR	**5**	12	3rd PM	16-N	9-W
SLAT	**4**	1	3rd PM	16-N	10-W
SLATTEN	**4**	2	3rd PM	16-N	10-W
" "	**9**	1	3rd PM	15-N	10-W
" "	**10**	1	3rd PM	15-N	9-W
" "	**5**	1	3rd PM	16-N	9-W
SLATTER	**10**	1	3rd PM	15-N	9-W
SLATTIN	**10**	4	3rd PM	15-N	9-W
SMADLEY	**17**	1	3rd PM	13-N	10-W
SMART	**7**	4	3rd PM	15-N	12-W
" "	**3**	2	3rd PM	16-N	11-W
" "	**2**	1	3rd PM	16-N	12-W
SMEDLEY	**13**	3	3rd PM	14-N	10-W
" "	**10**	3	3rd PM	15-N	9-W
SMIDLEY	**13**	4	3rd PM	14-N	10-W
SMITH	**5**	21	3rd PM	16-N	9-W
" "	**3**	18	3rd PM	16-N	11-W
" "	**13**	8	3rd PM	14-N	10-W
" "	**1**	8	3rd PM	16-N	13-W
" "	**12**	6	3rd PM	14-N	11-W
" "	**9**	6	3rd PM	15-N	10-W
" "	**7**	5	3rd PM	15-N	12-W
" "	**19**	4	3rd PM	13-N	8-W
" "	**4**	4	3rd PM	16-N	10-W
" "	**2**	4	3rd PM	16-N	12-W
" "	**17**	3	3rd PM	13-N	10-W
" "	**16**	2	3rd PM	13-N	11-W
" "	**8**	1	3rd PM	15-N	11-W
" "	**11**	1	3rd PM	15-N	8-W
" "	**10**	1	3rd PM	15-N	9-W
SNOW	**18**	2	3rd PM	13-N	9-W
SOLOMON	**9**	1	3rd PM	15-N	10-W
SOOY	**17**	1	3rd PM	13-N	10-W
SOWRY	**18**	1	3rd PM	13-N	9-W
SPAINHOWER	**14**	1	3rd PM	14-N	9-W
SPARKS	**5**	2	3rd PM	16-N	9-W
" "	**18**	1	3rd PM	13-N	9-W
SPATES	**2**	1	3rd PM	16-N	12-W
SPAULDING	**5**	1	3rd PM	16-N	9-W
SPEANHOWER	**14**	1	3rd PM	14-N	9-W
SPEARMAN	**4**	2	3rd PM	16-N	10-W
SPEARS	**9**	1	3rd PM	15-N	10-W
SPENCER	**9**	8	3rd PM	15-N	10-W
" "	**4**	4	3rd PM	16-N	10-W
" "	**17**	3	3rd PM	13-N	10-W
" "	**8**	2	3rd PM	15-N	11-W
" "	**2**	1	3rd PM	16-N	12-W

Surname	Map Group	Parcels of Land	Meridian/Township/Range
SPERRY	18	1	3rd PM 13-N 9-W
SPIRES	18	4	3rd PM 13-N 9-W
" "	14	2	3rd PM 14-N 9-W
" "	17	1	3rd PM 13-N 10-W
SPOTSWOOD	10	10	3rd PM 15-N 9-W
SPOTWOOD	10	2	3rd PM 15-N 9-W
SPRAGUE	8	1	3rd PM 15-N 11-W
SPRINGER	19	1	3rd PM 13-N 8-W
" "	13	1	3rd PM 14-N 10-W
ST LEWIS	19	2	3rd PM 13-N 8-W
STACY	4	2	3rd PM 16-N 10-W
" "	9	1	3rd PM 15-N 10-W
STAGNER	14	1	3rd PM 14-N 9-W
STAMPS	4	1	3rd PM 16-N 10-W
STANDLEY	3	2	3rd PM 16-N 11-W
STANLEY	3	2	3rd PM 16-N 11-W
STANLY	3	1	3rd PM 16-N 11-W
STAPLETON	5	2	3rd PM 16-N 9-W
STARMER	4	5	3rd PM 16-N 10-W
" "	3	2	3rd PM 16-N 11-W
STARR	1	2	3rd PM 16-N 13-W
STAUDLEY	8	1	3rd PM 15-N 11-W
STEBBINS	13	1	3rd PM 14-N 10-W
" "	9	1	3rd PM 15-N 10-W
STEEL	19	1	3rd PM 13-N 8-W
STEELE	19	1	3rd PM 13-N 8-W
STEIR	8	1	3rd PM 15-N 11-W
STEPHENSON	10	5	3rd PM 15-N 9-W
" "	4	1	3rd PM 16-N 10-W
STETTINIUS	13	3	3rd PM 14-N 10-W
STEWART	1	5	3rd PM 16-N 13-W
" "	18	2	3rd PM 13-N 9-W
" "	16	1	3rd PM 13-N 11-W
" "	8	1	3rd PM 15-N 11-W
" "	7	1	3rd PM 15-N 12-W
STICE	18	1	3rd PM 13-N 9-W
STILLWELL	12	1	3rd PM 14-N 11-W
STITES	2	5	3rd PM 16-N 12-W
" "	1	1	3rd PM 16-N 13-W
STITINIUS	13	1	3rd PM 14-N 10-W
STOCKTON	5	2	3rd PM 16-N 9-W
STODDARD	19	1	3rd PM 13-N 8-W
STONE	13	1	3rd PM 14-N 10-W
" "	9	1	3rd PM 15-N 10-W
STORY	17	18	3rd PM 13-N 10-W
STOUT	4	5	3rd PM 16-N 10-W
" "	5	4	3rd PM 16-N 9-W
" "	9	3	3rd PM 15-N 10-W
" "	6	1	3rd PM 16-N 8-W
STRAWN	12	38	3rd PM 14-N 11-W
" "	8	8	3rd PM 15-N 11-W
" "	13	3	3rd PM 14-N 10-W
" "	9	2	3rd PM 15-N 10-W
STRIBLING	4	1	3rd PM 16-N 10-W
STRODE	8	2	3rd PM 15-N 11-W
STRONER	17	1	3rd PM 13-N 10-W
STULL	19	1	3rd PM 13-N 8-W
STURGIS	18	9	3rd PM 13-N 9-W
" "	4	2	3rd PM 16-N 10-W
" "	15	1	3rd PM 14-N 8-W

Surname	Map Group	Parcels of Land	Meridian/Township/Range
SUMMERS	**18**	1	3rd PM 13-N 9-W
SUMMONS	**3**	1	3rd PM 16-N 11-W
SUSK	**1**	1	3rd PM 16-N 13-W
SUTER	**12**	1	3rd PM 14-N 11-W
SWALES	**8**	5	3rd PM 15-N 11-W
" "	**12**	4	3rd PM 14-N 11-W
" "	**2**	2	3rd PM 16-N 12-W
SWAN	**5**	4	3rd PM 16-N 9-W
SWEET	**13**	6	3rd PM 14-N 10-W
" "	**18**	1	3rd PM 13-N 9-W
SWIGERT	**13**	3	3rd PM 14-N 10-W
SWINNERTON	**8**	1	3rd PM 15-N 11-W
TAGGART	**9**	1	3rd PM 15-N 10-W
TAINTON	**2**	1	3rd PM 16-N 12-W
TALKINGTON	**18**	1	3rd PM 13-N 9-W
TANNEHILL	**18**	1	3rd PM 13-N 9-W
TANNER	**19**	5	3rd PM 13-N 8-W
" "	**15**	4	3rd PM 14-N 8-W
TATNALL	**6**	1	3rd PM 16-N 8-W
TAUMHILL	**18**	1	3rd PM 13-N 9-W
TAYLOR	**5**	11	3rd PM 16-N 9-W
" "	**7**	4	3rd PM 15-N 12-W
" "	**17**	1	3rd PM 13-N 10-W
" "	**19**	1	3rd PM 13-N 8-W
" "	**18**	1	3rd PM 13-N 9-W
" "	**14**	1	3rd PM 14-N 9-W
" "	**9**	1	3rd PM 15-N 10-W
" "	**3**	1	3rd PM 16-N 11-W
" "	**2**	1	3rd PM 16-N 12-W
TEAS	**4**	1	3rd PM 16-N 10-W
TENNISON	**18**	2	3rd PM 13-N 9-W
THOMAS	**19**	2	3rd PM 13-N 8-W
" "	**15**	1	3rd PM 14-N 8-W
" "	**3**	1	3rd PM 16-N 11-W
THOMPSON	**3**	10	3rd PM 16-N 11-W
" "	**2**	9	3rd PM 16-N 12-W
" "	**18**	5	3rd PM 13-N 9-W
" "	**1**	5	3rd PM 16-N 13-W
" "	**4**	4	3rd PM 16-N 10-W
" "	**6**	3	3rd PM 16-N 8-W
" "	**17**	2	3rd PM 13-N 10-W
" "	**19**	1	3rd PM 13-N 8-W
" "	**9**	1	3rd PM 15-N 10-W
" "	**7**	1	3rd PM 15-N 12-W
THOMSON	**15**	1	3rd PM 14-N 8-W
THORNBY	**3**	1	3rd PM 16-N 11-W
THORNLEY	**3**	5	3rd PM 16-N 11-W
THORNTON	**10**	9	3rd PM 15-N 9-W
TICKNOR	**8**	2	3rd PM 15-N 11-W
" "	**12**	1	3rd PM 14-N 11-W
TIFFT	**9**	1	3rd PM 15-N 10-W
TILTON	**9**	1	3rd PM 15-N 10-W
TINGLE	**13**	4	3rd PM 14-N 10-W
TINSLEY	**4**	1	3rd PM 16-N 10-W
TITUS	**9**	2	3rd PM 15-N 10-W
TODD	**12**	2	3rd PM 14-N 11-W
" "	**11**	2	3rd PM 15-N 8-W
" "	**10**	2	3rd PM 15-N 9-W
" "	**18**	1	3rd PM 13-N 9-W
TOLKINTON	**19**	2	3rd PM 13-N 8-W

Surname	Map Group	Parcels of Land	Meridian/Township/Range		
TOLKINTON (Cont'd)	**18**	1	3rd PM	13-N	9-W
TOLLY	**4**	1	3rd PM	16-N	10-W
TROTTER	**5**	1	3rd PM	16-N	9-W
TROY	**7**	11	3rd PM	15-N	12-W
" "	**8**	1	3rd PM	15-N	11-W
TUCKER	**17**	2	3rd PM	13-N	10-W
" "	**18**	2	3rd PM	13-N	9-W
" "	**12**	1	3rd PM	14-N	11-W
TUNNELL	**16**	6	3rd PM	13-N	11-W
" "	**17**	4	3rd PM	13-N	10-W
TURLEY	**3**	2	3rd PM	16-N	11-W
TURNBULL	**13**	3	3rd PM	14-N	10-W
" "	**14**	2	3rd PM	14-N	9-W
TURNER	**19**	17	3rd PM	13-N	8-W
" "	**3**	3	3rd PM	16-N	11-W
" "	**10**	1	3rd PM	15-N	9-W
" "	**1**	1	3rd PM	16-N	13-W
TURNEY	**3**	2	3rd PM	16-N	11-W
TURNHAM	**2**	2	3rd PM	16-N	12-W
TYLER	**3**	2	3rd PM	16-N	11-W
ULLERY	**2**	1	3rd PM	16-N	12-W
URBEAN	**2**	1	3rd PM	16-N	12-W
VALLENTINE	**2**	1	3rd PM	16-N	12-W
VANCE	**9**	3	3rd PM	15-N	10-W
" "	**14**	2	3rd PM	14-N	9-W
" "	**8**	1	3rd PM	15-N	11-W
VANCIL	**18**	2	3rd PM	13-N	9-W
" "	**19**	1	3rd PM	13-N	8-W
VANDEGRIFT	**1**	2	3rd PM	16-N	13-W
VANEATON	**3**	1	3rd PM	16-N	11-W
VANNEST	**10**	3	3rd PM	15-N	9-W
VANOATE	**18**	1	3rd PM	13-N	9-W
VANWINKLE	**15**	6	3rd PM	14-N	8-W
" "	**10**	3	3rd PM	15-N	9-W
" "	**18**	2	3rd PM	13-N	9-W
" "	**14**	2	3rd PM	14-N	9-W
" "	**9**	2	3rd PM	15-N	10-W
" "	**19**	1	3rd PM	13-N	8-W
VARNER	**13**	2	3rd PM	14-N	10-W
" "	**12**	2	3rd PM	14-N	11-W
VARY	**8**	1	3rd PM	15-N	11-W
VEACH	**19**	1	3rd PM	13-N	8-W
VENABLE	**5**	1	3rd PM	16-N	9-W
VERERS	**12**	1	3rd PM	14-N	11-W
VERRY	**13**	1	3rd PM	14-N	10-W
" "	**9**	1	3rd PM	15-N	10-W
VERTREES	**17**	1	3rd PM	13-N	10-W
VINSON	**15**	1	3rd PM	14-N	8-W
VOYLES	**17**	3	3rd PM	13-N	10-W
WACKERLE	**1**	1	3rd PM	16-N	13-W
WADDELL	**8**	1	3rd PM	15-N	11-W
WADE	**9**	1	3rd PM	15-N	10-W
WAFSON	**8**	1	3rd PM	15-N	11-W
WALDO	**1**	11	3rd PM	16-N	13-W
" "	**2**	1	3rd PM	16-N	12-W
WALKER	**6**	3	3rd PM	16-N	8-W
" "	**5**	2	3rd PM	16-N	9-W
" "	**17**	1	3rd PM	13-N	10-W
" "	**13**	1	3rd PM	14-N	10-W
" "	**14**	1	3rd PM	14-N	9-W

Surname	Map Group	Parcels of Land	Meridian/Township/Range
WALLER	**2**	2	3rd PM 16-N 12-W
WALSH	**17**	1	3rd PM 13-N 10-W
WALTON	**4**	1	3rd PM 16-N 10-W
WARD	**4**	2	3rd PM 16-N 10-W
WARE	**11**	2	3rd PM 15-N 8-W
" "	**6**	2	3rd PM 16-N 8-W
" "	**10**	1	3rd PM 15-N 9-W
" "	**5**	1	3rd PM 16-N 9-W
WARREN	**7**	2	3rd PM 15-N 12-W
" "	**2**	2	3rd PM 16-N 12-W
" "	**5**	2	3rd PM 16-N 9-W
" "	**9**	1	3rd PM 15-N 10-W
" "	**3**	1	3rd PM 16-N 11-W
WARRENS	**2**	1	3rd PM 16-N 12-W
WASHBURN	**4**	1	3rd PM 16-N 10-W
WASSON	**17**	1	3rd PM 13-N 10-W
" "	**8**	1	3rd PM 15-N 11-W
WATERS	**14**	4	3rd PM 14-N 9-W
" "	**18**	1	3rd PM 13-N 9-W
WATKINS	**19**	1	3rd PM 13-N 8-W
WATSON	**18**	1	3rd PM 13-N 9-W
" "	**9**	1	3rd PM 15-N 10-W
" "	**1**	1	3rd PM 16-N 13-W
WAY	**4**	1	3rd PM 16-N 10-W
WEATHERFORD	**18**	9	3rd PM 13-N 9-W
WEATHERS	**2**	2	3rd PM 16-N 12-W
WEBB	**6**	2	3rd PM 16-N 8-W
WEEKS	**2**	10	3rd PM 16-N 12-W
WELCH	**5**	1	3rd PM 16-N 9-W
WELTY	**4**	1	3rd PM 16-N 10-W
WESSON	**19**	1	3rd PM 13-N 8-W
WEST	**17**	2	3rd PM 13-N 10-W
" "	**18**	2	3rd PM 13-N 9-W
WESTFALL	**15**	1	3rd PM 14-N 8-W
" "	**11**	1	3rd PM 15-N 8-W
WESTHROPE	**13**	1	3rd PM 14-N 10-W
WESTROPE	**13**	6	3rd PM 14-N 10-W
" "	**17**	2	3rd PM 13-N 10-W
" "	**12**	1	3rd PM 14-N 11-W
WETHERFIELD	**15**	1	3rd PM 14-N 8-W
WETHERFORD	**15**	2	3rd PM 14-N 8-W
WHEELER	**17**	1	3rd PM 13-N 10-W
" "	**18**	1	3rd PM 13-N 9-W
" "	**5**	1	3rd PM 16-N 9-W
WHIPP	**4**	1	3rd PM 16-N 10-W
WHITE	**17**	2	3rd PM 13-N 10-W
" "	**3**	2	3rd PM 16-N 11-W
" "	**19**	1	3rd PM 13-N 8-W
" "	**18**	1	3rd PM 13-N 9-W
" "	**14**	1	3rd PM 14-N 9-W
" "	**4**	1	3rd PM 16-N 10-W
WHITEAKER	**19**	2	3rd PM 13-N 8-W
WHITEHEAD	**19**	3	3rd PM 13-N 8-W
WHITLEY	**7**	4	3rd PM 15-N 12-W
" "	**2**	2	3rd PM 16-N 12-W
WHITLOCK	**17**	10	3rd PM 13-N 10-W
" "	**13**	3	3rd PM 14-N 10-W
WHITWORTH	**18**	1	3rd PM 13-N 9-W
WHORTON	**7**	1	3rd PM 15-N 12-W
WIENSCHE	**3**	2	3rd PM 16-N 11-W

Surname	Map Group	Parcels of Land	Meridian/Township/Range
WILCOX	**17**	3	3rd PM 13-N 10-W
WILHELM	**15**	1	3rd PM 14-N 8-W
WILKERSON	**12**	1	3rd PM 14-N 11-W
WILKINSON	**18**	4	3rd PM 13-N 9-W
" "	**12**	2	3rd PM 14-N 11-W
" "	**17**	1	3rd PM 13-N 10-W
WILLARD	**7**	4	3rd PM 15-N 12-W
" "	**8**	3	3rd PM 15-N 11-W
" "	**9**	1	3rd PM 15-N 10-W
WILLETT	**5**	3	3rd PM 16-N 9-W
WILLHITE	**4**	1	3rd PM 16-N 10-W
WILLIAM	**1**	1	3rd PM 16-N 13-W
WILLIAMS	**17**	1	3rd PM 13-N 10-W
" "	**15**	1	3rd PM 14-N 8-W
" "	**3**	1	3rd PM 16-N 11-W
" "	**1**	1	3rd PM 16-N 13-W
" "	**5**	1	3rd PM 16-N 9-W
WILLSON	**2**	2	3rd PM 16-N 12-W
" "	**12**	1	3rd PM 14-N 11-W
" "	**4**	1	3rd PM 16-N 10-W
" "	**5**	1	3rd PM 16-N 9-W
WILSON	**16**	2	3rd PM 13-N 11-W
" "	**7**	2	3rd PM 15-N 12-W
" "	**4**	2	3rd PM 16-N 10-W
" "	**12**	1	3rd PM 14-N 11-W
" "	**9**	1	3rd PM 15-N 10-W
" "	**3**	1	3rd PM 16-N 11-W
WINEGAR	**1**	2	3rd PM 16-N 13-W
WING	**13**	3	3rd PM 14-N 10-W
WINNINGHAM	**1**	1	3rd PM 16-N 13-W
WINSLOW	**19**	1	3rd PM 13-N 8-W
WINTERS	**12**	1	3rd PM 14-N 11-W
WISE	**2**	3	3rd PM 16-N 12-W
WISNELL	**13**	1	3rd PM 14-N 10-W
WISWALL	**13**	2	3rd PM 14-N 10-W
" "	**9**	1	3rd PM 15-N 10-W
WISWELL	**9**	2	3rd PM 15-N 10-W
" "	**13**	1	3rd PM 14-N 10-W
WOLCOTT	**17**	15	3rd PM 13-N 10-W
" "	**13**	12	3rd PM 14-N 10-W
" "	**9**	5	3rd PM 15-N 10-W
" "	**18**	4	3rd PM 13-N 9-W
" "	**12**	4	3rd PM 14-N 11-W
" "	**14**	1	3rd PM 14-N 9-W
WOLF	**4**	5	3rd PM 16-N 10-W
" "	**3**	1	3rd PM 16-N 11-W
WOLFE	**4**	1	3rd PM 16-N 10-W
WOOD	**15**	5	3rd PM 14-N 8-W
" "	**19**	3	3rd PM 13-N 8-W
" "	**14**	1	3rd PM 14-N 9-W
" "	**9**	1	3rd PM 15-N 10-W
" "	**8**	1	3rd PM 15-N 11-W
" "	**11**	1	3rd PM 15-N 8-W
" "	**4**	1	3rd PM 16-N 10-W
" "	**5**	1	3rd PM 16-N 9-W
WOODS	**14**	2	3rd PM 14-N 9-W
" "	**19**	1	3rd PM 13-N 8-W
" "	**18**	1	3rd PM 13-N 9-W
" "	**12**	1	3rd PM 14-N 11-W
" "	**15**	1	3rd PM 14-N 8-W

Surname	Map Group	Parcels of Land	Meridian/Township/Range		
WOODWARD	**2**	3	3rd PM	16-N	12-W
" "	**10**	1	3rd PM	15-N	9-W
WOOLCOTT	**13**	1	3rd PM	14-N	10-W
" "	**9**	1	3rd PM	15-N	10-W
" "	**2**	1	3rd PM	16-N	12-W
WOOLLOMES	**14**	2	3rd PM	14-N	9-W
" "	**4**	1	3rd PM	16-N	10-W
WOOLMES	**14**	1	3rd PM	14-N	9-W
WOOLMS	**13**	1	3rd PM	14-N	10-W
WOOSTER	**4**	1	3rd PM	16-N	10-W
WORKMAN	**5**	1	3rd PM	16-N	9-W
WORTH	**10**	1	3rd PM	15-N	9-W
WRIGHT	**17**	11	3rd PM	13-N	10-W
" "	**18**	10	3rd PM	13-N	9-W
" "	**19**	5	3rd PM	13-N	8-W
" "	**9**	4	3rd PM	15-N	10-W
" "	**16**	2	3rd PM	13-N	11-W
" "	**15**	2	3rd PM	14-N	8-W
" "	**2**	1	3rd PM	16-N	12-W
WYATT	**9**	10	3rd PM	15-N	10-W
" "	**16**	5	3rd PM	13-N	11-W
" "	**5**	4	3rd PM	16-N	9-W
" "	**15**	3	3rd PM	14-N	8-W
" "	**14**	3	3rd PM	14-N	9-W
" "	**4**	3	3rd PM	16-N	10-W
" "	**18**	2	3rd PM	13-N	9-W
" "	**17**	1	3rd PM	13-N	10-W
" "	**7**	1	3rd PM	15-N	12-W
WYETH	**16**	1	3rd PM	13-N	11-W
YACK	**1**	3	3rd PM	16-N	13-W
YAPLE	**5**	3	3rd PM	16-N	9-W
" "	**4**	2	3rd PM	16-N	10-W
YATES	**17**	7	3rd PM	13-N	10-W
" "	**18**	3	3rd PM	13-N	9-W
" "	**13**	3	3rd PM	14-N	10-W
" "	**12**	1	3rd PM	14-N	11-W
YORK	**2**	3	3rd PM	16-N	12-W
" "	**19**	1	3rd PM	13-N	8-W
" "	**8**	1	3rd PM	15-N	11-W
YOUNG	**10**	1	3rd PM	15-N	9-W
YOUNGBLOOD	**18**	2	3rd PM	13-N	9-W

– Part II –

Township Map Groups

Map Group 1: Index to Land Patents

Township 16-North Range 13-West (3rd PM)

After you locate an individual in this Index, take note of the Section and Section Part then proceed to the Land Patent map on the pages immediately following. You should have no difficulty locating the corresponding parcel of land.

The "For More Info" Column will lead you to more information about the underlying Patents. See the *Legend* at right, and the "How to Use this Book" chapter, for more information.

```
┌─────────────────────────────────────────────────────┐
│                    LEGEND                             │
│          "For More Info . . . " column                │
├─────────────────────────────────────────────────────┤
│ G = Group  (Multi-Patentee Patent, see Appendix "C")  │
│ R = Residence                                         │
│ S = Social Status                                     │
│                                                       │
│                                                       │
│ See Appendix A for list of abbreviations used by the  │
│ Illinois State Archives in describing the place and   │
│ nature of these land patents.                         │
│                                                       │
│ Note: if the Abbreviations contain "L", "BL", "LOT",  │
│ or "BLOCK", the exact whereabouts of the parcel within│
│ the section is not known.                             │
└─────────────────────────────────────────────────────┘
```

ID	Individual in Patent	Sec.	Sec. Part	Purchase Date	Sale Type	IL Aliquot Part	For More Info . . .
115	ABBY, Lemuel	35	NE	1836-06-29	FD	NEPRE	R:MORGAN
3	ATTICK, Abraham	15	W2SE	1835-08-28	FD	W2SEPRE	R:SANGAMON
125	AUGUSTINE, Mary J	36	NESE	1849-09-07	FD	NESE	R:MORGAN S:F
142	AUSMUS, Philip	10	W2NE	1835-08-19	FD	W2NEPRE	R:MORGAN
141	" "	10	E2NW	1835-08-19	FD	E2NWPRE	R:MORGAN
107	AYLESWORTH, Philip	22	NW	1831-12-06	FD	NWFR	R:MORGAN G:3
143	" "	23	E2NW	1833-07-30	FD	E2NWPRE	R:MORGAN
26	BANNING, David	36	S½SE	1856-08-21	FD	S2SE	G:4
25	" "	28	E½SE	1856-08-21	FD	E2SE	G:4
26	BANNING, Jeremiah W	36	S½SE	1856-08-21	FD	S2SE	G:4
25	" "	28	E½SE	1856-08-21	FD	E2SE	G:4
126	BEAGLE, Mason	36	NWNE	1849-08-21	FD	NWNE	R:MORGAN
144	BENFER, Philip	3	SWNW	1835-10-27	FD	SWNW	R:GREENE
102	BENNINGER, John W	3	NWSW	1835-10-27	FD	NWSW	R:GREENE
7	BERNARD, Charles B	35	W½NE	1830-11-20	FD	W2NE	R:MORGAN
162	BOSWELL, Wenney	22	W½SW	1832-07-03	FD	W2SW	R:TAZEWELL
150	BROMLY, Samuel	36	SENE	1853-10-20	FD	SENE	
13	BURBANK, Daniel	15	W½SW	1832-09-24	FD	W2SWFRPRE	R:MORGAN
88	CARTER, John	27		1836-06-29	FD	E2NWFL	R:MORGAN G:24
89	" "	27	E½SW	1836-06-29	FD	E2SWFL	R:MORGAN G:24
101	CARTER, William B	4	SW	1835-10-03	FD	SWPRE	R:MORGAN G:25
5	CARTER, Zadock	4	NW	1835-10-03	FD	NWPRE	R:MORGAN G:26
55	CHAMBERS, George M	16	L2	1855-11-12	SC	LOT2	
9	CLOTFETTER, Charles	14		1835-08-14	FD	E2SEPREFL	R:MORGAN
70	" "	14		1835-08-14	FD	E2SEPREFL	R:MORGAN
8	" "	13	W2SE	1835-08-14	FD	W2SEPRE	R:MORGAN
69	CLOTFETTER, Jacob	13	E2SE	1835-08-14	FD	E2SEPRE	R:MORGAN
70	" "	14		1835-08-14	FD	W2SEPREFL	R:MORGAN
9	" "	14		1835-08-14	FD	W2SEPREFL	R:MORGAN
107	COBB, Jonathon	22	NW	1831-12-06	FD	NWFR	R:MORGAN G:3
106	" "	23	E2SE	1834-02-22	FD	E2SEPRE	R:MORGAN
136	COBB, Orran	23	NE	1831-12-06	FD	NE	R:MORGAN
58	CONN, William A	9	NW	1838-09-20	FD	NWFR	R:MORGAN G:46
57	" "	8	NE	1838-09-20	FD	NEFR	R:MORGAN G:46
56	" "	5	E½	1838-09-20	FD	EFR2	R:MORGAN G:46
59	" "	9	SW	1838-09-20	FD	SW	R:MORGAN G:46
164	" "	13	SENW	1839-07-24	FD	SENW	R:MORGAN
166	" "	33	W½SW	1839-08-01	FD	W2SW	R:MORGAN
165	" "	13	W½NW	1839-08-01	FD	W2NW	R:MORGAN
163	" "	13	NENW	1844-08-02	FD	NENW	R:MORGAN
175	COX, Abel Jr	15		1835-08-14	FD	E2SEPREFL	R:MORGAN
2	" "	15		1835-08-14	FD	E2SEPREFL	R:MORGAN
90	COX, John	23	W2SW	1835-08-14	FD	W2SWPRE	R:MORGAN
146	COX, William	4	SE	1835-10-03	FD	SEPRE	R:MORGAN G:50
167	CRAWFORD, William	24	SE	1831-12-06	FD	SE	R:MORGAN
134	CROMWELL, Oliver Ide	12	NENW	1847-06-26	FD	NENW	R:MORGAN

ID	Individual in Patent	Sec.	Sec. Part	Purchase Date	Sale Type	IL Aliquot Part	For More Info . . .
114	DAVIS, Joshua	36	SW	1834-07-04	FD	SW	R:MORGAN
124	DELAHAY, Mark W	32	SW	1838-10-27	FD	SWFR	R:MORGAN
123	" "	32	NE	1838-10-27	FD	NEFR	R:MORGAN
122	" "	29	SE	1838-10-27	FD	SEFR	R:MORGAN
168	DEW, William	24	W2NE	1832-10-04	FD	W2NEPRE	R:MORGAN
1	DICKERSON, Aaron	24	W2SW	1833-07-22	FD	W2SWPRE	R:MORGAN
46	DICKERSON, Eliza	24	E2NW	1833-07-22	FD	E2NWPRE	R:MORGAN S:F
49	EASTHAM, Marvillous	15	E½NE	1838-09-25	FD	E2NE	R:SANGAMON G:58
44	ELDRIDGE, Elias	3	NE	1846-07-02	FD	NEFR	R:MORGAN
45	" "	3	SE	1847-04-23	FD	SE	R:MORGAN
30	FOX, Edward A	3	SESW	1854-04-11	FD	SESWFR	R:MISSOURI
128	GASAWAY, Nicholas	2	SE	1846-08-31	FD	SE	R:MORGAN
129	" "	2	SWNE	1846-08-31	FD	SWNE	R:MORGAN
130	" "	9	E½NE	1846-08-31	FD	E2NEFR	R:MORGAN
146	GREEN, Reynolds	4	SE	1835-10-03	FD	SEPRE	R:MORGAN G:50
161	GREENE, Thomas Jr	34	SESE	1852-12-20	FD	SESE	
6	HAEFFNER, Anthony	33	NWNW	1851-03-04	FD	NWNW	R:MORGAN
172	HAMILTON, William	23	E½SW	1835-08-14	FD	E2SWPREFL	R:MORGAN
155	HARTWELL, Thomas	11	W2NE	1835-09-04	FD	W2NEPRE	R:MORGAN
49	HAWN, Frederick	15	E½NE	1838-09-25	FD	E2NE	R:SANGAMON G:58
147	HAYES, Richard	10	SW	1850-09-09	FD	SWFR	R:MORGAN
173	HICKEY, William	34	SWSW	1852-12-20	FD	SWSW	
174	HILHOUSE, William	11	E2NE	1835-09-04	FD	E2NEPRE	R:MORGAN
92	HILL, John	33	SESE	1853-01-10	FD	SESE	G:76
93	" "	34	NWSW	1853-01-10	FD	NWSW	G:76
91	" "	33	NESE	1853-01-10	FD	NESE	G:76
93	HILL, John Jr	34	NWSW	1853-01-10	FD	NWSW	G:76
92	" "	33	SESE	1853-01-10	FD	SESE	G:76
91	" "	33	NESE	1853-01-10	FD	NESE	G:76
93	HILL, Luther	34	NWSW	1853-01-10	FD	NWSW	G:76
91	" "	33	NESE	1853-01-10	FD	NESE	G:76
92	" "	33	SESE	1853-01-10	FD	SESE	G:76
157	HODGES, Thomas	28	NESW	1847-05-21	FD	NESWFR	R:MORGAN
158	" "	28	W½SW	1847-05-21	FD	W2SWFR	R:MORGAN
156	" "	16	L1	1855-11-12	SC	LOT1	
89	HOUSTON, Nicholas	27	E½SW	1836-06-29	FD	E2SWFL	R:MORGAN G:24
88	" "	27		1836-06-29	FD	E2NWFL	R:MORGAN G:24
135	HOVEY, Orlando D	25	NW	1835-07-22	FD	NWPRE	R:MORGAN
75	HOWELL, James	25	E2SE	1838-09-15	FD	E2SEPRE	R:MORGAN
149	HUDELSON, Robert L	36	NWSE	1839-06-17	FD	NWSE	R:MORGAN
132	IDE, Oliver C	12	NWNW	1845-01-01	FD	NWNW	R:MORGAN
131	" "	12	NESW	1845-08-25	FD	NESW	R:MORGAN
133	" "	12	SENW	1845-08-25	FD	SENW	R:MORGAN
152	JACKSON, Sina	26	NE	1835-07-17	FD	NE	R:MORGAN S:F
52	JAY, George	1	NENE	1850-08-27	FD	NENE	R:MORGAN
159	JAY, Thomas	2	SENW	1847-06-15	FD	SENW	R:MORGAN
160	" "	2	SWNW	1847-06-15	FD	SWNW	R:MORGAN
74	KEYES, James W	15	SWNW	1838-09-26	FD	SWFRNW	R:SANGAMON G:90
2	KIMBALL, William	15		1836-06-29	FD	E2NWFL	R:MORGAN
175	" "	15		1836-06-29	FD	E2NWFL	R:MORGAN
60	KROSA, Henrich W	11	W½SW	1847-07-13	FD	W2SW	R:MORGAN
11	KROZA, Christian W	11	SESW	1850-01-09	FD	SESW	R:MORGAN S:F
50	KRUSE, Frederick	11	NESW	1848-10-04	FD	NESW	R:MORGAN
68	LAKE, Israel	2	NENW	1848-06-16	FD	NENWFR	R:CASS
61	LOGSDON, Hiram	33	SWNW	1852-03-14	FD	SWNW	
53	LONG, George	11	E2SE	1835-09-04	FD	E2SEPRE	R:MORGAN
95	LONG, John	10	SE	1835-10-01	FD	SEPRE	R:MORGAN G:93
94	" "	14	SENE	1847-07-17	FD	SENE	R:MORGAN
117	LONG, Lewis B	14	NENE	1847-07-17	FD	NENE	R:MORGAN
95	LONG, William	10	SE	1835-10-01	FD	SEPRE	R:MORGAN G:93
171	LONG, William H	36	NENE	1838-10-01	FD	NENE	R:MORGAN
170	" "	12	W½SW	1846-07-07	FD	W2SW	R:MORGAN
169	" "	12	SWNW	1846-07-14	FD	SWNW	R:MORGAN
71	LOOSE, Jacob G	28	NWSE	1838-09-24	FD	NWSE	R:SANGAMON G:94
71	LOOSE, Joseph B	28	NWSE	1838-09-24	FD	NWSE	R:SANGAMON G:94
49	" "	15	E½NE	1838-09-25	FD	E2NE	R:SANGAMON G:58
139	LOYD, Peter	26	E2NW	1835-09-04	FD	E2NWPRE	R:MORGAN
54	LUCAS, George	14	SW	1835-09-02	FD	SWPRE	R:SANGAMON G:95
72	" "	14	SW	1835-09-02	FD	SWPRE	R:SANGAMON G:95
54	LUCAS, Hanah	14	SW	1835-09-02	FD	SWPRE	R:SANGAMON G:95
72	" "	14	SW	1835-09-02	FD	SWPRE	R:SANGAMON G:95
31	LUSK, Edward	33	SWNE	1853-01-08	FD	SWNE	
84	MALONEY, Jerry	2	SW	1846-08-22	FD	SW	R:MORGAN

ID	Individual in Patent	Sec.	Sec. Part	Purchase Date	Sale Type	IL Aliquot Part	For More Info . . .
105	MANARY, Jonas	33	E½NW	1830-11-08	FD	E2NW	R:MORGAN
62	MANNING, Horatio N	34	E½SW	1838-09-24	FD	E2SW	R:MORGAN
116	MARVIN, Levi C	28	SWSE	1854-05-22	FD	SWSE	
137	MATHIS, Perry	2	NENE	1843-12-05	FD	NENE	R:MORGAN
138	" "	2	SENE	1844-12-25	FD	SENEGLD	R:MORGAN
63	MATTHEWS, Isaac	1	NWNE	1838-12-26	FD	NWNE	R:MORGAN
178	MAY, William L	4	E½NE	1838-09-24	FD	E2NE	R:SANGAMON
177	" "	14	E½NW	1838-09-24	FD	E2NW	R:SANGAMON
176	" "	13	NE	1838-09-24	FD	NE	R:SANGAMON
5	MEEK, Allen	4	NW	1835-10-03	FD	NWPRE	R:MORGAN G:26
10	MILLAM, Charles K	34	NESE	1846-05-11	FD	NESE	R:MORGAN
32	MLODZIANOWSKI, Edward	14	W½NW	1838-09-20	FD	W2NW	R:MORGAN
97	MOORE, John	33	NWNE	1856-03-19	FD	NWNE	
96	" "	33	E½NE	1856-03-19	FD	E2NE	
145	MOORE, Reuben	4	W½NE	1835-10-03	FD	W2NE	R:MORGAN
98	MUSIC, John	15	E½SW	1835-08-27	FD	E2SWVOID	
99	MUSICK, John	15	E2SW	1835-08-28	FD	E2SWPRE	R:SANGAMON
72	NEWMAN, Jacob	14	SW	1835-10-24	FD	SW	R:MORGAN
54	" "	14	SW	1835-10-24	FD	SW	R:MORGAN
151	NEWMAN, Simon P	10	E½NE	1848-11-03	FD	E2NE	R:MORGAN
76	OGG, James	36	SWNE	1852-03-29	FD	SWNE	
27	PARK, David	34	W½SE	1838-09-24	FD	W2SE	R:TENNESSEE
179	PARKER, William	35	SE	1835-07-21	FD	SEPRE	R:MORGAN
180	PARKS, William	24	E2NE	1832-10-04	FD	E2NEPRE	R:MORGAN
118	PATTERSON, Lewis	35	W2NW	1835-09-04	FD	W2NWPRE	R:MORGAN
56	PLANTE, George P	5	E½	1838-09-20	FD	EFR2	R:MORGAN G:46
57	" "	8	NE	1838-09-20	FD	NEFR	R:MORGAN G:46
58	" "	9	NW	1838-09-20	FD	NWFR	R:MORGAN G:46
59	" "	9	SW	1838-09-20	FD	SW	R:MORGAN G:46
79	POINTER, James	26	W2SW	1835-09-04	FD	W2SWPRE	R:MORGAN
78	" "	1	SWNE	1838-09-25	FD	SWNE	R:MORGAN
77	" "	1	SENE	1838-09-25	FD	SENE	R:MORGAN
181	POINTER, William	11	W2SE	1835-09-04	FD	W2SEPRE	R:MORGAN
113	PRATT, Joseph S	2	NWNW	1845-06-02	FD	NWNW	R:MORGAN
100	PURVINE, John	34	W2NE	1835-09-04	FD	W2NEPRE	R:MORGAN
73	REED, James F	15	W½NE	1838-09-24	FD	W2NE	R:SANGAMON
49	" "	15	E½NE	1838-09-25	FD	E2NE	R:SANGAMON G:58
74	" "	15	SWNW	1838-09-26	FD	SWFRNW	R:SANGAMON G:90
47	RIEMAN, Francis	11	E½NW	1846-08-07	FD	E2NW	R:MORGAN
48	" "	11	W½NW	1846-08-22	FD	W2NW	R:MORGAN
80	ROUNDS, James	26	W½NW	1835-08-26	FD	W2NW	R:MORGAN
182	ROUNDS, William	22	E½SW	1835-08-26	FD	E2SWPREFL	R:MORGAN
51	RULON, Gabril W	15	NWNW	1851-11-26	FD	NWNW	R:MORGAN
4	SMITH, Absalom	25	NE	1832-03-16	FD	NEPRE	R:MORGAN G:113
12	SMITH, Clarke	22	W2SW	1833-01-23	FD	W2SWPRE	R:MORGAN G:116
28	SMITH, David	34	E2NE	1835-09-04	FD	E2NEPRE	R:MORGAN
64	SMITH, Isaac	25	W2SE	1832-10-04	FD	W2SEPRE	R:MORGAN G:119
12	" "	22	W2SW	1833-01-23	FD	W2SWPRE	R:MORGAN G:116
4	SMITH, James	25	NE	1832-03-16	FD	NEPRE	R:MORGAN G:113
81	" "	24	E2SW	1833-07-22	FD	E2SWPRE	R:MORGAN
12	SMITH, John	22	W2SW	1833-01-23	FD	W2SWPRE	R:MORGAN G:116
101	" "	4	SW	1835-10-03	FD	SWPRE	R:MORGAN G:25
127	SMITH, Michael	28	NW	1835-09-04	FD	NWFRPRE	R:MORGAN
148	SMITH, Richard	25	SW	1835-07-30	FD	SWPRE	R:MORGAN
64	SMITH, William	25	W2SE	1832-10-04	FD	W2SEPRE	R:MORGAN G:119
65	STARR, Isaac W	22	NE	1835-08-14	FD	NEPRE	R:MORGAN G:122
66	" "	26		1835-08-14	FD	SEPREFL	R:MORGAN G:122
82	STEWART, James	22		1835-08-14	FD	W2SEPREFL	R:MORGAN
83	" "	27	W2NE	1835-08-14	FD	W2NEPRE	R:MORGAN
121	STEWART, Mariah	23		1835-08-14	FD	W2NWPREFL	R:MORGAN S:F
140	STEWART, Peter	21		1831-12-13	FD	FRSEC	R:MORGAN G:124
140	STEWART, William	21		1831-12-13	FD	FRSEC	R:MORGAN G:124
183	" "	23	W½SE	1833-07-17	FD	W2SE	R:MORGAN
67	STITES, Isaiah	24	W½NW	1832-07-03	FD	W2NW	R:TAZEWELL
33	SUSK, Edward	16	L10	1855-11-12	SC	LOT10	
40	" "	16	L8	1855-11-12	SC	LOT8	
34	" "	16	L11	1855-11-12	SC	LOT11	
35	" "	16	L3	1855-11-12	SC	LOT3	
36	" "	16	L4	1855-11-12	SC	LOT4	
37	" "	16	L5	1855-11-12	SC	LOT5	
39	" "	16	L7	1855-11-12	SC	LOT7	
41	" "	16	L9	1855-11-12	SC	LOT9	
38	" "	16	L6	1855-11-12	SC	LOT6	

ID	Individual in Patent	Sec.	Sec. Part	Purchase Date	Sale Type	IL Aliquot Part	For More Info . . .
109	THOMPSON, Joseph C	1	W½	1839-07-24	FD	W2	R:MORGAN
108	" "	1	SE	1839-08-01	FD	SE	R:MORGAN
112	" "	34	SWNW	1852-10-28	FD	SWNW	G:127
110	" "	34	E½NW	1852-10-28	FD	E2NW	G:127
111	" "	34	NWNW	1852-10-28	FD	NWNW	R:MORGAN G:127
111	THOMPSON, Samuel P	34	NWNW	1852-10-28	FD	NWNW	R:MORGAN G:127
110	" "	34	E½NW	1852-10-28	FD	E2NW	G:127
112	" "	34	SWNW	1852-10-28	FD	SWNW	G:127
120	TURNER, Lydia	28	NE	1835-09-02	FD	NEFRPRE	R:SANGAMON S:F G:129
120	TURNER, Walter	28	NE	1835-09-02	FD	NEFRPRE	R:SANGAMON S:F G:129
66	VANDEGRIFT, Thomas	26		1835-08-14	FD	SEPREFL	R:MORGAN G:122
65	" "	22	NE	1835-08-14	FD	NEPRE	R:MORGAN G:122
184	WACKERLE, Williams	33	NENW	1854-03-25	FD	NENW	R:MORGAN
22	WALDO, Daniel	26	NESW	1847-05-17	FD	NESW	R:MORGAN G:131
23	" "	26	SESW	1848-04-18	FD	SESW	R:MORGAN G:131
24	" "	35	E½NW	1849-07-23	FD	E2NW	R:MORGAN G:131
15	" "	28	SESW	1852-11-24	FD	SESWFR	
21	" "	33	W½SE	1852-11-24	FD	W2SE	
18	" "	33	E½SW	1852-11-24	FD	E2SW	
17	" "	33	E½SW	1852-11-24	FD	E2SW	
16	" "	32	W½SE	1853-01-25	FD	W2SE	
14	" "	27	W½SW	1854-05-04	FD	W2SW	
18	" "	33	E½SW	1856-03-12	FD	E2SW	
19	" "	33	NWSE	1856-03-12	FD	NWSE	
17	" "	33	E½SW	1856-03-12	FD	E2SW	
20	" "	33	SWSE	1856-04-16	FD	SWSE	R:MORGAN
29	WALDO, David	33	SENW	1853-01-01	FD	SENW	
22	WALDO, James E	26	NESW	1847-05-17	FD	NESW	R:MORGAN G:131
23	" "	26	SESW	1848-04-18	FD	SESW	R:MORGAN G:131
24	" "	35	E½NW	1849-07-23	FD	E2NW	R:MORGAN G:131
42	WATSON, Edward	16	L12	1855-11-12	SC	LOT12	
43	" "	16	L13	1855-11-12	SC	LOT13	
85	WILLIAM, Jesse	27	W2NW	1835-09-07	FD	W2NWPRE	R:SANGAMON
103	WILLIAMS, John	14	W2NE	1835-09-07	FD	W2NEPRE	R:SANGAMON
154	WINEGAR, Stephen	12	SESW	1844-07-31	FD	SESW	R:MORGAN
153	" "	12	NWSE	1844-07-31	FD	NWSE	R:MORGAN
104	WINNINGHAM, John	2	NWNE	1844-04-15	FD	NWNESIL	R:MORGAN
87	YACK, John B	12	NENE	1844-11-28	FD	NENESIL	R:MORGAN
86	" "	12	NE	1844-11-28	FD	NESIL	R:MORGAN
119	YACK, Lewis	12	S½SE	1847-09-17	FD	S2SE	R:MENARD

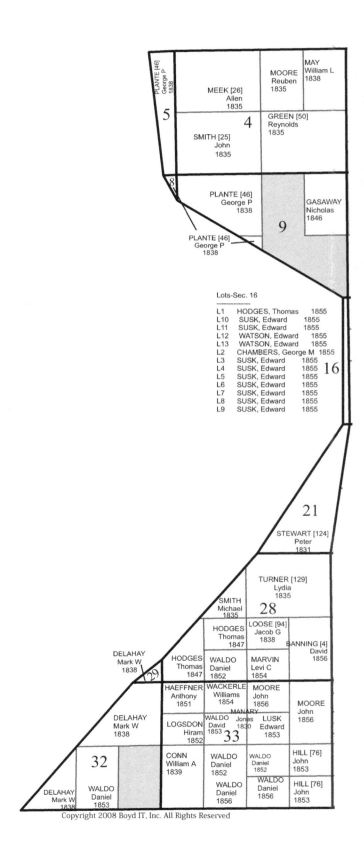

Patent Map

T16-N R13-W
3rd PM Meridian

Map Group 1

Township Statistics

Parcels Mapped	:	184
Number of Patents	:	1
Number of Individuals	:	139
Patentees Identified	:	127
Number of Surnames	:	102
Multi-Patentee Parcels	:	33
Oldest Patent Date	:	11/8/1830
Most Recent Patent	:	8/21/1856
Block/Lot Parcels	:	43
Cities and Towns	:	2
Cemeteries	:	5

Map (Township 16-N Range 13-W)

Section 3
- ELDRIDGE Elias 1846
- BENFER Philip 1835
- BENNINGER John W 1835
- FOX Edward A 1854
- ELDRIDGE Elias 1847

Section 2
- PRATT Joseph S 1845
- LAKE Israel 1848
- WINNINGHAM John 1844
- MATHIS Perry 1843
- JAY Thomas 1847
- JAY Thomas 1847
- GASAWAY Nicholas 1846
- MATHIS Perry 1844
- GASAWAY Nicholas 1846
- MALONEY Jerry 1846

Section 1
- MATTHEWS Isaac 1838
- JAY George 1850
- POINTER James 1838
- POINTER James 1838
- THOMPSON Joseph C 1839
- THOMPSON Joseph C 1839

Section 11
- AUSMUS Philip 1835
- AUSMUS Philip 1835
- NEWMAN Simon P 1848
- RIEMAN Francis 1846
- RIEMAN Francis 1846
- HILHOUSE William 1835
- HARTWELL Thomas 1835

Section 10
- HAYES Richard 1850
- LONG [93] John 1835

Section 12
- IDE Oliver C 1845
- CROMWELL Oliver Ide 1847
- YACK John B 1844
- LONG William H 1846
- IDE Oliver C 1845
- YACK John B 1844
- IDE Oliver C 1845
- WINEGAR Stephen 1844
- WINEGAR Stephen 1844
- YACK Lewis 1847

- KROSA Henrich W 1847
- KRUSE Frederick 1848
- KROZA Christian W 1850
- POINTER William 1835
- LONG George 1835
- LONG William H 1846

Section 15
- RULON Gabril W 1851
- REED [90] James F 1838
- KIMBALL William 1836
- REED James F 1838
- HAWN [58] Frederick 1838
- MUSICK John 1835
- MUSIC John 1835
- ATTICK Abraham 1835
- COX Abel Jr 1835
- BURBANK Daniel 1832

Section 14
- MLODZIANOWSKI Edward 1838
- MAY William L 1838
- WILLIAMS John 1835
- LUCAS [95] George 1835
- NEWMAN Jacob 1835
- CLOTFETTER Jacob 1835
- CLOTFETTER Charles 1835

Section 13
- LONG Lewis B 1847
- LONG John 1847
- CONN William A 1844
- CONN William A 1839
- CONN William A 1839
- MAY William L 1838
- CLOTFETTER Charles 1835
- CLOTFETTER Jacob 1835

Section 22
- COBB [3] Jonathon 1831
- STARR [122] Isaac W 1835
- BOSWELL Wenney 1832
- ROUNDS William 1835
- SMITH [116] Clarke 1833
- STEWART James 1835

Section 23
- STEWART Mariah 1835
- AYLESWORTH Philip 1833
- COBB Orran 1831
- HAMILTON William 1835
- STEWART William 1833
- COBB Jonathon 1834
- COX John 1835

Section 24
- STITES Isaiah 1832
- DICKERSON Eliza 1833
- DEW William 1832
- PARKS William 1832
- DICKERSON Aaron 1833
- SMITH James 1833
- CRAWFORD William 1831

Section 27
- CARTER [24] John 1836
- STEWART James 1835
- WILLIAM Jesse 1835
- CARTER [24] John 1836
- WALDO Daniel 1854

Section 26
- ROUNDS James 1835
- LOYD Peter 1835
- JACKSON Sina 1835
- WALDO [131] Daniel 1847
- STARR [122] Isaac W 1835
- POINTER James 1835
- WALDO [131] Daniel 1848

Section 25
- HOVEY Orlando D 1835
- SMITH [113] Absalom 1832
- SMITH Richard 1835
- SMITH [119] Isaac 1832
- HOWELL James 1838

Section 34
- THOMPSON [127] Joseph C 1852
- THOMPSON [127] Joseph C 1852
- THOMPSON [127] Joseph C 1852
- PURVINE John 1835
- SMITH David 1835
- HILL [76] John 1853
- MANNING Horatio N 1838
- PARK David 1838
- MILLAM Charles K 1846
- GREENE Thomas Jr 1852
- HICKEY William 1852

Section 35
- PATTERSON Lewis 1835
- WALDO [131] Daniel 1849
- BERNARD Charles B 1830
- ABBY Lemuel 1836
- PARKER William 1835

Section 36
- BEAGLE Mason 1849
- LONG William H 1838
- OGG James 1852
- BROMLY Samuel 1853
- AUGUSTINE Mary J 1849
- HUDELSON Robert L 1839
- DAVIS Joshua 1834
- BANNING [4] David 1856

Helpful Hints

1. This Map's INDEX can be found on the preceding pages.

2. Refer to Map "C" to see where this Township lies within Morgan County, Illinois.

3. Numbers within square brackets [ ] denote a multi-patentee land parcel (multi-owner). Refer to Appendix "C" for a full list of members in this group.

4. Areas that look to be crowded with Patentees usually indicate multiple sales of the same parcel (re-issues), cancellations or voided transactions (that we map, anyway) or overlapping parcels. We opt to show even these ambiguous parcels, which oftentimes lead to research avenues not yet taken.

Legend

- ——— Patent Boundary
- ▬▬▬ Section Boundary
- ▓ No Patents Found (or Outside County)
- 1., 2., 3., ... Lot Numbers (when beside a name)
- [ ] Group Number (see Appendix "C")

Scale: Section = 1 mile X 1 mile (generally, with some exceptions)

Road Map

T16-N R13-W
3rd PM Meridian

Map Group 1

Cities & Towns
Meredosia
Shady Acres

Cemeteries
Augustine Cemetery
Hodges Cemetery
Kiel Cemetery
New Salem Cemetery
Oakland Cemetery

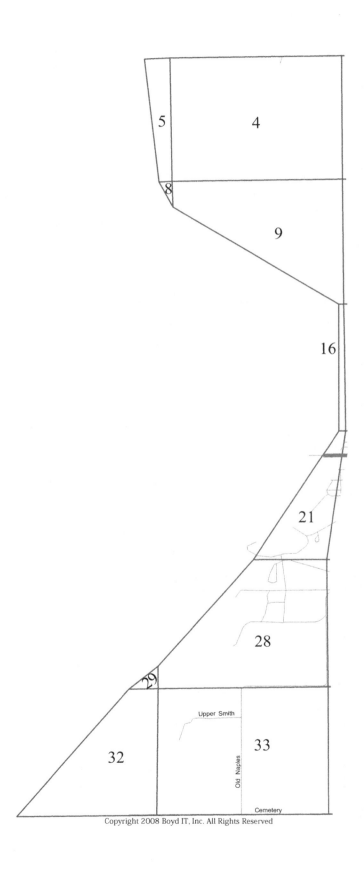

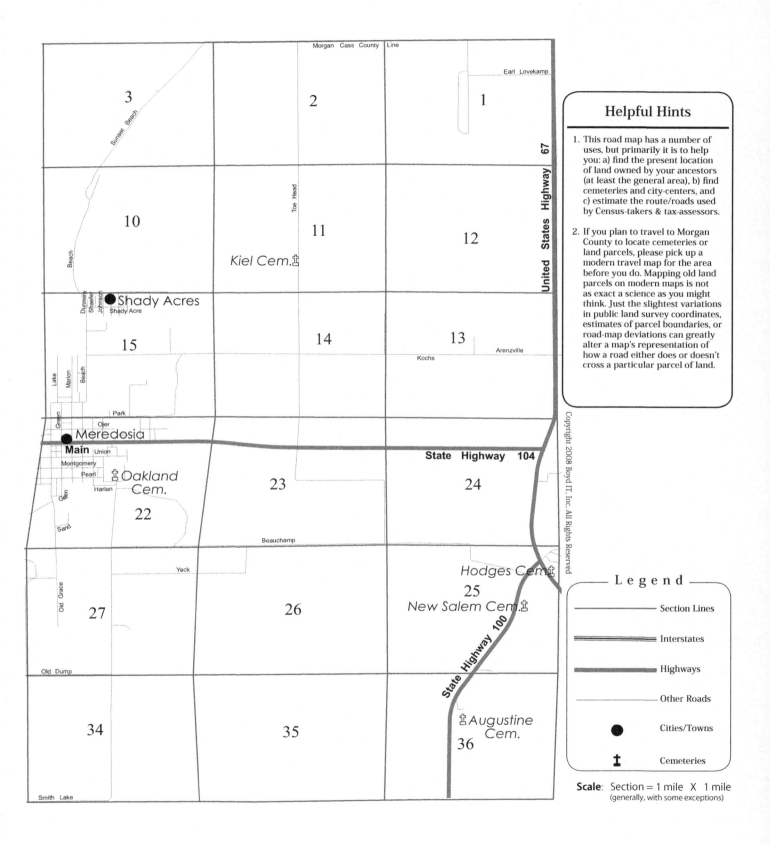

Morgan Cass County Line

Earl Lovekamp

3

2

1

United States Highway 67

Sunset Beach

Toe Head

10

11

12

Beach

Kiel Cem.

Dunmire
Shaefe
Johnson
Shady Acre

● Shady Acres

15

14

13

Arenzville

Kochs

Lake
Marion
Beach

Green

Park

Ojer

● Meredosia

Main Union

State Highway 104

Montgomery

Pearl

Green

✝ Oakland
Cem.

Harlan

23

24

22

Sand

Beauchamp

Yeck

Hodges Cem ✝

Old Grace

25

New Salem Cem. ✝

27

26

Old Dump

State Highway 100

✝ Augustine
Cem.

34

35

36

Smith Lake

Helpful Hints

1. This road map has a number of uses, but primarily it is to help you: a) find the present location of land owned by your ancestors (at least the general area), b) find cemeteries and city-centers, and c) estimate the route/roads used by Census-takers & tax-assessors.

2. If you plan to travel to Morgan County to locate cemeteries or land parcels, please pick up a modern travel map for the area before you do. Mapping old land parcels on modern maps is not as exact a science as you might think. Just the slightest variations in public land survey coordinates, estimates of parcel boundaries, or road-map deviations can greatly alter a map's representation of how a road either does or doesn't cross a particular parcel of land.

L e g e n d

————————	Section Lines
═══════════	Interstates
━━━━━━━━━	Highways
————————	Other Roads
●	Cities/Towns
✝	Cemeteries

Scale: Section = 1 mile X 1 mile
(generally, with some exceptions)

Historical Map

T16-N R13-W
3rd PM Meridian

Map Group 1

<u>Cities & Towns</u>
Meredosia
Shady Acres

<u>Cemeteries</u>
Augustine Cemetery
Hodges Cemetery
Kiel Cemetery
New Salem Cemetery
Oakland Cemetery

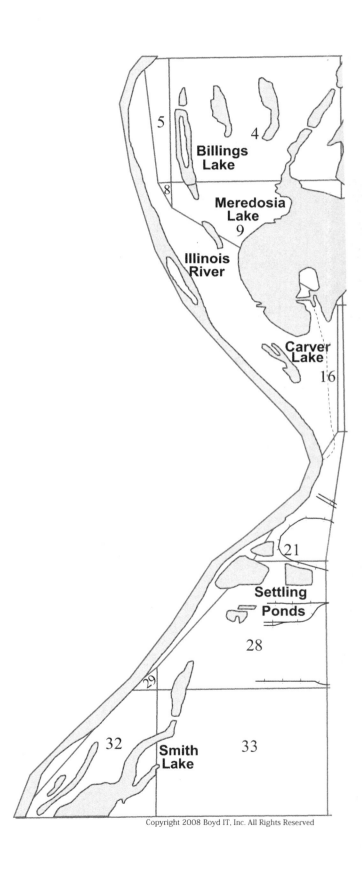

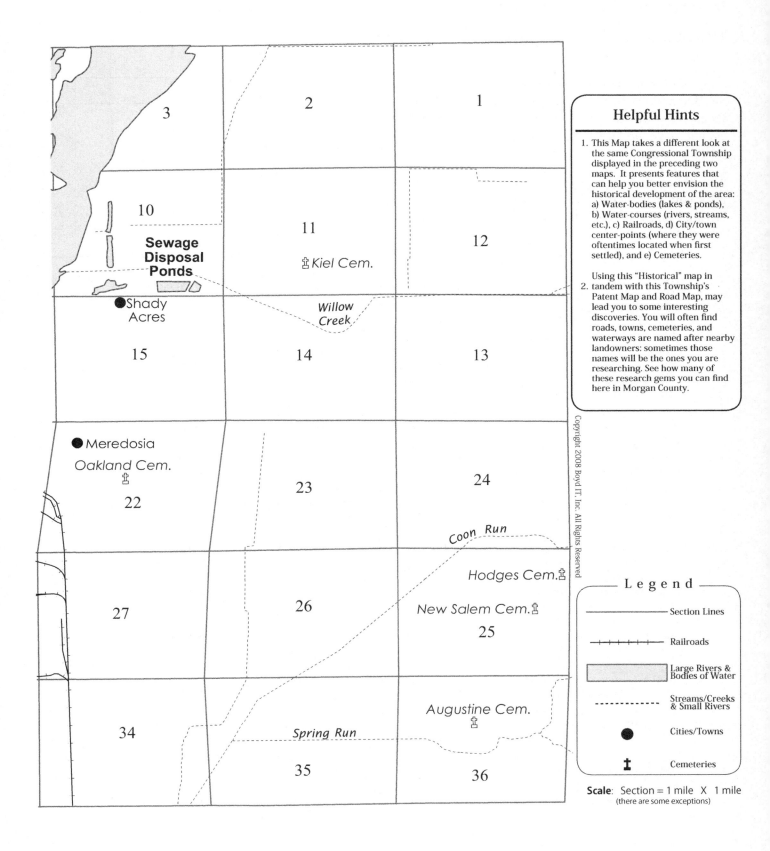

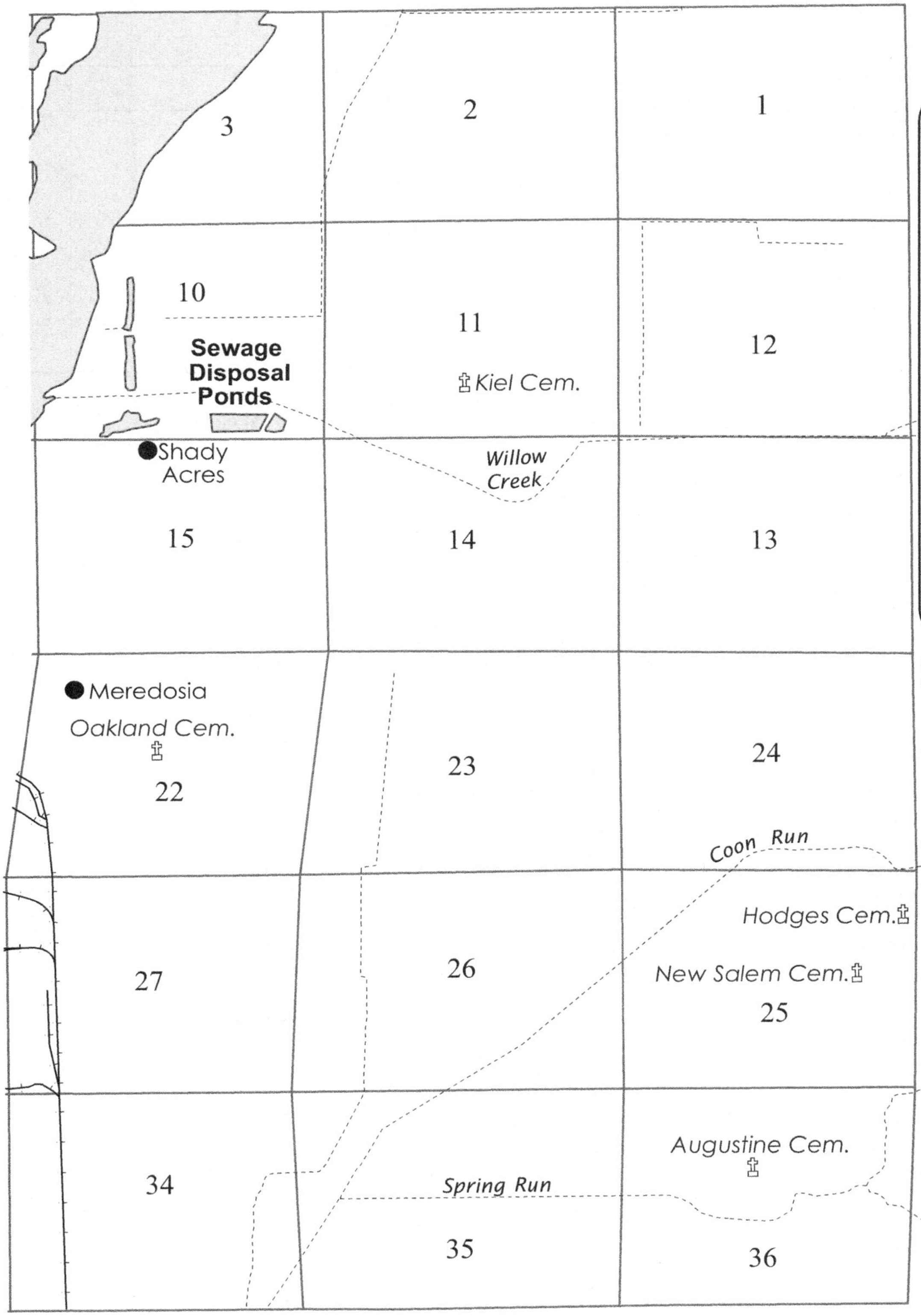
3
2
1
10
11
12
Sewage Disposal Ponds
Kiel Cem.
Shady Acres
Willow Creek
15
14
13
Meredosia
Oakland Cem.
22
23
24
Coon Run
Hodges Cem.
New Salem Cem.
27
26
25
Augustine Cem.
34
Spring Run
35
36

Helpful Hints

1. This Map takes a different look at the same Congressional Township displayed in the preceding two maps. It presents features that can help you better envision the historical development of the area: a) Water-bodies (lakes & ponds), b) Water-courses (rivers, streams, etc.), c) Railroads, d) City/town center-points (where they were oftentimes located when first settled), and e) Cemeteries.
2. Using this "Historical" map in tandem with this Township's Patent Map and Road Map, may lead you to some interesting discoveries. You will often find roads, towns, cemeteries, and waterways are named after nearby landowners: sometimes those names will be the ones you are researching. See how many of these research gems you can find here in Morgan County.

Legend

- Section Lines
- Railroads
- Large Rivers & Bodies of Water
- Streams/Creeks & Small Rivers
- Cities/Towns
- Cemeteries

Scale: Section = 1 mile X 1 mile
(there are some exceptions)

Map Group 2: Index to Land Patents

Township 16-North Range 12-West (3rd PM)

After you locate an individual in this Index, take note of the Section and Section Part then proceed to the Land Patent map on the pages immediately following. You should have no difficulty locating the corresponding parcel of land.

The "For More Info" Column will lead you to more information about the underlying Patents. See the *Legend* at right, and the "How to Use this Book" chapter, for more information.

```
                    LEGEND
         "For More Info . . . " column
G = Group   (Multi-Patentee Patent, see Appendix "C")
R = Residence
S = Social Status


See Appendix A for list of abbreviations used by the
Illinois State Archives in describing the place and
nature of these land patents.

Note: if the Abbreviations contain "L", "BL", "LOT",
or "BLOCK", the exact whereabouts of the parcel within
the section is not known.
```

ID	Individual in Patent	Sec.	Sec. Part	Purchase Date	Sale Type	IL Aliquot Part	For More Info . . .
428	ABBEY, Lemuel	31	SESW	1836-07-18	FD	SESW	R:MORGAN
539	ABRAMS, William G	11	E½SE	1831-06-01	FD	E2SE	R:SANGAMON
316	ALBIN, Isaac	34	SW	1828-12-08	FD	SW	R:MORGAN
315	" "	33	W½NE	1828-12-08	FD	W2NE	R:MORGAN
418	" "	33	W½NE	1828-12-08	FD	W2NE	R:MORGAN
317	" "	34	W½NE	1829-06-19	FD	W2NE	R:MORGAN
318	" "	35	SW	1829-06-19	FD	SW	R:MORGAN
225	ALDERSON, Charles	35	SENE	1850-10-21	FD	SENE	R:MORGAN
459	AVERITT, Nathan G	35	NWSE	1836-02-24	FD	NWSE	R:MORGAN
460	" "	35	SWNE	1836-02-24	FD	SWNE	R:MORGAN
471	AYLESWORTH, Philip	18	SWNW	1832-07-30	FD	SWNW	R:MORGAN
472	" "	30	W½SW	1835-07-23	FD	W2SW	R:MORGAN
256	BAKER, Francis	29	SESE	1836-11-01	FD	SESE	R:MORGAN
192	BAKER, Green H	32	SESW	1836-07-18	FD	SESW	R:MORGAN
289	" "	32	SESW	1836-07-18	FD	SESW	R:MORGAN
195	BALEY, Abraham R	2	SE	1828-04-03	FD	SE	R:MORGAN
194	" "	2	NE	1829-04-07	FD	NE	R:MORGAN
205	BARBER, Augustus K	25	SENE	1848-10-13	FD	SENE	R:MORGAN
337	BARRET, James A	25	S½NW	1849-05-28	FD	S2NW	
338	" "	26	SENE	1849-05-28	FD	SENE	
336	" "	25	NESW	1849-05-28	FD	NESW	
260	" "	26	SENE	1849-05-28	FD	SENE	
421	BARRICKLOW, Joseph	20	E½SE	1835-06-11	FD	E2SE	R:MORGAN
426	BATES, Joseph H	24	NWSE	1833-09-16	FD	NWSE	R:MORGAN
569	BATES, William T	25	NWNW	1844-06-14	FD	NWNW	R:MORGAN
248	BEAUCHAMP, Edward	6	L2 (S½)	1839-08-31	FD	S2LOT2SW	R:MORGAN
479	BEAUCHAMP, Richard	6	L1	1835-07-09	FD	LOT1SW	R:MORGAN
480	" "	6	L2 (N½)	1837-08-15	FD	N2LOT2SW	R:MORGAN
413	BERGHAUS, John W	17	SWSW	1854-03-06	FD	SWSW	R:MORGAN
414	" "	20	W½NW	1854-09-01	FD	W2NW	R:MORGAN
334	BLODGETT, Jacob	36	NW	1836-02-19	FD	NW	R:MORGAN
422	BONDURANT, Joseph	17	NE	1848-07-18	FD	NE	
430	" "	17	W½SE	1848-07-18	FD	W2SE	
424	" "	20	N½NE	1848-07-18	FD	N2NE	
423	" "	17	W½SE	1848-07-18	FD	W2SE	
457	BRADBURY, Nathan	33	E½NW	1826-10-06	FD	E2NW	R:MORGAN
458	" "	34	E½NW	1829-06-22	FD	E2NW	R:MORGAN
294	BRAYHAW, Harmon L	16	L2	1850-12-02	SC	L2W2NE	
209	BRENENK, Barney	14	SWSW	1851-11-01	FD	SWSW	R:MORGAN
206	BROCKENBROUGH, Austin	18	E½NW	1835-10-03	FD	E2NW	R:MORGAN
208	" "	32	W½NW	1835-10-26	FD	W2NW	R:MORGAN
207	" "	31	NE	1835-10-26	FD	NE	R:MORGAN
210	BROCKHOUSE, Barney	33	N½NE	1852-10-15	FD	N2NE	
293	BROCKHOUSE, Harmon G	16	L6	1848-06-17	SC	LOT6E2SW	
357	BROCKHOUSE, Jared H	16	L7	1847-12-11	SC	LOT7W2SE	
306	BROKHAUS, Herman G	25	SESW	1846-03-09	FD	SESW	R:MORGAN

ID	Individual in Patent	Sec.	Sec. Part	Purchase Date	Sale Type	IL Aliquot Part	For More Info . . .
487	BROMLY, Samuel	31	SWNW	1853-10-20	FD	SWNWFR	
198	BROTHERS, Alexander	22	NESW	1834-06-16	FD	NESW	R:MORGAN
515	BROWN, Thomas	36	E½SE	1830-01-01	FD	E2SE	R:MORGAN
516	"	36	E½SW	1830-01-01	FD	E2SW	R:MORGAN
371	BRUNING, John	16	L1	1846-05-23	SC	LOT1E2NE	
236	BURK, Daniel B Jr	21	NWNW	1852-05-21	FD	NWNW	
237	BUSH, Daniel B Jr	20	NE	1848-12-02	FD	NE	
536	CARRICK, William	2	S½NW	1831-07-16	FD	S2NW	R:MORGAN
368	CARTER, Job	19	E½SE	1831-04-01	FD	E2SE	R:MORGAN
376	CARTER, John	8	E½SW	1828-03-07	FD	E2SW	R:MORGAN
377	"	8	W½SW	1831-04-29	FD	W2SW	R:MORGAN
273	"	17	E½NW	1831-05-28	FD	E2NW	R:MORGAN
375	"	17	E½NW	1831-05-28	FD	E2NW	R:MORGAN
518	CARTER, Thomas	17	W½NE	1828-02-22	FD	W2NE	R:MORGAN
510	CAWOOD, Stephen B	1	SWSE	1853-05-10	FD	SWSE	
290	CHAMBER, Ain Griffing	35	SESE	1945-09-30	FD	SESE	R:MORGAN
292	"	35	SESE	1945-09-30	FD	SESE	R:MORGAN
197	"	35	SESE	1945-09-30	FD	SESE	R:MORGAN
292	CHAMBERLAIN, Griffin	35	SESE	1845-12-18	FD	SESE	
290	"	35	SESE	1845-12-18	FD	SESE	
197	"	35	SESE	1845-12-18	FD	SESE	
290	CHAMBERLAIN, Griffing	35	SESE	1845-08-12	FD	SESE	R:MORGAN
197	"	35	SESE	1845-08-12	FD	SESE	R:MORGAN
292	"	35	SESE	1845-08-12	FD	SESE	R:MORGAN
291	CHAMBERLIN, Griffin	35	NESE	1841-03-25	FD	NESE	R:MORGAN
335	CLOTFETTER, Jacob	19	W½NW	1830-04-07	FD	W2NW	R:MORGAN
227	COFFIN, Charles	10	E½NE	1830-08-05	FD	E2NE	R:MORGAN G:42
228	"	4	W½SE	1830-08-05	FD	W2SE	R:MORGAN G:42
226	"	4	SESW	1833-06-04	FD	SESW	R:MORGAN
473	COFFMAN, Philip	31	SENW	1849-09-15	FD	SENW	R:MORGAN
577	COGBURN, Zachariah	12	E½SW	1828-04-23	FD	E2SW	R:MORGAN
578	COGBURN, Zecheriah	14	E½NE	1831-05-24	FD	E2NE	R:MORGAN
343	COMER, James	19	NENE	1854-08-24	FD	NENE	R:MORGAN
189	COX, Abel	15	SW	1835-08-14	FD	SWPRE	R:MORGAN G:48
188	"	6	SENW	1837-08-09	FD	SENW	R:MORGAN
189	COX, John	15	SW	1835-08-14	FD	SWPRE	R:MORGAN G:48
378	"	6	SENE	1835-11-03	FD	SENE	R:MORGAN
478	COX, William	15	E2NE	1835-10-03	FD	E2NEPRE	R:MORGAN G:50
537	"	6	SESE	1839-06-14	FD	SESE	R:MORGAN
381	CRAWFORD, John	34	E½SW	1830-01-26	FD	E2SW	R:MORGAN
382	"	34	W½SW	1831-12-14	FD	W2SW	R:MORGAN
380	"	32	NWSE	1850-10-16	FD	NWSE	R:MORGAN
379	"	28	N½SW	1851-09-17	FD	N2SW	R:MORGAN
552	CRAWFORD, William P	30	SWNE	1837-07-17	FD	SWNE	R:MORGAN
551	"	30	NWSE	1837-07-17	FD	NWSE	R:MORGAN
372	CRISMAN, John C	29	SENW	1851-08-01	FD	SENW	R:MORGAN
373	"	29	SWNW	1853-02-21	FD	SWNW	R:MORGAN
374	"	29	SWSE	1853-05-05	FD	SWSE	
538	CRISMAN, William	30	SENE	1848-11-20	FD	SENE	R:MORGAN
251	CUREE, Elias	29	SWNE	1854-12-05	FD	SWNE	R:MORGAN
252	CURLL, Elias	29	E½NE	1851-07-29	FD	E2NE	R:MORGAN
340	CUTLER, James B	29	NESW	1854-12-06	FD	NESW	R:MORGAN
238	DEITRICK, Daniel	25	NESE	1845-05-07	FD	NESE	R:MORGAN
392	DRYER, John H	28	NWNW	1854-01-05	FD	NWNW	R:MORGAN
519	EDMUNDSON, Thomas	26	W½NW	1851-11-04	FD	W2NW	
263	ENGLEBACK, George	6	SWNE	1836-08-30	FD	SWNE	R:MORGAN
298	ERLER, Henry	23	SESW	1853-05-10	FD	SESW	R:MORGAN
344	ETHEL, James	35	SWSE	1836-07-23	FD	SWSE	R:MORGAN
345	FIKE, James	12	E½NW	1830-11-04	FD	E2NW	R:MORGAN
266	FILEY, George	27	SESE	1840-07-29	FD	SESE	R:MORGAN
265	"	26	SE	1840-07-29	FD	SE	R:MORGAN
425	FILEY, Joseph	26	NESW	1853-01-07	FD	NESW	
475	FUNK, Presley C	33	NWSW	1852-02-20	FD	NWSW	
299	GILBERT, Henry	25	NWSW	1846-03-09	FD	NWSW	R:MORGAN
300	"	25	SWSW	1849-05-28	FD	SWSW	R:MORGAN
431	GRAHAM, Lorenzo	5	SESE	1835-06-09	FD	SESE	R:MORGAN
423	GRAHAM, Lorenzo D	17	W½SE	1835-12-02	FD	W2SE	R:MORGAN
430	"	17	W½SE	1835-12-02	FD	W2SE	R:MORGAN
478	GREEN, Reynolds	15	E2NE	1835-10-03	FD	E2NEPRE	R:MORGAN G:50
540	GREEN, William	11	NWNE	1835-11-03	FD	NWNE	R:MORGAN
541	GREENE, William	10	SESE	1835-12-11	FD	SESE	R:MORGAN
319	GRIFFITTS, Isaac	11	E½NW	1829-12-28	FD	E2NW	R:MORGAN
385	GRIGG, John	5	NWSE	1836-04-15	FD	NWSE	R:PHILADELPHIA

ID	Individual in Patent	Sec.	Sec. Part	Purchase Date	Sale Type	IL Aliquot Part	For More Info . . .
386	GRIGG, John (Cont'd)	5	SENW	1836-04-15	FD	SENW	R:PHILADELPHIA
387	" "	5	L1	1836-04-15	FD	LOT1NE	R:PHILADELPHIA
388	" "	7	E½SE	1836-04-15	FD	E2SE	R:PHILADELPHIA
389	" "	7	NW	1836-04-15	FD	NW	R:PHILADELPHIA
390	" "	7	SENE	1836-04-15	FD	SENE	R:PHILADELPHIA
391	" "	7	W½NE	1836-04-15	FD	W2NE	R:PHILADELPHIA
384	" "	33	W½SE	1836-04-15	FD	W2SE	R:PHILADELPHIA
308	HALL, Hosea	12	E½SE	1829-12-07	FD	E2SE	R:MORGAN
394	HAM, John J	26	SWNE	1846-06-19	FD	SWNE	R:MORGAN
564	HAM, William R	24	SWNE	1833-09-17	FD	SWNE	R:MORGAN
563	" "	24	E½SE	1834-06-21	FD	E2SE	R:MORGAN
565	" "	26	E½NW	1846-03-04	FD	E2NW	R:MORGAN
488	HARRIS, Samuel	19	SENE	1852-05-25	FD	SENE	
467	HATCH, Ozias M	33	E½SW	1851-02-11	FD	E2SW	R:PIKE
466	" "	27	NW	1851-10-23	FD	NW	
489	HATFIELD, Samuel	32	SWSE	1836-07-18	FD	SWSE	R:MORGAN
511	HAYWARD, Stephen	32	N½SW	1844-07-10	FD	N2SWGLD	R:MORGAN
295	HEMMINGHAUS, Heinrich	28	N½NE	1855-02-16	FD	N2NE	R:MORGAN
393	HILL, John	26	SWSW	1852-08-10	FD	SWSW	
462	HILL, Nimrod	31	NWSW	1856-01-23	FD	NWSW	R:MORGAN
240	HODGES, David	19	NWNE	1845-01-08	FD	NWNE	R:MORGAN
246	HODGES, David L	30	NENW	1841-09-11	FD	NENW	R:MORGAN
245	" "	30	N½NE	1849-08-30	FD	N2NE	
244	" "	29	NWNE	1849-08-30	FD	NWNE	R:MORGAN
243	" "	29	N½NW	1849-08-30	FD	N2NW	
520	HODGES, Thomas	7	SESW	1847-04-07	FD	SESW	R:MORGAN
521	HOUGHAN, Thomas	18	NWNW	1836-02-04	FD	NWNW	R:SANGAMON
322	HOUSTON, Isaac	1	NWNW	1836-02-17	FD	NWNW	R:MORGAN
321	" "	1	NENW	1847-09-01	FD	NENWFR	R:CASS
320	" "	1	N½NE	1847-09-17	FD	N2NEFR	R:CASS
324	" "	1	L1	1851-02-18	FD	LOT1NE	
323	" "	1	SENW	1851-02-18	FD	SENW	
509	HOUSTON, Starett B	1	L1 (W½)	1855-05-22	FD	W2LOT1NWFR	R:CASS S:F G:80
509	HOUSTON, William T	1	L1 (W½)	1855-05-22	FD	W2LOT1NWFR	R:CASS S:F G:80
346	HUDELSON, James	30	SESE	1839-06-17	FD	SESE	R:MORGAN
347	" "	31	NWSE	1839-06-17	FD	NWSE	R:MORGAN
482	HUDELSON, Robert L	31	NESW	1839-06-17	FD	NESW	R:MORGAN
542	HUDELSON, William	30	SESW	1839-06-17	FD	SESW	R:MORGAN
543	" "	31	L2 (N½)	1839-06-17	FD	N2LOT2NW	R:MORGAN
242	HUDELSTON, David	31	L1 (N½)	1838-07-18	FD	N2LOT1NW	R:MORGAN
241	" "	30	NESW	1839-02-14	FD	NESW	R:MORGAN
349	HUMMER, James	29	SESW	1854-01-24	FD	SESW	R:MORGAN
348	" "	28	SESE	1855-01-10	FD	SESE	R:MORGAN
464	IDE, Oliver C	34	NWNW	1853-10-07	FD	NWNW	R:MORGAN
465	IDE, Oliver O	28	NESE	1853-01-18	FD	NESE	
468	JANUARY, Peter W	22	NWSE	1834-06-03	FD	NWSE	R:MORGAN
470	" "	33	E½SE	1835-10-01	FD	E2SE	R:MORGAN
469	" "	33	E½NE	1835-10-01	FD	E2NE	R:MORGAN
527	JANUARY, Thomas T	34	SWNW	1836-03-17	FD	SWNW	R:MORGAN
355	JOHNSON, Jane	4	SEN½	1831-03-16	FD	S2NE	R:MORGAN S:F G:89
257	KENNETT, Frank	28	SWNW	1844-07-10	FD	SWNWGLD	R:MORGAN
427	KENNETT, Joseph	31	NESE	1844-09-11	FD	NESE	R:MORGAN
544	KENNETT, William	28	E½NE	1844-07-10	FD	E2NE	R:MORGAN
432	KENNEY, Major	21	SWNW	1844-08-31	FD	SWNW	R:MORGAN
229	KIMBALL, Charles	6	NWSE	1833-06-04	FD	NWSE	R:MORGAN
312	KIMBALL, Ira	5	W½SW	1833-06-04	FD	W2SW	R:MORGAN
313	" "	6	NESE	1835-08-15	FD	NESE	R:MORGAN
311	" "	5	SWNW	1835-11-28	FD	SWNW	R:MORGAN
314	" "	9	NENE	1852-02-04	FD	NENE	
310	" "	3	SWSW	1852-02-04	FD	SWSW	
309	" "	10	N½NW	1852-02-04	FD	N2NW	
396	KINNEY, John	21	SENE	1845-02-24	FD	SENE	R:SANGAMON
433	KINNEY, Major	26	NWNE	1851-06-09	FD	NWNE	R:MORGAN
522	LEE, Thomas	20	NENW	1849-10-01	FD	NENW	R:MORGAN
429	LENARD, Levina R	25	SWSE	1844-05-13	FD	SWSESIL	R:MORGAN S:F
191	LEONARD, Abraham	36	NE	1835-11-10	FD	NE	R:MORGAN
190	" "	25	SESE	1844-05-08	FD	SESE	R:MORGAN
441	LESLIE, Miron	3	SEN½	1836-02-18	FD	S2NE	R:MORGAN
267	LOAR, George	24	E½NE	1833-06-28	FD	E2NE	R:MORGAN
268	LONG, George	12	W½NE	1829-11-10	FD	W2NE	R:MORGAN
270	" "	13	W½NE	1831-11-25	FD	W2NE	R:MORGAN
271	" "	13	W½SE	1835-07-20	FD	W2SE	R:MORGAN
272	" "	13	E2NE	1835-09-04	FD	E2NEPRE	R:MORGAN G:92

ID	Individual in Patent	Sec.	Sec. Part	Purchase Date	Sale Type	IL Aliquot Part	For More Info . . .
269	LONG, George (Cont'd)	12	W½SE	1836-12-08	FD	W2SE	R:MORGAN
302	LONG, Henry	13	NESW	1835-07-11	FD	NESW	R:MORGAN
297	LONG, Henry C	9	SWSW	1848-08-17	FD	SWSW	R:MORGAN
296	" "	17	NWSW	1851-12-22	FD	NWSW	R:MORGAN
301	LONG, Henry Jr	13	W½NW	1832-01-09	FD	W2NW	R:MORGAN
305	LONG, Henry Sen	11	W½SE	1831-12-07	FD	W2SE	R:MORGAN
304	" "	11	SWNE	1836-07-27	FD	SWNE	R:MORGAN
303	" "	11	E½SW	1836-12-08	FD	E2SW	R:MORGAN
325	LONG, Isaac	14	NWSW	1836-11-11	FD	NWSW	R:MORGAN
358	LONG, Jehu	14	NWNE	1833-05-20	FD	NWNE	R:MORGAN
400	LONG, John	12	W2SW	1835-10-01	FD	W2SWPRE	R:MORGAN G:93
397	" "	14	NESW	1836-08-22	FD	NESW	R:MORGAN
398	" "	9	SESW	1847-03-24	FD	SESW	R:MORGAN
399	" "	9	SWSE	1847-03-24	FD	SWSE	R:MORGAN
383	LONG, John F	23	NENE	1847-02-24	FD	NENE	R:MORGAN
461	LONG, Nicholas	14	NENW	1835-01-05	FD	NENW	R:MORGAN
400	LONG, William	12	W2SW	1835-10-01	FD	W2SWPRE	R:MORGAN G:93
545	LUND, William	6	L2(E½)	1839-12-23	FD	E2LOT2NE	R:MORGAN
223	" "	6	L2(E½)	1839-12-23	FD	E2LOT2NE	R:MORGAN
415	MADDOX, John W	25	NENE	1835-07-31	FD	NENE	R:MORGAN
315	MANARY, Jonas	33	W½NE	1830-11-20	FD	W2NE	R:MORGAN
418	" "	33	W½NE	1830-11-20	FD	W2NE	R:MORGAN
213	MANNING, Benjamin H	21	W½SW	1836-07-27	FD	W2SW	R:MORGAN
307	MANNING, Horatio N	28	S½SW	1836-07-13	FD	S2SW	R:MORGAN
402	MARA, John	30	NESE	1851-11-01	FD	NESE	R:MORGAN
401	" "	27	W½SW	1853-10-11	FD	W2SW	
491	MASON, Samuel	27	SWSE	1839-12-13	FD	SWSE	R:MORGAN
490	" "	27	SESW	1839-12-27	FD	SESW	R:MORGAN
363	MASTERSON, Jeremiah	8	W½NE	1831-04-29	FD	W2NELS	R:MORGAN
360	" "	17	E½SW	1831-04-29	FD	E2SWLS	R:MORGAN
362	" "	7	SESE	1835-05-06	FD	SESE	R:MORGAN
361	" "	17	NWNW	1835-05-06	FD	NWNW	R:MORGAN
359	" "	17		1845-02-03	FD	SWNWP	R:MORGAN
326	MATHEUS, Isaac	16	L4	1846-05-23	SC	LOT4W2NW	
327	MATTHEWS, Isaac	9	NWSW	1851-03-27	FD	NWSW	R:MORGAN
200	MCCONNEL, Amzi	1	E½SW	1854-01-28	FD	E2SW	R:MORGAN
201	" "	1	NWSE	1854-01-28	FD	NWSE	R:MORGAN
444	MCCONNEL, Murray	15	E½SW	1835-07-06	FD	E2SW	R:MORGAN
443	" "	15	E½NW	1835-07-06	FD	E2NW	R:MORGAN
445	" "	15	SE	1835-07-06	FD	SE	R:MORGAN
449	" "	24	SWSE	1835-07-06	FD	SWSE	R:MORGAN
446	" "	15	W½NE	1835-07-06	FD	W2NE	R:MORGAN
448	" "	22	E½NE	1836-04-19	FD	E2NE	R:MORGAN
442	" "	10	E½SW	1836-04-19	FD	E2SW	R:MORGAN
447	" "	21	SWSE	1852-08-27	FD	SWSE	
403	MCCONNELL, John	22	W½NW	1835-11-19	FD	W2NW	R:NEW JERSEY
455	MCCONNELL, Murray	23	W½NE	1835-07-20	FD	W2NE	R:MORGAN
450	" "	10	W½SE	1835-07-20	FD	W2SE	R:MORGAN
454	" "	22	W½NE	1835-07-20	FD	W2NE	R:MORGAN
456	" "	25	W½NE	1835-07-20	FD	W2NE	R:MORGAN
451	" "	12	W½NW	1835-11-11	FD	W2NW	R:MORGAN
452	" "	15	W½NW	1836-10-28	FD	W2NW	R:MORGAN
453	" "	22	E½NW	1836-10-28	FD	E2NW	R:MORGAN
481	MCPERSON, Richard F	5	L2(W½)	1847-08-18	FD	W2LOT2NE	R:MORGAN
215	MCPHERSON, Benjamin	28	SWSE	1836-07-30	FD	SWSE	R:MORGAN
214	" "	28	NWSE	1850-02-22	FD	NWSE	R:MORGAN
212	MCPHERSON, Benjamin G	32	SESE	1836-06-04	FD	SESE	R:MORGAN
284	MCPHERSON, George W	4	L2(E½)	1848-09-15	FD	E2LOT2NW	R:CASS
463	MCPHERSON, Nimrod	4	NWSW	1848-10-31	FD	NWSW	R:MORGAN
247	MILLER, Ebenezer T	35	NW	1835-10-19	FD	NW	R:MORGAN
350	MITCHELL, James	24	W½SW	1835-06-18	FD	W2SW	R:MORGAN
204	MOORE, Andrew	2	N½NW	1828-07-18	FD	N2NW	R:MORGAN
477	MOORE, Reuben	2	E½SW	1828-04-03	FD	E2SW	R:MORGAN
492	MOORE, Samuel	2	W½SW	1828-04-05	FD	W2SW	R:MORGAN
495	" "	3	S½NW	1828-07-14	FD	S2NW	R:MORGAN
493	" "	3	E½SE	1829-04-29	FD	E2SE	R:MORGAN
355	" "	4	SEN½	1831-03-16	FD	S2NE	R:MORGAN S:F G:89
498	" "	3	N½NW	1831-04-25	FD	N2NW	R:MORGAN
494	" "	3	N½NW	1831-04-25	FD	N2NW	R:MORGAN
483	MORRISON, Robert	1	SESE	1836-12-13	FD	SESE	R:MORGAN
395	MOSS, John Jr	13	E½NW	1831-05-30	FD	E2NW	R:MORGAN
220	NEWMAN, Benjamin	5	SWSE	1836-02-10	FD	SWSE	R:MORGAN
219	" "	5	NESW	1839-07-27	FD	NESW	R:MORGAN

ID	Individual in Patent	Sec.	Sec. Part	Purchase Date	Sale Type	IL Aliquot Part	For More Info . . .
218	NEWMAN, Benjamin (Cont'd)	5	NESE	1844-04-27	FD	NESE	R:MORGAN
224	" "	6	L2(W½)	1850-09-12	FD	W2LOT2NE	R:MORGAN
545	" "	6	L2(E½)	1850-09-12	FD	E2LOT2NW	R:MORGAN
223	" "	6	L2(E½)	1850-09-12	FD	E2LOT2NW	R:MORGAN
216	" "	10	NESE	1851-09-01	FD	NESE	R:MORGAN
274	" "	3	NESW	1851-09-01	FD	NESW	R:MORGAN
217	" "	3	NESW	1851-09-01	FD	NESW	R:MORGAN
221	" "	5	L2(E½)	1852-06-07	FD	E2LOT2NEFR	R:MORGAN
222	" "	5	L2	1852-06-08	FD	LOT2NWFR	
280	NEWMAN, George	9	NW	1831-03-19	FD	NW	R:MORGAN
277	" "	8	E½NE	1831-04-26	FD	E2NELS	R:MORGAN
279	" "	8	W½SE	1831-04-26	FD	W2SELS	R:MORGAN
375	" "	17	E½NW	1831-04-26	FD	E2NWLS	R:MORGAN
273	" "	17	E½NW	1831-04-26	FD	E2NWLS	R:MORGAN
278	" "	8	E½NW	1831-09-02	FD	E2NW	R:MORGAN
275	" "	3	NWSW	1832-10-27	FD	NWSW	R:MORGAN
281	" "	9	NWNW	1832-10-27	FD	NWNW	R:MORGAN
276	" "	4	N½NE	1835-06-08	FD	N2NE	R:MORGAN
217	" "	3	NESW	1837-05-04	FD	NESW	R:MORGAN
274	" "	3	NESW	1837-05-04	FD	NESW	R:MORGAN
351	NEWMAN, James	5	SESW	1836-02-24	FD	SESW	R:MORGAN
366	NEWMAN, Jesse T	4	L1(W½)	1845-11-08	FD	W2LOT1NW	R:MORGAN
367	" "	4	L2(W½)	1845-11-08	FD	W2LOT2NW	R:MORGAN
365	" "	4	SENW	1848-10-04	FD	SENW	R:MORGAN
419	NEWMAN, Jonathan	6	SWNW	1836-02-10	FD	SWNW	R:MORGAN
501	NEWMAN, Simon P	4	SWSW	1836-02-24	FD	SWSW	R:MORGAN
503	" "	9	NENW	1838-08-07	FD	NENW	R:MORGAN
499	" "	10	S½NW	1849-10-08	FD	S2NW	
500	" "	10	W½SW	1849-10-08	FD	W2SW	
502	" "	9	E½SE	1849-10-25	FD	E2SE	
505	" "	9	NWSE	1849-10-25	FD	NWSE	
504	" "	9	NESW	1849-10-25	FD	NESW	
506	NEWMAN, Simon T	9	SENE	1848-11-03	FD	SENE	
507	" "	9	SENW	1848-11-03	FD	SENW	
508	" "	9	W½NE	1848-11-03	FD	W2NE	
549	NEWMAN, William	3	E½SW	1835-12-30	FD	E2SW	R:MORGAN
550	" "	9	SWNW	1838-04-13	FD	SWNWLS	R:MORGAN
576	NEWMAN, Wingate	4	NESE	1833-03-04	FD	NESE	R:MORGAN
574	NEWMAN, Wingate J	4	NESW	1836-02-24	FD	NESW	R:MORGAN
573	" "	3	SWSE	1836-12-06	FD	SWSE	R:MORGAN
575	" "	4	SESE	1849-10-08	FD	SESE	R:MORGAN
404	ORTZ, John	8	NESE	1841-07-12	FD	NESE	R:MORGAN
186	PARKER, Aaron	29	W½SW	1837-08-15	FD	W2SW	R:MORGAN
187	" "	30	SWSE	1837-08-15	FD	SWSE	R:MORGAN
420	PERVIANCE, Jonathon	12	E½NE	1829-11-10	FD	E2NE	R:MORGAN
235	POINTER, Cornelius	13	NWSW	1832-11-29	FD	NWSW	R:MORGAN
352	POINTER, James	14	SWNE	1835-09-04	FD	SWNEPRE	R:MORGAN G:106
555	POINTER, William	14	NESE	1835-07-14	FD	NESE	R:MORGAN
352	" "	14	SWNE	1835-09-04	FD	SWNEPRE	R:MORGAN G:106
553	" "	1	NWSW	1835-12-08	FD	NWSW	R:MORGAN
554	" "	11	E½NE	1836-11-04	FD	E2NE	R:MORGAN
434	POND, Martin I	21	NWSE	1840-03-16	FD	NWSE	R:MORGAN
435	" "	22	NWSW	1840-03-16	FD	NWSW	R:MORGAN
439	POND, Martin J	22	SWSW	1840-10-06	FD	SWSW	R:MORGAN
437	" "	21	SESE	1846-01-22	FD	SESE	R:MORGAN
436	" "	21	NESE	1849-10-19	FD	NESE	R:MORGAN
438	" "	22	SESW	1852-09-01	FD	SESW	
282	POST, George	11	NWSW	1851-03-19	FD	NWSW	R:MORGAN
339	POST, James A	11	SWSW	1837-11-29	FD	SWSW	R:MORGAN
562	POST, William	23	NWSE	1835-07-20	FD	NWSE	R:MORGAN
558	" "	14	W½SE	1835-07-20	FD	W2SE	R:MORGAN
557	" "	14	SESE	1835-07-20	FD	SESE	R:MORGAN
561	" "	23	E½NW	1836-11-26	FD	E2NW	R:MORGAN
556	" "	10	W½NE	1836-11-26	FD	W2NE	R:MORGAN
559	" "	21		1845-01-22	FD	SENWP	R:SANGAMON
560	" "	21	SWNE	1845-02-10	FD	SWNE	R:SANGAMON
512	PREVOST, Theadezea	14	SESW	1843-04-24	FD	SESW	R:MORGAN
513	" "	23	W½NW	1843-04-24	FD	W2NW	R:MORGAN
193	PRICE, Abraham	32	W½NE	1835-03-16	FD	W2NE	R:SANGAMON
289	" "	32	SESW	1835-04-13	FD	SESW	R:MORGAN
192	" "	32	SESW	1835-04-13	FD	SESW	R:MORGAN
405	PRIEST, John	14	W½NW	1831-10-21	FD	W2NW	R:MORGAN
185	PROVOST, A J F	23	SWSE	1845-02-04	FD	SWSEGLD	R:MORGAN S:I

ID	Individual in Patent	Sec.	Sec. Part	Purchase Date	Sale Type	IL Aliquot Part	For More Info . . .
514	PROVOST, Theodore	23	SWSW	1845-02-04	FD	SWSW	R:MORGAN
264	PUCKETT, George F	23	N½SW	1843-04-24	FD	N2SW	R:MORGAN
406	PURVIANCE, John	13	E½SE	1831-08-19	FD	E2SE	R:MORGAN
272	PURVINE, John	13	E2NE	1835-09-04	FD	E2NEPRE	R:MORGAN G:92
408	" "	24	NWNE	1835-10-09	FD	NWNE	R:MORGAN
407	" "	1	NESE	1836-01-02	FD	NESE	R:MORGAN
354	RANSON, James	24	SWNW	1843-08-13	FD	SWNW	R:MORGAN
353	" "	23	SENE	1843-08-13	FD	SENE	R:MORGAN
484	RANSON, Robert	25	NENW	1835-07-20	FD	NENW	R:MORGAN
258	RAYBON, Franklin	25	NWSE	1849-10-02	FD	NWSE	R:MORGAN
410	REAKER, John	16	L5	1850-12-02	SC	L5W2SW	
409	" "	16	L3	1850-12-02	SC	LOT3E2NW	
250	REDDING, Eli W	32	E½NE	1829-12-05	FD	E2NE	R:MORGAN
496	ROBINSON, Samuel	22	NESE	1846-04-13	FD	NESE	R:MORGAN
568	SAXTON, William	24	SENW	1834-07-31	FD	SENW	R:MORGAN
567	" "	24	E½SW	1834-07-31	FD	E2SW	R:MORGAN
249	SHALDON, Edward	31	SWSW	1856-01-23	FD	SWSW	R:MORGAN
211	SHOEMAKER, Barney	21	NWNE	1851-11-03	FD	NWNE	R:MORGAN
287	SIBERT, Gideon	7	NWSW	1845-04-01	FD	N2W2SW	R:MORGAN
286	" "	7	NWSE	1845-04-01	FD	N2W2SE	R:MORGAN
288	" "	7	SWSW	1847-04-21	FD	SWSW	R:MORGAN
364	SIBERT, Jeremiah	8	SESE	1845-03-27	FD	SESEMP	R:MORGAN
523	SMART, Thomas	20	E½SW	1831-11-28	FD	E2SW	R:MORGAN
196	SMITH, Absalom	30	SWNW	1835-08-15	FD	SWNW	R:MORGAN
253	SMITH, Elias	22	SESE	1845-04-22	FD	SESE	R:MORGAN
328	SMITH, Isaac	1	SWSW	1835-12-04	FD	SWSW	R:MORGAN
566	SMITH, William R	36	W½SW	1835-11-19	FD	W2SW	R:MORGAN
476	SPATES, Reason	16	L8	1846-05-23	SC	LOT8E2SE	
524	SPENCER, Thomas	11	W½NW	1829-08-20	FD	W2NW	R:MORGAN
331	STITES, Isaiah	18	W½SW	1830-09-16	FD	W2SW	R:MORGAN
330	" "	18	W½SE	1831-03-28	FD	W2SE	R:CASS
333	" "	33	W½NW	1831-12-06	FD	W2NW	R:MORGAN
329	" "	18	E½SE	1832-05-02	FD	E2SE	R:MORGAN
332	" "	19	SW	1832-05-02	FD	SW	R:MORGAN
525	SWALES, Thomas	18	E½NE	1830-01-13	FD	E2NE	R:MORGAN
526	" "	33	W½SW	1830-01-18	FD	W2SW	R:MORGAN
474	TAINTON, Phineas W	27	NE	1850-02-22	FD	NE	
283	TAYLOR, George	32	SWSW	1852-04-01	FD	SWSW	
202	THOMPSON, Andrew J	21	NENW	1851-02-07	FD	NENW	R:MORGAN
203	" "	29	NESE	1853-11-11	FD	NESE	R:MORGAN
342	THOMPSON, James B	32	NENW	1851-02-11	FD	NENW	R:MORGAN
341	" "	29	NWSE	1853-11-11	FD	NWSE	R:MORGAN
412	THOMPSON, John	20	SWSW	1835-06-11	FD	SWSW	R:MORGAN
533	" "	20	SWSW	1835-06-11	FD	SWSW	R:MORGAN
411	" "	20	NWSE	1836-11-12	FD	NWSE	R:MORGAN
416	THOMPSON, John W	32	NESE	1851-02-26	FD	NESE	R:MORGAN
417	" "	33	SWSW	1853-08-18	FD	SWSW	R:MORGAN
486	THOMPSON, Robert	20	SENW	1846-01-02	FD	SENW	R:MORGAN
370	TURNHAM, John B	7	SWSE	1835-12-28	FD	SWSE	R:MORGAN
369	" "	7	NESE	1835-12-28	FD	NESE	R:MORGAN
497	ULLERY, Samuel	6	SWSE	1840-01-27	FD	SWSE	R:MORGAN
262	URBEAN, Gattliess	21	NENE	1850-05-28	FD	NENE	R:MORGAN
440	VALLENTINE, Michael	26	NWSW	1847-11-01	FD	NWSW	R:MORGAN
239	WALDO, Daniel	21	E½SW	1852-10-19	FD	E2SW	R:MORGAN
356	WALLER, Jane	3	S2NE	1836-06-04	FD	S2NEPRE	R:MORGAN S:F
517	WALLER, Thomas C	3	N½NE	1829-04-16	FD	N2NE	R:MORGAN
547	WARREN, William M	27	NWSE	1852-08-18	FD	NWSE	
546	" "	27	NESW	1852-08-18	FD	NESW	
548	WARRENS, William M	28	SEN½	1852-08-09	FD	S2NE	
285	WEATHERS, George	27	NESE	1849-03-16	FD	NESE	R:MORGAN
485	WEATHERS, Robert S	31	S½SE	1853-03-05	FD	S2SE	
228	WEEKS, W	4	W½SE	1830-08-05	FD	W2SE	R:MORGAN G:42
227	" "	10	E½NE	1830-08-05	FD	E2NE	R:MORGAN G:42
531	WEEKS, Washington	19	W½SE	1831-04-12	FD	W2SE	R:MORGAN
529	" "	19	E½NW	1831-06-27	FD	E2NW	R:MORGAN
528	" "	18	E½SW	1831-06-27	FD	E2SW	R:MORGAN
534	" "	30	NWNW	1836-09-26	FD	NWNW	R:MORGAN
535	" "	30	SENW	1837-01-06	FD	SENW	R:MORGAN
532	" "	20	NWSW	1837-01-06	FD	NWSW	R:MORGAN
530	" "	19	SWNE	1847-06-25	FD	SWNE	R:MORGAN
412	" "	20	SWSW	1851-11-19	FD	SWSW	
533	" "	20	SWSW	1851-11-19	FD	SWSW	
255	WHITLEY, Elisha	36		1829-06-15	FD	W2SEPTSK	R:MORGAN

ID	Individual in Patent	Sec.	Sec. Part	Purchase Date	Sale Type	IL Aliquot Part	For More Info . . .
494	WHITLEY, Samuel	3	N½NW	1831-04-25	FD	N2NWLS	R:MORGAN
498	"	3	N½NW	1831-04-25	FD	N2NWLS	R:MORGAN
231	WILLSON, Charles	8	W½NW	1836-03-25	FD	W2NW	R:MORGAN
230	" "	7	NENE	1836-03-25	FD	NENE	R:MORGAN
260	WISE, Frederick	26	SENE	1853-03-01	FD	SENEVOID	R:MORGAN
338	" "	26	SENE	1853-03-01	FD	SENEVOID	R:MORGAN
259	" "	26	NENE	1853-03-31	FD	NENE	R:MORGAN
261	" "	26	SESW	1853-12-20	FD	SESW	R:MORGAN
234	WOODWARD, Charles	24	N½NW	1836-08-03	FD	N2NW	R:OHIO
233	" "	23	E½SE	1836-08-03	FD	E2SE	R:OHIO
232	" "	13	S½SW	1836-08-03	FD	S2SW	R:OHIO
254	WOOLCOTT, Elihu	18	W½NE	1831-10-17	FD	W2NE	R:MORGAN
199	WRIGHT, Alfred	14	SENW	1835-07-23	FD	SENW	R:MORGAN
570	YORK, William	33	SE	1828-12-08	FD	SE	R:MORGAN
572	" "	34	SE	1829-06-19	FD	SE	R:MORGAN
571	" "	34	E½NE	1831-08-09	FD	E2NE	R:MORGAN

Patent Map

T16-N R12-W
3rd PM Meridian

Map Group 2

Township Statistics

Parcels Mapped	:	394
Number of Patents	:	1
Number of Individuals	:	230
Patentees Identified	:	231
Number of Surnames	:	154
Multi-Patentee Parcels	:	9
Oldest Patent Date	:	10/6/1826
Most Recent Patent	:	9/30/1945
Block/Lot Parcels	:	29
Cities and Towns	:	0
Cemeteries	:	13

Lots-Sec. 5
L1 GRIGG, John 1836
L2 NEWMAN, Benjamin 1852
L2(E½) NEWMAN, Benjamin 1852
L2(W½) MCPERSON, Richard F 1847

Lots-Sec. 4
L1(W½) NEWMAN, Jesse T 1845
L2(E½) MCPHERSON, George W 1848
L2(W½) NEWMAN, Jesse T 1845

NEWMAN George 1835

NEWMAN Jonathan 1836

COX Abel 1837

ENGLEBACK George 1836 **6**

COX John 1835

KIMBALL Ira 1835

GRIGG John 1836

NEWMAN Jesse T 1848

JOHNSON [89] Jane 1831

Lots-Sec. 6
L1 BEAUCHAMP, Richard 1835 1833
L2(E½) LUND, William 1839
L2(E½) NEWMAN, Benjamin 1850
L2(N½) BEAUCHAMP, Richard 1837
L2(S½) BEAUCHAMP, Edward 1839
L2(W½) NEWMAN, Benjamin 1850

KIMBALL Charles 1833

KIMBALL Ira 1835

KIMBALL Ira 1833

NEWMAN Benjamin 1839 **5**

GRIGG John 1836

NEWMAN Benjamin 1844

MCPHERSON Nimrod 1848

NEWMAN Wingate J 1836

4

NEWMAN Wingate 1833

ULLERY Samuel 1840

COX William 1839

NEWMAN James 1836

NEWMAN Benjamin 1836

GRAHAM Lorenzo 1835

NEWMAN Simon P 1836

COFFIN Charles 1833

COFFIN [42] Charles 1830

NEWMAN Wingate J 1849

GRIGG John 1836

GRIGG John 1836

WILLSON Charles 1836

WILLSON Charles 1836

NEWMAN George 1831

MASTERSON Jeremiah 1831

NEWMAN George 1831

NEWMAN George 1832

NEWMAN Simon P 1838

NEWMAN Simon T 1848

KIMBALL Ira 1852

7

GRIGG John 1836

8

NEWMAN William 1838

NEWMAN George 1831

NEWMAN Simon T 1848 **9**

NEWMAN Simon T 1848

SIBERT Gideon 1845

SIBERT Gideon 1845

TURNHAM John B GRIGG 1835 John 1836

CARTER John 1831

CARTER John 1828

NEWMAN George 1831

ORTZ John 1841

MATTHEWS Isaac 1851

NEWMAN Simon P 1849

NEWMAN Simon P 1849

NEWMAN Simon P 1849

SIBERT Gideon 1847

HODGES Thomas 1847

TURNHAM John B 1835

MASTERSON Jeremiah 1835

SIBERT Jeremiah 1845

LONG Henry C 1848

LONG John 1847

LONG John 1847

HOUGHAN Thomas 1836

BROCKENBROUGH Austin 1835

SWALES Thomas 1830

MASTERSON Jeremiah 1835

NEWMAN George 1831

CARTER Thomas 1828

BONDURANT Joseph 1848

Lots-Sec. 16
L1 BRUNING, John 1846
L2 BRAYHAW, Harmon L 1850
L3 REAKER, John 1850
L4 MATHEUS, Isaac 1846
L5 REAKER, John 1850
L6 BROCKHOUSE, Harmon G 1848
L7 BROCKHOUSE, Jared H 1847
L8 SPATES, Reason 1846

16

AYLESWORTH Philip 1832

WOOLCOTT Elihu 1831

MASTERSON Jeremiah 1845

CARTER John 1831

STITES Isaiah 1830

18

STITES Isaiah 1832

LONG Henry C 1851

17

BONDURANT Joseph 1848

MASTERSON Jeremiah 1831

GRAHAM Lorenzo D 1835

WEEKS Washington 1831

STITES Isaiah 1831

BERGHAUS John W 1854

WEEKS Washington 1831

HODGES David 1845

COMER James 1854

LEE Thomas 1849

BONDURANT Joseph 1848

BURK Daniel B Jr 1852

THOMPSON Andrew J 1851

SHOEMAKER Barney 1851

URBEAN Gattliess 1850

CLOTFETTER Jacob 1830

19

WEEKS Washington 1847

HARRIS Samuel 1852

BERGHAUS John W 1854

THOMPSON Robert 1846

BUSH Daniel B Jr 1848

KENNEY Major 1844

POST William 1845

POST William 1845

KINNEY John 1845

STITES Isaiah 1832

WEEKS Washington 1831

CARTER Job 1831

WEEKS Washington 1837

20

THOMPSON John 1836

BARRICKLOW Joseph 1835

MANNING Benjamin H 1836

21

WALDO Daniel 1852

POND Martin I 1840

MCCONNEL Murray 1852

POND Martin J 1849

POND Martin J 1846

THOMPSON John 1835 WEEKS Washington 1851

SMART Thomas 1831

WEEKS Washington 1836

HODGES David L 1841

HODGES David L 1849

HODGES David L 1849

HODGES David L 1849

CURLL Elias 1851

DRYER John H 1854

KENNETT William 1844

HEMMINGHAUS Heinrich 1855

SMITH Absalom 1835

WEEKS Washington 1837

CRAWFORD William P 1837 **30**

CRISMAN William 1848

CRISMAN John C 1853

CRISMAN John C 1851 **29**

CUREE Elias 1854

KENNETT Frank 1844

28

WARRENS William M 1852

AYLESWORTH Philip 1835

HUDELSTON David 1839

CRAWFORD William P 1837

MARA John 1851

PARKER Aaron 1837

CUTLER James B 1854

THOMPSON James B 1853

THOMPSON Andrew J 1853

CRAWFORD John 1851

MCPHERSON Benjamin 1850

IDE Oliver O 1853

HUDELSON William 1839

PARKER Aaron 1837

HUDELSON James 1839

HUMMER James 1854

CRISMAN John C 1853

BAKER Francis 1836

MANNING Horatio N 1836

MCPHERSON Benjamin 1836

HUMMER James 1855

Lots-Sec. 31
L1(N½) HUDELSTON, David 1838
L2(N½) HUDELSON, William 1839

BROCKENBROUGH Austin 1835

THOMPSON James B 1851

32

REDDING Eli W 1829

STITES Isaiah 1831

ALBIN Isaac 1828

BROCKHOUSE Barney 1852

BROMLY Samuel 1853

COFFMAN Philip 1849

BROCKENBROUGH Austin 1835

PRICE Abraham 1835

BRADBURY Nathan 1826

MANARY Jonas 1830

JANUARY Peter W 1835

HILL Nimrod 1856

HUDELSON Robert L 1839

HUDELSON James 1839 **31**

KENNETT Joseph 1844

HAYWARD Stephen 1844

CRAWFORD John 1850

THOMPSON John W 1851

FUNK Presley C SWALES 1852 Thomas 1830

33

HATCH Ozias M 1851

GRIGG John 1836

JANUARY Peter W 1835

SHALDON Edward 1856

ABBEY Lemuel 1836

WEATHERS Robert S 1853

TAYLOR George 1852

BAKER Green H 1836 PRICE Abraham 1835

HATFIELD Samuel 1836

MCPHERSON Benjamin G 1836

THOMPSON John W 1853

YORK William 1828

Section 3
- MOORE Samuel 1831
- WHITLEY Samuel 1831
- WALLER Thomas C 1829
- MOORE Samuel 1828
- LESLIE Miron 1836
- WALLER Jane 1836
- NEWMAN George 1832
- NEWMAN George 1837 / NEWMAN Benjamin 1851
- MOORE Samuel 1829
- KIMBALL Ira 1852
- NEWMAN William 1835
- NEWMAN Wingate J 1836

Section 2
- CARRICK William 1831
- MOORE Andrew 1828
- BALEY Abraham R 1829
- MOORE Samuel 1828
- MOORE Reuben 1828
- BALEY Abraham R 1828

Section 1
- HOUSTON Isaac 1836
- HOUSTON Isaac 1847
- HOUSTON Isaac 1847
- HOUSTON IsaacLots-Sec. 1 1851 L1   HOUSTON, Isaac 1851   L1(W½) HOUSTON, Starett[80]1855
- POINTER William 1835
- MCCONNEL Amzi 1854
- PURVINE John 1836
- SMITH Isaac 1835
- MCCONNEL Amzi 1854
- CAWOOD Stephen B 1853
- MORRISON Robert 1836

Section 10
- KIMBALL Ira 1852
- POST William 1836
- COFFIN [42] Charles 1830
- NEWMAN Simon P 1849
- SPENCER Thomas 1829
- MCCONNEL Murray 1836
- MCCONNELL Murray 1835
- NEWMAN Benjamin 1851
- GREENE William 1835
- NEWMAN Simon P 1849
- POST George 1851
- POST James A 1837

Section 11
- GRIFFITTS Isaac 1829
- GREEN William 1835
- LONG Henry Sen 1836
- LONG Henry Sen 1836
- LONG Henry Sen 1831
- ABRAMS William G 1831
- POINTER William 1836

Section 12
- FIKE James 1830
- LONG George 1829
- PERVIANCE Jonathon 1829
- LONG George 1836
- COGBURN Zachariah 1828
- LONG [93] John 1835
- HALL Hosea 1829

Section 15
- MCCONNELL Murray 1836
- MCCONNEL Murray 1835
- MCCONNELL Murray 1835
- GREEN [50] Reynolds 1835
- MCCONNELL Murray 1836
- COX [48] Abel 1835
- MCCONNEL Murray 1835
- MCCONNEL Murray 1835

Section 14
- PRIEST John 1831
- LONG Nicholas 1835
- WRIGHT Alfred 1835
- LONG Jehu 1833
- POINTER [106] James 1835
- COGBURN Zecheriah 1831
- LONG Henry Jr 1832
- LONG Isaac 1836
- LONG John 1836
- POST William 1835
- BRENENK Barney 1851
- PREVOST Theadezea 1843
- POINTER William 1835
- POST William 1835

Section 13
- LONG Henry Jr 1832
- MOSS John Jr 1831
- LONG George 1831
- LONG [92] George 1835
- POINTER Cornelius 1832
- LONG Henry 1835
- LONG George 1835
- PURVIANCE John 1831
- WOODWARD Charles 1836

Section 22
- MCCONNELL John 1835
- MCCONNELL Murray 1836
- MCCONNELL Murray 1835
- MCCONNEL Murray 1836
- POND Martin I 1840
- BROTHERS Alexander 1834
- JANUARY Peter W 1834
- ROBINSON Samuel 1846
- POND Martin J 1840
- POND Martin J 1852
- SMITH Elias 1845

Section 23
- PREVOST Theadezea 1843
- POST William 1836
- MCCONNELL Murray 1835
- PUCKETT George F 1843
- POST William 1835
- PROVOST Theodore 1845
- ERLER Henry 1853
- PROVOST A J F 1845

Section 24
- LONG John F 1847
- WOODWARD Charles 1836
- RANSON James 1843
- RANSON James 1843
- SAXTON William 1834
- HAM William R 1833
- MITCHELL James 1835
- WOODWARD Charles 1836
- BATES Joseph H 1833
- SAXTON William 1834
- MCCONNEL Murray 1835

Section 27
- HATCH Ozias M 1851
- TAINTON Phineas W 1850
- MARA John 1853
- WARREN William M 1852
- WARREN George 1849
- WEATHERS George 1849
- MASON Samuel 1839
- MASON Samuel 1839
- FILEY George 1840

Section 26
- EDMUNDSON Thomas 1851
- HAM William R 1846
- KINNEY Major 1851
- WISE Frederick 1853
- HAM John J 1846
- WISE Frederick 1853
- BARRET James A 1849
- VALLENTINE Michael 1847
- FILEY Joseph 1853
- HILL John 1852
- WISE Frederick 1853
- FILEY George 1840

Section 25
- BATES William T 1844
- RANSON Robert 1835
- MCCONNELL Murray 1835
- MADDOX John W 1835
- BARRET James A 1849
- BARBER Augustus K 1848
- GILBERT Henry 1846
- BARRET James A 1849
- RAYBON Franklin 1849
- DEITRICK Daniel 1845
- GILBERT Henry 1849
- BROKHAUS Herman G 1846
- LENARD Levina R 1844
- LEONARD Abraham 1844
- LOAR George 1833

Section 34
- IDE Oliver C 1853
- BRADBURY Nathan 1829
- ALBIN Isaac 1829
- YORK William 1831
- JANUARY Thomas T 1836
- CRAWFORD John 1831
- CRAWFORD John 1830
- ALBIN Isaac 1828
- YORK William 1829

Section 35
- MILLER Ebenezer T 1835
- AVERITT Nathan G 1836
- ALDERSON Charles 1850
- ALBIN Isaac 1829
- AVERITT Nathan G 1836
- CHAMBERLIN Griffin 1841
- ETHEL James 1836
- CHAMBERLAIN Griffin
- CHAMBER 1845 Ain Griffin 1945

Section 36
- BLODGETT Jacob 1836
- LEONARD Abraham 1835
- WHITLEY Elisha 1829
- BROWN Thomas 1830
- SMITH William R 1835
- BROWN Thomas 1830

Helpful Hints

1. This Map's INDEX can be found on the preceding pages.

2. Refer to Map "C" to see where this Township lies within Morgan County, Illinois.

3. Numbers within square brackets [ ] denote a multi-patentee land parcel (multi-owner). Refer to Appendix "C" for a full list of members in this group.

4. Areas that look to be crowded with Patentees usually indicate multiple sales of the same parcel (re-issues), cancellations or voided transactions (that we map, anyway) or overlapping parcels. We opt to show even these ambiguous parcels, which oftentimes lead to research avenues not yet taken.

Legend

- ———— Patent Boundary
- ▬▬▬▬ Section Boundary
- No Patents Found (or Outside County)
- 1., 2., 3., ... Lot Numbers (when beside a name)
- [ ] Group Number (see Appendix "C")

Scale: Section = 1 mile X 1 mile (generally, with some exceptions)

Road Map

T16-N R12-W
3rd PM Meridian

Map Group 2

Cities & Towns
None

Cemeteries
Burrus Cemetery
Charles Schlickers Cemetery
Grace Cemetery
Graham Cemetery
Heffner Cemetery
Hemminghaus Cemetery
Houston Cemetery
Nergenah Cemetery
Newman Cemetery
Sibert Cemetery
Tippet William Cemetery
Weeks Cemetery

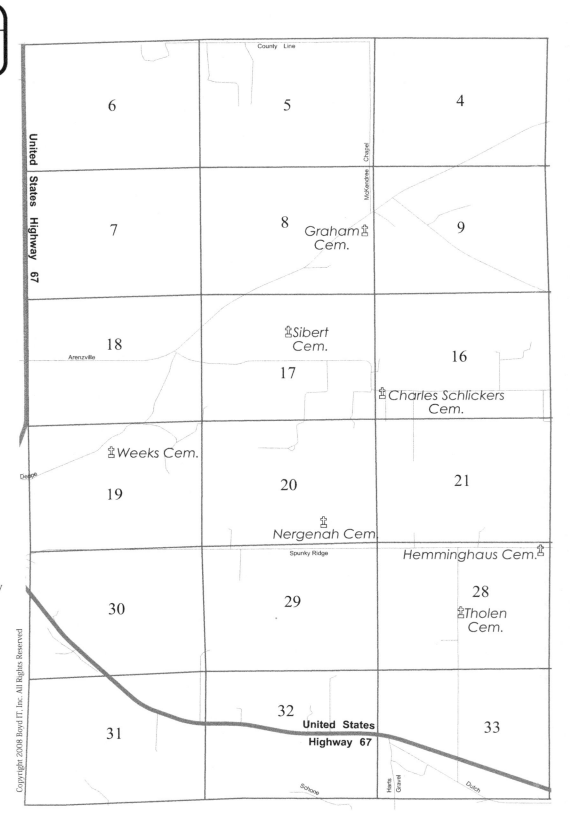

3

Newman
Cem.

🕆 Burrus Cem.   🕆
          Heffner
          Cem.   2

🕆 Houston
   Cem.   1

10

11

12

Thomas

Trones

15

Musch   14

Triopia

13

Trinity
Church

Fricke

22   23   24

Hefner Hills

27   26   25

Slaake

Grace 🕆
Cem.   Schumacher

Saint Pauls Church

34   35   36

Aufdenkamp

Tippet
William Cem.
🕆

Copyright 2008 Boyd IT, Inc. All Rights Reserved

Helpful Hints

1. This road map has a number of uses, but primarily it is to help you: a) find the present location of land owned by your ancestors (at least the general area), b) find cemeteries and city-centers, and c) estimate the route/roads used by Census-takers & tax-assessors.

2. If you plan to travel to Morgan County to locate cemeteries or land parcels, please pick up a modern travel map for the area before you do. Mapping old land parcels on modern maps is not as exact a science as you might think. Just the slightest variations in public land survey coordinates, estimates of parcel boundaries, or road-map deviations can greatly alter a map's representation of how a road either does or doesn't cross a particular parcel of land.

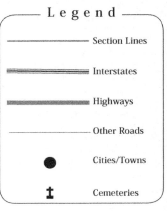

L e g e n d

———————— Section Lines

════════ Interstates

▬▬▬▬▬▬ Highways

———————— Other Roads

● Cities/Towns

🕆 Cemeteries

Scale: Section = 1 mile X 1 mile
(generally, with some exceptions)

Historical Map

T16-N R12-W
3rd PM Meridian

Map Group 2

<u>Cities & Towns</u>
None

<u>Cemeteries</u>
Burrus Cemetery
Charles Schlickers Cemetery
Grace Cemetery
Graham Cemetery
Heffner Cemetery
Hemminghaus Cemetery
Houston Cemetery
Nergenah Cemetery
Newman Cemetery
Sibert Cemetery
Tholen Cemetery
Tippet William Cemetery
Weeks Cemetery

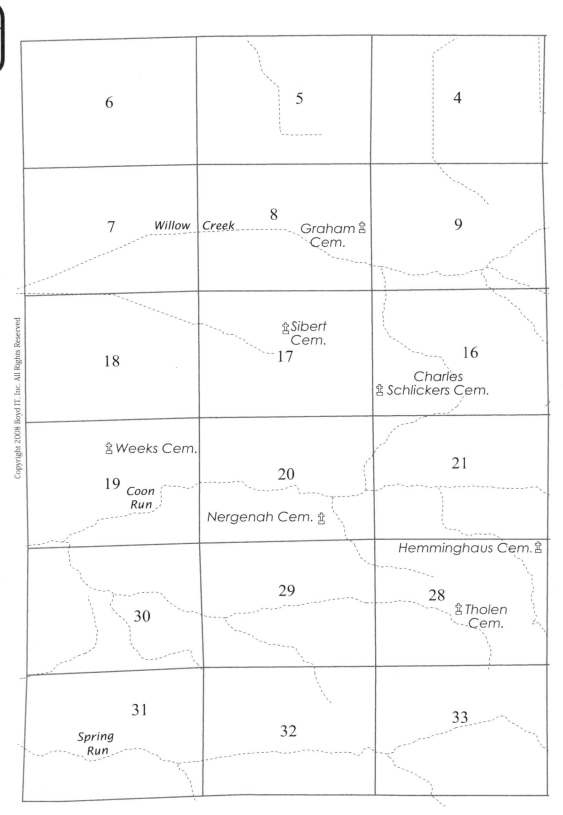

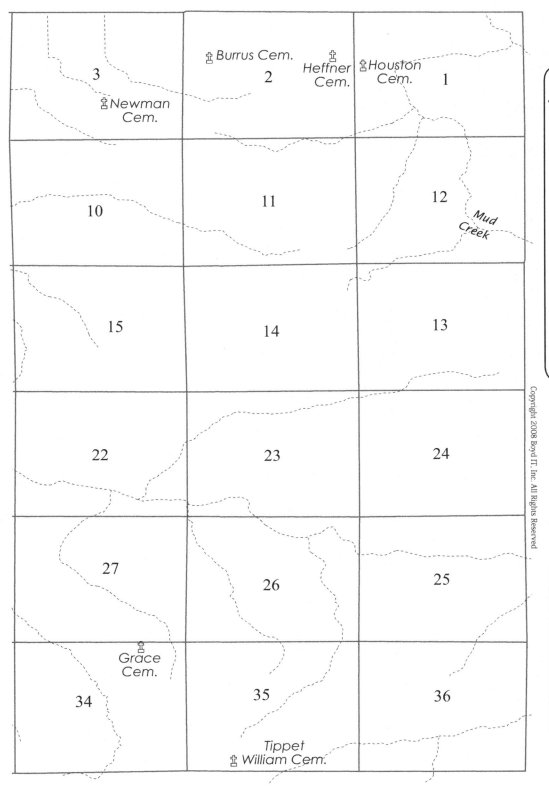

3

🪦 Burrus Cem.
2

🪦 Heffner Cem.

🪦 Houston Cem.
1

🪦 Newman Cem.

10

11

12

Mud Creek

15

14

13

22

23

24

27

26

25

🪦 Grace Cem.

34

35

36

Tippet
🪦 William Cem.

Helpful Hints

1. This Map takes a different look at the same Congressional Township displayed in the preceding two maps. It presents features that can help you better envision the historical development of the area: a) Water-bodies (lakes & ponds), b) Water-courses (rivers, streams, etc.), c) Railroads, d) City/town center-points (where they were oftentimes located when first settled), and e) Cemeteries.

2. Using this "Historical" map in tandem with this Township's Patent Map and Road Map, may lead you to some interesting discoveries. You will often find roads, towns, cemeteries, and waterways are named after nearby landowners: sometimes those names will be the ones you are researching. See how many of these research gems you can find here in Morgan County.

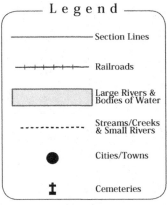

L e g e n d

——————— Section Lines

+—+—+—+—+ Railroads

Large Rivers & Bodies of Water

- - - - - - - Streams/Creeks & Small Rivers

● Cities/Towns

🪦 Cemeteries

Scale: Section = 1 mile X 1 mile
(there are some exceptions)

Map Group 3: Index to Land Patents

Township 16-North Range 11-West (3rd PM)

After you locate an individual in this Index, take note of the Section and Section Part then proceed to the Land Patent map on the pages immediately following. You should have no difficulty locating the corresponding parcel of land.

The "For More Info" Column will lead you to more information about the underlying Patents. See the *Legend* at right, and the "How to Use this Book" chapter, for more information.

ID	Individual in Patent	Sec.	Sec. Part	Purchase Date	Sale Type	IL Aliquot Part	For More Info . . .
828	ADALMAN, Leopold	8	SENE	1847-12-11	FD	SENE	R:MORGAN
823	ADDINGTON, Labird	31	S½SW	1835-11-07	FD	S2SW	R:MORGAN
601	ALFKIN, Alfred	6	N½NW	1851-10-27	FD	N2NW	
602	" "	6	NWNE	1851-10-27	FD	NWNE	
595	ALLINSON, Adam	35	E½NW	1827-11-13	FD	E2NW	R:MORGAN
754	ALTMANN, John J	6	NESE	1837-07-12	FD	NESE	R:CASS
668	ANGEL, George	14	NESW	1832-12-07	FD	NESW	R:MORGAN
670	" "	15	SESE	1832-12-07	FD	SESE	R:MORGAN
669	"	15	N½SE	1837-05-31	FD	N2SE	R:MORGAN
730	ANGEL, John	5	NWSE	1851-10-11	FD	NWSE	R:MORGAN
664	ARENZ, Francis	6	E½NE	1832-05-29	FD	E2NE	R:MORGAN
663	" "	5	W½NE	1833-06-25	FD	W2NE	R:MORGAN
665	"	9	NWNE	1854-03-02	FD	NWNE	R:CASS
661	ARNZ, Frances	5	NENE	1833-03-23	FD	NENE	R:MORGAN
662	" "	5	NENW	1833-03-23	FD	NENW	R:MORGAN
624	ATER, Bazzel	2	NESE	1835-12-29	FD	NESE	R:MORGAN
623	" "	1	L1(W½)	1850-06-01	FD	W2LOT1NW	R:MORGAN
642	" "	1	L1(W½)	1850-06-01	FD	W2LOT1NW	R:MORGAN
731	AUSEMUS, John	34	E½NE	1830-12-04	FD	E2NE	R:MORGAN
863	AUSEMUS, Peter	35	W½NE	1828-01-02	FD	W2NE	R:MORGAN
871	AUSEMUS, Philip	36	W½SW	1827-06-08	FD	W2SW	R:MORGAN
870	" "	35	E½SE	1828-09-26	FD	E2SE	R:MORGAN
925	AUSEMUS, Thomas	36	W½NW	1826-09-19	FD	W2NW	R:MORGAN
864	AUSMUS, Peter	35	W½NW	1830-12-16	FD	W2NW	R:MORGAN
872	AUSMUS, Philip	21	NESW	1835-08-31	FD	NESW	R:MORGAN
873	" "	21	NWSE	1835-08-31	FD	NWSE	R:MORGAN
850	AVERITT, Nathan	31	SENE	1833-04-08	FD	SENE	R:MORGAN
647	BAKER, Edward D	33	NWNW	1837-02-10	FD	NWNW	R:SANGAMON
725	BALLARD, Jeremiah	19	E½SE	1833-06-24	FD	E2SE	R:MORGAN
726	" "	30	NWNW	1835-07-04	FD	NWNW	R:MORGAN
735	BALLARD, John	19	SENE	1835-12-14	FD	SENE	R:NEW YORK
927	BALLARD, Thomas	19	SW	1833-06-24	FD	SWFR	R:MORGAN
928	" "	19	W½SE	1833-06-28	FD	W2SE	R:MORGAN
930	" "	4	NWSW	1833-07-03	FD	NWSW	R:MORGAN
929	" "	30	SENW	1835-10-14	FD	SENW	R:MORGAN
806	BANCROFT, Joseph H	28	SW	1848-11-24	FD	SW	
600	BARBER, Agusta Kent	30	SWNW	1838-06-04	FD	SWNW	R:MORGAN
940	BARNETT, Vina	4	NESE	1835-11-14	FD	NESEPRE	R:MORGAN S:F G:5
940	BARNETT, William	4	NESE	1835-11-14	FD	NESEPRE	R:MORGAN S:F G:5
810	BATES, Joseph H	7	NWSW	1835-10-29	FD	NWSW	R:MORGAN
807	" "	18	SESE	1840-06-11	FD	SESE	R:MORGAN
808	" "	19	NENE	1840-06-11	FD	NENE	R:MORGAN
809	" "	20	NWNW	1840-06-11	FD	NWNW	R:MORGAN
949	BATES, William T	18	SWSE	1844-06-14	FD	SWSE	R:MORGAN
685	BERGEN, Gotlieb	6	SWNE	1837-05-08	FD	SWNE	R:MORGAN
641	BLACK, David	1	N½NW	1829-11-10	FD	N2NW	R:MORGAN

ID	Individual in Patent	Sec.	Sec. Part	Purchase Date	Sale Type	IL Aliquot Part	For More Info . . .
736	BOX, John	36	W½NE	1826-11-27	FD	W2NE	R:MORGAN
709	BOZARTH, James	34	NESW	1836-11-11	FD	NESW	R:MORGAN
710	" "	34	NWNE	1836-11-11	FD	NWNE	R:MORGAN
629	BRACKENRIDGE, Caleb	8	E½SW	1835-02-18	FD	E2SW	R:KENTUCKY G:11
629	BRACKENRIDGE, John B	8	E½SW	1835-02-18	FD	E2SW	R:KENTUCKY G:11
835	BRACKENRIDGE, Marcus	.20	E½NW	1835-10-09	FD	E2NW	R:KENTUCKY G:12
835	BRACKENRIDGE, Robert	20	E½NW	1835-10-09	FD	E2NW	R:KENTUCKY G:12
729	BRADSHAW, Joel	19	E½NW	1833-08-30	FD	E2NW	R:MORGAN
737	BRANER, John	10	E½SE	1851-01-28	FD	E2SE	
739	" "	14	NWNW	1851-01-28	FD	NWNW	
738	" "	11	SWSW	1851-01-28	FD	SWSW	
625	BRATTAIN, Benjamin	35	E½NE	1827-11-30	FD	E2NE	R:MORGAN
862	BRATTON, Paul	35	W½SE	1831-05-28	FD	W2SE	R:MORGAN
740	BRAUR, John	11	SE	1830-12-16	FD	SE	R:MONTGOMERY
666	BRIDGEMAN, Franklin	4	SESW	1847-11-04	FD	SESW	R:MORGAN
667	" "	4	SWSW	1854-02-20	FD	SWSW	R:MORGAN
692	BRIDGEMAN, Hezekiah	14	NWSW	1836-01-09	FD	NWSW	R:MORGAN
693	" "	14	SESW	1836-01-09	FD	SESW	R:MORGAN
695	" "	3	SESW	1844-09-11	FD	SESW	R:MORGAN
694	" "	3	NESW	1847-04-30	FD	NESW	R:MORGAN
614	BROCKENBROUGH, Austin	15	W½NW	1833-10-18	FD	W2NW	R:MORGAN
620	" "	20	E½NE	1833-10-18	FD	E2NE	R:MORGAN
618	" "	17	E½SE	1833-10-18	FD	E2SE	R:MORGAN
619	" "	17	SWSE	1833-10-18	FD	SWSE	R:MORGAN
621	" "	20	NWNE	1833-10-18	FD	NWNE	R:MORGAN
622	" "	21	NW	1833-10-18	FD	NW	R:MORGAN
617	" "	17	E½NE	1835-12-15	FD	E2NE	R:MORGAN
615	" "	16	L6	1837-01-19	SC	LOT6SEMA	
616	" "	16	L7	1837-01-19	SC	LOT7SEMA	
582	BROKENBROUGH, A	16	L4	1835-11-21	SC	LOT4	S:I
581	" "	16	L3	1835-11-21	SC	LOT3	S:I
583	" "	16	L8	1835-11-21	SC	LOT8	S:I
580	" "	16	L2	1835-11-21	SC	LOT2	S:I
579	" "	16	L1	1835-11-21	SC	LOT1	S:I
711	BURBAGE, James	3	NWSW	1843-02-04	FD	NWSW	R:MORGAN
911	BURBANK, Edwin S	22	NESE	1857-07-29	FD	NESE	
655	" "	22	NESE	1857-07-29	FD	NESE	
788	BURTON, John W	11	E½NE	1831-11-23	FD	E2NE	R:MORGAN
822	BURTON, Katharine	12	W½NW	1831-11-23	FD	W2NW	R:MORGAN S:F
866	BUTLER, Peter	36	E½NE	1829-12-12	FD	E2NE	R:MORGAN
865	" "	14	E½NE	1830-08-07	FD	E2NE	R:MORGAN
742	CARTER, John	13	W½NW	1828-09-16	FD	W2NW	R:MORGAN
779	CARTER, William B	9	W2SE	1835-10-03	FD	W2SEPRE	R:MORGAN G:25
603	CARTER, Zadock	4	NW	1835-10-03	FD	NWPRE	R:MORGAN G:27
628	CASTLEBERRY, Elizabet	5	SESE	1835-10-17	FD	SESEPRE	R:MORGAN S:F G:29
659	CLAY, Elizabeth	34	N½NW	1851-07-11	FD	N2NW	S:F
834	CLAYTON, Madison	25	SWSW	1836-08-30	FD	SWSW	R:MORGAN
833	" "	25	SENW	1837-08-01	FD	SENW	R:MORGAN
832	" "	25	NESW	1851-06-28	FD	NESW	
898	COMBS, Samuel	8	W½SW	1830-09-11	FD	W2SW	R:MORGAN
610	COOPER, Armstong	23	NENW	1850-12-02	FD	NENW	R:MORGAN
613	COOPER, Asa D	31	SESE	1833-08-09	FD	SESE	R:MORGAN
671	COOPER, George	32	W½NW	1831-05-30	FD	W2NW	R:MORGAN
743	COOPER, John D	31	NESE	1835-07-25	FD	NESE	R:MORGAN
672	COULTER, George	24	E½SW	1830-02-02	FD	E2SW	R:MORGAN
628	COX, Beverly	5	SESE	1835-10-17	FD	SESEPRE	R:MORGAN S:F G:29
631	DALTON, Charles	18	NWNE	1839-02-09	FD	NWNE	R:MORGAN
712	DAVIS, James	23	NWNW	1834-06-24	FD	NWNW	R:MORGAN
713	" "	23	SWNW	1835-12-21	FD	SWNW	R:MORGAN
727	DAVIS, Jeremiah	17	SWSW	1836-01-01	FD	SWSW	R:MORGAN
728	" "	6	SWSE	1836-01-01	FD	SWSE	R:MORGAN
744	DEAN, John	22	NWSE	1844-11-05	FD	NWSE	R:MORGAN
830	DEANE, Lewis	28	N½SE LS	1838-11-06	FD	N2SELS	R:MORGAN
829	" "	27	NWSW	1850-06-20	FD	NWSW	R:MORGAN
831	DEATON, Littleberry H	18	L2 (N½)	1851-03-17	FD	N2LOT2NW	R:MORGAN
638	DEITRICK, Daniel	30	NWSW	1845-05-07	FD	NWSW	R:MORGAN
681	DEWEESE, George W	32	NENE	1835-10-30	FD	NENE	R:MORGAN
853	DEWEESE, Nimrod	24	E½NW	1830-07-05	FD	E2NW	R:MORGAN
852	" "	23	W½SW	1832-01-20	FD	W2SW	R:MORGAN
855	" "	32	W½NE	1832-02-01	FD	W2NE	R:MORGAN
854	" "	32	SENE	1832-08-04	FD	SENE	R:MORGAN
857	" "	33	SWNW	1835-06-15	FD	SWNW	R:MORGAN
856	" "	33	E½NW	1837-02-10	FD	E2NW	R:MORGAN

ID	Individual in Patent	Sec.	Sec. Part	Purchase Date	Sale Type	IL Aliquot Part	For More Info . . .
605	DUNCAN, Anna Maria	22	SWSW	1843-06-14	FD	SWSW	R:MORGAN S:F
802	DUNCAN, Joseph	32	E½SW	1833-06-21	FD	E2SWSK	R:MORGAN
801	" "	32		1833-06-21	FD	SESK	R:MORGAN
805	" "	33	W½SW	1833-06-26	FD	W2SW	R:MORGAN
804	" "	33	E½SW	1835-06-11	FD	E2SW	R:MORGAN
803	" "	32	SWSW	1835-06-11	FD	SWSW	R:MORGAN
800	" "	27	W½NE	1836-08-09	FD	W2NE	R:MORGAN
798	" "	27	E½NW	1836-08-09	FD	E2NW	R:MORGAN
799	" "	27	NWNW	1837-07-29	FD	NWNW	R:MORGAN
903	DURANT, Samuel	29	E½SW	1833-06-24	FD	E2SW	R:MORGAN
901	" "	20	W½SE	1833-06-24	FD	W2SE	R:MORGAN
902	" "	29	E½NW	1833-06-24	FD	E2NW	R:MORGAN
900	" "	20	SW	1833-06-27	FD	SW	R:MORGAN
904	" "	5	SENE	1833-07-03	FD	SENE	R:MORGAN
941	DYER, William A	9	SWNE	1844-09-12	FD	SWNE	R:MORGAN
656	EVANS, Elijah	29	W½SW	1831-08-22	FD	W2SW	R:MORGAN
658	EVANS, Elijan	32	E½NW	1831-08-05	FD	E2NW	R:MORGAN
723	EVANS, James Sen	17	NWSE	1833-08-22	FD	NWSE	R:MORGAN
745	EVANS, John	29	SWSE	1834-11-03	FD	SWSE	R:MORGAN
789	EVANS, John W	16	L5	1835-11-21	SC	LOT5	
790	" "	16	L9	1835-11-21	SC	LOT9	
657	EVENS, Elijah	14	S½NW	1835-07-31	FD	S2NW	R:MORGAN
649	FLETCHER, Edward	4	NESW	1835-02-24	FD	NESW	R:MORGAN
648	" "	3	SWNW	1839-01-22	FD	SWNW	R:MORGAN
660	FLETCHER, Ernest	3	SENW	1839-01-22	FD	SENW	R:MORGAN
597	GADDIS, Adam	26	NWNE	1836-08-17	FD	NWNE	R:MORGAN
596	" "	26	N½SW	1836-08-17	FD	N2SW	R:MORGAN
599	" "	27	W½SE	1836-08-17	FD	W2SE	R:MORGAN
598	" "	26	SENW	1836-08-17	FD	SENW	R:MORGAN
942	GADDIS, William H	27	SENE	1851-07-26	FD	SENE	R:MORGAN
935	GILLHAM, Thomas M	15	SESW	1851-12-17	FD	SESW	
673	GINTHER, George	6	SENW	1854-01-06	FD	SENWFR	R:MORGAN
905	GISH, Samuel	22	E½NE	1827-10-22	FD	E2NE	R:MORGAN
591	GOODPASTURE, Abram	22	SWNE	1855-11-13	FD	SWNE	R:MORGAN
604	GOODPASTURE, Andrew A	8	NESE	1840-11-06	FD	NESE	R:MORGAN
954	GREEN, Willie B	1	E½SE	1830-02-27	FD	E2SE	R:MORGAN
813	GROUT, Joseph M	28	NENW	1850-03-05	FD	NENW	R:MORGAN
814	" "	28	SENW	1851-01-17	FD	SENW	R:MORGAN
906	HAGGARD, Samuel	14	E½SE	1830-08-16	FD	E2SE	R:MORGAN
907	" "	35	E½SW	1830-11-20	FD	E2SW	R:MORGAN
895	HALL, Robert W	2	W½NW	1835-09-23	FD	W2NW	R:SANGAMON
955	HAM, Willis C	9	E½NW	1848-11-10	FD	E2NW	
847	" "	9	E½SW	1848-11-10	FD	E2SW	
956	" "	9	E½SW	1848-11-10	FD	E2SW	
642	HARNAKER, David	1	L1 (W½)	1845-12-12	FD	W2LOT1NE	R:CASS
623	" "	1	L1 (W½)	1845-12-12	FD	W2LOT1NE	R:CASS
752	HARRIS, John	2	SESW	1838-09-14	FD	SESW	R:MORGAN
750	" "	11	NENW	1838-09-14	FD	NENW	R:MORGAN
751	" "	12	SENW	1838-09-14	FD	SENW	R:MORGAN
732	HARRIS, John B	31	SWNW	1836-08-10	FD	SWNW	R:MORGAN
588	HENDERSON, Aaron	24	W½SE	1830-05-31	FD	W2SE	R:MORGAN
611	HENDERSON, Aron	25	NENW	1833-09-21	FD	NENW	R:MORGAN
636	HENDERSON, John	8	SWNW	1835-03-07	FD	SWNW	R:MORGAN
753	" "	8	SWNW	1835-03-07	FD	SWNW	R:MORGAN
851	HENDERSON, Nathaniel	13	E½NE	1827-03-20	FD	E2NE	R:MORGAN
919	HENDERSON, Silas	24	NENE	1836-01-19	FD	NENE	R:MORGAN
924	HENDERSON, Stephen	12	W½SE	1830-10-18	FD	W2SE	R:MORGAN
923	" "	12	SESW	1833-10-28	FD	SESW	R:MORGAN
943	HENDERSON, William	11	W½NW	1830-11-04	FD	W2NW	R:MORGAN
696	HODGE, Isaac	25	SESW	1835-09-09	FD	SESW	R:MORGAN
944	HOPPER, William	21	S½SE	1836-01-18	FD	S2SE	R:MORGAN
697	HOUSTON, Isaac	6	SWNW	1851-02-18	FD	SWNW	
932	HOUSTON, Thomas	10	NWNE	1833-07-22	FD	NWNE	R:MORGAN
933	" "	3	SWSW	1836-07-16	FD	SWSW	R:MORGAN
908	HUDDLESTON, Samuel M	25	E½SE	1827-11-07	FD	E2SE	R:MORGAN
909	" "	36	E½SE	1827-11-07	FD	E2SE	R:MORGAN
945	HUDDLESTON, William J	36	E½NW	1827-11-23	FD	E2NW	R:MORGAN
950	HUDDLESTON, William T	36	W½SE	1827-11-07	FD	W2SE	R:MORGAN
626	HUMPHREY, Benjamin N	25	SENE	1851-10-13	FD	SENE	
715	HUSSEY, James	28	SWSE	1853-08-10	FD	SWSE	R:MARSHALL
797	HUSTON, Jonas	4	W½SE	1835-10-19	FD	W2SE	R:MORGAN G:83
797	HUSTON, Squire	4	W½SE	1835-10-19	FD	W2SE	R:MORGAN G:83
721	JAY, James P	33	E½SE	1838-10-30	FD	E2SE	R:MORGAN

ID	Individual in Patent	Sec.	Sec. Part	Purchase Date	Sale Type	IL Aliquot Part	For More Info . . .
722	JAY, James P (Cont'd)	33	W½SE	1838-10-30	FD	W2SE	R:MORGAN
793	JOHNSON, John W	8	NENE	1837-01-05	FD	NENE	R:MORGAN
792	" "	7	L1 (S½)	1852-04-10	FD	S2LOT1SW	
791	" "	18	L1 (N½)	1852-10-26	FD	N2LOT1NW	
880	JOHNSON, Reuben	17	E½SW	1831-12-03	FD	E2SW	R:MORGAN
881	" "	17	NWSW	1834-02-25	FD	NWSW	R:MORGAN
882	" "	18	NESE	1835-07-15	FD	NESE	R:MORGAN
633	JOY, Charles	33	NWNE	1851-06-13	FD	NWNE	
634	" "	34	SWNW	1851-06-13	FD	SWNW	
632	" "	33	E½NE	1851-06-13	FD	E2NE	
886	KERSHAW, Robert	27	NESW	1852-08-23	FD	NESW	
915	KING, Sandy	29	NWSE	1835-06-05	FD	NWSE	R:MORGAN S:F
755	KIRKPATRICK, John	31	N½SW	1836-03-08	FD	N2SW	R:MORGAN
812	KIRKPATRICK, Joseph L	1	N½NE	1829-10-22	FD	N2NE	R:MORGAN
811	KLEIN, Joseph	23	E½SE	1830-03-22	FD	E2SE	R:SANGAMON
612	LAUGHERY, Arthur	15	NWNE	1844-08-23	FD	NWNE	R:MORGAN
934	LAYCOCK, Thomas	15	NESW	1839-02-04	FD	NESW	R:MORGAN
948	LAYTON, William M	22	SWNW	1839-06-10	FD	SWNW	R:MORGAN
947	" "	21	SWNE	1839-06-10	FD	SWNE	R:MORGAN
951	LAYTON, William W	18	SWNE	1849-09-22	FD	SWNE	R:MORGAN
592	LEFFLER, Absalom	30	NWNE	1834-07-18	FD	NWNE	R:MORGAN
593	" "	30	NWSE	1834-07-18	FD	NWSE	R:MORGAN
756	LEFFLER, John	17	W½NE	1835-02-02	FD	W2NE	R:MORGAN
761	" "	31	W½SE	1835-02-02	FD	W2SE	R:MORGAN
757	" "	19	W½NE	1835-02-02	FD	W2NE	R:MORGAN
760	" "	31	W½NE	1835-07-04	FD	W2NE	R:MORGAN
758	" "	30	SWNE	1835-07-04	FD	SWNE	R:MORGAN
759	" "	30	SWSE	1835-07-04	FD	SWSE	R:MORGAN
590	LEONARD, Abraham	31	NWNW	1835-11-10	FD	NWNW	R:MORGAN
674	LOAR, George	19	W½NW	1833-06-28	FD	W2NW	R:MORGAN
675	" "	5	NESE	1833-07-03	FD	NESE	R:MORGAN
899	LOCKWOOD, Samuel D	14	W½SE	1830-11-20	FD	W2SE	R:MORGAN
794	LOHR, John W	9	SWNW	1854-05-27	FD	SWNW	R:OHIO
795	" "	9	W½SW	1854-05-27	FD	W2SW	R:OHIO
708	LOWRANCE, Jacob	4	W½NE	1836-02-24	FD	W2NE	R:MORGAN
707	" "	3	NWNW	1837-05-31	FD	NWNW	R:MORGAN
946	LOWRENCE, William	4	E½NE	1836-02-18	FD	E2NE	R:MORGAN
717	MACKEY, James	13	E½SE	1826-11-11	FD	E2SE	R:MORGAN
796	MARSHALL, John W	20	SWNE	1835-10-26	FD	SWNE	R:MORGAN
889	MARTIN, Robert	15	SWNE	1835-12-19	FD	SWNE	R:MORGAN
888	" "	15	E½NW	1835-12-19	FD	E2NW	R:MORGAN
887	" "	11	NWSW	1836-01-12	FD	NWSW	R:MORGAN
883	MATHEWS, Richard	3	W½NE	1852-01-09	FD	W2NEFR	R:MORGAN
910	MATHEWS, Samuel	15		1845-01-07	FD	NWSWGLDMP	R:MORGAN
706	MCCOMB, Jacob E	30	NESE	1835-02-18	FD	NESE	R:MORGAN
842	MCCONNEL, Murray	31	E½NW	1835-07-06	FD	E2NW	R:MORGAN
841	" "	30	E½SW	1835-07-06	FD	E2SW	R:MORGAN
844	" "	7	E½SE	1835-07-06	FD	E2SE	R:MORGAN
843	" "	31	NENE	1835-07-06	FD	NENE	R:MORGAN
845	" "	8	W½SE	1835-07-06	FD	W2SE	R:MORGAN
847	MCCONNELL, Murray	9	E½SW	1835-08-18	FD	E2SW	R:MORGAN
846	" "	10	E½SW	1835-08-18	FD	E2SW	R:MORGAN
956	" "	9	E½SW	1835-08-18	FD	E2SW	R:MORGAN
848	MCCONNELL, Murry	10	E½NW	1835-08-14	FD	E2NW	R:MORGAN
764	MCFADDEN, John	12	W½SW	1829-12-05	FD	W2SW	R:MORGAN
763	" "	12	NESW	1836-01-12	FD	NESW	R:MORGAN
718	MCGEE, James	30	SESE	1833-07-31	FD	SESE	R:MORGAN
719	" "	30	SWSW	1835-01-05	FD	SWSW	R:MORGAN
720	" "	9	NWNW	1849-09-08	FD	NWNW	R:MORGAN
603	MEEKS, Allen	4	NW	1835-10-03	FD	NWPRE	R:MORGAN G:27
606	MILLEN, Archabald Jr	35	SWSW	1835-08-25	FD	SWSW	R:MORGAN
608	MILLEN, Archibald	25	W½SE	1831-10-06	FD	W2SE	R:MORGAN
607	" "	25	W½NE	1832-01-20	FD	W2NE	R:MORGAN
609	" "	34	SE	1832-01-20	FD	SE	R:MORGAN
766	MILLEN, John	34	SWNE	1833-06-27	FD	SWNE	R:MORGAN
765	" "	34	SESW	1835-08-25	FD	SESW	R:MORGAN
892	MORRISON, Robert	18	W½SW	1831-08-31	FD	W2SW	R:MORGAN
890	" "	18	NESW	1835-07-14	FD	NESW	R:MORGAN
891	" "	18	NWSE	1845-03-14	FD	NWSE	R:MORGAN
885	MORRISON, Robert Jr	18	SENW	1835-11-09	FD	SENW	R:MORGAN
747	MOSES, John H	26	SWNW	1851-08-19	FD	SWNW	R:MORGAN
769	MOSS, John	28	SESE	1838-01-05	FD	SESE	R:MORGAN
767	" "	26	SWSE	1838-01-05	FD	SWSE	R:MORGAN

ID	Individual in Patent	Sec.	Sec. Part	Purchase Date	Sale Type	IL Aliquot Part	For More Info . . .
768	MOSS, John (Cont'd)	27	NESE	1851-07-14	FD	NESE	
733	MOSS, John B	26	NENE	1845-02-01	FD	NENE	R:MORGAN
734	" "	26	SENE	1848-11-09	FD	SENE	R:MORGAN
748	MOSS, John H	22	S½SE	1852-07-13	FD	S2SE	
749	" "	27	NENE	1852-08-20	FD	NENE	
639	NILSON, Daniel	22	SENW	1848-06-12	FD	SENW	R:MORGAN
594	OGLE, Abslem	24	W½NE	1829-03-23	FD	W2NE	R:KENTUCKY
920	OSBORN, Silas	14	SWSW	1855-11-06	FD	SWSW	R:MORGAN
686	PARK, Henry M	27	SESW	1838-05-05	FD	SESW	R:MORGAN
687	" "	34	SENW	1851-07-26	FD	SENW	R:MORGAN
938	PARK, Thomas	35	NWSW	1833-12-05	FD	NWSW	R:MORGAN
936	" "	26	E½SE	1836-01-18	FD	E2SE	R:MORGAN
937	" "	27		1845-02-06	FD	SWSWP	R:MORGAN
776	PARKS, John S	34	W½SW	1835-08-25	FD	W2SW	R:SANGAMON
753	PERVINE, Charles	8	SWNW	1836-03-25	FD	SWNW	R:MORGAN
636	" "	8	SWNW	1836-03-25	FD	SWNW	R:MORGAN
589	PETERS, Aaron	11	E½SW	1836-01-12	FD	E2SW	R:MORGAN
688	PFEIL, Henry	6	SESE	1846-03-03	FD	SESE	R:MORGAN
746	PFEIL, John G	6	NWSE	1853-12-30	FD	NWSE	R:MORGAN
655	PHEASANT, Samuel	22	NESE	1857-04-14	FD	NESE	
911	"	22	NESE	1857-04-14	FD	NESE	
741	PHIEL, John C	5	SWSW	1844-03-21	FD	SWSW	R:MORGAN
630	PHILIPPI, Ceasar	5	NWNW	1835-02-16	FD	NWNW	R:MORGAN
819	PHILIPPI, Julius	5	E½SW	1835-07-31	FD	E2SW	R:MORGAN
821	" "	5	SWSE	1835-07-31	FD	SWSE	R:MORGAN
820	" "	5	SENW	1835-07-31	FD	SENW	R:MORGAN
584	PREVOST, A J F	29	NWNW	1834-07-15	FD	NWNW	R:MORGAN S:I
586	" "	30	NENE	1834-07-15	FD	NENE	R:MORGAN S:I
585	" "	29	SWNW	1834-07-18	FD	SWNW	R:MORGAN S:I
587	" "	30	SENE	1834-07-18	FD	SENE	R:MORGAN S:I
689	PRICE, Henry	1	SWSW	1834-06-24	FD	SWSW	R:MORGAN
690	" "	22	NWNE	1834-06-24	FD	NWNE	R:MORGAN
678	PURKITT, George T	22	NWSW	1835-12-31	FD	NWSW	R:MORGAN
677	" "	21	NESE	1835-12-31	FD	NESE	R:MORGAN
679	" "	28	NE	1835-12-31	FD	NE	R:MORGAN
680	" "	6	SW	1836-02-10	FD	SW	R:MORGAN
772	PURVINE, John	7	L2(S½)	1836-12-08	FD	S2LOT2SW	R:MORGAN
770	" "	7	W½NE	1837-01-13	FD	W2NE	R:MORGAN
771	" "	7	W½SE	1837-01-13	FD	W2SE	R:MORGAN
893	RANSON, Robert	7	NESW	1835-11-19	FD	NESW	R:MORGAN
849	RATLIFF, Nancy	23	NESW	1850-12-14	FD	NESW	R:MORGAN S:F
884	RATLIFF, Richard	15	SWSE	1836-01-01	FD	SWSE	R:MORGAN
894	RATLIFF, Robert	26	NWNW	1847-01-04	FD	NWNW	R:MORGAN
926	RATLIFF, Thomas B	24	W½SW	1831-11-11	FD	W2SW	R:MORGAN
931	RATLIFFE, Thomas H	23	W½SE	1830-08-26	FD	W2SE	R:MORGAN
682	REID, George W	20	SWNW	1835-11-28	FD	SWNW	R:MORGAN
957	REXROTE, Zachariah	12	NENE	1846-04-14	FD	NENE	R:MORGAN
918	RICHARDSON, Shadrick	25	W½NW	1834-02-07	FD	W2NW	R:MORGAN
916	" "	24	E½SE	1834-02-07	FD	E2SE	R:MORGAN
917	" "	24	SENE	1836-03-07	FD	SENE	R:MORGAN
635	ROBERTSON, Charles M	3	E½NE	1831-07-16	FD	E2NE	R:MORGAN
698	RUBART, Isaac	23	SENW	1851-04-28	FD	SENW	R:MORGAN
774	RUBART, John	13	E½NW	1827-10-13	FD	E2NW	R:SANGAMON
775	" "	13	E½SW	1828-06-10	FD	E2SW	R:MORGAN
773	" "	12	SENE	1845-11-19	FD	SENE	R:MORGAN
777	SAMMONS, John	26	SESW	1837-12-08	FD	SESW	R:MORGAN
651	SHARP, Edward M	1	W½SE	1832-03-07	FD	W2SE	R:MORGAN
650	" "	1	E½SW	1832-03-07	FD	E2SW	R:MORGAN
699	SHEETS, Isaac	14	NENW	1837-08-23	FD	NENW	R:MORGAN
867	SHEPHERD, Peter	23	W½NE	1830-05-10	FD	W2NE	R:MORGAN
837	SHEWSBERRY, Michael	8	E½NW	1835-05-05	FD	E2NW	R:MORGAN
838	" "	8	W½NE	1835-05-23	FD	W2NE	R:MORGAN
640	SHORT, Daniel	14	W½NE	1836-02-02	FD	W2NE	R:MORGAN
839	SHREWSBERRY, Michael	7	E½NE	1836-02-17	FD	E2NE	R:MORGAN
836	SILES, Mary	25	NWSW	1856-01-08	FD	NWSW	R:MORGAN S:F
627	SMART, Bennet	13	W½SE	1826-11-01	FD	W2SE	R:MORGAN
724	SMART, James	13	W½NE	1827-01-04	FD	W2NE	R:MORGAN
645	SMITH, David	10	W½SW	1827-01-24	FD	W2SW	R:MORGAN
644	" "	10	W½NW	1830-07-09	FD	W2NW	R:MORGAN
646	" "	10	E2SW	1835-09-04	FD	E2SWPRE	R:MORGAN G:117
643	" "	10	SWSE	1836-11-15	FD	SWSE	R:MORGAN
676	SMITH, George	10	NWSE	1836-08-22	FD	NWSE	R:MORGAN
703	SMITH, Isaac	29	E½NE	1834-10-27	FD	E2NE	R:NEW YORK

ID	Individual in Patent	Sec.	Sec. Part	Purchase Date	Sale Type	IL Aliquot Part	For More Info . . .
700	SMITH, Isaac (Cont'd)	20	E½SE	1834-10-27	FD	E2SE	R:NEW YORK
701	" "	21	W½SW	1834-10-27	FD	W2SW	R:NEW YORK
702	" "	28	W½NW	1834-10-27	FD	W2NW	R:NEW YORK
704	" "	29	W½NE	1834-10-28	FD	W2NE	R:NEW YORK
705	" "	8	NWNW	1836-02-10	FD	NWNW	R:MORGAN
779	SMITH, John	9	W2SE	1835-10-03	FD	W2SEPRE	R:MORGAN G:25
778	" "	26	NENW	1836-01-09	FD	NENW	R:MORGAN
826	SMITH, Larkin	22	NWNW	1845-01-24	FD	NWNWP	R:MORGAN
825	SMITH, Larkin B	21	NENE	1850-12-23	FD	NENE	R:MORGAN
646	SMITH, Michael	10	E2SW	1835-09-04	FD	E2SWPRE	R:MORGAN G:117
869	SMITH, Peter	27	SESE	1836-01-09	FD	SESE	R:MORGAN
868	" "	25	NENE	1852-09-28	FD	NENE	
952	SMITH, William W	21	NWNE	1847-06-15	FD	NWNE	R:MORGAN
815	STANDLEY, Joseph	17	W½NW	1828-04-23	FD	W2NW	R:MORGAN
840	STANDLEY, Moses	18	NENE	1835-06-13	FD	NENE	R:MORGAN
816	STANLEY, Joseph	18	SENE	1836-01-01	FD	SENE	R:MORGAN
858	STANLEY, Noble	26	SWNE	1851-07-26	FD	SWNE	
817	STANLY, Joseph	17	E½NW	1829-12-07	FD	E2NW	R:MORGAN
781	STARMER, John	23	E½NE	1828-12-31	FD	E2NE	R:TENNESSEE
780	" "	13	W½SW	1828-12-31	FD	W2SW	R:TENNESSEE
782	SUMMONS, John	26	SWSW	1835-10-20	FD	SWSW	R:MORGAN
783	TAYLOR, John	1	L1(E½)	1855-01-16	FD	E2LOT1NWFR	R:MORGAN
827	THOMAS, Lawson	33	SWNE	1845-06-04	FD	SWNE	R:SANGAMON
683	THOMPSON, George W	2	NENW	1834-06-09	FD	NENW	R:MORGAN
684	" "	2	SENW	1836-02-24	FD	SENW	R:MORGAN
786	THOMPSON, John	11	W½NE	1832-12-17	FD	W2NE	R:MORGAN G:126
784	" "	10	SEN½	1835-12-29	FD	S2NE	R:MORGAN
785	" "	2	SWSW	1838-10-20	FD	SWSW	R:MORGAN
874	THOMPSON, John M	2	NWSW	1845-01-23	FD	NWSWMPGLD	R:MORGAN
762	" "	2	NWSW	1845-01-23	FD	NWSWMPGLD	R:MORGAN
859	THOMPSON, Oswald Jr	10	NENE	1835-11-17	FD	NENE	R:MORGAN
860	THOMPSON, Oswell	1	SENE	1836-03-04	FD	SENE	R:MORGAN
861	THOMPSON, Ozel	2	S½SE	1832-12-17	FD	S2SE	R:MORGAN
786	THOMPSON, Phillip	11	W½NE	1832-12-17	FD	W2NE	R:MORGAN G:126
912	THOMPSON, Samuel	12	E½SE	1831-09-15	FD	E2SE	R:MORGAN
762	THORNBY, Ralph	2	NWSW	1845-01-24	FD	NWSWGLD	R:MORGAN
874	" "	2	NWSW	1845-01-24	FD	NWSWGLD	R:MORGAN
878	THORNLEY, Ralph	3	NENW	1848-04-08	FD	NENWFR	R:MORGAN
879	" "	3	SE	1849-08-23	FD	SE	
875	" "	2	NESW	1854-12-05	FD	NESW	R:MORGAN
876	" "	2	NWSE	1854-12-05	FD	NWSE	R:MORGAN
877	" "	2	L1(W½)	1854-12-05	FD	W2LOT1NE	R:MORGAN
637	TURLEY, Cornelius	22	NENW	1849-02-17	FD	NENW	R:MORGAN
787	TURLEY, John	21	SENE	1850-05-21	FD	SENE	R:MORGAN
654	TURNER, Edward W	2	SENE	1835-12-19	FD	SENE	R:MORGAN
652	" "	12	NENW	1835-12-19	FD	NENW	R:MORGAN
653	" "	2	N½NE	1835-12-19	FD	N2NE	R:MORGAN
896	TURNEY, Russell	4	SESE	1833-06-10	FD	SESE	R:MORGAN
897	" "	9	E½NE	1835-06-22	FD	E2NE	R:MORGAN
921	TYLER, Stephen H Jr	22	NESW	1836-02-08	FD	NESW	R:MORGAN
922	" "	27	SWNW	1836-02-08	FD	SWNW	R:MORGAN
818	VANEATON, Joseph	30	NENW	1834-07-23	FD	NENW	R:MORGAN
953	WARREN, William	36	E½SW	1829-10-02	FD	E2SW	R:MORGAN
714	WHITE, James Henry	21		1844-05-09	FD	SESWTYNT	R:MORGAN
939	WHITE, Thomas	26	NWSE	1854-07-18	FD	NWSE	
913	WIENSCHE, Samuel	5	NWSW	1837-04-27	FD	NWSW	R:MORGAN
914	" "	5	SWNW	1837-04-27	FD	SWNW	R:MORGAN
824	WILLIAMS, Landon	29	E½SE	1835-12-04	FD	E2SE	R:MISSOURI
716	WILSON, James M	1	NWSW	1837-09-29	FD	NWSW	R:MORGAN
691	WOLF, Henry	24	W½NW	1828-12-25	FD	W2NW	R:MORGAN

Patent Map

T16-N R11-W
3rd PM Meridian

Map Group 3

Township Statistics

Parcels Mapped	:	379
Number of Patents	:	1
Number of Individuals	:	239
Patentees Identified	:	233
Number of Surnames	:	161
Multi-Patentee Parcels	:	9
Oldest Patent Date	:	9/19/1826
Most Recent Patent	:	7/29/1857
Block/Lot Parcels	:	19
Cities and Towns	:	1
Cemeteries	:	6

Section 6
ALFKIN Alfred 1851 | ALFKIN Alfred 1851
HOUSTON Isaac 1851 | GINTHER George 1854 | BERGEN Gotlieb 1837 | ARENZ Francis 1832
PFEIL John G 1853 | ALTMANN John J 1837
PURKITT George T 1836 | DAVIS Jeremiah 1836 | PFEIL Henry 1846

Section 5
PHILIPPI Ceasar 1835 | ARNZ Frances 1833
WIENSCHE Samuel 1837 | PHILIPPI Julius 1835 | ARENZ Francis 1833
WIENSCHE Samuel 1837 | ANGEL John 1851
PHIEL John C 1844 | PHILIPPI Julius 1835 | PHILIPPI Julius 1835

Section 4
ARNZ Frances 1833 | DURANT Samuel 1833
MEEKS [27] Allen 1835 | LOWRANCE Jacob 1836 | LOWRENCE William 1836
LOAR George 1833 | BALLARD Thomas 1833 | FLETCHER Edward 1835 | BARNETT [5] Vina 1835
COX [29] Beverly 1835 | BRIDGEMAN Franklin 1854 | BRIDGEMAN Franklin 1847 | HUSTON [83] Jonas 1835 | TURNEY Russell 1833

Section 7
Lots-Sec. 7
L1(S½) JOHNSON, John W 1852
L2(S½) PURVINE, John 1836
PURVINE John 1837
BATES Joseph H 1835 | RANSON Robert 1835
PURVINE John 1837

Section 8
SMITH Isaac 1836
SHREWSBERRY Michael 1836 | HENDERSON John PERVINE 1835 Charles 1836 | SHEWSBERRY Michael 1835
MCCONNEL Murray 1835 | COMBS Samuel 1830 | BRACKENRIDGE [11] Caleb 1835

Section 9
SHEWSBERRY Michael 1835
JOHNSON John W 1837 | MCGEE James 1849 | HAM Willis C 1848 | ARENZ Francis 1854 | TURNEY Russell 1835
ADALMAN Leopold 1847 | LOHR John W 1854 | DYER William A 1844
MCCONNEL Murray 1835 | GOODPASTURE Andrew A 1840 | LOHR John W 1854 | MCCONNELL Murray 1835 | SMITH [25] John 1835
HAM Willis C 1848

Section 18
Lots-Sec. 18
L1(N½) JOHNSON, John W 1852 1839
L2(N½) DEATON, Littleberry 1851
DALTON Charles 1839 | STANDLEY Moses 1835
MORRISON Robert Jr 1835 | LAYTON William W 1849 | STANLEY Joseph 1836
18
MORRISON Robert 1831 | MORRISON Robert 1835 | MORRISON Robert 1845 | JOHNSON Reuben 1835
BATES William T 1844 | BATES Joseph H 1840 | DAVIS Jeremiah 1836

Section 17
STANDLEY Joseph 1828 | STANLY Joseph 1829 | LEFFLER John 1835
17 | BROCKENBROUGH Austin 1833
JOHNSON Reuben 1834 | EVANS James Sen 1833
JOHNSON Reuben 1831 | BROCKENBROUGH Austin 1835

Section 16
Lots-Sec. 16 | 16
L1 BROKENBROUGH, A 1835
L2 BROKENBROUGH, A 1835
L3 BROKENBROUGH, A 1835
L4 BROKENBROUGH, A 1835
L5 EVANS, John W 1835
L6 BROCKENBROUGH, Austi 1837
L7 BROCKENBROUGH, Austi 1837
L8 BROKENBROUGH, A 1835
L9 EVANS, John W 1835

Section 19
LOAR George 1833 | BRADSHAW Joel 1833 | LEFFLER John 1835 | BATES Joseph H 1840 | BATES Joseph H 1840
BALLARD John 1835 | REID George W 1835
19 | BALLARD Thomas 1833 | BALLARD Jeremiah 1833
BALLARD Thomas 1833

Section 20
20
DURANT Samuel 1833

Section 21
BROCKENBROUGH Austin 1833
BRACKENRIDGE [12] Marcus 1835 | BROCKENBROUGH Austin 1833
MARSHALL John W 1835 | BROCKENBROUGH Austin 1833
DURANT Samuel 1833 | SMITH Isaac 1834
BROCKENBROUGH Austin 1833 | SMITH William W 1847 | SMITH Larkin B 1850
LAYTON William M 1839 | TURLEY John 1850
SMITH Isaac 1834 | AUSMUS Philip 1835 | AUSMUS Philip 1835 | PURKITT George T 1835
WHITE James Henry 1844 | HOPPER William 1836

Section 30
BALLARD Jeremiah 1835 | VANEATON Joseph 1834 | LEFFLER Absalom 1834 | PREVOST A J F 1834
BARBER Agusta Kent 1838 | BALLARD Thomas 1835 | LEFFLER John 1835 | PREVOST A J F 1834
DEITRICK Daniel 1845 | 30 | LEFFLER Absalom 1834 | MCCOMB Jacob E 1835
MCGEE James 1835 | MCCONNEL Murray 1835 | LEFFLER John 1835 | MCGEE James 1833

Section 29
PREVOST A J F 1834 | DURANT Samuel 1833
PREVOST A J F 1834 | 29
DURANT Samuel 1833

Section 28
SMITH Isaac 1834 | SMITH Isaac 1834 | GROUT Joseph M 1850
SMITH Isaac 1834 | GROUT Joseph M 1851 | 28 | PURKITT George T 1835
DEANE Lewis 1838
BANCROFT Joseph H 1848 | HUSSEY James 1853 | MOSS John 1838

Section 32
KING Sandy 1835 | WILLIAMS Landon 1835
DURANT Samuel 1833 | EVANS John 1834
EVANS Elijan 1831 | 32
COOPER George 1831

Section 31
LEONARD Abraham 1835 | MCCONNEL Murray 1835 | MCCONNEL Murray 1835
HARRIS John B 1836 | 31 | LEFFLER John 1835 | AVERITT Nathan 1833
KIRKPATRICK John 1836 | LEFFLER John 1835 | COOPER John D 1835
ADDINGTON Labird 1835 | COOPER Asa D 1833 | DUNCAN Joseph 1835

Section 33
DEWEESE Nimrod 1832 | DEWEESE George W 1835 | BAKER Edward D 1837 | DEWEESE Nimrod 1837 | JOY Charles 1851 | JOY Charles 1851
DEWEESE Nimrod 1832 | DEWEESE Nimrod 1835 | THOMAS Lawson 1845
DUNCAN Joseph 1833 | DUNCAN Joseph 1833 | DUNCAN Joseph 1833 | DUNCAN Joseph 1835 | 33 | JAY James P 1838
JAY James P 1838

Section 3 (and surrounding NW area)

- LOWRANCE Jacob 1837
- THORNLEY Ralph 1848
- ROBERTSON Charles M 1831
- HALL Robert W 1835
- FLETCHER Edward 1839
- FLETCHER Ernest 1839
- MATHEWS Richard 1852
- BURBAGE James 1843
- BRIDGEMAN Hezekiah 1847
- **3**
- THORNLEY Ralph 1849
- HOUSTON Thomas 1836
- BRIDGEMAN Hezekiah 1844

Section 2

- THOMPSON George W 1834
- TURNER Edward W 1835
- THOMPSON George W 1836
- **2**
- TURNER Edward W 1835
- THORNBY Ralph 1845 / THOMPSON John M 1845
- THORNLEY Ralph 1854
- THORNLEY Ralph 1854
- ATER Bazzel 1835
- THOMPSON John 1838
- HARRIS John 1838 — Lots-Sec. 2
- L1(W½) THORNLEY, Ralph 1854
- THOMPSON Ozel 1832

Section 1

- BLACK David 1829
- KIRKPATRICK Joseph L 1829
- Lots-Sec. 1
- L1(E½) TAYLOR, John 1855
- L1(W½) ATER, Bazzel 1850
- L1(W½) HARNAKER, David 1845
- THOMPSON Oswell 1836
- WILSON James M 1837
- SHARP Edward M 1832
- **1**
- GREEN Willie B 1830
- PRICE Henry 1834
- SHARP Edward M 1832

Section 10

- SMITH David 1830
- MCCONNELL Murry 1835
- HOUSTON Thomas 1833
- THOMPSON Oswald Jr 1835
- THOMPSON John 1835
- **10**
- SMITH David 1827
- SMITH George 1836
- BRANER John 1851
- SMITH David 1836
- SMITH [117] David 1835
- MCCONNELL Murray 1835

Section 11

- HENDERSON William 1830
- HARRIS John 1838
- **11**
- THOMPSON [126] John 1832
- MARTIN Robert 1836
- PETERS Aaron 1836
- BRANER John 1851
- BRAUR John 1830

Section 12

- BURTON John W 1831
- BURTON Katharine 1831
- TURNER Edward W 1835
- HARRIS John 1838
- **12**
- REXROTE Zachariah 1846
- RUBART John 1845
- MCFADDEN John 1829
- MCFADDEN John 1836
- HENDERSON Stephen 1830
- HENDERSON Stephen 1833
- THOMPSON Samuel 1831

Section 15

- BROCKENBROUGH Austin 1833
- MARTIN Robert 1835
- LAUGHERY Arthur 1844
- **15**
- MARTIN Robert 1835
- MATHEWS Samuel 1845
- LAYCOCK Thomas 1839
- ANGEL George 1837
- GILLHAM Thomas M 1851
- RATLIFF Richard 1836
- ANGEL George 1832

Section 14

- BRANER John 1851
- SHEETS Isaac 1837
- SHORT Daniel 1836
- BUTLER Peter 1830
- **14**
- EVENS Elijah 1835
- BRIDGEMAN Hezekiah 1836
- ANGEL George 1832
- OSBORN Silas 1855
- BRIDGEMAN Hezekiah 1836
- LOCKWOOD Samuel D 1830
- HAGGARD Samuel 1830

Section 13

- CARTER John 1828
- RUBART John 1827
- SMART James 1827
- HENDERSON Nathaniel 1827
- **13**
- STARMER John 1828
- RUBART John 1828
- SMART Bennet 1826
- MACKEY James 1826

Section 22

- SMITH Larkin 1845
- TURLEY Cornelius 1849
- PRICE Henry 1834
- GISH Samuel 1827
- LAYTON William M 1839
- NILSON Daniel 1848
- GOODPASTURE Abram 1855
- **22**
- PURKITT George T 1835
- TYLER Stephen H Jr 1836
- DEAN John 1844
- BURBANK Edwin S / PHEASANT Samuel 1857
- DUNCAN Anna Maria 1843
- MOSS John H 1852

Section 23

- DAVIS James 1834
- COOPER Armstong 1850
- SHEPHERD Peter 1830
- DAVIS James 1835
- RUBART Isaac 1851
- **23**
- STARMER John 1828
- WOLF Henry 1828
- RATLIFF Nancy 1850
- DEWEESE Nimrod 1832
- RATLIFFE Thomas H 1830
- KLEIN Joseph 1830

Section 24

- DEWEESE Nimrod 1830
- OGLE Abslem 1829
- HENDERSON Silas 1836
- RICHARDSON Shadrick 1836
- **24**
- RATLIFF Thomas B 1831
- COULTER George 1830
- HENDERSON Aaron 1830
- RICHARDSON Shadrick 1834

Section 27

- DUNCAN Joseph 1837
- DUNCAN Joseph 1836
- MOSS John H 1852
- RATLIFF Robert 1847
- TYLER Stephen H Jr 1836
- DUNCAN Joseph 1836
- **27**
- GADDIS William H 1851
- MOSES John H 1851
- DEANE Lewis 1850
- KERSHAW Robert 1852
- GADDIS Adam 1836
- MOSS John 1851
- GADDIS Adam 1836
- PARK Thomas 1845
- PARK Henry M 1838
- SMITH Peter 1836
- SUMMONS John 1835

Section 26

- SMITH John 1836
- GADDIS Adam 1836
- STANLEY Noble 1851
- MOSS John B 1845
- MOSS John B 1848
- GADDIS Adam 1836
- **26**
- WHITE Thomas 1854
- PARK Thomas 1836
- SAMMONS John 1837
- MOSS John 1838

Section 25

- HENDERSON Aron 1833
- RICHARDSON Shadrick 1834
- SMITH Peter 1852
- HUMPHREY Benjamin N 1851
- CLAYTON Madison 1837
- MILLEN Archibald 1832
- SILES Mary 1856
- CLAYTON Madison 1851
- HUDDLESTON Samuel M 1827
- **25**
- CLAYTON Madison 1836
- HODGE Isaac 1835
- MILLEN Archibald 1831

Section 34

- CLAY Elizabeth 1851
- BOZARTH James 1836
- AUSEMUS John 1830
- JOY Charles 1851
- PARK Henry M 1851
- MILLEN John 1833
- PARKS John S 1835
- BOZARTH James 1836
- **34**
- MILLEN Archibald 1832
- MILLEN John 1835

Section 35

- AUSMUS Peter 1830
- ALLINSON Adam 1827
- AUSEMUS Peter 1828
- BRATTAIN Benjamin 1827
- PARK Thomas 1833
- **35**
- HAGGARD Samuel 1830
- BRATTON Paul 1831
- AUSEMUS Philip 1828
- MILLEN Archabald Jr 1835

Section 36

- AUSEMUS Thomas 1826
- HUDDLESTON William J 1827
- BOX John 1826
- BUTLER Peter 1829
- AUSEMUS Philip 1827
- **36**
- WARREN William 1829
- HUDDLESTON William T 1827
- HUDDLESTON Samuel M 1827

Helpful Hints

1. This Map's INDEX can be found on the preceding pages.

2. Refer to Map "C" to see where this Township lies within Morgan County, Illinois.

3. Numbers within square brackets [ ] denote a multi-patentee land parcel (multi-owner). Refer to Appendix "C" for a full list of members in this group.

4. Areas that look to be crowded with Patentees usually indicate multiple sales of the same parcel (re-issues), cancellations or voided transactions (that we map, anyway) or overlapping parcels. We opt to show even these ambiguous parcels, which oftentimes lead to research avenues not yet taken.

Legend

- Patent Boundary
- Section Boundary
- No Patents Found (or Outside County)
- 1., 2., 3., ... Lot Numbers (when beside a name)
- [ ] Group Number (see Appendix "C")

Scale: Section = 1 mile X 1 mile (generally, with some exceptions)

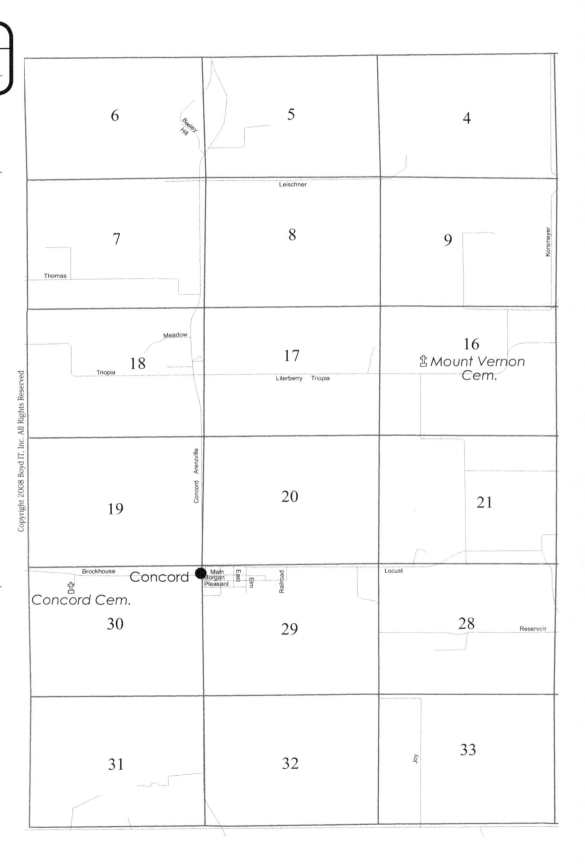

Road Map

T16-N R11-W
3rd PM Meridian

Map Group 3

Cities & Towns
Concord

Cemeteries
Angel Cemetery
Concord Cemetery
Crum Cemetery
Mount Vernon Cemetery
Smith Cemetery
Walnut Grove Cemetery

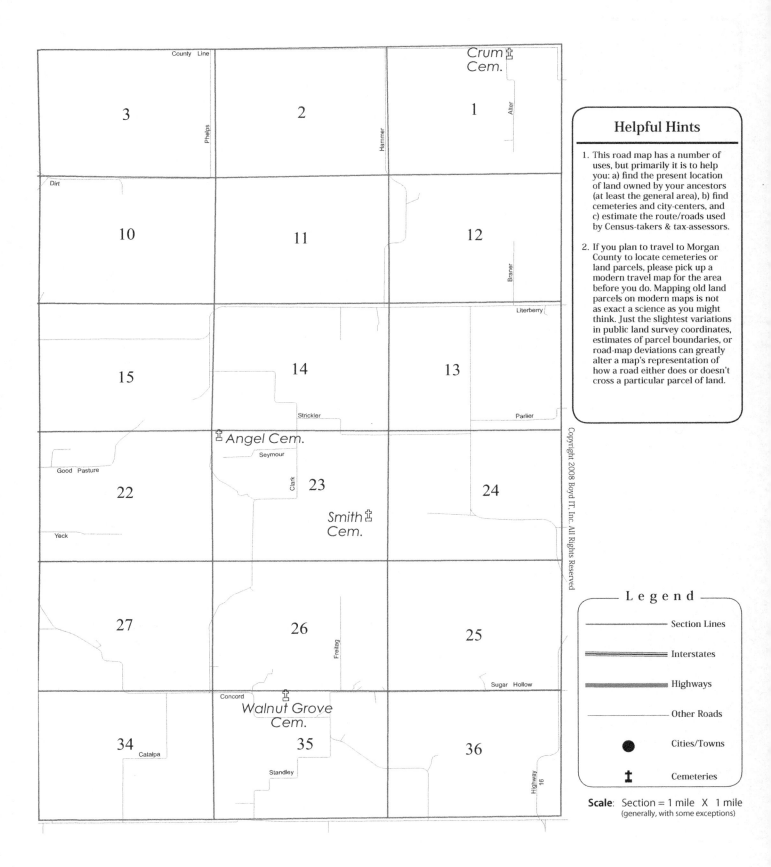

County Line

3

Crum Cem.

2

1

Alter

Phelps

Hammer

Dirt

10

11

12

Braner

Literberry

15

14

13

Strickler

Parlier

Angel Cem.

Seymour

Good Pasture

22

Clark

23

24

Yeck

Smith Cem.

27

26

Freitag

25

Sugar Hollow

Concord

Walnut Grove Cem.

34

Catalpa

35

Standley

36

Highway 16

Helpful Hints

1. This road map has a number of uses, but primarily it is to help you: a) find the present location of land owned by your ancestors (at least the general area), b) find cemeteries and city-centers, and c) estimate the route/roads used by Census-takers & tax-assessors.

2. If you plan to travel to Morgan County to locate cemeteries or land parcels, please pick up a modern travel map for the area before you do. Mapping old land parcels on modern maps is not as exact a science as you might think. Just the slightest variations in public land survey coordinates, estimates of parcel boundaries, or road-map deviations can greatly alter a map's representation of how a road either does or doesn't cross a particular parcel of land.

Legend

————	Section Lines
═══════	Interstates
▬▬▬▬▬	Highways
————	Other Roads
●	Cities/Towns
✝	Cemeteries

Scale: Section = 1 mile X 1 mile
(generally, with some exceptions)

95

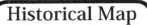

Historical Map

T16-N R11-W
3rd PM Meridian

Map Group 3

Cities & Towns
Concord

Cemeteries
Angel Cemetery
Concord Cemetery
Crum Cemetery
Mount Vernon Cemetery
Smith Cemetery
Walnut Grove Cemetery

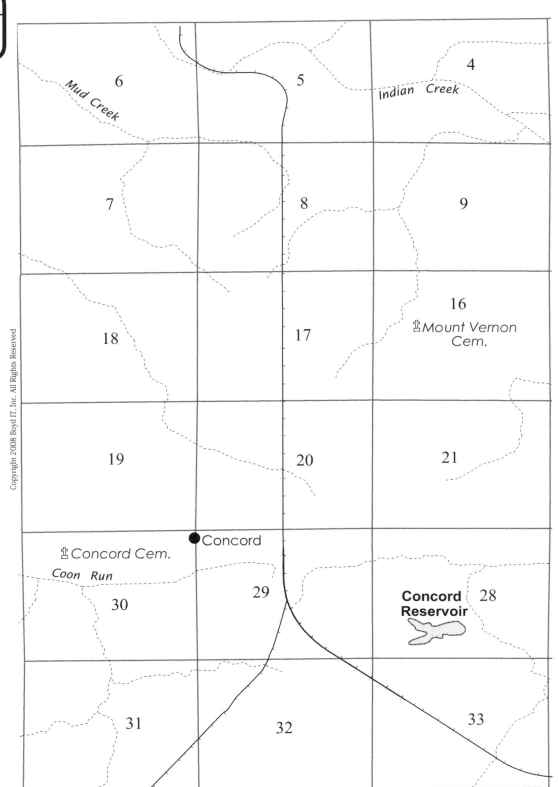

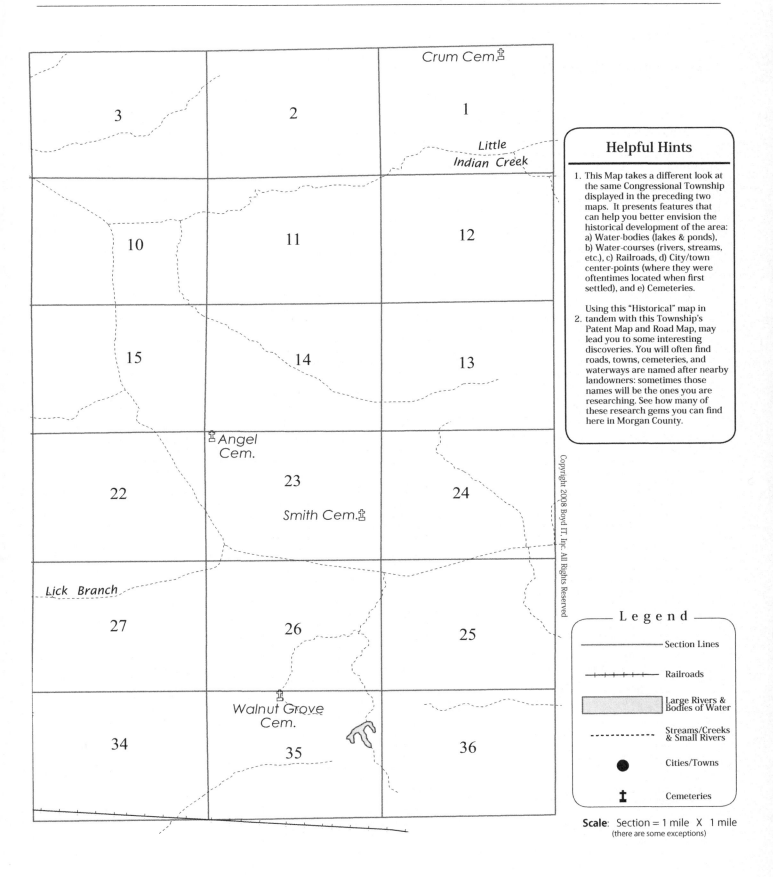

Crum Cem.⚓

3

2

1

Little
Indian Creek

10

11

12

15

14

13

⚓Angel
Cem.

23

Smith Cem.⚓

22

24

Lick Branch

27

26

25

Walnut Grove
Cem.⚓

34

35

36

Helpful Hints

1. This Map takes a different look at the same Congressional Township displayed in the preceding two maps. It presents features that can help you better envision the historical development of the area: a) Water-bodies (lakes & ponds), b) Water-courses (rivers, streams, etc.), c) Railroads, d) City/town center-points (where they were oftentimes located when first settled), and e) Cemeteries.

2. Using this "Historical" map in tandem with this Township's Patent Map and Road Map, may lead you to some interesting discoveries. You will often find roads, towns, cemeteries, and waterways are named after nearby landowners: sometimes those names will be the ones you are researching. See how many of these research gems you can find here in Morgan County.

L e g e n d

————————	Section Lines
‑+‑+‑+‑+‑+‑+‑	Railroads
▭	Large Rivers & Bodies of Water
‑ ‑ ‑ ‑ ‑ ‑ ‑	Streams/Creeks & Small Rivers
⬤	Cities/Towns
⚓	Cemeteries

Scale: Section = 1 mile X 1 mile
(there are some exceptions)

Map Group 4: Index to Land Patents

Township 16-North Range 10-West (3rd PM)

After you locate an individual in this Index, take note of the Section and Section Part then proceed to the Land Patent map on the pages immediately following. You should have no difficulty locating the corresponding parcel of land.

The "For More Info" Column will lead you to more information about the underlying Patents. See the *Legend* at right, and the "How to Use this Book" chapter, for more information.

```
                        LEGEND
             "For More Info . . . " column
   G = Group   (Multi-Patentee Patent, see Appendix "C")
   R = Residence
   S = Social Status


   See Appendix A for list of abbreviations used by the
   Illinois State Archives in describing the place and
   nature of these land patents.

   Note: if the Abbreviations contain "L", "BL", "LOT",
   or "BLOCK", the exact whereabouts of the parcel within
   the section is not known.
```

ID	Individual in Patent	Sec.	Sec. Part	Purchase Date	Sale Type	IL Aliquot Part	For More Info . . .
1163	AKERS, Peter	28	NWSW	1832-07-24	FD	NWSW	R:MORGAN
1164	" "	29	SESE	1832-07-24	FD	SESE	R:MORGAN
1165	AKIRS, Peter	32	W½NW	1835-06-09	FD	W2NW	R:MORGAN
962	ALLINSON, Adam	35	W½NE	1826-09-18	FD	W2NE	R:MORGAN
963	" "	35	W½SE	1828-04-07	FD	W2SE	R:MORGAN
1085	ANGEL, John	15		1845-01-21	FD	SENEGLDMP	R:MORGAN
1204	ARCHER, Sharp B	29	NENE	1835-08-01	FD	NENE	R:MORGAN
1268	BABB, William W	13	W½NE	1828-03-13	FD	W2NE	R:MORGAN
1267	" "	12	E½SW	1828-05-30	FD	E2SW	R:MORGAN
1008	BADGER, Edmund W	34	NWSW	1823-11-08	FD	NWSW	R:MORGAN
1009	" "	34	SENW	1833-01-01	FD	SENW	R:MORGAN
1090	BADGER, John	27	W½SW	1830-07-20	FD	W2SW	R:MORGAN
1021	BARBER, Henry	22	SWSE	1836-07-19	FD	SWSE	R:MORGAN
1022	" "	28	SENE	1836-07-19	FD	SENE	R:MORGAN
1218	BARBER, Thomas	22	NWSE	1836-07-12	FD	NWSE	R:MORGAN
1219	" "	28	NENE	1836-07-12	FD	NENE	R:MORGAN
1220	BARKER, Thomas	32	E½NW	1837-05-06	FD	E2NW	R:MORGAN
1224	BARLAND, Thomas	34	W½NW	1835-07-20	FD	W2NW	R:MORGAN
1223	" "	34	SWSW	1835-12-03	FD	SWSW	R:MORGAN
1222	" "	28	W½NE	1835-12-03	FD	W2NE	R:MORGAN
1250	" "	21	SWSE	1835-12-03	FD	SWSE	R:MORGAN
1221	" "	21	SWSE	1835-12-03	FD	SWSE	R:MORGAN
973	BATEMAN, Burgen	30	W½SE	1835-11-12	FD	W2SE	R:MORGAN
977	BEGGS, Charles	2	NE	1826-10-11	FD	NEFR	R:INDIANA
976	" "	1	SW	1827-05-22	FD	SW	R:CLARK
974	" "	1	NW	1829-05-12	FD	NWFR	R:INDIANA
975	" "	1	SE	1831-06-17	FD	SE	R:MORGAN
1096	BERGEN, John G	11	E½SE	1829-01-07	FD	E2SE	R:SANGAMON
1097	" "	6	E½SW	1830-03-19	FD	E2SW	R:SANGAMON
968	BERRY, Benjamin	24	SWNW	1835-03-08	FD	SWNW	R:MORGAN
1113	BERRY, John M	24	SWNE	1853-08-09	FD	SWNE	R:MORGAN
1112	" "	13	SESE	1853-08-09	FD	SESE	R:MORGAN
1260	BERRY, William M	36	W½NE	1831-07-19	FD	W2NE	R:MORGAN
1175	BIBB, Richard	24	NWNW	1836-01-30	FD	NWNW	R:MORGAN
1173	" "	13	E½SW	1836-01-30	FD	E2SW	R:MORGAN
1174	" "	23	NENE	1836-01-30	FD	NENE	R:MORGAN
987	BLACK, David	9	E½NE	1826-10-25	FD	E2NE	R:MORGAN
986	" "	4	SE	1826-10-25	FD	SE	R:MORGAN
1185	BLACK, Samuel	33	SENE	1835-07-18	FD	SENE	R:MORGAN
1183	" "	23	SENW	1835-07-23	FD	SENW	R:MORGAN
1184	" "	27	SWNW	1836-05-30	FD	SWNW	R:MORGAN
1210	BOX, Stephen	26	E½SE	1826-10-31	FD	E2SE	R:MORGAN
1234	BRISTOE, Thomas Jr	20	SENE	1833-12-02	FD	SENE	R:MORGAN
1235	" "	21	SWNW	1833-12-02	FD	SWNW	R:MORGAN
1082	BRISTOW, Joab P	7	NWNW	1849-06-25	FD	NWNWFR	R:MORGAN
1149	BRISTOW, Mathias	34	E½SW	1830-11-29	FD	E2SW	R:SCHUYLER

ID	Individual in Patent	Sec.	Sec. Part	Purchase Date	Sale Type	IL Aliquot Part	For More Info . . .
1225	BRISTOW, Thomas	17	E½SE	1826-09-18	FD	E2SE	R:MORGAN
1227	" "	8	SWNW	1835-09-02	FD	SWNW	R:MORGAN
1226	" "	7	SWSW	1849-06-25	FD	SWSWFR	R:MORGAN
1236	BRISTOW, Thomas Jr	21	SENW	1835-12-19	FD	SENWPRE	R:MORGAN
1091	BROADHEAD, John	29	SWNW	1835-07-30	FD	SWNW	R:MORGAN
1228	BROADHEAD, Thomas	21	SESE	1836-07-07	FD	SESE	R:MORGAN
1247	BROWN, William	32	NWSE	1836-07-30	FD	NWSE	R:MORGAN
1248	" "	33	SESW	1836-07-30	FD	SESW	R:MORGAN
1161	BUCKINGHAM, Nathan	33	SENW	1835-07-18	FD	SENW	R:MORGAN
1160	" "	33	NESW	1835-07-18	FD	NESW	R:MORGAN
1166	BUCKSTON, Peter	6	W½SE	1835-02-06	FD	W2SE	R:MORGAN
1119	CLARK, John S	16	L3	1832-04-16	SC	LOT3E2NW16	
1120	" "	16	L6	1833-02-16	SC	LOT6E2SW16	
1121	" "	21	SESW	1835-12-15	FD	SESW	R:MORGAN
1122	" "	28	NWNW	1835-12-15	FD	NWNW	R:MORGAN
1250	CLARKE, William	21	SWSE	1835-12-09	FD	SENWVOID	R:MORGAN
1249	" "	21	NESW	1835-12-09	FD	NESW	R:MORGAN
1221	" "	21	SWSE	1835-12-09	FD	SENWVOID	R:MORGAN
1031	COEN, Hugh	26	E½SW	1828-03-18	FD	E2SW	R:MORGAN
1030	" "	24	W½SE	1828-03-18	FD	W2SE	R:MORGAN
1029	" "	24	SENW	1836-05-23	FD	SENW	R:MORGAN
1012	COLE, Elijah	21	W½NE	1829-12-04	FD	W2NE	R:MORGAN
1133	COLE, Joseph	35	E½SW	1828-12-25	FD	E2SW	R:MORGAN
1146	COONS, Martin	21	NESE	1833-01-04	FD	NESE	R:MORGAN
1147	" "	21	NWSE	1835-12-15	FD	NWSE	R:MORGAN
1052	CORRINGTON, James B	28	W½SE	1830-06-21	FD	W2SE	R:MORGAN
969	COUCHMAN, Benjamin	20	W½SE	1829-02-19	FD	W2SE	R:MORGAN
970	" "	7	S½SW	1834-02-24	FD	S2SW	R:MORGAN
1157	COUCHMAN, Milesent	7	NESW	1837-05-09	FD	NESW	R:MORGAN
1167	COWNOVER, Peter	2	E½SW	1826-09-18	FD	E2SW	R:MORGAN
1168	" "	2	W½SW	1826-12-06	FD	W2SW	R:MORGAN
978	COX, Charles	23	SESE	1835-03-24	FD	SESE	R:MORGAN
1077	COX, Jeremiah	35	E½SE	1829-10-26	FD	E2SE	R:MORGAN
1078	" "	36	E½SW	1831-07-25	FD	E2SW	R:MORGAN
1027	CRABTREE, Hiram	17	W½SE	1827-10-08	FD	W2SE	R:MORGAN
1158	CRAIG, Moses H	20	NWNW	1835-11-30	FD	NWNW	R:MORGAN
1150	CRUM, Mathias	12	NW	1830-09-28	FD	NW	R:INDIANA
1244	DANIELS, Verin	20	E½SE	1831-02-25	FD	E2SE	R:MORGAN
1148	DAWSON, Elijah	29	E½SW	1835-07-29	FD	E2SW	R:MORGAN
1013	" "	29	E½SW	1835-07-29	FD	E2SW	R:MORGAN
1229	DINWIDDIE, Thomas	17	E½NW	1826-09-18	FD	E2NW	R:MORGAN
1134	DOBSON, Joseph	30	NENE	1837-07-04	FD	NENE	R:MORGAN
979	DRAKE, Charles	20	W½SW	1836-08-11	FD	W2SW	R:MORGAN
1028	ELLISTON, Hiram	11	W½SE	1829-04-10	FD	W2SE	R:MORGAN
1092	ELMER, John	19	E½SE	1836-08-11	FD	E2SE	R:NEW JERSEY
1093	ELMORE, John	30	W½NW	1835-11-12	FD	W2NW	R:NEW JERSEY
1042	EMRICK, Jacob	3	SE	1826-10-16	FD	SE	R:MORGAN
1041	" "	10	E½NE	1826-10-16	FD	E2NE	R:MORGAN
1094	EPLER, John	1	NE	1830-07-30	FD	NE	R:INDIANA
1095	FORSYTHE, John	29	NWNW	1851-05-09	FD	NWNW	R:SANGAMON
1177	GAINES, Richard	27	E½SE	1828-11-10	FD	E2SE	R:MORGAN
1176	" "	26	W½SW	1829-01-05	FD	W2SW	R:SANGAMON
1178	GAINS, Richard	25	W½NE	1829-12-12	FD	W2NE	R:MORGAN
1252	GEERS, William	36	W½SE	1831-07-22	FD	W2SE	R:MORGAN
1251	" "	24	W½SW	1831-07-25	FD	W2SW	R:MORGAN
1253	GENTRY, William	22	E½SW	1830-07-19	FD	E2SW	R:MORGAN
1254	GILLIAM, William	11	W½NE	1830-07-24	FD	W2NE	R:OHIO
1049	GRAVES, James A	36	SESE	1834-07-31	FD	SESE	R:MORGAN
1048	" "	36	NESE	1835-06-05	FD	NESE	R:MORGAN
1141	GRAVES, Lewis	6	W½NW	1829-12-18	FD	W2NWFR	R:MORGAN
1101	GREEN, John	31	W½SE	1830-11-26	FD	W2SE	R:MORGAN
1104	GRIGG, John	33	W½NW	1836-02-09	FD	W2NW	R:SANGAMON
1103	" "	33	NENW	1836-02-09	FD	NENW	R:SANGAMON
1102	" "	32	NE	1836-02-09	FD	NE	R:SANGAMON
1106	HALL, John	16	L9	1835-07-14	SC	LOT9	
1105	" "	16	L8	1835-07-14	SC	LOT8	
990	HAMAKER, David	6	W½SW	1830-10-21	FD	W2SW	R:MORGAN
1107	HARDIN, John J	31	NE	1833-06-03	FD	NE	R:MORGAN
1083	HARGROVE, Joel	9	E½SW	1827-08-15	FD	E2SW	R:MORGAN
1255	HARRISON, William	15	E½NE	1827-10-19	FD	E2NE	R:MORGAN
1202	HEMSTED, Seth	23	SENE	1838-07-28	FD	SENELS	R:MORGAN
993	HENDERSHOT, David	9	W½SE	1826-09-18	FD	W2SE	R:MORGAN
992	" "	17	W½NE	1826-09-18	FD	W2NE	R:MORGAN

ID	Individual in Patent	Sec.	Sec. Part	Purchase Date	Sale Type	IL Aliquot Part	For More Info . . .
991	HENDERSHOT, David (Cont'd)	17	E½NE	1827-01-15	FD	E2NE	R:MORGAN
994	HENDERSON, David	18	W½SW	1826-10-23	FD	W2SW	R:MORGAN
988	HENDERSON, David G	16	L5	1832-04-16	SC	LOT5W2SW16	
1006	HENDERSON, David W	8	E½SE	1828-07-11	FD	E2SE	R:MORGAN
1005	" "	8	E½NW	1830-10-01	FD	E2NW	R:MORGAN
1002	" "	16	L4	1832-04-16	SC	LOT4W2NW	
1003	" "	20	SENW	1833-09-17	FD	SENW	R:MORGAN
1004	" "	8	E½NE	1835-11-17	FD	E2NE	R:MORGAN
1079	HENDERSON, Jeremiah	19	E½NE	1836-11-26	FD	E2NELS	R:MORGAN
1206	HENDERSON, Silas	19	NWSW	1835-10-06	FD	NWSW	R:MORGAN
1207	" "	19	L2 (S½)	1850-05-01	FD	S2LOT2NW	R:MORGAN
1186	HUDDLESTON, Samuel M	31	W½NW	1826-09-18	FD	W2NWFR	R:MORGAN
1187	" "	31	W½SW	1826-09-18	FD	W2SWFR	R:MORGAN
1256	HUDDLESTON, William J	30	W½SW	1829-04-03	FD	W2SW	R:MORGAN
1035	HUDSON, Isaac	21	NENW	1834-07-23	FD	NENW	R:MORGAN
1036	"	21	NWNW	1835-12-15	FD	NWNW	R:MORGAN
1020	JAYNE, Gersham	33	E½SE	1829-12-05	FD	E2SE	R:SANGAMON
1058	JENKINS, James	34	E½SE	1827-10-05	FD	E2SE	R:MORGAN
1179	JOHNSON, Richard	8	W½SE	1827-11-29	FD	W2SE	R:MORGAN
1272	JOHNSON, Zachariah	8	SESW	1835-02-02	FD	SESW	R:MORGAN
959	JONES, Abraham	29	W½SE	1830-11-11	FD	W2SE	R:MORGAN
1043	KEPLINGER, Jacob	22	E½NE	1828-12-22	FD	E2NE	R:MORGAN
1230	LARIMORE, Thomas J	27	E½SW	1830-07-19	FD	E2SW	R:MORGAN
1232	" "	34	NENW	1836-01-08	FD	NENW	R:MORGAN
1233	" "	34	SWNE	1836-01-08	FD	SWNE	R:MORGAN
1231	" "	27	W½SE	1836-07-04	FD	W2SE	R:MORGAN
1111	LAURIE, John	34	E½NE	1836-01-08	FD	E2NE	R:MORGAN
1084	LEWIS, John A	14	W½SE	1831-05-30	FD	W2SE	R:MORGAN
965	LINDSEY, Allen	12	E½SE	1826-12-02	FD	E2SE	R:MORGAN
1257	LINDSEY, William	13	NESE	1837-02-25	FD	NESE	R:MORGAN
1055	LURTON, James H	15	W½SW	1835-12-03	FD	W2SW	R:MORGAN
1259	LURTON, William	16	L2	1833-05-27	SC	LOT2W2NE16	
1258	" "	16	L1	1833-05-27	SC	LOT1E2NE16	
1023	MADISON, Henry	13	E½NE	1826-09-18	FD	E2NE	R:MORGAN
1024	" "	14	NW	1826-09-18	FD	NW	R:MORGAN
1025	" "	4	NE	1826-12-11	FD	NEFR	R:MORGAN
1172	MARTIN, Preston	31	E½SE	1830-09-18	FD	E2SE	R:MORGAN
1205	MATTINGLY, Shelton	9	E½NW	1827-10-06	FD	E2NW	R:SANGAMON
1034	MCCLURE, Hugh	11	W½SW	1826-10-13	FD	W2SW	R:MORGAN
1032	" "	10	W½NE	1826-10-13	FD	W2NE	R:MORGAN
1033	" "	10	W½SE	1827-09-18	FD	W2SE	R:MORGAN
1115	MCCLURE, John	16	L7	1833-05-27	SC	LOT7W2SE16	
1159	MCCONNEL, Murry	28	E½SE	1835-08-01	FD	E2SE	R:MORGAN
1188	MCCONNELL, Samuel	33	N½NE	1835-07-20	FD	N2NE	R:MORGAN
995	MCCOY, David	36	W½SW	1831-03-08	FD	W2SW	R:MORGAN
983	MCDONALD, Daniel	35	W½NW	1830-01-20	FD	W2NW	R:MORGAN
1116	MCELFRESH, John	32	SWSE	1836-02-01	FD	SWSE	R:MORGAN
1060	MCFILLON, James	5	W½SW	1835-11-03	FD	W2SW	R:MORGAN G:102
1061	" "	6	E½NW	1835-11-03	FD	E2NW	R:MORGAN G:102
1059	" "	7	NENE	1836-02-05	FD	NENE	R:MORGAN
996	MCKNIGHT, David	20	SWNW	1832-10-06	FD	SWNW	R:MORGAN
1162	MCLAUGHLIN, Patrick	7	SENW	1838-05-26	FD	SENW	R:MORGAN
1014	METCALF, Emanuel	23	SWNE	1835-07-24	FD	SWNE	R:MORGAN
1180	MITCHELL, Robert	33	SWSE	1835-07-20	FD	SWSE	R:MORGAN
1062	MORRISON, James	20	NENE	1835-11-03	FD	NENE	R:MORGAN
1108	MOSELY, John J	13	E½NW	1831-07-14	FD	E2NW	R:MORGAN
1109	MOSS, John Jr	31	E½SW	1828-06-11	FD	E2SW	R:MORGAN
1007	MURRAY, Edmund	28	SWSW	1836-08-26	FD	SWSW	R:MORGAN
1074	NISBIT, Jane	10	W½SW	1826-09-29	FD	W2SW	R:MORGAN S:F
1237	NUNNS, Thomas	23	NESE	1840-08-27	FD	NESE	R:MORGAN
960	OGLE, Absolem	19	W½SW	1829-11-30	FD	W2SWFR	R:MORGAN
961	OGLE, Absolum	19	NESW	1834-02-20	FD	NESW	R:MORGAN
1264	OGLE, William	19	SESW	1837-01-18	FD	SESW	R:MORGAN
1263	" "	19	SENW	1837-01-18	FD	SENW	R:MORGAN
1238	PARK, Thomas	32	W½SW	1830-09-23	FD	W2SW	R:SANGAMON
1239	PARKER, Thomas	30	E½SW	1831-08-24	FD	E2SW	R:MORGAN
1265	PATRICK, William	25	SESW	1861-02-27	FD	SESW	R:OHIO
998	PATTERSON, David	33	SWNE	1835-07-18	FD	SWNE	R:MORGAN
997	" "	33	NWSE	1835-07-18	FD	NWSE	R:MORGAN
989	PATTERSON, David H	28	E½SW	1836-04-02	FD	E2SW	R:KENTUCKY
1261	PATTERSON, William M	29	SWSW	1836-02-25	FD	SWSW	R:MORGAN
1262	" "	30	SWNE	1836-02-25	FD	SWNE	R:MORGAN
966	PATTON, Andrew V	10	NW	1826-09-18	FD	NW	R:MORGAN

ID	Individual in Patent	Sec.	Sec. Part	Purchase Date	Sale Type	IL Aliquot Part	For More Info . . .
1241	PATTON, Andrew V (Cont'd)	3	W½SW	1830-02-12	FD	W2SW	R:MORGAN
967	" "	3	W½SW	1830-02-12	FD	W2SW	R:MORGAN
981	PENSON, Daniel C	30	SENE	1835-11-12	FD	SENE	R:MORGAN
980	" "	30	E½SE	1835-11-12	FD	E2SE	R:MORGAN
1209	PERKINS, Solomon	27	W½NE	1827-01-05	FD	W2NE	R:MORGAN
1016	PORTER, Gavin	35	W½SW	1826-12-23	FD	W2SW	R:MORGAN
971	PRATHER, Benjamin	32	E½SE	1830-11-16	FD	E2SE	R:MORGAN
964	PRICE, Adam	4	NW	1835-12-07	FD	NW	R:MORGAN
1241	PROCTOR, Thomas	3	W½SW	1828-05-30	FD	W2SW	R:MORGAN
967	" "	3	W½SW	1828-05-30	FD	W2SW	R:MORGAN
1240	" "	12	W½SE	1828-06-12	FD	W2SE	R:MORGAN
1100	PURVIANCE, John G	26	E½NW	1827-11-14	FD	E2NW	R:SANGAMON
1099	" "	23	E½SW	1827-11-14	FD	E2SW	R:SANGAMON
1098	" "	22	E½SE	1827-11-14	FD	E2SE	R:SANGAMON
1189	PURVIANCE, Samuel	23	W½SW	1827-11-14	FD	W2SW	R:SANGAMON
1190	" "	26	W½NW	1827-11-14	FD	W2NW	R:SANGAMON
1037	PYLE, Isaac	24	NWNE	1853-08-02	FD	NWNE	R:MORGAN
1117	REAM, John	5	E½SW	1830-06-08	FD	E2SW	R:MORGAN
1110	REAM, John Jr	5	SENW	1835-02-13	FD	SENW	R:MORGAN
1154	REAM, Michael	5	SENE	1835-07-20	FD	SENE	R:MORGAN
1155	"	5	SWNE	1835-10-12	FD	SWNE	R:MORGAN
1011	REDING, Eli W	5	E½SE	1827-10-25	FD	E2SE	R:MORGAN
1010	" "	4	W½SW	1827-10-25	FD	W2SW	R:MORGAN
1211	REED, Stephen H	32	E½SE	1835-07-17	FD	E2SE	R:MORGAN
1191	REID, Samuel	10	E½SW	1828-02-06	FD	E2SW	R:SANGAMON
1212	REID, Stephen H	21	W½SW	1826-09-18	FD	W2SW	R:MORGAN
1213	" "	22	W½NW	1827-04-02	FD	W2NW	R:MORGAN
1214	" "	29	W½NE	1827-04-02	FD	W2NE	R:MORGAN
1215	" "	33	W½SW	1835-08-04	FD	W2SW	R:MORGAN
1274	REXROOT, Zachariah	6	SENE	1833-02-15	FD	SENE	R:MORGAN
1273	" "	6	SENE	1833-02-15	FD	SENE	R:MORGAN
1274	REXROTE, Zachariah	6	SENE	1835-10-22	FD	SENE	R:MORGAN
1273	" "	6	SENE	1835-10-22	FD	SENE	R:MORGAN
1276	REXROUT, Zachariah	7	SWNE	1836-05-20	FD	SWNE	R:MORGAN
1275	" "	7	NENW	1836-05-20	FD	NENW	R:MORGAN
1056	RICHARDS, James H	24	E½SW	1828-12-06	FD	E2SW	R:MORGAN
1057	" "	25	E½NW	1829-07-08	FD	E2NW	R:MORGAN
1118	ROACH, John	22	E2SW	1831-04-15	FD	E2SWPRE	R:MORGAN
1050	ROBERTS, James A	7	E½SE	1837-12-08	FD	E2SE	R:MORGAN
1051	" "	8	SWSW	1837-12-08	FD	SWSW	R:MORGAN
1193	ROBERTS, Samuel	8	NESW	1835-04-23	FD	NESW	R:MORGAN
1194	" "	8	W½NE	1835-10-20	FD	W2NE	R:MORGAN
1192	" "	7	SENE	1837-12-08	FD	SENE	R:MORGAN
1061	ROBERTSON, Kirker	6	E½NW	1835-11-03	FD	E2NW	R:MORGAN G:102
1060	" "	5	W½SW	1835-11-03	FD	W2SW	R:MORGAN G:102
1139	ROBESSON, Kisher	8	NWNW	1836-02-22	FD	NWNW	R:MORGAN
1039	ROBINSON, Israel	34	W½SE	1827-11-20	FD	W2SE	R:MORGAN
1038	" "	27	E½NW	1828-03-17	FD	E2NW	R:MORGAN
1040	ROLL, Jacob C	12	NE	1826-12-06	FD	NE	R:SANGAMON
1064	ROSS, James	2	NW	1826-11-07	FD	NWFR	R:MORGAN
1063	" "	2	E½SE	1826-11-07	FD	E2SE	R:MORGAN
1075	ROSS, Janus	11	E½NE	1830-08-04	FD	E2NE	R:MORGAN
958	RUBLE, Aaron	23	W½NW	1832-01-20	FD	W2NW	R:MORGAN
1080	RUBLE, Jesse	3	NE	1829-01-03	FD	NEFR	R:MORGAN
1171	RUCKER, Pressley W	14	E½SW	1835-08-07	FD	E2SW	R:MORGAN
982	RUDISELL, Daniel H	19	W½NE	1830-05-12	FD	W2NE	R:MORGAN
1124	SACKETT, John	26	W½NE	1827-11-14	FD	W2NE	R:SANGAMON
1123	" "	23	W½SE	1827-11-14	FD	W2SE	R:SANGAMON
1216	SALLEE, Stephen	25	W½NW	1828-03-21	FD	W2NW	R:MORGAN
1200	SCOGGINS, Seburn J	22	NWSW	1836-05-09	FD	NWSW	R:MORGAN
1144	SCOTT, Lyman	9	SE	1826-10-04	FD	SE	R:MISSOURI
1143	" "	21	E½NE	1828-02-14	FD	E2NE	R:MISSOURI
1142	" "	15	W½NW	1828-04-21	FD	W2NW	R:MORGAN
1201	SCROGGINS, Seburn J	22	SWSW	1836-05-28	FD	SWSW	R:MORGAN
1181	SEDGWICK, Robert	16	L10	1835-07-27	SC	LOT10	
1266	SHARP, William	23	NWNE	1836-06-04	FD	NWNE	R:MORGAN
1170	SHEPHERD, Peter	27	E½NE	1826-09-18	FD	E2NE	R:MORGAN
1169	" "	22	W½NE	1830-07-20	FD	W2NE	R:MORGAN
1182	SHEPHERD, Rowland	26	E½NE	1828-12-20	FD	E2NE	R:MORGAN
1156	SHREWBURY, Michael	6	E½SE	1830-02-17	FD	E2SE	R:MORGAN G:111
1065	SIMS, James	14	E½NE	1826-09-25	FD	E2NE	R:SANGAMON
1066	" "	15	E½SE	1826-10-02	FD	E2SE	R:SANGAMON
1068	" "	18	E½SW	1826-10-20	FD	E2SW	R:SANGAMON

ID	Individual in Patent	Sec.	Sec. Part	Purchase Date	Sale Type	IL Aliquot Part	For More Info . . .
1067	SIMS, James (Cont'd)	18	E½NW	1826-10-20	FD	E2NW	R:SANGAMON
1208	SLAT,	24	NENE	1836-07-04	FD	NENE	R:MORGAN S:A
1069	SLATTEN, James	24	E½SE	1827-12-29	FD	E2SE	R:MORGAN
1070	" "	24	SENE	1836-05-12	FD	SENE	R:MORGAN
1140	SMITH, Larkin B	15	SWSW	1851-10-27	FD	SWSW	R:MORGAN
1152	SMITH, Matthias	13	W½SE	1838-02-05	FD	W2SE	R:MORGAN
1153	"	24	NENW	1838-02-05	FD	NENW	R:MORGAN
1242	SMITH, Thomas	36		1832-10-05	FD	E2NESK	R:MORGAN
1053	SPEARMAN, James D	17	W½NW	1828-01-23	FD	W2NW	R:SANGAMON
1054	" "	27	NWNE	1835-11-23	FD	NWNE	R:MORGAN
1125	SPENCER, John	28	E½NW	1836-08-11	FD	E2NW	R:MORGAN
1126	" "	28	SWNW	1836-08-11	FD	SWNW	R:MORGAN
1127	" "	29	NESE	1836-08-11	FD	NESE	R:MORGAN
1128	" "	29	SENE	1836-08-11	FD	SENE	R:MORGAN
1148	STACY, Mathew	29	E½SW	1828-11-01	FD	E2SW	R:MORGAN
1013	" "	29	E½SW	1828-11-01	FD	E2SW	R:MORGAN
1151	STACY, Matthew	27	NWNW	1836-05-28	FD	NWNW	R:MORGAN
1145	STAMPS, Manly	10	E½SE	1826-09-18	FD	E2SE	R:MORGAN
985	STARMER, Daniel	25	W½SE	1828-12-22	FD	W2SE	R:MORGAN
984	" "	25	E½SE	1831-05-14	FD	E2SE	R:MORGAN
1195	STARMER, Samuel	12	W½SW	1827-11-28	FD	W2SW	R:MORGAN
1197	" "	14	W½SW	1827-11-28	FD	W2SW	R:MORGAN
1196	" "	13	W½NW	1828-12-22	FD	W2NW	R:MORGAN
1129	STEPHENSON, John	35	E½NW	1826-09-18	FD	E2NW	R:MORGAN
1000	STOUT, David	35	E½NE	1826-11-20	FD	E2NE	R:MORGAN
999	" "	25	SW	1826-11-20	FD	SW	R:MORGAN
1001	" "	36	NW	1826-11-20	FD	NW	R:MORGAN
1015	STOUT, Ezra	34	NWNW	1835-07-29	FD	NWNW	R:MORGAN
1081	STOUT, Jesse	26	W½SE	1827-03-24	FD	W2SE	R:MORGAN
972	STRIBLING, Benjamin	11	NW	1827-10-17	FD	NW	R:MORGAN
1131	STURGIS, John	9	W½NE	1827-10-08	FD	W2NE	R:MORGAN
1130	" "	4	E½SW	1827-10-15	FD	E2SW	R:MORGAN
1018	TEAS, George W	17	W½SW	1827-03-07	FD	W2SW	R:SANGAMON
1088	THOMPSON, John B	5	W½NW	1835-11-25	FD	W2NW	R:MORGAN G:125
1087	" "	5	NENW	1836-01-20	FD	NENW	R:MORGAN G:125
1086	" "	5	N½NE	1836-01-20	FD	N2NE	R:MORGAN G:125
1089	" "	6	N½NE	1836-02-18	FD	N2NE	R:MORGAN G:125
1088	THOMPSON, Richard D	5	W½NW	1835-11-25	FD	W2NW	R:MORGAN G:125
1087	" "	5	NENW	1836-01-20	FD	NENW	R:MORGAN G:125
1086	" "	5	N½NE	1836-01-20	FD	N2NE	R:MORGAN G:125
1089	" "	6	N½NE	1836-02-18	FD	N2NE	R:MORGAN G:125
1203	TINSLEY, Seth M	15	E½NW	1836-01-01	FD	E2NW	R:SANGAMON
1071	TOLLY, James	31	E½NW	1830-01-28	FD	E2NW	R:MORGAN
1017	WALTON, George H	20	E½SW	1829-12-05	FD	E2SW	R:MORGAN
1044	WARD, Jacob	17	E½SW	1829-03-23	FD	E2SW	R:KENTUCKY
1045	" "	9	W½NW	1830-06-16	FD	W2NW	R:MORGAN
1217	WASHBURN, Susan	15	E½SW	1827-10-17	FD	E2SW	R:MORGAN S:F
1198	WAY, Samuel	5	W½SE	1828-06-16	FD	W2SE	R:MORGAN
1199	WELTY, Samuel	20	W½NE	1829-09-18	FD	W2NE	R:MORGAN
1269	WHIPP, William	30	E½NW	1838-06-29	FD	E2NW	R:MORGAN
1072	WHITE, James	2	W½SE	1826-09-18	FD	W2SE	R:SANGAMON
1245	WILLHITE, Washington	23	NENW	1835-12-24	FD	NENW	R:MORGAN
1076	WILLSON, Janus	14	E½SE	1830-02-15	FD	E2SE	R:SANGAMON
1073	WILSON, James	14	W½NE	1826-10-20	FD	W2NE	R:MORGAN
1114	WILSON, John M	20	NENW	1850-05-01	FD	NENW	R:MORGAN
1019	WOLF, George	19	NENW	1832-11-24	FD	NENW	R:MORGAN
1026	WOLF, Henry	7	W½SE	1828-12-30	FD	W2SE	R:MORGAN
1135	WOLF, Joseph	18	E½	1832-12-06	FD	E2SEC	R:MORGAN
1136	" "	18	W½NW	1826-12-11	FD	W2NW	R:MORGAN
1137	" "	19	W½SE	1831-03-24	FD	W2SE	R:MORGAN
1138	WOLFE, Joseph	7	L1 (N½)	1851-12-01	FD	N2LOT1SW	R:MORGAN
1246	WOOD, Wheatley	30	NWNE	1836-08-03	FD	NWNE	R:MORGAN
1243	WOOLLOMES, Thomas	15	W½NE	1836-04-21	FD	W2NE	R:MORGAN
1156	WOOSTER, Sheldon	6	E½SE	1830-02-17	FD	E2SE	R:MORGAN G:111
1132	WYATT, John	22	E½NW	1828-04-15	FD	E2NW	R:MORGAN
1271	WYATT, William	15	W½SE	1827-09-03	FD	W2SE	R:MORGAN
1270	" "	11	E½SW	1827-09-03	FD	E2SW	R:MORGAN
1047	YAPLE, Jacob	3	NW	1827-11-28	FD	NWFR	R:MORGAN
1046	" "	3	E½SW	1828-01-19	FD	E2SW	R:MORGAN

Patent Map

T16-N R10-W
3rd PM Meridian

Map Group 4

Township Statistics

Parcels Mapped	:	319
Number of Patents	:	1
Number of Individuals	:	214
Patentees Identified	:	212
Number of Surnames	:	169
Multi-Patentee Parcels	:	7
Oldest Patent Date	:	11/8/1823
Most Recent Patent	:	2/27/1861
Block/Lot Parcels	:	13
Cities and Towns	:	2
Cemeteries	:	5

Copyright 2008 Boyd IT. Inc. All Rights Reserved

Section 3
YAPLE Jacob 1827
RUBLE Jesse 1829

Section 2
ROSS James 1826
BEGGS Charles 1826

Section 1
BEGGS Charles 1829
EPLER John 1830

PATTON Andrew V 1830 / PROCTOR Thomas 1828
YAPLE Jacob 1828
EMRICK Jacob 1826
COWNOVER Peter 1826
COWNOVER Peter 1826
WHITE James 1826
ROSS James 1826
BEGGS Charles 1827
BEGGS Charles 1831

Section 10
PATTON Andrew V 1826
MCCLURE Hugh 1826
EMRICK Jacob 1826

GILLIAM William 1830
ROSS Janus 1830

Section 12
CRUM Mathias 1830
ROLL Jacob C 1826

STRIBLING Benjamin 1827

NISBIT Jane 1826
REID Samuel 1828
MCCLURE Hugh 1827
STAMPS Manly 1826

Section 11
MCCLURE Hugh 1826
WYATT William 1827
ELLISTON Hiram 1829
BERGEN John G 1829
STARMER Samuel 1827
BABB William W 1828
PROCTOR Thomas 1828
LINDSEY Allen 1826

Section 15
SCOTT Lyman 1828
TINSLEY Seth M 1836
WOOLLOMES Thomas 1828
HARRISON William 1827 / ANGEL John 1845

Section 14
MADISON Henry 1826
WILSON James 1826
SIMS James 1826
STARMER Samuel 1828
MOSELY John J 1831
BABB William W 1828
MADISON Henry 1826

LURTON James H 1835 / SMITH Larkin B 1851
WASHBURN Susan 1827
WYATT William 1827
SIMS James 1826
STARMER Samuel 1827
RUCKER Pressley W 1835
LEWIS John A 1831
WILLSON Janus 1830

Section 13
BIBB Richard 1836
SMITH Matthias 1838
LINDSEY William 1837
BERRY John M 1853

Section 22
REID Stephen H 1827
WYATT John 1828
SHEPHERD Peter 1830
KEPLINGER Jacob 1828
RUBLE Aaron 1832

WILLHITE Washington 1835
SHARP William 1836
BIBB Richard 1836
BIBB Richard 1836
SMITH Matthias 1838
PYLE Isaac 1853
SLAT 1836

BLACK Samuel 1835
METCALF Emanuel 1835
HEMSTED Seth 1838
BERRY Benjamin 1835
COEN Hugh 1836
BERRY John M 1853
SLATTEN James 1836

Section 23
SCOGGINS Seburn J 1836
GENTRY William 1830
BARBER Thomas 1836
PURVIANCE John G 1827
PURVIANCE Samuel 1827
PURVIANCE John G 1827
SACKETT John 1827
NUNNS Thomas 1840
COX Charles 1835
GEERS William 1831

Section 24
RICHARDS James H 1828
COEN Hugh 1828
SLATTEN James 1827

SCROGGINS Seburn J 1836
ROACH John 1831
BARBER Henry 1836

Section 26
STACY Matthew 1836
ROBINSON Israel 1828
SPEARMAN James D 1835
PERKINS Solomon 1827
SHEPHERD Peter 1826
PURVIANCE Samuel 1827
PURVIANCE John G 1827
SACKETT John 1827
SHEPHERD Rowland 1828
SALLEE Stephen 1828

Section 25
RICHARDS James H 1829
GAINS Richard 1829

BLACK Samuel 1836

Section 27
BADGER John 1830
LARIMORE Thomas J 1830
LARIMORE Thomas J 1836
GAINES Richard 1828
GAINES Richard 1829
COEN Hugh 1828
STOUT Jesse 1827
BOX Stephen 1826
STOUT David 1826
PATRICK William 1861
STARMER Daniel 1828
STARMER Daniel 1831

Section 34
STOUT Ezra 1835
BARLAND Thomas 1835
BADGER Edmund W 1823
LARIMORE Thomas J 1836
BADGER Edmund W 1833
LARIMORE Thomas J 1836
BRISTOW Mathias 1830
ROBINSON Israel 1827
LAURIE John 1836
JENKINS James 1827

Section 35
MCDONALD Daniel 1830
STEPHENSON John 1826
ALLINSON Adam 1826
STOUT David 1826
PORTER Gavin 1826
COLE Joseph 1828
ALLINSON Adam 1828
COX Jeremiah 1829

Section 36
STOUT David 1826
BERRY William M 1831
SMITH Thomas 1832
MCCOY David 1831
COX Jeremiah 1831
GEERS William 1831
GRAVES James A 1835
GRAVES James A 1834

Copyright 2008 Boyd IT, Inc. All Rights Reserved

Helpful Hints

1. This Map's INDEX can be found on the preceding pages.

2. Refer to Map "C" to see where this Township lies within Morgan County, Illinois.

3. Numbers within square brackets [ ] denote a multi-patentee land parcel (multi-owner). Refer to Appendix "C" for a full list of members in this group.

4. Areas that look to be crowded with Patentees usually indicate multiple sales of the same parcel (re-issues), cancellations or voided transactions (that we map, anyway) or overlapping parcels. We opt to show even these ambiguous parcels, which oftentimes lead to research avenues not yet taken.

Legend

——— Patent Boundary

━━━ Section Boundary

▨ No Patents Found (or Outside County)

1., 2., 3., ... Lot Numbers (when beside a name)

[ ] Group Number (see Appendix "C")

Scale: Section = 1 mile X 1 mile (generally, with some exceptions)

Road Map

T16-N R10-W
3rd PM Meridian

Map Group 4

Cities & Towns
Arcadia
Literberry

Cemeteries
Arcadia Cemetery
Henderson-McFadden
  Cemetery
Liter Cemetery
Phillips Cemetery
Rucker Cemetery

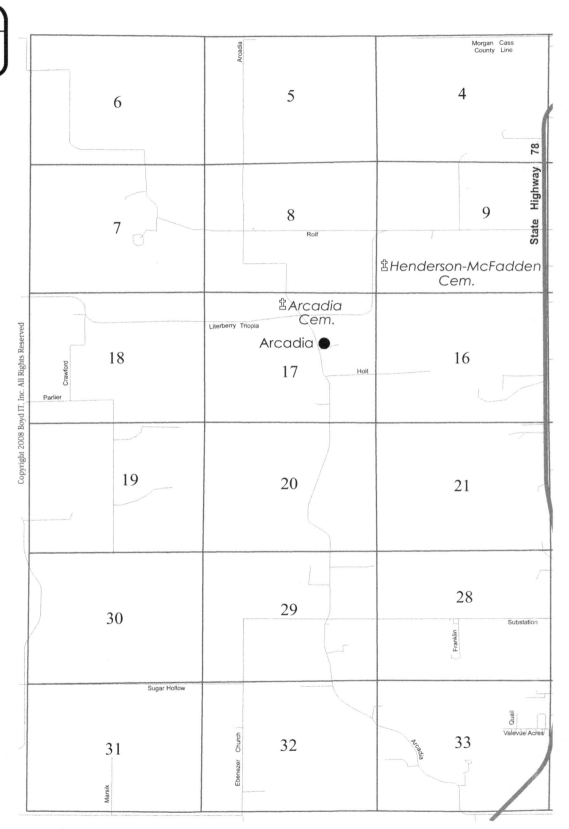

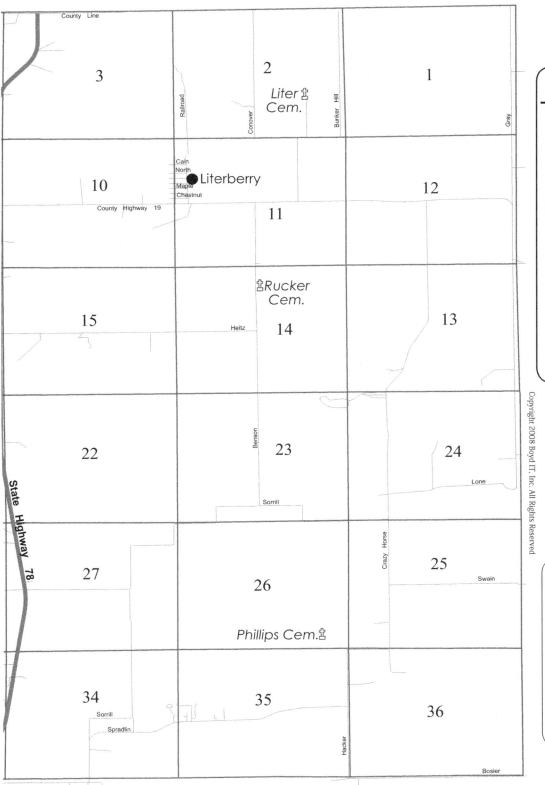

Helpful Hints

1. This road map has a number of uses, but primarily it is to help you: a) find the present location of land owned by your ancestors (at least the general area), b) find cemeteries and city-centers, and c) estimate the route/roads used by Census-takers & tax-assessors.

2. If you plan to travel to Morgan County to locate cemeteries or land parcels, please pick up a modern travel map for the area before you do. Mapping old land parcels on modern maps is not as exact a science as you might think. Just the slightest variations in public land survey coordinates, estimates of parcel boundaries, or road-map deviations can greatly alter a map's representation of how a road either does or doesn't cross a particular parcel of land.

Legend

——————— Section Lines

═══════ Interstates

▬▬▬▬▬▬ Highways

——————— Other Roads

● Cities/Towns

✝ Cemeteries

Scale: Section = 1 mile X 1 mile
(generally, with some exceptions)

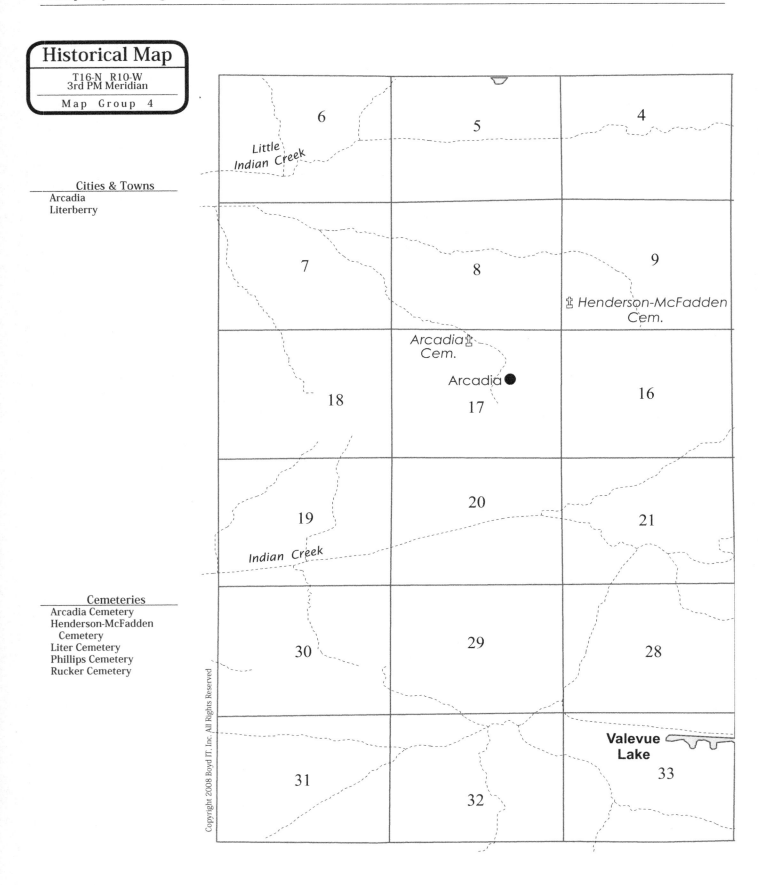

Historical Map

T16-N R10-W
3rd PM Meridian

Map Group 4

Cities & Towns
Arcadia
Literberry

Cemeteries
Arcadia Cemetery
Henderson-McFadden
  Cemetery
Liter Cemetery
Phillips Cemetery
Rucker Cemetery

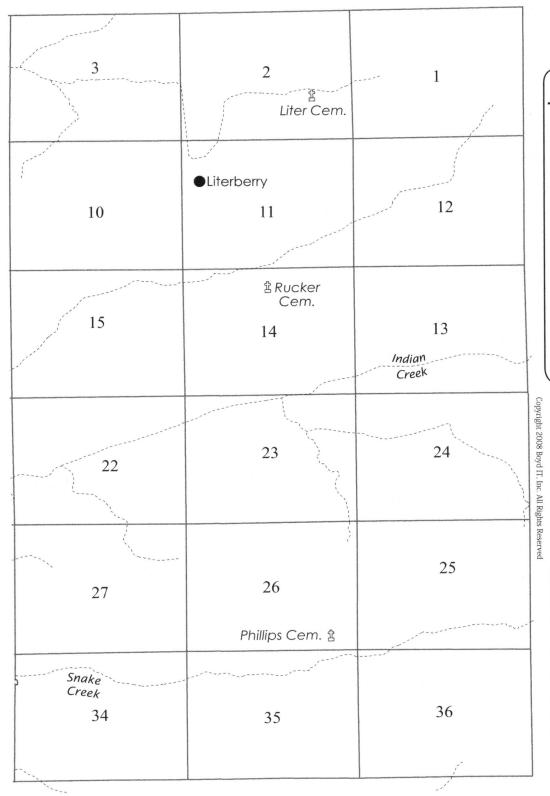

| 3 | 2 | 1 |

Liter Cem.

●Literberry

| 10 | 11 | 12 |

Rucker Cem.

| 15 | 14 | 13 |

Indian Creek

| 22 | 23 | 24 |

| 27 | 26 | 25 |

Phillips Cem.

Snake Creek

| 34 | 35 | 36 |

Helpful Hints

1. This Map takes a different look at the same Congressional Township displayed in the preceding two maps. It presents features that can help you better envision the historical development of the area: a) Water-bodies (lakes & ponds), b) Water-courses (rivers, streams, etc.), c) Railroads, d) City/town center-points (where they were oftentimes located when first settled), and e) Cemeteries.

2. Using this "Historical" map in tandem with this Township's Patent Map and Road Map, may lead you to some interesting discoveries. You will often find roads, towns, cemeteries, and waterways are named after nearby landowners: sometimes those names will be the ones you are researching. See how many of these research gems you can find here in Morgan County.

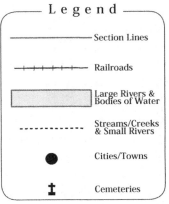

Legend

———————— Section Lines

+++++++ Railroads

Large Rivers & Bodies of Water

- - - - - - Streams/Creeks & Small Rivers

● Cities/Towns

✝ Cemeteries

Scale: Section = 1 mile X 1 mile
(there are some exceptions)

Map Group 5: Index to Land Patents

Township 16-North Range 9-West (3rd PM)

After you locate an individual in this Index, take note of the Section and Section Part then proceed to the Land Patent map on the pages immediately following. You should have no difficulty locating the corresponding parcel of land.

The "For More Info" Column will lead you to more information about the underlying Patents. See the *Legend* at right, and the "How to Use this Book" chapter, for more information.

```
                    LEGEND
         "For More Info . . . " column
G = Group  (Multi-Patentee Patent, see Appendix "C")
R = Residence
S = Social Status


See Appendix A for list of abbreviations used by the
Illinois State Archives in describing the place and
nature of these land patents.

Note: if the Abbreviations contain "L", "BL", "LOT",
or "BLOCK", the exact whereabouts of the parcel within
the section is not known.
```

ID	Individual in Patent	Sec.	Sec. Part	Purchase Date	Sale Type	IL Aliquot Part	For More Info . . .
1324	ADAMS, Elijah	25	NESW	1832-12-17	FD	NESW	R:MORGAN
1325	" "	36	NWNW	1833-07-02	FD	NWNW	R:MORGAN
1366	ADAMS, Jacob	26	SE	1826-09-15	FD	SE	R:MASSAC
1367	" "	35	E½NE	1830-03-12	FD	E2NE	R:MORGAN
1368	" "	35	NESE	1833-05-27	FD	NESE	R:MORGAN
1370	" "	36	SWNW	1833-05-27	FD	SWNW	R:MORGAN
1371	" "	36	W½SW	1835-08-12	FD	W2SW	R:MORGAN
1369	" "	36	E½SW	1836-02-22	FD	E2SW	R:MORGAN
1505	ALLEN, Robert	4	E½SW	1831-05-31	FD	E2SW	R:SANGAMON
1506	" "	9	E½NW	1831-05-31	FD	E2NW	R:SANGAMON
1495	ANDERSON, Richard	16	L31	1836-03-05	SC	LOT31MA	
1495	" "	16	L31	1836-03-05	SC	LOT31	
1496	" "	21	NWSE	1836-11-16	FD	NWSE	R:MORGAN
1497	" "	21	SENW	1836-11-16	FD	SENW	R:MORGAN
1281	APLER, Abram	2	E½SE	1832-04-06	FD	E2SE	R:MORGAN
1299	ARMSTRONG, Andrew	3	NW	1826-09-15	FD	PT1NW	R:MORGAN
1567	ARMSTRONG, William	10	W½NW	1831-09-27	FD	W2NW	R:MORGAN
1380	BAKER, James	10	E½NW	1831-10-03	FD	E2NW	R:MORGAN
1356	BALDWIN, Ira	11	NWNW	1851-11-24	FD	NWNW	R:MORGAN S:F
1545	BALL, Strother	1	NE	1826-09-15	FD	NEFR	R:MORGAN
1415	BARNET, John	34	NESE	1833-07-03	FD	NESE	R:MORGAN
1571	BEAVERS, William	18	L1 (S½)	1851-02-17	FD	S2LOT1NW	R:MORGAN
1364	BENNET, Isaac R	12	SW	1826-09-15	FD	SW	R:MASSAC
1304	BENNETT, Arthur F	12	W½SE	1827-10-03	FD	W2SE	R:MORGAN
1365	BENNETT, Isaac R	12	E½SE	1831-12-10	FD	E2SE	R:MORGAN
1345	BERGEN, George L	9	NESW	1835-11-16	FD	NESW	R:MORGAN
1427	BERGEN, John G	6	N½NW	1831-06-28	FD	N2NW	R:SANGAMON
1428	" "	8	E½NW	1835-11-16	FD	E2NW	R:SANGAMON
1372	BINGMAN, Jacob	22	SESE	1835-03-13	FD	SESE	R:MORGAN
1416	BIRKBY, John	29	W½SE	1831-09-05	FD	W2SE	R:MORGAN
1300	BOWEN, Andrew	33	E½NE	1830-11-20	FD	E2NE	R:MORGAN
1305	BOYCE, Bartholomew T	21	SWNE	1836-04-25	FD	SWNE	R:MORGAN
1558	BOYCE, Thomas T	21	W½SE	1831-02-25	FD	W2SE	R:MORGAN
1560	BOYER, Thomas T	29	E½NE	1830-11-03	FD	E2NE	R:MORGAN
1559	" "	21	W½NW	1830-11-03	FD	W2NW	R:MORGAN
1355	BRADLEY, Hezekiah P	2	W½SE	1829-10-21	FD	W2SE	R:MORGAN
1572	BRISBY, William	31	SENW	1834-06-30	FD	SENW	R:MORGAN
1486	BROWN, Peyton	21	E½SW	1827-11-08	FD	E2SW	R:MORGAN
1487	" "	21	W½SW	1829-07-30	FD	W2SW	R:MORGAN
1574	BROWN, William	26	W½NE	1836-12-06	FD	W2NE	R:MORGAN
1573	" "	11	NESW	1854-06-13	FD	NESW	R:MORGAN
1417	BRYAMT, John	16	L114	1833-12-23	SC	LOT114	G:17
1422	BRYANT, John	16	L115	1833-12-23	SC	LOT115	G:20
1417	" "	16	L114	1833-12-23	SC	LOT114	G:17
1418	" "	16	L116	1833-12-23	SC	LOT116	G:19
1421	" "	16	L111	1833-12-23	SC	LOT111	G:20

ID	Individual in Patent	Sec.	Sec. Part	Purchase Date	Sale Type	IL Aliquot Part	For More Info . . .
1419	BRYANT, John (Cont'd)	16	L109	1833-12-23	SC	LOT109	G:20
1420	"	16	L110	1833-12-23	SC	LOT110	G:20
1311	CAMREN, Constant	15	NESW	1851-06-03	FD	NESW	R:MASON
1312	"	15	NWSW	1851-11-01	FD	NWSW	R:MASON
1342	CANNON, Richard	3	E½SW	1828-12-08	FD	E2SW	R:MORGAN
1499	"	3	E½SW	1828-12-08	FD	E2SW	R:MORGAN
1498	"	3	E½SE	1829-10-19	FD	E2SE	R:MORGAN
1604	CARR, William P	11	W½SW	1853-06-14	FD	W2SW	
1381	CHALLEN, James	18	NENW	1835-11-03	FD	NENW	R:KENTUCKY
1543	CHAPMAN, Sidney S	10	SWNE	1855-11-08	FD	SWNE	R:OHIO
1326	CLARK, Elisha	1	W½SW	1827-11-14	FD	W2SW	R:SANGAMON
1314	CLOPTON, David	12	E½NE	1831-09-27	FD	E2NE	R:SANGAMON
1319	COKER, Dennis	19	W½SE	1827-12-25	FD	W2SE	R:MORGAN
1320	"	30	W½NE	1830-10-02	FD	W2NE	R:MORGAN
1425	COKER, John	15	SESW	1855-02-10	FD	SESW	R:MORGAN
1470	COOPER, George	32	NWSW	1833-01-22	FD	NWSW	R:MORGAN
1340	"	32	NWSW	1833-01-22	FD	NWSW	R:MORGAN
1576	COOPER, William	13	W½NW	1829-09-19	FD	W2NW	R:MORGAN
1577	"	14	E½NE	1829-10-12	FD	E2NE	R:MORGAN
1322	COWNOVER, Dominicus	6	W½SE	1827-10-27	FD	W2SE	R:MORGAN
1321	"	6	E½SW	1827-10-27	FD	E2SW	R:MORGAN
1484	COWNOVER, Peter Jr	7		1826-09-15	FD	PT2SW	R:MASSAC
1483	"	18		1826-09-15	FD	PT2NW	R:MASSAC
1578	COWNOVER, William	5	NW	1826-09-15	FD	PT1NW	R:MORGAN
1414	CREED, John A	15	SENE	1836-07-20	FD	SENE	R:MORGAN
1580	CROW, William	7	E½SE	1826-09-15	FD	E2SE	R:MORGAN
1579	"	6	E½SE	1826-11-25	FD	E2SE	R:MORGAN
1463	DANIEL, Joseph	2	SESW	1853-11-28	FD	SESW	R:MORGAN
1287	DECK, Allen	16	L30	1833-06-24	SC	LOT30	
1423	DENNIS, John C	9	NWSE	1844-09-06	FD	NWSE	R:MORGAN
1500	DODSWORTH, Richard	18	NESE	1834-10-22	FD	NESE	R:MORGAN
1501	"	18	SESW	1834-10-22	FD	SESW	R:MORGAN
1464	DUNCAN, Joseph	31	W½NE	1833-04-23	FD	W2NE	R:MORGAN
1426	DUVAL, John	10	E½SW	1851-08-18	FD	E2SW	
1387	EADS, James M	20	W½NW	1829-06-16	FD	W2NW	R:MORGAN
1502	EDWARDS, Richard	25	W½SW	1828-07-17	FD	W2SW	R:MORGAN
1382	ELDER, James	23	S½NW	1853-03-30	FD	S2NW	
1478	ELDER, Mathew	7	E½SW	1826-12-02	FD	E2SW	R:MORGAN
1383	ELDRIDGE, James	15	SWNW	1836-11-01	FD	SWNW	R:MORGAN
1619	ELDRIDGE, Zachariah	11	SESW	1854-07-11	FD	SESW	R:MORGAN
1548	EMMERSON, Thomas	31	S½	1834-10-22	FD	S2	R:MORGAN
1552	"	33	SW	1834-10-22	FD	SW	R:MORGAN
1551	"	32	SWSW	1834-10-22	FD	SWSW	R:MORGAN
1550	"	32	SE	1834-10-22	FD	SE	R:MORGAN
1549	"	32	E½SW	1834-10-22	FD	E2SW	R:MORGAN
1547	"	17	W½SW	1835-11-09	FD	W2SW	R:MORGAN
1546	"	17	E½SW	1836-03-17	FD	E2SW	R:MORGAN
1280	ENYART, Abner	3		1826-09-15	FD	PT2NW	R:MORGAN
1591	"	3		1826-09-15	FD	PT2NW	R:MORGAN
1278	"	17	W½NW	1827-10-02	FD	W2NW	R:MORGAN
1279	"	18	E½NE	1828-02-16	FD	E2NE	R:MORGAN
1471	FARNUN, Lucian	16	L100	1834-01-15	SC	LOT100	
1472	"	16	L112	1834-01-15	SC	LOT112	
1473	"	16	L89	1834-01-15	SC	LOT089	
1508	FITZHUGH, Robert	4	NE	1826-09-15	FD	NEFR	R:MORGAN
1513	FLIN, Royal	23	NWNE	1851-12-09	FD	NWNE	
1620	FLIN, Zadoc W	5	N½NW	1826-12-02	FD	N2NW	R:MORGAN
1468	FLINN, Josiah	1	NW	1826-09-15	FD	NWFR	R:MORGAN
1621	FLINN, Zadoc W	5	SW	1826-09-15	FD	SW	R:MORGAN
1622	FLINN, Zadock W	15	W½NE	1832-02-09	FD	W2NE	R:MORGAN
1329	FOX, Elisha	27	NWNE	1850-06-14	FD	NWNE	R:MORGAN
1328	"	22	SWSE	1850-06-14	FD	SWSE	R:MORGAN
1327	"	22	SESW	1851-02-11	FD	SESW	R:MORGAN
1570	FRENCH, William	21	E½NE	1836-11-15	FD	E2NE	R:MORGAN G:64
1568	"	23	E½NE	1836-11-21	FD	E2NE	R:MORGAN G:63
1412	GESFORD, Joel	20	W½SW	1826-09-15	FD	W2SW	R:MORGAN
1411	"	20	E½SW	1829-06-06	FD	E2SW	R:MORGAN
1424	GORE, John C	10	NESE	1853-11-02	FD	NESE	
1581	GRAY, William	16	L29	1833-04-16	SC	LOT29	
1333	HALL, Equillar	24	NE	1826-09-15	FD	NE	R:MORGAN
1332	"	23	NENW	1852-01-17	FD	NENW	
1431	HARDIN, John	35	NESW	1832-11-24	FD	NESW	R:MORGAN
1432	"	35	W½SE	1832-11-24	FD	W2SE	R:MORGAN

ID	Individual in Patent	Sec.	Sec. Part	Purchase Date	Sale Type	IL Aliquot Part	For More Info . . .
1437	HARDIN, John J	35	NWSW	1833-01-02	FD	NWSW	R:MORGAN
1438	" "	35	S½SW	1833-08-30	FD	S2SW	R:MORGAN
1436	" "	33	W½NE	1833-09-09	FD	W2NE	R:MORGAN
1435	" "	33	NW	1833-09-09	FD	NW	R:MORGAN
1434	" "	33		1833-09-23	FD	SESK	R:MORGAN
1433	" "	23	SW	1835-08-26	FD	SW	R:MORGAN
1459	HARDING, Jonathan	11	NENE	1838-11-16	FD	NENE	R:SANGAMON
1474	HARDING, Martin	4	SWNW	1833-12-05	FD	SWNW	R:MORGAN
1341	HARRISON, George	18	SESE	1836-03-17	FD	SESE	R:MORGAN
1460	HAYNES, Jonathan	16	L22	1832-04-16	SC	LOT22	
1542	HAYNES, Sarah	9	NWSW	1833-05-20	FD	NWSW	R:MORGAN S:F
1310	HENDRICK, Claudius T	11	E½SE	1837-12-02	FD	E2SE	R:MORGAN
1349	HOAGLAND, George W	6	NE	1829-06-08	FD	NE	R:MORGAN G:77
1347	" "	7	E½NE	1831-08-23	FD	E2NE	R:MORGAN
1348	" "	8	W½NW	1831-08-23	FD	W2NW	R:MORGAN
1349	HOAGLAND, John	6	NE	1829-06-08	FD	NE	R:MORGAN G:77
1475	HOAGLAND, Martin	6	W2SW	1831-03-08	FD	W2SWPRE	R:MORGAN
1476	" "	9	SESE	1836-03-18	FD	SESE	R:MORGAN
1584	HOAGLAND, William	20	E½NW	1828-10-18	FD	E2NW	R:MORGAN
1554	HOBIN, Thomas	8	W½NE	1854-03-17	FD	W2NE	
1586	HOGLIN, William	8	E½SW	1827-10-31	FD	E2SW	R:MORGAN
1585	" "	17	E½NW	1827-11-20	FD	E2NW	R:MORGAN
1363	HOLMES, Isaac	27	E½NE	1829-01-07	FD	E2NE	R:MORGAN
1362	" "	26	W½NW	1830-10-02	FD	W2NW	R:MORGAN
1359	HOLMES, Isaac G	10	SWSE	1852-01-03	FD	SWSE	R:MORGAN
1357	" "	10	NWSE	1854-02-18	FD	NWSE	R:MORGAN
1360	" "	15	NWNW	1854-02-23	FD	NWNW	R:MORGAN
1361	" "	17	NENE	1854-04-22	FD	NENE	
1358	" "	10	SENE	1854-04-22	FD	SENE	R:MORGAN
1454	HOLMES, John W	19	NWNE	1847-03-27	FD	NWNE	R:MORGAN
1514	HOLMES, Samuel	16	L6	1853-08-26	SC	LOT6	
1492	HUDSPETH, Ralph	1	E½SW	1826-09-15	FD	E2SW	R:MORGAN
1284	HUGHES, Allen B	16	L26	1832-04-16	SC	LOT26	
1285	" "	29	SESE	1834-06-05	FD	SESE	R:MORGAN
1499	HUGHES, George	3	E½SW	1829-12-21	FD	E2SW	R:MORGAN
1342	" "	3	E½SW	1829-12-21	FD	E2SW	R:MORGAN
1344	" "	4	E½SE	1829-12-21	FD	E2SE	R:MORGAN
1343	" "	3	W½SW	1830-07-08	FD	W2SW	R:MORGAN
1286	HUGHS, Allen B	29	NESE	1832-09-08	FD	NESE	R:MORGAN
1337	HUNTER, Francis	21	SWNW	1836-11-16	FD	SWNW	R:MORGAN
1338	" "	22	N½SE	1836-11-19	FD	N2SE	R:MORGAN
1339	" "	22	SWNE	1837-10-10	FD	SWNE	R:MORGAN
1465	JACKSON, Joseph W	28	E½NE	1826-11-10	FD	E2NE	R:MORGAN
1466	" "	28	E½SW	1826-11-10	FD	E2SW	R:MORGAN
1330	JAMES, Enoch	11	SWSE	1850-03-12	FD	SWSE	R:SANGAMON
1331	" "	14	SWNW	1850-03-12	FD	SWNW	R:SANGAMON
1561	JANUARY, Thomas T	16	L9	1832-04-16	SC	LOT9	
1323	JONES, Edward	18	W½SE	1830-09-25	FD	W2SE	R:SANGAMON
1352	KELTNER, Henry	3	SEN½	1830-06-26	FD	S2NE	R:MORGAN
1373	KEPLINGER, Jacob	30	E½SW	1830-11-20	FD	E2SW	R:MORGAN
1353	KETTNER, Henry	9	W½NE	1831-06-29	FD	W2NE	R:MORGAN
1491	LANHAM, Plesant	16	L7	1854-02-23	SC	LOT7	S:F
1515	LEWIS, Samuel	22	E½NE	1837-05-02	FD	E2NE	R:MORGAN
1587	LEWIS, William M	22	NWNE	1844-03-02	FD	NWNE	R:MORGAN
1288	LINDSEY, Allen F	18	NESW	1833-02-04	FD	NESW	R:MORGAN
1469	LINDSEY, Landy And Co	18	W½NE	1829-12-21	FD	W2NE	R:MORGAN
1307	LITTON, Burton	5	NE	1826-09-15	FD	NEFR	R:MORGAN
1308	" "	5	NWSE	1835-02-12	FD	NWSE	R:MORGAN
1309	LITTON, Cager	5	NESE	1836-01-09	FD	NESE	R:MORGAN
1455	MADDOX, John W	16	L8	1836-02-19	SC	L8MA	
1457	" "	9	SWSW	1836-02-23	FD	SWSW	R:MORGAN
1456	" "	16	L27	1837-03-28	SC	L27MA	
1282	MALONE, Alexander	4	NWSW	1835-11-25	FD	NWSW	R:MORGAN
1315	MANCHESTER, David	11	NWSE	1851-12-22	FD	NWSE	
1443	MATHERS, John	16	L16	1851-09-13	SC	LOT16PTE2	
1447	" "	16	L20	1851-09-13	SC	LOT20PTE2	
1440	" "	16	L13	1851-09-13	SC	LOT13PTE2	
1441	" "	16	L14	1851-09-13	SC	LOT14PTE2	
1442	" "	16	L15	1851-09-13	SC	LOT15PTE2	
1446	" "	16	L19	1851-09-13	SC	LOT19PTE2	
1444	" "	16	L17	1851-09-13	SC	LOT17PTE2	
1445	" "	16	L18	1851-09-13	SC	LOT18PTE2	
1477	MATHEWS, Mary	26	W½SW	1829-07-09	FD	W2SW	R:MORGAN S:F

ID	Individual in Patent	Sec.	Sec. Part	Purchase Date	Sale Type	IL Aliquot Part	For More Info . . .
1504	MATHEWS, Richard	26	E½SW	1826-09-15	FD	E2SW	R:MORGAN
1516	MATHEWS, Samuel	26	E½NE	1830-11-20	FD	E2NE	R:MORGAN
1519	" "	35	W½NE	1830-12-13	FD	W2NE	R:MORGAN
1518	" "	35	E½NW	1831-07-01	FD	E2NW	R:MORGAN
1517	" "	26	E½NW	1832-03-22	FD	E2NW	R:MORGAN
1588	MCCAMMON, William	29	W½SW	1831-09-19	FD	W2SW	R:MORGAN
1589	MCCLURR, William	2	NW	1830-11-13	FD	NW	R:VIRGINIA
1509	MICKEY, Robert	11	E½NW	1837-10-07	FD	E2NW	R:MORGAN
1511	" "	11	W½NE	1837-10-07	FD	W2NE	R:MORGAN
1510	" "	11	SENE	1837-10-07	FD	SENE	R:MORGAN
1374	MILLER, Jacob	10	NWSW	1855-01-18	FD	NWSW	
1375	MILLER, Jacob N	9	NESE	1855-01-16	FD	NESE	R:MORGAN
1568	MORGAN, William B	23	E½NE	1836-11-21	FD	E2NE	R:MORGAN G:63
1439	MOSELY, John J	6	S½NW	1830-11-26	FD	S2NW	R:MORGAN
1590	MUNDAY, William	2	W2SW	1830-11-13	FD	W2SWPRE	R:MORGAN
1493	MURPHY, Renex	28	W½NW	1826-09-15	FD	W2NW	R:MORGAN
1494	MURPHY, Rennex	28	E½NW	1828-03-08	FD	E2NW	R:MORGAN
1389	NAULTY, James	21	NENW	1854-04-05	FD	NENW	R:MORGAN
1538	NILES, Samuel V	23	SE	1852-02-03	FD	SE	
1354	NORTHCUT, Hezekiah	16	L32	1837-06-24	SC	L32MA	
1335	OBANION, Evin	13	E½SE	1826-09-15	FD	E2SE	R:MORGAN
1592	OKEAR, William	36	NE	1835-02-04	FD	NE	R:MORGAN
1555	OKEEFFE, Thomas	5	SESE	1835-12-07	FD	SESE	R:MORGAN
1556	" "	5	SWSE	1836-01-18	FD	SWSE	R:MORGAN
1346	OREAR, George	35	SESE	1836-02-09	FD	SESE	R:MORGAN
1594	OREAR, William	24	E½SE	1826-09-15	FD	E2SE	R:MORGAN
1593	" "	24	E½NW	1827-11-19	FD	E2NW	R:MORGAN
1599	" "	25	E½NW	1829-01-05	FD	E2NW	R:MORGAN
1595	" "	24	E½SW	1830-01-05	FD	E2SW	R:MORGAN
1600	" "	25	W½SE	1830-03-26	FD	W2SE	R:MORGAN
1598	" "	25		1833-05-27	FD	SESWSK	R:MORGAN
1598	" "	25		1833-05-27	FD	SESESK	R:MORGAN
1601	" "	36	E½NW	1835-07-14	FD	E2NW	R:MORGAN
1602	" "	36	SE	1836-02-22	FD	SE	R:MORGAN
1597	" "	24	SWSW	1846-05-07	FD	SWSW	R:MORGAN
1596	" "	24	NWSW	1848-01-05	FD	NWSW	R:MORGAN
1603	OSCAR, William	25	W½NW	1835-12-22	FD	W2NW	R:MORGAN
1448	PARR, John	4	SWSW	1835-02-12	FD	SWSW	R:MORGAN
1507	PARROTT, Robert D	23	NWNW	1851-03-22	FD	NWNW	R:MORGAN
1605	PEARSON, William	14	NWNW	1855-01-01	FD	NWNW	R:MORGAN
1390	PERVIANCE, James	13	E½NW	1830-09-29	FD	E2NW	R:MORGAN
1293	PHILIPS, Amos G	29	W½NE	1830-11-08	FD	W2NE	R:MORGAN
1292	" "	16	L25	1832-04-16	SC	LOT25	
1388	PHILIPS, James M	16	L11	1833-04-13	SC	LOT11	
1303	POINDEXTER, Arche	12	W½NE	1829-06-22	FD	W2NE	R:MORGAN
1302	" "	12	E½NW	1829-12-31	FD	E2NW	R:MORGAN
1488	PRICE, Philemon B	23	SWNE	1853-03-31	FD	SWNE	
1283	PURVIANCE, Alexander	7	W½NE	1826-09-25	FD	W2NE	R:SANGAMON
1334	PURVIANCE, Evan	4	W½SE	1828-10-06	FD	W2SE	R:MORGAN
1391	PURVIANCE, James	13	W½NE	1830-05-22	FD	W2NE	R:MORGAN
1430	PURVIANCE, John G	8	W½SW	1826-09-25	FD	W2SW	R:SANGAMON
1429	" "	7	W½SE	1826-09-25	FD	W2SE	R:SANGAMON
1520	PURVIANCE, Samuel	7	NW	1826-09-25	FD	NWFR	R:SANGAMON
1336	RAY, Felix	13	W½SE	1826-09-15	FD	W2SE	R:MORGAN
1392	REDMAN, James	27	W½SW	1826-09-15	FD	W2SW	R:MORGAN
1393	" "	28	E½SE	1826-09-15	FD	E2SE	R:MORGAN
1409	REDMON, Janus	28	W½SE	1830-03-11	FD	W2SE	R:MORGAN
1418	REEVES, Lazarus	16	L116	1833-12-23	SC	LOT116	G:19
1420	REEVIS, Lazarus	16	L110	1833-12-23	SC	LOT110	G:20
1421	" "	16	L111	1833-12-23	SC	LOT111	G:20
1422	" "	16	L115	1833-12-23	SC	LOT115	G:20
1417	" "	16	L114	1833-12-23	SC	LOT114	G:17
1419	" "	16	L109	1833-12-23	SC	LOT109	G:20
1461	ROBERTSON, Jonathan J	15	SWSW	1836-05-20	FD	SWSW	R:MORGAN
1413	ROBINSON, Joel	13	E½SW	1829-10-14	FD	E2SW	R:MORGAN
1522	ROBINSON, Samuel	24	W½NW	1829-12-22	FD	W2NW	R:MORGAN
1521	" "	13	W½SW	1829-12-25	FD	W2SW	R:MORGAN
1606	ROBINSON, William	28	W½SW	1831-09-20	FD	W2SW	R:MORGAN
1277	RUBLE, Aaron	30	N½SW	1832-01-20	FD	N2SW	R:MORGAN
1316	RUDE, David	14	E½SE	1830-11-22	FD	E2SE	R:MORGAN
1451	RUSK, John	17	SE	1826-11-10	FD	SE	R:MORGAN
1452	" "	20	E½SE	1826-11-10	FD	E2SE	R:MORGAN
1607	RUTHERFORD, William	19	E½SE	1826-09-15	FD	E2SE	R:MORGAN

ID	Individual in Patent	Sec.	Sec. Part	Purchase Date	Sale Type	IL Aliquot Part	For More Info . . .
1317	RUYNKLE, David	22	NENW	1855-07-16	FD	NENW	R:MORGAN
1523	SACKETT, Samuel	2	NE	1827-11-14	FD	NEFR	R:OHIO
1608	SAGE, William	1	E½SE	1826-09-15	FD	E2SE	R:MORGAN
1376	SAMPLE, Jacob	10	NENE	1852-03-05	FD	NENE	
1313	SCOTT, Daniel	13	E½NE	1831-10-05	FD	E2NE	R:MORGAN
1609	SEWALL, William	30	E½SE	1830-11-27	FD	E2SE	R:MORGAN
1485	SHEPHERD, Peter	14	W½SW	1830-09-08	FD	W2SW	R:MORGAN G:109
1394	SHORT, James	1	W½SE	1826-09-15	FD	W2SE	R:MORGAN
1544	SHORT, Stephen	12	W½NW	1830-01-06	FD	W2NW	R:MORGAN
1395	SIMS, James	14	W½NE	1827-12-08	FD	W2NE	R:MORGAN
1297	SINCLAIR, Amos	32	NWNE	1823-11-15	FD	NWNE	R:MORGAN
1294	" "	16	L23	1832-04-16	SC	LOT23	
1295	" "	16	L24	1832-04-16	SC	LOT24	
1296	" "	32		1833-11-27	FD	E2NWSK	R:MORGAN
1296	" "	32		1833-11-27	FD	SWNWSK	R:MORGAN
1530	SINCLAIR, Samuel	32	E½NE	1833-08-31	FD	E2NE	R:VIRGINIA
1529	" "	28	W½NE	1833-08-31	FD	W2NE	R:VIRGINIA
1525	" "	21	SESE	1833-09-16	FD	SESE	R:VIRGINIA
1531	" "	32	W½NE	1833-09-16	FD	W2NE	R:VIRGINIA
1528	" "	27	E½NW	1836-05-14	FD	E2NW	R:MORGAN
1524	" "	21	NESE	1846-05-07	FD	NESE	R:MORGAN
1527	" "	22	W½SW	1846-05-07	FD	W2SW	R:MORGAN
1526	" "	22	NESW	1853-03-28	FD	NESW	R:MORGAN
1565	SINCLAIR, Watson	31	E½NE	1833-11-18	FD	E2NE	R:MORGAN
1396	SLATTEN, James	19	SWNE	1832-06-18	FD	SWNE	R:MORGAN
1298	SMITH, Anderson	14	E½SW	1830-07-26	FD	E2SW	R:MORGAN G:114
1351	SMITH, Hannah	30	W½NW	1830-10-21	FD	W2NW	R:MORGAN S:F G:118
1397	SMITH, James	16	L12	1833-04-08	SC	LOT12	G:120
1398	" "	16	L3	1833-04-08	SC	LOT3	G:120
1470	SMITH, Levi	32	NWSW	1834-07-29	FD	NWSW	R:MORGAN
1340	" "	32	NWSW	1834-07-29	FD	NWSW	R:MORGAN
1479	SMITH, Matthias	19	SENW	1837-05-29	FD	SENW	R:MORGAN
1298	SMITH, Pleasant	14	E½SW	1830-07-26	FD	E2SW	R:MORGAN G:114
1397	" "	16	L12	1833-04-08	SC	LOT12	G:120
1398	" "	16	L3	1833-04-08	SC	LOT3	G:120
1351	SMITH, Ruth	30	W½NW	1830-10-21	FD	W2NW	R:MORGAN S:F G:118
1534	SMITH, Samuel	20	E½NE	1826-09-15	FD	E2NE	R:MORGAN
1533	" "	16	L28	1832-04-16	SC	LOT28	
1532	" "	16	L21	1832-04-16	SC	LOT21	
1535	" "	30	NWSE	1832-06-11	FD	NWSE	R:MORGAN
1536	" "	30	SWSE	1832-10-05	FD	SWSE	R:MORGAN
1485	SMITH, Thomas	14	W½SW	1830-09-08	FD	W2SW	R:MORGAN G:109
1557	" "	31	L2	1832-10-05	FD	LOT2NWSK	R:MORGAN
1566	SMITH, Westly	30	E½NW	1830-08-24	FD	E2NW	R:MORGAN G:121
1613	SMITH, William	19	SW	1826-09-15	FD	SWFR	R:MORGAN
1611	" "	19	E½NE	1828-01-30	FD	E2NE	R:MORGAN
1614	" "	19	W½NW	1828-01-30	FD	W2NWFR	R:MORGAN
1615	" "	20	W½SE	1829-06-15	FD	W2SE	R:MORGAN
1618	" "	29	W½NW	1829-10-12	FD	W2NW	R:MORGAN
1616	" "	29	E½NW	1830-08-24	FD	E2NW	R:MORGAN
1617	" "	29	E½SW	1832-07-17	FD	E2SW	R:MORGAN
1610	" "	18	W½SW	1836-03-04	FD	W2SW	R:MORGAN
1612	" "	19	NENW	1837-05-04	FD	NENW	R:MORGAN
1575	SMITH, William C	10	NWNE	1836-06-01	FD	NWNE	R:MORGAN
1566	SMITH, William Jr	30	E½NW	1830-08-24	FD	E2NW	R:MORGAN G:121
1450	SPARKS, John R	35	W½NW	1831-07-01	FD	W2NW	R:MORGAN
1449	" "	27	SWNE	1833-07-02	FD	SWNE	R:MORGAN
1350	SPAULDING, H	16	L4	1854-06-10	SC	LOT4	
1583	STAPLETON, William H	22	SENW	1836-11-04	FD	SENW	R:MORGAN
1582	" "	22	NWNW	1836-11-04	FD	NWNW	R:MORGAN
1291	STOCKTON, Allen	9	SESW	1836-01-09	FD	SESW	R:MORGAN
1289	" "	16	L5	1836-02-29	SC	L5MA	
1290	" "	16	L2	1837-04-05	SC	L2MA	
1301	STOUT, Andrew	20	W½NE	1828-12-18	FD	W2NE	R:MORGAN
1490	STOUT, Philemon	14	W½SE	1830-10-20	FD	W2SE	R:MORGAN
1489	" "	14	E½NW	1830-10-20	FD	E2NW	R:MORGAN
1553	STOUT, Thomas F	25	NESE	1833-05-25	FD	NESE	R:MORGAN
1410	SWAN, Jesse	16	L1	1854-06-10	SC	LOT1	
1453	SWAN, John	9	SWSE	1854-09-08	FD	SWSE	R:MORGAN
1462	SWAN, Jonathan	10	SWSW	1836-02-11	FD	SWSW	R:MORGAN
1512	SWAN, Robert	30	E½NE	1829-10-14	FD	E2NE	R:MORGAN
1402	TAYLOR, James	34	E½NW	1826-09-15	FD	E2NW	R:MASSAC
1406	" "	34	W½NE	1826-09-15	FD	W2NE	R:MASSAC

ID	Individual in Patent	Sec.	Sec. Part	Purchase Date	Sale Type	IL Aliquot Part	For More Info . . .
1407	TAYLOR, James (Cont'd)	34	W½NW	1826-10-25	FD	W2NW	R:MORGAN
1399	" "	27	E½SW	1827-01-26	FD	E2SW	R:MORGAN
1400	" "	27	W½NW	1830-01-02	FD	W2NW	R:MORGAN
1403	" "	34	E½SW	1831-06-24	FD	E2SW	R:MORGAN
1408	" "	34	W½SE	1831-06-24	FD	W2SE	R:MORGAN
1401	" "	34	E½NE	1831-07-01	FD	E2NELS	R:MORGAN
1405	" "	34	SESE	1833-06-10	FD	SESE	R:MORGAN
1404	" "	34	NWSW	1833-07-12	FD	NWSW	R:MORGAN
1537	TAYLOR, Samuel	34	SWSW	1833-10-15	FD	SWSW	R:MORGAN
1318	TROTTER, David	4	SENW	1832-11-24	FD	SENW	R:MORGAN
1384	VENABLE, James H	9		1831-05-30	FD	E2NEPTLS	R:MORGAN
1386	WALKER, James H	8	SENE	1836-02-19	FD	SENE	R:MORGAN
1385	" "	8	NENE	1836-06-04	FD	NENE	R:MORGAN
1481	WARE, Milton	2	NESW	1835-10-19	FD	NESW	R:MORGAN
1570	WARREN, William B	21	E½NE	1836-11-15	FD	E2NE	R:MORGAN G:64
1569	" "	11	SWNW	1853-11-30	FD	SWNW	
1458	WELCH, John	31	NENW	1833-11-19	FD	NENW	R:MORGAN
1280	WHEELER, William O	3		1830-11-19	FD	W2SEPTSK	R:IOWA
1591	" "	3		1830-11-19	FD	W2SEPTSK	R:IOWA
1541	WILLETT, Samuel	15	SENW	1836-01-02	FD	SENW	R:MORGAN
1540	" "	15	NENW	1837-03-02	FD	NENW	R:MORGAN
1539	" "	15	NENE	1846-11-09	FD	NENE	R:MORGAN
1482	WILLIAMS, Page A	3	N½NE	1830-06-05	FD	N2NE	R:MORGAN
1467	WILLSON, Joseph	15	SE	1832-03-15	FD	SE	R:VIRGINIA
1480	WOOD, Milo	27	SE	1826-09-15	FD	SE	R:MORGAN
1306	WORKMAN, Benjamin	4	N½NW	1831-03-21	FD	N2NW	R:MORGAN
1503	WYATT, Richard H	8	W½SE	1828-10-24	FD	W2SE	R:MORGAN
1564	WYATT, Walter	9	W½NW	1828-10-22	FD	W2NW	R:MORGAN
1562	" "	17	W½NE	1828-11-05	FD	W2NE	R:MORGAN
1563	" "	8	E½SE	1831-06-10	FD	E2SE	R:MORGAN
1377	YAPLE, Jacob	24	W½SE	1826-09-15	FD	W2SE	R:MORGAN
1378	" "	25	E½NE	1827-01-20	FD	E2NE	R:MORGAN
1379	" "	25	W½NE	1827-11-09	FD	W2NE	R:MORGAN

Patent Map

T16-N R9-W
3rd PM Meridian

Map Group 5

Township Statistics

Parcels Mapped	:	346
Number of Patents	:	1
Number of Individuals	:	216
Patentees Identified	:	212
Number of Surnames	:	154
Multi-Patentee Parcels	:	15
Oldest Patent Date	:	11/15/1823
Most Recent Patent	:	11/8/1855
Block/Lot Parcels	:	44
Cities and Towns	:	4
Cemeteries	:	3

Section 6
BERGEN John G 1831
MOSELY John J 1830
HOAGLAND [77] George W 1829
HOAGLAND Martin 1831
COWNOVER Dominicus 1827
COWNOVER Dominicus 1827
CROW William 1826

Section 5
FLIN Zadoc W 1826
COWNOVER William 1826
FLINN Zadoc W 1826
LITTON Burton 1826
LITTON Burton 1835
LITTON Cager 1836
OKEEFFE Thomas 1836
OKEEFFE Thomas 1835

Section 4
WORKMAN Benjamin 1831
FITZHUGH Robert 1826
HARDING Martin 1833
TROTTER David 1832
MALONE Alexander 1835
ALLEN Robert 1831
PARR John
PURVIANCE Evan 1828
HUGHES George 1829

Section 7
PURVIANCE Samuel 1826
PURVIANCE Alexander 1826
HOAGLAND George W 1831
COWNOVER Peter Jr 1826
ELDER Mathew 1826
PURVIANCE John G 1826
CROW William 1826

Section 8
HOAGLAND George W 1831
BERGEN John G 1835
HOBIN Thomas 1854
WALKER James H 1836
WALKER James H 1836
PURVIANCE John G 1826
HOGLIN William 1827
WYATT Richard H 1828

Section 9
WYATT Walter 1828
ALLEN Robert 1831
KETTNER Henry 1831
VENABLE James H 1831
WYATT Walter 1831
HAYNES Sarah 1833
BERGEN George L 1835
DENNIS John C 1844
MILLER Jacob N 1855
MADDOX John W 1836
STOCKTON Allen 1836
SWAN John 1854
HOAGLAND Martin 1836

Section 18
CHALLEN James 1835
LINDSEY Landy And Co 1829
ENYART Abner 1828
COWNOVER Peter Jr 1826
Lots-Sec. 18
L1(S½) BEAVERS, William 1851
SMITH William 1836
LINDSEY Allen F 1833
DODSWORTH Richard 1834
DODSWORTH Richard 1834
JONES Edward 1830
HARRISON George 1836

Section 17
ENYART Abner 1827
HOGLIN William 1827
EMMERSON Thomas 1835
EMMERSON Thomas 1836
RUSK John 1826

Section 16
WYATT Walter 1828
HOLMES Isaac G 1854

Lots-Sec. 16
L1	SWAN, Jesse	1854	L23	SINCLAIR, Amos	1832
L2	STOCKTON, Allen	1837	L24	SINCLAIR, Amos	1832
L3	SMITH, James [120]	1833	L25	PHILIPS, Amos G	1832
L4	SPAULDING, H	1854	L26	HUGHES, Allen B	1832
L5	STOCKTON, Allen	1836	L27	MADDOX, John W	1837
L6	HOLMES, Samuel	1853	L28	SMITH, Samuel	1832
L7	LANHAM, Plesant	1854	L29	GRAY, William	1833
L8	MADDOX, John W	1836	L30	DECK, Allen	1833
L9	JANUARY, Thomas T	1832	L31	ANDERSON, Richard	1836
L11	PHILIPS, James M	1833	L32	NORTHCUT, Hezekiah	183
L12	SMITH, James [120]	1833	L89	FARNUN, Lucian	1834
L13	MATHERS, John	1851	L100	FARNUN, Lucian	1834
L14	MATHERS, John	1851	L109	BRYANT, John [20]	1833
L15	MATHERS, John	1851	L110	BRYANT, John [20]	1833
L16	MATHERS, John	1851	L111	BRYANT, John [20]	1833
L17	MATHERS, John	1851	L112	FARNUN, Lucian	1834
L18	MATHERS, John	1851	L114	BRYAMT, John [17]	1833
L19	MATHERS, John	1851	L115	BRYANT, John	1833
L20	MATHERS, John	1851	L116	BRYANT, John [19]	1833
L21	SMITH, Samuel	1832			
L22	HAYNES, Jonathan	1832			

Section 19
SMITH William 1828
SMITH William 1837
SMITH Matthias 1837
HOLMES John W 1847
SLATTEN James 1832
SMITH William 1828
SMITH William 1826
COKER Dennis 1827
RUTHERFORD William 1826

Section 20
EADS James M 1829
HOAGLAND William 1828
STOUT Andrew 1828
SMITH Samuel 1826
GESFORD Joel 1826
GESFORD Joel 1829
SMITH William 1829
RUSK John 1826

Section 21
BOYER Thomas T 1830
NAULTY James 1854
HUNTER Francis 1836
ANDERSON Richard 1836
BOYCE Bartholomew T 1836
WARREN [64] William B 1836
BROWN Peyton 1829
ANDERSON Richard 1836
SINCLAIR Samuel 1846
BROWN Peyton 1827
BOYCE Thomas T 1831
SINCLAIR Samuel 1833

Section 30
SMITH [118] Hannah 1830
SMITH [121] Westly 1830
COKER Dennis 1830
SWAN Robert 1829
RUBLE Aaron 1832
SMITH Samuel 1832
KEPLINGER Jacob 1830
SEWALL William 1830
SMITH Samuel 1832

Section 29
SMITH William 1829
SMITH William 1830
PHILIPS Amos G 1830
BOYER Thomas T 1830
MCCAMMON William 1831
SMITH William 1832
BIRKBY John 1831
HUGHS Allen B 1832
HUGHES Allen B 1834

Section 28
MURPHY Renex 1826
MURPHY Rennex 1828
SINCLAIR Samuel 1833
ROBINSON William 1831
JACKSON Joseph W 1826
REDMON Janus 1830
JACKSON Joseph W 1826
REDMAN James 1826

Section 31
WELCH John 1833
BRISBY William 1834
DUNCAN Joseph 1833
SINCLAIR Watson 1833
EMMERSON Thomas 1834
Lots-Sec. 31
L2 SMITH, Thomas 1832

Section 32
SINCLAIR Amos 1833
SINCLAIR Amos 1833
SINCLAIR Samuel 1833
COOPER George 1833
SMITH Levi 1834
EMMERSON Thomas 1834
EMMERSON Thomas 1834
SINCLAIR Amos 1823
SINCLAIR Samuel 1833
EMMERSON Thomas 1834

Section 33
HARDIN John J 1833
HARDIN John J 1833
BOWEN Andrew 1830
EMMERSON Thomas 1834
HARDIN John J 1833

Section 3
- ARMSTRONG Andrew 1826
- ENYART Abner 1826
- WILLIAMS Page A 1830
- KELTNER Henry 1830

Section 2
- MCCLURR William 1830
- SACKETT Samuel 1827

Section 1
- FLINN Josiah 1826
- BALL Strother 1826

(below Section 3)
- HUGHES George 1830
- CANNON Richard 1828
- HUGHES George 1829
- WHEELER William O 1830
- CANNON Richard 1829

(below Section 2)
- MUNDAY William 1830
- WARE Milton 1835
- DANIEL Joseph 1853
- BRADLEY Hezekiah P 1829
- APLER Abram 1832

(below Section 1)
- CLARK Elisha 1827
- HUDSPETH Ralph 1826
- SHORT James 1826
- SAGE William 1826

Section 10
- ARMSTRONG William 1831
- BAKER James 1831
- SMITH William C 1836
- SAMPLE Jacob 1852
- CHAPMAN Sidney S 1855
- HOLMES Isaac G 1854
- MILLER Jacob 1855
- DUVAL John 1851
- HOLMES Isaac G 1854
- GORE John C 1853
- HOLMES Isaac G 1852
- SWAN Jonathan 1836

Section 11
- BALDWIN Ira 1851
- WARREN William B 1853
- MICKEY Robert 1837
- MICKEY Robert 1837
- CARR William P 1853
- BROWN William 1854
- ELDRIDGE Zachariah 1854
- MANCHESTER David 1851
- JAMES Enoch 1850

Section 12
- HARDING Jonathan 1838
- MICKEY Robert 1837
- SHORT Stephen 1830
- POINDEXTER Arche 1829
- POINDEXTER Arche 1829
- CLOPTON David 1831
- HENDRICK Claudius T 1837
- BENNET Isaac R 1826
- BENNETT Arthur F 1827
- BENNETT Isaac R 1831

Section 15
- HOLMES Isaac G 1854
- WILLETT Samuel 1837
- WILLETT Samuel 1846
- FLINN Zadock W 1832
- CREED John A 1836
- ELDRIDGE James 1836
- WILLETT Samuel 1836
- CAMREN Constant 1851
- CAMREN Constant 1851
- WILLSON Joseph 1832
- ROBERTSON Jonathan J 1836
- COKER John 1855

Section 14
- PEARSON William 1855
- STOUT Philemon 1830
- JAMES Enoch 1850
- SHEPHERD [109] Peter 1830
- SMITH [114] Anderson 1830
- SIMS James 1827
- STOUT Philemon 1830
- RUDE David 1830

Section 13
- COOPER William 1829
- PERVIANCE James 1830
- COOPER William 1829
- PURVIANCE James 1830
- SCOTT Daniel 1831
- ROBINSON Samuel 1829
- ROBINSON Joel 1829
- RAY Felix 1826
- OBANION Evin 1826

Section 22
- STAPLETON William H 1836
- RUYNKLE David 1855
- LEWIS William M 1844
- LEWIS Samuel 1837
- STAPLETON William H 1836
- HUNTER Francis 1837
- SINCLAIR Samuel 1853
- HUNTER Francis 1836
- SINCLAIR Samuel 1846
- FOX Elisha 1851
- FOX Elisha 1850
- BINGMAN Jacob 1835

Section 23
- PARROTT Robert D 1851
- HALL Equillar 1852
- FLIN Royal 1851
- ELDER James 1853
- PRICE Philemon B 1853
- MORGAN [63] William B 1836
- HARDIN John J 1835
- NILES Samuel V 1852

Section 24
- ROBINSON Samuel 1829
- OREAR William 1827
- HALL Equillar 1826
- OREAR William 1848
- OREAR William 1846
- OREAR William 1830
- YAPLE Jacob 1826
- OREAR William 1826

Section 27
- TAYLOR James 1830
- SINCLAIR Samuel 1836
- FOX Elisha 1850
- HOLMES Isaac 1829
- SPARKS John R 1833
- REDMAN James 1826
- TAYLOR James 1827
- WOOD Milo 1826

Section 26
- HOLMES Isaac 1830
- MATHEWS Samuel 1832
- BROWN William 1836
- MATHEWS Samuel 1830
- MATHEWS Richard 1826
- MATHEWS Mary 1829
- ADAMS Jacob 1826

Section 25
- OREAR William 1829
- YAPLE Jacob 1827
- YAPLE Jacob 1827
- OSCAR William 1835
- OREAR William 1829
- EDWARDS Richard 1828
- ADAMS Elijah 1832
- OREAR William 1833
- OREAR William 1830
- STOUT Thomas F 1833
- OREAR William 1833

Section 34
- TAYLOR James 1826
- TAYLOR James 1826
- TAYLOR James 1826
- TAYLOR James 1831
- TAYLOR James 1833
- TAYLOR James 1831
- TAYLOR James 1831
- BARNET John 1833
- TAYLOR James 1833
- TAYLOR Samuel 1833

Section 35
- SPARKS John R 1831
- MATHEWS Samuel 1831
- MATHEWS Samuel 1830
- ADAMS Jacob 1830
- HARDIN John J 1833
- HARDIN John 1832
- HARDIN John 1832
- HARDIN John J 1833
- ADAMS Jacob 1833
- OREAR George 1836

Section 36
- ADAMS Elijah 1833
- ADAMS Jacob 1833
- OREAR William 1835
- OKEAR William 1835
- ADAMS Jacob 1835
- OREAR William 1836
- ADAMS Jacob 1836
- ADAMS Jacob 1835

Helpful Hints

1. This Map's INDEX can be found on the preceding pages.

2. Refer to Map "C" to see where this Township lies within Morgan County, Illinois.

3. Numbers within square brackets [ ] denote a multi-patentee land parcel (multi-owner). Refer to Appendix "C" for a full list of members in this group.

4. Areas that look to be crowded with Patentees usually indicate multiple sales of the same parcel (re-issues), cancellations or voided transactions (that we map, anyway) or overlapping parcels. We opt to show even these ambiguous parcels, which oftentimes lead to research avenues not yet taken.

Legend

- Patent Boundary
- Section Boundary
- No Patents Found (or Outside County)
- 1., 2., 3., ... Lot Numbers (when beside a name)
- [ ] Group Number (see Appendix "C")

Scale: Section = 1 mile X 1 mile (generally, with some exceptions)

Road Map

T16-N R9-W
3rd PM Meridian

Map Group 5

<u>Cities & Towns</u>
Jordanville (historical)
Sinclair
Strawns Crossing
Yatesville

<u>Cemeteries</u>
Hebron Cemetery
Oak Ridge Cemetery
Yatesville Cemetery

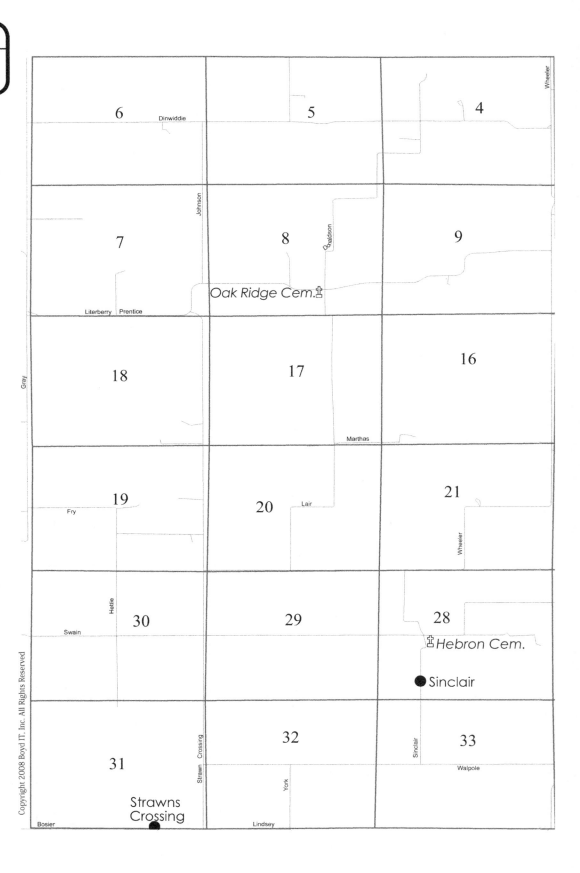

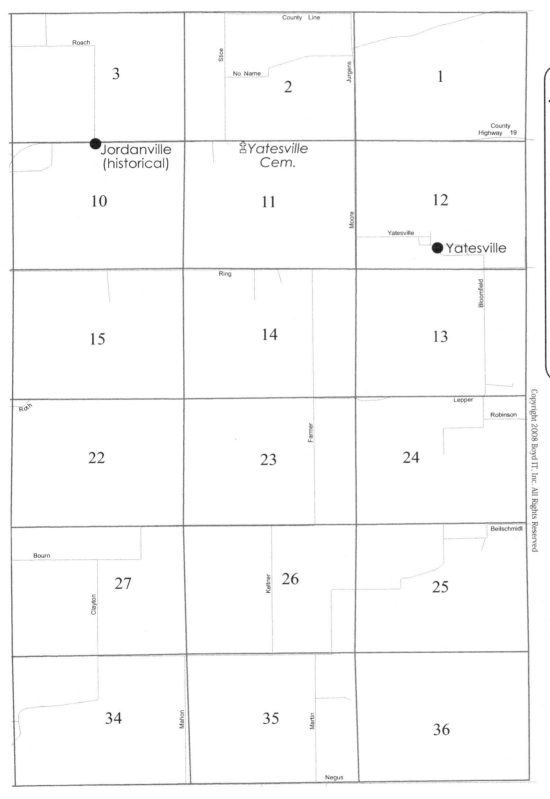

Helpful Hints

1. This road map has a number of uses, but primarily it is to help you: a) find the present location of land owned by your ancestors (at least the general area), b) find cemeteries and city-centers, and c) estimate the route/roads used by Census-takers & tax-assessors.

2. If you plan to travel to Morgan County to locate cemeteries or land parcels, please pick up a modern travel map for the area before you do. Mapping old land parcels on modern maps is not as exact a science as you might think. Just the slightest variations in public land survey coordinates, estimates of parcel boundaries, or road-map deviations can greatly alter a map's representation of how a road either does or doesn't cross a particular parcel of land.

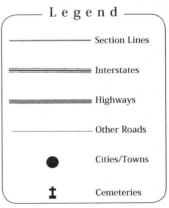

Legend

——— Section Lines

═══ Interstates

▬▬▬ Highways

——— Other Roads

● Cities/Towns

☨ Cemeteries

Scale: Section = 1 mile X 1 mile
(generally, with some exceptions)

Historical Map

T16-N R9-W
3rd PM Meridian

Map Group 5

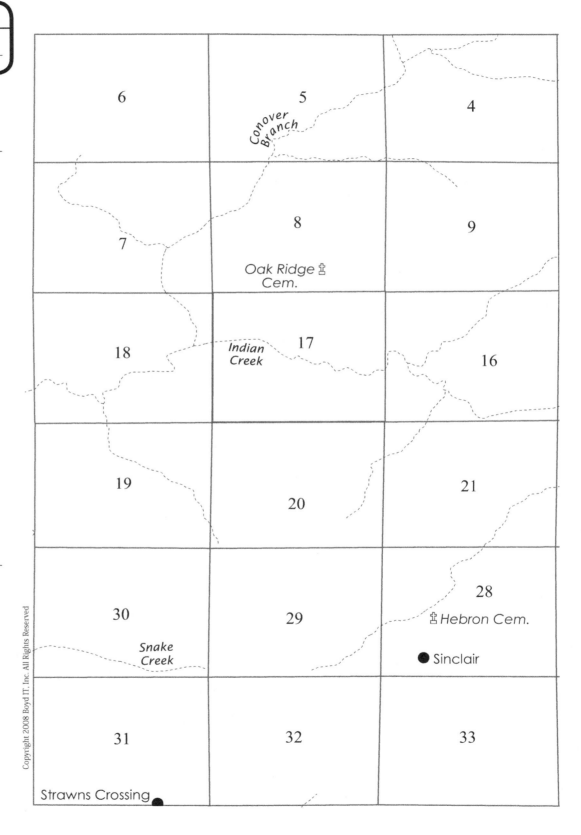

Cities & Towns
Jordanville (historical)
Sinclair
Strawns Crossing
Yatesville

Cemeteries
Hebron Cemetery
Oak Ridge Cemetery
Yatesville Cemetery

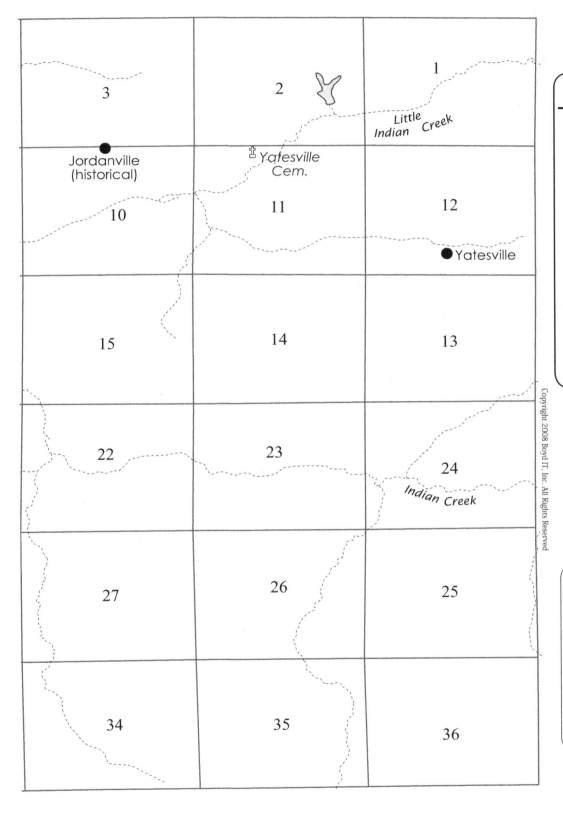

3

2

1

Little
Indian Creek

Jordanville
(historical)

✝ Yatesville
Cem.

10

11

12

● Yatesville

15

14

13

22

23

24

Indian Creek

27

26

25

34

35

36

Helpful Hints

1. This Map takes a different look at the same Congressional Township displayed in the preceding two maps. It presents features that can help you better envision the historical development of the area: a) Water-bodies (lakes & ponds), b) Water-courses (rivers, streams, etc.), c) Railroads, d) City/town center-points (where they were oftentimes located when first settled), and e) Cemeteries.

2. Using this "Historical" map in tandem with this Township's Patent Map and Road Map, may lead you to some interesting discoveries. You will often find roads, towns, cemeteries, and waterways are named after nearby landowners: sometimes those names will be the ones you are researching. See how many of these research gems you can find here in Morgan County.

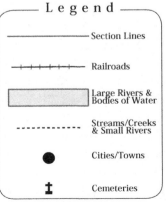

L e g e n d

——————— Section Lines

+–+–+–+–+–+ Railroads

Large Rivers & Bodies of Water

- - - - - - - - Streams/Creeks & Small Rivers

● Cities/Towns

✝ Cemeteries

Scale: Section = 1 mile X 1 mile
(there are some exceptions)

Map Group 6: Index to Land Patents

Township 16-North Range 8-West (3rd PM)

After you locate an individual in this Index, take note of the Section and Section Part then proceed to the Land Patent map on the pages immediately following. You should have no difficulty locating the corresponding parcel of land.

The "For More Info" Column will lead you to more information about the underlying Patents. See the *Legend* at right, and the "How to Use this Book" chapter, for more information.

ID	Individual in Patent	Sec.	Sec. Part	Purchase Date	Sale Type	IL Aliquot Part	For More Info . . .
1646	ALLEN, James	30	SENE	1835-07-20	FD	SENE	R:MORGAN
1644	BENNETT, Isaac R	7	SWSW	1835-11-09	FD	SWSW	R:MORGAN
1625	CATLIN, Charles	16	L2	1855-10-19	SC	LOT2N2NW	
1626	" "	16	L3	1855-10-19	SC	LOT3S2NW	
1624	CATLIN, Charles As	16	L4	1855-11-10	SC	L4S2NE	
1627	" "	16	L4	1855-11-10	SC	L4S2NE	
1627	CATLIN, Charles H	16	L4	1855-11-10	SC	LOT4S2NE	
1624	" "	16	L4	1855-11-10	SC	LOT4S2NE	
1686	CATLIN, Margaret E	16	L1	1855-10-19	SC	L1N2NE	S:F
1713	CATLIN, Thomas W	16	L8	1855-10-19	SC	LOT8S2SE	
1623	CAUBY, Merit	5	NENE	1839-07-11	FD	NENE	R:DELAWARE G:31
1649	CORRINGTON, Joel	29	E½NW	1835-07-20	FD	E2NW	R:MORGAN
1650	" "	29	NE	1835-07-20	FD	NE	R:MORGAN
1647	COX, James	5	SENE	1834-06-03	FD	SENE	R:MORGAN
1648	" "	5	SWNE	1835-03-10	FD	SWNE	R:MORGAN G:49
1717	COX, John	6		1826-09-13	FD	PT1NE	R:MORGAN
1656	" "	6		1826-09-13	FD	PT1NE	R:MORGAN
1655	" "	5	S½NW	1829-01-05	FD	S2NW	R:MORGAN
1648	COX, Warren	5	SWNE	1835-03-10	FD	SWNE	R:MORGAN G:49
1656	CROW, William	6		1826-09-13	FD	PT2NE	R:MORGAN
1717	" "	6		1826-09-13	FD	PT2NE	R:MORGAN
1715	" "	5		1826-12-02	FD	PT2NW	R:MORGAN
1716	" "	5	NWNE	1833-04-13	FD	NWNE	R:MORGAN
1685	FLIN, Josiah	7	W½NE	1826-09-13	FD	W2NE	R:MORGAN
1724	FLINN, Zaddock W	7	SESE	1835-06-26	FD	SESELS	R:MORGAN
1725	FLINN, Zadoc W	6	W½SE	1826-09-13	FD	W2SE	R:MORGAN
1729	FLINN, Zadock W	7	W½SE	1831-12-10	FD	W2SE	R:MORGAN
1728	" "	7	NESE	1833-06-07	FD	NESE	R:MORGAN
1730	" "	8	E½SW	1835-07-18	FD	E2SW	R:MORGAN
1731	" "	8	W½SE	1835-07-18	FD	W2SE	R:MORGAN
1727	" "	18	NE	1835-12-15	FD	NE	R:MORGAN
1726	" "	17	NW	1835-12-15	FD	NW	R:MORGAN
1628	GILTNER, Daniel	29	SW	1835-07-09	FD	SW	R:MORGAN
1684	GREEN, Joseph	16	L5	1855-11-10	SC	LOT5N2SE	
1665	GRIGG, John	33	W½	1835-10-31	FD	W2	R:PHILADELPHIA
1660	" "	30	SE	1835-10-31	FD	SE	R:PHILADELPHIA
1663	" "	31	SW	1835-10-31	FD	SW	R:PHILADELPHIA
1658	" "	28	SW	1835-10-31	FD	SW	R:PHILADELPHIA
1659	" "	29	SE	1835-10-31	FD	SE	R:PHILADELPHIA
1661	" "	31	E½	1835-10-31	FD	E2	R:PHILADELPHIA
1664	" "	32		1835-10-31	FD	SEC	R:PHILADELPHIA
1662	" "	31	E½NW	1835-10-31	FD	E2NW	R:PHILADELPHIA
1671	GRIGGS, John	28	SE	1835-11-14	FD	SE	R:PHILADELPHIA
1676	" "	9		1835-11-14	FD	SEC	R:PHILADELPHIA
1675	" "	8	E½SE	1835-11-14	FD	E2SE	R:PHILADELPHIA
1674	" "	8	E½NE	1835-11-14	FD	E2NE	R:PHILADELPHIA

ID	Individual in Patent	Sec.	Sec. Part	Purchase Date	Sale Type	IL Aliquot Part	For More Info . . .
1672	GRIGGS, John (Cont'd)	33	E½	1835-11-14	FD	E2	R:PHILADELPHIA
1670	" "	28	E½NE	1835-11-14	FD	E2NE	R:PHILADELPHIA
1669	" "	21	N½	1835-11-14	FD	N2	R:PHILADELPHIA
1668	" "	21	E½SE	1835-11-14	FD	E2SE	R:PHILADELPHIA
1667	" "	20	E½NE	1835-11-14	FD	E2NE	R:PHILADELPHIA
1666	" "	17	E½	1835-11-14	FD	E2	R:PHILADELPHIA
1673	" "	4		1835-11-14	FD	SEC	R:PHILADELPHIA
1633	HALL, Equilar	17	E½SW	1835-12-15	FD	E2SW	R:MORGAN
1634	HALL, Equilla	18	E½SW	1833-05-18	FD	E2SW	R:MORGAN
1636	HALL, Equillar	19	NW	1826-09-13	FD	NWFR	R:MORGAN
1635	" "	18	W½SW	1830-07-01	FD	W2SW	R:MORGAN
1637	" "	20	E½NW	1835-07-29	FD	E2NW	R:MORGAN
1638	" "	20	SWNW	1835-07-29	FD	SWNW	R:MORGAN
1639	HALL, Equiller	17	W½SW	1835-07-25	FD	W2SW	R:MORGAN
1640	" "	18	N½SE	1835-07-25	FD	N2SE	R:MORGAN
1681	HENRY, John	28	W½NE	1835-07-25	FD	W2NE	R:MORGAN
1680	" "	28	NW	1835-07-25	FD	NW	R:MORGAN
1679	" "	21	W½SE	1835-07-25	FD	W2SE	R:MORGAN
1678	" "	21	SW	1835-07-25	FD	SW	R:MORGAN
1677	" "	20	SE	1835-07-25	FD	SE	R:MORGAN
1629	HOGAN, Daniel	6	SW	1826-09-13	FD	SWFR	R:MORGAN
1630	HOGIN, Daniel	7	E½NW	1830-11-29	FD	E2NW	R:MORGAN
1682	HUDSPETH, John	8	NWNE	1835-02-10	FD	NWNE	R:MORGAN
1683	" "	8	SWNE	1835-06-26	FD	SWNELS	R:MORGAN
1695	HUDSPETH, Ralph	5	SW	1826-09-13	FD	SW	R:MORGAN
1694	" "	5	NWSE	1833-05-07	FD	NWSE	R:MORGAN
1696	" "	5	SWSE	1835-06-29	FD	SWSE	R:MORGAN
1693	" "	5	E½SE	1835-06-29	FD	E2SE	R:MORGAN
1697	" "	5	SWSE	1835-06-29	FD	SWSE	R:MORGAN
1692	" "	5	E½SE	1835-06-29	FD	E2SE	R:MORGAN
1697	" "	5	SWSE	1853-06-29	FD	SWSE	R:MORGAN
1696	" "	5	SWSE	1853-06-29	FD	SWSE	R:MORGAN
1692	" "	5	E½SE	1853-06-29	FD	E2SE	R:MORGAN
1693	" "	5	E½SE	1853-06-29	FD	E2SE	R:MORGAN
1657	LEWIS, John F	7	W½NW	1836-06-01	FD	W2NW	R:OHIO
1623	MANDAIN, Arnold	5	NENE	1839-07-11	FD	NENE	R:DELAWARE G:31
1631	MORRIS, Edmund	20	NWNW	1835-07-25	FD	NWNW	R:MORGAN
1701	MORRISON, Robert	18	SESW	1834-07-19	FD	SESW	R:MORGAN
1632	MORRISS, Edmund	19	W½NE	1832-02-25	FD	W2NELS	R:MORGAN
1641	OBANION, Garrett	18	W½NW	1831-10-05	FD	W2NW	R:MORGAN
1643	OREAR, George	31	W½NW	1835-06-29	FD	W2NW	R:MORGAN
1642	" "	30	S½SW	1835-07-02	FD	S2SW	R:MORGAN
1720	OREAR, William	30	W½NW	1829-12-14	FD	W2NW	R:MORGAN
1714	PARROTT, Tyre	7	NWSW	1833-05-20	FD	NWSW	R:MORGAN
1704	ROBESON, Samuel	8	W½NW	1826-09-13	FD	W2NW	R:MORGAN
1703	" "	7	E½NE	1826-09-13	FD	E2NE	R:MORGAN
1702	" "	6	E½SE	1826-09-13	FD	E2SE	R:MORGAN
1645	ROBINSON, Isaac	30		1832-09-24	FD	NWNEPTSK	R:MORGAN
1653	ROBINSON, Joel	19	W½SE	1826-09-13	FD	W2SE	R:MORGAN
1652	" "	19	E½SE	1832-02-29	FD	E2SE	R:MORGAN
1651	" "	19	E½NE	1832-02-29	FD	E2NE	R:MORGAN
1654	" "	30	NENE	1835-02-17	FD	NENE	R:MORGAN
1689	ROBINSON, Peter	30	E½NW	1830-06-14	FD	E2NW	R:MORGAN
1691	" "	30	SWNE	1833-05-22	FD	SWNE	R:MORGAN
1690	" "	30	NESW	1833-05-22	FD	NESW	R:MORGAN
1706	ROBISON, Samuel	8	NWSW	1833-05-30	FD	NWSW	R:MORGAN
1705	" "	8	NENW	1833-05-30	FD	NENW	R:MORGAN
1709	SHORT, Stephen	6	NW	1826-09-13	FD	NWFR	R:MORGAN
1723	SIMS, William	19	SW	1826-09-13	FD	SWFR	R:MORGAN
1722	" "	18	SWSE	1835-07-17	FD	SWSE	R:MORGAN
1721	" "	18	SESE	1835-07-17	FD	SESE	R:MORGAN
1710	STOUT, Thomas F	30	NWSW	1833-05-25	FD	NWSW	R:MORGAN
1623	TATNALL, Edward	5	NENE	1839-07-11	FD	NENE	R:DELAWARE G:31
1711	THOMPSON, Thomas R	8	SENW	1835-06-30	FD	SENW	R:MORGAN
1712	" "	8	SWSW	1835-06-30	FD	SWSW	R:MORGAN
1719	THOMPSON, William M	16	L7	1855-10-19	SC	LOT7S2SW	
1718	" "	16	L6	1855-10-19	SC	LOT6N2SW	
1700	WALKER, Richard	20	W½NE	1835-08-25	FD	W2NE	R:MORGAN
1698	WALKER, Richard S	20	SW	1835-07-20	FD	SW	R:MORGAN
1699	" "	29	W½NW	1835-07-20	FD	W2NW	R:MORGAN
1688	WARE, Nathaniel A	7	E½SW	1833-06-14	FD	E2SW	R:ST. LOUIS
1687	" "	18	E½NW	1833-06-14	FD	E2NW	R:ST. LOUIS
1707	WEBB, Simeon	7	NWNW	1834-03-17	FD	NWNW	R:MORGAN

ID	Individual in Patent	Sec.	Sec. Part	Purchase Date	Sale Type	IL Aliquot Part	For More Info . . .
1708	WEBB, Simeon (Cont'd)	7	SWNW	1835-02-10	FD	SWNW	R:MORGAN

Patent Map

T16-N R8-W
3rd PM Meridian

Map Group 6

Township Statistics

Parcels Mapped	:	109
Number of Patents	:	1
Number of Individuals	:	54
Patentees Identified	:	52
Number of Surnames	:	37
Multi-Patentee Parcels	:	2
Oldest Patent Date	:	9/13/1826
Most Recent Patent	:	11/10/1855
Block/Lot Parcels	:	12
Cities and Towns	:	1
Cemeteries	:	2

Note: the area contained in this map amounts to far less than a full Township. Therefore, its contents are completely on this single page (instead of a "normal" 2-page spread).

Map parcels

Section 6
SHORT Stephen 1826
COX John 1826
CROW William 1826
HOGAN Daniel 1826
FLINN Zadoc W 1826
ROBESON Samuel 1826

Section 5
CROW William 1826
CROW William 1833
MANDAIN [31] Arnold 1839
COX John 1829
COX [49] James 1835
COX James 1834
HUDSPETH Ralph 1833
HUDSPETH Ralph 1826
HUDSPETH Ralph 1853
HUDSPETH Ralph 1835
HUDSPETH Ralph 1853
HUDSPETH Ralph 1835

Section 4
GRIGGS John 1835

Section 7
WEBB Simeon 1834
LEWIS John F
WEBB Simeon 1836
HOGIN Daniel 1830
FLIN Josiah 1826
ROBESON Samuel 1826
PARROTT Tyre 1833
WARE Nathaniel A 1833
BENNETT Isaac R 1835
FLINN Zadock W 1831
FLINN Zadock W 1833
FLINN Zaddock W 1835

Section 8
ROBESON Samuel 1826
ROBISON Samuel 1833
THOMPSON Thomas R 1835
ROBISON Samuel 1833
THOMPSON Thomas R 1835
ROBISON Samuel 1833
HUDSPETH John 1835
HUDSPETH John 1835
FLINN Zadock W 1835
FLINN Zadock W 1835

Section 9
GRIGGS John 1835
GRIGGS John 1835
GRIGGS John 1835
FLINN Zadock W 1835
GRIGGS John 1835

Section 18
OBANION Garrett 1831
WARE Nathaniel A 1833
FLINN Zadock W 1835
HALL Equilla 1833
HALL Equiller 1835
HALL Equillar 1830
MORRISON Robert 1834
SIMS William 1835
SIMS William 1835

Section 17
FLINN Zadock W 1835
HALL Equiller 1835
HALL Equilar 1835
GRIGGS John 1835

Section 16
Lots-Sec. 16
L1 CATLIN, Margaret E 1855
L2 CATLIN, Charles 1855
L3 CATLIN, Charles 1855
L4 CATLIN, Charles H 1855
L4 CATLIN, Charles As 1855
L5 GREEN, Joseph 1855
L6 THOMPSON, William M 1855
L7 THOMPSON, William M 1855
L8 CATLIN, Thomas W 1855

Section 19
HALL Equillar 1826
MORRISS Edmund 1832
ROBINSON Joel 1832
SIMS William 1826
ROBINSON Joel 1826
ROBINSON Joel 1832

Section 20
MORRIS Edmund 1835
HALL Equiller 1835
HALL Equillar 1835
WALKER Richard 1835
WALKER Richard S 1835

Section 21
GRIGGS John 1835
HENRY John 1835
HENRY John 1835
GRIGGS John 1835
GRIGGS John 1835

Section 30
OREAR William 1829
ROBINSON Peter 1830
ROBINSON Peter 1833
ROBINSON Joel 1835
ROBINSON Isaac 1832
ALLEN James 1835
STOUT Thomas F 1833
ROBINSON Peter 1833
GRIGG John 1835
OREAR George 1835

Section 29
WALKER Richard S 1835
CORRINGTON Joel 1835
CORRINGTON Joel 1835

Section 28
HENRY John 1835
HENRY John 1835
GRIGGS John 1835
GRIG John 1835
GRIGGS John 1835

Section 31
OREAR George 1835
GRIGG John 1835
GRIGG John 1835
GRIGG John 1835

Section 32
GILTNER Daniel 1835
GRIGG John 1835
GRIGG John 1835

Section 33
GRIGG John 1835
GRIGGS John 1835
GRIGG John 1835

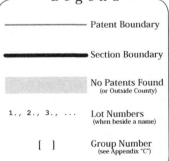

Legend

—— Patent Boundary

━━ Section Boundary

▓▓ No Patents Found (or Outside County)

1., 2., 3., ... Lot Numbers (when beside a name)

[ ] Group Number (see Appendix "C")

Scale: Section = 1 mile X 1 mile (generally, with some exceptions)

Road Map

T16-N R8-W
3rd PM Meridian

Map Group 6

Note: the area contained in this map amounts to far less than a full Township. Therefore, its contents are completely on this single page (instead of a "normal" 2-page spread).

Cities & Towns
Prentice

Cemeteries
Berea Cemetery
Flinn Cemetery

Legend
Section Lines
Interstates
Highways
Other Roads
Cities/Towns
Cemeteries

Scale: Section = 1 mile X 1 mile
(generally, with some exceptions)

6

County Highway 123

5

Donnan

4

Creed

County Line

Clay
Co Hwy 19
Adkins
Beard
Prentice
Anderson

Flinn Cem.

Rieken

7

8

9

Yatesville

Buelah

18

17

16

Robinson

Berea
Berea Cem.

19

Hog Barn

20

21

Thornley

Davenport

Beilschmidt

30

County Highway 123

29

28

31

32

Kern

33

Negus

126

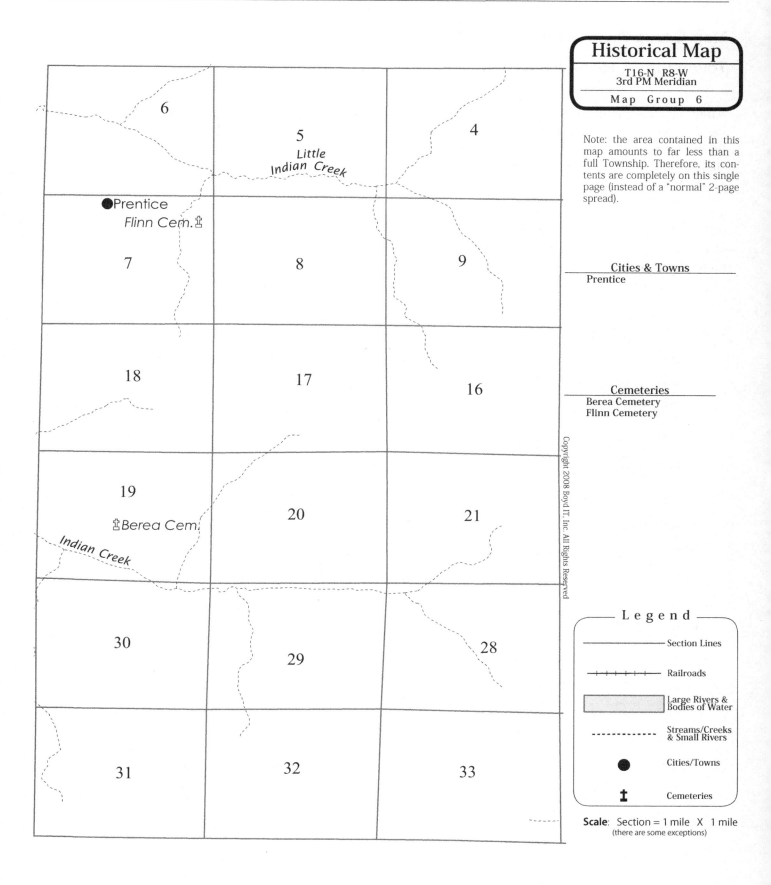

Map Group 7: Index to Land Patents

Township 15-North Range 12-West (3rd PM)

After you locate an individual in this Index, take note of the Section and Section Part then proceed to the Land Patent map on the pages immediately following. You should have no difficulty locating the corresponding parcel of land.

The "For More Info" Column will lead you to more information about the underlying Patents. See the *Legend* at right, and the "How to Use this Book" chapter, for more information.

```
                    LEGEND
        "For More Info . . . " column
G = Group  (Multi-Patentee Patent, see Appendix "C")
R = Residence
S = Social Status


See Appendix A for list of abbreviations used by the
Illinois State Archives in describing the place and
nature of these land patents.

Note: if the Abbreviations contain "L", "BL", "LOT",
or "BLOCK", the exact whereabouts of the parcel within
the section is not known.
```

ID	Individual in Patent	Sec.	Sec. Part	Purchase Date	Sale Type	IL Aliquot Part	For More Info . . .
1816	ABBEY, Orsemus	3	L3 (W½)	1835-08-06	FD	W2LOT3NW	R:MORGAN
1781	ABBOTT, John	6	L3	1855-02-20	FD	NELOT3NEFR	
1836	" "	6	L3	1855-02-20	FD	NELOT3NEFR	
1749	" "	6	L3	1855-02-20	FD	NELOT3NEFR	
1826	ALLINSON, Thomas	1		1831-12-28	FD	N03NW	R:MORGAN
1758	" "	1		1831-12-28	FD	N03NW	R:MORGAN
1786	BARTON, John H	1	E½SW	1833-05-01	FD	E2SW	R:MORGAN
1788	" "	12	E½NW	1833-05-01	FD	E2NW	R:MORGAN
1787	" "	1	SWSE	1833-11-14	FD	SWSE	R:MORGAN
1789	" "	12	NESW	1836-02-19	FD	NESW	R:MORGAN
1790	" "	12	W½SW	1836-02-19	FD	W2SW	R:MORGAN
1774	BOZARTH, James	11	E½NE	1830-07-13	FD	E2NE	R:MORGAN
1747	BRADBURY, Nathan	4		1826-10-06	FD	PT2NW	R:MORGAN
1746	" "	4		1826-10-06	FD	PT2NW	R:MORGAN
1760	" "	4		1826-10-06	FD	PT2NW	R:MORGAN
1812	" "	4		1826-10-06	FD	PT2NW	R:MORGAN
1813	" "	4	NW	1829-10-27	FD	PT1NW	R:MORGAN
1835	BRISBIN, William	3	W½SE	1828-12-12	FD	W2SE	R:MORGAN
1744	BROADWELL, Baxter	9	NW	1823-11-14	FD	NW	R:MORGAN
1742	" "	4	W½SW	1828-12-20	FD	W2SW	R:MORGAN
1743	" "	8	E½NW	1829-04-07	FD	E2NW	R:MORGAN
1745	" "	9	W½NE	1829-04-18	FD	W2NE	R:MORGAN
1785	" "	9	W½NE	1829-04-18	FD	W2NE	R:MORGAN
1740	" "	4	E½SW	1830-05-22	FD	E2SW	R:MORGAN
1741	" "	4	W½SE	1831-05-23	FD	W2SE	R:MORGAN
1766	CHAMBERLIN, Griffin	3	L3	1835-10-06	FD	LOT3NE	R:MORGAN G:32
1766	CHAMBERLIN, James	3	L3	1835-10-06	FD	LOT3NE	R:MORGAN G:32
1772	COBB, Orson P	7	W½SE	1836-07-02	FD	W2SE	R:MORGAN G:40
1770	" "	7	NESE	1836-07-02	FD	NESE	R:MORGAN G:40
1771	" "	7	SW	1836-07-02	FD	SW	R:MORGAN G:40
1773	" "	8	W½SW	1836-07-02	FD	W2SW	R:MORGAN G:40
1750	COLLINS, Charles	12	S½SE	1836-07-18	FD	S2SE	R:ST. LOUIS
1754	" "	6	L2 (W½)	1836-07-28	FD	W2LOT2NE	R:MORGAN G:45
1751	" "	5	NW	1836-07-28	FD	NW	R:MORGAN G:45
1752	" "	5	L3	1836-07-28	FD	LOT3NE	R:MORGAN G:45
1753	" "	6	L1 (W½)	1836-07-28	FD	W2LOT1NE	R:MORGAN G:45
1783	COONRAD, Woolery	2		1831-08-31	FD	N01NE	R:MORGAN
1795	" "	2		1831-08-31	FD	N01NE	R:MORGAN
1849	" "	2		1831-08-31	FD	N01NE	R:MORGAN
1764	" "	2		1831-08-31	FD	N01NE	R:MORGAN
1818	DANIELS, Samuel	9	E½SW	1836-02-19	FD	E2SW	R:MORGAN
1798	DANIELS, Verin	3		1831-05-05	FD	PT2NE	R:MORGAN
1821	" "	3		1831-05-05	FD	PT2NE	R:MORGAN
1784	" "	3		1831-05-05	FD	PT2NE	R:MORGAN
1831	" "	2	E½SW	1831-05-05	FD	E2SW	R:MORGAN
1832	" "	3		1831-05-05	FD	PT2NE	R:MORGAN

ID	Individual in Patent	Sec.	Sec. Part	Purchase Date	Sale Type	IL Aliquot Part	For More Info . . .
1751	DUNCAN, Thomas O	5	NW	1836-07-28	FD	NW	R:MORGAN G:45
1752	" "	5	L3	1836-07-28	FD	LOT3NE	R:MORGAN G:45
1753	" "	6	L1 (W½)	1836-07-28	FD	W2LOT1NE	R:MORGAN G:45
1754	" "	6	L2 (W½)	1836-07-28	FD	W2LOT2NE	R:MORGAN G:45
1734	DUNLAP, Alexander	6	L1	1836-12-10	FD	LOT1NW	R:MORGAN
1733	" "	6	N½SW	1836-12-10	FD	N2SW	R:MORGAN
1828	EDMONSON, Thomas	6	L3 (W½)	1836-07-18	FD	W2LOT3NE	R:MORGAN
1827	" "	6	L1 (E½)	1836-07-18	FD	E2LOT1NE	R:MORGAN
1780	ETHEL, Janus	10	W½NW	1831-10-14	FD	W2NWLS	R:MORGAN S:F
1847	ETHEL, Willis J	12	SESW	1836-07-18	FD	SESW	R:MORGAN
1846	" "	12	N½SE	1836-07-18	FD	N2SE	R:MORGAN
1848	" "	5	L1 (W½)	1836-07-23	FD	W2LOT1NE	R:MORGAN
1824	FARTHING, Solomon	6	L2 (E½)	1835-08-29	FD	E2LOT2NE	R:MORGAN
1775	FIKE, James	5	NWSE	1835-08-26	FD	NWSE	R:MORGAN
1815	FISK, Nathaniel	1	NWSE	1835-03-17	FD	NWSE	R:MORGAN
1814	" "	1	NESE	1835-09-26	FD	NESE	R:MORGAN
1821	FOX, John	3		1830-05-08	FD	NO3NE	R:MORGAN
1798	" "	3		1830-05-08	FD	NO3NE	R:MORGAN
1784	" "	3		1830-05-08	FD	NO3NE	R:MORGAN
1832	" "	3		1830-05-08	FD	NO3NE	R:MORGAN
1795	" "	2		1831-03-22	FD	PT3NE	R:MORGAN
1849	" "	2		1831-03-22	FD	PT3NE	R:MORGAN
1764	" "	2		1831-03-22	FD	PT3NE	R:MORGAN
1783	" "	2		1831-03-22	FD	PT3NE	R:MORGAN
1834	FRENCH, William	7	W½NW	1836-11-15	FD	W2NW	R:MORGAN G:64
1833	" "	6	L2	1836-11-21	FD	LOT2NW	R:MORGAN G:63
1808	GOODPASTURE, Madison	2	E½SE	1831-12-29	FD	E2SE	R:MORGAN
1807	" "	1	SESE	1834-06-10	FD	SESE	R:MORGAN
1745	GRIGG, John	9	W½NE	1835-07-01	FD	W2NE	R:PENNSYLVANIA
1785	" "	9	W½NE	1835-07-01	FD	W2NE	R:PENNSYLVANIA
1837	HAMILTON, William	8	W2NE	1835-08-14	FD	W2NEPRE	R:MORGAN
1781	" "	6	L3	1852-10-29	FD	SELOT3NEFR	
1836	" "	6	L3	1852-10-29	FD	SELOT3NEFR	
1749	" "	6	L3	1852-10-29	FD	SELOT3NEFR	
1776	HILLARD, William	1	L1 (E½)	1835-03-17	FD	E2LOT1NW	R:MORGAN
1838	" "	1	L1 (E½)	1835-03-17	FD	E2LOT1NW	R:MORGAN
1739	HOSKINS, Barnet	9	E2SE	1836-05-27	FD	E2SEPRE	R:MORGAN G:78
1791	HOSKINS, John	9	E½NE	1831-05-28	FD	E2NE	R:MORGAN
1739	" "	9	E2SE	1836-05-27	FD	E2SEPRE	R:MORGAN G:78
1821	KIRKPATRICK, John L	3		1831-03-22	FD	PT1NE	R:MORGAN
1784	" "	3		1831-03-22	FD	PT1NE	R:MORGAN
1832	" "	3		1831-03-22	FD	PT1NE	R:MORGAN
1796	" "	2	NW	1831-03-22	FD	PT1NW	R:MORGAN
1798	" "	3		1831-03-22	FD	PT1NE	R:MORGAN
1849	" "	2		1831-05-30	FD	NO3NW	R:MORGAN
1764	" "	2		1831-05-30	FD	NO3NW	R:MORGAN
1783	" "	2		1831-05-30	FD	NO3NW	R:MORGAN
1795	" "	2		1831-05-30	FD	NO3NW	R:MORGAN
1797	" "	2	W½SE	1831-12-12	FD	W2SE	R:MORGAN
1817	KIRKPATRICK, Polly	2	W½SW	1831-03-22	FD	W2SW	R:MORGAN S:F
1799	LEWIS, John	3	E½SE	1830-08-28	FD	E2SE	R:MORGAN
1773	LUDWICK, Kennedy	8	W½SW	1836-07-02	FD	W2SW	R:MORGAN G:40
1772	" "	7	W½SE	1836-07-02	FD	W2SE	R:MORGAN G:40
1771	" "	7	SW	1836-07-02	FD	SW	R:MORGAN G:40
1770	" "	7	NESE	1836-07-02	FD	NESE	R:MORGAN G:40
1772	MANCHESTER, John	7	W½SE	1836-07-02	FD	W2SE	R:MORGAN G:40
1771	" "	7	SW	1836-07-02	FD	SW	R:MORGAN G:40
1773	" "	8	W½SW	1836-07-02	FD	W2SW	R:MORGAN G:40
1770	" "	7	NESE	1836-07-02	FD	NESE	R:MORGAN G:40
1768	MANNING, Horatio A	5	L2	1836-07-18	FD	LOT2NE	R:MORGAN
1772	MCKEE, Jesse	7	W½SE	1836-07-02	FD	W2SE	R:MORGAN G:40
1770	" "	7	NESE	1836-07-02	FD	NESE	R:MORGAN G:40
1773	" "	8	W½SW	1836-07-02	FD	W2SW	R:MORGAN G:40
1771	" "	7	SW	1836-07-02	FD	SW	R:MORGAN G:40
1747	MCPHERSON, Benjamin G	4		1829-08-17	FD	PT3NWFR	R:MORGAN
1760	" "	4		1829-08-17	FD	PT3NWFR	R:MORGAN
1746	" "	4		1829-08-17	FD	PT3NWFR	R:MORGAN
1812	" "	4		1829-08-17	FD	PT3NWFR	R:MORGAN
1747	" "	4		1829-11-09	FD	PT3NE	R:MORGAN
1746	" "	4		1829-11-09	FD	PT3NE	R:MORGAN
1812	" "	4		1829-11-09	FD	PT3NE	R:MORGAN
1760	" "	4		1829-11-09	FD	PT3NE	R:MORGAN
1769	MILNOR, Isaac	3	L3 (E½)	1835-11-28	FD	E2LOT3NW	R:MORGAN

ID	Individual in Patent	Sec.	Sec. Part	Purchase Date	Sale Type	IL Aliquot Part	For More Info . . .
1777	MILSTEAD, James	11	W½SE	1831-10-19	FD	W2SE	R:MORGAN
1833	MORGAN, William B	6	L2	1836-11-21	FD	LOT2NW	R:MORGAN G:63
1763	MORRELL, Elfonso	9	W½SE	1829-06-23	FD	W2SE	R:MORGAN
1800	MURPHEY, John	12	W½NE	1831-10-13	FD	W2NE	R:MORGAN
1801	MURPHY, John	12	E½NE	1830-11-20	FD	E2NE	R:MORGAN
1738	NEW, Asa C	10	W½SW	1836-03-08	FD	W2SW	R:MORGAN
1737	"	10	SESW	1836-03-08	FD	SESW	R:MORGAN
1819	OSBOURN, Samuel	8	SESW	1835-04-20	FD	SESW	R:MORGAN
1820	OSBURN, Samuel	8	NESW	1836-06-04	FD	NESW	R:MORGAN
1765	PREWITT, Fields	2	L2	1832-04-17	FD	LOT2NWPRE	R:MORGAN
1735	REED, Andrew	10	E½NW	1831-11-30	FD	E2NW	R:MORGAN
1736	"	10	W½NE	1831-11-30	FD	W2NE	R:MORGAN
1825	REID, Stephen H	1	L1 (W½)	1835-09-18	FD	W2LOT1NW	R:MORGAN
1845	"	1	L1 (W½)	1835-09-18	FD	W2LOT1NW	R:MORGAN
1778	ROUNDS, James	6	SE	1835-08-26	FD	SEPRE	R:MORGAN G:108
1778	ROUNDS, William	6	SE	1835-08-26	FD	SEPRE	R:MORGAN G:108
1840	SAIGHMAN, William	3	E½SW	1830-06-02	FD	E2SW	R:MORGAN
1841	"	7	E½NE	1830-06-02	FD	E2NE	R:MORGAN
1779	SIMMONS, James	8	W½NW	1829-12-30	FD	W2NW	R:MORGAN
1767	SIMPLOT, Henry	5	L1 (E½)	1833-05-13	FD	E2LOT1NE	R:MORGAN
1806	SMART, Josiah	5	E½SE	1828-11-24	FD	E2SE	R:MORGAN
1805	SMART, Josiah H	5	SWSE	1823-11-05	FD	SWSE	R:MORGAN
1830	SMART, Thomas	11	W½SW	1823-11-14	FD	W2SW	R:MORGAN
1829	"	11	E½NW	1824-12-01	FD	E2NW	R:MORGAN
1770	SMITH, Isaac R	7	NESE	1836-07-02	FD	NESE	R:MORGAN G:40
1772	"	7	W½SE	1836-07-02	FD	W2SE	R:MORGAN G:40
1773	"	8	W½SW	1836-07-02	FD	W2SW	R:MORGAN G:40
1771	"	7	SW	1836-07-02	FD	SW	R:MORGAN G:40
1839	SMITH, William R	1	L2	1835-11-18	FD	LOT2NE	R:MORGAN
1809	STEWART, Mariah	8		1835-08-14	FD	E2NEPREFL	R:MORGAN S:F
1792	TAYLOR, John Jr	8	E½SE	1830-11-09	FD	E2SE	R:MORGAN
1794	"	9	W½SW	1830-11-09	FD	W2SW	R:MORGAN
1793	"	8	NWSE	1835-11-26	FD	NWSE	R:MORGAN
1804	TAYLOR, Jonathan	5	SW	1836-04-25	FD	SW	R:MORGAN
1749	THOMPSON, Bernard	6	L3	1852-01-17	FD	LOT3NWFR	
1836	"	6	L3	1852-01-17	FD	LOT3NWFR	
1781	"	6	L3	1852-01-17	FD	LOT3NWFR	
1748	TROY, Benjamin	7	NWNE	1833-05-20	FD	NWNE	R:MORGAN
1756	TROY, Charles	10	SE	1823-11-14	FD	SE	R:MORGAN
1755	"	10	E½NE	1823-11-14	FD	E2NE	R:MORGAN
1757	"	11	W½NW	1825-12-22	FD	W2NW	R:MORGAN
1746	TROY, Daniel	4		1823-11-14	FD	PT1NE	R:MORGAN
1812	"	4		1823-11-14	FD	PT1NE	R:MORGAN
1762	"	4	L2	1823-11-14	FD	PT2NE	R:MORGAN
1760	"	4		1823-11-14	FD	PT1NE	R:MORGAN
1747	"	4		1823-11-14	FD	PT1NE	R:MORGAN
1826	"	1		1830-07-23	FD	N02NW	R:MORGAN
1758	"	1		1830-07-23	FD	N02NW	R:MORGAN
1761	"	4	E½SE	1831-06-28	FD	E2SE	R:MORGAN
1759	"	10	NESW	1835-09-11	FD	NESW	R:MORGAN
1811	TROY, Nancy	7	SWNE	1836-06-04	FD	SWNE	R:MORGAN S:F
1810	"	7	E½NW	1836-06-04	FD	E2NW	R:MORGAN S:F
1782	WARREN, John F	6	S½SW	1836-11-15	FD	S2SW	R:MORGAN
1834	WARREN, William B	7	W½NW	1836-11-15	FD	W2NW	R:MORGAN G:64
1849	WHITLEY, Elisha	2		1832-03-05	FD	PT2NE	R:MORGAN
1795	"	2		1832-03-05	FD	PT2NE	R:MORGAN
1783	"	2		1832-03-05	FD	PT2NE	R:MORGAN
1764	"	2		1832-03-05	FD	PT2NE	R:MORGAN
1822	WHITLEY, Samuel	3	NW	1828-10-30	FD	PT1NW	R:MORGAN
1823	"	3	W½SW	1828-10-30	FD	W2SW	R:MORGAN
1832	"	3		1830-02-18	FD	N02NW	R:MORGAN
1821	"	3		1830-02-18	FD	N02NW	R:MORGAN
1784	"	3		1830-02-18	FD	N02NW	R:MORGAN
1798	"	3		1830-02-18	FD	N02NW	R:MORGAN
1802	WHORTON, John	8	SWSE	1832-04-17	FD	SWSEPRE	R:MORGAN
1838	WILLARD, James M	1	L1 (E½)	1835-09-26	FD	E2LOT1NE	R:MORGAN
1776	"	1	L1 (E½)	1835-09-26	FD	E2LOT1NE	R:MORGAN
1844	WILLARD, William	12	W½NW	1830-06-25	FD	W2NW	R:MORGAN
1843	"	11	E½SE	1830-06-25	FD	E2SE	R:MORGAN
1842	"	1	W½SW	1831-10-31	FD	W2SWLS	R:MORGAN
1732	WILSON, Aaron	7	SESE	1835-12-04	FD	SESE	R:MORGAN
1825	WILSON, William	1	L1 (W½)	1835-07-16	FD	W2LOT1NE	R:MORGAN
1845	"	1	L1 (W½)	1835-07-16	FD	W2LOT1NE	R:MORGAN

ID	Individual in Patent	Sec.	Sec. Part	Purchase Date	Sale Type	IL Aliquot Part	For More Info . . .
1803	WYATT, John	11	E½SW	1830-11-16	FD	E2SW	R:MORGAN

Patent Map

T15-N R12-W
3rd PM Meridian

Map Group 7

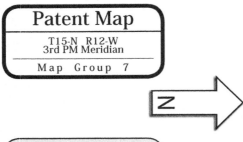

N

Township Statistics

Parcels Mapped	:	118
Number of Patents	:	1
Number of Individuals	:	79
Patentees Identified	:	72
Number of Surnames	:	62
Multi-Patentee Parcels	:	13
Oldest Patent Date	:	11/5/1823
Most Recent Patent	:	2/20/1855
Block/Lot Parcels	:	26
Cities and Towns	:	3
Cemeteries	:	1

Note: the area contained in this map amounts to far less than a full Township. Therefore, its contents are completely on this single page (instead of a "normal" 2-page spread).

Legend

— Patent Boundary

━ Section Boundary

▨ No Patents Found
(or Outside County)

1., 2., 3., ... Lot Numbers
(when beside a name)

[ ] Group Number
(see Appendix "C")

Scale: Section = 1 mile X 1 mile
(generally, with some exceptions)

Map Grid

Section 18

Section 6
Lots-Sec. 6
L1 DUNLAP Alexander 1836
L1(E½) EDMONSON, Thomas 1836
L1(W½) COLLINS, Charles[45]1836
L2 FRENCH, William [63]1836
L2(E½) FARTHING, Solomon 1835
L2(W½) COLLINS, Charles[45]1836
L3 THOMPSON, Bernard 1852
L3 HAMILTON, William 1852
L3 ABBOTT, John 1855
L3(W½) EDMONSON, Thomas 1836

WARREN William B [64] 1836
SMITH [40] Isaac R 1836
WARREN John F 1836
DUNLAP Alexander 1836
7
TROY Nancy 1836
SMITH [40] Isaac R 1836
TROY Benjamin 1833
WARREN James 1835
6
ROUNDS [108]
SMITH [40] Isaac R 1836
TROY Nancy 1836
SAIGHMAN William 1830
WILSON Aaron 1835

Section 17

Section 5
Lots-Sec. 5
L1 SIMPLOT, Henry 1833
L1(E½) ETHEL, Willis J 1836
L2 MANNING, Horatio A 1836
L3 COLLINS, Charles[45]1836

SMITH [40] Isaac R 1836
SIMMONS James 1829
COLLINS Charles 1836
OSBURN Samuel 1836
BROADWELL Baxter 1829
TAYLOR Jonathan 1836
8
OSBOURN Samuel 1835
WHORTON John 1832
TAYLOR John Jr 1835
HAMILTON William 1835
FIKE James 1835
5
SMART Josiah H 1823
TAYLOR John Jr 1830
STEWART Mariah 1835
SMART Josiah 1828

Section 16
Scott

Section 4
TAYLOR John Jr 1830
BROADWELL Baxter 1823
L2 TROY Daniel 1823
Lots-Sec. 4
BRADBURY Nathan 1826
BROADWELL Baxter 1828
MCPHERSON Benjamin G 1829
DANIELS Samuel 1836
9
BROADWELL Baxter 1830
BRADBURY Nathan 1829
4
MORRELL Elfonso 1829
GRIGG John 1835
BROADWELL Baxter 1831
BROADWELL Baxter 1831
MCPHERSON Benjamin G 1829
HOSKINS Daniel 1836
HOSKINS John 1831
TROY Daniel 1823

Section 15

Section 10
NEW Asa C 1836
ETHEL Janus 1831
Lots-Sec. 3
WHITLEY Samuel 1828
WHITLEY Samuel 1828
KIRKPATRICK John L 1831
FOX John 1830
NEW Asa C 1836
TROY Daniel 1835
REED Andrew 1831
L3 CHAMBERLIN, Griffin[32]1835
L3(E½) MILNOR, Isaac 1835
L3(W½) ABBEY, Orsemus 1835
SAIGHMAN William 1830
3
DANIELS Venn 1831
Morgan
REED Andrew 1831
TROY Charles 1823
BRISBIN William 1828
LEWIS John 1830

Section 14

Section 11
SMART Thomas 1823
TROY Charles 1825
L2 PREWITT, Fields 1836
KIRKPATRICK Polly 1831
KIRKPATRICK John L 1831
KIRKPATRICK John L 1831
WYATT John 1830
SMART Thomas 1824
11
DANIELS Venn 1831
KIRKPATRICK John L 1831
2
WHITLEY Elisha 1832
MILSTEAD James 1831
WILLARD William 1830
BOZARTH James 1830
GOODPASTURE Madison 1831
COONRAD Wooley 1831

Section 13

Section 12
BARTON John H 1836
WILLARD William 1830
WILLARD William 1831
BARTON John H 1833
TROY Daniel 1830
ALLINSON Thomas 1831
BARTON John H 1836
BARTON John H 1833
L1(E½) WILLARD, James M 1835
L1(E½) HILLARD, William 1835
L1(W½) WILSON, William 1835
L2 REID, Stephen H 1835
Lots-Sec. 1
FISK Nathaniel 1835
MURPHEY John 1831
ETHEL Willis J 1836
MURPHY John 1830
BARTON John H 1836
12
COLLINS Charles 1836
GOODPASTURE Madison 1834
SMITH, William R 1835
FISK Nathaniel 1835

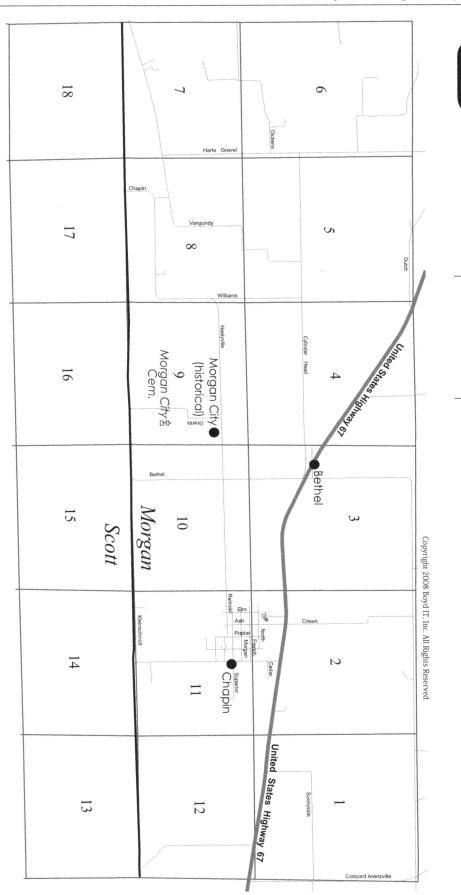

Road Map
T15-N R12-W
3rd PM Meridian
Map Group 7

Note: the area contained in this map amounts to far less than a full Township. Therefore, its contents are completely on this single page (instead of a "normal" 2-page spread).

Cities & Towns
Bethel
Chapin
Morgan City (historical)

Cemeteries
Morgan City Cemetery

N

Legend
— Section Lines
═ Interstates
▬ Highways
— Other Roads
● Cities/Towns
✝ Cemeteries

Scale: Section = 1 mile X 1 mile
(generally, with some exceptions)

Copyright 2008 Boyd IT, Inc. All Rights Reserved

Historical Map

T15-N R12-W
3rd PM Meridian

Map Group 7

Note: the area contained in this map amounts to far less than a full Township. Therefore, its contents are completely on this single page (instead of a "normal" 2-page spread).

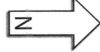

Cities & Towns
Bethel
Chapin
Morgan City (historical)

Cemeteries
Morgan City Cemetery

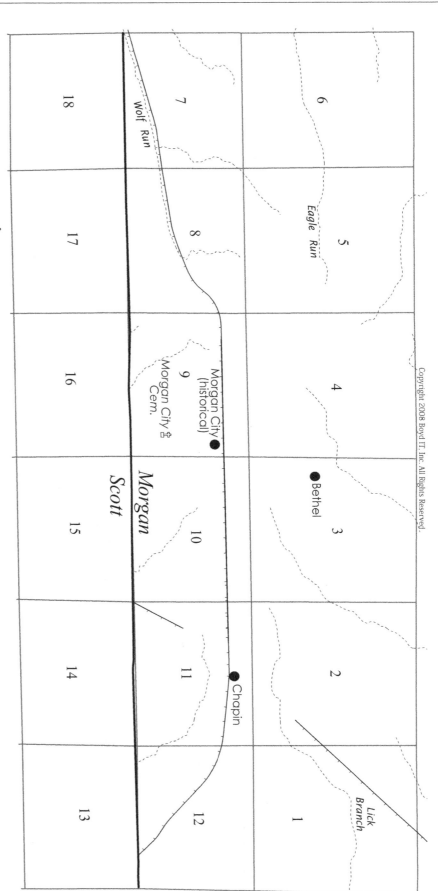

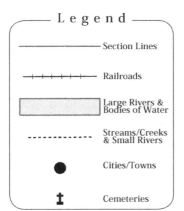

Legend

—————— Section Lines

┼┼┼┼┼┼ Railroads

▭ Large Rivers & Bodies of Water

------------ Streams/Creeks & Small Rivers

● Cities/Towns

† Cemeteries

Scale: Section = 1 mile X 1 mile
(there are some exceptions)

Map Group 8: Index to Land Patents

Township 15-North Range 11-West (3rd PM)

After you locate an individual in this Index, take note of the Section and Section Part then proceed to the Land Patent map on the pages immediately following. You should have no difficulty locating the corresponding parcel of land.

The "For More Info" Column will lead you to more information about the underlying Patents. See the *Legend* at right, and the "How to Use this Book" chapter, for more information.

ID	Individual in Patent	Sec.	Sec. Part	Purchase Date	Sale Type	IL Aliquot Part	For More Info . . .
1969	ADAMS, John	31	SW	1823-11-13	FD	SWFR	R:MORGAN
1968	" "	29	W½SE	1823-11-13	FD	W2SE	R:MORGAN
1970	" "	32	NW	1823-11-13	FD	NW	R:MORGAN
1861	ALLINSON, Adam	36	E½SE	1823-11-13	FD	E2SE	R:MORGAN
1862	" "	36	E½SW	1823-11-13	FD	E2SW	R:MORGAN
1856	" "	10	E½SE	1823-11-13	FD	E2SE	R:MORGAN
1858	" "	29	E½SW	1824-03-10	FD	E2SW	R:MORGAN
1857	" "	21	E½NE	1824-08-24	FD	E2NE	R:MORGAN
1860	" "	31	E½NE	1824-12-18	FD	E2NE	R:MORGAN
1859	" "	29	W½NW	1827-11-23	FD	W2NW	R:MORGAN
1854	" "	1	E½SW	1829-11-26	SM	E2SWDD	R:MORGAN
1855	" "	1	W½SW	1829-11-26	SM	W2SWDD	R:MORGAN
2095	ALLINSON, Thomas	30	E½SE	1825-11-05	FD	E2SE	R:MORGAN
2096	" "	30	W½NW	1828-10-28	FD	W2NW	R:MORGAN
2094	" "	2	W½SE	1829-11-26	SM	W2SEDD	R:MORGAN
2093	" "	2	E½SE	1829-11-26	SM	E2SEDD	R:MORGAN
2097	" "	33	E½NE	1830-08-03	FD	E2NE	R:MORGAN
1876	AUSEMNS, F	1	NWNE	1830-08-16	SM	NWNEDD	R:MORGAN G:1
2035	AUSTIN, Joshua D	31	SE	1823-11-13	FD	SE	R:MORGAN
2034	" "	26	W½NW	1829-07-13	FD	W2NW	R:MORGAN
2030	" "	17	W½NW	1829-08-29	FD	W2NW	R:MORGAN
1906	" "	26	E½NW	1830-08-03	FD	E2NW	R:MORGAN
2031	" "	26	E½NW	1830-08-03	FD	E2NW	R:MORGAN
2033	" "	26	W½NE	1830-08-03	FD	W2NE	R:MORGAN
2032	" "	26	E½SW	1831-05-05	FD	E2SW	R:MORGAN
2070	AYLESWORTH, Philip	3	L3	1835-08-01	FD	LOT3NW	R:MORGAN
1976	BARTON, John H	13	W½SE	1830-03-19	SM	W2SEDD	R:MORGAN
1964	BELLAMMY, Jesse	29	W½SW	1823-11-13	FD	W2SW	R:MORGAN
1874	BENTON, Asa	17	E½SE	1827-09-25	FD	E2SE	R:MORGAN
2080	BOGART, Samuel	21	E½SE	1824-03-05	FD	E2SE	R:MORGAN
2046	BROADWELL, Moses	14	W½NE	1825-11-12	FD	W2NE	R:SANGAMON
1904	CADWELL, George	32	E½NE	1823-11-13	FD	E2NE	R:MORGAN
1903	" "	29	E½SE	1823-11-13	FD	E2SE	R:MORGAN
1905	" "	32	E½SE	1825-12-12	FD	E2SE	R:MORGAN
1971	CARLOCK, John	15	W½NE	1828-11-10	FD	W2NE	R:MORGAN
1972	"	9	W½SW	1829-12-03	FD	W2SW	R:MORGAN
2047	CARLOCK, Moses	17	E½NE	1827-01-08	FD	E2NE	R:MORGAN
1963	CARTER, Richard P	3		1827-10-18	FD	PT1NE	R:MORGAN
2072	" "	3		1827-10-18	FD	PT1NE	R:MORGAN
2127	" "	3		1827-10-18	FD	PT1NE	R:MORGAN
2071	CAUDLE, Ransom	1	L3	1830-06-23	SM	LOT3NWDD	R:MORGAN
1927	" "	1	L3	1830-06-23	SM	LOT3NWDD	R:MORGAN
2067	CHRISMAN, Peter	31	W½NE	1829-11-20	FD	W2NE	R:MORGAN
1973	CHRISTMAN, John	30	W½SE	1826-12-18	FD	W2SE	R:MORGAN
1922	COBB, Hart L	25	E½SW	1826-01-09	FD	E2SW	R:MORGAN
2008	COBB, Jonathon	35	E½SE	1824-09-21	FD	E2SE	R:MORGAN

ID	Individual in Patent	Sec.	Sec. Part	Purchase Date	Sale Type	IL Aliquot Part	For More Info . . .
2009	CODDINGTON, Joseph	36	W½NW	1828-11-27	FD	W2NW	R:MORGAN
1885	COLLINS, Charles	4	L2	1836-07-18	FD	LOT2NE	R:ST. LOUIS
1884	"	4	L1	1836-07-18	FD	LOT1NE	R:ST. LOUIS
1883	"	4	W½SE	1836-07-18	FD	W2SE	R:ST. LOUIS
2019	"	4	L1	1836-07-18	FD	LOT1NE	R:ST. LOUIS
1882	"	4	SWSW	1836-07-18	FD	SWSW	R:ST. LOUIS
1879	"	3	E½SW	1836-07-18	FD	E2SW	R:ST. LOUIS
1880	"	3	SE	1836-07-18	FD	SE	R:ST. LOUIS
1881	"	4	E½SW	1836-07-18	FD	E2SW	R:ST. LOUIS
1878	"	18	N½NW	1836-07-18	FD	N2NW	R:ST. LOUIS
1889	"	7	W½SE	1836-07-18	FD	W2SE	R:ST. LOUIS
1887	"	7	NESW	1836-07-18	FD	NESW	R:ST. LOUIS
1888	"	7	SEN½	1836-07-18	FD	S2NE	R:ST. LOUIS
1890	"	7	W½SW	1836-07-18	FD	W2SW	R:ST. LOUIS
1886	"	5	SESE	1836-07-18	FD	SESE	R:ST. LOUIS
1891	"	8	NESW	1836-07-18	FD	NESW	R:ST. LOUIS
1920	COWARD, Godfry	33	W½SE	1831-06-06	FD	W2SE	R:MORGAN
2081	DANIELS, Samuel	18	N½SW	1836-07-07	FD	N2SW	R:MORGAN
2082	"	8	NWNE	1848-07-18	FD	NWNE	R:MORGAN
1942	DEATON, James	12	E½SW	1829-11-26	SM	E2SWDD	R:MORGAN
1943	"	12	W½NW	1829-11-26	SM	W2NWDD	R:MORGAN
1944	"	12	W½SW	1829-11-26	SM	W2SWDD	R:MORGAN
1961	DEATON, James Sen	14	E½NE	1828-11-18	FD	E2NE	R:MORGAN
2040	DEATON, Levi	13	W½NW	1829-11-26	SM	W2NWDD	R:MORGAN
2039	"	13	E½NW	1829-11-26	SM	E2NWDD	R:MORGAN
2073	DEATON, Robert H	11	E½SE	1829-11-26	SM	E2SEDD	R:MORGAN
2098	DENNIS, Thomas	19	SESE	1835-10-31	FD	SESE	R:MORGAN
2051	DEWEESE, Nimrod	1	L1	1829-11-26	SM	LOT1NWDD	R:MORGAN
2054	"	2	W½SW	1829-11-26	SM	W2SWDD	R:MORGAN
2053	"	1	L2	1830-08-10	SM	LOT2NEDD	R:MORGAN
2052	"	1	L2	1830-08-10	SM	LOT2NEDD	R:MORGAN
2063	"	2	L3	1830-08-16	SM	LOT3NEDD	R:MORGAN
2053	"	1	L2	1830-08-16	SM	LOT2NWDD	R:MORGAN
2052	"	1	L2	1830-08-16	SM	LOT2NWDD	R:MORGAN
2055	"	2	L3	1830-08-16	SM	LOT3NEDD	R:MORGAN
1926	DIAL, Isaac	36	W½SW	1823-11-13	FD	W2SW	R:MORGAN
1925	"	25	W½SE	1825-03-18	FD	W2SE	R:MORGAN
2042	DIAL, Martin	35	W½SE	1831-07-02	FD	W2SE	R:MORGAN
2038	DOWNER, Lawson	15	E½NW	1826-03-02	FD	E2NW	R:MORGAN
2071	DOYAL, Isaac	1	L3	1183-02-11	SM	LOT3NEDP	R:MORGAN
1927	"	1	L3	1183-02-11	SM	LOT3NEDP	
1906	DUFF, George	26	E½NW	1828-11-18	FD	E2NW	R:SANGAMON
2031	"	26	E½NW	1828-11-18	FD	E2NW	R:SANGAMON
2012	DUNCAN, Joseph	23	E½SE	1830-08-03	FD	E2SE	R:MORGAN
2017	"	25	W½NW	1830-08-03	FD	W2NW	R:MORGAN
2018	"	26	E½NE	1830-08-03	FD	E2NE	R:MORGAN
2011	"	23	E½NE	1830-09-08	FD	E2NE	R:MORGAN
2016	"	24	W½NW	1830-09-08	FD	W2NW	R:MORGAN
2014	"	23	W½NE	1830-10-12	FD	W2NE	R:MORGAN
2010	"	14	E½SE	1830-10-12	FD	E2SE	R:MORGAN
2013	"	23	NW	1831-01-18	FD	NW	R:MORGAN
2015	"	23	W½SW	1831-03-31	FD	W2SW	R:MORGAN
2022	"	6		1833-06-22	FD	PT2NWSK	R:MORGAN
2021	"	6		1833-06-22	FD	PT2NWSK	R:MORGAN
2021	"	6		1833-06-22	FD	PT3NEPTSK	R:MORGAN
2022	"	6		1833-06-22	FD	PT3NEPTSK	R:MORGAN
2022	"	6		1834-11-06	FD	PT2NE	R:MORGAN
2021	"	6		1834-11-06	FD	PT2NE	R:MORGAN
2021	"	6		1834-11-06	FD	PT1NE	R:MORGAN
2022	"	6		1834-11-06	FD	PT1NE	R:MORGAN
2023	"	6	NW	1834-11-06	FD	PT1NW	R:MORGAN
2020	"	5	S½SW	1835-06-11	FD	S2SW	R:MORGAN
2019	"	4	L1	1835-12-04	FD	LOT1NW	R:MORGAN
1884	"	4	L1	1835-12-04	FD	LOT1NW	R:MORGAN
1892	DUNSMORE, Daniel	32	W½NE	1823-11-13	FD	W2NE	R:MORGAN
2118	EARLL, Willbur	35	E½NW	1826-06-10	FD	E2NW	R:MORGAN
2099	EDMONDSON, Thomas	20	E½SE	1828-12-03	FD	E2SE	R:MORGAN
2057	EDWARDS, Ninian	13	E½NE	1829-11-26	SM	E2NEDD	R:ST. CLAIR
2058	"	13	E½SE	1833-07-17	SM	E2SEDD	R:ST. CLAIR
2060	"	13	W½SW	1833-07-17	SM	W2SWDD	R:ST. CLAIR
2059	"	13	E½SW	1833-07-17	SM	E2SWDD	R:ST. CLAIR
2048	FISK, Nathaniel	6	N½SW	1834-10-24	FD	N2SW	R:MORGAN
2056	FUNK, Nimrod	32	W½SW	1827-11-24	FD	W2SW	R:MORGAN

ID	Individual in Patent	Sec.	Sec. Part	Purchase Date	Sale Type	IL Aliquot Part	For More Info . . .
2119	GADDES, William F	18	NWNE	1832-11-21	FD	NWNE	R:MORGAN
2120	GADDIS, William F	7	SESW	1832-12-18	FD	SESW	R:MORGAN
1850	GOODPASTURE, Abraham	8	E½NE	1831-01-24	FD	E2NE	R:MORGAN
1921	GOODPASTURE, Hamilton	5	L2 (E½)	1833-10-11	FD	E2LOT2NE	R:MORGAN
2121	GOODPASTURE, William	5	NESE	1823-11-06	FD	NESE	R:MORGAN
2122	" "	5	W½SE	1832-01-05	FD	W2SE	R:MORGAN
1946	GORHAM, James H	27	W½NW	1829-11-11	FD	W2NW	R:MORGAN
2089	GORHAM, Stephen	28	W½NW	1823-11-13	FD	W2NW	R:GREENE
2088	" "	28	W½NE	1823-11-13	FD	W2NE	R:GREENE
2087	" "	28	E½NE	1825-09-05	FD	E2NE	R:MORGAN
2100	GRAHAM, Thomas	4	L2 (W½)	1833-08-09	FD	W2LOT2NW	R:MORGAN
1918	GRAVES, George W	20	E½NE	1829-07-15	FD	E2NE	R:MORGAN
1919	" "	22	W½SW	1829-07-15	FD	W2SW	R:MORGAN
1975	GRIGG, John	4	L3	1836-04-15	FD	LOT3NE	R:PHILADELPHIA
2123	HALL, William	16	L7	1833-06-11	SC	LOT7W2SE16	
1977	HAMBROUGH, John	11	E½NE	1829-11-26	SM	E2NEDD	R:MORGAN
2129	HAMILTON, William L	25	E½SE	1823-11-13	FD	E2SE	R:MORGAN G:68
1929	HARVY, J	12	E½NW	1829-11-26	SM	E2NWDD	R:MORGAN S:I G:72
1980	HEMBROUGH, John	24	E½SE	1829-08-19	FD	E2SE	R:MORGAN
1978	" "	15	E½SE	1829-08-19	FD	E2SE	R:MORGAN
1979	" "	22	E½NE	1830-01-13	FD	E2NE	R:MORGAN
1941	HENRY, James D	33	E½SW	1830-01-18	FD	E2SW	R:SANGAMON
2024	HENRY, Joseph	14	W½SE	1829-10-15	FD	W2SE	R:MORGAN
2101	HENSON, Thomas	20	W½SE	1829-01-05	FD	W2SE	R:MORGAN
1898	HIBARD, Davison	28	E½SE	1825-06-03	FD	E2SE	R:MORGAN
1947	HOLIDAY, James	10	E½NE	1828-07-07	FD	E2NE	R:MORGAN
1948	" "	15	E½SW	1828-11-10	FD	E2SW	R:MORGAN
1949	" "	15	W½SE	1829-03-13	FD	W2SE	R:MORGAN
1950	" "	9	W½NE	1830-01-16	FD	W2NE	R:MORGAN
2026	HOLIDAY, Joseph	3	L2 (E½)	1835-11-04	FD	E2LOT2NW	R:MORGAN
2025	" "	3	W½SW	1835-11-04	FD	W2SW	R:MORGAN
2027	" "	3	L1 (E½)	1850-02-06	FD	E2LOT1NW	R:MORGAN
1951	HOLME, James	34	E½NE	1830-08-11	FD	E2NE	R:MORGAN
1933	" "	34	E½SE	1830-08-11	FD	E2SE	R:MORGAN
1952	" "	34	E½SE	1830-08-11	FD	E2SE	R:MORGAN
1953	" "	35	W½NW	1830-08-11	FD	W2NW	R:MORGAN
1954	" "	35	W½SW	1830-08-11	FD	W2SW	R:MORGAN
1937	" "	35	W½SW	1830-08-11	FD	W2SW	R:MORGAN
2076	JAMES, Robert	13	W½NE	1829-11-26	SM	W2NEDD	R:MORGAN
2074	" "	12	W½NE	1829-11-26	SM	W2NEDD	R:MORGAN
2075	" "	12	W½SE	1829-11-26	SM	W2SEDD	R:MORGAN
2124	JARRED, William	12	E½NE	1829-11-26	SM	E2NEDD	R:MORGAN
2125	" "	12	E½SE	1829-11-26	SM	E2SEDD	R:MORGAN
1981	JOETT, John	2	L2	1829-11-26	SM	LOT2NEDD	R:MORGAN
2062	" "	2	L2	1829-11-26	SM	LOT2NEDD	R:MORGAN
1853	JOHNSON, Abraham	14	E½NW	1826-08-16	FD	E2NW	R:MORGAN
1852	" "	11	W½SE	1829-11-26	SM	W2SEDD	R:MORGAN
1851	" "	11	W½NE	1829-11-26	SM	W2NEDD	R:MORGAN
1893	JONES, Daniel R	18	NWSE	1832-12-03	FD	NWSE	R:MORGAN
1894	" "	6	W½SE	1835-07-01	FD	W2SE	R:MORGAN
1956	JONES, James	5	L1 (E½)	1832-10-16	FD	E2LOT1NW	R:MORGAN
1955	" "	5	NESW	1832-10-16	FD	NESW	R:MORGAN
1966	JONES, Joel	20	NENW	1834-03-06	FD	NENW	R:MORGAN
1967	" "	20	SENW	1835-11-14	FD	SENW	R:MORGAN
1965	" "	19	E½NE	1836-01-21	FD	E2NE	R:MORGAN
2077	JONES, Samuel B	17	E½NW	1827-01-08	FD	E2NW	R:MORGAN
2078	" "	5	L1 (W½)	1832-10-16	FD	W2LOT1NW	R:MORGAN
2079	" "	8	SESW	1835-10-27	FD	SESW	R:MORGAN
2084	JONES, Samuel R	17	W½NE	1828-01-02	FD	W2NE	R:MORGAN
2102	JONES, Thomas	17	E½SW	1828-01-02	FD	E2SW	R:MORGAN
2103	" "	18	E½NE	1828-12-26	FD	E2NE	R:MORGAN
2126	JONES, William	18	SWSE	1836-01-21	FD	SWSE	R:MORGAN
2061	JOUETT, John	2	L1	1829-11-26	SM	LOT1NEDD	R:MORGAN
1982	" "	2	L1	1829-11-26	SM	LOT1NEDD	R:MORGAN
1988	KILLAM, John	27	NE	1829-08-08	FD	NE	R:MORGAN
1986	" "	19	NW	1829-08-15	FD	NWFR	R:MORGAN
1987	" "	20	E½SW	1830-01-13	FD	E2SW	R:MORGAN
1984	" "	16	W½NW	1835-02-26	SC	W2NWMA	
1985	" "	16	W½SW	1835-02-26	SC	W2SWMA	
2050	KING, Nicholas	27	W½SE	1830-12-01	FD	W2SE	R:MORGAN
2049	" "	27	E½SW	1830-12-01	FD	E2SW	R:MORGAN
2128	KING, William	31	NW	1827-10-05	FD	NWFR	R:MORGAN
2072	" "	3		1829-01-05	FD	PT2NE	R:MORGAN

ID	Individual in Patent	Sec.	Sec. Part	Purchase Date	Sale Type	IL Aliquot Part	For More Info . . .
2127	KING, William (Cont'd)	3		1829-01-05	FD	PT2NE	R:MORGAN
1963	" "	3		1829-01-05	FD	PT2NE	R:MORGAN
1909	KIRKMAN, George	2	E½SW	1829-11-26	SM	E2SWDD	R:MORGAN
1901	LAW, Edmund	18	S½SW	1836-12-07	FD	S2SW	R:MORGAN
1989	LAZEMBY, John	24	E½NE	1829-08-19	FD	E2NE	R:MORGAN
2083	LEE, Samuel Jr	28	E½NW	1823-11-13	FD	E2NW	R:GREENE
1991	LEICH, John	23	N½SE	1830-08-12	FD	N2SE	R:MORGAN
1990	" "	23	E½SW	1830-08-12	FD	E2SW	R:MORGAN
2045	LESLIE, Miron	5	L3	1835-06-08	FD	LOT3NE	R:MORGAN
2045	" "	5	L3	1835-06-08	FD	LOT3NW	R:MORGAN
2043	" "	5	L2	1835-06-08	FD	LOT2NW	R:MORGAN
2044	" "	5	L2 (W½)	1835-06-08	FD	W2LOT2NE	R:MORGAN
1992	LEWIS, John	28	NW	1828-11-18	FD	NW	R:MORGAN
2037	LODWICK, Kennedy	18	SWNE	1836-07-16	FD	SWNE	R:OHIO
1902	MARKHAM, Edward	16	L3	1832-03-12	SC	LOT3E2NW16	
1911	MARKHAM, George	16	L2	1832-03-12	SC	LOT2W2NE16	
1912	" "	16	L1	1832-05-07	SC	LOT1E2NE16	
2007	MARSHALL, John W	8	SENW	1835-09-11	FD	SENW	R:MORGAN
2131	MARSHALL, William	16	L8	1832-06-12	SC	LOT8E2SE16	
2132	" "	19	W½SE	1836-03-14	FD	W2SE	R:MORGAN
2085	MASSEY, Silas	25	W½NE	1829-11-17	FD	W2NE	R:MORGAN
2104	MASTERS, Thomas	24	E½NW	1830-08-03	FD	E2NW	R:MORGAN
1931	MCGINNIS, J S	11	W½SW	1829-11-26	SM	W2SWDD	R:MORGAN S:I
1930	" "	11	W½NW	1829-11-26	SM	W2NWDD	R:MORGAN S:I
1993	MCGINNIS, John	14	W½NW	1828-10-30	FD	W2NW	R:MORGAN
1994	" "	15	E½NE	1828-10-30	FD	E2NE	R:MORGAN
2136	MCKEE, William P	33	E½NW	1823-11-13	FD	E2NW	R:MADISON
2133	" "	28	E½SW	1823-11-13	FD	E2SW	R:MADISON
2135	" "	29	W½NE	1824-04-21	FD	W2NE	R:MADISON
2134	" "	28	W½SE	1825-06-01	FD	W2SE	R:MADISON
2091	MCKINNEY, Stephen	30	E½NE	1828-06-09	FD	E2NE	R:MORGAN
2090	" "	20	W½NW	1828-12-26	FD	W2NW	R:MORGAN
1872	MILLEN, Archibald	25	E½NE	1829-10-19	FD	E2NE	R:MORGAN
1995	MILLEN, John	4		1831-10-05	FD	N03NW	R:MORGAN
1873	MILLER, Archibald Sen	4	L2 (E½)	1835-09-17	FD	E2LOT2NW	R:MORGAN
1907	MILLER, George F	17	SW	1828-05-14	FD	SW	R:KENTUCKY
1974	MILLER, John E	10	W½NE	1828-10-15	FD	W2NE	R:MORGAN
1957	MILLS, James	10	W½SE	1823-11-13	FD	W2SE	R:MORGAN
2105	MORRIS, Thomas P	5	NWSW	1833-06-20	FD	NWSW	R:MORGAN
1996	MOSS, John	4	NWSW	1835-05-25	FD	NWSW	R:MORGAN
1983	MOSS, John Jr	5		1829-12-11	FD	PT1NE	R:MORGAN
1997	MURPHEY, John	7	NW	1832-01-14	FD	NW	R:MORGAN
1998	MURPHY, John	8	E½SE	1829-12-03	FD	E2SE	R:MORGAN
1913	NEWMAN, George	18	E½SE	1830-01-09	FD	E2SE	R:MORGAN
1914	" "	24	W½NE	1830-07-29	FD	W2NE	R:MORGAN
1915	" "	8	W½SW	1831-09-02	FD	W2SW	R:MORGAN
1908	NEWMAN, George Jr	15	W½SW	1829-10-28	FD	W2SW	R:MORGAN
1917	NEWMAN, George Sen	14	W½SW	1829-10-28	FD	W2SW	R:MORGAN
1916	" "	14	E½SW	1829-11-25	FD	E2SW	R:MORGAN
2106	NORISS, Thomas P	6	E½SE	1831-10-05	FD	E2SE	R:MORGAN
2092	OLMSTEAD, Stephen	32	W½SE	1824-02-10	FD	W2SE	R:MORGAN
1958	PALMER, James	30	SW	1823-11-13	FD	SWFR	R:MORGAN
2002	PARK, John S	3	L2 (W½)	1835-08-06	FD	W2LOT2NW	R:MORGAN
1959	PARKASON, James	24	W½SW	1830-01-11	FD	W2SW	R:MORGAN
1960	PARKINSON, James	1	E½SE	1829-11-26	SM	E2SEDD	R:MORGAN
1871	PATTEN, Andrew V	33	W½NE	1824-08-02	FD	W2NE	R:MORGAN
2127	POCKLINGTON, Janus	3		1830-08-11	FD	N03NE	R:MORGAN S:F
1963	" "	3		1830-08-11	FD	N03NE	R:MORGAN S:F
2072	" "	3		1830-08-11	FD	N03NE	R:MORGAN S:F
2086	POWELL, Starkey R	6	S½SW	1833-05-23	FD	S2SW	R:MORGAN
1866	REED, Andrew	10	E½SW	1827-03-07	FD	E2SW	R:MORGAN
1867	" "	22	W½NW	1829-08-05	FD	W2NW	R:MORGAN
1868	" "	16	L6	1833-06-06	SC	LOT6E2SW16	G:107
1869	REID, Andrew	21	W½NW	1829-01-28	FD	W2NW	R:MORGAN
1895	RICHARDS, Daniel	20	W½SW	1829-05-06	FD	W2SW	R:MORGAN
1896	" "	32	E½SW	1829-08-10	FD	E2SW	R:MORGAN
1910	RICHARDS, George M	25	W½SW	1828-10-22	FD	W2SW	R:MORGAN
2001	RICHARDSON, John	34	W½NE	1831-11-01	FD	W2NELS	R:MORGAN
2000	" "	34	SW	1831-11-01	FD	SWLS	R:MORGAN
1999	" "	34	E½NW	1831-11-01	FD	E2NWLS	R:MORGAN
2116	RICHARDSON, Vincent	34	W½NW	1831-08-12	FD	W2NW	R:MORGAN
1899	ROCKWELL, Dennis	26	W½SW	1830-10-27	FD	W2SW	R:MORGAN
1900	" "	27	E½SE	1830-10-27	FD	E2SE	R:MORGAN

ID	Individual in Patent	Sec.	Sec. Part	Purchase Date	Sale Type	IL Aliquot Part	For More Info . . .
2005	SARGEANT, John	7	E½SE	1829-10-29	FD	E2SE	R:MORGAN
2004	" "	11	E½SW	1829-11-26	SM	E2SWDD	R:MORGAN
2003	" "	11	E½NW	1829-11-26	SM	E2NWDD	R:MORGAN
2138	SARGEANT, William	9	E½SE	1826-11-08	FD	E2SE	R:MORGAN
2137	" "	4	E½SE	1835-11-04	FD	E2SE	R:MORGAN
1940	SARGENT, James B	8	SWNW	1835-02-14	FD	SWNW	R:MORGAN
2130	SARGENT, William L	3	L1 (W½)	1835-09-11	FD	W2LOT1NW	R:MORGAN
1929	SAVAGE, P	12	E½NW	1829-11-26	SM	E2NWDD	R:MORGAN S:I G:72
2069	SAVAGE, Peter	24	E½SW	1829-10-15	FD	E2SW	R:MORGAN
2068	SAVAGE, Peter S	25	E½NW	1830-01-11	FD	E2NW	R:MORGAN
2108	SERALES, Thomas	22	W½SE	1831-03-05	FD	W2SE	R:MORGAN
2107	" "	22	E½SW	1831-03-05	FD	E2SW	R:MORGAN
1875	SHARTZER, Ben	1	W½SE	1829-11-26	SM	W2SEDD	R:MORGAN
1876	" "	1	NWNE	1830-08-16	SM	NWNEDD	R:MORGAN G:1
1962	SIMMONS, James	21	W½NE	1825-12-26	FD	W2NE	R:MORGAN
2140	SIMMONS, William	21	W½SW	1826-02-18	FD	W2SW	R:MORGAN
2139	" "	21	E½SW	1826-12-11	FD	E2SW	R:MORGAN
1924	SIMMS, Ignatius R	36	W½NE	1829-04-28	FD	W2NE	R:MORGAN
1923	" "	36	E½NW	1829-05-04	FD	E2NW	R:MORGAN
1928	SMITH, Isaac	24	W½SE	1824-12-18	FD	W2SE	R:MORGAN
2110	SPENCER, Thomas	27	W½SW	1829-08-15	FD	W2SW	R:MORGAN
2109	" "	19	SW	1829-10-30	FD	SW	R:MORGAN
2036	SPRAGUE, Joshua	29	E½NE	1823-11-20	FD	E2NE	R:MORGAN
2061	STAUDLEY, Noble	2	L1	1829-11-26	SM	LOT1NWDD	R:MORGAN
1981	" "	2	L2	1829-11-26	SM	LOT2NWDD	R:MORGAN
1982	" "	2	L1	1829-11-26	SM	LOT1NWDD	R:MORGAN
2062	" "	2	L2	1829-11-26	SM	LOT2NWDD	R:MORGAN
2063	" "	2	L3	1830-10-13	SM	LOT3NWDD	R:MORGAN
2055	" "	2	L3	1830-10-13	SM	LOT3NWDD	R:MORGAN
1870	STEIR, Andrew	21	E½NW	1826-01-09	FD	E2NW	R:MORGAN
2006	STEWART, John W H	19	NESE	1836-03-21	FD	NESE	R:MORGAN
1939	STRAWN, Jacob	36	W½SE	1829-11-09	FD	W2SE	R:OHIO
1936	" "	35	NE	1829-11-09	FD	NE	R:OHIO
1938	" "	36	E½NE	1829-11-18	FD	E2NE	R:OHIO
1932	" "	26	SE	1830-08-05	FD	SE	R:OHIO
1935	" "	35	E½SW	1831-06-01	FD	E2SW	R:MORGAN
1934	" "	34	W½SE	1831-07-11	FD	W2SE	R:MORGAN
1933	" "	34	E½SE	1831-10-21	FD	E2SE	R:MORGAN
1954	" "	35	W½SW	1831-10-21	FD	W2SW	R:MORGAN
1952	" "	34	E½SE	1831-10-21	FD	E2SE	R:MORGAN
1937	" "	35	W½SW	1831-10-21	FD	W2SW	R:MORGAN
2041	STRODE, Mahlon	20	W½NE	1829-12-22	FD	W2NE	R:MORGAN
1868	" "	16	L6	1833-06-06	SC	LOT6E2SW16	G:107
2112	SWALES, Thomas	22	E½NW	1830-01-05	FD	E2NW	R:MORGAN
2114	" "	22	W½NE	1830-01-05	FD	W2NE	R:MORGAN
2111	" "	17	W½SW	1830-01-05	FD	W2SW	R:MORGAN
2115	" "	27	E½NW	1830-08-27	FD	E2NW	R:MORGAN
2113	" "	22	E½SE	1830-08-27	FD	E2SE	R:MORGAN
1945	SWINNERTON, James G	33	W½NW	1823-11-13	FD	W2NW	R:MORGAN
2066	TICKNOR, Olney	30	W½NE	1826-12-18	FD	W2NE	R:MORGAN
2065	" "	19	W½NE	1830-01-29	FD	W2NE	R:MORGAN
1897	TROY, Daniel	17	W½SE	1828-11-18	FD	W2SE	R:MORGAN
2064	" "	17	W½SE	1828-11-18	FD	W2SE	R:MORGAN
1877	VANCE, Bradley	9	E½NW	1827-10-16	FD	E2NW	R:MORGAN
2129	VARY, William	25	E½SE	1823-11-13	FD	E2SE	R:MORGAN G:68
2064	WADDELL, Obediah	17	W½SE	1829-05-16	FD	W2SE	R:MORGAN
1897	" "	17	W½SE	1829-05-16	FD	W2SE	R:MORGAN
2028	WAFSON, Joseph	28	W½SW	1823-11-17	FD	W2SW	R:MORGAN
2029	WASSON, Joseph	33	E½SE	1831-08-01	FD	E2SE	R:MORGAN
1863	WILLARD, Alexander	15	W½NW	1828-10-26	FD	W2NW	R:MORGAN
1865	" "	9	W½NW	1828-10-30	FD	W2NW	R:MORGAN
1864	" "	8	SWNE	1833-06-10	FD	SWNE	R:MORGAN
2117	WOOD, Whitley	18	S½NW	1832-11-21	FD	S2NW	R:MORGAN
2141	YORK, William	10	W½NW	1827-03-20	FD	W2NW	R:MORGAN

Patent Map

T15-N R11-W
3rd PM Meridian

Map Group 8

Township Statistics

Parcels Mapped	:	292
Number of Patents	:	1
Number of Individuals	:	159
Patentees Identified	:	158
Number of Surnames	:	124
Multi-Patentee Parcels	:	4
Oldest Patent Date	:	2/11/1183
Most Recent Patent	:	2/6/1850
Block/Lot Parcels	:	34
Cities and Towns	:	2
Cemeteries	:	11

Section 6
DUNCAN Joseph 1834
DUNCAN Joseph 1833
DUNCAN Joseph 1834
DUNCAN Joseph 1833

Section 5 — Lots
L1(E½)	JONES, James	1832
L1(W½)	JONES, Samuel B	1832
L2	LESLIE, Miron	1835
L2(E½)	GOODPASTURE, Hamilto	1833
L2(W½)	LESLIE, Miron	1835
L3	LESLIE, Miron	1835

MOSS John Jr 1829

Section 4 — Lots
L1	DUNCAN, Joseph	1835
L1	COLLINS, Charles	1836
L2	COLLINS, Charles	1836
L2(E½)	MILLER, Archibald Se	1835
L2(W½)	GRAHAM, Thomas	1833
L3	GRIGG, John	1836

MILLEN John 1831

Section 6 (lower)
FISK Nathaniel 1834
POWELL Starkey R 1833
JONES Daniel R 1835
NORISS Thomas P 1831

Section 5
MORRIS Thomas P 1833
JONES James 1832
DUNCAN Joseph 1835
GOODPASTURE William 1823
GOODPASTURE William 1832
MOSS John 1835
COLLINS Charles 1836
COLLINS Charles 1836

Section 4
COLLINS Charles 1836
COLLINS Charles 1836
SARGEANT William 1835

Section 7
MURPHEY John 1832
COLLINS Charles 1836
SARGENT James B 1835
MARSHALL John W 1835
DANIELS Samuel 1848
WILLARD Alexander 1833

Section 8
GOODPASTURE Abraham 1831
WILLARD Alexander 1828
VANCE Bradley 1827
HOLIDAY James 1830

Section 7 (lower)
COLLINS Charles 1836
COLLINS Charles 1836
GADDIS William F 1832
COLLINS Charles 1836
SARGEANT John 1829
NEWMAN George 1831

Section 8 (lower)
COLLINS Charles 1836
JONES Samuel B 1835
MURPHY John 1829

Section 9
CARLOCK John 1829
SARGEANT William 1826

Section 18
COLLINS Charles 1836
GADDES William F 1832
WOOD Whitley 1832
LODWICK Kennedy 1836
JONES Thomas 1828
DANIELS Samuel 1836
JONES Daniel R 1832
LAW Edmund 1836
JONES William 1836
NEWMAN George 1830

Section 17
JONES Samuel B 1827
AUSTIN Joshua D 1829
JONES Samuel R 1828
SWALES Thomas 1830
MILLER George F 1828
JONES Thomas 1828

Section 16 — Lots
L1	MARKHAM, George	1832
L2	MARKHAM, George	1832
L3	MARKHAM, Edward	1832
L6	REED, Andrew	[107]1833
L7	HALL, William	1833
L8	MARSHALL, William	1832

CARLOCK Moses 1827
JONES Samuel R 1828
TROY Daniel 1828
WADDELL Obediah 1829
BENTON Asa 1827
KILLAM John 1835
KILLAM John 1835

Section 19
KILLAM John 1829
TICKNOR Olney 1830
JONES Joel 1836
SPENCER Thomas 1829
MARSHALL William 1836
STEWART John W H 1836
DENNIS Thomas 1835

Section 20
MCKINNEY Stephen 1828
JONES Joel 1834
JONES Joel 1835
STRODE Mahlon 1829
GRAVES George W 1829
RICHARDS Daniel 1829
KILLAM John 1830
HENSON Thomas 1829
EDMONDSON Thomas 1828

Section 21
REID Andrew 1829
STEIR Andrew 1826
SIMMONS James 1825
ALLINSON Adam 1824
SIMMONS William 1826
SIMMONS William 1826
BOGART Samuel 1824

Section 30
ALLINSON Thomas 1828
TICKNOR Olney 1826
MCKINNEY Stephen 1828

Section 29
ALLINSON Adam 1827

Section 28
MCKEE William P 1824
SPRAGUE Joshua 1823
GORHAM Stephen 1823
LEWIS John 1828
LEE Samuel Jr 1823
GORHAM Stephen 1823
GORHAM Stephen 1825

Section 31
PALMER James 1823
CHRISTMAN John 1826
ALLINSON Thomas 1825

Section 32
BELLAMMY Jesse 1823
ALLINSON Adam 1824
ADAMS John 1823
CADWELL George 1823
WAFSON Joseph 1823
MCKEE William P 1823
MCKEE William P 1825
HIBARD Davison 1825

Section 31 (lower)
KING William 1827
CHRISMAN Peter 1829
ALLINSON Adam 1824

Section 32 (lower)
ADAMS John 1823
DUNSMORE Daniel 1823
CADWELL George 1823
SWINNERTON James G 1823
MCKEE William P 1823
PATTEN Andrew V 1824
ALLINSON Thomas 1830

Section 33
ADAMS John 1823
AUSTIN Joshua D 1823
FUNK Nimrod 1827
RICHARDS Daniel 1829
OLMSTEAD Stephen 1824
CADWELL George 1825
HENRY James D 1830
COWARD Godfry 1831
WASSON Joseph 1831

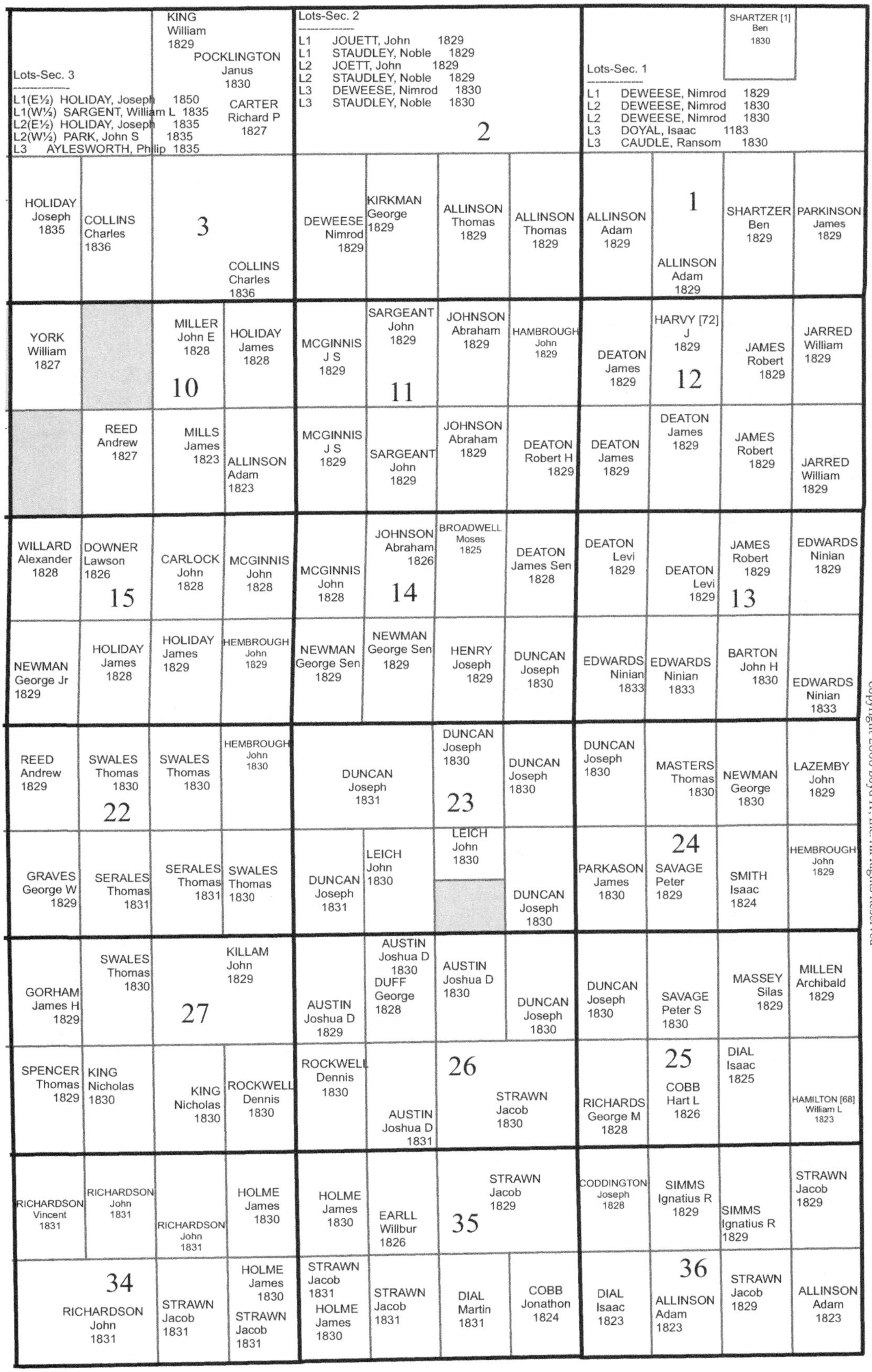
KING William 1829
POCKLINGTON Janus 1830
CARTER Richard P 1827
Lots-Sec. 3
L1(E½) HOLIDAY, Joseph 1850
L1(W½) SARGENT, William L 1835
L2(E½) HOLIDAY, Joseph 1835
L2(W½) PARK, John S 1835
L3 AYLESWORTH, Philip 1835
Lots-Sec. 2
L1 JOUETT, John 1829
L1 STAUDLEY, Noble 1829
L2 JOETT, John 1829
L2 STAUDLEY, Noble 1829
L3 DEWEESE, Nimrod 1830
L3 STAUDLEY, Noble 1830
2
SHARTZER [1] Ben 1830
Lots-Sec. 1
L1 DEWEESE, Nimrod 1829
L2 DEWEESE, Nimrod 1830
L2 DEWEESE, Nimrod 1830
L3 DOYAL, Isaac 1183
L3 CAUDLE, Ransom 1830
HOLIDAY Joseph 1835
COLLINS Charles 1836
3
COLLINS Charles 1836
DEWEESE Nimrod 1829
KIRKMAN George 1829
ALLINSON Thomas 1829
ALLINSON Thomas 1829
ALLINSON Adam 1829
1
ALLINSON Adam 1829
SHARTZER Ben 1829
PARKINSON James 1829
YORK William 1827
MILLER John E 1828
HOLIDAY James 1828
10
MCGINNIS J S 1829
SARGEANT John 1829
11
JOHNSON Abraham 1829
HAMBROUGH John 1829
DEATON James 1829
HARVY [72] J 1829
12
JAMES Robert 1829
JARRED William 1829
REED Andrew 1827
MILLS James 1823
ALLINSON Adam 1823
MCGINNIS J S 1829
SARGEANT John 1829
JOHNSON Abraham 1829
DEATON Robert H 1829
DEATON James 1829
DEATON James 1829
JAMES Robert 1829
JARRED William 1829
WILLARD Alexander 1828
DOWNER Lawson 1826
15
CARLOCK John 1828
MCGINNIS John 1828
MCGINNIS John 1828
JOHNSON Abraham 1826
14
BROADWELL Moses 1825
DEATON James Sen 1828
DEATON Levi 1829
DEATON Levi 1829
JAMES Robert 1829
13
EDWARDS Ninian 1829
NEWMAN George Jr 1829
HOLIDAY James 1828
HOLIDAY James 1829
HEMBROUGH John 1829
NEWMAN George Sen 1829
NEWMAN George Sen 1829
HENRY Joseph 1829
DUNCAN Joseph 1830
EDWARDS Ninian 1833
EDWARDS Ninian 1833
BARTON John H 1830
EDWARDS Ninian 1833
REED Andrew 1829
SWALES Thomas 1830
22
SWALES Thomas 1830
HEMBROUGH John 1830
DUNCAN Joseph 1831
DUNCAN Joseph 1830
23
DUNCAN Joseph 1830
DUNCAN Joseph 1830
MASTERS Thomas 1830
NEWMAN George 1830
LAZEMBY John 1829
GRAVES George W 1829
SERALES Thomas 1831
SERALES Thomas 1831
SWALES Thomas 1830
DUNCAN Joseph 1831
LEICH John 1830
LEICH John 1830
DUNCAN Joseph 1830
PARKASON James 1830
24
SAVAGE Peter 1829
SMITH Isaac 1824
HEMBROUGH John 1829
GORHAM James H 1829
SWALES Thomas 1830
KILLAM John 1829
27
AUSTIN Joshua D 1829
AUSTIN Joshua D 1830
DUFF George 1828
AUSTIN Joshua D 1830
DUNCAN Joseph 1830
DUNCAN Joseph 1830
SAVAGE Peter S 1830
MASSEY Silas 1829
MILLEN Archibald 1829
SPENCER Thomas 1829
KING Nicholas 1830
KING Nicholas 1830
ROCKWELL Dennis 1830
ROCKWELL Dennis 1830
26
AUSTIN Joshua D 1831
STRAWN Jacob 1830
RICHARDS George M 1828
25
COBB Hart L 1826
DIAL Isaac 1825
HAMILTON [68] William L 1823
RICHARDSON Vincent 1831
RICHARDSON John 1831
RICHARDSON John 1831
HOLME James 1830
HOLME James 1830
EARLL Willbur 1826
STRAWN Jacob 1829
35
CODDINGTON Joseph 1828
SIMMS Ignatius R 1829
SIMMS Ignatius R 1829
STRAWN Jacob 1829
34
RICHARDSON John 1831
STRAWN Jacob 1831
HOLME James 1830
STRAWN Jacob 1831
STRAWN Jacob 1831
HOLME James 1830
STRAWN Jacob 1831
DIAL Martin 1831
COBB Jonathon 1824
DIAL Isaac 1823
36
ALLINSON Adam 1823
STRAWN Jacob 1829
ALLINSON Adam 1823

Helpful Hints

1. This Map's INDEX can be found on the preceding pages.
2. Refer to Map "C" to see where this Township lies within Morgan County, Illinois.
3. Numbers within square brackets [ ] denote a multi-patentee land parcel (multi-owner). Refer to Appendix "C" for a full list of members in this group.
4. Areas that look to be crowded with Patentees usually indicate multiple sales of the same parcel (re-issues), cancellations or voided transactions (that we map, anyway) or overlapping parcels. We opt to show even these ambiguous parcels, which oftentimes lead to research avenues not yet taken.

Legend

- Patent Boundary
- Section Boundary
- No Patents Found (or Outside County)
- 1., 2., 3., ... Lot Numbers (when beside a name)
- [ ] Group Number (see Appendix "C")

Scale: Section = 1 mile X 1 mile (generally, with some exceptions)

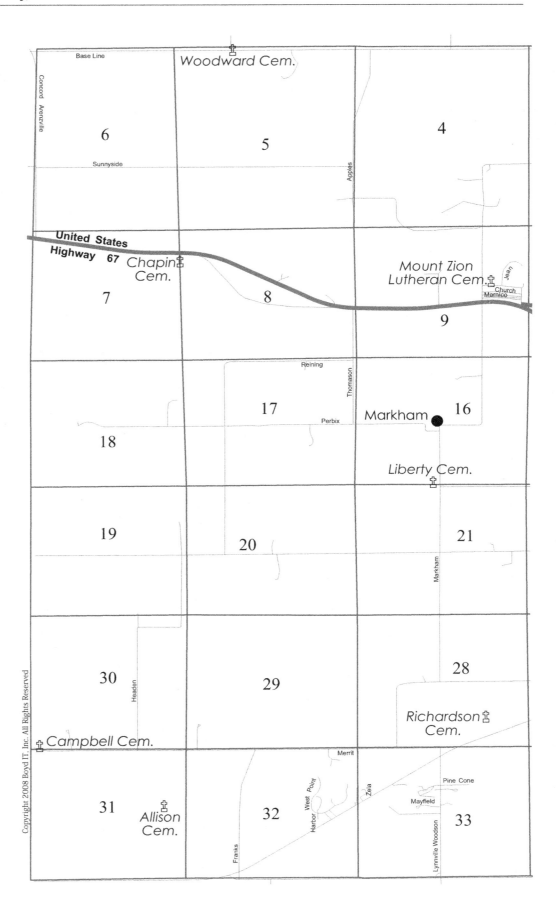

Road Map

T15-N R11-W
3rd PM Meridian

Map Group 8

Cities & Towns
Joy Prairie
Markham

Cemeteries
Allison Cemetery
Caldwell Cemetery
Campbell Cemetery
Chapin Cemetery
Liberty Cemetery
Morgan County Farm Cemetery
Morgan County Poor Farm
  Cemetery
Mount Zion Lutheran Cemetery
Richardson Cemetery
Wood Cemetery
Woodward Cemetery

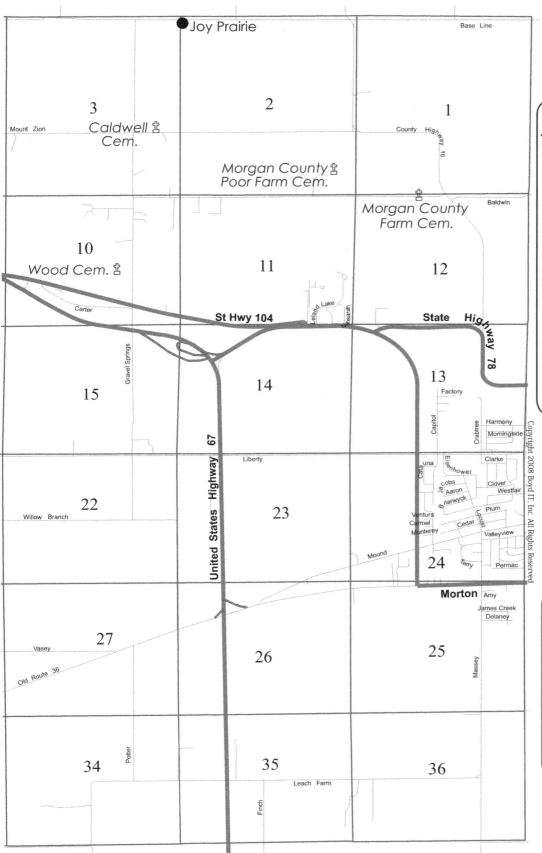

Joy Prairie

Base Line

3

2

1

Mount Zion

Caldwell ⚔
Cem.

County Highway 16

Morgan County ⚔
Poor Farm Cem.

Baldwin

⚔
Morgan County
Farm Cem.

10

11

12

Wood Cem. ⚔

Carter

St Hwy 104

Leland Lake

Nasarah

State   Highway

78

15

14

Gravel Springs

13

Factory

Capitol

Crabtree

Harmony
Morningside

Liberty

United States Highway 67

Catalina

Eisenhower

Clarke

Clover
Westfair

22

Jacobs
Aaron
Briarwyck

Plum

Willow Branch

Ventura
Carmel
Monterey

Cedar

Locust

Valleyview

23

Mound

24

Terry

Permac

27

26

25

Morton   Amy

James Creek
Delaney

Vasey

Old Route 36

Massey

34

Potter

35

36

Leach Farm

Finch

Helpful Hints

1. This road map has a number of uses, but primarily it is to help you: a) find the present location of land owned by your ancestors (at least the general area), b) find cemeteries and city-centers, and c) estimate the route/roads used by Census-takers & tax-assessors.

2. If you plan to travel to Morgan County to locate cemeteries or land parcels, please pick up a modern travel map for the area before you do. Mapping old land parcels on modern maps is not as exact a science as you might think. Just the slightest variations in public land survey coordinates, estimates of parcel boundaries, or road-map deviations can greatly alter a map's representation of how a road either does or doesn't cross a particular parcel of land.

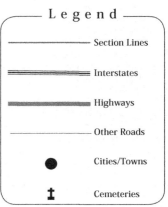

Legend

——————— Section Lines

═══════════ Interstates

━━━━━━━━━ Highways

——————— Other Roads

● Cities/Towns

⚔ Cemeteries

Scale: Section = 1 mile X 1 mile
(generally, with some exceptions)

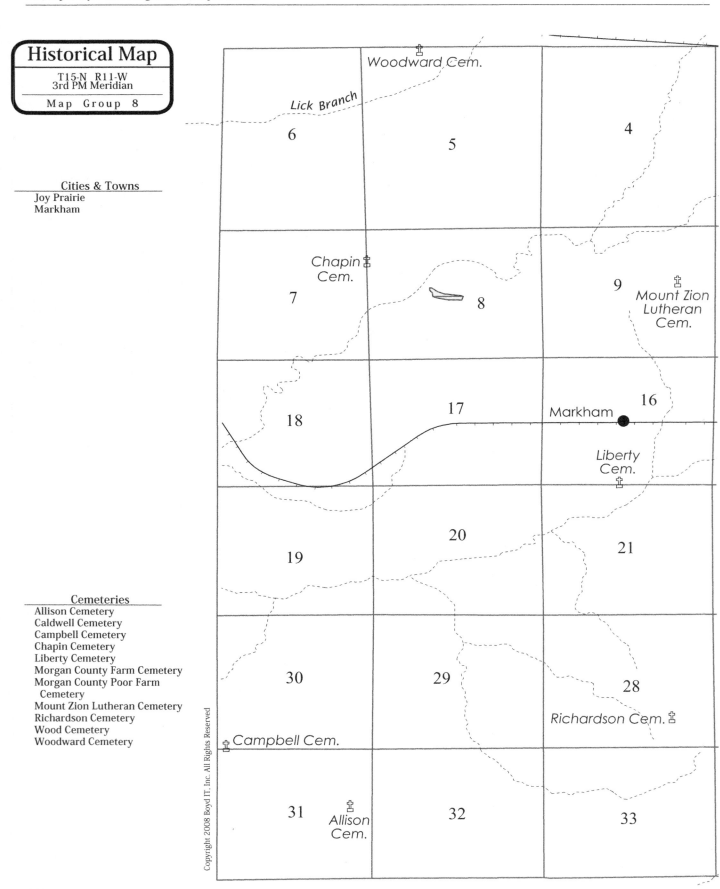

Historical Map

T15-N R11-W
3rd PM Meridian

Map Group 8

Cities & Towns
Joy Prairie
Markham

Cemeteries
Allison Cemetery
Caldwell Cemetery
Campbell Cemetery
Chapin Cemetery
Liberty Cemetery
Morgan County Farm Cemetery
Morgan County Poor Farm
 Cemetery
Mount Zion Lutheran Cemetery
Richardson Cemetery
Wood Cemetery
Woodward Cemetery

Woodward Cem.

Lick Branch

6

5

4

Chapin
Cem.

7

8

9

Mount Zion
Lutheran
Cem.

18

17

Markham

16

Liberty
Cem.

19

20

21

30

29

28

Richardson Cem.

Campbell Cem.

31

Allison
Cem.

32

33

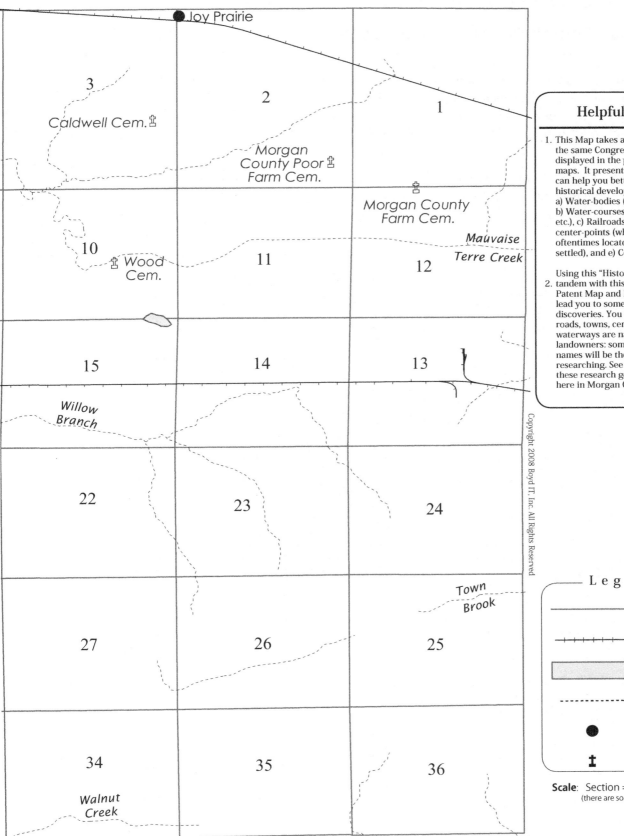

Joy Prairie

3

2

1

Caldwell Cem. ⚱

Morgan
County Poor ⚱
Farm Cem.

⚱

Morgan County
Farm Cem.

10

⚱ Wood
Cem.

11

12

Mauvaise
Terre Creek

15

14

13

Willow
Branch

22

23

24

Town
Brook

27

26

25

34

35

36

Walnut
Creek

Helpful Hints

1. This Map takes a different look at the same Congressional Township displayed in the preceding two maps. It presents features that can help you better envision the historical development of the area: a) Water-bodies (lakes & ponds), b) Water-courses (rivers, streams, etc.), c) Railroads, d) City/town center-points (where they were oftentimes located when first settled), and e) Cemeteries.

2. Using this "Historical" map in tandem with this Township's Patent Map and Road Map, may lead you to some interesting discoveries. You will often find roads, towns, cemeteries, and waterways are named after nearby landowners: sometimes those names will be the ones you are researching. See how many of these research gems you can find here in Morgan County.

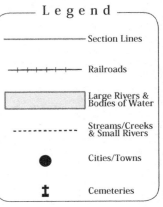

Legend

————————	Section Lines
+++++++++	Railroads
▭	Large Rivers & Bodies of Water
- - - - - -	Streams/Creeks & Small Rivers
●	Cities/Towns
⚱	Cemeteries

Scale: Section = 1 mile X 1 mile
(there are some exceptions)

Map Group 9: Index to Land Patents

Township 15-North Range 10-West (3rd PM)

After you locate an individual in this Index, take note of the Section and Section Part then proceed to the Land Patent map on the pages immediately following. You should have no difficulty locating the corresponding parcel of land.

The "For More Info" Column will lead you to more information about the underlying Patents. See the *Legend* at right, and the "How to Use this Book" chapter, for more information.

```
┌─────────────────────────────────────────────────────┐
│                      LEGEND                           │
│          "For More Info . . . " column                │
│ ───────────────────────────────────────────────────  │
│ G = Group  (Multi-Patentee Patent, see Appendix "C")  │
│ R = Residence                                         │
│ S = Social Status                                     │
│                                                       │
│                                                       │
│ See Appendix A for list of abbreviations used by the  │
│ Illinois State Archives in describing the place and   │
│ nature of these land patents.                         │
│                                                       │
│ Note: if the Abbreviations contain "L", "BL", "LOT",  │
│ or "BLOCK", the exact whereabouts of the parcel within│
│ the section is not known.                             │
└─────────────────────────────────────────────────────┘
```

ID	Individual in Patent	Sec.	Sec. Part	Purchase Date	Sale Type	IL Aliquot Part	For More Info . . .
2420	ABRAM, William G	28	W½SE	1823-12-02	FD	W2SE	R:MORGAN
2421	ABRAMS, William G	28	E½SW	1825-03-05	FD	E2SW	R:MORGAN
2165	ALLINSON, Adam	8	E½SW	1823-11-12	FD	E2SW	R:MORGAN
2158	" "	17	E½NW	1823-11-12	FD	E2NW	R:MORGAN
2161	" "	19	NW	1823-11-12	FD	NWFR	R:MORGAN
2162	" "	31	SW	1823-11-12	FD	SWFR	R:MORGAN
2166	" "	9	E½SW	1824-03-10	FD	E2SW	R:MORGAN
2157	" "	15	E½SW	1824-08-24	FD	E2SW	R:MORGAN
2163	" "	7	NW	1825-02-15	FD	NWFR	R:MORGAN
2159	" "	18	E½SE	1825-03-29	FD	E2SE	R:MORGAN
2160	" "	19	E½NE	1825-04-25	FD	E2NE	R:MORGAN
2164	" "	8	E½NW	1825-11-03	FD	E2NW	R:MORGAN
2392	ALLINSON, Thomas	21	E½NE	1823-11-12	FD	E2NE	R:MORGAN
2394	" "	22	W½NW	1823-11-12	FD	W2NW	R:MORGAN
2393	" "	21	W½NE	1823-11-17	FD	W2NE	R:MORGAN
2172	ALLYN, Benjamin	16	L10	1831-11-09	SC	LOT10	
2239	ARNETT, James	21	E½SW	1827-12-14	FD	E2SW	R:MORGAN
2268	ARNETT, Janus	29	W½NW	1829-10-10	FD	W2NW	R:MORGAN
2396	ARNETT, Thomas	21	E½SE	1823-11-12	FD	E2SE	R:MORGAN
2397	" "	21	W½SE	1823-11-17	FD	W2SE	R:MORGAN
2395	" "	20	E½NE	1825-02-25	FD	E2NE	R:MORGAN
2400	" "	7	SW	1825-04-04	FD	SWFR	R:MORGAN
2398	" "	32	E½NE	1828-10-06	FD	E2NE	R:MORGAN
2399	" "	33	W½NW	1828-10-06	FD	W2NW	R:MORGAN
2401	BALLARD, Thomas	29	E½NE	1828-09-30	FD	E2NE	R:MORGAN
2334	BARTLETT, Milton	35	W½NE	1831-06-29	FD	W2NE	R:MORGAN G:8
2332	" "	26	E½SW	1831-06-29	FD	E2SW	R:MORGAN G:7
2333	" "	35	E½NW	1831-06-29	FD	E2NW	R:MORGAN G:7
2231	BARTON, Jacob	17		1828-12-09	FD	E2NEPTSK	R:MORGAN
2230	" "	16	L5	1831-09-10	SC	LOT5	
2383	BELL, Robert	5		1827-03-24	FD	PT2NW	R:MORGAN
2360	" "	5		1827-03-24	FD	PT2NW	R:MORGAN
2216	" "	5		1827-03-24	FD	PT2NW	R:MORGAN
2319	" "	5		1827-03-24	FD	PT2NW	R:MORGAN
2341	BENNETT, Moses R	16	L38	1831-12-08	SC	LOT38	
2402	BENTLEY, Thomas	16	L3	1831-10-07	SC	LOT3	
2208	BIDWELL, George	7	E½SE	1823-11-12	FD	E2SE	R:MORGAN
2274	BIRKBY, John	16	L15	1833-04-26	SC	LOT15	
2377	BIRKLEY, John	16	L16	1832-04-16	SC	LOT16	
2275	" "	16	L16	1832-04-16	SC	LOT16	
2209	BLAIR, George	20	W½NW	1825-10-31	FD	W2NW	R:MORGAN
2277	BRADSHAW, John	27	NW	1823-11-12	FD	NW	R:MORGAN
2278	" "	27	W½NE	1827-05-23	FD	W2NE	R:MORGAN
2276	" "	27	E½NE	1829-06-08	FD	E2NE	R:MORGAN
2280	BRICH, John	22	SW	1825-02-14	FD	SW	R:CHAMPAIGN
2279	" "	15	W½NW	1825-02-14	FD	W2NW	R:CHAMPAIGN

ID	Individual in Patent	Sec.	Sec. Part	Purchase Date	Sale Type	IL Aliquot Part	For More Info . . .
2228	BRISTOW, Samuel	3		1829-01-19	FD	PT2NW	R:MORGAN
2246	" "	3		1829-01-19	FD	PT2NW	R:MORGAN
2227	" "	3		1829-01-19	FD	PT2NW	R:MORGAN
2370	" "	3		1829-01-19	FD	PT2NW	R:MORGAN
2412	" "	3		1829-01-19	FD	PT2NW	R:MORGAN
2374	BROADHEAD, Thomas	4		1829-10-26	FD	PT2NW	R:MORGAN
2403	" "	4		1829-10-26	FD	PT2NW	R:MORGAN
2366	" "	4		1829-10-26	FD	PT2NW	R:MORGAN
2343	" "	4		1829-10-26	FD	PT2NW	R:MORGAN
2245	BROWN, Preston M	16	L37	1833-05-23	SC	LOT37	G:16
2240	BUCY, James	10	W½NE	1828-10-27	FD	W2NE	R:MORGAN
2210	CAMP, George	35	W½SE	1824-09-29	FD	W2SE	R:MORGAN
2358	CANDLE, Ransom	18	SW	1829-12-18	FD	SW	R:MORGAN
2244	CASSELL, John T	16	L22	1833-05-23	SC	LOT22	G:28
2351	CAULKINS, Nehemiah	16	L34	1831-09-19	SC	LOT34	
2143	CHAPMAN, Abner Jr	34	W½SW	1831-03-15	FD	W2SW	R:MORGAN
2404	CHURCH, Thomas	20	E½SE	1827-10-10	FD	E2SE	R:MORGAN
2405	" "	21	W½SW	1828-01-30	FD	W2SW	R:MORGAN
2406	" "	3	W½SW	1830-02-04	FD	W2SW	R:MORGAN
2407	" "	9	NE	1831-11-15	FD	NELS	R:MORGAN
2357	CLARY, Porter	1		1832-06-20	FD	SEC	R:KENTUCKY
2312	CODDINGTON, Joseph	20	W½SW	1828-10-07	FD	W2SW	R:MORGAN
2171	"	29	E½NW	1829-10-06	FD	E2NW	R:MORGAN G:41
2355	COFFMAN, Philip	16	L49	1833-05-22	SC	LOT49	
2356	" "	16	L19	1833-05-23	SC	LOT19	
2408	COGER, Thomas	25	W½SW	1825-11-03	FD	W2SW	R:MORGAN
2361	COLE, Robert	11	E½SW	1823-11-12	FD	E2SW	R:MORGAN
2168	COUCHMAN, Ann	35	E½NE	1828-10-27	FD	E2NE	R:MORGAN S:F
2362	COWNOVER, Robert	10	E½NE	1824-04-15	FD	E2NE	R:MORGAN
2364	" "	2	W½SW	1824-06-22	FD	W2SW	R:SANGAMON
2365	" "	3	E½SE	1824-06-22	FD	E2SE	R:SANGAMON
2363	" "	2	E½SW	1825-09-13	FD	E2SW	R:SANGAMON
2322	CROW, Joshua	20	W½NE	1825-10-17	FD	W2NE	R:MORGAN G:51
2232	DEEDS, Jacob	31	W½SE	1829-11-17	FD	W2SE	R:MORGAN
2146	DEWIT, Abraham B	16	L11	1831-09-10	SC	LOT11	
2147	" "	16	L32	1831-09-10	SC	LOT32	
2154	DEWITT, Abram P	16	L12	1832-04-16	SC	LOT12	
2155	" "	16	L13	1832-04-16	SC	LOT13	
2156	" "	16	L14	1832-04-16	SC	LOT14	
2223	DIAL, Isaac	21	W½NW	1825-02-25	FD	W2NW	R:MORGAN
2372	DIXON, Samuel	36	W½NW	1825-09-24	FD	W2NW	R:MORGAN
2264	EVANS, James Sen	26	W½SW	1828-12-30	FD	W2SW	R:MORGAN
2243	EVENS, James	23	E½SE	1829-06-09	FD	E2SE	R:MORGAN
2212	FAIRFIELD, Joseph M	19	W½NE	1826-05-31	FD	W2NE	R:MORGAN G:60
2309	FARRIS, Jonathon	8	E½NE	1830-11-18	FD	E2NE	R:MORGAN
2338	FINDLEY, Moses	22	E½NE	1823-11-12	FD	E2NE	R:MORGAN
2173	GEAR, William	16	L6	1831-09-10	SC	LOT6	
2422	" "	16	L36	1831-09-10	SC	LOT36	
2423	" "	16	L6	1831-09-10	SC	LOT6	
2345	GEST, Nathan	10	W½SW	1825-02-26	FD	W2SW	R:MORGAN
2346	GEST, Nathan H	10	E½SE	1823-11-22	FD	E2SE	R:SANGAMON
2347	" "	3	S½NW	1828-01-15	FD	S2NW	R:MORGAN
2449	GIBBON, Zachariah	28	W½SW	1828-10-01	FD	W2SW	R:MORGAN
2448	" "	10	W½NW	1828-10-01	FD	W2NW	R:MORGAN
2310	GIBBONS, Jonathon	10	E½NW	1828-10-27	FD	E2NW	R:MORGAN
2311	" "	3	E½SW	1830-02-12	FD	E2SW	R:MORGAN
2171	GILLETT, Bazateil	29	E½NW	1829-10-06	FD	E2NW	R:MORGAN G:41
2148	GOODPASTURE, Abraham	14	E½NW	1826-12-20	FD	E2NW	R:MORGAN
2149	" "	23	W½NE	1827-03-12	FD	W2NE	R:MORGAN
2359	GRAHAM, William	6		1829-11-28	FD	PT2NEFR	R:MORGAN
2424	" "	6		1829-11-28	FD	PT2NEFR	R:MORGAN
2167	" "	6		1829-11-28	FD	PT2NEFR	R:MORGAN
2425	" "	6		1829-11-28	FD	PT2NEFR	R:MORGAN
2359	" "	6		1829-11-30	FD	PT3NEFR	R:MORGAN
2167	" "	6		1829-11-30	FD	PT3NEFR	R:MORGAN
2425	" "	6		1829-11-30	FD	PT3NEFR	R:MORGAN
2424	" "	6		1829-11-30	FD	PT3NEFR	R:MORGAN
2450	GRAHAM, Zachariah	16	L17	1833-02-08	SC	LOT17	
2333	GRAVES, William	35	E½NW	1831-06-29	FD	E2NW	R:MORGAN G:7
2332	" "	26	E½SW	1831-06-29	FD	E2SW	R:MORGAN G:7
2334	GRAVES, William H	35	W½NE	1831-06-29	FD	W2NE	R:MORGAN G:8
2173	GREEN, Benjamin	16	L6	1833-05-27	SC	LOT6	
2174	" "	16	L7	1833-05-27	SC	LOT7	

ID	Individual in Patent	Sec.	Sec. Part	Purchase Date	Sale Type	IL Aliquot Part	For More Info . . .
2423	GREEN, Benjamin (Cont'd)	16	L6	1833-05-27	SC	LOT6	
2190	" "	16	L7	1833-05-27	SC	LOT7	
2282	GREEN, John	24	E½NW	1824-09-28	FD	E2NW	R:MORGAN
2281	" "	13	W½SE	1824-12-16	FD	W2SE	R:MORGAN
2313	GREEN, Joseph	24	E½SE	1829-05-21	FD	E2SE	R:MORGAN
2376	GREEN, Sephen	24	E½SW	1828-12-23	FD	E2SW	R:MORGAN
2265	GREEN, William B	24	W½SW	1829-04-30	FD	W2SW	R:MORGAN G:67
2414	" "	26	E½NW	1830-12-17	FD	E2NW	R:MORGAN
2283	GREENE, John	24	NE	1823-11-12	FD	NE	R:MORGAN
2284	" "	24	W½NW	1823-11-12	FD	W2NW	R:MORGAN
2426	GRIMSLEY, William	33	SE	1831-05-26	FD	SE	R:MORGAN
2212	HACKETT, George	19	W½NE	1826-05-31	FD	W2NE	R:MORGAN G:60
2211	" "	9	E½NW	1835-02-02	FD	E2NW	R:MORGAN
2176	HAMILTON, Benjamin	11	W½NE	1827-08-24	FD	W2NE	R:MORGAN
2175	" "	11	E½NE	1829-10-24	FD	E2NE	R:MORGAN
2427	HAMILTON, William	29	SW	1823-11-12	FD	SW	R:SANGAMON
2391	HAMILTON, William S	32	W½NW	1823-11-12	FD	W2NW	R:MORGAN G:69
2435	" "	32	E½NW	1823-11-12	FD	E2NW	R:SANGAMON
2269	HANDY, Jesse B	5	L3 (E½)	1834-10-15	FD	E2LOT3NE	R:MORGAN
2285	HANDY, John	5	E½SE	1829-06-23	FD	E2SE	R:MORGAN
2409	HARTMORE, Thomas J	2	L2	1832-10-19	FD	LOT2NESK	R:MORGAN G:71
2207	HAYES, William	24	W½SE	1829-05-27	FD	W2SE	R:MORGAN G:73
2266	HEDENBERG, James V	29	W½NE	1828-10-01	FD	W2NE	R:MORGAN
2219	HOFFMAN, Herman L	32	W½NE	1826-06-24	FD	W2NE	R:MISSOURI
2428	HURST, William	5	E½SW	1829-06-26	FD	E2SW	R:MORGAN
2179	INGALES, Darius	8	W½SW	1830-09-07	FD	W2SW	R:MORGAN
2181	INGALLS, Darius	17	W½SW	1828-09-09	FD	W2SW	R:MORGAN
2180	" "	10	W½SE	1829-01-10	FD	W2SE	R:MORGAN
2224	ISRAEL, Isaac G	16	L9	1833-04-17	SC	LOT9	G:84
2430	JACKSON, William	14	W½NE	1823-11-12	FD	W2NE	R:MORGAN
2429	" "	11	W½SE	1823-11-12	FD	W2SE	R:MORGAN
2431	" "	2	L1	1832-08-18	FD	LOT1NELS	R:MORGAN
2216	JAYNE, Gershom	5		1829-06-15	FD	W2SWSK	R:SANGAMON
2383	" "	5		1829-06-15	FD	W2SWSK	R:SANGAMON
2319	" "	5		1829-06-15	FD	W2SWSK	R:SANGAMON
2360	" "	5		1829-06-15	FD	W2SWSK	R:SANGAMON
2246	JENKINS, James	3		1825-04-13	FD	PT3NW	R:MORGAN
2227	" "	3		1825-04-13	FD	PT3NW	R:MORGAN
2370	" "	3		1825-04-13	FD	PT3NW	R:MORGAN
2228	" "	3		1825-04-13	FD	PT3NW	R:MORGAN
2412	" "	3		1825-04-13	FD	PT3NW	R:MORGAN
2286	JOHNSON, John Jr	18	W½NE	1826-03-03	FD	W2NE	R:MORGAN
2150	JONES, Abraham	5	W½SE	1829-10-05	FD	W2SE	R:MORGAN
2433	JORDEN, William	21	E½NW	1823-11-12	FD	E2NW	R:MORGAN
2432	" "	14	E½SE	1823-11-21	FD	E2SE	R:MORGAN
2434	JORDEN, William L	15	W½SW	1823-11-12	FD	W2SW	R:MORGAN
2436	JOURDAN, William S	16	L29	1831-12-06	SC	LOT29	
2437	"	16	L30	1831-12-06	SC	LOT30	
2438	JOURDON, William S	16	L27	1833-04-23	SC	LOT27	
2439	" "	16	L28	1833-04-23	SC	LOT28	
2440	" "	16	L41	1833-04-23	SC	LOT41	
2248	KERR, James	15	SE	1823-11-12	FD	SE	R:MORGAN
2249	" "	22	W½NE	1823-11-12	FD	W2NE	R:MORGAN
2247	" "	14	W½SW	1823-11-12	FD	W2SW	R:MORGAN
2250	" "	23	W½NW	1823-11-12	FD	W2NW	R:MORGAN
2215	KIRKMAN, George	35	W½NW	1830-11-09	FD	W2NW	R:MORGAN
2214	" "	35	E½SW	1831-05-10	FD	E2SW	R:MORGAN
2315	KLEIN, Joseph	33	E½SE	1829-02-02	FD	E2SE	R:SANGAMON
2314	KLEIN, Joseph Jr	29	W½SE	1824-01-01	FD	W2SE	R:MORGAN
2411	LARIMORE, Thomas J	2		1830-07-15	FD	N03NW	R:MORGAN
2178	" "	2		1830-07-15	FD	N03NW	R:MORGAN
2412	" "	3		1830-07-15	FD	N03NE	R:MORGAN
2370	" "	3		1830-07-15	FD	N03NE	R:MORGAN
2228	" "	3		1830-07-15	FD	N03NE	R:MORGAN
2227	" "	3		1830-07-15	FD	N03NE	R:MORGAN
2246	" "	3		1830-07-15	FD	N03NE	R:MORGAN
2410	" "	2		1830-07-15	FD	N03NW	R:MORGAN
2410	" "	2		1830-11-15	FD	PT3NE	R:MORGAN
2411	" "	2		1830-11-15	FD	PT3NE	R:MORGAN
2178	" "	2		1830-11-15	FD	PT3NE	R:MORGAN
2409	" "	2	L2	1832-10-19	FD	LOT2NESK	R:MORGAN G:71
2251	LEEPER, James	34	E½SE	1830-07-19	FD	E2SE	R:MORGAN
2288	LEEPER, John	28	NE	1823-11-12	FD	NE	R:MORGAN

ID	Individual in Patent	Sec.	Sec. Part	Purchase Date	Sale Type	IL Aliquot Part	For More Info . . .
2287	LEEPER, John (Cont'd)	28	E½NW	1823-11-12	FD	E2NW	R:MORGAN
2289	" "	28	W½NW	1827-05-23	FD	W2NW	R:MORGAN
2371	LOCKWOOD, Samuel D	18	W½SE	1829-04-27	FD	W2SE	R:SANGAMON
2290	LOWRIE, John	4	L3 (E½)	1833-11-21	FD	E2LOT3NE	R:MORGAN
2256	MAGILL, James	25	SE	1823-11-12	FD	SE	R:MORGAN
2259	" "	36	E½NE	1823-11-12	FD	E2NE	R:MORGAN
2257	" "	25	W½NE	1823-11-12	FD	W2NE	R:MORGAN
2255	" "	25	E½SW	1823-11-12	FD	E2SW	R:MORGAN
2253	" "	14	E½NE	1823-11-12	FD	E2NE	R:MORGAN
2252	" "	11	E½SE	1823-11-12	FD	E2SE	R:MORGAN
2254	" "	25	E½NW	1823-11-12	FD	E2NW	R:MORGAN
2258	" "	25	W½NW	1829-06-19	FD	W2NW	R:MORGAN
2260	" "	36	SE	1829-07-07	FD	SE	R:MORGAN
2261	" "	36	W½NE	1829-07-07	FD	W2NE	R:MORGAN
2292	MAJORS, John	12	E½SE	1828-12-22	FD	E2SE	R:MORGAN
2291	" "	12	E½NE	1831-06-10	FD	E2NE	R:MORGAN
2221	MASSES, Ira	16	L44	1832-10-26	SC	LOT44	
2222	" "	16	L43	1833-05-22	SC	LOT43	
2342	MCCONNEL, Murry	19	E½SE	1825-11-03	FD	E2SE	R:MORGAN
2344	MCCONNELL, Murry	4	W½SW	1828-12-31	FD	W2SW	R:MORGAN
2366	" "	4		1830-01-16	FD	NO1NW	R:MORGAN
2343	" "	4		1830-01-16	FD	NO1NW	R:MORGAN
2403	" "	4		1830-01-16	FD	NO1NW	R:MORGAN
2374	" "	4		1830-01-16	FD	NO1NW	R:MORGAN
2177	MCDONALD, Daniel	14	E½SW	1823-11-12	FD	E2SW	R:MORGAN
2178	" "	2		1830-05-29	FD	N02NW	R:MORGAN
2410	" "	2		1830-05-29	FD	N02NW	R:MORGAN
2411	" "	2		1830-05-29	FD	N02NW	R:MORGAN
2186	MEARS, Edwin A	27	W½SW	1828-10-11	FD	W2SW	R:MORGAN
2187	" "	34	W½NW	1828-10-11	FD	W2NW	R:MORGAN
2262	MEARS, James	33	E½NE	1828-10-20	FD	E2NE	R:MORGAN
2366	MEDCALF, Robert	4		1828-09-24	FD	PT3NWFR	R:MORGAN
2374	" "	4		1828-09-24	FD	PT3NWFR	R:MORGAN
2343	" "	4		1828-09-24	FD	PT3NWFR	R:MORGAN
2403	" "	4		1828-09-24	FD	PT3NWFR	R:MORGAN
2368	" "	4	E½SW	1828-11-22	FD	E2SW	R:MORGAN
2367	" "	4	E½SE	1829-03-23	FD	E2SE	R:MORGAN
2369	METCALF, Robert	4	L3 (W½)	1835-07-20	FD	W2LOT3NE	R:MORGAN
2169	MILLEN, Archibald	30	W½NE	1829-10-19	FD	W2NE	R:MORGAN
2322	MILLER, William	20	W½NE	1825-10-17	FD	W2NE	R:MORGAN G:51
2207	MONDON, Frederick	24	W½SE	1829-05-27	FD	W2SE	R:MORGAN G:73
2316	MORTON, Joseph	22	E½NW	1823-11-17	FD	E2NW	R:MORGAN
2317	" "	22	W½SE	1824-04-19	FD	W2SE	R:MORGAN
2340	NASH, Moses	30	SE	1823-11-12	FD	SE	R:MORGAN G:103
2339	" "	30	E½NE	1823-11-12	FD	E2NE	R:MORGAN
2275	NEWLON, Smithson	16	L16	1845-02-03	SC	LOT16	
2377	" "	16	L16	1845-02-03	SC	LOT16	
2326	NEWMAN, Levi	3	W½SE	1825-11-26	FD	W2SE	R:MORGAN
2325	" "	2	NW	1825-11-26	FD	PT1NW	R:MORGAN
2324	" "	13	W½SW	1825-11-30	FD	W2SW	R:MORGAN
2263	PARKINSON, James	16	L39	1831-09-10	SC	LOT39	
2335	PITNER, Montgomery	15	E½NW	1825-10-31	FD	E2NW	R:MORGAN
2336	" "	23	E½NW	1826-01-26	FD	E2NW	R:MORGAN
2337	" "	23	E½SW	1829-06-25	FD	E2SW	R:MORGAN
2417	POSEY, William C	22	E½SE	1826-08-30	FD	E2SE	R:KENTUCKY
2418	" "	23	W½SW	1826-08-30	FD	W2SW	R:KENTUCKY
2373	POWERS, Samuel	6	SWNE	1834-06-13	FD	SWNE	R:SANGAMON
2354	PRICE, Philemon B	16	L23	1833-05-22	SC	LOT23	
2353	" "	16	L18	1833-05-22	SC	LOT18	
2233	REDDING, Jacob	14	W½SE	1823-11-12	FD	W2SE	R:MORGAN
2235	" "	6	E½SE	1828-02-08	FD	E2SE	R:MORGAN
2234	" "	23	E½NE	1828-05-05	FD	E2NE	R:MORGAN
2225	REEVE, Isaac	13	E½NE	1824-09-21	FD	E2NE	R:MORGAN
2323	REEVE, Lazarus	29	E½SE	1828-08-25	FD	E2SE	R:MORGAN
2359	REID, Andrew	6		1828-02-04	FD	PT1NE	R:MORGAN
2424	" "	6		1828-02-04	FD	PT1NE	R:MORGAN
2167	" "	6		1828-02-04	FD	PT1NE	R:MORGAN
2425	" "	6		1828-02-04	FD	PT1NE	R:MORGAN
2386	REID, Stephen H	8	W½NW	1825-10-28	FD	W2NW	R:KENTUCKY
2381	" "	20	E½NW	1825-10-28	FD	E2NW	R:KENTUCKY
2385	" "	6	W½SE	1825-10-28	FD	W2SE	R:KENTUCKY
2380	" "	17	W½NE	1825-10-28	FD	W2NE	R:KENTUCKY
2382	" "	20	E½SW	1825-11-03	FD	E2SW	R:KENTUCKY

ID	Individual in Patent	Sec.	Sec. Part	Purchase Date	Sale Type	IL Aliquot Part	For More Info . . .
2378	REID, Stephen H (Cont'd)	17	E½SW	1826-05-22	FD	E2SW	R:MORGAN
2384	" "	6	SW	1826-05-22	FD	SWFR	R:MORGAN
2319	" "	5		1827-04-02	FD	PT3NW	R:MORGAN
2216	" "	5		1827-04-02	FD	PT3NW	R:MORGAN
2360	" "	5		1827-04-02	FD	PT3NW	R:MORGAN
2383	" "	5		1827-04-02	FD	PT3NW	R:MORGAN
2379	" "	17	SE	1827-04-02	FD	SE	R:MORGAN
2387	" "	8	W½SE	1856-10-28	FD	W2SE	R:KENTUCKY
2227	ROBINSON, Israel	3		1825-10-25	FD	PT1NE	R:MORGAN
2412	" "	3		1825-10-25	FD	PT1NE	R:MORGAN
2246	" "	3		1825-10-25	FD	PT1NE	R:MORGAN
2229	" "	9	E½SE	1825-10-25	FD	E2SE	R:MORGAN
2370	" "	3		1825-10-25	FD	PT1NE	R:MORGAN
2228	" "	3		1825-10-25	FD	PT1NE	R:MORGAN
2228	" "	3		1829-06-25	FD	PT2NE	R:MORGAN
2412	" "	3		1829-06-25	FD	PT2NE	R:MORGAN
2370	" "	3		1829-06-25	FD	PT2NE	R:MORGAN
2227	" "	3		1829-06-25	FD	PT2NE	R:MORGAN
2246	" "	3		1829-06-25	FD	PT2NE	R:MORGAN
2217	ROBLEY, Henry	33	W½NE	1824-01-23	FD	W2NE	R:MORGAN
2327	ROLLINS, Lloyd	18	NW	1829-10-12	FD	NWFR	R:MORGAN
2238	RUARK, James A	9	W½NW	1830-09-25	FD	W2NW	R:MORGAN
2273	RUBLE, Jesse	13	W½NW	1823-11-12	FD	W2NW	R:MORGAN
2271	" "	12	W½SW	1823-11-26	FD	W2SW	R:MORGAN
2270	" "	12	E½NW	1830-07-22	FD	E2NW	R:MORGAN
2272	" "	13	W½NE	1830-10-11	FD	W2NE	R:MORGAN
2295	RUSK, John	13	E½SE	1823-11-21	FD	E2SE	R:MORGAN
2167	SADDLER, Richard	6		1829-08-10	FD	NWFRPTNW	R:MORGAN
2359	" "	6		1829-08-10	FD	NWFRPTNW	R:MORGAN
2424	" "	6		1829-08-10	FD	NWFRPTNW	R:MORGAN
2425	" "	6		1829-08-10	FD	NWFRPTNW	R:MORGAN
2296	SAMPLE, John	15	E½NE	1830-10-21	FD	E2NE	R:MORGAN
2297	" "	2	W½SE	1830-10-21	FD	W2SE	R:MORGAN
2441	SAMPLE, William	2	E½SE	1830-10-26	FD	E2SE	R:MORGAN
2299	SAMPLES, John	11	W½NW	1824-01-14	FD	W2NW	R:MORGAN
2298	" "	11	E½NW	1825-07-18	FD	E2NW	R:MORGAN
2442	SAXTON, William	5	L3 (W½)	1836-02-01	FD	W2LOT3NE	R:MORGAN
2242	SCOTT, James D	16	L35	1831-11-28	SC	LOT35	
2241	" "	16	L31	1831-11-28	SC	LOT31	
2300	SCROGGIN, John	26	W½NE	1828-12-06	FD	W2NE	R:MORGAN
2301	" "	26	W½SE	1830-11-25	FD	W2SE	R:MORGAN
2220	SIMMS, Ignatius R	30	NW	1828-12-15	FD	NWFR	R:MORGAN
2265	SLATTEN, James	24	W½SW	1829-04-30	FD	W2SW	R:MORGAN G:67
2226	SMITH, Isaac	9	W½SE	1824-12-18	FD	W2SE	R:MORGAN
2321	SMITH, Joseph	5	NE	1825-01-20	FD	PT1NE	R:MORGAN
2320	" "	5	NE	1825-01-20	FD	PT1NE	R:MORGAN
2321	" "	5	NE	1825-10-20	FD	PT2NE	R:MORGAN
2320	" "	5	NE	1825-10-20	FD	PT2NE	R:MORGAN
2318	" "	4	NE	1826-10-28	FD	PT2NE	R:MORGAN
2383	" "	5		1830-01-11	FD	NO1NW	R:MORGAN
2319	" "	5		1830-01-11	FD	NO1NW	R:MORGAN
2360	" "	5		1830-01-11	FD	NO1NW	R:MORGAN
2216	" "	5		1830-01-11	FD	NO1NW	R:MORGAN
2352	SMITH, Patrick	7	W½SE	1826-03-03	FD	W2SE	R:MORGAN
2415	SMITH, William B	16	L33	1831-12-07	SC	LOT33	
2218	SOLOMON, Henry	27	W½SE	1827-11-12	FD	W2SE	R:MORGAN
2213	SPEARS, George Jr	10	E½SW	1825-03-14	FD	E2SW	R:MORGAN
2200	SPENCER, Enoch W	27	E½SW	1825-03-15	FD	E2SW	R:MORGAN
2202	" "	33	E½NW	1825-10-24	FD	E2NW	R:MORGAN
2201	" "	28	E½SE	1825-10-31	FD	E2SE	R:MORGAN
2391	SPENCER, Stephen W	32	W½NW	1823-11-12	FD	W2NW	R:MORGAN G:69
2389	" "	31	NE	1823-11-12	FD	NE	R:MORGAN
2390	" "	31	NW	1823-11-12	FD	NWFR	R:MORGAN
2340	" "	30	SE	1823-11-12	FD	SE	R:MORGAN G:103
2388	" "	30	SW	1823-11-12	FD	SWFR	R:MORGAN
2328	STACY, Mathew	16	L4	1831-09-09	SC	LOT4	
2330	" "	16	L26	1833-06-15	SC	LOT26	
2329	" "	16	L25	1833-06-15	SC	LOT25	
2293	STEBBINS, John O	34	E½NE	1827-04-07	FD	E2NE	R:MORGAN
2170	STONE, Barton W	35	W½SW	1830-10-18	FD	W2SW	R:MORGAN
2348	STOUT, Nathaniel	17	W½NW	1825-11-03	FD	W2NW	R:MORGAN
2350	" "	7	W½NE	1825-11-03	FD	W2NE	R:MORGAN
2349	" "	18	E½NE	1826-11-20	FD	E2NE	R:MORGAN

ID	Individual in Patent	Sec.	Sec. Part	Purchase Date	Sale Type	IL Aliquot Part	For More Info . . .
2237	STRAWN, Jacob	20	W½SE	1828-02-20	FD	W2SE	R:OHIO
2236	"	13	E½SW	1831-05-21	FD	E2SW	R:MORGAN
2224	TAGGART, Joseph J	16	L9	1833-04-17	SC	LOT9	G:84
2302	TAYLOR, John	16	L40	1831-12-07	SC	LOT40	
2194	THOMPSON, Elijah	34	W½NE	1829-12-30	FD	W2NE	R:MORGAN
2294	TIFFT, John P	9	W½SW	1825-10-31	FD	W2SW	R:MORGAN
2244	TILTON, James J	16	L22	1833-05-23	SC	LOT22	G:28
2245	" "	16	L37	1833-05-23	SC	LOT37	G:16
2375	TITUS, Samuel	4	W½SE	1828-07-21	FD	W2SE	R:MORGAN
2374	" "	4		1829-11-25	FD	PT1NE	R:MORGAN
2343	" "	4		1829-11-25	FD	PT1NE	R:MORGAN
2403	" "	4		1829-11-25	FD	PT1NE	R:MORGAN
2366	" "	4		1829-11-25	FD	PT1NE	R:MORGAN
2153	VANCE, Abraham	14	W½NW	1823-11-17	FD	W2NW	R:SANGAMON
2151	" "	11	W½SW	1823-11-17	FD	W2SW	R:SANGAMON
2152	" "	12	W½NW	1830-07-27	FD	W2NW	R:MORGAN
2145	VANWINKLE, Abner	26	E½SE	1826-11-27	FD	E2SE	R:MORGAN
2144	" "	26	E½NE	1828-11-22	FD	E2NE	R:MORGAN
2419	VERRY, William C	32	W½SE	1825-04-24	FD	W2SE	R:MORGAN
2443	WADE, William	32	E½SE	1828-10-24	FD	E2SE	R:MORGAN
2416	WARREN, William B	7	E½NE	1834-01-03	FD	E2NE	R:MORGAN
2184	WATSON, David	16	L24	1831-11-28	SC	LOT24	
2183	" "	16	L21	1831-11-28	SC	LOT21	
2185	" "	16	L42	1831-11-28	SC	LOT42	
2182	" "	16	L20	1831-11-28	SC	LOT20	
2267	WILLARD, James	26	W½NW	1829-08-05	FD	W2NW	R:MORGAN
2142	WILSON, Aaron	19	W½SE	1823-11-12	FD	W2SE	R:MORGAN
2413	WISWALL, Thomas	33	W½SW	1828-07-31	FD	W2SW	R:MORGAN
2195	WISWELL, Elijah	31	E½SE	1823-11-12	FD	E2SE	R:MORGAN
2196	" "	32	SW	1823-11-12	FD	SW	R:MORGAN
2188	WOLCOTT, Elihu	16	L1	1831-09-09	SC	LOT1	
2189	" "	16	L2	1831-09-09	SC	LOT2	
2190	" "	16	L7	1831-09-10	SC	LOT7	
2174	" "	16	L7	1831-09-10	SC	LOT7	
2191	" "	16	L8	1831-09-10	SC	LOT8	
2193	WOLCOTT, Elihue	8	E½SE	1830-11-23	FD	E2SE	R:MORGAN
2198	WOLCOTT, Elisha	34	E½SW	1831-04-11	FD	E2SW	R:MORGAN
2199	" "	34	W½SE	1831-04-11	FD	W2SE	R:MORGAN
2197	" "	34	E½NW	1831-04-11	FD	E2NW	R:MORGAN
2331	WOOD, Milo	15	W½NE	1824-10-19	FD	W2NE	R:MORGAN
2192	WOOLCOTT, Elihu	8	W½NE	1830-12-25	FD	W2NE	R:MORGAN
2205	WRIGHT, Erastus	15	SESW	1854-12-06	FD	SESW	R:SANGAMON
2203	" "	15	E½SE	1854-12-06	FD	E2SE	R:SANGAMON
2206	" "	15	SWSE	1854-12-06	FD	SWSE	R:SANGAMON
2204	" "	15	NE	1854-12-06	FD	NE	R:SANGAMON
2305	WYATT, John	35	E½SE	1823-11-12	FD	E2SE	R:MORGAN
2308	" "	36	W½SW	1823-11-12	FD	W2SW	R:MORGAN
2306	" "	36	E½NW	1826-02-06	FD	E2NW	R:MORGAN
2304	" "	27	E½SE	1828-10-16	FD	E2SE	R:MORGAN
2303	" "	25	E½NE	1828-12-22	FD	E2NE	R:MORGAN
2307	" "	36	E½SW	1829-06-19	FD	E2SW	R:MORGAN
2444	WYATT, William	12	E½SW	1823-11-12	FD	E2SW	R:MORGAN
2447	" "	13	E½NW	1823-11-12	FD	E2NW	R:MORGAN
2446	" "	12	W½SE	1829-06-13	FD	W2SE	R:MORGAN
2445	" "	12	W½NE	1830-10-14	FD	W2NE	R:MORGAN

Patent Map

T15-N R10-W
3rd PM Meridian

Map Group 9

Township Statistics

Parcels Mapped	:	309
Number of Patents	:	1
Number of Individuals	:	177
Patentees Identified	:	174
Number of Surnames	:	150
Multi-Patentee Parcels	:	14
Oldest Patent Date	:	11/12/1823
Most Recent Patent	:	10/28/1856
Block/Lot Parcels	:	55
Cities and Towns	:	5
Cemeteries	:	8

Section 6

SADDLER Richard 1829

GRAHAM William 1829
REID Andrew 1828

GRAHAM William 1829
POWERS Samuel 1834

REID Stephen H 1826

REDDING Jacob 1828
REID Stephen H 1825

Section 5

SMITH Joseph 1830

BELL Robert 1827
REID Stephen H 1827
SMITH Joseph 1825
SMITH Joseph 1825

JAYNE Gershom 1829
HURST William 1829
HANDY John 1829
JONES Abraham 1829

Lots-Sec. 5
L3(E½) HANDY, Jesse B 1834
L3(W½) SAXTON, William 1836

Section 4

MCCONNELL Murry 1830
MEDCALF Robert 1828
SMITH Joseph 1826
BROADHEAD Thomas 1829
TITUS Samuel 1829

MCCONNELL Murry 1828
MEDCALF Robert 1828
TITUS Samuel 1828
MEDCALF Robert 1829

Lots-Sec. 4
L3(E½) LOWRIE, John 1833
L3(W½) METCALF, Robert 1835

Section 7

ALLINSON Adam 1825

STOUT Nathaniel 1825
WARREN William B 1834

ARNETT Thomas 1825

SMITH Patrick 1826
BIDWELL George 1823

Section 8

REID Stephen H 1825
ALLINSON Adam 1825
WOOLCOTT Elihu 1830
FARRIS Jonathon 1830

INGALES Darius 1830
ALLINSON Adam 1823
REID Stephen H 1856
WOLCOTT Elihue 1830

Section 9

RUARK James A 1830
HACKETT George 1835
CHURCH Thomas 1831

TIFFT John P 1825
ALLINSON Adam 1824
SMITH Isaac 1824
ROBINSON Israel 1825

Section 18

ROLLINS Lloyd 1829
JOHNSON John Jr 1826
STOUT Nathaniel 1826

CANDLE Ransom 1829
LOCKWOOD Samuel D 1829
ALLINSON Adam 1825

Section 17

STOUT Nathaniel 1825
ALLINSON Adam 1823
REID Stephen H 1825
BARTON Jacob 1828

INGALLS Darius 1828
REID Stephen H 1826
REID Stephen H 1827

Section 16

Lots-Sec. 16
L1/2 WOLCOTT, Elihu 1831
L3 BENTLEY, Thomas 1831
L4 STACY, Mathew 1831
L5 BARTON, Jacob 1831
L6 GREEN, Benjamin 1833
L6 GEAR, William 1831
L7 GREEN, Benjamin 1833
L7/8 WOLCOTT, Elihu 1831
L9 ISRAEL, Isaac G [84]1833
L10 ALLYN, Benjamin 1831
L11 DEWITT, Abraham B 1831
L12-14 DEWITT, Abram P 1832
L15 BIRKBY, John 1833
L16 BIRKLEY, John 1832
L16 NEWLON, Smithson 1845
L17 GRAHAM, Zachariah1833
L18 PRICE, Philemon B 1833
L19 COFFMAN, Philip 1833
L20/21 WATSON, David 1831
L22 CASSELL, John T [28]1833

L23 PRICE, Philemon B1833
L24 WATSON, David 1831
L25 STACY, Mathew 1833
L26 STACY, Mathew 1833
L27/28JOURDON, William S1833
L29/30 JOURDAN, William S1831
L31 SCOTT, James D 1831
L32 DEWIT, Abraham B 1831
L33 SMITH, William B 1831
L34 CAULKINS, Nehemiah1831
L35 SCOTT, James D 1831
L36 GEAR, William 1831
L37 BROWN, Preston M[16]1833
L38 BENNETT, Moses R 1831
L39 PARKINSON, James 1831
L40 TAYLOR, John 1831
L41 JOURDON, William S1833
L42 WATSON, David 1831
L43 MASSES, Ira 1833
L44 MASSES, Ira 1832
L49 COFFMAN, Philip 1833

Section 19

ALLINSON Adam 1823
HACKETT [60] George 1826
ALLINSON Adam 1825

WILSON Aaron 1823
MCCONNEL Murry 1825
CODDINGTON Joseph 1828

Section 20

BLAIR George 1825
REID Stephen H 1825
CROW [51] Joshua 1825
ARNETT Thomas 1825

REID Stephen H 1825
STRAWN Jacob 1828
CHURCH Thomas 1827

Section 21

DIAL Isaac 1825
JORDEN William 1823
ALLINSON Thomas 1823
ALLINSON Thomas 1823

CHURCH Thomas 1828
ARNETT James 1827
ARNETT Thomas 1823
ARNETT Thomas 1823

Section 30

SIMMS Ignatius R 1828
MILLEN Archibald 1829
NASH Moses 1823

SPENCER Stephen W 1823
NASH [103] Moses 1823

Section 29

ARNETT Janus 1829
GILLETT [41] Bazateil 1829
HEDENBERG James V 1828
BALLARD Thomas 1828

HAMILTON William 1823
REEVE Lazarus 1828
KLEIN Joseph Jr 1824

Section 28

LEEPER John 1827
LEEPER John 1823
LEEPER John 1823

GIBBON Zachariah 1828
ABRAMS William G 1825
ABRAM William G 1823
SPENCER Enoch W 1825

Section 31

SPENCER Stephen W 1823
SPENCER Stephen W 1823

Section 32

SPENCER [69] Stephen W 1823
HAMILTON William S 1823
HOFFMAN Herman L 1826
ARNETT Thomas 1828

Section 33

ARNETT Thomas 1828
SPENCER Enoch W 1825
ROBLEY Henry 1824
MEARS James 1828

WISWALL Thomas 1828
KLEIN Joseph 1829
GRIMSLEY William 1831

ALLINSON Adam 1823
DEEDS Jacob 1829
WISWELL Elijah 1823
WISWELL Elijah 1823
VERRY William C 1825
WADE William 1828

Section 3
- BRISTOW Samuel 1829
- JENKINS James 1825
- ROBINSON Israel 1829
- LARIMORE Thomas J 1830
- ROBINSON Israel 1825
- GEST Nathan H 1828
- **3**
- CHURCH Thomas 1830
- GIBBONS Jonathon 1830
- NEWMAN Levi 1825
- COWNOVER Robert 1824

Section 2
- LARIMORE Thomas J 1830
- LARIMORE Thomas J 1830
- MCDONALD Daniel 1830
- NEWMAN Levi 1825
- **2**
- COWNOVER Robert 1824
- COWNOVER Robert 1825
- SAMPLE John 1830
- SAMPLE William 1830
- Lots-Sec. 2
  - L1 JACKSON, William 1832
  - L2 HARTMORE, Thomas [71]1832

Section 1
- CLARY Porter 1832
- **1**

Section 10
- GIBBON Zachariah 1828
- GIBBONS Jonathon 1828
- BUCY James 1828
- COWNOVER Robert 1824
- GEST Nathan 1825
- **10**
- SPEARS George Jr 1825
- INGALLS Darius 1829
- GEST Nathan H 1823

Section 11
- SAMPLES John 1824
- SAMPLES John 1825
- HAMILTON Benjamin 1827
- HAMILTON Benjamin 1829
- VANCE Abraham 1823
- COLE Robert 1823
- **11**
- MAGILL James 1823
- JACKSON William 1823

Section 12
- MAJORS John 1831
- WYATT William 1830
- VANCE Abraham 1830
- RUBLE Jesse 1830
- RUBLE Jesse 1823
- WYATT William 1823
- **12**
- WYATT William 1829
- MAJORS John 1828

Section 15
- BRICH John 1825
- PITNER Montgomery 1825
- WOOD Milo 1824
- WRIGHT Erastus 1854
- SAMPLE John 1830
- **15**
- JORDEN William L 1823
- ALLINSON Adam 1824
- WRIGHT Erastus 1854
- KERR James 1823
- WRIGHT Erastus 1854
- WRIGHT Erastus 1854

Section 14
- VANCE Abraham 1823
- GOODPASTURE Abraham 1826
- JACKSON William 1823
- MAGILL James 1823
- **14**
- KERR James 1823
- MCDONALD Daniel 1823
- REDDING Jacob 1823
- JORDEN William 1823

Section 13
- RUBLE Jesse 1830
- WYATT William 1823
- RUBLE Jesse 1823
- REEVE Isaac 1824
- **13**
- NEWMAN Levi 1825
- STRAWN Jacob 1831
- GREEN John 1824
- RUSK John 1823

Section 22
- ALLINSON Thomas 1823
- MORTON Joseph 1823
- KERR James 1823
- FINDLEY Moses 1823
- BRICH John 1825
- **22**
- MORTON Joseph 1824
- POSEY William C 1826

Section 23
- KERR James 1823
- PITNER Montgomery 1826
- GOODPASTURE Abraham 1827
- **23**
- POSEY William C 1826
- PITNER Montgomery 1829
- REDDING Jacob 1828
- EVENS James 1829

Section 24
- GREENE John 1823
- GREEN John 1824
- GREENE John 1823
- **24**
- GREENE John 1823
- SLATTEN [67] James 1829
- GREEN Sephen 1828
- MONDON [73] Frederick 1829
- GREEN Joseph 1829

Section 27
- BRADSHAW John 1823
- BRADSHAW John 1829
- BRADSHAW John 1827
- **27**
- MEARS Edwin A 1828
- SOLOMON Henry 1827
- SPENCER Enoch W 1825
- WYATT John 1828

Section 26
- WILLARD James 1829
- GREEN William B 1830
- SCROGGIN John 1828
- MAGILL James 1829
- **26**
- EVANS James Sen 1828
- BARTLETT [7] Milton 1831
- SCROGGIN John 1830
- VANWINKLE Abner 1828
- VANWINKLE Abner 1826

Section 25
- MAGILL James 1823
- MAGILL James 1823
- WYATT John 1828
- **25**
- COGER Thomas 1825
- MAGILL James 1823

Section 34
- MEARS Edwin A 1828
- WOLCOTT Elisha 1831
- THOMPSON Elijah 1829
- STEBBINS John O 1827
- **34**
- CHAPMAN Abner Jr 1831
- WOLCOTT Elisha 1831
- WOLCOTT Elisha 1831
- LEEPER James 1830

Section 35
- BARTLETT [7] Milton 1831
- BARTLETT [8] Milton 1831
- COUCHMAN Ann 1828
- KIRKMAN George 1830
- **35**
- STONE Barton W 1830
- KIRKMAN George 1831
- CAMP George 1824
- WYATT John 1823

Section 36
- DIXON Samuel 1825
- WYATT John 1826
- MAGILL James 1829
- MAGILL James 1823
- WYATT John 1823
- **36**
- WYATT John 1829
- MAGILL James 1829

Helpful Hints

1. This Map's INDEX can be found on the preceding pages.

2. Refer to Map "C" to see where this Township lies within Morgan County, Illinois.

3. Numbers within square brackets [ ] denote a multi-patentee land parcel (multi-owner). Refer to Appendix "C" for a full list of members in this group.

4. Areas that look to be crowded with Patentees usually indicate multiple sales of the same parcel (re-issues), cancellations or voided transactions (that we map, anyway) or overlapping parcels. We opt to show even these ambiguous parcels, which oftentimes lead to research avenues not yet taken.

Legend

- ———— Patent Boundary
- ▬▬▬▬ Section Boundary
- (shaded) No Patents Found (or Outside County)
- 1., 2., 3., ... Lot Numbers (when beside a name)
- [ ] Group Number (see Appendix "C")

Scale: Section = 1 mile X 1 mile (generally, with some exceptions)

Road Map

T15-N R10-W
3rd PM Meridian

Map Group 9

Cities & Towns
Brownton (historical)
Jacksonville
Portuguese Hill
Savage (historical)
South Jacksonville

Cemeteries
Calvary Cemetery
Diamond Grove Cemetery
East Cemetery
Ebenezer Cemetery
Hazel Green Cemetery
Sample Cemetery
Scott Cemetery
South Fork Mauvaise Terre
  Cemetery

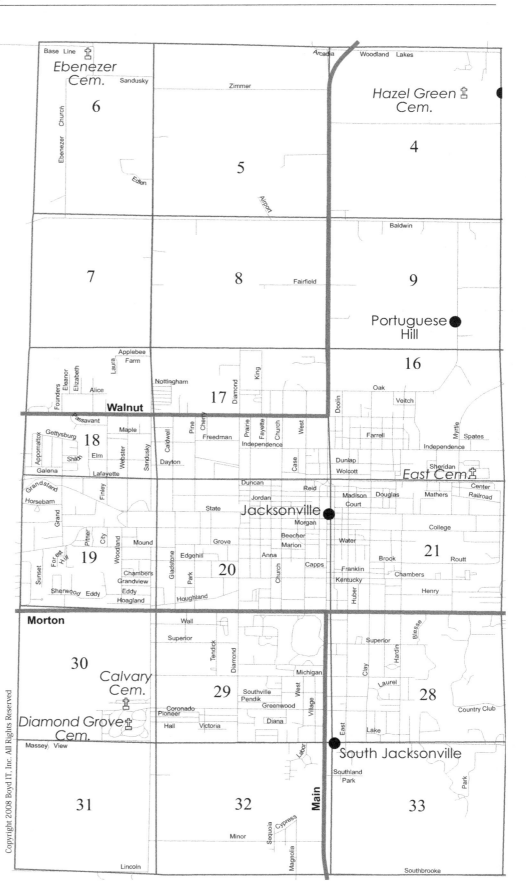

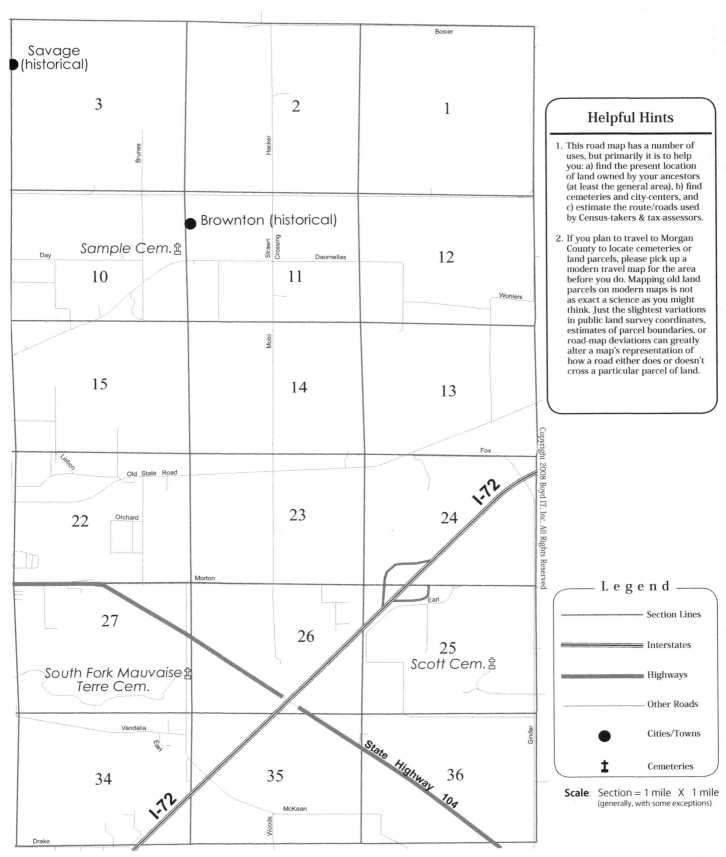

Savage
(historical)

3

Bosier

2

1

Brunes

Hacker

Brownton (historical)

Sample Cem. ⚱

Day

Strawn Crossing

Deornellas

12

10

11

Wohlers

Mobil

15

14

13

Lisbon

Old State Road

Fox

I-72

22

Orchard

23

24

Morton

Earl

27

26

25

Scott Cem. ⚱

South Fork Mauvaise ⚱
Terre Cem.

Vandalia

Easy

Ginder

34

I-72

35

State Highway 104

36

McKean

Woods

Drake

Helpful Hints

1. This road map has a number of uses, but primarily it is to help you: a) find the present location of land owned by your ancestors (at least the general area), b) find cemeteries and city-centers, and c) estimate the route/roads used by Census-takers & tax-assessors.

2. If you plan to travel to Morgan County to locate cemeteries or land parcels, please pick up a modern travel map for the area before you do. Mapping old land parcels on modern maps is not as exact a science as you might think. Just the slightest variations in public land survey coordinates, estimates of parcel boundaries, or road-map deviations can greatly alter a map's representation of how a road either does or doesn't cross a particular parcel of land.

Legend

———————	Section Lines
═══════════	Interstates
━━━━━━━━━	Highways
—————	Other Roads
●	Cities/Towns
⚱	Cemeteries

Scale: Section = 1 mile X 1 mile
(generally, with some exceptions)

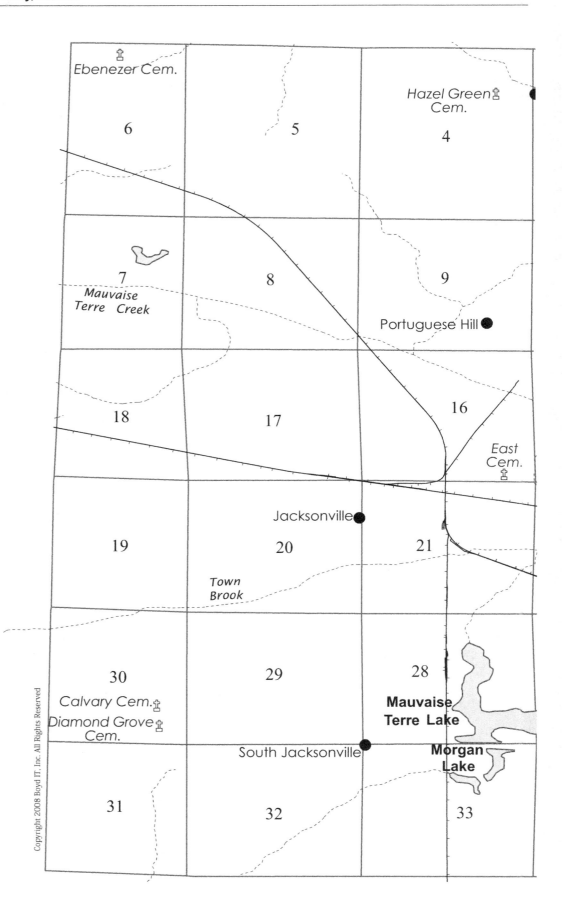

Historical Map

T15-N R10-W
3rd PM Meridian

Map Group 9

Cities & Towns

Brownton (historical)
Jacksonville
Portuguese Hill
Savage (historical)
South Jacksonville

Cemeteries

Calvary Cemetery
Diamond Grove Cemetery
East Cemetery
Ebenezer Cemetery
Hazel Green Cemetery
Sample Cemetery
Scott Cemetery
South Fork Mauvaise Terre
  Cemetery

Ebenezer Cem.

Hazel Green
Cem.

6

5

4

7

8

9

Mauvaise
Terre Creek

Portuguese Hill

18

17

16

East
Cem.

Jacksonville

19

20

21

Town
Brook

30

29

28

Mauvaise
Terre Lake

Calvary Cem.

Diamond Grove
Cem.

South Jacksonville

Morgan
Lake

31

32

33

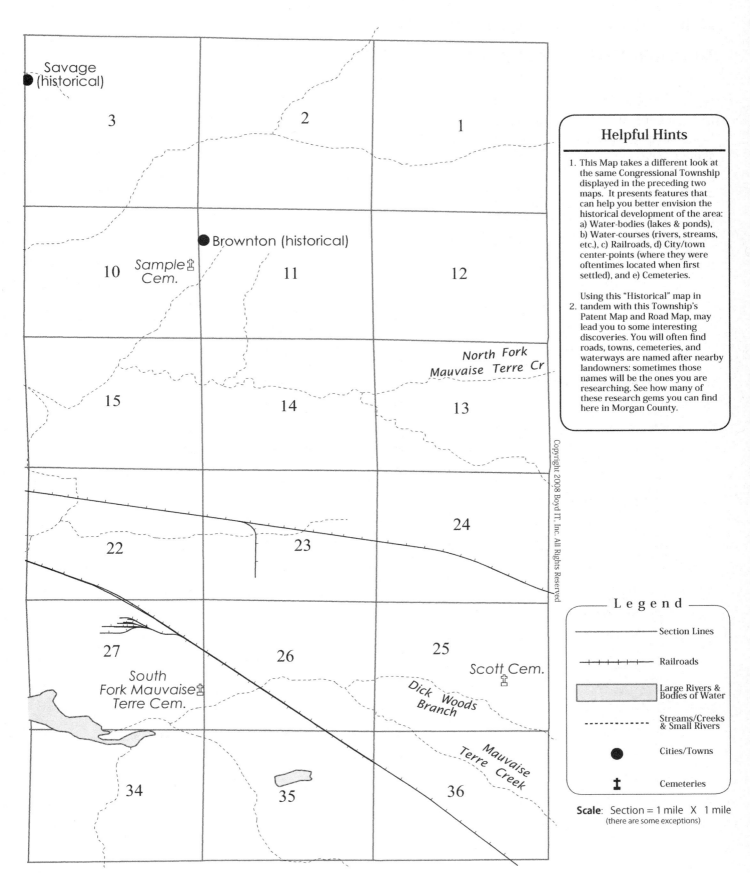

Savage (historical)

3

2

1

Brownton (historical)

10

Sample ⚔ Cem.

11

12

15

North Fork
Mauvaise Terre Cr

14

13

22

23

24

27

26

25

Scott Cem. ⚔

South
Fork Mauvaise ⚔
Terre Cem.

Dick Woods Branch

34

35

Mauvaise
Terre Creek

36

Helpful Hints

1. This Map takes a different look at
the same Congressional Township
displayed in the preceding two
maps. It presents features that
can help you better envision the
historical development of the area:
a) Water-bodies (lakes & ponds),
b) Water-courses (rivers, streams,
etc.), c) Railroads, d) City/town
center-points (where they were
oftentimes located when first
settled), and e) Cemeteries.

2. Using this "Historical" map in
tandem with this Township's
Patent Map and Road Map, may
lead you to some interesting
discoveries. You will often find
roads, towns, cemeteries, and
waterways are named after nearby
landowners: sometimes those
names will be the ones you are
researching. See how many of
these research gems you can find
here in Morgan County.

Legend

————	Section Lines
+++++	Railroads
▭	Large Rivers & Bodies of Water
- - - - -	Streams/Creeks & Small Rivers
●	Cities/Towns
⚔	Cemeteries

Scale: Section = 1 mile X 1 mile
(there are some exceptions)

Map Group 10: Index to Land Patents

Township 15-North Range 9-West (3rd PM)

After you locate an individual in this Index, take note of the Section and Section Part then proceed to the Land Patent map on the pages immediately following. You should have no difficulty locating the corresponding parcel of land.

The "For More Info" Column will lead you to more information about the underlying Patents. See the *Legend* at right, and the "How to Use this Book" chapter, for more information.

```
                        LEGEND
              "For More Info . . . " column
  G = Group  (Multi-Patentee Patent, see Appendix "C")
  R = Residence
  S = Social Status

  See Appendix A for list of abbreviations used by the
  Illinois State Archives in describing the place and
  nature of these land patents.

  Note: if the Abbreviations contain "L", "BL", "LOT",
  or "BLOCK", the exact whereabouts of the parcel within
  the section is not known.
```

ID	Individual in Patent	Sec.	Sec. Part	Purchase Date	Sale Type	IL Aliquot Part	For More Info . . .
2521	ANDERSON, James	17	W½NW	1825-11-22	FD	W2NW	R:MORGAN
2522	" "	9	W½SE	1825-11-22	FD	W2SE	R:MORGAN
2540	ANDERSON, John	18	E½NE	1823-11-12	FD	E2NE	R:MORGAN
2542	" "	7	E½SE	1823-11-12	FD	E2SE	R:MORGAN
2541	" "	19	W½SE	1824-06-29	FD	W2SE	R:MORGAN
2576	BALLARD, Theophilas	32	W½NW	1825-11-02	FD	W2NW	R:MORGAN
2689	" "	32	W½NW	1825-11-02	FD	W2NW	R:MORGAN
2671	BERRY, Samuel	9	E½NW	1825-02-23	FD	E2NW	R:MORGAN
2645	" "	9	W½NW	1825-11-03	FD	W2NW	R:MORGAN G:10
2669	" "	4	E½SW	1831-05-13	FD	E2SW	R:MORGAN
2636	" "	4	W½SW	1831-05-13	FD	W2SW	R:MORGAN G:9
2670	" "	4	SENW	1834-02-07	FD	SENW	R:MORGAN
2543	BLANEY, John	19	SW	1825-08-31	FD	SWFR	R:GREENE
2546	" "	31	W½SE	1825-08-31	FD	W2SE	R:GREENE
2545	" "	31	E½NE	1825-08-31	FD	E2NE	R:GREENE
2544	" "	30	NW	1825-12-26	FD	NWFR	R:MORGAN
2457	BROCKENBROUGH, Austin	16	L3	1836-06-04	SC	LOT3	
2698	BROWN, William	22	E½SW	1833-06-18	FD	E2SW	R:KENTUCKY
2697	" "	21	NE	1833-06-18	FD	NE	R:KENTUCKY
2693	" "	1	S½	1833-06-18	FD	S2SEC	R:KENTUCKY
2694	" "	13	E½SE	1833-06-18	FD	E2SE	R:KENTUCKY
2696	" "	21	E½SE	1833-06-18	FD	E2SE	R:KENTUCKY
2695	" "	21	E½NW	1833-06-18	FD	E2NW	R:KENTUCKY
2700	" "	27	NE	1833-06-25	FD	NE	R:KENTUCKY
2699	" "	22	SE	1833-06-25	FD	SE	R:KENTUCKY
2701	BRUTON, William	32	E½NE	1832-01-02	FD	E2NE	R:MORGAN
2548	BUCHANAN, John	32	W½SE	1829-04-04	FD	W2SE	R:MORGAN
2547	" "	32	W½NE	1831-12-27	FD	W2NE	R:MORGAN
2630	BUTLER, Nathan	12	W½SE	1823-11-18	FD	W2SE	R:MORGAN
2629	" "	12	E½SW	1824-04-07	FD	E2SW	R:MORGAN
2631	" "	13	W½NE	1831-04-14	FD	W2NELS	R:MORGAN
2458	CASSEL, Benjamin	16	L2	1836-06-04	SC	LOT2	
2582	CASSEL, John T	16	L12	1836-06-04	SC	LOT12	
2583	" "	16	L13	1836-06-04	SC	LOT13	
2584	" "	16	L18	1836-06-04	SC	LOT18	
2585	" "	16	L19	1836-06-04	SC	LOT19	
2581	" "	16	L11	1836-06-04	SC	LOT11	
2662	CASSELL, Robert	14	W½NW	1831-04-27	FD	W2NW	R:MORGAN
2663	" "	15	E½NE	1831-04-27	FD	E2NE	R:MORGAN
2664	" "	22	E½NW	1831-06-14	FD	E2NW	R:MORGAN
2665	" "	22	W½NE	1831-06-14	FD	W2NE	R:MORGAN
2666	CASTLE, Robert	14	E½NW	1830-11-26	FD	E2NW	R:MORGAN
2523	CAVE, James	12	E½SE	1828-10-30	FD	E2SE	R:MORGAN
2524	" "	12	W½NE	1830-03-17	FD	W2NE	R:MORGAN
2612	CLARKE, Lancelot	7	W½SW	1829-11-09	FD	W2SW	R:MORGAN
2624	CLARKE, Mathew	15		1831-06-04	FD	E2SEPTLS	R:MORGAN G:37

ID	Individual in Patent	Sec.	Sec. Part	Purchase Date	Sale Type	IL Aliquot Part	For More Info . . .
2592	CLARKE, Mathew (Cont'd)	15		1831-06-04	FD	E2SEPTLS	R:MORGAN G:37
2593	" "	15		1831-06-04	FD	E2SEPTLS	R:MORGAN G:37
2617	CLARKE, Mathew S	15	E½SW	1831-04-28	FD	E2SW	R:DIST. OF COLUMBIA
2618	" "	9	E½SW	1831-06-03	FD	E2SWPTLS	R:DIST. OF COLUMBIA
2593	" "	15		1831-06-03	FD	W2SEPTLS	R:MORGAN G:36
2592	" "	15		1831-06-03	FD	W2SEPTLS	R:MORGAN G:36
2591	" "	9	E½SW	1831-06-03	FD	E2SWPTLS	R:DIST. OF COLUMBIA
2624	" "	15		1831-06-03	FD	W2SEPTLS	R:MORGAN G:36
2647	COFFMAN, Philip	12	E½NE	1831-04-30	FD	E2NE	R:MORGAN G:44
2646	" "	29	E½NW	1831-06-01	FD	E2NW	R:MORGAN
2648	" "	27	W½NW	1831-06-02	FD	W2NW	R:MORGAN G:44
2649	" "	22	W½SW	1831-06-14	FD	W2SW	R:MORGAN G:43
2467	COKER, Clabourn	32	W½SW	1826-12-13	FD	W2SW	R:MORGAN
2468	COKER, Claibourne	29	W½SW	1830-11-24	FD	W2SW	R:MORGAN
2684	COLE, Stephen	27	SWSE	1833-06-17	FD	SWSE	R:MORGAN
2506	CONNAWAY, Hugh	30	W½NE	1825-12-08	FD	W2NE	R:MORGAN
2667	COWNOVER, Robert	10	W½NW	1824-04-12	FD	W2NW	R:MORGAN
2456	COX, Ancil	35	W½NW	1833-11-12	FD	W2NW	R:MORGAN
2633	COX, Nathaniel	34	SENE	1833-11-12	FD	SENE	R:MORGAN
2510	CROSS, Israel	27	E½SE	1833-06-24	FD	E2SE	R:MORGAN
2706	CROSS, William	34	W½NW	1831-12-17	FD	W2NW	R:MORGAN
2705	" "	33	SENE	1833-06-24	FD	SENE	R:MORGAN
2489	CURTS, George	16	L8	1836-06-04	SC	LOT8	
2488	" "	16	L7	1836-06-04	SC	LOT7	
2619	CYRUS, Matthew	33	W½SE	1829-02-20	FD	W2SE	R:MORGAN
2526	DODD, James	28	W½NW	1828-07-09	FD	W2NW	R:MORGAN
2525	" "	21	W½SW	1829-12-17	FD	W2SW	R:MORGAN
2653	DODSWORTH, Richard	5	NWNE	1834-10-22	FD	NWNE	R:MORGAN
2652	" "	5	NW	1834-10-22	FD	NW	R:MORGAN
2527	DOOD, James	21	E½SW	1831-08-10	FD	E2SW	R:MORGAN
2492	DRURY, George W	27	NWSE	1833-06-18	FD	NWSE	R:MORGAN
2613	DRURY, Lawson	27	E½NW	1831-08-23	FD	E2NW	R:MORGAN
2593	DUNCAN, Joseph	15		1831-06-03	FD	W2SEPTLS	R:MORGAN G:36
2592	" "	15		1831-06-03	FD	W2SEPTLS	R:MORGAN G:36
2591	" "	9	E½SW	1831-06-03	FD	E2SW	R:MORGAN
2624	" "	15		1831-06-03	FD	W2SEPTLS	R:MORGAN G:36
2618	" "	9	E½SW	1831-06-03	FD	E2SW	R:MORGAN
2592	" "	15		1831-06-04	FD	E2SEPTLS	R:MORGAN G:37
2624	" "	15		1831-06-04	FD	E2SEPTLS	R:MORGAN G:37
2593	" "	15		1831-06-04	FD	E2SEPTLS	R:MORGAN G:37
2590	" "	22	W½NW	1832-08-10	FD	W2NWLS	R:MORGAN
2589	" "	22	E½NE	1832-08-10	FD	E2NELS	R:MORGAN
2528	DUNLAP, James	24	SWSW	1836-02-03	FD	SWSW	R:MORGAN
2616	EASTHAM, Marvillous	1	L3	1838-09-20	FD	LOT3NW	R:SANGAMON
2616	" "	1	L3	1838-09-20	FD	LOT3NE	R:SANGAMON
2615	" "	1	L2	1838-09-20	FD	LOT2NE	R:SANGAMON
2615	" "	1	L2	1838-09-20	FD	LOT2NW	R:SANGAMON
2614	" "	1	L1	1838-09-20	FD	LOT1NW	R:SANGAMON
2614	" "	1	L1	1838-09-20	FD	LOT1NE	R:SANGAMON
2502	EDWARDS, Henry	28	E½NW	1826-06-16	FD	E2NW	R:MORGAN
2503	" "	28	E½SW	1828-09-05	FD	E2SW	R:MORGAN
2504	" "	28	W½SW	1831-09-15	FD	W2SW	R:MORGAN
2509	EDWARDS, Isaac	17	E½NE	1827-11-24	FD	E2NE	R:MORGAN
2642	EDWARDS, Peter	28	W½NE	1828-03-28	FD	W2NE	R:MORGAN
2641	" "	28	E½NE	1828-12-15	FD	E2NE	R:MORGAN
2640	" "	21	SWSE	1832-07-20	FD	SWSE	R:MORGAN
2624	FERIS, Moses A	15		1832-10-15	FD	W2SWSK	R:KENTUCKY
2625	" "	16		1832-10-15	FD	E2ESK	R:KENTUCKY
2626	" "	5		1832-10-15	FD	W2SWSK	R:KENTUCKY
2627	" "	6		1832-10-15	FD	E2SEDK	R:KENTUCKY
2593	" "	15		1832-10-15	FD	W2SWSK	R:KENTUCKY
2592	" "	15		1832-10-15	FD	W2SWSK	R:KENTUCKY
2707	FILSON, William	33	NENE	1833-05-17	FD	NENE	R:MORGAN
2628	FINDLEY, Moses	19	E½SE	1825-07-13	FD	E2SE	R:MORGAN
2469	FITZHUGH, Cole	33	NENW	1833-02-18	FD	NENW	R:MORGAN
2709	FRASER, William J	20	NE	1831-10-06	FD	NELS	R:MORGAN
2708	" "	17	SE	1831-10-06	FD	SELS	R:MORGAN
2710	" "	21	W½NW	1832-03-02	FD	W2NW	R:MORGAN
2505	GODDARD, Henry W	1	S½NW	1837-05-08	FD	S2NW	R:MORGAN
2685	GREEN, Stephen	31	W½SW	1829-10-21	FD	W2SW	R:MORGAN G:66
2685	GREEN, William	31	W½SW	1829-10-21	FD	W2SW	R:MORGAN G:66
2549	GREGORY, John	25	W½SW	1836-01-08	FD	W2SW	R:MORGAN
2553	" "	35	E½NE	1836-01-08	FD	E2NE	R:MORGAN

ID	Individual in Patent	Sec.	Sec. Part	Purchase Date	Sale Type	IL Aliquot Part	For More Info . . .
2552	GREGORY, John (Cont'd)	26	W½NE	1836-01-08	FD	W2NE	R:MORGAN
2551	" "	26	SE	1836-01-08	FD	SE	R:MORGAN
2550	" "	26	N½SW	1836-01-08	FD	N2SW	R:MORGAN
2554	" "	36	W½NW	1836-01-08	FD	W2NW	R:MORGAN
2558	HARDIN, John J	6	W½	1833-04-27	FD	W2SEC	R:MORGAN
2559	" "	6	W½SE	1833-04-27	FD	W2SE	R:MORGAN
2562	" "	7	E½NW	1833-05-21	FD	E2NW	R:MORGAN
2560	" "	6	L1	1833-08-19	FD	LOT1NE	R:MORGAN
2561	" "	6	L2	1833-09-09	FD	LOT2NE	R:MORGAN
2555	" "	3	L2	1833-10-16	FD	LOT2NW	R:MORGAN
2556	" "	3	L2	1833-10-16	FD	LOT2NW	R:MORGAN
2557	" "	4	L2	1833-10-16	FD	LOT2NE	R:MORGAN
2557	" "	4	L2	1833-10-16	FD	LOT2NW	R:MORGAN
2556	" "	3	L2	1835-08-26	FD	LOT2NEFR	R:MORGAN
2555	" "	3	L2	1835-08-26	FD	LOT2NEFR	R:MORGAN
2475	HENDERSON, David P	23	S½SW	1835-07-07	FD	S2SW	R:MORGAN
2529	HENDERSON, James	16	L4	1836-06-04	SC	LOT4	
2600	HEWETT, Josephus	34		1831-07-20	FD	E2SESK	R:MORGAN
2604	" "	35		1831-07-20	FD	W2SWSK	R:MORGAN
2602	" "	34	E½SW	1831-08-03	FD	E2SW	R:MORGAN
2601	" "	34	E½NW	1833-06-06	FD	E2NW	R:MORGAN
2603	" "	34	W½NE	1833-06-06	FD	W2NE	R:MORGAN
2605	HEWITT, Josephus	34	NENE	1833-11-18	FD	NENE	R:MORGAN
2606	" "	35	E½NW	1833-11-18	FD	E2NW	R:MORGAN
2594	HICKENBOTTOM, Joseph	26	S½SW	1835-03-18	FD	S2SW	R:MORGAN
2564	HILL, John M	20	E½NW	1831-04-12	FD	E2NW	R:MORGAN
2511	HODGEN, Jacob	23	W½NE	1833-06-11	FD	W2NE	R:MORGAN
2532	HOLMES, James T	35	E½SW	1835-06-18	FD	E2SW	R:KENTUCKY
2533	" "	35	W½NE	1835-06-18	FD	W2NE	R:KENTUCKY
2514	HUFFAKER, Jacob	19	NW	1824-10-14	FD	NWFR	R:KENTUCKY
2513	" "	18	SW	1824-10-14	FD	SWFR	R:KENTUCKY
2512	" "	16	L6	1836-06-04	SC	LOT6	
2516	HUFFAKER, Jacob Jr	8	SE	1825-10-15	FD	SE	R:MORGAN
2515	" "	17	W½NE	1831-06-06	FD	W2NE	R:MORGAN
2518	HUFFAKER, Jacob Sen	18	W½SE	1825-10-15	FD	W2SE	R:MORGAN
2517	" "	18	E½SE	1829-12-26	FD	E2SE	R:MORGAN
2520	" "	7	W½NW	1831-11-28	FD	W2NW	R:MORGAN
2519	" "	7	E½SW	1833-05-22	FD	E2SW	R:MORGAN
2621	HUFFAKER, Michael	19	NE	1824-03-06	FD	NE	R:MORGAN
2622	" "	20	W½NW	1829-11-18	FD	W2NW	R:MORGAN
2620	" "	17	W½SW	1831-06-08	FD	W2SW	R:MORGAN
2476	JOHNSON, Dosha	31	E½SE	1828-08-18	FD	E2SE	R:MORGAN
2608	JONES, Joshua	14	W½NE	1831-03-24	FD	W2NE	R:MORGAN
2607	" "	14	SW	1831-05-09	FD	SWLS	R:MORGAN
2609	" "	14	W½SE	1831-06-14	FD	W2SE	R:MORGAN
2611	" "	23	NW	1831-06-14	FD	NW	R:MORGAN
2610	" "	23	N½SW	1833-06-18	FD	N2SW	R:MORGAN
2686	JONES, Stephen	11	E½SE	1823-11-12	FD	E2SE	R:MORGAN
2687	" "	12	W½SW	1823-12-31	FD	W2SW	R:MORGAN
2688	" "	28	W½SE	1825-09-05	FD	W2SE	R:MORGAN
2658	" "	28	W½SE	1825-09-05	FD	W2SE	R:MORGAN
2634	LATIMER, Nathaniel	11	W½NW	1825-01-22	FD	W2NW	R:MORGAN
2649	LINDSEY, William	22	W½SW	1831-06-14	FD	W2SW	R:MORGAN G:43
2647	LINDSEY, William K	12	E½NE	1831-04-30	FD	E2NE	R:MORGAN G:44
2648	" "	27	W½NW	1831-06-02	FD	W2NW	R:MORGAN G:44
2668	LOGAN, Robert	2	NW	1836-10-14	FD	NW	R:KENTUCKY
2530	MAGILL, James	33	E½SE	1829-02-24	FD	E2SE	R:MORGAN
2531	" "	33	E½SW	1829-05-16	FD	E2SW	R:MORGAN
2672	MAGILL, Samuel	32	E½NW	1830-11-04	FD	E2NW	R:MORGAN
2565	MAJORS, John	18	NW	1825-11-01	FD	NWFR	R:MORGAN
2638	MARCH, Oliver	25	W½NW	1835-12-08	FD	W2NW	R:MORGAN
2639	" "	26	E½NE	1835-12-08	FD	E2NE	R:MORGAN
2656	MATHEWS, Richard	3	SW	1823-11-12	FD	SW	R:MORGAN
2655	" "	10	NE	1823-11-12	FD	NE	R:MORGAN
2654	" "	10	E½NW	1823-11-12	FD	E2NW	R:MORGAN
2657	" "	3	W½SE	1830-09-14	FD	W2SE	R:MORGAN
2678	MATHEWS, Samuel T	4	SE	1823-11-12	FD	SE	R:MORGAN
2680	" "	9	E½NE	1823-11-12	FD	E2NE	R:MORGAN
2577	" "	9	W½NE	1825-12-27	FD	W2NE	R:MORGAN G:97
2679	" "	4	L1	1835-08-12	FD	LOT1NE	R:MORGAN
2677	" "	2	NWSW	1835-08-12	FD	NWSW	R:MORGAN
2473	MATTHEWS, Cyrus	3	E½SE	1833-04-23	FD	E2SE	R:MORGAN
2566	" "	3	L1	1835-11-02	FD	LOT1NE	R:MORGAN

ID	Individual in Patent	Sec.	Sec. Part	Purchase Date	Sale Type	IL Aliquot Part	For More Info . . .
2474	MATTHEWS, Cyrus (Cont'd)	3	L1	1835-11-02	FD	LOT1NE	R:MORGAN
2470	" "	16	L14	1836-06-04	SC	LOT14	
2472	" "	16	L9	1836-06-04	SC	LOT9	
2471	" "	16	L17	1836-06-04	SC	LOT17	
2474	MATTHEWS, John	3	L1	1835-11-02	FD	LOT1NW	R:MORGAN G:99
2566	" "	3	L1	1835-11-02	FD	LOT1NW	R:MORGAN G:99
2566	MATTHEWS, Richard	3	L1	1835-11-02	FD	LOT1NW	R:MORGAN G:99
2474	" "	3	L1	1835-11-02	FD	LOT1NW	R:MORGAN G:99
2682	MATTHEWS, Samuel T	16	L5	1836-06-04	SC	LOT5	
2681	" "	16	L10	1836-06-04	SC	LOT10	
2711	MCMURRAY, William	5	W½SE	1830-10-26	FD	W2SE	R:MORGAN
2715	MCMURRY, William	8	W½NE	1824-07-10	FD	W2NE	R:MORGAN
2712	" "	5	E½SW	1831-06-21	FD	E2SW	R:MORGAN
2714	" "	5	L1	1833-06-15	FD	LOT1NE	R:MORGAN
2713	" "	5	NENE	1834-02-07	FD	NENE	R:MORGAN
2477	MOORE, Edmund	28	E½SE	1828-09-05	FD	E2SE	R:MORGAN
2479	" "	29	SE	1831-11-17	FD	SE	R:MORGAN
2478	" "	29	E½SW	1831-11-17	FD	E2SWLS	R:MORGAN
2595	MORTON, Joseph	30	E½NE	1830-02-02	FD	E2NE	R:MORGAN
2651	MURPHY, Renex	14	E½NE	1825-06-14	FD	E2NE	R:MORGAN
2691	ONEAL, Thomas	30	W½SE	1829-01-22	FD	W2SE	R:MORGAN
2690	" "	30	E½SE	1830-10-11	FD	E2SE	R:MORGAN
2501	OSBORNE, Harrison	14	E½SE	1831-05-09	FD	E2SE	R:MORGAN
2688	PEMBERTON, Richard	28	W½SE	1827-11-19	FD	W2SE	R:MORGAN
2658	" "	28	W½SE	1827-11-19	FD	W2SE	R:MORGAN
2659	" "	32	E½SE	1829-10-20	FD	E2SE	R:MORGAN
2660	" "	32	E½SW	1829-10-20	FD	E2SW	R:MORGAN
2717	PEMBERTON, William	33	W½SW	1830-10-08	FD	W2SW	R:MORGAN
2716	" "	33	W½NW	1832-01-10	FD	W2NW	R:MORGAN
2567	PORTER, John	13	W½NW	1825-01-22	FD	W2NW	R:MORGAN
2508	REEVE, Huran	18	W½NE	1825-11-14	FD	W2NE	R:MORGAN
2563	RICE, John J	16	L1	1836-06-04	SC	LOT1	
2661	RIGGIN, Right	27	W½SW	1827-12-04	FD	W2SW	R:MORGAN
2636	ROACH, Nedom	4	W½SW	1831-05-13	FD	W2SW	R:MORGAN G:9
2635	" "	2	S½SW	1833-07-11	FD	S2SW	R:MORGAN
2637	ROACH, Nedun	11	E½NW	1831-05-05	FD	E2NW	R:MORGAN
2451	ROBERTSON, Alexander	11	E½NE	1823-12-31	FD	E2NE	R:MORGAN
2453	" "	2	SESE	1833-03-16	FD	SESE	R:MORGAN
2454	" "	2	SWSE	1833-07-18	FD	SWSE	R:MORGAN
2452	" "	2	N½SE	1833-11-12	FD	N2SE	R:MORGAN
2455	ROBISON, Alexander	11	W½NE	1831-05-05	FD	W2NE	R:MORGAN
2570	ROGERS, John	36	W½SE	1836-04-25	FD	W2SE	R:KENTUCKY
2568	" "	35	W½SE	1836-04-25	FD	W2SE	R:KENTUCKY
2569	" "	36	E½SE	1836-04-29	FD	E2SE	R:KENTUCKY
2572	ROGES, John	35	E½SE	1836-04-22	FD	E2SE	R:MORGAN
2718	" "	30	SW	1836-04-22	FD	SW	R:MORGAN
2571	" "	30	SW	1836-04-22	FD	SW	R:MORGAN
2623	RUBART, Milton B	11	W½SW	1826-01-16	FD	W2SW	R:MORGAN
2673	RUBART, Samuel	10	E½SE	1824-08-19	FD	E2SE	R:KENTUCKY
2574	RUSK, John	8	NW	1823-11-12	FD	NW	R:MORGAN
2573	" "	7	E½NE	1831-06-21	FD	E2NE	R:MORGAN
2650	RUTHERFORD, Prudence	12	NW	1823-11-18	FD	NW	R:MORGAN S:F
2575	RUYLE, John	31	E½SW	1829-02-04	FD	E2SW	R:MORGAN
2576	" "	32	W½NW	1829-07-07	FD	W2NW	R:MORGAN
2689	" "	32	W½NW	1829-07-07	FD	W2NW	R:MORGAN
2577	SCOTT, John	9	W½NE	1825-12-27	FD	W2NE	R:MORGAN G:97
2676	SCOTT, Samuel	9	W½SW	1823-11-12	FD	W2SW	R:MORGAN
2675	" "	8	SW	1823-11-12	FD	SW	R:MORGAN
2674	" "	31	W½NE	1825-03-21	FD	W2NE	R:MORGAN
2683	SCOTT, Solomon	17	E½NW	1831-06-10	FD	E2NW	R:MORGAN
2719	SCOTT, William	31	NW	1823-11-12	FD	NWFR	R:MORGAN
2718	" "	30	SW	1827-06-09	FD	SWFR	R:MORGAN
2571	" "	30	SW	1827-06-09	FD	SWFR	R:MORGAN
2461	SHIBE, Casper	20	W½SW	1823-11-12	FD	W2SW	R:MORGAN
2460	" "	20	E½SW	1825-08-04	FD	E2SW	R:MORGAN
2578	SHUFF, John	16	L15	1836-06-04	SC	LOT15	
2579	" "	16	L16	1836-06-04	SC	LOT16	
2580	SLATTEN, John	15	E½NW	1831-06-03	FD	E2NW	R:MORGAN
2596	SLATTER, Joseph	15	W½NE	1831-05-04	FD	W2NE	R:MORGAN
2459	SLATTIN, Benjamin	15	W½NW	1829-10-16	FD	W2NW	R:MORGAN
2597	SLATTIN, Joseph	10	SW	1823-11-12	FD	SW	R:MORGAN
2598	" "	10	W½SE	1823-11-12	FD	W2SE	R:MORGAN
2599	" "	9	E½SE	1823-11-12	FD	E2SE	R:MORGAN

ID	Individual in Patent	Sec.	Sec. Part	Purchase Date	Sale Type	IL Aliquot Part	For More Info . . .
2466	SMEDLEY, Christopher	29	W½NW	1830-10-23	FD	W2NW	R:MORGAN
2465	" "	29	E½NE	1830-12-03	FD	E2NE	R:MORGAN
2692	SMEDLEY, Thomas	29	W½NE	1831-02-02	FD	W2NE	R:MORGAN
2507	SMITH, Hugh	11	E½SW	1828-11-05	FD	E2SW	R:MORGAN
2463	SPOTSWOOD, Charles F	24	NWNE	1835-07-07	FD	NWNE	R:MORGAN
2490	SPOTSWOOD, George R	24	E½NW	1835-07-06	FD	E2NW	R:MORGAN
2496	SPOTSWOOD, George W	25	E½SW	1835-01-02	FD	E2SWLS	R:MORGAN
2493	" "	24	E½SW	1835-01-02	FD	E2SWLS	R:MORGAN
2500	" "	36	NE	1835-01-02	FD	NELS	R:MORGAN
2498	" "	25	SE	1835-01-02	FD	SELS	R:MORGAN
2497	" "	25	NE	1835-01-02	FD	NELS	R:MORGAN
2494	" "	24	SE	1835-01-02	FD	SELS	R:MORGAN
2495	" "	25	E½NW	1835-01-02	FD	E2NWLS	R:MORGAN
2499	" "	36	E½NW	1835-01-04	FD	E2NWLS	R:MORGAN
2462	SPOTWOOD, Charles F M	24	NENE	1835-07-18	FD	NENE	R:MORGAN
2491	SPOTWOOD, George R	20	SEN½	1835-08-13	FD	S2NE	R:MORGAN
2480	STEPHENSON, Elliott	21	NWSE	1835-07-27	FD	NWSE	R:MORGAN S:F
2720	STEPHENSON, William	20	W½SE	1829-11-03	FD	W2SE	R:MORGAN
2703	STEPHENSON, William C	20	E½SE	1831-05-03	FD	E2SE	R:MORGAN
2704	" "	27	E½SW	1831-08-23	FD	E2SW	R:MORGAN
2702	" "	17	E½SW	1831-10-17	FD	E2SW	R:MORGAN
2482	THORNTON, Fitzhugh	13	E½NE	1831-06-06	FD	E2NELS	R:MORGAN
2483	" "	13	SW	1831-06-06	FD	SWLS	R:MORGAN
2484	" "	13	W½SE	1831-06-06	FD	W2SELS	R:MORGAN
2485	THORNTON, Francis	23	E½NE	1831-05-09	FD	E2NE	R:MORGAN
2487	" "	24	W½NW	1831-05-09	FD	W2NWLS	R:MORGAN
2486	" "	24	NWSW	1833-06-14	FD	NWSW	R:MORGAN
2534	THORNTON, James T	7	W½NE	1831-06-07	FD	W2NE	R:MORGAN
2535	" "	7	W½SE	1831-06-07	FD	W2SE	R:MORGAN
2721	THORNTON, William T	2	L1	1837-04-26	FD	LOTINE	R:MORGAN
2722	" "	2	L2	1837-05-01	FD	LOT2NE	R:MORGAN
2537	TODD, James	23	W½SE	1831-06-02	FD	W2SE	R:MORGAN
2536	" "	23	E½SE	1831-06-06	FD	E2SE	R:MORGAN
2588	TURNER, Jonathon	4	SWNW	1833-05-20	FD	SWNW	R:MORGAN
2643	VANNEST, Peter	5	E½SE	1824-12-01	FD	E2SE	R:MORGAN
2644	" "	8	E½NE	1824-12-01	FD	E2NE	R:MORGAN
2645	" "	9	W½NW	1825-11-03	FD	W2NW	R:MORGAN G:10
2539	VANWINKLE, Jason	33	W½NE	1831-11-07	FD	W2NE	R:MORGAN
2587	VANWINKLE, John	34	W½SE	1831-06-11	FD	W2SE	R:MORGAN
2586	" "	33	SENW	1833-09-30	FD	SENW	R:MORGAN
2632	WARE, Nathaniel A	34	W½SW	1833-06-06	FD	W2SW	R:ST. LOUIS
2464	WOODWARD, Charles	26	NW	1835-12-09	FD	NW	R:OHIO
2481	WORTH, Evan B	2	NESW	1836-04-25	FD	NESW	R:MORGAN
2538	YOUNG, James	13	E½NW	1829-12-14	FD	E2NW	R:MORGAN

Patent Map

T15-N R9-W
3rd PM Meridian

Map Group 10

Township Statistics

Parcels Mapped	:	272
Number of Patents	:	1
Number of Individuals	:	138
Patentees Identified	:	139
Number of Surnames	:	99
Multi-Patentee Parcels	:	10
Oldest Patent Date	:	11/12/1823
Most Recent Patent	:	9/20/1838
Block/Lot Parcels	:	33
Cities and Towns	:	2
Cemeteries	:	1

Section 6
HARDIN John J 1833
HARDIN John J 1833
FERIS Moses A 1832
Lots-Sec. 6
L1 HARDIN, John J 1833
L2 HARDIN, John J 1833

Section 5
DODSWORTH Richard 1834
DODSWORTH Richard 1834
FERIS Moses A 1832
MCMURRAY William 1831
MCMURRAY William 1830
VANNEST Peter 1824
Lots-Sec. 5
L1 MCMURRY, William 1833

Section 4
DODSWORTH Richard 1834
MCMURRY William 1834
Lots-Sec. 4
L1 MATHEWS, Samuel T 1835
L2 HARDIN, John J 1833
TURNER Jonathon 1833
BERRY Samuel 1834
ROACH [9] Nedom 1831
BERRY Samuel 1831
MATHEWS Samuel T 1823

Section 7
HUFFAKER Jacob Sen 1831
HARDIN John J 1833
THORNTON James T 1831
RUSK John 1831
HUFFAKER Jacob Sen 1833
CLARKE Lancelot 1829
THORNTON James T 1831
ANDERSON John 1823

Section 8
RUSK John 1823
MCMURRY William 1824
VANNEST Peter 1824
SCOTT Samuel 1823
HUFFAKER Jacob Jr 1825

Section 9
VANNEST [10] Peter 1825
BERRY Samuel 1825
SCOTT [97] John 1825
MATHEWS Samuel T 1823
SCOTT Samuel 1823
DUNCAN Joseph 1831
CLARKE Mathew S 1831
ANDERSON James 1825
SLATTIN Joseph 1823

Section 18
MAJORS John 1825
REEVE Huran 1825
ANDERSON John 1823
HUFFAKER Jacob 1824
HUFFAKER Jacob Sen 1825
HUFFAKER Jacob Sen 1829

Section 17
ANDERSON James 1825
SCOTT Solomon 1831
HUFFAKER Jacob Jr 1831
EDWARDS Isaac 1827
HUFFAKER Michael 1831
STEPHENSON William C 1831
FRASER William J 1831

Section 16
Lots-Sec. 16
L1 RICE, John J 1836
L2 CASSEL, Benjamin 1836
L3 BROCKENBROUGH, Austin 1836
L4 HENDERSON, James 1836
L5 MATTHEWS, Samuel T 1836
L6 HUFFAKER, Jacob 1836
L7 CURTS, George 1836
L8 CURTS, George 1836
L9 MATTHEWS, Cyrus 1836
L10 MATTHEWS, Samuel T 1836
L11 CASSEL, John T 1836
L12 CASSEL, John T 1836
L13 CASSEL, John T 1836
L14 MATTHEWS, Cyrus 1836
L15 SHUFF, John 1836
L16 SHUFF, John 1836
L17 MATTHEWS, Cyrus 1836
L18 CASSEL, John T 1836
L19 CASSEL, John T 1836
FERIS Moses A 1832

Section 19
HUFFAKER Jacob 1824
HUFFAKER Michael 1824
BLANEY John 1825
ANDERSON John 1824
FINDLEY Moses 1825

Section 20
HUFFAKER Michael 1829
HILL John M 1831
SHIBE Casper 1823
SHIBE Casper 1825
STEPHENSON William 1829
FRASER William J 1831
SPOTWOOD George R 1835
STEPHENSON William C 1831

Section 21
FRASER William J 1832
BROWN William 1833
BROWN William 1833
DODD James 1829
DOOD James 1831
STEPHENSON Elliott 1835
EDWARDS Peter 1832
BROWN William 1833

Section 30
BLANEY John 1825
CONNAWAY Hugh 1825
MORTON Joseph 1830
ROGES John 1836
SCOTT William 1827
ONEAL Thomas 1829
ONEAL Thomas 1830

Section 29
SMEDLEY Christopher 1830
COFFMAN Philip 1831
SMEDLEY Thomas 1831
SMEDLEY Christopher 1830
COKER Claibourne 1830
MOORE Edmund 1831
MOORE Edmund 1831

Section 28
DODD James 1828
EDWARDS Henry 1826
EDWARDS Peter 1828
EDWARDS Peter 1828
EDWARDS Henry 1831
EDWARDS Henry 1828
JONES Stephen 1825
PEMBERTON Richard 1827
MOORE Edmund 1828

Section 31
SCOTT William 1823
SCOTT Samuel 1825
BLANEY John 1825
GREEN [66] Stephen 1829
RUYLE John 1829
BLANEY John 1825
JOHNSON Dosha 1828

Section 32
BALLARD Theophilas 1825
RUYLE John 1829
MAGILL Samuel 1830
BUCHANAN John 1831
BRUTON William 1832
COKER Claibourn 1826
PEMBERTON Richard 1829
BUCHANAN John 1829
PEMBERTON Richard 1829

Section 33
PEMBERTON William 1832
FITZHUGH Cole 1833
VANWINKLE Jason 1831
FILSON William 1833
VANWINKLE John 1833
CROSS William 1833
PEMBERTON William 1830
MAGILL James 1830
CYRUS Matthew 1829
MAGILL James 1829

Lots-Sec. 3
L1 MATTHEWS, John [99]1835
L1 MATTHEWS, Cyrus 1835
L2 HARDIN, John J 1835
L2 HARDIN, John J 1833

3

Lots-Sec. 2
L1 THORNTON, William T 1837
L2 THORNTON, William T 1837

LOGAN
Robert
1836

2

GODDARD
Henry W
1837

1

Helpful Hints

1. This Map's INDEX can be found on the preceding pages.

2. Refer to Map "C" to see where this Township lies within Morgan County, Illinois.

3. Numbers within square brackets [ ] denote a multi-patentee land parcel (multi-owner). Refer to Appendix "C" for a full list of members in this group.

4. Areas that look to be crowded with Patentees usually indicate multiple sales of the same parcel (re-issues), cancellations or voided transactions (that we map, anyway) or overlapping parcels. We opt to show even these ambiguous parcels, which oftentimes lead to research avenues not yet taken.

MATHEWS
Richard
1823

MATHEWS
Richard
1830

MATTHEWS
Cyrus
1833

MATHEWS
Samuel T
1835

WORTH
Evan B
1836

ROBERTSON
Alexander
1833

BROWN
William
1833

ROACH
Nedom
1833

ROBERTSON
Alexander
1833

ROBERTSON
Alexander
1833

Lots-Sec. 1
L1 EASTHAM, Marvillous 1838
L2 EASTHAM, Marvillous 1838
L3 EASTHAM, Marvillous 1838

COWNOVER
Robert
1824

MATHEWS
Richard
1823

MATHEWS
Richard
1823

LATIMER
Nathaniel
1825

ROACH
Nedun
1831

ROBISON
Alexander
1831

ROBERTSON
Alexander
1823

RUTHERFORD
Prudence
1823

CAVE
James
1830

COFFMAN [44]
Philip
1831

12

SLATTIN
Joseph
1823

SLATTIN
Joseph
1823

RUBART
Samuel
1824

RUBART
Milton B
1826

SMITH
Hugh
1828

11

JONES
Stephen
1823

JONES
Stephen
1823

BUTLER
Nathan
1824

BUTLER
Nathan
1823

CAVE
James
1828

10

SLATTIN
Benjamin
1829

SLATTEN
John
1831

SLATTER
Joseph
1831

CASSELL
Robert
1831

CASSELL
Robert
1831

CASTLE
Robert
1830

JONES
Joshua
1831

MURPHY
Renex
1825

PORTER
John
1825

YOUNG
James
1829

BUTLER
Nathan
1831

THORNTON
Fitzhugh
1831

15

FERIS
Moses A
1832

CLARKE
Mathew S
1831

DUNCAN [36]
Joseph
1831

DUNCAN [37]
Joseph
1831

14

JONES
Joshua
1831

JONES
Joshua
1831

OSBORNE
Harrison
1831

THORNTON
Fitzhugh
1831

THORNTON
Fitzhugh
1831

BROWN
William
1833

13

DUNCAN
Joseph
1832

CASSELL
Robert
1831

CASSELL
Robert
1831

DUNCAN
Joseph
1832

JONES
Joshua
1831

23

HODGEN
Jacob
1833

THORNTON
Francis
1831

THORNTON
Francis
1831

SPOTSWOOD
George R
1835

SPOTSWOOD
Charles F
1835

SPOTWOOD
Charles F M
1835

24

COFFMAN [43]
Philip
1831

BROWN
William
1833

22

BROWN
William
1833

JONES
Joshua
1833

HENDERSON
David P
1835

TODD
James
1831

TODD
James
1831

THORNTON
Francis
1833

DUNLAP
James
1836

SPOTSWOOD
George W
1835

SPOTSWOOD
George W
1835

COFFMAN [44]
Philip
1831

DRURY
Lawson
1831

BROWN
William
1833

27

WOODWARD
Charles
1835

GREGORY
John
1836

MARCH
Oliver
1835

MARCH
Oliver
1835

SPOTSWOOD
George W
1835

SPOTSWOOD
George W
1835

RIGGIN
Right
1827

STEPHENSON
William C
1831

DRURY
George W
1833

COLE
Stephen
1833

CROSS
Israel
1833

GREGORY
John
1836

HICKENBOTTOM
Joseph
1835

26

GREGORY
John
1836

GREGORY
John
1836

SPOTSWOOD
George W
1835

25

SPOTSWOOD
George W
1835

CROSS
William
1831

HEWETT
Josephus
1833

HEWETT
Josephus
1833

HEWITT
Josephus
1833

COX
Nathaniel
1833

COX
Ancil
1833

HEWITT
Josephus
1833

HOLMES
James T
1835

GREGORY
John
1836

GREGORY
John
1836

SPOTSWOOD
George W
1835

SPOTSWOOD
George W
1835

34

35

WARE
Nathaniel A
1833

HEWETT
Josephus
1831

VANWINKLE
John
1831

HEWITT
Josephus
1831

HEWETT
Josephus
1831

HOLMES
James T
1835

ROGERS
John
1836

ROGES
John
1836

36

ROGERS
John
1836

ROGERS
John
1836

Copyright 2008 Boyd IT, Inc. All Rights Reserved

Legend

— Patent Boundary

— Section Boundary

No Patents Found
(or Outside County)

1., 2., 3., ... Lot Numbers
(when beside a name)

[ ] Group Number
(see Appendix "C")

Scale: Section = 1 mile X 1 mile
(generally, with some exceptions)

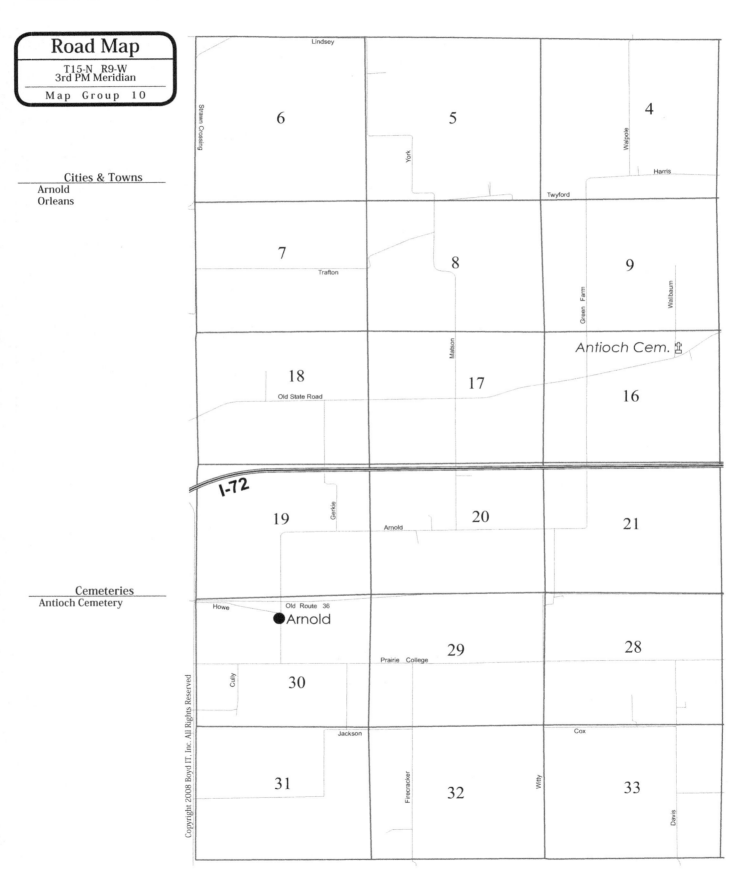

Road Map

T15-N R9-W
3rd PM Meridian

Map Group 10

Cities & Towns
Arnold
Orleans

Cemeteries
Antioch Cemetery

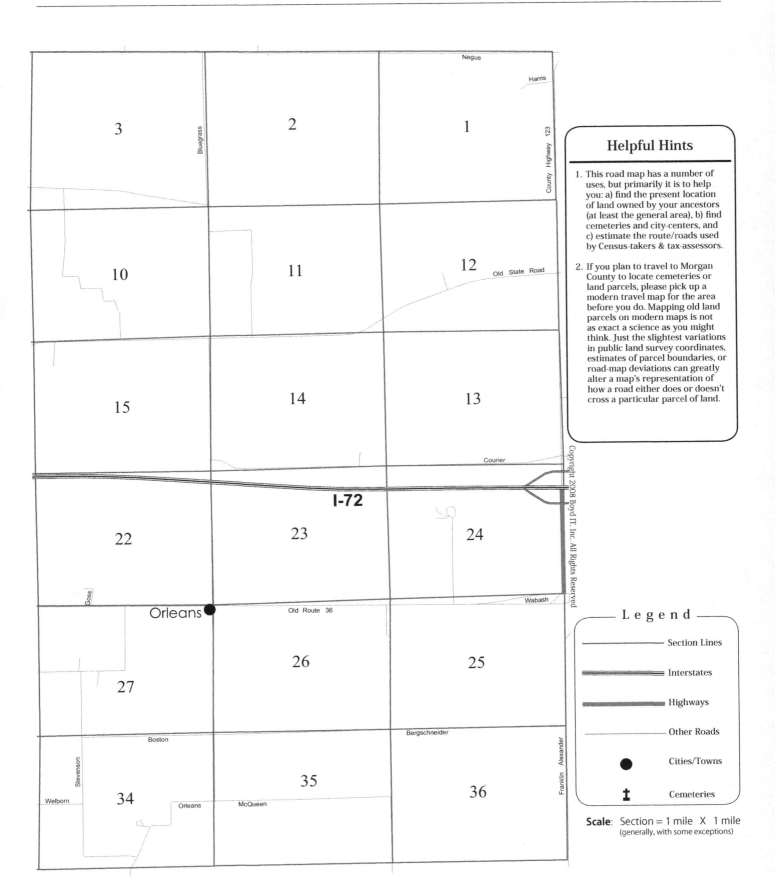

Helpful Hints

1. This road map has a number of uses, but primarily it is to help you: a) find the present location of land owned by your ancestors (at least the general area), b) find cemeteries and city-centers, and c) estimate the route/roads used by Census-takers & tax-assessors.

2. If you plan to travel to Morgan County to locate cemeteries or land parcels, please pick up a modern travel map for the area before you do. Mapping old land parcels on modern maps is not as exact a science as you might think. Just the slightest variations in public land survey coordinates, estimates of parcel boundaries, or road-map deviations can greatly alter a map's representation of how a road either does or doesn't cross a particular parcel of land.

Legend

—————	Section Lines
══════	Interstates
▬▬▬▬▬	Highways
—————	Other Roads
●	Cities/Towns
⛭	Cemeteries

Scale: Section = 1 mile X 1 mile
(generally, with some exceptions)

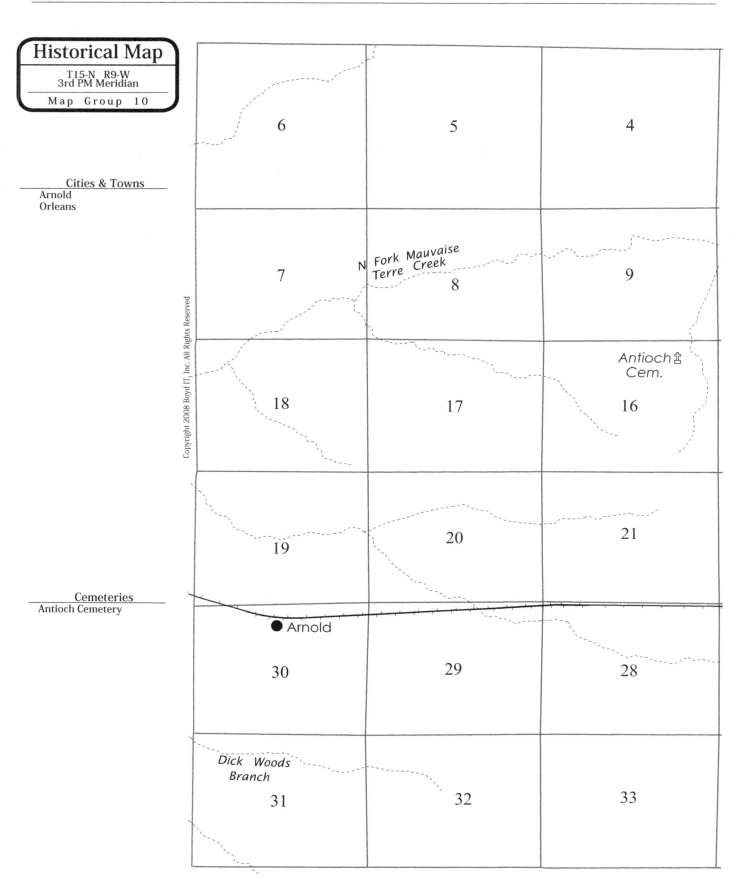

Historical Map

T15-N R9-W
3rd PM Meridian

Map Group 10

Cities & Towns
Arnold
Orleans

Cemeteries
Antioch Cemetery

N Fork Mauvaise Terre Creek

Antioch Cem.

Arnold

Dick Woods Branch

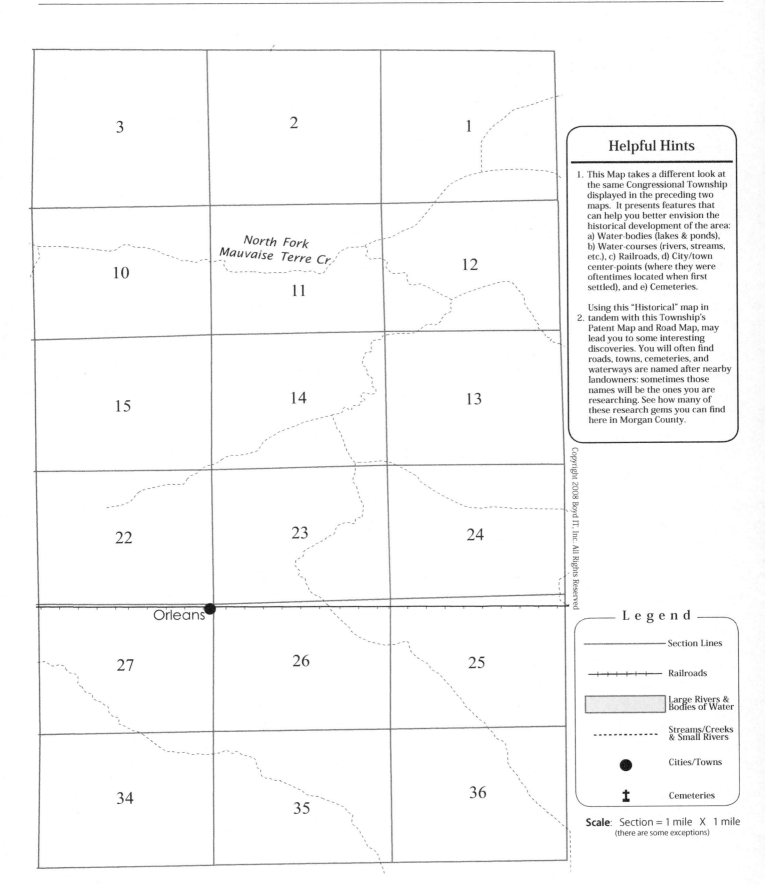

Helpful Hints

1. This Map takes a different look at the same Congressional Township displayed in the preceding two maps. It presents features that can help you better envision the historical development of the area: a) Water-bodies (lakes & ponds), b) Water-courses (rivers, streams, etc.), c) Railroads, d) City/town center-points (where they were oftentimes located when first settled), and e) Cemeteries.

2. Using this "Historical" map in tandem with this Township's Patent Map and Road Map, may lead you to some interesting discoveries. You will often find roads, towns, cemeteries, and waterways are named after nearby landowners: sometimes those names will be the ones you are researching. See how many of these research gems you can find here in Morgan County.

Legend

————————	Section Lines
+++++++++	Railroads
▭	Large Rivers & Bodies of Water
- - - - - - -	Streams/Creeks & Small Rivers
●	Cities/Towns
✝	Cemeteries

Scale: Section = 1 mile X 1 mile
(there are some exceptions)

Map Group 11: Index to Land Patents

Township 15-North Range 8-West (3rd PM)

After you locate an individual in this Index, take note of the Section and Section Part then proceed to the Land Patent map on the pages immediately following. You should have no difficulty locating the corresponding parcel of land.

The "For More Info" Column will lead you to more information about the underlying Patents. See the *Legend* at right, and the "How to Use this Book" chapter, for more information.

```
                    LEGEND
          "For More Info . . . " column
G = Group (Multi-Patentee Patent, see Appendix "C")
R = Residence
S = Social Status


See Appendix A for list of abbreviations used by the
Illinois State Archives in describing the place and
nature of these land patents.

Note: if the Abbreviations contain "L", "BL", "LOT",
or "BLOCK", the exact whereabouts of the parcel within
the section is not known.
```

ID	Individual in Patent	Sec.	Sec. Part	Purchase Date	Sale Type	IL Aliquot Part	For More Info . . .
2753	ADAMS, John	33	NE	1838-11-10	FD	NE	R:MORGAN
2772	ALEXANDER, John T	32	NW	1849-09-12	FD	NW	
2768	" "	31	NE	1849-09-12	FD	NE	
2769	" "	31	NW	1849-09-12	FD	NWFR	
2771	" "	31	SW	1849-09-12	FD	SWFR	
2773	" "	32	SW	1849-09-12	FD	SW	
2770	" "	31	SE	1849-09-12	FD	SE	
2725	ASHER, Bartlet	7	SENE	1832-07-11	FD	SENELS	R:MORGAN
2726	" "	7	SENW	1832-07-11	FD	SENWLS	R:MORGAN
2728	BARRET, James A	34	SEN½	1848-12-30	FD	S2NE	
2784	BARRETT, Richard F	28	E½SE	1837-07-29	FD	E2SE	R:SANGAMON
2783	" "	27	SW	1837-07-29	FD	SW	R:SANGAMON
2782	" "	27	NE	1837-07-29	FD	NE	R:SANGAMON
2746	BROWN, James N	16	L16	1848-10-30	SC	LOT16PTSWSE	G:14
2747	" "	16	L17	1848-10-30	SC	LOT17N2SESE	G:14
2790	" "	16	L10	1848-10-30	SC	L10S2NESE	
2751	" "	16	L9	1848-10-30	SC	L9N2NESE	G:14
2750	" "	16	L8	1848-10-30	SC	LOT8SENE	G:14
2748	" "	16	L18	1848-10-30	SC	LOT18S2SESE	G:14
2735	" "	16	L10	1848-10-30	SC	L10S2NESE	
2749	" "	16	L7	1848-10-30	SC	LOT7PTSWNE	G:14
2745	" "	16	L11	1848-10-30	SC	LOT11PTNWSE	G:14
2738	" "	16	L13	1848-12-14	SC	L13NWSW	
2794	" "	16	L14	1848-12-14	SC	L14SWSW	
2792	" "	16	L12	1848-12-14	SC	L12NESW	
2741	" "	16	L2	1848-12-14	SC	L2PTNWNE	
2736	" "	16	L1	1848-12-14	SC	L1NENE	
2791	" "	16	L1	1848-12-14	SC	L1NENE	
2796	" "	16	L2	1848-12-14	SC	L2PTNWNE	
2793	" "	16	L13	1848-12-14	SC	L13NWSW	
2737	" "	16	L12	1848-12-14	SC	L12NESW	
2795	" "	16	L15	1848-12-14	SC	L15PTSESW	
2798	" "	16	L5	1848-12-14	SC	L5SWNW	
2799	" "	16	L6	1848-12-14	SC	L6PTSENW	
2739	" "	16	L14	1848-12-14	SC	L14SWSW	
2744	" "	16	L6	1848-12-14	SC	L6PTSENW	
2740	" "	16	L15	1848-12-14	SC	L15PTSESW	
2743	" "	16	L5	1848-12-14	SC	L5SWNW	
2742	" "	16	L3	1848-12-14	SC	L3PTNENW	
2797	" "	16	L3	1848-12-14	SC	L3PTNENW	
2776	BROWN, Loyd W	33	W½NW	1844-08-03	FD	W2NW	R:MORGAN
2777	" "	34	NW	1848-12-12	FD	NW	
2779	" "	34	N½NE	1848-12-12	FD	N2NE	G:15
2775	" "	27	SE	1848-12-12	FD	SE	
2778	" "	34	SW	1849-01-26	FD	SW	R:SANGAMON
2805	BROWN, William	27	SWNW	1833-06-13	FD	SWNW	R:KENTUCKY

ID	Individual in Patent	Sec.	Sec. Part	Purchase Date	Sale Type	IL Aliquot Part	For More Info . . .
2809	BROWN, William (Cont'd)	28	W½SE	1833-06-13	FD	W2SE	R:KENTUCKY
2808	" "	28	W½NE	1833-06-13	FD	W2NE	R:KENTUCKY
2807	" "	28	SENE	1833-06-13	FD	SENE	R:KENTUCKY
2803	" "	21	W½SE	1833-06-13	FD	W2SE	R:KENTUCKY
2802	" "	21	W½NE	1833-06-13	FD	W2NE	R:KENTUCKY
2806	" "	28	E½SW	1833-06-13	FD	E2SW	R:KENTUCKY
2816	" "	8	SW	1833-06-18	FD	SW	R:KENTUCKY
2815	" "	8	E½NW	1833-06-18	FD	E2NW	R:KENTUCKY
2810	" "	33	E½NW	1833-06-18	FD	E2NW	R:KENTUCKY
2812	" "	6	W½SW	1833-06-18	FD	W2SW	R:KENTUCKY
2801	" "	18	W½SW	1833-06-18	FD	W2SW	R:KENTUCKY
2800	" "	18	W½NW	1833-06-18	FD	W2NW	R:KENTUCKY
2814	" "	7	NENW	1834-07-09	FD	NENW	R:MORGAN
2813	" "	7	NENE	1834-07-09	FD	NENE	R:MORGAN
2818	" "	8	W½SE	1835-02-03	FD	W2SE	R:MORGAN
2817	" "	8	W½NE	1835-02-03	FD	W2NE	R:MORGAN
2804	" "	27	E½NW	1836-03-26	FD	E2NW	R:MORGAN
2811	" "	4	NE	1838-01-12	FD	NE	R:MORGAN
2746	" "	16	L16	1848-10-30	SC	LOT16PTSWSE	G:14
2750	" "	16	L8	1848-10-30	SC	LOT8SENE	G:14
2748	" "	16	L18	1848-10-30	SC	LOT18S2SESE	G:14
2745	" "	16	L11	1848-10-30	SC	LOT11PTNWSE	G:14
2749	" "	16	L7	1848-10-30	SC	LOT7PTSWNE	G:14
2735	" "	16	L10	1848-10-30	SC	LOT10S2NESE	
2747	" "	16	L17	1848-10-30	SC	LOT17N2SESE	G:14
2790	" "	16	L10	1848-10-30	SC	LOT10S2NESE	
2751	" "	16	L9	1848-10-30	SC	L9N2NESE	G:14
2779	" "	34	N½NE	1848-12-12	FD	N2NE	G:15
2791	" "	16	L1	1848-12-14	SC	LOT1NENE	
2799	" "	16	L6	1848-12-14	SC	LOT6PTSENW	
2798	" "	16	L5	1848-12-14	SC	LOT5SWNW	
2797	" "	16	L3	1848-12-14	SC	LOT3PTNENW	
2796	" "	16	L2	1848-12-14	SC	LOT2PTNWNE	
2795	" "	16	L15	1848-12-14	SC	LOT15PTSESW	
2794	" "	16	L14	1848-12-14	SC	LOT14SWSW	
2793	" "	16	L13	1848-12-14	SC	LOT13NWSW	
2737	" "	16	L12	1848-12-14	SC	LOT12NESW	
2792	" "	16	L12	1848-12-14	SC	LOT12NESW	
2741	" "	16	L2	1848-12-14	SC	LOT2PTNWNE	
2736	" "	16	L1	1848-12-14	SC	LOT1NENE	
2738	" "	16	L13	1848-12-14	SC	LOT13NWSW	
2744	" "	16	L6	1848-12-14	SC	LOT6PTSENW	
2739	" "	16	L14	1848-12-14	SC	LOT14SWSW	
2740	" "	16	L15	1848-12-14	SC	LOT15PTSESW	
2743	" "	16	L5	1848-12-14	SC	LOT5SWNW	
2742	" "	16	L3	1848-12-14	SC	LOT3PTNENW	
2823	BROWN, William Jr	7	SW	1833-06-18	FD	SW	R:MORGAN
2822	" "	7	NWNE	1833-06-18	FD	NWNE	R:MORGAN
2821	" "	7	E½SE	1833-06-18	FD	E2SE	R:MORGAN
2824	" "	7	SWSE	1833-06-18	FD	SWSE	R:MORGAN
2825	" "	7	W½NW	1833-06-18	FD	W2NW	R:MORGAN
2819	" "	18	E½NW	1833-07-30	FD	E2NW	R:MORGAN
2820	" "	6	E½SW	1833-08-26	FD	E2SW	R:MORGAN
2789	CLARK, William B	32	E½	1838-11-14	FD	E2LS	R:MARYLAND
2774	DUNCAN, Joseph	8	W½NW	1832-08-10	FD	W2NWLS	R:MORGAN
2786	GORHAM, Stephen	29	E½NW	1825-02-03	FD	E2NW	R:MORGAN
2730	GRAY, James	17		1836-03-26	FD	SEC	R:PHILADELPHIA
2731	" "	18	NE	1836-03-26	FD	NE	R:PHILADELPHIA
2732	" "	20		1836-03-26	FD	SEC	R:PHILADELPHIA
2733	" "	21	W½	1836-03-26	FD	W2	R:PHILADELPHIA
2734	" "	9	E½	1836-03-26	FD	E2	R:PHILADELPHIA
2767	GRIGG, John	9	W½	1835-10-31	FD	W2	R:PHILADELPHIA
2755	" "	18	SE	1835-10-31	FD	SE	R:PHILADELPHIA
2762	" "	5		1835-10-31	FD	SEC	R:PHILADELPHIA
2756	" "	19		1835-10-31	FD	SEC	R:PHILADELPHIA
2760	" "	30		1835-10-31	FD	SEC	R:PHILADELPHIA
2761	" "	4	W½	1835-10-31	FD	W2	R:PHILADELPHIA
2754	" "	18	E½SW	1835-10-31	FD	E2SW	R:PHILADELPHIA
2763	" "	6	E½	1835-10-31	FD	E2	R:PHILADELPHIA
2764	" "	6	NW	1835-10-31	FD	NW	R:PHILADELPHIA
2765	" "	8	E½NE	1835-10-31	FD	E2NE	R:PHILADELPHIA
2766	" "	8	E½SE	1835-10-31	FD	E2SE	R:PHILADELPHIA
2759	" "	29		1836-02-09	FD	SEC	R:SANGAMON

ID	Individual in Patent	Sec.	Sec. Part	Purchase Date	Sale Type	IL Aliquot Part	For More Info . . .
2757	GRIGG, John (Cont'd)	28	NW	1836-02-09	FD	NW	R:SANGAMON
2758	" "	28	W½SW	1836-02-09	FD	W2SW	R:SANGAMON
2787	ONEAL, Thomas	27	NWNW	1832-07-02	FD	NWNW	R:SANGAMON
2788	" "	28	NENE	1833-03-28	FD	NENE	R:SANGAMON
2826	RHEA, William	4	SWSW	1833-06-12	FD	SWSW	R:SANGAMON
2752	RUBLE, Jesse	16	L4	1848-10-30	SC	LOT4NWNW	
2729	SMITH, James D	4	SE	1838-01-10	FD	SE	R:SANGAMON
2724	TODD, Augustus	7	SWNE	1832-07-03	FD	SWNE	R:MORGAN
2723	" "	7	NWSE	1832-07-09	FD	NWSE	R:MORGAN
2780	WARE, Nathaniel A	21	E½NE	1833-06-06	FD	E2NE	R:ST. LOUIS
2781	" "	21	E½SE	1833-06-06	FD	E2SE	R:ST. LOUIS
2785	WESTFALL, Samuel	34	SE	1848-01-04	FD	SE	
2727	WOOD, Eli	19	NWNW	1846-08-22	FD	NWNWFR	R:INDIANA

Patent Map

T15-N R8-W
3rd PM Meridian

Map Group 11

Township Statistics

Parcels Mapped	:	104
Number of Patents	:	1
Number of Individuals	:	22
Patentees Identified	:	24
Number of Surnames	:	19
Multi-Patentee Parcels	:	8
Oldest Patent Date	:	2/3/1825
Most Recent Patent	:	9/12/1849
Block/Lot Parcels	:	34
Cities and Towns	:	1
Cemeteries	:	0

6
GRIGG John 1835
GRIGG John 1835
BROWN William 1833
BROWN William Jr 1833

5
GRIGG John 1835
RHEA William 1833

4
GRIGG John 1835
BROWN William 1838
SMITH James D 1838

7
BROWN William Jr 1833
BROWN William 1834
BROWN William Jr 1833
BROWN William 1834
ASHER Bartlet 1832
TODD Augustus 1832
ASHER Bartlet 1832
TODD Augustus 1832
BROWN William Jr 1833
BROWN William Jr 1833
DUNCAN Joseph 1832

8
BROWN William 1833
BROWN William 1835
GRIGG John 1835
BROWN William 1833
BROWN William Jr 1833
BROWN William 1835
GRIGG John 1835

9
Morgan
GRIGG John 1835
GRAY James 1836

18
BROWN William Jr 1833
BROWN William 1833
BROWN William 1833
GRIGG John 1835
GRAY James 1836
GRIGG John 1835

17
GRAY James 1836

16
Lots-Sec. 16
L1 BROWN, James N 1848
L1 BROWN, William 1848
L2 BROWN, James N 1848
L2/3 BROWN, William 1848
L3 BROWN, James N 1848
L4 RUBLE, Jesse 1848
L5 BROWN, William 1848
L5 BROWN, James N 1848
L6 BROWN, William 1848
L6 BROWN, James N 1848
L7-9 BROWN, James N [14]1848
L10 BROWN, James N 1848
L10 BROWN, William 1848
L11 BROWN, James N [14]1848
L12 BROWN, William 1848
L12 BROWN, James N 1848
L13 BROWN, William 1848
L13/14 BROWN, James N 1848
L14 BROWN, William 1848
L15 BROWN, William 1848
L15 BROWN, James N 1848
L16-18 BROWN, James N [14]1848

19
WOOD Eli 1846
GRIGG John 1835

20
GRAY James 1836

21
GRAY James 1836
BROWN William 1833
BROWN William 1833
WARE Nathaniel A 1833
WARE Nathaniel A 1833

30
GRIGG John 1835

29
GORHAM Stephen 1825
GRIGG John 1836

28
GRIGG John 1836
BROWN William 1833
GRIGG John 1836
BROWN William 1833
BROWN William 1833
ONEAL Thomas 1833
BROWN William 1833
BROWN William 1833
BARRETT Richard F 1837

31
ALEXANDER John T 1849
ALEXANDER John T 1849
ALEXANDER John T 1849
ALEXANDER John T 1849

32
ALEXANDER John T 1849
ALEXANDER John T 1849
CLARK William B 1838

33
BROWN Loyd W 1844
BROWN William 1833
ADAMS John 1838

| 3 | 2 | 1 |

Sangamon

| 10 | 11 | 12 |

| 15 | 14 | 13 |

| 22 | 23 | 24 |

Section 27:
ONEAL Thomas 1832 / BROWN William 1833 | BROWN William 1836 | BARRETT Richard F 1837 / **27**
BARRETT Richard F 1837 | BROWN Loyd W 1848

| 26 | 25 |

Section 34:
BROWN Loyd W 1848 | BROWN [15] Loyd W 1848 / **34** / BARRET James A 1848
WESTFALL Samuel 1848

| 35 | 36 |

Helpful Hints

1. This Map's INDEX can be found on the preceding pages.

2. Refer to Map "C" to see where this Township lies within Morgan County, Illinois.

3. Numbers within square brackets [ ] denote a multi-patentee land parcel (multi-owner). Refer to Appendix "C" for a full list of members in this group.

4. Areas that look to be crowded with Patentees usually indicate multiple sales of the same parcel (re-issues), cancellations or voided transactions (that we map, anyway) or overlapping parcels. We opt to show even these ambiguous parcels, which oftentimes lead to research avenues not yet taken.

Legend

——— Patent Boundary

▬▬▬ Section Boundary

▓▓▓ No Patents Found (or Outside County)

1., 2., 3., ... Lot Numbers (when beside a name)

[ ] Group Number (see Appendix "C")

Scale: Section = 1 mile X 1 mile (generally, with some exceptions)

Road Map

T15-N R8-W
3rd PM Meridian

Map Group 11

Cities & Towns
Alexander

Cemeteries
None

6

5

4

7

8

9

18

17

16

I-72

19

20

Morgan
21

Alexander

30

29

28

31

32

33

Old State Road

Bloom

Cockin

Robin

Kennett

Owen Long

Sangamon Morgan County Road

County Highway 123

Ludwig

Park

School

Ridder

Wabash

Old Route 36

Wabash

Franklin

Alexander

Contrary

Old Route 36

Dr Donovan

Owen Long

3

2

1

10

11

12

15

14

13

Sangamon

22

23

24

27

26

25

34

35

36

Helpful Hints

1. This road map has a number of uses, but primarily it is to help you: a) find the present location of land owned by your ancestors (at least the general area), b) find cemeteries and city-centers, and c) estimate the route/roads used by Census-takers & tax-assessors.

2. If you plan to travel to Morgan County to locate cemeteries or land parcels, please pick up a modern travel map for the area before you do. Mapping old land parcels on modern maps is not as exact a science as you might think. Just the slightest variations in public land survey coordinates, estimates of parcel boundaries, or road-map deviations can greatly alter a map's representation of how a road either does or doesn't cross a particular parcel of land.

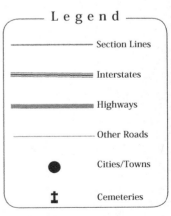

— L e g e n d —

———— Section Lines

════════ Interstates

━━━━━━ Highways

———— Other Roads

● Cities/Towns

☩ Cemeteries

Scale: Section = 1 mile X 1 mile
(generally, with some exceptions)

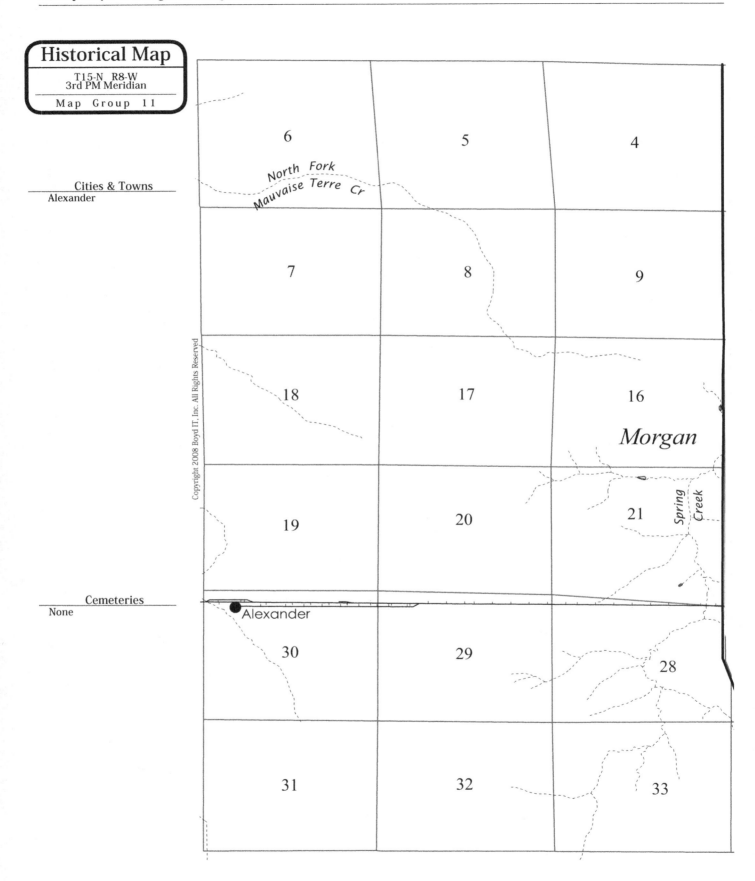

Historical Map

T15-N R8-W
3rd PM Meridian

Map Group 11

Cities & Towns
Alexander

Cemeteries
None

6

5

4

North Fork
Mauvaise Terre Cr

7

8

9

18

17

16

Morgan

19

20

21

Spring Creek

Alexander

30

29

28

31

32

33

3	2	1
10	11	12
15	14	13
22	23	24
27	26	25
34	35	36

Sangamon

Helpful Hints

1. This Map takes a different look at the same Congressional Township displayed in the preceding two maps. It presents features that can help you better envision the historical development of the area: a) Water-bodies (lakes & ponds), b) Water-courses (rivers, streams, etc.), c) Railroads, d) City/town center-points (where they were oftentimes located when first settled), and e) Cemeteries.

2. Using this "Historical" map in tandem with this Township's Patent Map and Road Map, may lead you to some interesting discoveries. You will often find roads, towns, cemeteries, and waterways are named after nearby landowners: sometimes those names will be the ones you are researching. See how many of these research gems you can find here in Morgan County.

L e g e n d

——————	Section Lines
‡‡‡‡‡‡	Railroads
▭	Large Rivers & Bodies of Water
- - - - - -	Streams/Creeks & Small Rivers
●	Cities/Towns
‡	Cemeteries

Scale: Section = 1 mile X 1 mile
(there are some exceptions)

181

Map Group 12: Index to Land Patents

Township 14-North Range 11-West (3rd PM)

After you locate an individual in this Index, take note of the Section and Section Part then proceed to the Land Patent map on the pages immediately following. You should have no difficulty locating the corresponding parcel of land.

The "For More Info" Column will lead you to more information about the underlying Patents. See the *Legend* at right, and the "How to Use this Book" chapter, for more information.

```
                    LEGEND
             "For More Info . . . " column
  G = Group  (Multi-Patentee Patent, see Appendix "C")
  R = Residence
  S = Social Status


  See Appendix A for list of abbreviations used by the
  Illinois State Archives in describing the place and
  nature of these land patents.

  Note: if the Abbreviations contain "L", "BL", "LOT",
  or "BLOCK", the exact whereabouts of the parcel within
  the section is not known.
```

ID	Individual in Patent	Sec.	Sec. Part	Purchase Date	Sale Type	IL Aliquot Part	For More Info . . .
2924	ADAMS, John	6	NW	1823-11-13	FD	NWFR	R:MORGAN
3006	ALLEN, William	21	SENW	1837-03-04	FD	SENW	R:MAINE
3004	" "	21	E½SW	1837-03-04	FD	E2SW	R:MAINE
3005	" "	21	S½SE	1837-03-04	FD	S2SE	R:MAINE
3007	" "	21	W½SW	1839-01-22	FD	W2SW	R:MAINE
2828	ALLINSON, Adam	5		1824-09-07	FD	PT2NW	R:MORGAN
2989	ALLINSON, Thomas	5	NE	1829-08-20	FD	NEFR	R:MORGAN
2990	" "	5	W½SW	1830-02-24	FD	W2SW	R:MORGAN
2988	" "	3	W½SW	1831-08-16	FD	W2SW	R:MORGAN
2836	ANGELO, Benjamin	14	W½NE	1830-05-17	FD	W2NE	R:MORGAN
2925	ANGELO, John	25	SWNW	1852-10-08	FD	SWNW	
2926	" "	26	SENE	1852-10-08	FD	SENE	
2912	ANGELON, James	13	W½SE	1836-01-22	FD	W2SE	R:MORGAN
2837	ANGELOW, Benjamin	14	E½NW	1828-12-05	FD	E2NW	R:MORGAN
2838	" "	14	SENE	1835-07-07	FD	SENE	R:MORGAN
2914	ANGELOW, James	13	W½NE	1835-07-07	FD	W2NE	R:MORGAN
2913	" "	13	NENW	1835-08-11	FD	NENW	R:MORGAN
2915	ANGELOW, James B	14	NENE	1836-02-23	FD	NENE	R:MORGAN
2928	ANGELOW, John	15	E½SE	1828-12-22	FD	E2SE	R:MORGAN
2927	" "	14	NWSW	1835-07-07	FD	NWSW	R:MORGAN
2929	" "	26	SWNE	1852-02-03	FD	SWNE	R:MORGAN
2834	ARNETT, Andrew	14	W½NW	1828-11-15	FD	W2NW	R:MORGAN
2991	ARNETT, Thomas B	13	E½SE	1829-07-09	FD	E2SE	R:MORGAN
2952	AUSTIN, Joshua D	6	NE	1823-11-13	FD	NE	R:MORGAN
2947	BANCROFT, Joseph H	15	W½SE	1836-02-22	FD	W2SE	R:MORGAN
2946	" "	15	SESW	1836-02-22	FD	SESW	R:MORGAN
2992	BATTY, Thomas	8	E½NE	1830-08-18	FD	E2NE	R:MORGAN
3008	BATTY, William	9	E½NW	1829-08-15	FD	E2NW	R:MORGAN
3009	BEASLEY, William	24	SESW	1835-07-14	FD	SESW	R:MORGAN
3010	" "	24	SWSE	1836-02-01	FD	SWSE	R:MORGAN
2839	BEAVERS, Benjamin	21	NENW	1836-10-31	FD	NENW	R:MORGAN
2858	BERRY, Garrison W	7	E½SE	1824-01-29	FD	E2SE	R:MORGAN
2857	" "	7	E½NE	1828-11-25	FD	E2NE	R:MORGAN
2944	BERRY, Joseph	14	E½SW	1829-04-04	FD	E2SW	R:MORGAN
2953	BERRY, Lucian	8	W½SW	1828-01-05	FD	W2SW	R:MORGAN
2993	BERRY, Thomas	14	SWSW	1835-10-19	FD	SWSW	R:MORGAN
2994	" "	26	NENW	1835-10-19	FD	NENW	R:MORGAN
2916	BRIEDEN, James	21	NESE	1836-03-08	FD	NESE	R:MORGAN
3011	BRISBIN, William	7	NW	1828-07-05	FD	NWFR	R:MORGAN
2975	BROWN, Robert	22	SENE	1835-06-30	FD	SENE	R:MORGAN
2845	CARTER, Ebenezer	25	SENW	1836-08-29	FD	SENW	R:MORGAN
2936	CARTER, John	8	W½SE	1828-11-17	FD	W2SE	R:MORGAN
2935	" "	8	E½SE	1829-01-08	FD	E2SE	R:MORGAN
2937	" "	9	NWSW	1836-04-15	FD	NWSW	R:MORGAN
2933	" "	16	L4	1839-03-13	SC	LOT4MA	
2931	" "	16	L2	1839-03-13	SC	LOT2MA	

ID	Individual in Patent	Sec.	Sec. Part	Purchase Date	Sale Type	IL Aliquot Part	For More Info . . .
2932	CARTER, John (Cont'd)	16	L3	1839-03-13	SC	LOT3MA	
2934	" "	25	NWNE	1852-08-31	FD	NWNE	
2859	CLARK, George	21	NWNW	1846-12-01	FD	NWNW	R:MORGAN
2942	COBB, Jonathon	1	NW	1824-09-21	FD	NWFR	R:MORGAN
2943	" "	2	NW	1828-11-28	FD	NWFR	R:MORGAN
2945	CODDINGTON, Joseph	12	E½NE	1828-10-07	FD	E2NE	R:MORGAN
2964	COFFIN, Nathaniel	9	SWSW	1837-03-04	FD	SWSW	R:MORGAN
2960	" "	26	E½SE	1837-05-15	FD	E2SE	R:MORGAN
2957	" "	25	E½SE	1837-05-15	FD	E2SE	R:MORGAN
2959	" "	25	SWSE	1837-05-15	FD	SWSE	R:MORGAN
2961	" "	26	SW	1837-05-15	FD	SW	R:MORGAN
2962	" "	36	E½SW	1837-05-15	FD	E2SW	R:MORGAN
2963	" "	36	W½NE	1837-05-15	FD	W2NE	R:MORGAN
2958	" "	25	SW	1837-05-15	FD	SW	R:MORGAN
3012	CRAGGS, William	4	W½SW	1831-06-09	FD	W2SW	R:MORGAN
2868	DANIEL, Hatch	25	SWNE	1836-11-18	FD	SWNE	R:MORGAN
2872	DOAK, Herrel	26	NWSE	1836-06-10	FD	NWSE	R:MORGAN
3013	EDWARDS, William	9	SESW	1837-02-28	FD	SESW	R:MORGAN
2842	EONIGER, David	5	L1	1853-10-29	FD	LOT1NWFR	R:EDGAR
2840	FUNK, Martin	6	E½SE	1829-07-15	FD	E2SE	R:MORGAN G:65
2968	FUNK, Nimrod	5	NW	1828-02-06	FD	PT1NW	R:MORGAN
2967	" "	5	E½SW	1830-08-31	FD	E2SW	R:MORGAN
2860	GARMAN, George	16	L12	1836-08-22	SC	LOT12N2W2SW	
2938	GARMAN, John	16	L5	1836-09-13	SC	L5MA	
2939	GRIGG, John	35	NE	1836-02-09	FD	NE	R:PHILADELPHIA
2940	" "	36	NW	1836-03-17	FD	NW	R:PHILADELPHIA
2831	HANEY, Alden	15	NESW	1835-11-19	FD	NESW	R:MORGAN
2832	HANEY, Aldon	15	W½SW	1833-10-15	FD	W2SW	R:MORGAN
2833	HANEY, Alldon	21	SWNE	1833-12-13	FD	SWNE	R:MORGAN G:70
2873	HATCHER, Ichabird W	26	NENE	1836-07-09	FD	NENE	R:MORGAN
2973	HATCHER, Richard	23	SWSE	1835-06-29	FD	SWSE	R:MORGAN
2974	" "	26	NWNE	1835-07-18	FD	NWNE	R:MORGAN
2949	HENDERSON, Joseph	15	E½NE	1828-10-10	FD	E2NE	R:MORGAN
2948	" "	13	E½NE	1830-11-08	FD	E2NE	R:MORGAN
2976	HILL, Robert	22	SWSW	1835-08-26	FD	SWSW	R:MORGAN
2977	HILLS, Robert	10	NWNW	1836-01-18	FD	NWNW	R:MORGAN
2917	HOLME, James	5	W½SE	1831-06-09	FD	W2SE	R:MORGAN
2922	HOLME, Janus	9	W½NW	1831-10-14	FD	W2NW	R:MORGAN
2923	" "	9	W½SE	1831-10-14	FD	W2SE	R:MORGAN
2918	HORRELL, James L	6	W½SE	1827-11-21	FD	W2SE	R:MORGAN
3003	HORTON, Urias	14	W½SE	1835-07-11	FD	W2SE	R:MORGAN
2871	HOWARD, Reubin	8	W½NE	1831-07-27	FD	W2NE	R:MORGAN G:81
3014	JAMES, William	36	W½SW	1853-11-12	FD	W2SW	R:MORGAN
2864	JAYNE, Gershom	7	SW	1823-11-17	FD	SWFR	R:SANGAMON
2869	JOHNSON, Henry	25	NENW	1836-01-15	FD	NENW	R:MORGAN
2870	" "	25	NWSE	1837-01-27	FD	NWSE	R:MORGAN
2965	KING, Nicholas	3	N½NW	1830-12-01	FD	N2NW	R:MORGAN
2966	" "	4	NE	1830-12-01	FD	NE	R:MORGAN
2950	KLEIN, Joseph	15	W½NE	1829-12-23	FD	W2NE	R:SANGAMON
2854	LANDRUM, F A	16	L10	1836-08-22	SC	L10N2W2SE	S:I
2855	LANDRUM, Francis A	16	L6	1836-09-13	SC	L6MA	G:91
2995	LEACH, Thomas	5	E½SE	1830-10-12	FD	E2SE	R:MORGAN
2843	LEWIS, David G	26	SENW	1838-07-17	FD	SENW	R:MORGAN
2984	LEWIS, Samuel	25	NWNW	1837-01-24	FD	NWNW	R:MORGAN
2856	LUNDAY, Gabriel	35	SW	1835-06-25	FD	SW	R:MORGAN
2979	MARSHALL, Robert	10	SENE	1835-09-14	FD	SENE	R:MORGAN
2978	" "	10	NESE	1835-09-14	FD	NESE	R:MORGAN
2987	MASSEY, Silas	1	E½SE	1835-11-28	FD	E2SE	R:MORGAN
2863	MAXFIELD, George W	16	L11	1836-08-22	SC	LOT11N2E2SW	
2955	MCCONNELL, Murry	8	W½NW	1829-01-08	FD	W2NW	R:MORGAN
2867	MILLER, Harrison	16	L1	1836-08-22	SC	LOT1N2E2NE	
2985	MONTGOMERY, Samuel	35	SE	1852-02-10	FD	SE	
2844	MOORE, David	9	W½NE	1829-08-18	FD	W2NE	R:MORGAN
3015	MORSE, William L	7	W½SE	1823-11-13	FD	W2SE	R:MORGAN
3016	MOSS, William L	8	E½SW	1829-01-12	FD	E2SW	R:MORGAN
2841	MURRY, Daniel	21	NWNE	1833-12-07	FD	NWNE	R:MORGAN
2829	PRENTICE, Agnes	10	NENE	1836-03-09	FD	NENE	R:MORGAN S:F
2830	" "	11	NWNW	1836-03-17	FD	NWNW	R:MORGAN S:F
2997	PRENTICE, Thomas	2	W½SW	1829-11-14	FD	W2SW	R:MORGAN
2998	" "	3	E½SE	1829-11-14	FD	E2SE	R:MORGAN
2996	" "	2	E½SW	1829-11-25	FD	E2SW	R:MORGAN
2970	RAFFERTY, Pachall H	26	SWSE	1854-11-11	FD	SWSEVOID	R:MORGAN
2920	" "	26	SWSE	1854-11-11	FD	SWSEVOID	R:MORGAN

ID	Individual in Patent	Sec.	Sec. Part	Purchase Date	Sale Type	IL Aliquot Part	For More Info . . .
2930	RANSON, John B	22	N½SW	1836-03-07	FD	N2SW	R:MORGAN
2980	RAUGH, Robert	16	L15	1836-08-22	SC	LOT15S2W2SE	
2981	REAUGH, Robert	13	NWNW	1834-02-07	FD	NWNW	R:MORGAN
2982	"	13	SENW	1836-04-11	FD	SENW	R:MORGAN
2951	RHODES, Joseph	4	E½SW	1831-09-22	FD	E2SWLS	R:MORGAN
2862	SHEPARD, George	36	NENE	1853-10-17	FD	NENE	R:MORGAN
2846	SHIRTCLIFF, Edward	10	NENW	1836-08-11	FD	NENW	R:MORGAN
2954	SHUMAKER, Michael	36	SWSE	1853-11-10	FD	SWSE	
2835	SMITH, Arnton	15	W½NW	1830-11-18	FD	W2NW	R:MORGAN
2833	SMITH, George	21	SWNE	1833-12-13	FD	SWNE	R:MORGAN G:70
2866	SMITH, Green	22	SWNW	1835-11-12	FD	SWNW	R:MORGAN
2865	"	16	L8	1836-08-22	SC	LOT8S2E2NE	
2919	SMITH, James P	36	SENE	1836-03-26	FD	SENE	R:MORGAN
2983	SMITH, Robert	21	NWSE	1833-12-25	FD	NWSE	R:MORGAN
2849	STILLWELL, Elender	22	NWNW	1835-11-13	FD	NWNW	R:MORGAN
2874	STRAWN, Jacob	1	NE	1829-11-18	FD	NE	R:OHIO
2893	"	2	NE	1831-06-01	FD	NEFR	R:MORGAN
2910	"	3	SEN½	1831-07-07	FD	S2NE	R:MORGAN
2908	"	3	N½NE	1831-07-11	FD	N2NE	R:MORGAN
2909	"	3	S½NW	1831-07-11	FD	S2NW	R:MORGAN
2911	"	9	E½NE	1831-10-28	FD	E2NELS	R:MORGAN
2875	"	1	SW	1835-11-05	FD	SW	R:MORGAN
2887	"	12	NW	1835-11-05	FD	NW	R:MORGAN
2894	"	2	SE	1835-11-05	FD	SE	R:MORGAN
2883	"	11	NE	1835-11-05	FD	NE	R:MORGAN
2876	"	1	W½SE	1835-11-16	FD	W2SE	R:MORGAN
2889	"	12	W½NE	1835-11-16	FD	W2NE	R:MORGAN
2888	"	12	S½	1835-12-21	FD	S2	R:MORGAN
2884	"	11	SE	1835-12-21	FD	SE	R:MORGAN
2885	"	11	SW	1836-11-02	FD	SW	R:MORGAN
2886	"	11	SWNW	1836-11-02	FD	SWNW	R:MORGAN
2882	"	11	E½NW	1836-11-02	FD	E2NW	R:MORGAN
2881	"	10	W½SE	1836-11-02	FD	W2SE	R:MORGAN
2880	"	10	SWNE	1836-11-02	FD	SWNE	R:MORGAN
2879	"	10	SW	1836-11-02	FD	SW	R:MORGAN
2878	"	10	SESE	1836-11-02	FD	SESE	R:MORGAN
2877	"	10	S½NW	1836-11-02	FD	S2NW	R:MORGAN
2892	"	15	E½NW	1836-12-02	FD	E2NW	R:MORGAN
2907	"	24	W½SW	1837-01-09	FD	W2SW	R:MORGAN
2906	"	24	W½NE	1837-01-09	FD	W2NE	R:MORGAN
2890	"	13	SW	1837-01-09	FD	SW	R:MORGAN
2905	"	24	NWSE	1837-01-09	FD	NWSE	R:MORGAN
2904	"	24	NWNE	1837-01-09	FD	NWNE	R:MORGAN
2901	"	23	NWSE	1837-01-09	FD	NWSE	R:MORGAN
2891	"	14	E½SE	1837-01-09	FD	E2SE	R:MORGAN
2902	"	23	SW	1837-01-09	FD	SW	R:MORGAN
2895	"	22	E½NW	1837-01-09	FD	E2NW	R:MORGAN
2899	"	23	E½SE	1837-01-09	FD	E2SE	R:MORGAN
2896	"	22	NE	1837-01-09	FD	NE	R:MORGAN
2897	"	22	SE	1837-01-09	FD	SE	R:MORGAN
2898	"	22	SESW	1837-01-09	FD	SESW	R:MORGAN
2903	"	24	NESW	1837-01-09	FD	NESW	R:MORGAN
2900	"	23	N½	1837-01-09	FD	N2	R:MORGAN
2941	SUTER, John	21	SWNW	1844-09-06	FD	SWNW	R:SCOTT
2999	SWALES, Thomas	21	E½NE	1830-01-13	FD	E2NE	R:MORGAN
3001	"	4	S½NW	1830-11-23	FD	S2NW	R:MORGAN
3000	"	4	E½SE	1831-08-04	FD	E2SE	R:MORGAN
3002	"	4	W½SE	1831-08-04	FD	W2SE	R:MORGAN
2969	TICKNOR, Olney	4	N½NW	1830-01-29	FD	N2NW	R:MORGAN
2840	TODD, Coleman	6	E½SE	1829-07-15	FD	E2SE	R:MORGAN G:65
2871	TODD, Henry	8	W½NE	1831-07-27	FD	W2NE	R:MORGAN G:81
2855	TUCKER, James	16	L6	1836-09-13	SC	L6MA	G:91
2971	VARNER, Peter	26	NWNW	1835-09-21	FD	NWNW	R:MORGAN
2972	"	26	SWNW	1836-01-18	FD	SWNW	R:MORGAN
2970	VERERS, James	26	SWSE	1854-12-14	FD	SWSE	R:MORGAN
2920	"	26	SWSE	1854-12-14	FD	SWSE	R:MORGAN
2986	WESTROPE, Samuel	36	N½SE	1836-12-02	FD	N2SE	R:MORGAN
3017	WILKERSON, William	9	NESW	1836-12-08	FD	NESW	R:MORGAN
3019	WILKINSON, William	3	W½SE	1830-08-21	FD	W2SE	R:MORGAN
3018	"	10	NWNE	1836-03-09	FD	NWNE	R:MORGAN S:F
2847	WILLSON, Edward	8	E½NW	1830-01-07	FD	E2NW	R:MORGAN
2848	WILSON, Edward	16	L13	1836-08-22	SC	LOT13S2W2SW	
2861	WILSON, George M	16	L16	1836-08-22	SC	LOT16S2E2SE	

ID	Individual in Patent	Sec.	Sec. Part	Purchase Date	Sale Type	IL Aliquot Part	For More Info . . .
2956	WINTERS, Nathan	6	SW	1823-12-23	FD	SW	R:MORGAN
2850	WOLCOTT, Elihu	35	NW	1836-02-09	FD	NW	R:MORGAN
2853	WOLCOTT, Elisha	25	E½NE	1836-02-13	FD	E2NE	R:MORGAN
2852	" "	24	E½SE	1836-02-13	FD	E2SE	R:MORGAN
2851	" "	24	E½NE	1836-02-13	FD	E2NE	R:MORGAN
2921	WOODS, James	3	E½SW	1829-10-02	FD	E2SW	R:MORGAN
2827	YATES, Abner	36	SESE	1854-03-09	FD	SESE	R:MORGAN

Patent Map

T14-N R11-W
3rd PM Meridian

Map Group 12

Township Statistics

Parcels Mapped	:	193
Number of Patents	:	1
Number of Individuals	:	112
Patentees Identified	:	108
Number of Surnames	:	85
Multi-Patentee Parcels	:	4
Oldest Patent Date	:	11/13/1823
Most Recent Patent	:	12/14/1854
Block/Lot Parcels	:	14
Cities and Towns	:	1
Cemeteries	:	1

Section 6
- ADAMS John 1823
- AUSTIN Joshua D 1823
- WINTERS Nathan 1823
- HORRELL James L 1827
- TODD [65] Coleman 1829

Section 5
- ALLINSON Adam 1824
- FUNK Nimrod 1828
- ALLINSON Thomas 1829
- ALLINSON Thomas 1830
- FUNK Nimrod 1830
- HOLME James 1831
- LEACH Thomas 1830
- Lots-Sec. 5
- L1   EONIGER, David   1853

Section 4
- TICKNOR Olney 1830
- KING Nicholas 1830
- SWALES Thomas 1830
- CRAGGS William 1831
- RHODES Joseph 1831
- SWALES Thomas 1831
- SWALES Thomas 1831

Section 7
- BRISBIN William 1828
- BERRY Garrison W 1828
- JAYNE Gershom 1823
- MORSE William L 1823
- BERRY Garrison W 1824

Section 8
- MCCONNELL Murry 1829
- WILLSON Edward 1830
- TODD [81] Henry 1831
- BATTY Thomas 1830
- BERRY Lucian 1828
- MOSS William L 1829
- CARTER John 1828
- CARTER John 1829

Section 9
- HOLME Janus 1831
- BATTY William 1829
- MOORE David 1829
- STRAWN Jacob 1831
- CARTER John 1836
- WILKERSON William 1836
- HOLME Janus 1831
- COFFIN Nathaniel 1837
- EDWARDS William 1837

Section 18 — 18

Section 17 — *Scott* — 17

Morgan

Section 16 — 16
- Lots-Sec. 16
- L1   MILLER, Harrison   1836
- L2   CARTER, John   1839
- L3   CARTER, John   1839
- L4   CARTER, John   1839
- L5   GARMAN, John   1836
- L6   LANDRUM, Francis[91] 1836
- L8   SMITH, Green   1836
- L10 LANDRUM, F A   1836
- L11 MAXFIELD, George W 1836
- L12 GARMAN, George   1836
- L13 WILSON, Edward   1836
- L15 RAUGH, Robert   1836
- L16 WILSON, George M   1836

Section 19 — 19

Section 20 — 20

Section 21 — 21
- CLARK George 1846
- BEAVERS Benjamin 1836
- MURRY Daniel 1833
- SWALES Thomas 1830
- SUTER John 1844
- ALLEN William 1837
- HANEY [70] Alldon 1833
- ALLEN William 1839
- ALLEN William 1837
- SMITH Robert 1833
- BRIEDEN James 1836
- ALLEN William 1837

Section 30 — 30

Section 29 — 29

Section 28 — 28

Section 31 — 31

Section 32 — 32

Section 33 — 33

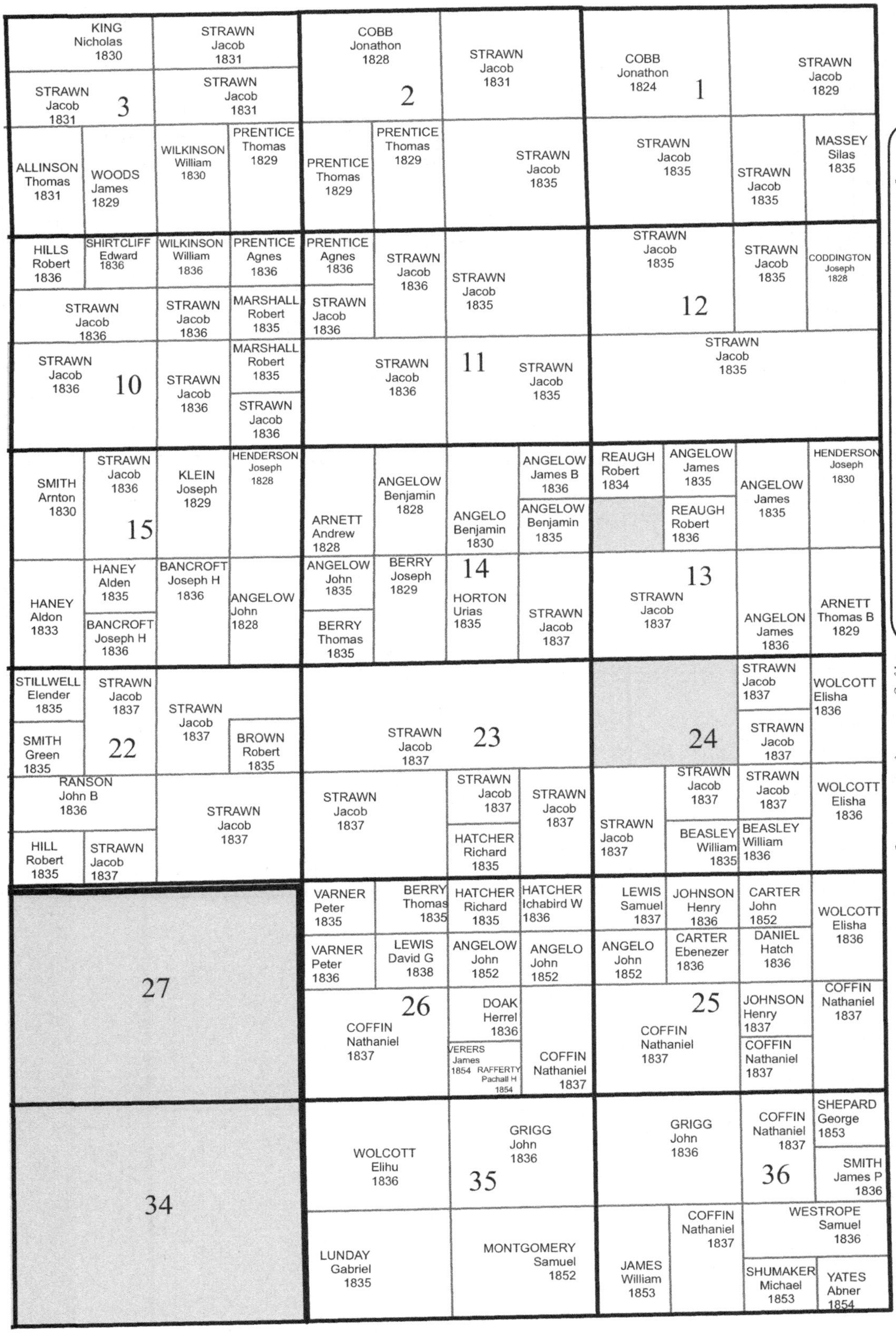
KING Nicholas 1830
STRAWN Jacob 1831
STRAWN Jacob 1831
STRAWN Jacob 1831
3
ALLINSON Thomas 1831
WOODS James 1829
WILKINSON William 1830
PRENTICE Thomas 1829
COBB Jonathon 1828
2
STRAWN Jacob 1831
PRENTICE Thomas 1829
PRENTICE Thomas 1829
STRAWN Jacob 1835
COBB Jonathon 1824
1
STRAWN Jacob 1829
STRAWN Jacob 1835
STRAWN Jacob 1835
MASSEY Silas 1835
HILLS Robert 1836
SHIRTCLIFF Edward 1836
WILKINSON William 1836
PRENTICE Agnes 1836
STRAWN Jacob 1836
STRAWN Jacob 1836
MARSHALL Robert 1835
STRAWN Jacob 1836
10
STRAWN Jacob 1836
MARSHALL Robert 1835
STRAWN Jacob 1836
PRENTICE Agnes 1836
STRAWN Jacob 1836
STRAWN Jacob 1836
STRAWN Jacob 1835
STRAWN Jacob 1836
11
STRAWN Jacob 1835
STRAWN Jacob 1835
STRAWN Jacob 1835
CODDINGTON Joseph 1828
12
STRAWN Jacob 1835
SMITH Arnton 1830
STRAWN Jacob 1836
15
KLEIN Joseph 1829
HENDERSON Joseph 1828
HANEY Aldon 1833
HANEY Alden 1835
BANCROFT Joseph H 1836
BANCROFT Joseph H 1836
ANGELOW John 1828
ARNETT Andrew 1828
ANGELOW Benjamin 1828
ANGELO Benjamin 1830
ANGELOW James B 1836
ANGELOW Benjamin 1835
ANGELOW John 1835
BERRY Joseph 1829
14
HORTON Urias 1835
BERRY Thomas 1835
STRAWN Jacob 1837
REAUGH Robert 1834
ANGELOW James 1835
REAUGH Robert 1836
ANGELOW James 1835
HENDERSON Joseph 1830
13
STRAWN Jacob 1837
ANGELON James 1836
ARNETT Thomas B 1829
STILLWELL Elender 1835
STRAWN Jacob 1837
SMITH Green 1835
22
STRAWN Jacob 1837
BROWN Robert 1835
RANSON John B 1836
STRAWN Jacob 1837
HILL Robert 1835
STRAWN Jacob 1837
STRAWN Jacob 1837
23
STRAWN Jacob 1837
STRAWN Jacob 1837
STRAWN Jacob 1837
HATCHER Richard 1835
24
STRAWN Jacob 1837
WOLCOTT Elisha 1836
STRAWN Jacob 1837
STRAWN Jacob 1837
STRAWN Jacob 1837
STRAWN Jacob 1837
WOLCOTT Elisha 1836
BEASLEY William 1835
BEASLEY William 1836
27
VARNER Peter 1835
BERRY Thomas 1835
HATCHER Richard 1835
HATCHER Ichabird W 1836
VARNER Peter 1836
LEWIS David G 1838
ANGELOW John 1852
ANGELO John 1852
26
COFFIN Nathaniel 1837
DOAK Herrel 1836
VERERS James 1854
RAFFERTY Pachall H 1854
COFFIN Nathaniel 1837
LEWIS Samuel 1837
JOHNSON Henry 1836
CARTER John 1852
WOLCOTT Elisha 1836
ANGELO John 1852
CARTER Ebenezer 1836
DANIEL Hatch 1836
25
COFFIN Nathaniel 1837
JOHNSON Henry 1837
COFFIN Nathaniel 1837
COFFIN Nathaniel 1837
34
WOLCOTT Elihu 1836
GRIGG John 1836
35
LUNDAY Gabriel 1835
MONTGOMERY Samuel 1852
GRIGG John 1836
COFFIN Nathaniel 1837
SHEPARD George 1853
36
SMITH James P 1836
COFFIN Nathaniel 1837
JAMES William 1853
WESTROPE Samuel 1836
SHUMAKER Michael 1853
YATES Abner 1854

Helpful Hints

1. This Map's INDEX can be found on the preceding pages.
2. Refer to Map "C" to see where this Township lies within Morgan County, Illinois.
3. Numbers within square brackets [ ] denote a multi-patentee land parcel (multi-owner). Refer to Appendix "C" for a full list of members in this group.
4. Areas that look to be crowded with Patentees usually indicate multiple sales of the same parcel (re-issues), cancellations or voided transactions (that we map, anyway) or overlapping parcels. We opt to show even these ambiguous parcels, which oftentimes lead to research avenues not yet taken.

Legend

- Patent Boundary
- Section Boundary
- No Patents Found (or Outside County)
- 1., 2., 3., ... Lot Numbers (when beside a name)
- [ ] Group Number (see Appendix "C")

Scale: Section = 1 mile X 1 mile (generally, with some exceptions)

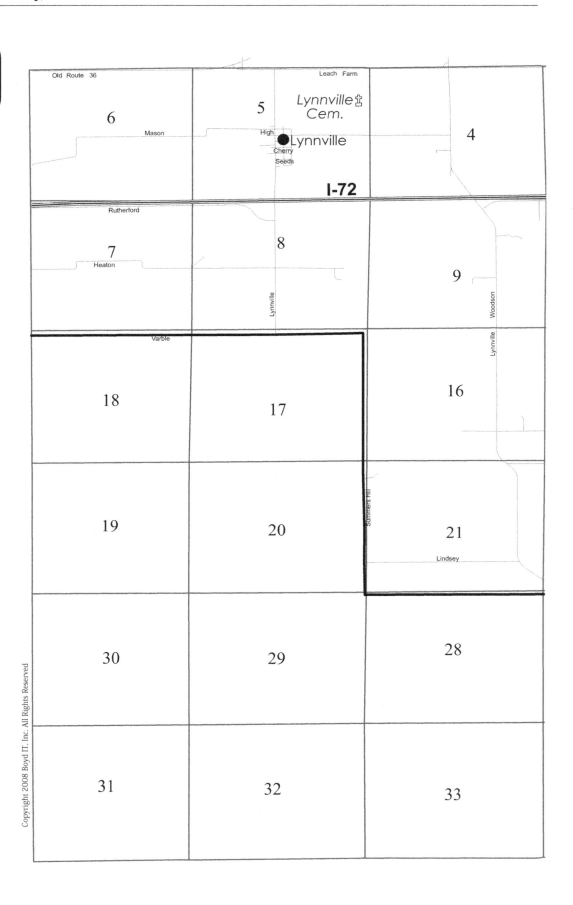

Road Map

T14-N R11-W
3rd PM Meridian

Map Group 12

Cities & Towns
Lynnville

Cemeteries
Lynnville Cemetery

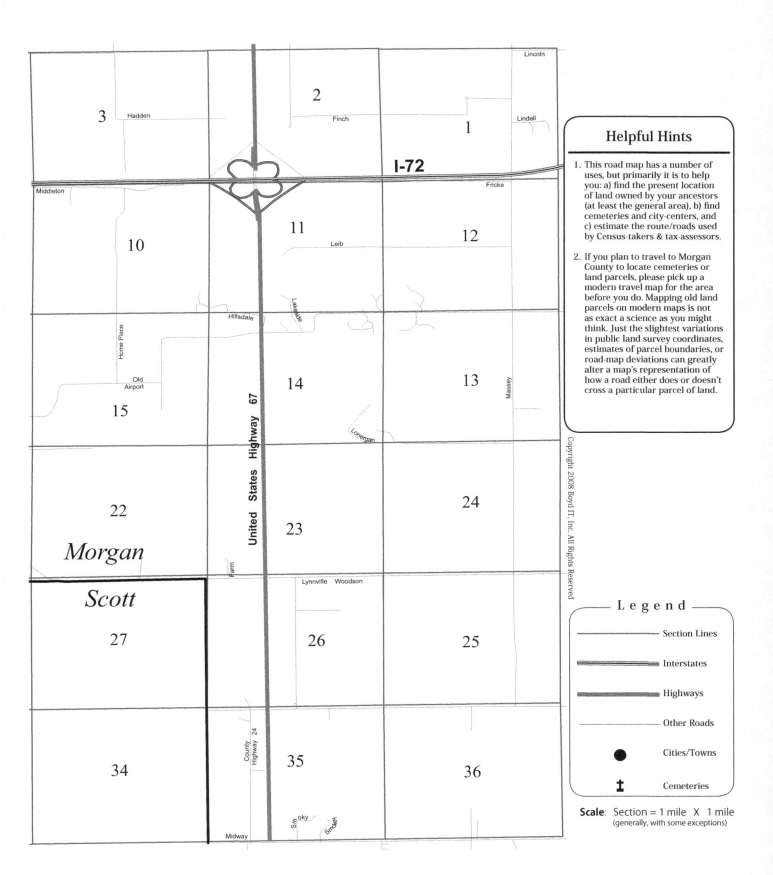

Helpful Hints

1. This road map has a number of uses, but primarily it is to help you: a) find the present location of land owned by your ancestors (at least the general area), b) find cemeteries and city-centers, and c) estimate the route/roads used by Census-takers & tax-assessors.

2. If you plan to travel to Morgan County to locate cemeteries or land parcels, please pick up a modern travel map for the area before you do. Mapping old land parcels on modern maps is not as exact a science as you might think. Just the slightest variations in public land survey coordinates, estimates of parcel boundaries, or road-map deviations can greatly alter a map's representation of how a road either does or doesn't cross a particular parcel of land.

L e g e n d

————	Section Lines
═══════	Interstates
▬▬▬▬▬	Highways
————	Other Roads
●	Cities/Towns
♰	Cemeteries

Scale: Section = 1 mile X 1 mile
(generally, with some exceptions)

189

Historical Map

T14-N R11-W
3rd PM Meridian

Map Group 12

Cities & Towns
Lynnville

Walnut Creek

6

Lynnville ● Cem.

Lynnville ● 5

4

7

Big
Branch

8

9

18

17

16

Sandy
Creek

Scott

Morgan

19

20

21

Cemeteries
Lynnville Cemetery

30

29

28

31

32

33

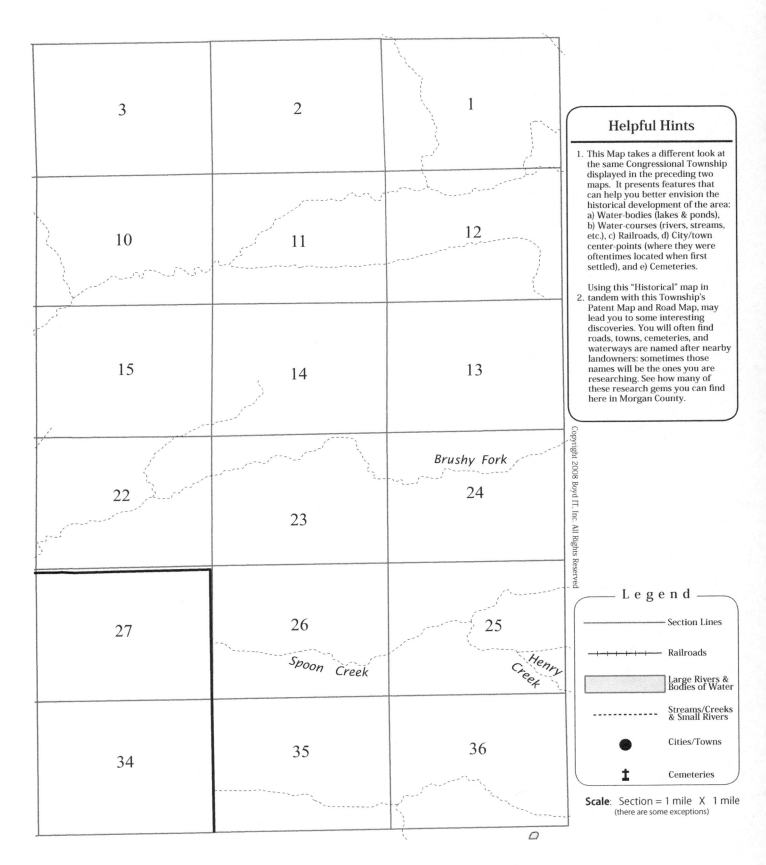

Helpful Hints

1. This Map takes a different look at the same Congressional Township displayed in the preceding two maps. It presents features that can help you better envision the historical development of the area: a) Water-bodies (lakes & ponds), b) Water-courses (rivers, streams, etc.), c) Railroads, d) City/town center-points (where they were oftentimes located when first settled), and e) Cemeteries.

2. Using this "Historical" map in tandem with this Township's Patent Map and Road Map, may lead you to some interesting discoveries. You will often find roads, towns, cemeteries, and waterways are named after nearby landowners: sometimes those names will be the ones you are researching. See how many of these research gems you can find here in Morgan County.

L e g e n d

———————— Section Lines

-+-+-+-+-+- Railroads

▭ Large Rivers & Bodies of Water

- - - - - - - Streams/Creeks & Small Rivers

● Cities/Towns

✝ Cemeteries

Scale: Section = 1 mile X 1 mile
(there are some exceptions)

Map Group 13: Index to Land Patents

Township 14-North Range 10-West (3rd PM)

After you locate an individual in this Index, take note of the Section and Section Part then proceed to the Land Patent map on the pages immediately following. You should have no difficulty locating the corresponding parcel of land.

The "For More Info" Column will lead you to more information about the underlying Patents. See the *Legend* at right, and the "How to Use this Book" chapter, for more information.

ID	Individual in Patent	Sec.	Sec. Part	Purchase Date	Sale Type	IL Aliquot Part	For More Info . . .
3089	ADAMS, Elijah	32	E½NW	1829-10-16	FD	E2NW	R:MORGAN
3090	" "	33	W½NW	1830-03-12	FD	W2NW	R:MORGAN
3199	ADAMS, Joseph	33	SEN½	1833-11-14	FD	S2NE	R:MORGAN
3198	" "	33	E½NW	1835-10-27	FD	E2NW	R:MORGAN
3296	ADAMS, William	32	E½NE	1828-11-01	FD	E2NE	R:MORGAN
3068	ANDERSON, Dickey	12	E½NE	1827-05-25	FD	E2NE	R:MORGAN
3067	" "	1	W½SW	1828-12-05	FD	W2SW	R:MORGAN
3041	ANGDANO, Benjamin	31	NWNW	1837-05-10	FD	NWNW	R:MORGAN
3161	ANGELO, John	18	W½NE	1829-10-27	FD	W2NE	R:MORGAN
3160	" "	17	E½NE	1830-11-08	FD	E2NE	R:MORGAN
3162	ANGELOW, John	7	E½SW	1835-07-07	FD	E2SW	R:MORGAN
3163	" "	7	SWSW	1835-07-07	FD	SWSW	R:MORGAN
3278	ARNETT, Thomas B	18	NW	1830-10-27	FD	NW	R:MORGAN
3277	" "	18	E½NE	1831-05-30	FD	E2NE	R:MORGAN
3279	" "	7	E½SE	1831-05-30	FD	E2SE	R:MORGAN
3298	BAILEY, William	30	SWSE	1835-01-05	FD	SWSE	R:MORGAN
3297	" "	29	SW	1835-01-05	FD	SW	R:MORGAN
3033	BARROWS, Barnabas	25	NE	1831-05-14	FD	NE	R:MORGAN G:6
3124	BARROWS, Isaac R	36	E½SE	1831-02-16	FD	E2SE	R:MORGAN
3033	" "	25	NE	1831-05-14	FD	NE	R:MORGAN G:6
3120	" "	25	E½NW	1832-10-11	FD	E2NW	R:MORGAN
3121	" "	25	NWSE	1835-07-06	FD	NWSE	R:MORGAN
3123	" "	26	W½SE	1835-11-13	FD	W2SE	R:MORGAN
3122	" "	26	E½NW	1835-11-13	FD	E2NW	R:MORGAN
3280	BENTLEY, Thomas	5		1828-12-05	FD	W2SEPTSK	R:MORGAN
3284	BERRY, Thomas H	8	E½SW	1835-07-18	FD	E2SW	R:SANGAMON
3034	BOTTS, Barnett	32	W½NE	1828-10-22	FD	W2NE	R:MORGAN
3048	BOTTS, Bernard	28	E½SW	1831-05-09	FD	E2SW	R:MORGAN
3047	" "	28	E½SE	1831-05-30	FD	E2SE	R:MORGAN
3049	" "	28	W½SE	1836-02-06	FD	W2SE	R:MORGAN
3299	BRISBIN, William	1	E½SW	1828-12-12	FD	E2SW	R:MORGAN
3300	" "	1	W½SE	1828-12-12	FD	W2SE	R:MORGAN
3036	BROWN, Beaford	24	NESW	1835-06-19	FD	NESW	R:SANGAMON
3037	BROWN, Bedford	24	E½SE	1830-10-13	FD	E2SE	R:MORGAN
3039	" "	24	W½SE	1831-03-24	FD	W2SE	R:MORGAN
3038	" "	24	W½NW	1831-03-24	FD	W2NW	R:MORGAN
3040	" "	24	W½SW	1833-06-05	FD	W2SW	R:MORGAN
3099	BROWN, Elizabeth	24	SESW	1834-07-14	FD	SESW	R:MORGAN S:F
3102	BROWN, Franklin	34	NESW	1835-08-11	FD	NESW	R:MORGAN
3103	" "	34	NWSE	1835-08-11	FD	NWSE	R:MORGAN
3133	BROWN, James	26	NE	1835-07-08	FD	NE	R:MORGAN
3219	BROWN, Liner	34	W½SW	1828-11-05	FD	W2SW	R:MORGAN
3218	" "	33	E½SE	1830-11-29	FD	E2SE	R:MORGAN
3239	BROWN, Parmelia	34	SWSE	1835-11-09	FD	SWSE	R:MORGAN S:F
3238	" "	34	SESW	1835-11-09	FD	SESW	R:MORGAN S:F
3258	BROWN, Robert	23	SWNW	1835-06-29	FD	SWNW	R:MORGAN

ID	Individual in Patent	Sec.	Sec. Part	Purchase Date	Sale Type	IL Aliquot Part	For More Info . . .
3257	BROWN, Robert (Cont'd)	23	SWNW	1835-06-29	FD	SWNW	R:MORGAN
3258	" "	23	SWNW	1835-06-30	FD	SWNW	R:MORGAN
3257	" "	23	SWNW	1835-06-30	FD	SWNW	R:MORGAN
3256	" "	22	SENE	1835-06-30	FD	SENE	R:MORGAN
3320	BROWN, William S	22	NWNW	1834-06-10	FD	NWNW	R:MORGAN
3319	" "	22	E½NW	1834-06-10	FD	E2NW	R:MORGAN
3032	BRYANT, Arthur	11	W½SW	1831-07-02	FD	W2SW	R:MORGAN G:18
3032	BRYANT, John H	11	W½SW	1831-07-02	FD	W2SW	R:MORGAN G:18
3125	BURROWS, Isaac R	26	W½NW	1835-11-17	FD	W2NW	R:MORGAN
3069	CARTER, Ebenezer	6	SESE	1835-06-09	FD	SESE	R:MORGAN
3070	" "	8	E½NE	1835-06-09	FD	E2NE	R:MORGAN
3166	CLARK, John	3	E½SE	1828-10-16	FD	E2SE	R:MORGAN
3165	" "	10	E½NE	1829-01-02	FD	E2NE	R:MORGAN
3228	COFFIN, Nathaniel	18	S½SW	1837-05-15	FD	S2SW	R:MORGAN
3229	" "	18	SWSE	1837-05-15	FD	SWSE	R:MORGAN
3230	" "	19	E½NE	1837-05-15	FD	E2NE	R:MORGAN
3231	" "	20	W½NW	1837-05-15	FD	W2NW	R:MORGAN
3232	" "	30	SE	1837-05-15	FD	SE	R:MORGAN
3233	" "	30	SW	1837-05-15	FD	SW	R:MORGAN
3234	" "	30	W½NE	1837-05-15	FD	W2NE	R:MORGAN
3135	CRAIG, James	24	W½NE	1830-06-14	FD	W2NE	R:MORGAN
3134	" "	13	E½SE	1830-10-14	FD	E2SE	R:MORGAN
3136	" "	25	SWSE	1835-07-04	FD	SWSE	R:MORGAN
3301	CRAIG, William	25	E½SE	1833-05-31	FD	E2SE	R:KENTUCKY
3126	DEEDS, Jacob	6	NW	1830-02-23	FD	NW	R:MORGAN
3302	DELANY, William	10	W½NE	1830-11-22	FD	W2NE	R:MORGAN
3303	" "	3	W½SE	1831-03-22	FD	W2SE	R:MORGAN
3249	DEW, Peter	9	W½NW	1828-12-05	FD	W2NW	R:MORGAN
3167	DOWLING, John	20	NESW	1839-08-19	FD	NESW	R:MORGAN G:57
3060	DUDHOPE, David	15	E½SW	1835-06-29	FD	E2SW	R:MORGAN
3061	" "	15	E½SW	1835-06-29	FD	E2SW	R:MORGAN
3061	" "	15	E½SW	1835-06-30	FD	E2SW	R:MORGAN
3060	" "	15	E½SW	1835-06-30	FD	E2SW	R:MORGAN
3281	DUDHOPE, Thomas	12	E½SE	1835-03-09	FD	E2SE	R:MORGAN
3168	EADS, John	36	NE	1830-11-04	FD	NE	R:MORGAN
3323	ENNOS, Williams	13	E½NW	1823-12-04	FD	E2NW	R:MORGAN
3042	FAHNESTOCK, Benjamin	31	W½NE	1854-12-15	FD	W2NE	
3215	FANNING, Levi	10	E½SW	1830-10-29	FD	E2SW	R:MORGAN
3216	" "	15	E½NW	1830-12-14	FD	E2NW	R:MORGAN
3236	FATHERKILE, Nicholas	33	W½SW	1828-10-23	FD	W2SW	R:MORGAN
3235	" "	32	E½SE	1828-10-23	FD	E2SE	R:MORGAN
3304	FOLDON, William	21	W½NW	1835-02-03	FD	W2NW	R:MORGAN
3308	FRENCH, William	33	N½NE	1834-05-16	FD	N2NE	R:MORGAN
3305	" "	27	E½SE	1835-07-27	FD	E2SE	R:MORGAN
3306	" "	27	SWSE	1835-08-25	FD	SWSE	R:MORGAN
3311	" "	34	W½NE	1835-08-25	FD	W2NE	R:MORGAN
3309	" "	33	NWSE	1835-11-17	FD	NWSE	R:MORGAN
3307	" "	27	W½NW	1836-02-20	FD	W2NW	R:MORGAN
3310	" "	34	E½NE	1836-07-01	FD	E2NE	R:MORGAN
3202	FRY, Joseph	26	E½SE	1835-07-18	FD	E2SE	R:MORGAN
3200	" "	25	N½SW	1835-09-10	FD	N2SW	R:MORGAN
3201	" "	25	S½SW	1835-09-26	FD	S2SW	R:MORGAN
3313	GEERS, William	13	W½SW	1833-11-06	FD	W2SW	R:MORGAN
3147	GENTRY, James M	18	NWSE	1834-01-20	FD	NWSE	R:MORGAN
3283	GILLILAND, Thomas	13	W½SE	1828-01-04	FD	W2SE	R:MORGAN
3282	" "	13	E½SW	1828-10-24	FD	E2SW	R:MORGAN
3111	GILMORE, Henry	2	NE	1828-12-08	FD	NE	R:MORGAN
3139	GREEN, James	12	W½NW	1824-05-10	FD	W2NW	R:MORGAN
3137	" "	11	E½SW	1828-12-31	FD	E2SW	R:MORGAN
3138	" "	12	E½NW	1830-01-04	FD	E2NW	R:MORGAN
3141	" "	2	N½NW	1830-10-27	FD	N2NW	R:MORGAN
3140	" "	12	W½SE	1830-12-01	FD	W2SE	R:MORGAN
3157	GREEN, Janus	12	W½NE	1831-10-21	FD	W2NE	R:MORGAN S:F
3169	GREGORY, John	22	NWNE	1836-01-08	FD	NWNE	R:MORGAN
3179	GRIGG, John	9	SE	1836-02-09	FD	SE	R:PHILADELPHIA
3174	" "	30	E½SE	1836-02-09	FD	E2SE	R:PHILADELPHIA
3178	" "	9	E½SW	1836-02-09	FD	E2SW	R:PHILADELPHIA
3175	" "	7	NENE	1836-02-09	FD	NENE	R:PHILADELPHIA
3173	" "	30	E½NE	1836-02-09	FD	E2NE	R:PHILADELPHIA
3172	" "	29	W½SE	1836-02-09	FD	W2SE	R:PHILADELPHIA
3177	" "	8	W½NE	1836-02-09	FD	W2NE	R:PHILADELPHIA
3171	" "	29	W½NE	1836-02-09	FD	W2NE	R:PHILADELPHIA
3170	" "	29	NW	1836-02-09	FD	NW	R:PHILADELPHIA

ID	Individual in Patent	Sec.	Sec. Part	Purchase Date	Sale Type	IL Aliquot Part	For More Info . . .
3176	GRIGG, John (Cont'd)	8	E½NW	1836-02-09	FD	E2NW	R:PHILADELPHIA
3314	GRIMSLEY, William	16	L6	1837-02-13	SC	L6E2SWMA	
3321	GRIMSLEY, William Sen	10	E½NW	1831-03-07	FD	E2NW	R:MORGAN
3180	GUM, John	21	NENW	1835-08-05	FD	NENW	R:MORGAN
3182	GUNN, John	21	W½NE	1830-10-12	FD	W2NE	R:MORGAN
3181	" "	21	SENW	1833-12-23	FD	SENW	R:MORGAN
3164	HAMILTON, John C	36	W½SE	1831-11-08	FD	W2SE	R:CASS
3029	HARNEY, Alfred G	35	SESE	1835-03-17	FD	SESE	R:MORGAN
3030	" "	36	SWSW	1835-03-17	FD	SWSW	R:MORGAN
3055	HARNEY, Conrad	2	E½SE	1831-10-28	FD	E2SELS	R:MORGAN
3142	HARNEY, James	35	NESE	1835-09-25	FD	NESE	R:MORGAN
3221	HARNEY, Margaret	36	E½SW	1830-11-12	FD	E2SW	R:MORGAN S:F
3056	HARVEY, Conrad	11	W½NE	1830-12-01	FD	W2NE	R:MORGAN
3269	HARVEY, Sophronia	11	E2NE	1831-05-03	FD	E2NEPRE	R:MORGAN S:F
3155	HEDENBERG, James V	3	SEN½	1830-09-30	FD	S2NE	R:MORGAN
3106	HENRY, George	35	W½SE	1835-07-20	FD	W2SE	R:MORGAN
3252	HENRY, Richard	12	W½SW	1829-05-04	FD	W2SW	R:KENTUCKY
3250	" "	11	E½SE	1829-05-04	FD	E2SE	R:KENTUCKY
3251	" "	12	E½SW	1829-08-31	FD	E2SW	R:MORGAN
3253	" "	28	SENW	1851-02-13	FD	SENW	R:MORGAN
3254	" "	28	SWNW	1852-12-23	FD	SWNW	
3071	HOAG, Ebenezer	14	E½NE	1829-01-13	FD	E2NE	R:MORGAN
3072	" "	23	NENW	1834-06-03	FD	NENW	R:MORGAN
3245	HOLMES, Peris	2	W½SW	1829-10-24	FD	W2SW	R:MORGAN
3244	" "	2	S½NW	1830-01-15	FD	S2NW	R:MORGAN
3242	" "	11	W½NW	1830-09-20	FD	W2NW	R:MORGAN
3248	" "	3	N½NE	1830-11-11	FD	N2NE	R:MORGAN
3243	" "	15	W½SE	1835-06-29	FD	W2SE	R:MORGAN
3246	" "	22	NENE	1835-06-29	FD	NENE	R:MORGAN
3247	" "	23	NWNW	1835-06-29	FD	NWNW	R:MORGAN
3227	HOUGHAN, Thomas	36	NWSW	1836-02-08	FD	NWSW	R:SANGAMON G:79
3025	HOWARD, Alanson	14	SESW	1833-11-04	FD	SESW	R:MORGAN
3026	" "	15	E½SE	1835-03-12	FD	E2SE	R:MORGAN
3024	" "	14	NESW	1835-03-12	FD	NESW	R:MORGAN
3078	HOWARD, Ehakim	14	W½SE	1827-08-07	FD	W2SE	R:MORGAN
3195	HOWARD, Jordan	23	NWNE	1833-11-12	FD	NWNE	R:MORGAN
3237	HOWARD, Palmer	25		1834-06-27	FD	W2NWSK	R:MORGAN
3276	HOWARD, Sylvester	14	W½NE	1830-01-05	FD	W2NE	R:MORGAN
3291	HOWARD, Tilton	23	SWNE	1835-03-03	FD	SWNE	R:MORGAN
3290	" "	23	SENW	1835-06-25	FD	SENW	R:MORGAN
3054	HUNTER, Colladon	4	W½SE	1829-12-26	FD	W2SE	R:MORGAN
3077	HUNTER, Edward	4	SW	1829-12-26	FD	SW	R:MORGAN
3143	HURST, James	1	NE	1829-06-13	FD	NE	R:MORGAN G:82
3143	HURST, John	1	NE	1829-06-13	FD	NE	R:MORGAN G:82
3206	JANUARY, Thomas	17	SE	1835-10-12	FD	SE	R:MORGAN G:87
3207	" "	20	NE	1835-10-12	FD	NE	R:MORGAN G:87
3208	" "	9	W½SW	1835-10-12	FD	W2SW	R:MORGAN G:87
3209	JANUARY, Thomas T	17	E½SW	1835-10-24	FD	E2SW	R:MORGAN G:86
3285	" "	20	E½NW	1836-02-25	FD	E2NWLS	R:MORGAN
3053	JENKINS, Christopher	16	L8	1836-09-02	SC	L8E2SEMA	
3052	" "	16	L7	1836-09-02	SC	L7W2SEMA	
3051	" "	16	L2	1836-09-02	SC	L2W2NEMA	
3050	" "	16	L1	1836-09-02	SC	L1E2NEMA	
3043	JOHNSON, Benjamin	17	W½SW	1831-02-01	FD	W2SW	R:MORGAN
3044	" "	21	NESW	1834-11-12	FD	NESW	R:MORGAN
3045	" "	21	NWSW	1835-10-26	FD	NWSW	R:MORGAN
3312	JOHNSON, William G	30	NWSE	1853-12-13	FD	NWSE	
3079	KEATH, Eleazer	18	E½SE	1830-10-29	FD	E2SE	R:MORGAN
3203	KLEIN, Joseph	17	W½NE	1830-10-01	FD	W2NE	R:SANGAMON
3204	" "	8	W½SE	1830-10-01	FD	W2SE	R:SANGAMON
3268	LEFFLER, Shepherd	27	NWSE	1198-02-03	FD	NWSE	R:MORGAN
3267	" "	27	NE	1835-02-02	FD	NE	R:MORGAN
3266	" "	27	E½NW	1835-02-02	FD	E2NW	R:MORGAN
3265	" "	22	E½SW	1835-02-02	FD	E2SW	R:MORGAN
3146	LITTON, James	1	E½SE	1829-09-21	FD	E2SE	R:MORGAN
3148	MAGILL, James	1	NW	1824-10-20	FD	NWFR	R:MORGAN
3027	MASON, Alexander	19	E½SE	1830-11-01	FD	E2SE	R:MORGAN
3028	" "	19	W½SE	1831-03-29	FD	W2SELS	R:MORGAN
3149	MCALISTER, James	8	NWNW	1835-12-21	FD	NWNW	R:MORGAN
3196	MCALISTER, Jordan W	28	NWSW	1852-12-18	FD	NWSW	
3197	" "	32	W½SW	1852-12-18	FD	W2SW	
3259	MCALLISTER, Robert H	32	NWSE	1853-02-24	FD	NWSE	
3315	MCAVOY, William	16	L4	1849-03-12	SC	LOT4W2NW	

ID	Individual in Patent	Sec.	Sec. Part	Purchase Date	Sale Type	IL Aliquot Part	For More Info . . .
3183	MCCORMAC, John	20	SESE	1835-08-05	FD	SESE	R:MORGAN
3184	" "	29	NENE	1835-08-05	FD	NENE	R:MORGAN
3295	MCCORMICK, Walter	23	SWSW	1833-07-25	FD	SWSW	R:KENTUCKY
3292	" "	22	SE	1833-07-25	FD	SE	R:KENTUCKY
3294	" "	23	NWSW	1835-06-29	FD	NWSW	R:MORGAN
3293	" "	23	NWSW	1835-06-29	FD	NWSW	R:MORGAN
3294	" "	23	NWSW	1835-06-30	FD	NWSW	R:MORGAN
3293	" "	23	NWSW	1835-06-30	FD	NWSW	R:MORGAN
3167	MCCOY, William	20	NESW	1839-08-19	FD	NESW	R:MORGAN G:57
3185	MCDONALD, John	11	E½NE	1830-10-26	FD	E2NE	R:MORGAN
3156	MCKEAND, Jannet	32	E½SW	1852-11-11	FD	E2SW	S:F
3316	MCWAIN, William	7	W½SE	1829-11-03	FD	W2SE	R:MORGAN
3092	MILLEN, Elijah F	22	W½SW	1835-02-02	FD	W2SW	R:MORGAN
3091	" "	21	E½SE	1835-02-02	FD	E2SE	R:MORGAN
3270	MILLER, Squire B	33	SWSE	1835-09-03	FD	SWSE	R:MORGAN
3220	MILLION, Marcus	28	SWNE	1839-08-26	FD	SWNE	R:MORGAN
3271	MILLION, Squire B	28	SENE	1835-08-07	FD	SENE	R:MORGAN
3227	MOBLEY, Mordecai	36	NWSW	1836-02-08	FD	NWSW	R:SANGAMON G:79
3205	MORTEN, Joseph	9	W½NE	1828-10-22	FD	W2NE	R:MORGAN
3186	MURRAY, John	28	NWNE	1835-11-18	FD	NWNE	R:MORGAN
3150	NELSON, James	32	SWSE	1852-11-09	FD	SWSE	
3100	NORTHCUT, Elnor	18	N½SW	1835-06-29	FD	N2SW	R:MORGAN S:F
3104	PATTERSON, Franklin H	7	SENE	1835-12-14	FD	SENE	R:MORGAN
3105	" "	8	SWNW	1835-12-14	FD	SWNW	R:MORGAN
3260	REAUGH, Robert	13	SWNW	1835-11-16	FD	SWNW	R:MORGAN
3214	REEVE, Lazarus	6	W½SE	1828-12-27	FD	W2SE	R:MORGAN
3227	RIDGLEY, Nicholas	36	NWSW	1836-02-08	FD	NWSW	R:SANGAMON G:79
3210	ROBINSON, Kirker	15	W½SW	1835-06-05	FD	W2SW	R:MORGAN
3211	" "	21	E½NE	1835-06-05	FD	E2NE	R:MORGAN
3212	" "	22	SWNW	1835-06-25	FD	SWNW	R:MORGAN
3213	" "	31	E½NE	1835-06-30	FD	E2NE	R:MORGAN
3113	ROBLEY, Henry	5	E½SE	1823-11-12	FD	E2SE	R:MORGAN
3112	" "	14	E½SE	1827-08-24	FD	E2SE	R:MORGAN
3066	ROCKWELL, Dennis	9	E½NW	1828-10-18	FD	E2NW	R:MORGAN
3065	" "	4	NW	1828-12-05	FD	NWFR	R:MORGAN
3108	ROUTT, Harvey	23	NESE	1198-02-04	FD	NESE	R:MORGAN
3110	" "	24	E½NW	1834-10-08	FD	E2NW	R:MORGAN
3109	" "	23	NWSE	1835-05-08	FD	NWSE	R:MORGAN
3107	" "	23	E½SW	1835-10-05	FD	E2SW	R:MORGAN
3223	RUSSELL, Mary M	35	W½SW	1835-12-31	FD	W2SW	R:MORGAN S:F
3222	" "	34	E½SE	1835-12-31	FD	E2SE	R:MORGAN S:F
3151	SHEPARD, Benjamin	31	NWSW	1853-10-17	FD	NWSWFR	R:MORGAN
3046	" "	31	NWSW	1853-10-17	FD	NWSWFR	R:MORGAN
3217	SHEPHERD, Lewis J	16	L3	1849-03-12	SC	LOT3E2NW	
3272	SHEPHERD, Stephen	21	NWSE	1198-02-02	FD	NWSE	R:MORGAN
3275	" "	32	W½NW	1831-04-25	FD	W2NW	R:MORGAN
3273	" "	21	SWSW	1834-01-01	FD	SWSW	R:MORGAN
3274	" "	28	NENE	1836-02-22	FD	NENE	R:MORGAN
3288	SHEPHERD, Thornton	15	NWNW	1833-10-05	FD	NWNW	R:MORGAN
3289	SHEPPARD, Thornton	15	SWNW	1835-11-09	FD	SWNW	R:MORGAN
3117	SIMMS, Ignatius R	8	E½SE	1829-06-08	FD	E2SE	R:MORGAN
3063	SMEDLEY, David	6	NESE	1833-12-09	FD	NESE	R:MORGAN
3062	" "	5	NWSW	1833-12-09	FD	NWSW	R:MORGAN
3116	SMEDLEY, Hiram	33	NESW	1835-11-10	FD	NESW	R:MORGAN
3058	SMIDLEY, Daniel	34	NW	1835-04-11	FD	NW	R:MORGAN
3057	" "	27	SW	1835-04-11	FD	SW	R:MORGAN
3059	" "	35	E½SW	1835-07-17	FD	E2SW	R:MORGAN
3064	SMIDLEY, David	35	NW	1835-07-17	FD	NW	R:MORGAN
3031	SMITH, Arnton	33	SESW	1835-03-03	FD	SESW	R:MORGAN G:115
3151	SMITH, James P	31	NWSW	1836-03-26	FD	NWSW	R:MORGAN
3046	" "	31	NWSW	1836-03-26	FD	NWSW	R:MORGAN
3158	SMITH, Jesse	31	E½SW	1836-03-26	FD	E2SW	R:MORGAN
3189	SMITH, John	17	W½NW	1830-01-18	FD	W2NW	R:MORGAN
3188	" "	16	L5	1849-03-12	SC	LOT5W2SW	
3191	" "	29	SENE	1851-10-04	FD	SENE	
3190	" "	29	NESE	1851-10-04	FD	NESE	
3261	SMITH, Robert	13	W½NE	1829-12-26	FD	W2NE	R:MORGAN
3031	SMITH, Samuel	33	SESW	1835-03-03	FD	SESW	R:MORGAN G:115
3224	SPRINGER, Mary R	22	SWNE	1835-06-30	FD	SWNE	R:MORGAN S:F
3187	STEBBINS, John O	4	NE	1831-05-23	FD	NE	R:MORGAN
3208	STETTINIUS, Joseph	9	W½SW	1835-10-12	FD	W2SW	R:MORGAN G:87
3206	" "	17	SE	1835-10-12	FD	SE	R:MORGAN G:87
3207	" "	20	NE	1835-10-12	FD	NE	R:MORGAN G:87

ID	Individual in Patent	Sec.	Sec. Part	Purchase Date	Sale Type	IL Aliquot Part	For More Info . . .
3209	STITINIUS, Joseph	17	E½SW	1835-10-24	FD	E2SW	R:MORGAN G:86
3035	STONE, Barton	26	SW	1835-07-17	FD	SW	R:MORGAN
3129	STRAWN, Jacob	7	NWSW	1835-01-06	FD	NWSW	R:MORGAN
3128	" "	7	NW	1835-01-06	FD	NW	R:MORGAN
3127	" "	6	SW	1835-12-21	FD	SW	R:MORGAN
3101	SWEET, Francis	23	E½NE	1831-11-25	FD	E2NE	R:MORGAN
3159	SWEET, Joel	23	S½SE	1835-02-14	FD	S2SE	R:MORGAN
3193	SWEET, Jonathon	11	W½SE	1823-11-12	FD	W2SE	R:MORGAN
3194	" "	2	W½SE	1823-11-12	FD	W2SE	R:MORGAN
3241	SWEET, Peleg	2	E½SW	1828-12-31	FD	E2SW	R:MORGAN
3240	" "	11	E½NW	1831-10-29	FD	E2NWLS	R:MORGAN
3264	SWIGERT, Samuel	24	E½NE	1830-10-07	FD	E2NE	R:MORGAN
3262	" "	13	E½NE	1830-10-07	FD	E2NE	R:MORGAN
3263	" "	13	W½NW	1830-10-18	FD	W2NW	R:MORGAN
3073	TINGLE, Ebenezer	35	SEN½	1835-02-10	FD	S2NE	R:MORGAN
3075	" "	36	W½NW	1835-02-10	FD	W2NW	R:MORGAN
3074	" "	36	E½NW	1835-08-17	FD	E2NW	R:MORGAN
3076	TINGLE, Ebiner	35	N½NE	1835-04-03	FD	N2NE	R:SANGAMON
3153	TURNBULL, James	14	SWNW	1835-03-14	FD	SWNW	R:MORGAN
3152	" "	14	E½NW	1835-03-14	FD	E2NW	R:MORGAN
3154	" "	14	W½SW	1835-06-13	FD	W2SW	R:MORGAN
3115	VARNER, Henry	20	W½SW	1830-12-10	FD	W2SW	R:MORGAN
3114	" "	20	SESW	1836-06-04	FD	SESW	R:MORGAN
3287	VERRY, William C	7	W½NE	1827-01-03	FD	W2NE	R:MORGAN G:130
3322	WALKER, William	31	W½SE	1835-10-06	FD	W2SE	R:MORGAN
3144	WESTHROPE, James L	20	W½SE	1835-12-16	FD	W2SE	R:MORGAN
3145	WESTROPE, James L	21	SWSE	1835-02-14	FD	SWSE	R:MORGAN
3226	WESTROPE, Mary	19	W½NE	1830-01-18	FD	W2NE	R:MORGAN S:F
3225	" "	17	E½NW	1830-01-18	FD	E2NW	R:MORGAN S:F
3255	WESTROPE, Richard	28	NWNW	1835-12-22	FD	NWNW	R:MORGAN
3317	WESTROPE, William P	21	SESW	1835-02-14	FD	SESW	R:MORGAN
3318	" "	28	NENW	1835-12-22	FD	NENW	R:MORGAN
3119	WHITLOCK, Ira	29	SESE	1835-12-14	FD	SESE	R:MORGAN
3118	" "	28	SWSW	1835-12-14	FD	SWSW	R:MORGAN
3192	WHITLOCK, John	9	E½NE	1830-11-04	FD	E2NE	R:MORGAN
3132	WING, Jacob	15	E½NE	1829-11-17	FD	E2NE	R:MORGAN
3130	" "	10	W½SE	1830-10-28	FD	W2SE	R:MORGAN
3131	" "	14	NWNW	1835-12-22	FD	NWNW	R:MORGAN
3093	WISNELL, Elijah	6	NE	1823-11-12	FD	NEFR	R:MORGAN
3287	WISWALL, Thomas	7	W½NE	1827-01-03	FD	W2NE	R:MORGAN G:130
3286	" "	5	SWSW	1836-01-30	FD	SWSW	R:MORGAN
3094	WISWELL, Elijah	5	NW	1823-11-12	FD	NWFR	R:MORGAN
3085	WOLCOTT, Elihu	3	W½SW	1831-03-07	FD	W2SW	R:MORGAN
3087	" "	8	W½SW	1831-03-07	FD	W2SW	R:MORGAN
3080	" "	10	E½SE	1831-04-14	FD	E2SE	R:MORGAN
3084	" "	3	E½SW	1831-04-14	FD	E2SW	R:MORGAN
3082	" "	15	W½NE	1831-04-23	FD	W2NE	R:MORGAN
3086	" "	4	E½SE	1831-05-25	FD	E2SE	R:MORGAN
3081	" "	10	W½NW	1835-05-13	FD	W2NW	R:MORGAN
3083	" "	19	W½	1836-01-22	FD	W2	R:MORGAN
3097	WOLCOTT, Elisha	3	NW	1831-04-11	FD	NWFR	R:MORGAN
3095	" "	10	W½SW	1831-04-11	FD	W2SWLS	R:MORGAN
3096	" "	20	NENE	1836-02-13	FD	NENE	R:MORGAN
3098	" "	30	NW	1836-02-13	FD	NW	R:MORGAN
3088	WOOLCOTT, Elihu	5	E½SW	1830-12-25	FD	E2SW	R:MORGAN
3023	WOOLMS, Absolem	5	NE	1823-11-12	FD	NEFR	R:MORGAN
3022	YATES, Abner	31	S½NW	1853-10-06	FD	S2NWFR	R:MORGAN
3021	" "	31	NENW	1854-03-09	FD	NENWFR	R:MORGAN
3020	" "	31	E½SE	1854-03-09	FD	E2SE	R:MORGAN

Patent Map

T14-N R10-W
3rd PM Meridian

Map Group 13

Township Statistics

Parcels Mapped	:	304
Number of Patents	:	1
Number of Individuals	:	170
Patentees Identified	:	163
Number of Surnames	:	119
Multi-Patentee Parcels	:	11
Oldest Patent Date	:	2/2/1198
Most Recent Patent	:	12/15/1854
Block/Lot Parcels	:	9
Cities and Towns	:	2
Cemeteries	:	7

Patent map grid (Sections 4–9, 16–21, 28–33):

Section 6: DEEDS Jacob 1830; WISNELL Elijah 1823; REEVE Lazarus 1828; SMEDLEY David 1833; CARTER Ebenezer 1835

Section 5: WISWELL Elijah 1823; SMEDLEY David 1833; WOOLCOTT Elihu 1830; WISWALL Thomas 1836; BENTLEY Thomas 1828; ROBLEY Henry 1823

Section 4: WOOLMS Absolem 1823; ROCKWELL Dennis 1828; HUNTER Edward 1829; HUNTER Colladon 1829; WOLCOTT Elihu 1831; STEBBINS John O 1831

Section 7: STRAWN Jacob 1835; WISWALL [130] Thomas 1827; GRIGG John 1836; PATTERSON Franklin H 1835; STRAWN Jacob 1835; ANGELOW John 1835; ANGELOW John 1835; MCWAIN William 1829; ARNETT Thomas B 1831; WOLCOTT Elihu 1831

Section 8: MCALISTER James 1835; PATTERSON Franklin H 1835; GRIGG John 1836; GRIGG John 1836; BERRY Thomas H 1835; KLEIN Joseph 1830; CARTER Ebenezer 1835; SIMMS Ignatius R 1829

Section 9: DEW Peter 1828; ROCKWELL Dennis 1828; MORTEN Joseph 1828; WHITLOCK John 1830; STETTINIUS [87] Joseph 1835; GRIGG John 1836; GRIGG John 1836

Section 18: ARNETT Thomas B 1830; ANGELO John 1829; ARNETT Thomas B 1831; NORTHCUT Elnor 1835; GENTRY James M 1834; COFFIN Nathaniel 1837; COFFIN Nathaniel 1837

Section 17: SMITH John 1830; WESTROPE Mary 1830; KLEIN Joseph 1830; KEATH Eleazer 1830; JOHNSON Benjamin 1831; STITINIUS [86] Joseph 1835; STETTINIUS [87] Joseph 1835

Section 16: ANGELO John 1830; Lots-Sec. 16
- L1 JENKINS, Christopher 1836
- L2 JENKINS, Christopher 1836
- L3 SHEPHERD, Lewis J 1849
- L4 MCAVOY, William 1849
- L5 SMITH, John 1849
- L6 GRIMSLEY, William 1837
- L7 JENKINS, Christopher 1836
- L8 JENKINS, Christopher 1836

Section 19: WOLCOTT Elihu 1836; WESTROPE Mary 1830; COFFIN Nathaniel 1837; MASON Alexander 1831; MASON Alexander 1830

Section 20: COFFIN Nathaniel 1837; JANUARY Thomas T 1836; STETTINIUS [87] Joseph 1835; WOLCOTT Elisha 1836; DOWLING [57] John 1839; WESTHROPE James L 1835; VARNER Henry 1830; VARNER Henry 1836; MCCORMAC John 1835

Section 21: FOLDON William 1835; GUM John 1835; GUNN John 1830; GUNN John 1833; ROBINSON Kirker 1835; JOHNSON Benjamin 1835; JOHNSON Benjamin 1834; SHEPHERD Stephen 1198; SHEPHERD Stephen 1834; WESTROPE William P 1835; WESTROPE James L 1835; MILLEN Elijah F 1835

Section 30: WOLCOTT Elisha 1836; COFFIN Nathaniel 1837; GRIGG John 1836; COFFIN Nathaniel 1837; JOHNSON William G 1853; GRIGG John 1836; BAILEY William 1835; COFFIN Nathaniel 1837

Section 29: GRIGG John 1836; BAILEY William 1835; GRIGG John 1836

Section 28: MCCORMAC John 1835; SMITH John 1851; GRIGG John 1836; SMITH John 1851; WHITLOCK Ira 1835; HENRY Richard 1852; MCALISTER Jordan W 1852; WHITLOCK Ira 1835; WESTROPE Richard 1835; HENRY Richard 1852; BOTTS Bernard 1835; BOTTS Bernard 1836

Section 21/28 east: WESTROPE William P 1835; MURRAY John 1835; MILLION Marcus 1839; SHEPHERD Stephen 1836; MILLION Squire B 1835; BOTTS Bernard 1831

Section 31: ANGDANO Benjamin 1837; YATES Abner 1854; YATES Abner 1853; FAHNESTOCK Benjamin 1854; ROBINSON Kirker 1835; SHEPARD Benjamin 1853; SMITH James P 1836; SMITH Jesse 1836; WALKER William 1835; YATES Abner 1854

Section 32: SHEPHERD Stephen 1831; ADAMS Elijah 1829; BOTTS Barnett 1828; ADAMS William 1828; MCALISTER Jordan W 1852; MCKEAND Jannet 1852; MCALLISTER Robert H 1853; NELSON James 1852; FATHERKILE Nicholas 1828

Section 33: ADAMS Elijah 1830; ADAMS Joseph 1835; ADAMS Joseph 1833; FRENCH William 1834; FATHERKILE Nicholas 1828; SMEDLEY Hiram 1835; FRENCH William 1835; SMITH [115] Arnton 1835; MILLER Squire B 1835; BROWN Liner 1830

Section 3 / 2 / 1 row

WOLCOTT Elisha 1831

HOLMES Peris 1830
HEDENBERG James V 1830

GREEN James 1830
HOLMES Peris 1830

GILMORE Henry 1828

2

MAGILL James 1824

1

HURST [82] James 1829

WOLCOTT Elihu 1831 | WOLCOTT Elihu 1831 **3**
DELANY William 1831 | CLARK John 1828
HOLMES Peris 1829 | SWEET Peleg 1828
SWEET Jonathon 1823 | HARNEY Conrad 1831
ANDERSON Dickey 1828 | BRISBIN William 1828
BRISBIN William 1828 | LITTON James 1829

Section 10 / 11 / 12

WOLCOTT Elihu 1835 | GRIMSLEY William Sen 1831 | DELANY William 1830 | CLARK John 1829
HOLMES Peris 1830 | SWEET Peleg 1831 | HARVEY Conrad 1830
HARVEY Sophronia 1831 | MCDONALD John 1830
GREEN James 1824 | GREEN James 1830 | GREEN Janus 1831 | ANDERSON Dickey 1827

WOLCOTT Elisha 1831 | FANNING Levi 1830 **10** WING Jacob 1830 | WOLCOTT Elihu 1831
BRYANT [18] Arthur 1831 **11** GREEN James 1828 | SWEET Jonathon 1823 | HENRY Richard 1829
HENRY Richard 1829 **12** HENRY Richard 1829 | GREEN James 1830 | DUDHOPE Thomas 1835

Section 15 / 14 / 13

SHEPHERD Thornton 1833 / SHEPPARD Thornton 1835 | FANNING Levi 1830 | WOLCOTT Elihu 1831 | WING Jacob 1829
WING Jacob 1835 | TURNBULL James 1835 / TURNBULL James 1835
HOWARD Sylvester 1830 | HOAG Ebenezer 1829
SWIGERT Samuel 1830 / REAUGH Robert 1835 | ENNOS Williams 1823 **13** | SMITH Robert 1829 | SWIGERT Samuel 1830

ROBINSON Kirker 1835 | DUDHOPE David 1835 / DUDHOPE David 1835 **15** HOLMES Peris 1835 | HOWARD Alanson 1835
HOWARD Alanson 1835 **14** TURNBULL James 1835 | HOWARD Alanson 1833
HOWARD Ehakim 1827 | ROBLEY Henry 1827
GEERS William 1833 | GILLILAND Thomas 1828 | GILLILAND Thomas 1828 | CRAIG James 1830

Section 22 / 23 / 24

BROWN William S 1834 | GREGORY John 1836 | HOLMES Peris 1835
ROBINSON Kirker 1835 | BROWN William S 1834 | SPRINGER Mary R 1835 | BROWN Robert 1835
HOLMES Peris 1835 | HOAG Ebenezer 1834 | BROWN Robert 1835 BROWN Robert 1835 | HOWARD Tilton 1835
HOWARD Jordan 1833 | SWEET Francis 1831 | HOWARD Tilton 1835
ROUTT Harvey 1834 | BROWN Bedford 1831 **24** | CRAIG James 1830 | SWIGERT Samuel 1830

MILLEN Elijah F 1835 | LEFFLER Shepherd 1835 **22** MCCORMICK Walter 1833
MCCORMICK Walter 1835 MCCORMICK Walter 1835 / MCCORMICK Walter 1833 | ROUTT Harvey 1835 **23** SWEET Joel 1835
ROUTT Harvey 1835 | ROUTT Harvey 1198
BROWN Bedford 1833 | BROWN Beaford 1835 / BROWN Elizabeth 1834 | BROWN Bedford 1831 | BROWN Bedford 1830

Section 27 / 26 / 25

FRENCH William 1836 | LEFFLER Shepherd 1835 | LEFFLER Shepherd 1835
BURROWS Isaac R 1835 | BARROWS Isaac R 1835 | BROWN James 1835
HOWARD Palmer 1834 | BARROWS Isaac R 1832 | BARROWS [6] Barnabas 1831 **25**

27 | LEFFLER Shepherd 1198 | FRENCH William 1835 | FRENCH William 1835
SMIDLEY Daniel 1835 **26** STONE Barton 1835 | BARROWS Isaac R 1835 | FRY Joseph 1835
FRY Joseph 1835 | BARROWS Isaac R 1835 | FRY Joseph 1835 | CRAIG William 1833 | CRAIG James 1835

Section 34 / 35 / 36

SMIDLEY Daniel 1835 | FRENCH William 1835 **34** FRENCH William 1836
SMIDLEY David 1835 **35** | TINGLE Ebiner 1835 / TINGLE Ebenezer 1835
TINGLE Ebenezer 1835 | TINGLE Ebenezer 1835
EADS John 1830 **36**

BROWN Liner 1828 | BROWN Franklin 1835 / BROWN Parmelia 1835 | BROWN Franklin 1835 / BROWN Parmelia 1835 | RUSSELL Mary M 1835
RUSSELL Mary M 1835 | SMIDLEY Daniel 1835
HENRY George 1835 | HARNEY James 1835 / HARNEY Alfred G 1835
MOBLEY [79] Mordecai 1836 | HARNEY Margaret 1830 / HARNEY Alfred G 1835 | HAMILTON John C 1831 | BARROWS Isaac R 1831

Helpful Hints

1. This Map's INDEX can be found on the preceding pages.

2. Refer to Map "C" to see where this Township lies within Morgan County, Illinois.

3. Numbers within square brackets [ ] denote a multi-patentee land parcel (multi-owner). Refer to Appendix "C" for a full list of members in this group.

4. Areas that look to be crowded with Patentees usually indicate multiple sales of the same parcel (re-issues), cancellations or voided transactions (that we map, anyway) or overlapping parcels. We opt to show even these ambiguous parcels, which oftentimes lead to research avenues not yet taken.

Legend

— Patent Boundary
— Section Boundary
No Patents Found (or Outside County)
1., 2., 3., ... Lot Numbers (when beside a name)
[ ] Group Number (see Appendix "C")

Scale: Section = 1 mile X 1 mile (generally, with some exceptions)

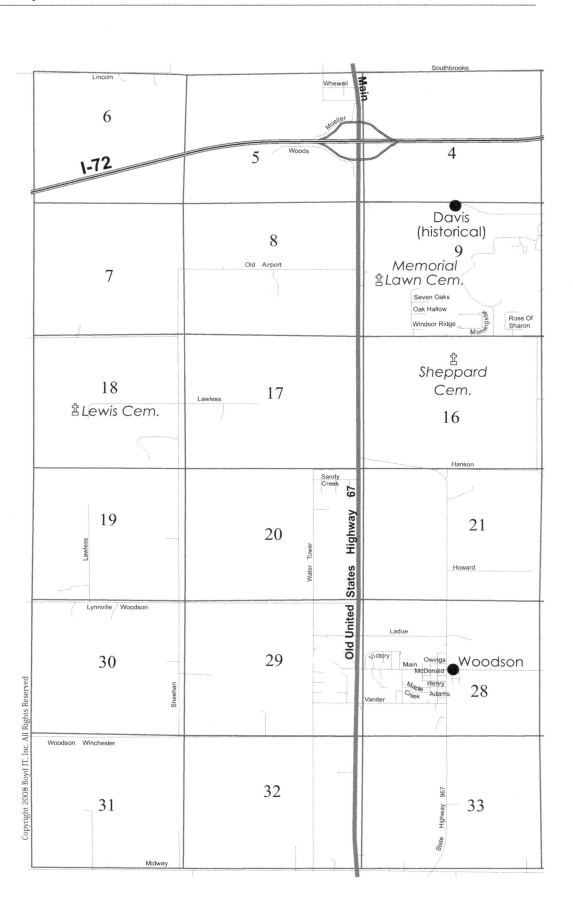

Road Map

T14-N R10-W
3rd PM Meridian

Map Group 13

Cities & Towns
Davis (historical)
Woodson

Cemeteries
Asbury Cemetery
Craig-Burrows Cemetery
Hoag Cemetery
Holmes Daniel D Cemetery
Lewis Cemetery
Memorial Lawn Cemetery
Sheppard Cemetery

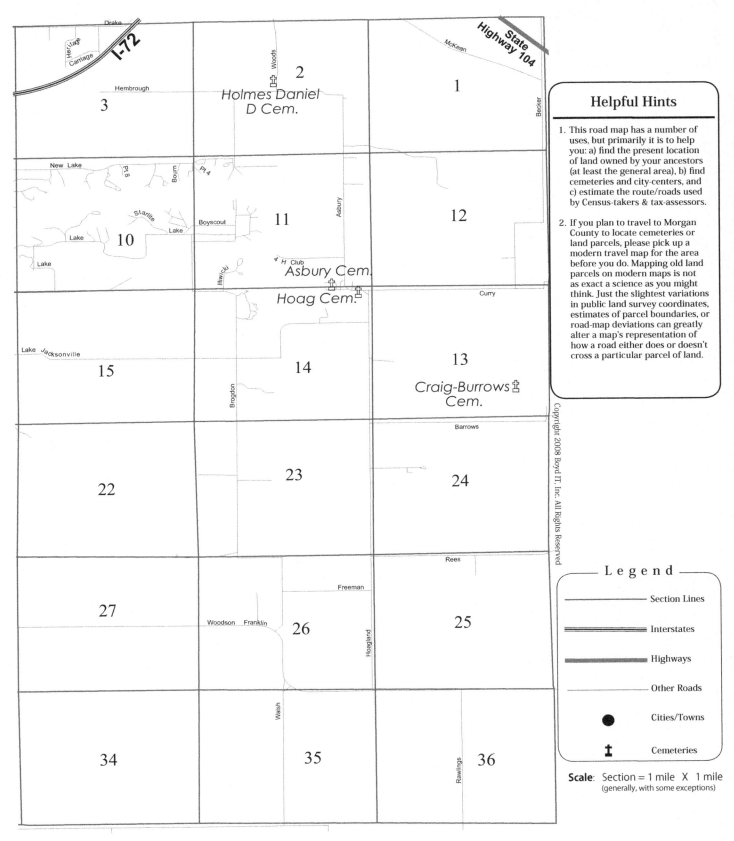

Helpful Hints

1. This road map has a number of uses, but primarily it is to help you: a) find the present location of land owned by your ancestors (at least the general area), b) find cemeteries and city-centers, and c) estimate the route/roads used by Census-takers & tax-assessors.

2. If you plan to travel to Morgan County to locate cemeteries or land parcels, please pick up a modern travel map for the area before you do. Mapping old land parcels on modern maps is not as exact a science as you might think. Just the slightest variations in public land survey coordinates, estimates of parcel boundaries, or road-map deviations can greatly alter a map's representation of how a road either does or doesn't cross a particular parcel of land.

Copyright 2008 Boyd IT, Inc. All Rights Reserved

Legend

———— Section Lines

══════ Interstates

▬▬▬▬ Highways

———— Other Roads

● Cities/Towns

✝ Cemeteries

Scale: Section = 1 mile X 1 mile
(generally, with some exceptions)

Historical Map

T14-N R10-W
3rd PM Meridian

Map Group 13

Cities & Towns
Davis (historical)
Woodson

Cemeteries
Asbury Cemetery
Craig-Burrows Cemetery
Hoag Cemetery
Holmes Daniel D Cemetery
Lewis Cemetery
Memorial Lawn Cemetery
Sheppard Cemetery

6	5		4
7	8	● Davis (historical) / Memorial Lawn Cem.	9
18 / Lewis Cem.	17	Sheppard Cem. / Sandy Creek	16
19	20	Brushy Fork	21
30	29 / Spoon Creek	28 ● Woodson	
31	32 / Henry Creek	33 / Henry Creek	

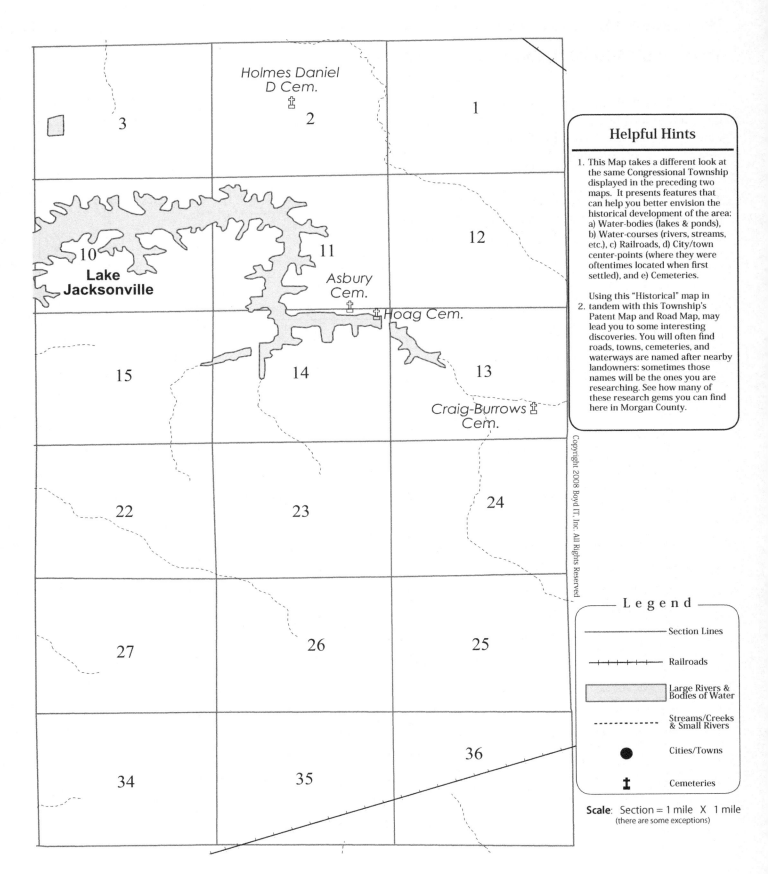

3

Holmes Daniel
D Cem.
✝
2

1

10
Lake
Jacksonville

11

12

Asbury
Cem.
✝

✝ Hoag Cem.

15

14

13

Craig-Burrows ✝
Cem.

22

23

24

27

26

25

34

35

36

Helpful Hints

1. This Map takes a different look at the same Congressional Township displayed in the preceding two maps. It presents features that can help you better envision the historical development of the area: a) Water-bodies (lakes & ponds), b) Water-courses (rivers, streams, etc.), c) Railroads, d) City/town center-points (where they were oftentimes located when first settled), and e) Cemeteries.

   Using this "Historical" map in
2. tandem with this Township's Patent Map and Road Map, may lead you to some interesting discoveries. You will often find roads, towns, cemeteries, and waterways are named after nearby landowners: sometimes those names will be the ones you are researching. See how many of these research gems you can find here in Morgan County.

Legend

———————— Section Lines

+–+–+–+–+– Railroads

▭ Large Rivers & Bodies of Water

– – – – – – Streams/Creeks & Small Rivers

● Cities/Towns

✝ Cemeteries

Scale: Section = 1 mile X 1 mile
(there are some exceptions)

Map Group 14: Index to Land Patents

Township 14-North Range 9-West (3rd PM)

After you locate an individual in this Index, take note of the Section and Section Part then proceed to the Land Patent map on the pages immediately following. You should have no difficulty locating the corresponding parcel of land.

The "For More Info" Column will lead you to more information about the underlying Patents. See the *Legend* at right, and the "How to Use this Book" chapter, for more information.

ID	Individual in Patent	Sec.	Sec. Part	Purchase Date	Sale Type	IL Aliquot Part	For More Info . . .
3366	ANDERSON, Dickey	7	E½SE	1831-10-28	FD	E2SELS	R:MORGAN
3542	ANTLE, Michael	10	E½NE	1828-03-25	FD	E2NE	R:MORGAN
3543	AUTLE, Michael	11	W½NW	1826-10-27	FD	W2NW	R:MORGAN
3334	BARROWS, Barnabas	19	SESW	1835-06-22	FD	SESW	R:MORGAN
3335	BARROWS, Barnabus	30	NE	1835-10-19	FD	NE	R:MORGAN
3404	BARROWS, Isaac R	18		1831-12-10	FD	N02SW	R:MORGAN
3545	" "	18		1831-12-10	FD	N02SW	R:MORGAN
3405	" "	19		1831-12-10	FD	N02SW	R:MORGAN
3405	" "	19		1831-12-10	FD	N02NW	R:MORGAN
3406	" "	31	SWNW	1835-03-25	FD	SWNW	R:MORGAN
3379	BERRY, Garrison W	25	W½NW	1829-11-03	FD	W2NW	R:MORGAN
3456	BERRY, Jesse	7	NESW	1823-10-29	FD	NESW	R:MORGAN
3544	BOURLAND, Miles	35	NWSW	1833-03-20	FD	NWSW	R:MORGAN
3412	BOYER, Jacob	10	W½SW	1828-01-18	FD	W2SW	R:MORGAN
3413	" "	16	L8	1836-02-13	SC	LOT8	
3458	BOYER, John	9	E½SE	1829-03-06	FD	E2SE	R:MORGAN
3457	" "	16	L1	1836-02-13	SC	LOT1	
3564	BRISBIN, William	7	W½NE	1825-02-23	FD	W2NE	R:SANGAMON
3599	" "	7	W½NE	1825-02-23	FD	W2NE	R:SANGAMON
3598	" "	7	E½NE	1828-12-12	FD	E2NE	R:MORGAN
3336	BROWN, Bedford	30	E½SE	1831-07-26	FD	E2SE	R:MORGAN
3426	BROWN, James L	19	E½NE	1834-08-23	FD	E2NE	R:MORGAN
3427	" "	19	NENW	1834-08-23	FD	NENW	R:MORGAN
3428	" "	19	NWNE	1834-08-23	FD	NWNE	R:MORGAN
3600	BRUTON, William	5	NE	1828-01-01	FD	NEFR	R:MORGAN
3328	BUCHANAN, Alexander	11	W½SW	1833-10-18	FD	W2SW	R:MORGAN
3339	BUCHANAN, Benjamin	3	E½SE	1827-03-12	FD	E2SE	R:MORGAN
3337	" "	2	N½NW	1833-10-18	FD	N2NW	R:MORGAN
3338	" "	2	SWNE	1835-09-26	FD	SWNE	R:MORGAN
3507	BUCHANAN, Joseph	2	W½SW	1825-03-23	FD	W2SW	R:MORGAN
3504	" "	10	W½NE	1828-07-22	FD	W2NE	R:MORGAN
3506	" "	2	E½SW	1831-07-23	FD	E2SW	R:MORGAN
3505	" "	11	E½NW	1831-07-23	FD	E2NW	R:MORGAN
3340	BUCHANNON, Benjamin	2	S½NW	1829-10-10	FD	S2NW	R:MORGAN
3459	BUCKHANAN, John	2	N½NE	1835-09-29	FD	N2NE	R:MORGAN
3588	BULLARD, Theophilus	31	E½SE	1831-11-03	FD	E2SELS	R:MORGAN
3589	" "	32	W½SW	1831-11-03	FD	W2SW	R:MORGAN
3341	BURCH, Benjamin	36	E½NW	1828-01-02	FD	E2NW	R:MORGAN
3496	BURCH, John W	36	W½NE	1826-12-12	FD	W2NE	R:MORGAN
3495	" "	25	W½SE	1828-06-18	FD	W2SE	R:MORGAN
3416	CARNES, James	7	NWSW	1833-03-19	FD	NWSW	R:MORGAN
3332	CARNS, Andrew	5	W½SW	1829-06-18	FD	W2SW	R:MORGAN
3333	" "	7	E½NW	1831-07-25	FD	E2NW	R:MORGAN
3514	CARSELL, Joseph J	6	N½NE	1846-09-15	FD	N2NE	R:MORGAN
3465	CHALLEN, John	24	S½SW	1834-10-02	FD	S2SW	R:MORGAN
3466	" "	25	SENE	1834-10-03	FD	SENE	R:MORGAN

ID	Individual in Patent	Sec.	Sec. Part	Purchase Date	Sale Type	IL Aliquot Part	For More Info . . .
3467	CHALLEN, John (Cont'd)	35	SE	1836-02-06	FD	SE	R:MORGAN
3609	CHILTON, William P	6	E½SE	1829-11-02	FD	E2SE	R:MORGAN
3470	CLARK, John D B	15	S½	1834-06-06	FD	S2	R:KENTUCKY
3469	"	14	W½SW	1834-06-06	FD	W2SW	R:KENTUCKY
3471	"	22	W½NE	1834-06-06	FD	W2NE	R:KENTUCKY
3529	CLARKE, Lancelot	5	E½NW	1835-12-11	FD	E2NW	R:MORGAN
3468	CLAYTON, John	26	SWSE	1835-02-21	FD	SWSE	R:MORGAN
3602	CLAYTON, William	26	W½NE	1831-03-26	FD	W2NE	R:MORGAN G:39
3601	CLAYTON, William C	24	NESW	1835-06-09	FD	NESW	R:MORGAN
3602	CLAYTON, William R	26	W½NE	1831-03-26	FD	W2NE	R:MORGAN G:39
3349	COKER, Claibourn	5	NWNW	1836-01-07	FD	NWNW	R:MORGAN
3559	COUNTY, Morgan	16	L6	1836-02-13	SC	LOT6	
3558	"	16	L11	1836-02-13	SC	LOT11	
3477	COURTIS, John H	19	NESW	1834-10-02	FD	NESW	R:MORGAN
3577	COWNOVER, Robert	25	SW	1826-01-26	FD	SW	R:SANGAMON
3329	COX, Anciel	3	W½SE	1827-11-10	FD	W2SE	R:MORGAN
3331	COX, Ancil	3	SEN½	1829-09-21	FD	S2NE	R:MORGAN
3330	"	3	N½NE	1831-07-23	FD	N2NE	R:MORGAN
3530	COX, Lee W	5	SWNW	1850-10-28	FD	SWNWFR	R:MORGAN
3560	COX, Nathaniel	3	NW	1829-01-07	FD	NWFR	R:MORGAN
3361	CRAIG, David	30	E½NW	1832-02-25	FD	E2NW	R:MORGAN
3369	CRAIG, Edward	18	SWNW	1833-04-15	FD	SWNW	R:MORGAN
3402	CRAIG, Hugh G	18	SESW	1834-08-27	FD	SESW	R:MORGAN
3603	CRAIG, William	19	W½SE	1833-05-31	FD	W2SE	R:KENTUCKY
3606	CRAIG, William H	19	SENW	1833-04-04	FD	SENW	R:MORGAN
3607	"	19	SWNE	1833-04-15	FD	SWNE	R:MORGAN
3566	CUNNINGHAM, Peyton	5	W½SE	1829-07-17	FD	W2SE	R:MORGAN
3540	CYRUS, Mathew	36	W½SE	1830-03-04	FD	W2SE	R:MORGAN
3539	"	25	SENW	1833-01-30	FD	SENW	R:MORGAN
3538	"	25	NWNE	1834-10-02	FD	NWNE	R:MORGAN
3537	"	25	NENW	1834-10-02	FD	NENW	R:MORGAN
3541	CYRUS, Matthew	25	SWNE	1833-07-27	FD	SWNE	R:MORGAN
3385	DAVENPORT, Henry	17	NWNE	1832-10-06	FD	NWNE	R:MORGAN
3386	DEVANPORT, Henry	8	W½NE	1829-06-29	FD	W2NE	R:MORGAN
3387	DEVENPORT, Henry	8	W½SE	1828-09-19	FD	W2SE	R:MORGAN
3472	DEVORE, John	21	SW	1835-11-28	FD	SW	R:MORGAN
3479	DEVORE, John Jr	20	N½SE	1835-12-07	FD	N2SE	R:MORGAN
3579	DEVORE, Samuel	7	NWSE	1832-10-11	FD	NWSE	R:MORGAN
3371	DODD, Elijah	11	NWNE	1833-03-05	FD	NWNE	R:MORGAN
3417	DODD, James	2	SWSE	1833-06-05	FD	SWSE	R:MORGAN
3593	DODD, Uriah	5	E½SW	1829-05-14	FD	E2SW	R:MORGAN
3595	"	8	W½SW	1830-06-21	FD	W2SW	R:MORGAN
3594	"	8	W½NW	1832-03-27	FD	W2NW	R:SANGAMON
3481	DRENNAN, John L	20	E½SE	1828-11-06	FD	E2SE	R:SANGAMON
3362	DUDHOPE, David	21	NE	1835-06-25	FD	NE	R:MORGAN
3590	DUDHOPE, Thomas	18	NWNW	1835-03-14	FD	NWNW	R:MORGAN
3575	DUNCAN, Rice	10	W½NW	1826-10-16	FD	W2NW	R:MORGAN
3587	DUNCAN, Sidney P	16	L7	1836-02-13	SC	LOT7	
3363	DUNLAP, David	21	NW	1835-06-13	FD	NW	R:MORGAN
3473	EADS, John	31	W½SE	1830-11-04	FD	W2SE	R:MORGAN
3388	EDWARDS, Henry	3	W½SW	1826-06-16	FD	W2SW	R:MORGAN
3325	FANNING, Abraham	33	W½NE	1829-04-03	FD	W2NE	R:MORGAN
3324	"	29	E½SE	1831-08-22	FD	E2SE	R:MORGAN
3365	FANNING, Davis	29	W½SE	1831-09-08	FD	W2SE	R:MORGAN
3380	FANNING, George	30	W½SW	1829-04-04	FD	W2SW	R:MORGAN
3381	"	31	NWNW	1835-10-26	FD	NWNW	R:MORGAN
3384	FANNING, George W	33	E½NW	1828-11-06	FD	E2NW	R:MORGAN
3414	FANNING, Jacob	33	NENE	1836-03-01	FD	NENE	R:MORGAN
3475	FANNING, John	28	W½SW	1831-09-01	FD	W2SW	R:MORGAN
3476	"	33	W½NW	1831-11-02	FD	W2NWLS	R:MORGAN
3474	"	28	SESW	1834-10-09	FD	SESW	R:MORGAN
3508	FANNING, Joseph	33	E½SE	1828-02-26	FD	E2SE	R:MORGAN
3510	"	33	W½SE	1830-09-25	FD	W2SE	R:MORGAN
3509	"	33	E½SW	1831-08-22	FD	E2SW	R:MORGAN
3511	"	34	W½SW	1831-08-22	FD	W2SW	R:MORGAN
3512	FARMING, Joseph	30	E½SW	1825-09-04	FD	E2SW	R:MORGAN
3513	"	31	E½NW	1825-09-04	FD	E2NW	R:MORGAN
3347	FOSTER, Caleb	36	SWSW	1849-10-23	FD	SWSWVOID	
3346	"	36	NWSE	1849-10-23	FD	NWSEVOID	
3345	"	36	E½SW	1849-10-23	FD	E2SWVOID	
3615	"	36	E½SW	1849-10-23	FD	E2SWVOID	
3418	FOSTER, James	1	SE	1851-11-15	FD	SE	
3545	FRY, Milton	18		1833-11-22	FD	NENWSK	R:MORGAN

ID	Individual in Patent	Sec.	Sec. Part	Purchase Date	Sale Type	IL Aliquot Part	For More Info . . .
3551	FRY, Milton (Cont'd)	7		1833-11-22	FD	SWSESK	R:MORGAN
3404	" "	18		1833-11-22	FD	W2NESK	R:MORGAN
3545	" "	18		1833-11-22	FD	W2NESK	R:MORGAN
3612	" "	7		1833-11-22	FD	SWSESK	R:MORGAN
3404	" "	18		1833-11-22	FD	NENWSK	R:MORGAN
3612	" "	7		1833-11-22	FD	S2SWPTSK	R:MORGAN
3551	" "	7		1833-11-22	FD	S2SWPTSK	R:MORGAN
3549	" "	28	W½SE	1835-11-17	FD	W2SE	R:MORGAN
3550	" "	34	W½NW	1835-11-17	FD	W2NW	R:MORGAN
3548	" "	27	W½NW	1835-11-28	FD	W2NW	R:MORGAN
3546	" "	21	SE	1835-11-28	FD	SE	R:MORGAN
3547	" "	22	SW	1835-11-28	FD	SW	R:MORGAN
3605	FRY, William	29	NWSW	1835-02-12	FD	NWSW	R:MORGAN
3604	" "	20	SESW	1835-02-16	FD	SESW	R:MORGAN
3423	GREEN, James	4	W½SE	1827-01-10	FD	W2SE	R:MORGAN
3419	" "	19	SESE	1835-02-17	FD	SESE	R:MORGAN
3420	" "	20	W½NW	1835-03-17	FD	W2NW	R:MORGAN
3421	" "	28	E½NE	1835-06-22	FD	E2NE	R:MORGAN
3422	" "	28	W½NE	1835-07-03	FD	W2NE	R:MORGAN
3497	GREEN, John W	19	NESE	1835-03-20	FD	NESE	R:MORGAN
3535	GRIDER, Martin	9	E½NE	1828-09-27	FD	E2NE	R:MORGAN
3464	HAMILTON, John C	30	W½NW	1831-11-08	FD	W2NW	R:CASS
3463	" "	18	SENE	1834-10-27	FD	SENE	R:MORGAN
3462	" "	18	SE	1834-10-27	FD	SE	R:MORGAN
3461	" "	17	NWSW	1834-10-27	FD	NWSW	R:MORGAN
3460	" "	17	E½SW	1835-02-02	FD	E2SW	R:MORGAN
3351	HARP, Conrad	27	E½SW	1834-10-29	FD	E2SW	R:KENTUCKY
3352	" "	27	SE	1834-10-29	FD	SE	R:KENTUCKY
3353	" "	27	W½NE	1834-10-29	FD	W2NE	R:KENTUCKY
3354	" "	28	E½SE	1834-10-29	FD	E2SE	R:KENTUCKY
3355	" "	34	E½NW	1834-10-29	FD	E2NW	R:KENTUCKY
3356	" "	34	E½SW	1834-10-29	FD	E2SW	R:KENTUCKY
3350	" "	27	E½NW	1834-10-29	FD	E2NW	R:KENTUCKY
3357	HARP, Coonrod	27	W½SW	1835-11-13	FD	W2SW	R:MORGAN
3564	HEDENBERG, Peter	7	W½NE	1829-10-24	FD	W2NE	R:MORGAN
3599	" "	7	W½NE	1829-10-24	FD	W2NE	R:MORGAN
3565	HEDENBURG, Peter	6	W½SE	1829-10-24	FD	W2SE	R:MORGAN
3452	HEDINBERG, James V	6	SEN½	1829-10-14	FD	S2NE	R:MORGAN
3425	HOBBS, James	6	E½SW	1827-05-02	FD	E2SW	R:MORGAN
3424	" "	4	W½SW	1827-05-02	FD	W2SW	R:MORGAN
3557	HOUGHAN, Thomas	24	N½NW	1836-02-08	FD	N2NW	R:SANGAMON G:79
3555	" "	17	SWNE	1836-02-08	FD	SWNE	R:SANGAMON G:79
3556	" "	2	SENE	1836-02-08	FD	SENE	R:SANGAMON G:79
3554	" "	17	SESE	1836-02-08	FD	SESE	R:SANGAMON G:79
3360	HUEY, Daniel	24	NE	1835-10-17	FD	NE	R:MISSISSIPPI
3359	" "	13	SE	1835-10-17	FD	SE	R:MISSISSIPPI
3358	" "	12	E½	1835-10-17	FD	E2SEC	R:MISSISSIPPI
3374	HUNTER, Elizabeth	31	E½NE	1824-11-09	FD	E2NE	R:MORGAN S:F
3478	JOHNSON, John	10	E½NW	1827-12-11	FD	E2NW	R:MORGAN
3372	JOLLY, Elisha	35	E½SW	1832-05-03	FD	E2SW	R:MORGAN
3561	KELLOGG, Orville E	29	SWSW	1833-02-16	FD	SWSW	R:MORGAN
3391	KING, Henry	11	SE	1835-07-18	FD	SE	R:PENNSYLVANIA
3390	" "	11	E½NE	1835-07-18	FD	E2NE	R:PENNSYLVANIA
3389	" "	1	SW	1835-07-18	FD	SW	R:PENNSYLVANIA
3392	" "	11	SWNE	1835-07-18	FD	SWNE	R:PENNSYLVANIA
3393	" "	12	W½	1835-07-18	FD	W2	R:PENNSYLVANIA
3394	" "	2	E½SE	1835-07-18	FD	E2SE	R:PENNSYLVANIA
3395	" "	2	NWSE	1835-07-18	FD	NWSE	R:PENNSYLVANIA
3480	KING, John	26	E½NW	1830-11-18	FD	E2NW	R:MORGAN
3453	LEEPER, Janus	17	E½NW	1831-08-25	FD	E2NW	R:MORGAN S:F
3454	" "	8	E½SW	1831-08-25	FD	E2SW	R:MORGAN S:F
3553	LESLIE, Miron	14	E½	1835-06-20	FD	E2	R:MORGAN
3552	" "	13	W½	1835-07-15	FD	W2	R:MORGAN
3429	LITTON, James	6	W½NW	1830-01-01	FD	W2NW	R:MORGAN
3411	LUSK, J H	16	L9	1836-02-13	SC	LOT9	S:I
3410	" "	16	L16	1836-02-13	SC	LOT16	S:I
3533	LUTRELL, Lot	10	W½SE	1826-10-27	FD	W2SE	R:MORGAN
3534	LUTTRELL, Lott	10	E½SE	1831-08-04	FD	E2SE	R:MORGAN
3608	LUTTRELL, William	26	E½SE	1827-11-19	FD	E2SE	R:MORGAN
3430	LYNCH, James	32	E½NW	1827-01-23	FD	E2NW	R:MORGAN
3431	" "	32	W½SE	1830-02-10	FD	W2SE	R:MORGAN
3432	MACAIN, James	18	NESW	1835-06-13	FD	NESW	R:MORGAN
3433	" "	18	SENW	1835-06-13	FD	SENW	R:MORGAN

ID	Individual in Patent	Sec.	Sec. Part	Purchase Date	Sale Type	IL Aliquot Part	For More Info . . .
3485	MACAIN, John	20	E½NW	1835-03-14	FD	E2NW	R:MORGAN
3434	MAGILL, James	4	E½SE	1826-09-28	FD	E2SE	R:MORGAN
3435	" "	4	NE	1826-10-30	FD	NEFR	R:MORGAN
3375	MAYFIELD, Enness	23	E½SW	1830-11-23	FD	E2SW	R:MORGAN G:100
3375	MAYFIELD, Manning	23	E½SW	1830-11-23	FD	E2SW	R:MORGAN G:100
3436	MCCORMICK, James	17	SWSE	1833-04-09	FD	SWSE	R:MORGAN
3437	" "	20	NWNE	1833-04-09	FD	NWNE	R:MORGAN
3573	MCCORMICK, Ralph	18	NENE	1833-11-16	FD	NENE	R:MORGAN
3571	" "	16	L4	1836-02-13	SC	LOT4	
3572	" "	16	L5	1836-02-13	SC	LOT5	
3596	MCCORMICK, Valentine	17	NWSE	1834-05-18	FD	NWSE	R:MORGAN
3439	MCKEE, James	14	W½NW	1833-07-25	FD	W2NW	R:MORGAN
3438	" "	14	E½NW	1833-10-05	FD	E2NW	R:MORGAN
3344	MILLER, Bradshaw	34	E½SE	1830-10-30	FD	E2SE	R:MORGAN
3555	MOBLEY, Mordecai	17	SWNE	1836-02-08	FD	SWNE	R:SANGAMON G:79
3556	" "	2	SENE	1836-02-08	FD	SENE	R:SANGAMON G:79
3557	" "	24	N½NW	1836-02-08	FD	N2NW	R:SANGAMON G:79
3554	" "	17	SESE	1836-02-08	FD	SESE	R:SANGAMON G:79
3440	MOODY, James	32	W½NE	1831-04-06	FD	W2NE	R:MORGAN
3367	MOORE, Edmund	4	E½SW	1831-11-17	FD	E2SW	R:MORGAN
3368	" "	5	E½SE	1832-01-05	FD	E2SE	R:MORGAN
3515	MORTON, Joseph	26	E½NE	1832-01-02	FD	E2NE	R:MORGAN
3516	" "	27	E½NE	1833-10-07	FD	E2NE	R:MORGAN
3520	" "	36	W½SW	1835-07-02	FD	W2SW	R:MORGAN
3517	" "	34	NE	1835-07-02	FD	NE	R:MORGAN
3518	" "	35	SWNE	1835-07-02	FD	SWNE	R:MORGAN
3519	" "	35	SWSW	1835-07-02	FD	SWSW	R:MORGAN
3444	PARKINSON, James	23		1833-09-23	FD	W2SWSK	R:MORGAN
3445	" "	23		1833-09-23	FD	W2SWSK	R:MORGAN
3443	" "	22	SENE	1833-09-23	FD	SENE	R:MORGAN
3441	" "	22		1833-09-23	FD	E2SESK	R:MORGAN
3446	" "	23	W½NW	1833-09-23	FD	W2NW	R:MORGAN
3445	" "	23		1834-03-24	FD	E2NESK	R:MORGAN
3447	" "	35		1834-03-24	FD	E2NESK	R:MORGAN
3444	" "	23		1834-03-24	FD	E2NWSK	R:MORGAN
3445	" "	23		1834-03-24	FD	E2NWSK	R:MORGAN
3444	" "	23		1834-03-24	FD	E2NESK	R:MORGAN
3442	" "	22	NENE	1834-06-21	FD	NENE	R:MORGAN
3448	PARKISON, James	22	W½SE	1835-06-22	FD	W2SE	R:MORGAN
3610	PEMBERTON, William	33	W½SW	1828-01-01	FD	W2SW	R:MORGAN
3611	" "	4	S½NW	1829-06-15	FD	S2NW	R:MORGAN
3484	PETER, John M	11	E½SW	1198-02-03	FD	E2SW	R:MORGAN
3376	PETREE, Francis	10	E½SW	1827-03-30	FD	E2SW	R:MORGAN
3378	" "	15	W½NE	1829-12-26	FD	W2NE	R:MORGAN
3377	" "	15	E½NW	1831-08-04	FD	E2NW	R:MORGAN
3397	PEXTON, Henry	20	W½SW	1835-02-25	FD	W2SW	R:MORGAN
3396	" "	20	NESW	1835-12-08	FD	NESW	R:MORGAN
3551	PORTER, William	7		1826-09-27	FD	PT2NW	R:SANGAMON
3612	" "	7		1826-09-27	FD	PT2NW	R:SANGAMON
3584	PROSSEE, Samuel	13	NE	1835-07-20	FD	NE	R:MORGAN
3613	RANNELLS, William	17	W½NW	1832-02-04	FD	W2NW	R:MORGAN
3370	RANSDELL, Eli C	28	NESW	1836-01-07	FD	NESW	R:MORGAN
3382	RANSDELL, George	28	NENW	1836-01-07	FD	NENW	R:MORGAN
3570	RANSDELL, Presley	32	E½NE	1834-11-03	FD	E2NE	R:MORGAN
3569	" "	28	SWNW	1835-02-12	FD	SWNW	R:MORGAN
3568	" "	28	SENW	1835-03-25	FD	SENW	R:MORGAN
3591	RANSDELL, Thomas T	28	NWNW	1835-07-18	FD	NWNW	R:MORGAN
3536	RAWLIN, Mary	29	E½NW	1198-02-02	FD	E2NW	R:MORGAN S:F
3581	RAWNELLS, Samuel M	16	L13	1836-02-13	SC	LOT13	
3582	" "	16	L14	1836-02-13	SC	LOT14	
3583	" "	16	L15	1836-02-13	SC	LOT15	
3580	" "	16	L12	1836-02-13	SC	LOT12	
3521	REYNOLDS, Joseph	26	E½SW	1826-11-20	FD	E2SW	R:GREENE
3523	" "	35	E½NW	1829-12-07	FD	E2NW	R:MORGAN
3524	" "	35	NWNE	1833-03-25	FD	NWNE	R:MORGAN
3522	" "	26	SWSW	1835-03-09	FD	SWSW	R:MORGAN
3531	REYNOLDS, Lewis	26	NWSW	1834-06-06	FD	NWSW	R:MORGAN
3407	RICHARDSON, Isaac	3	E½SW	1826-09-09	FD	E2SW	R:MORGAN
3486	RICHARDSON, John	29	NWNW	1835-02-25	FD	NWNW	R:MORGAN
3487	" "	29	SWNW	1835-11-03	FD	SWNW	R:MORGAN
3563	RICHARDSON, Peter D	29	E½NE	1198-02-02	FD	E2NE	R:MORGAN
3562	" "	20	S½SE	1835-11-10	FD	S2SE	R:MORGAN
3597	RICHARDSON, Vincent S	29	W½NE	1835-02-11	FD	W2NE	R:MORGAN

ID	Individual in Patent	Sec.	Sec. Part	Purchase Date	Sale Type	IL Aliquot Part	For More Info . . .
3554	RIDGLEY, Nicholas	17	SESE	1836-02-08	FD	SESE	R:SANGAMON G:79
3555	" "	17	SWNE	1836-02-08	FD	SWNE	R:SANGAMON G:79
3556	" "	2	SENE	1836-02-08	FD	SENE	R:SANGAMON G:79
3557	" "	24	N½NW	1836-02-08	FD	N2NW	R:SANGAMON G:79
3576	RIGGIN, Right	36	E½SE	1828-11-24	FD	E2SE	R:MORGAN
3348	RUSSEL, Caswell	36	E½NE	1826-11-06	FD	E2NE	R:MORGAN
3483	RUYLE, John L	9	W½SE	1829-03-06	FD	W2SE	R:MORGAN
3482	" "	9	E½NE	1829-03-06	FD	E2NE	R:MORGAN
3532	SAMPLE, Light	15	E½NE	1831-10-08	FD	E2NE	R:MORGAN
3567	SAMPLES, Polly	15	W½NW	1829-07-21	FD	W2NW	R:MORGAN S:F
3489	SAPPINGTON, John	36	W½NW	1828-01-02	FD	W2NW	R:MORGAN
3488	" "	24	W½SE	1835-06-09	FD	W2SE	R:MORGAN
3398	SAUNDERSON, Henry	22	NW	1835-02-25	FD	NW	R:MORGAN
3399	" "	23	NE	1835-02-25	FD	NE	R:MORGAN
3400	" "	24	NWSW	1835-02-25	FD	NWSW	R:MORGAN
3401	" "	24	SWNW	1835-02-25	FD	SWNW	R:MORGAN
3578	SCARTH, Robert	24	SENW	1835-11-19	FD	SENW	R:MORGAN
3409	SCOTT, Isaac W	1	N½	1836-06-02	FD	N2	R:KENTUCKY
3408	" "	1	N½	1836-06-02	FD	N2	R:KENTUCKY
3409	" "	1	N½	1836-06-04	FD	N2	R:KENTUCKY
3408	" "	1	N½	1836-06-04	FD	N2	R:KENTUCKY
3449	SCOTT, James	26	NWSE	1835-02-18	FD	NWSE	R:MORGAN
3490	SCROGGIN, John	6	E½NW	1829-12-29	FD	E2NW	R:MORGAN
3503	SHELTON, Johnston	9	W½NE	1827-11-29	FD	W2NE	R:MORGAN
3501	" "	16	L10	1836-02-13	SC	LOT10	
3502	" "	16	L2	1836-02-13	SC	LOT2	
3403	SIMMS, Ignatius R	35	W½NW	1829-05-21	FD	W2NW	R:MORGAN
3585	SIMMS, Samuel R	14	E½SW	1835-06-17	FD	E2SW	R:MORGAN
3415	SPAINHOWER, Jacob	8	NENW	1836-07-19	FD	NENW	R:MORGAN
3491	SPEANHOWER, John	17	NESE	1834-10-08	FD	NESE	R:MORGAN
3492	SPIRES, John	32	E½SE	1830-09-28	FD	E2SE	R:MORGAN
3493	" "	33	SENE	1833-12-30	FD	SENE	R:MORGAN
3455	STAGNER, Jeremiah	8	SENW	1835-07-10	FD	SENW	R:MORGAN
3383	TAYLOR, George	31	L1	1847-10-06	FD	LOT1SW	R:MORGAN
3450	TURNBULL, James	20	E½NE	1835-03-09	FD	E2NE	R:MORGAN
3451	" "	20	SWNE	1835-03-14	FD	SWNE	R:MORGAN
3342	VANCE, Bradly	9	E½SW	1826-10-28	FD	E2SW	R:MORGAN
3343	" "	9	W½NW	1826-10-28	FD	W2NW	R:MORGAN
3494	VANWINKLE, John	4	N½NW	1829-10-22	FD	N2NW	R:MORGAN
3574	VANWINKLE, Ransom	34	W½SE	1830-11-06	FD	W2SE	R:SANGAMON
3364	WALKER, David P	32	E½SW	1831-11-03	FD	E2SWLS	R:MORGAN
3526	WATERS, Joseph	8	E½NE	1825-11-05	FD	E2NE	R:MORGAN
3527	" "	8	E½SE	1825-11-05	FD	E2SE	R:MORGAN
3525	" "	17	E½NE	1829-03-17	FD	E2NE	R:MORGAN
3616	WATERS, Zacheriah	9	W½SW	1830-11-30	FD	W2SW	R:MORGAN
3528	WHITE, Joseph	25	NENE	1833-11-06	FD	NENE	R:MORGAN
3373	WOLCOTT, Elisha	23	W½SE	1831-04-11	FD	W2SELS	R:MORGAN
3586	WOOD, Samuel	16	L3	1836-02-13	SC	LOT3	
3614	WOODS, William	25	E½SE	1830-03-22	FD	E2SE	R:MORGAN
3345	" "	36	E½SW	1831-08-03	FD	E2SW	R:MORGAN
3615	" "	36	E½SW	1831-08-03	FD	E2SW	R:MORGAN
3326	WOOLLOMES, Absalom	30	W½SE	1828-04-08	FD	W2SE	R:MORGAN
3592	WOOLLOMES, Thomas	31	W½NE	1827-03-20	FD	W2NE	R:MORGAN
3327	WOOLMES, Absolem	31	W½SW	1829-10-12	FD	W2SW	R:MORGAN
3500	WYATT, John	29	E½SW	1831-07-29	FD	E2SW	R:MORGAN
3499	" "	26	W½NW	1833-10-03	FD	W2NW	R:MORGAN
3498	" "	24	E½SE	1835-06-17	FD	E2SE	R:MORGAN

Patent Map

T14-N R9-W
3rd PM Meridian

Map Group 14

Township Statistics

Parcels Mapped	:	293
Number of Patents	:	1
Number of Individuals	:	175
Patentees Identified	:	171
Number of Surnames	:	122
Multi-Patentee Parcels	:	6
Oldest Patent Date	:	2/2/1198
Most Recent Patent	:	11/15/1851
Block/Lot Parcels	:	17
Cities and Towns	:	5
Cemeteries	:	5

Section 6
LITTON James 1830
SCROGGIN John 1829
CARSELL Joseph J 1846
HEDINBERG James V 1829
HOBBS James 1827
HEDENBURG Peter 1829
CHILTON William P 1829

Section 5
COKER Claibourn 1836
COX Lee W 1850
CLARKE Lancelot 1835
BRUTON William 1828
CARNS Andrew 1829
DODD Uriah 1829
CUNNINGHAM Peyton 1829
MOORE Edmund 1832

Section 4
VANWINKLE John 1829
PEMBERTON William 1829
MAGILL James 1826
HOBBS James 1827
MOORE Edmund 1831
GREEN James 1827
MAGILL James 1826

Section 7
PORTER William 1826
CARNS Andrew 1831
HEDENBERG Peter 1829
BRISBIN William 1825
BRISBIN William 1828
CARNES James 1833
BERRY Jesse 1823
DEVORE Samuel 1832
FRY Milton 1833
FRY Milton 1833
ANDERSON Dickey 1831

Section 8
DODD Uriah 1832
SPAINHOWER Jacob 1836
STAGNER Jeremiah 1835
DEVANPORT Henry 1829
WATERS Joseph 1825
DODD Uriah 1830
LEEPER Janus 1831
DEVENPORT Henry 1828
WATERS Joseph 1825

Section 9
VANCE Bradly 1826
GRIDER Martin 1828
SHELTON Johnston 1827
RUYLE John L 1829
WATERS Zacheriah 1830
VANCE Bradly 1826
RUYLE John L 1829
BOYER John 1829

Section 18
DUDHOPE Thomas 1835
FRY Milton 1833
MCCORMICK Ralph 1833
CRAIG Edward 1833
MACAIN James 1835
FRY Milton 1833
HAMILTON John C 1834
MACAIN James 1835
BARROWS Isaac R 1831
CRAIG Hugh G 1834
HAMILTON John C 1834

Section 17
RANNELLS William 1832
LEEPER Janus 1831
HAMILTON John C 1834
HAMILTON John C 1835
DAVENPORT Henry 1832
MOBLEY [79] Mordecai 1836
MCCORMICK Valentine 1834
MCCORMICK James 1833
WATERS Joseph 1829
SPEANHOWER John 1834
MOBLEY [79] Mordecai 1836

Section 16
Lots-Sec. 16
L1	BOYER, John	1836
L2	SHELTON, Johnston	1836
L3	WOOD, Samuel	1836
L4	MCCORMICK, Ralph	1836
L5	MCCORMICK, Ralph	1836
L6	COUNTY, Morgan	1836
L7	DUNCAN, Sidney P	1836
L8	BOYER, Jacob	1836
L9	LUSK, J H	1836
L10	SHELTON, Johnston	1836
L11	COUNTY, Morgan	1836
L12	RAWNELLS, Samuel M	1836
L13	RAWNELLS, Samuel M	1836
L14	RAWNELLS, Samuel M	1836
L15	RAWNELLS, Samuel M	1836
L16	LUSK, J H	1836

Section 19
BARROWS Isaac R 1831
BROWN James L 1834
BROWN James L 1834
BROWN James L 1834
CRAIG William H 1833
CRAIG William H 1833
COURTIS John H 1834
CRAIG William 1833
GREEN John W 1835
GREEN James 1835
BARROWS Isaac R 1831
BARROWS Barnabas 1835

Section 20
GREEN James 1835
MACAIN John 1835
MCCORMICK James 1833
TURNBULL James 1835
TURNBULL James 1835
PEXTON Henry 1835
DEVORE John Jr 1835
DRENNAN John L 1828
PEXTON Henry 1835
FRY William 1835
RICHARDSON Peter D 1835

Section 21
DUNLAP David 1835
DUDHOPE David 1835
DEVORE John 1835
FRY Milton 1835

Section 30
HAMILTON John C 1831
CRAIG David 1832
BARROWS Barnabas 1835
FANNING George 1829
FARMING Joseph 1825
WOOLLOMES Absalom 1828
BROWN Bedford 1831

Section 29
RICHARDSON John 1835
RICHARDSON John 1835
RAWLIN Mary 1198
RICHARDSON Vincent S 1835
RICHARDSON Peter D 1198
FRY William 1835
WYATT John 1831
KELLOGG Orville E 1833
FANNING Davis 1831
FANNING Abraham 1831

Section 28
RANSDELL Thomas T 1835
RANSDELL George 1836
RANSDELL Presley 1835
RANSDELL Presley 1835
FANNING John 1831
RANSDELL Eli C 1836
FANNING John 1834
GREEN James 1835
GREEN James 1835
FRY Milton 1835
HARP Conrad 1834

Section 31
FANNING George 1835
BARROWS Isaac R 1835
FARMING Joseph 1825
WOOLLOMES Thomas 1827
HUNTER Elizabeth 1824
WOOLMES Absolem 1829
EADS John 1830
BULLARD Theophilus 1831

Lots-Sec. 31
| L1 | TAYLOR, George | 1847 |

Section 32
LYNCH James 1827
MOODY James 1831
RANSDELL Presley 1834
BULLARD Theophilus 1831
WALKER David P 1831
LYNCH James 1830
SPIRES John 1830

Section 33
FANNING John 1831
FANNING George W 1828
FANNING Abraham 1829
FANNING Jacob 1836
SPIRES John 1833
PEMBERTON William 1828
FANNING Joseph 1831
FANNING Joseph 1830
FANNING Joseph 1828

Section 3
COX Nathaniel 1829
COX Ancil 1831
COX Ancil 1829
3
EDWARDS Henry 1826
RICHARDSON Isaac 1826
COX Anciel 1827
BUCHANAN Benjamin 1827

Section 2
BUCHANAN Benjamin 1833
BUCHANNON Benjamin 1829
2
BUCHANAN Joseph 1825
BUCHANAN Joseph 1831
BUCKHANAN John 1835
BUCHANAN Benjamin 1835
MOBLEY [79] Mordecai 1836
KING Henry 1835
KING Henry 1835
DODD James 1833

Section 1
SCOTT Isaac W 1836
SCOTT Isaac W 1836
1
KING Henry 1835
FOSTER James 1851

Section 10
DUNCAN Rice 1826
JOHNSON John 1827
BUCHANAN Joseph 1828
ANTLE Michael 1828
10
BOYER Jacob 1828
PETREE Francis 1827
LUTRELL Lot 1826
LUTTRELL Lott 1831

Section 11
AUTLE Michael 1826
BUCHANAN Joseph 1831
11
BUCHANAN Alexander 1833
PETER John M 1198
KING Henry 1835

Section 12
DODD Elijah 1833
KING Henry 1835
KING Henry 1835
12
KING Henry 1835
HUEY Daniel 1835

Section 15
SAMPLES Polly 1829
PETREE Francis 1831
PETREE Francis 1829
SAMPLE Light 1831
15
CLARK John D B 1834

Section 14
MCKEE James 1833
MCKEE James 1833
14
CLARK John D B 1834
SIMMS Samuel R 1835
LESLIE Miron 1835

Section 13
PROSSEE Samuel 1835
13
LESLIE Miron 1835
HUEY Daniel 1835

Section 22
SAUNDERSON Henry 1835
CLARK John D B 1834
PARKINSON James 1834
PARKINSON James 1833
22
FRY Milton 1835
PARKISON James 1835
PARKINSON James 1833

Section 23
PARKINSON James 1833
PARKINSON James 1834
SAUNDERSON Henry 1835
23
PARKINSON James 1834
PARKINSON James 1833
WOLCOTT Elisha 1831
MAYFIELD [100] Enness 1830

Section 24
MOBLEY [79] Mordecai 1836
HUEY Daniel 1835
SAUNDERSON Henry 1835
SCARTH Robert 1835
24
SAUNDERSON Henry 1835
CLAYTON William C 1835
CHALLEN John 1834
SAPPINGTON John 1835
WYATT John 1835

Section 27
FRY Milton 1835
HARP Conrad 1834
HARP Conrad 1834
MORTON Joseph 1833
27
HARP Coonrod 1835
HARP Conrad 1834
HARP Conrad 1834

Section 26
WYATT John 1833
KING John 1830
26
CLAYTON [39] William 1831
MORTON Joseph 1832
REYNOLDS Lewis 1834
REYNOLDS Joseph 1826
SCOTT James 1835
REYNOLDS Joseph 1835
CLAYTON John 1835
LUTTRELL William 1827

Section 25
BERRY Garrison W 1829
CYRUS Mathew 1834
CYRUS Mathew 1834
WHITE Joseph 1833
CYRUS Mathew 1833
CYRUS Matthew 1833
CHALLEN John 1834
25
COWNOVER Robert 1826
BURCH John W 1828
WOODS William 1830

Section 34
FRY Milton 1835
HARP Conrad 1834
MORTON Joseph 1835
34
FANNING Joseph 1831
VANWINKLE Ransom 1830
HARP Conrad 1834
MILLER Bradshaw 1830

Section 35
SIMMS Ignatius R 1829
REYNOLDS Joseph 1829
REYNOLDS Joseph 1833
MORTON Joseph 1835
PARKINSON James 1834
BOURLAND Miles 1833
MORTON Joseph 1835
JOLLY Elisha 1832
35
CHALLEN John 1836

Section 36
SAPPINGTON John 1828
BURCH Benjamin 1828
BURCH John W 1826
RUSSEL Caswell 1826
36
MORTON Joseph 1835
WOODS William 1831
FOSTER Caleb 1849
FOSTER Caleb 1849
FOSTER Caleb 1849
RIGGIN Right 1828
CYRUS Mathew 1830

Helpful Hints

1. This Map's INDEX can be found on the preceding pages.

2. Refer to Map "C" to see where this Township lies within Morgan County, Illinois.

3. Numbers within square brackets [ ] denote a multi-patentee land parcel (multi-owner). Refer to Appendix "C" for a full list of members in this group.

4. Areas that look to be crowded with Patentees usually indicate multiple sales of the same parcel (re-issues), cancellations or voided transactions (that we map, anyway) or overlapping parcels. We opt to show even these ambiguous parcels, which oftentimes lead to research avenues not yet taken.

Legend

— Patent Boundary

▬ Section Boundary

No Patents Found (or Outside County)

1., 2., 3., ...   Lot Numbers (when beside a name)

[ ]   Group Number (see Appendix "C")

Scale: Section = 1 mile X 1 mile (generally, with some exceptions)

Road Map

T14-N R9-W
3rd PM Meridian

Map Group 14

State Highway 104

Cities & Towns
Clements
Franklin
Pisgah
Rees
Yeomans

Cemeteries
Davis Cemetery
Franklin Cemetery
Pisgah Cemetery
Sulphur Springs Cemetery
Union Cemetery

6
5
4
Firecracker
Davis
Pisgah Cem.
Jd Turner
Loami
7
8
9
Gordon
Pisgah
Union Cem.
Cully
18
17
16
Pisgah
Barrows
Wood
19
20
21
Yording
Rees
Darley
Ransdell
30
29
28
Bills
Clements
31
Davis Cem.
32
33
Woodson Franklin
Wohlers
County Highway 14
Durbin

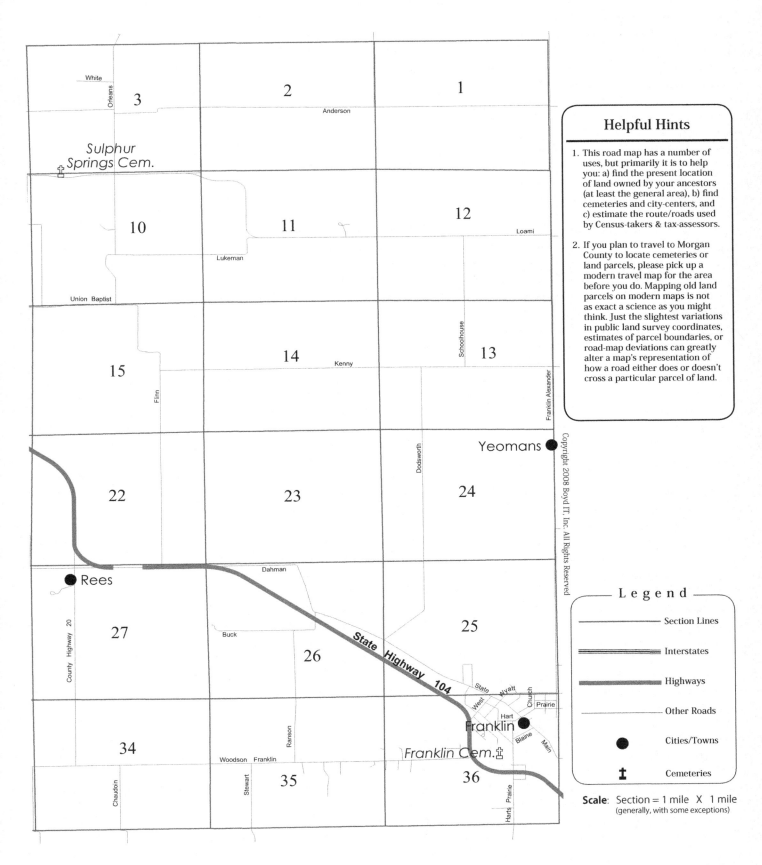

Helpful Hints

1. This road map has a number of uses, but primarily it is to help you: a) find the present location of land owned by your ancestors (at least the general area), b) find cemeteries and city-centers, and c) estimate the route/roads used by Census-takers & tax-assessors.

2. If you plan to travel to Morgan County to locate cemeteries or land parcels, please pick up a modern travel map for the area before you do. Mapping old land parcels on modern maps is not as exact a science as you might think. Just the slightest variations in public land survey coordinates, estimates of parcel boundaries, or road-map deviations can greatly alter a map's representation of how a road either does or doesn't cross a particular parcel of land.

Legend

—————— Section Lines

══════ Interstates

━━━━━━ Highways

—————— Other Roads

● Cities/Towns

✝ Cemeteries

Scale: Section = 1 mile X 1 mile
(generally, with some exceptions)

213

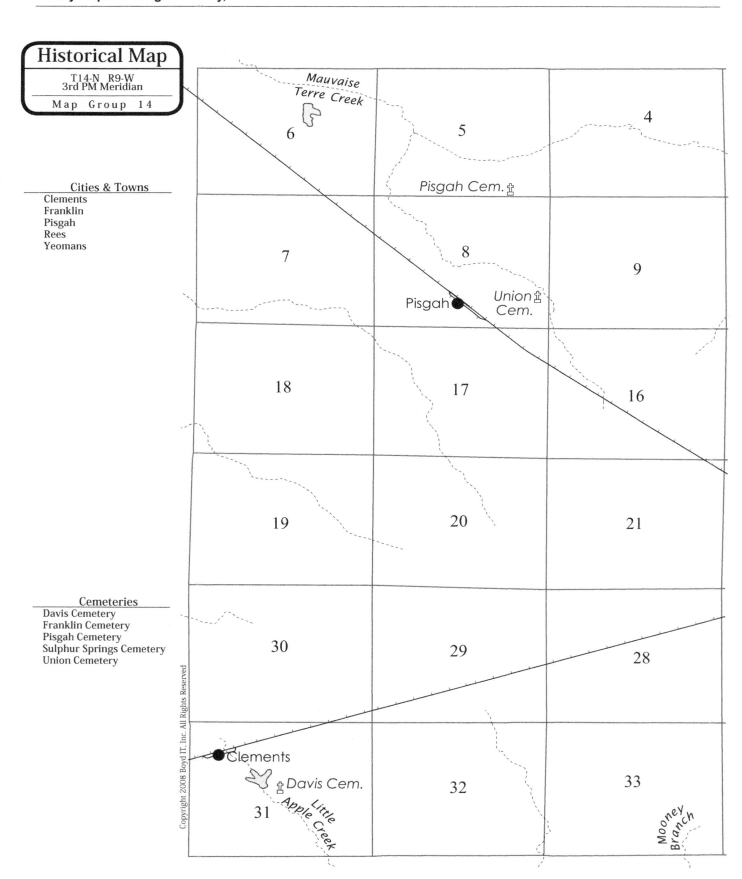

Historical Map

T14-N R9-W
3rd PM Meridian

Map Group 14

Cities & Towns
Clements
Franklin
Pisgah
Rees
Yeomans

Cemeteries
Davis Cemetery
Franklin Cemetery
Pisgah Cemetery
Sulphur Springs Cemetery
Union Cemetery

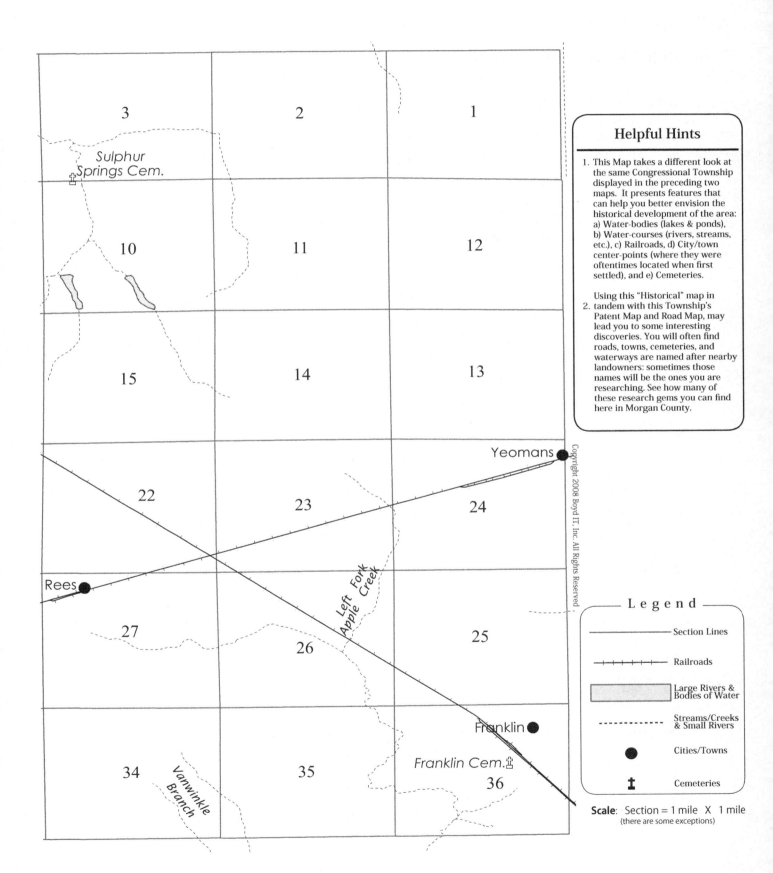

3

2

1

Sulphur
Springs Cem.

10

11

12

15

14

13

22

23

Yeomans ●

24

Rees ●

Left Fork
Apple Creek

27

26

25

34

Vanwinkle
Branch

35

Franklin ●

Franklin Cem. ⚱

36

Copyright 2008 Boyd IT, Inc. All Rights Reserved

Helpful Hints

1. This Map takes a different look at the same Congressional Township displayed in the preceding two maps. It presents features that can help you better envision the historical development of the area: a) Water-bodies (lakes & ponds), b) Water-courses (rivers, streams, etc.), c) Railroads, d) City/town center-points (where they were oftentimes located when first settled), and e) Cemeteries.

2. Using this "Historical" map in tandem with this Township's Patent Map and Road Map, may lead you to some interesting discoveries. You will often find roads, towns, cemeteries, and waterways are named after nearby landowners: sometimes those names will be the ones you are researching. See how many of these research gems you can find here in Morgan County.

Legend

———————— Section Lines

+–+–+–+–+ Railroads

▭ Large Rivers & Bodies of Water

----------- Streams/Creeks & Small Rivers

● Cities/Towns

⚱ Cemeteries

Scale: Section = 1 mile X 1 mile
(there are some exceptions)

Map Group 15: Index to Land Patents

Township 14-North Range 8-West (3rd PM)

After you locate an individual in this Index, take note of the Section and Section Part then proceed to the Land Patent map on the pages immediately following. You should have no difficulty locating the corresponding parcel of land.

The "For More Info" Column will lead you to more information about the underlying Patents. See the *Legend* at right, and the "How to Use this Book" chapter, for more information.

```
┌─────────────────────────────────────────────────────┐
│                      LEGEND                           │
│            "For More Info . . . " column              │
│  G = Group (Multi-Patentee Patent, see Appendix "C")  │
│  R = Residence                                        │
│  S = Social Status                                    │
│                                                       │
│  See Appendix A for list of abbreviations used by the │
│  Illinois State Archives in describing the place and  │
│  nature of these land patents.                        │
│                                                       │
│  Note: if the Abbreviations contain "L", "BL", "LOT", │
│  or "BLOCK", the exact whereabouts of the parcel within│
│  the section is not known.                             │
└─────────────────────────────────────────────────────┘
```

ID	Individual in Patent	Sec.	Sec. Part	Purchase Date	Sale Type	IL Aliquot Part	For More Info . . .
3654	ANDERSON, Dickey	30	SWNE	1836-08-09	FD	SWNE	R:TAZEWELL
3712	ARNOLD, John	32	E½SW	1828-12-04	FD	E2SW	R:MORGAN
3714	" "	32	SWNE	1832-10-09	FD	SWNE	R:MORGAN
3713	" "	32	NWNE	1835-02-02	FD	NWNE	R:MORGAN
3711	" "	28	E½NW	1835-07-08	FD	E2NW	R:MORGAN
3649	AYERS, David B	20	E½NW	1834-05-15	FD	E2NW	R:MORGAN
3652	AYRES, David B	30	E½NE	1834-10-30	FD	E2NE	R:MORGAN
3651	" "	20	W½NW	1834-10-30	FD	W2NW	R:MORGAN
3650	" "	19	SENE	1835-07-30	FD	SENE	R:MORGAN
3689	BARRET, James A	3	NWSE	1849-06-27	FD	NWSE	
3688	" "	3	E½SE	1849-06-27	FD	E2SE	
3628	BEACRAFT, Aquilla	16	L1	1849-11-03	SC	LOT1NENE	S:F
3629	" "	16	L7	1849-11-03	SC	L7SWNE	S:F
3630	" "	16	L8	1849-11-03	SC	L8SENE	S:F
3631	BEARCRAFT, Aquilla	16	L2	1849-11-03	SC	LOT2NWNE	S:F
3760	BOULWARD, Philip P	31		1830-03-04	FD	N01SW	R:MORGAN
3766	" "	31		1830-03-04	FD	N01SW	R:MORGAN
3761	BOULWARE, Philip P	31	W½SE	1835-02-18	FD	W2SE	R:MORGAN
3784	BOWYER, William	34	SESW	1835-02-03	FD	SESW	R:MORGAN
3702	BROWN, James N	3	NESW	1849-10-08	FD	NESW	G:14
3703	" "	3	S½SW	1849-10-08	FD	S2SW	G:14
3704	" "	3	SWSE	1849-10-08	FD	SWSE	G:14
3740	BROWN, Loyd W	4	NESE	1849-10-20	FD	NESE	
3739	" "	3	NWSW	1849-10-20	FD	NWSW	
3741	" "	4	S½SE	1849-10-20	FD	S2SE	
3785	BROWN, William	3	NW	1849-04-05	FD	NWFR	R:MORGAN
3703	" "	3	S½SW	1849-10-08	FD	S2SW	G:14
3704	" "	3	SWSE	1849-10-08	FD	SWSE	G:14
3702	" "	3	NESW	1849-10-08	FD	NESW	G:14
3772	BURCH, Shelby M	30	NESW	1835-10-08	FD	NESW	R:MORGAN
3680	BURNETT, Isham	32	SWNW	1832-10-23	FD	SWNW	R:MORGAN
3679	" "	29	NWSE	1833-12-02	FD	NWSE	R:MORGAN
3681	BURNETT, Ishom	29	E½NE	1831-10-20	FD	E2NELS	R:MORGAN
3692	BURNETT, James	33	E½NW	1831-07-25	FD	E2NW	R:MORGAN
3694	" "	33	SWNE	1835-06-05	FD	SWNE	R:MORGAN
3691	" "	29	SWSE	1835-07-08	FD	SWSE	R:MORGAN
3693	" "	33	NWNE	1835-07-18	FD	NWNE	R:MORGAN
3781	BUTLER, Walter	19	SESW	1833-07-31	FD	SESW	R:MORGAN
3782	" "	19	SWSE	1833-07-31	FD	SWSE	R:MORGAN
3780	" "	19	NESW	1834-10-08	FD	NESW	R:MORGAN
3665	COREY, Hamilton F	33	SWSW	1835-12-11	FD	SWSW	R:MORGAN
3715	COWAN, John	19	NWNE	1833-12-13	FD	NWNE	R:MORGAN
3653	COWEN, David	31	SWNE	1835-02-25	FD	SWNE	R:MORGAN
3682	CROSS, Israel	32	W½SE	1831-10-12	FD	W2SE	R:MORGAN
3758	CUNNINGHAM, Payton	19	SWSW	1834-10-27	FD	SWSW	R:MORGAN
3759	CUNNINGHAM, Peyton	30	NWNE	1835-03-11	FD	NWNE	R:MORGAN

ID	Individual in Patent	Sec.	Sec. Part	Purchase Date	Sale Type	IL Aliquot Part	For More Info . . .
3786	CUNNINGHAM, William D	19	SESE	1848-02-24	FD	SESE	R:MORGAN
3765	DAVIS, Richard T	16	L9	1850-01-15	SC	LOT9NESE	
3762	"	16	L10	1850-01-15	SC	LOT10NWSE	
3764	"	16	L16	1850-01-15	SC	LOT16SESE	
3763	"	16	L15	1850-01-15	SC	LOT15SWSE	
3672	DILLER, Isaac	4	NW	1849-10-09	FD	NWFR	R:SANGAMON
3674	DILLER, Isaac R	4	NE	1849-10-09	FD	NEFR	
3676	"	5	NW	1849-10-09	FD	NWFR	
3675	"	5	NE	1849-10-09	FD	NEFR	
3744	DYERS, Martin W	19	NESE	1835-03-11	FD	NESE	R:MORGAN
3662	EASTMAN, George	28	E½SE	1835-11-18	FD	E2SE	R:MORGAN
3755	ENGLISH, Nathaniel	6	SE	1849-11-14	FD	SE	
3757	"	8	SWNW	1850-01-23	FD	SWNW	
3756	"	8	E½NW	1850-01-23	FD	E2NW	
3754	"	5	SESW	1850-01-23	FD	SESW	
3706	EVANS, Janus	31	E½NE	1831-08-17	FD	E2NE	R:MORGAN S:F
3800	FLINN, Zadoc W	8	W½SW	1826-01-21	FD	W2SW	R:MORGAN
3710	GILLELAND, Joel	32	W½SW	1829-12-30	FD	W2SW	R:SANGAMON
3709	"	29	W½NE	1831-04-25	FD	W2NELS	R:MORGAN
3794	GIVENS, William T	30	SESW	1833-08-03	FD	SESW	R:MORGAN
3716	GRIGG, John	14	E½	1835-09-22	FD	E2	R:PHILADELPHIA
3721	"	17	SE	1835-10-06	FD	SE	R:PHILADELPHIA
3720	"	17	N½	1835-10-06	FD	N2	R:PHILADELPHIA
3719	"	17	E½SW	1835-10-06	FD	E2SW	R:PHILADELPHIA
3717	"	14	W½	1835-10-06	FD	W2	R:PHILADELPHIA
3718	"	15		1835-10-06	FD	SEC	R:PHILADELPHIA
3655	HAGGARD, Edmund	33	E½SW	1830-02-25	FD	E2SW	R:MORGAN
3769	HAGGARD, Samuel	34	SWNW	1834-11-01	FD	SWNW	R:MORGAN
3768	"	33	SENE	1835-06-09	FD	SENE	R:MORGAN
3658	HALL, Eliza	32	NWNW	1835-07-01	FD	NWNW	R:MORGAN S:F
3657	"	32	E½NW	1835-07-01	FD	E2NW	R:MORGAN S:F
3656	"	20	NE	1835-07-01	FD	NE	R:MORGAN S:F
3722	HAM, John H	29	SESW	1834-11-14	FD	SESW	R:MORGAN
3726	HAM, John S	28	W½NW	1835-02-02	FD	W2NW	R:MORGAN
3777	HARRIS, Thomas J	29	E½SE	1835-09-23	FD	E2SE	R:MORGAN
3776	"	28	W½SW	1835-09-23	FD	W2SW	R:MORGAN
3774	HOUGHAN, Thomas	23	NWSW	1836-02-04	FD	NWSW	R:SANGAMON
3775	"	26	SWNW	1836-02-04	FD	SWNW	R:SANGAMON
3640	HUEY, Daniel	22	NE	1835-10-17	FD	NE	R:MISSISSIPPI
3637	"	10		1835-10-17	FD	SEC	R:MISSISSIPPI
3638	"	18	NE	1835-10-17	FD	NE	R:MISSISSIPPI
3648	"	9		1835-10-17	FD	SEC	R:MISSISSIPPI
3639	"	20	W½SW	1835-10-17	FD	W2SW	R:MISSISSIPPI
3641	"	23	E½	1835-10-17	FD	E2SEC	R:MISSISSIPPI
3642	"	23	E½SW	1835-10-17	FD	E2SW	R:MISSISSIPPI
3643	"	23	NW	1835-10-17	FD	NW	R:MISSISSIPPI
3644	"	29	NWSW	1835-10-17	FD	NWSW	R:MISSISSIPPI
3645	"	7		1835-10-17	FD	SEC	R:MISSISSIPPI
3646	"	8	NE	1835-10-19	FD	NE	R:MISSISSIPPI
3647	"	8	S½	1835-10-19	FD	S2	R:MISSISSIPPI
3687	HUFFAKER, Jacob M	5	SE	1850-05-08	FD	SE	
3685	"	4	SW	1850-05-08	FD	SW	
3684	"	4	NWSE	1850-05-10	FD	NWSE	R:MORGAN
3686	"	5	N½SW	1850-05-10	FD	N2SW	R:MORGAN
3683	"	30	NWSE	1850-05-10	FD	NWSE	R:MORGAN
3632	JACKSON, Brice B	33	W½SE	1831-04-12	FD	W2SE	R:MORGAN
3633	"	34	NWSW	1834-11-01	FD	NWSW	R:MORGAN
3696	JOHNSTON, James	16	L5	1849-11-03	SC	L5SWNW	
3695	"	16	L4	1849-11-03	SC	L4NWNW	
3666	JONES, Henry	18	SW	1834-05-15	FD	SW	R:MORGAN
3667	"	19	NW	1835-05-08	FD	NW	R:MORGAN
3668	"	19	SWNE	1835-05-08	FD	SWNE	R:MORGAN
3770	KEPLINGER, Samuel	30	SESE	1832-12-03	FD	SESE	R:MORGAN
3724	KERR, John	18	E½SE	1835-07-30	FD	E2SE	R:MORGAN
3723	"	17	W½SW	1835-07-30	FD	W2SW	R:MORGAN
3701	LAMB, James L	35	SE	1835-07-11	FD	SE	R:SANGAMON
3700	"	35	E½SW	1835-07-11	FD	E2SW	R:SANGAMON
3699	"	35	E½NW	1835-07-11	FD	E2NW	R:SANGAMON
3698	"	27	SEN½	1835-12-15	FD	S2NE	R:SANGAMON
3697	"	27	SE	1835-12-15	FD	SE	R:SANGAMON
3749	LESLIE, Miron	27	SW	1835-06-20	FD	SW	R:MORGAN
3750	"	34	E½	1835-06-20	FD	E2	R:MORGAN
3751	"	34	N½NW	1835-06-20	FD	N2NW	R:MORGAN

ID	Individual in Patent	Sec.	Sec. Part	Purchase Date	Sale Type	IL Aliquot Part	For More Info . . .
3659	MAYFIELD, Enness	20	NWSE	1835-09-10	FD	NWSE	R:MORGAN
3660	" "	29	SWNW	1835-09-10	FD	SWNW	R:MORGAN
3742	MAYFIELD, Manning	20	SESW	1834-06-06	FD	SESW	R:MORGAN
3743	" "	29	NWNW	1834-06-06	FD	NWNW	R:MORGAN
3748	MAYFIELD, Milton	20	SWSE	1835-03-28	FD	SWSE	R:MORGAN
3705	MCCORMICK, Jane	18	W½SE	1835-06-06	FD	W2SE	R:MORGAN S:F
3725	MCCORMICK, John	19	NENE	1835-05-11	FD	NENE	R:MORGAN
3621	MINER, Amos	21		1835-07-04	FD	SEC	R:MORGAN
3623	" "	22	W½	1835-07-04	FD	W2	R:MORGAN
3626	" "	27	NW	1835-07-04	FD	NW	R:MORGAN
3627	" "	28	E½NE	1835-07-04	FD	E2NE	R:MORGAN
3622	" "	22	SE	1835-08-19	FD	SE	R:MORGAN
3625	" "	26	NWNW	1835-08-19	FD	NWNW	R:MORGAN
3624	" "	23	SWSW	1835-08-19	FD	SWSW	R:MORGAN
3620	MINER, Amos Jr	20	NESE	1835-07-08	FD	NESE	R:MORGAN
3661	MINER, Franklin	27	N½NE	1835-09-23	FD	N2NE	R:MORGAN
3778	NIX, Thomas	29	E½NW	1829-10-17	FD	E2NW	R:MORGAN
3788	PACKER, William Jr	26	E½SW	1835-09-22	FD	E2SW	R:NEW YORK
3790	" "	26	W½NE	1835-09-22	FD	W2NE	R:NEW YORK
3787	" "	26	E½NW	1835-09-22	FD	E2NW	R:NEW YORK
3789	" "	26	SE	1835-09-22	FD	SE	R:NEW YORK
3793	PACKER, William S	26	W½SW	1835-10-28	FD	W2SW	R:NEW YORK
3792	PACKER, William S Jr	26	E½NE	1835-09-30	FD	E2NE	R:NEW YORK
3664	PEMBERTON, Giddeon	34	SENW	1835-06-15	FD	SENW	R:MORGAN
3673	POOL, Isaac	30	SWSE	1834-06-09	FD	SWSE	R:MORGAN
3771	PROSSEE, Samuel	18	W½NW	1835-07-20	FD	W2NW	R:MORGAN
3634	RUSSEL, Caswell	32	E½NE	1827-05-29	FD	E2NE	R:MORGAN
3783	SAMPLES, Washington	34	SWSW	1835-09-02	FD	SWSW	R:MORGAN
3677	SCOTT, Isaac	6	N½	1842-10-07	FD	N2FR	R:KENTUCKY
3678	"	6	N½	1842-10-07	FD	N2FR	R:KENTUCKY
3677	SCOTT, Isaac W	6	N½	1836-06-29	FD	N2	R:KENTUCKY
3678	" "	6	N½	1836-06-29	FD	N2	R:KENTUCKY
3791	SCOTT, William N	20	NESW	1834-11-15	FD	NESW	R:MORGAN
3767	SEARTH, Robert	30	NESE	1835-10-16	FD	NESE	R:MORGAN
3707	SHEARER, Jester	5	SWSW	1849-09-17	FD	SWSW	R:MORGAN
3708	" "	8	NWNW	1849-09-17	FD	NWNW	R:MORGAN
3690	STURGIS, James B	32	E½SE	1828-02-11	FD	E2SE	R:MORGAN
3635	TANNER, Cyrus	33	NENE	1835-07-18	FD	NENE	R:MORGAN
3736	TANNER, Joseph A	35	W½NW	1835-07-10	FD	W2NW	R:MORGAN
3737	" "	35	W½SW	1835-07-10	FD	W2SW	R:MORGAN
3735	" "	35	NE	1835-07-10	FD	NE	R:MORGAN
3795	THOMAS, William	18	E½NW	1849-11-21	FD	E2NW	R:MORGAN
3636	THOMSON, D R	16	L13	1850-12-21	SC	LOT13SWSW	S:I
3779	THOMSON, W H	16	L12	1850-12-21	SC	LOT12NWSW	S:I
3670	VANWINKLE, Hiram	33	E½SE	1834-06-09	FD	E2SE	R:MORGAN
3671	" "	34	NESW	1835-05-25	FD	NESW	R:MORGAN
3728	VANWINKLE, John	33	NWSW	1834-06-10	FD	NWSW	R:MORGAN
3727	" "	28	W½NE	1835-07-02	FD	W2NE	R:MORGAN
3753	VANWINKLE, Napoleon	29	NESW	1835-07-07	FD	NESW	R:MORGAN
3752	VANWINKLE, Napoleon B	20	SESE	1834-11-15	FD	SESE	R:MORGAN
3738	VINSON, Littlebury	33	W½NW	1829-12-15	FD	W2NW	R:MORGAN
3669	WESTFALL, Henry	3	NE	1848-12-21	FD	NEFR	
3733	WETHERFIELD, Jonas	31	NWNE	1835-07-10	FD	NWNE	R:MORGAN
3734	WETHERFORD, Jonas	30	NENW	1834-10-02	FD	NENW	R:MORGAN
3796	WETHERFORD, William	30	SENW	1835-09-07	FD	SENW	R:MORGAN
3766	WILHELM, Richard	31		1827-01-11	FD	PT2SW	R:MORGAN
3760	" "	31		1827-01-11	FD	PT2SW	R:MORGAN
3729	WILLIAMS, John	6	SW	1850-02-09	FD	SWFR	
3747	WOOD, Mason	29	SWSW	1835-10-08	FD	SWSW	R:MORGAN
3745	" "	28	E½SW	1835-10-08	FD	E2SW	R:MORGAN
3746	" "	28	W½SE	1835-10-08	FD	W2SE	R:MORGAN
3773	WOOD, Sterling	31	E½NW	1835-10-10	FD	E2NW	R:MORGAN
3797	WOOD, William	31	W½NW	1827-12-15	FD	W2NW	R:MORGAN
3798	WOODS, William	30	W½SW	1830-05-07	FD	W2SW	R:MORGAN
3619	WRIGHT, Alexander M	16	L6	1849-11-03	SC	L6SENW	
3617	" "	16	L11	1849-11-03	SC	LOT11NESW	
3618	" "	16	L3	1849-11-03	SC	L3NENW	
3663	WRIGHT, George W	16	L14	1851-01-15	SC	LOT14SESW	
3799	WRIGHT, William	30		1832-01-19	FD	N02NW	R:MORGAN
3732	WYATT, John	31	E½SE	1831-08-17	FD	E2SE	R:MORGAN
3731	" "	19	NWSW	1835-06-17	FD	NWSW	R:MORGAN
3730	" "	19	NWSE	1835-07-20	FD	NWSE	R:MORGAN

Patent Map

T14-N R8-W
3rd PM Meridian

Map Group 15

Township Statistics

Parcels Mapped	:	184
Number of Patents	:	1
Number of Individuals	:	99
Patentees Identified	:	99
Number of Surnames	:	71
Multi-Patentee Parcels	:	3
Oldest Patent Date	:	1/21/1826
Most Recent Patent	:	1/15/1851
Block/Lot Parcels	:	21
Cities and Towns	:	0
Cemeteries	:	3

Section 6
- SCOTT Isaac 1842
- SCOTT Isaac W 1836
- WILLIAMS John 1850
- ENGLISH Nathaniel 1849

Section 5
- DILLER Isaac R 1849
- DILLER Isaac R 1849
- HUFFAKER Jacob M 1850
- SHEARER Jester 1849
- ENGLISH Nathaniel 1850
- HUFFAKER Jacob M 1850

Section 4
- DILLER Isaac R 1849
- DILLER Isaac 1849
- HUFFAKER Jacob M 1850
- HUFFAKER Jacob M 1850
- BROWN Loyd W 1849
- BROWN Loyd W 1849

Section 7
- PROSSEE Samuel 1835
- THOMAS William 1849
- HUEY Daniel 1835
- HUEY Daniel 1835

Section 8
- SHEARER Jester 1849
- ENGLISH Nathaniel 1850
- ENGLISH Nathaniel 1850
- HUEY Daniel 1835
- FLINN Zadoc W 1826
- HUEY Daniel 1835

Section 9
- HUEY Daniel 1835

Section 18
- JONES Henry 1834
- MCCORMICK Jane 1835
- KERR John 1835

Section 17
- GRIGG John 1835
- KERR John 1835
- GRIGG John 1835
- GRIGG John 1835

Lots-Sec. 16
L1	BEACRAFT, Aquilla	1849
L2	BEARCRAFT, Aquilla	1849
L3	WRIGHT, Alexander M	1849
L4	JOHNSTON, James	1849
L5	JOHNSTON, James	1849
L6	WRIGHT, Alexander M	1849
L7	BEACRAFT, Aquilla	1849
L8	BEACRAFT, Aquilla	1849
L9	DAVIS, Richard T	1850
L10	DAVIS, Richard T	1850
L11	WRIGHT, Alexander M	1849
L12	THOMSON, W H	1850
L13	THOMSON, D R	1850
L14	WRIGHT, George W	1851
L15	DAVIS, Richard T	1850
L16	DAVIS, Richard T	1850

Section 16

Section 19
- JONES Henry 1835
- COWAN John 1833
- MCCORMICK John 1835
- JONES Henry 1835
- AYRES David B 1835
- WYATT John 1835
- BUTLER Walter 1834
- WYATT John 1835
- DYERS Martin W 1835
- CUNNINGHAM Payton 1834
- BUTLER Walter 1833
- BUTLER Walter 1833
- CUNNINGHAM William D 1848

Section 20
- AYRES David B 1834
- AYERS David B 1834
- HALL Eliza 1835
- SCOTT William N 1834
- MAYFIELD Enness 1835
- MINER Amos Jr 1835
- HUEY Daniel 1835
- MAYFIELD Manning 1834
- MAYFIELD Milton 1835
- VANWINKLE Napoleon B 1834

Section 21
- MINER Amos 1835

Section 30
- WRIGHT William 1832
- WETHERFORD Jonas 1834
- WETHERFORD William 1835
- CUNNINGHAM Peyton 1835
- AYRES David B 1834
- ANDERSON Dickey 1836
- WOODS William 1830
- BURCH Shelby M 1835
- HUFFAKER Jacob M 1850
- SEARTH Robert 1835
- GIVENS William T 1833
- POOL Isaac 1834
- KEPLINGER Samuel 1832

Section 29
- MAYFIELD Manning 1834
- MAYFIELD Enness 1835
- NIX Thomas 1829
- GILLELAND Joel 1831
- BURNETT Ishom 1831
- HUEY Daniel 1835
- VANWINKLE Napoleon 1835
- BURNETT Isham 1833
- WOOD Mason 1835
- HAM John H 1834
- BURNETT James 1835

Section 28
- HAM John S 1835
- ARNOLD John 1835
- VANWINKLE John 1835
- MINER Amos 1835
- HARRIS Thomas J 1835
- HARRIS Thomas J 1835
- WOOD Mason 1835
- WOOD Mason 1835
- EASTMAN George 1835

Section 31
- WOOD William 1827
- WOOD Sterling 1835
- WETHERFIELD Jonas 1835
- COWEN David 1835
- EVANS Janus 1831
- BOULWARD Philip P 1830
- BOULWARE Philip P 1835
- WYATT John 1831
- WILHELM Richard 1827

Section 32
- HALL Eliza 1835
- BURNETT Isham 1832
- HALL Eliza 1835
- ARNOLD John 1835
- ARNOLD John 1832
- RUSSEL Caswell 1827
- GILLELAND Joel 1829
- ARNOLD John 1828
- CROSS Israel 1831
- STURGIS James B 1828

Section 33
- VINSON Littlebury 1829
- BURNETT James 1831
- BURNETT James 1835
- BURNETT James 1835
- TANNER Cyrus 1835
- HAGGARD Samuel 1835
- VANWINKLE John 1834
- HAGGARD Edmund 1830
- COREY Hamilton F 1835
- JACKSON Brice B 1831
- VANWINKLE Hiram 1834

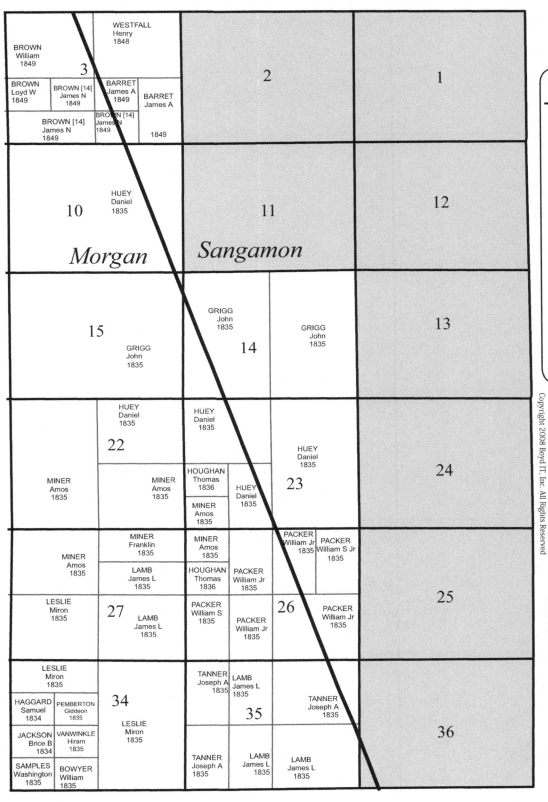

Helpful Hints

1. This Map's INDEX can be found on the preceding pages.

2. Refer to Map "C" to see where this Township lies within Morgan County, Illinois.

3. Numbers within square brackets [ ] denote a multi-patentee land parcel (multi-owner). Refer to Appendix "C" for a full list of members in this group.

4. Areas that look to be crowded with Patentees usually indicate multiple sales of the same parcel (re-issues), cancellations or voided transactions (that we map, anyway) or overlapping parcels. We opt to show even these ambiguous parcels, which oftentimes lead to research avenues not yet taken.

L e g e n d

———————— Patent Boundary

━━━━━━━ Section Boundary

No Patents Found (or Outside County)

1., 2., 3., ... Lot Numbers (when beside a name)

[ ] Group Number (see Appendix "C")

Scale: Section = 1 mile X 1 mile (generally, with some exceptions)

Road Map

T14-N R8-W
3rd PM Meridian

Map Group 15

Cities & Towns
None

Cemeteries
Little York Cemetery
Luken Cemetery
Sacred Heart Cemetery

6

Hermes

5

4

7

Loami

8

⚑Luken Cem.

9

McCarty

18

17

Kenny

16

Contrary

Burnett

Franklin Alexander

19

20

21

Pauls

Colwell

McNeely

30

29

28

Sacred Heart ⚑
Cem.

Austif

Prairie

31

33

Lake

Clevenger

32

North

St Hwy 104

Sou

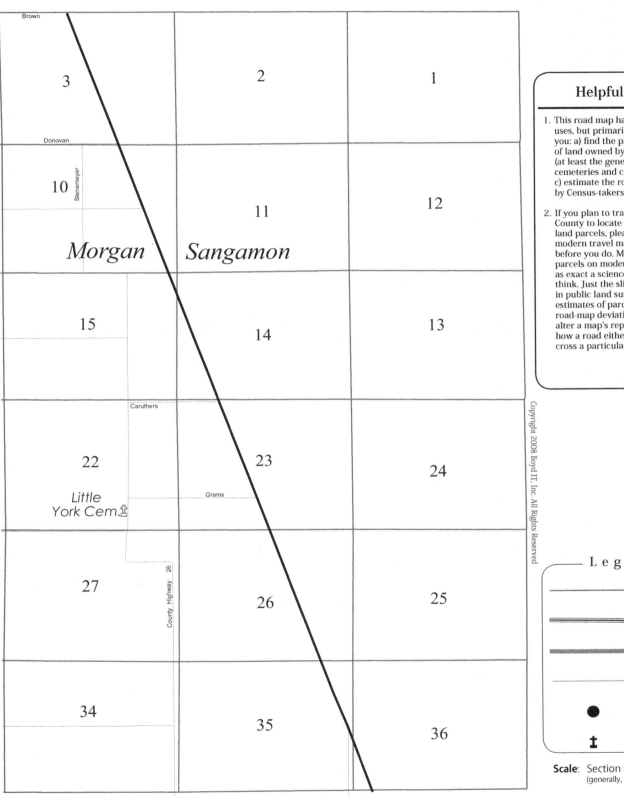

Brown

3

2

1

Donovan

10

Stenemeyer

11

12

Morgan

Sangamon

15

14

13

Caruthers

22

23

24

Grams

Little
York Cem.

27

County Highway 26

26

25

34

35

36

Helpful Hints

1. This road map has a number of uses, but primarily it is to help you: a) find the present location of land owned by your ancestors (at least the general area), b) find cemeteries and city-centers, and c) estimate the route/roads used by Census-takers & tax-assessors.

2. If you plan to travel to Morgan County to locate cemeteries or land parcels, please pick up a modern travel map for the area before you do. Mapping old land parcels on modern maps is not as exact a science as you might think. Just the slightest variations in public land survey coordinates, estimates of parcel boundaries, or road-map deviations can greatly alter a map's representation of how a road either does or doesn't cross a particular parcel of land.

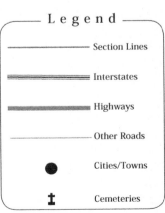

L e g e n d

—————————— Section Lines

══════════ Interstates

━━━━━━━━━━ Highways

—————————— Other Roads

● Cities/Towns

✝ Cemeteries

Scale: Section = 1 mile X 1 mile
(generally, with some exceptions)

Historical Map

T14-N R8-W
3rd PM Meridian

Map Group 15

Cities & Towns
None

Cemeteries
Little York Cemetery
Luken Cemetery
Sacred Heart Cemetery

6	5	4
7	8	⚱ Luken Cem.
		9
18	17	16
		Lick Creek
19	20	21
30	29	28
Woods Creek		
Sacred Heart ⚱ Cem.		
31	32	33
	Waverly Lake	

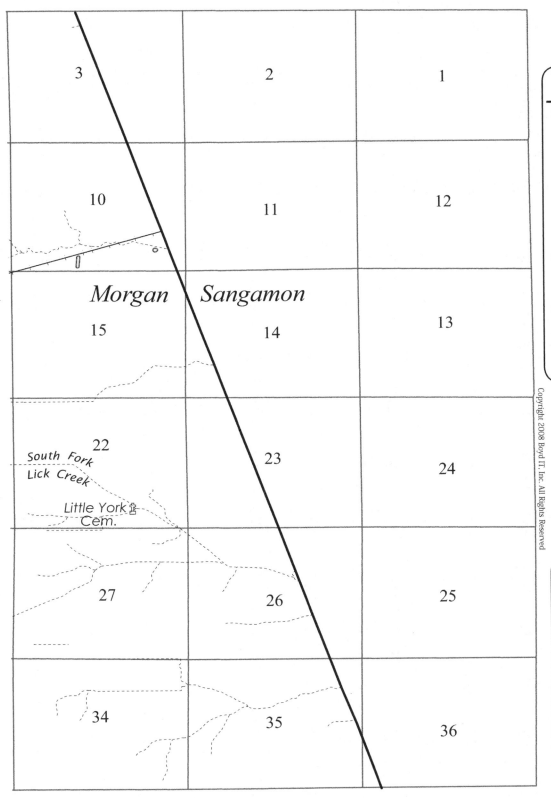

3

2

1

10

11

12

Morgan   *Sangamon*

15

14

13

22

South Fork
Lick Creek

23

24

Little York ⚓
Cem.

27

26

25

34

35

36

Helpful Hints

1. This Map takes a different look at the same Congressional Township displayed in the preceding two maps. It presents features that can help you better envision the historical development of the area: a) Water-bodies (lakes & ponds), b) Water-courses (rivers, streams, etc.), c) Railroads, d) City/town center-points (where they were oftentimes located when first settled), and e) Cemeteries.

2. Using this "Historical" map in tandem with this Township's Patent Map and Road Map, may lead you to some interesting discoveries. You will often find roads, towns, cemeteries, and waterways are named after nearby landowners: sometimes those names will be the ones you are researching. See how many of these research gems you can find here in Morgan County.

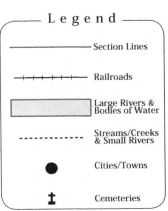

Legend

———— Section Lines

–+–+–+– Railroads

�▭ Large Rivers & Bodies of Water

------- Streams/Creeks & Small Rivers

● Cities/Towns

⚓ Cemeteries

Scale: Section = 1 mile X 1 mile
(there are some exceptions)

Map Group 16: Index to Land Patents

Township 13-North Range 11-West (3rd PM)

After you locate an individual in this Index, take note of the Section and Section Part then proceed to the Land Patent map on the pages immediately following. You should have no difficulty locating the corresponding parcel of land.

The "For More Info" Column will lead you to more information about the underlying Patents. See the *Legend* at right, and the "How to Use this Book" chapter, for more information.

```
┌─────────────────────────────────────────────────────┐
│                    LEGEND                            │
│       "For More Info . . . " column                  │
│ ───────────────────────────────────────────────     │
│ G = Group (Multi-Patentee Patent, see Appendix "C")  │
│ R = Residence                                        │
│ S = Social Status                                    │
│                                                      │
│                                                      │
│ See Appendix A for list of abbreviations used by the │
│ Illinois State Archives in describing the place and  │
│ nature of these land patents.                        │
│                                                      │
│ Note: if the Abbreviations contain "L", "BL", "LOT", │
│ or "BLOCK", the exact whereabouts of the parcel within│
│ the section is not known.                            │
└─────────────────────────────────────────────────────┘
```

ID	Individual in Patent	Sec.	Sec. Part	Purchase Date	Sale Type	IL Aliquot Part	For More Info . . .
3854	ABBOTT, John	26	SESE	1855-11-01	FD	SESE	R:SCOTT
3840	ASH, James	11	SENE	1851-02-07	FD	SENE	R:MORGAN
3841	" "	2	E½SE	1851-10-30	FD	E2SE	R:MORGAN
3914	ASHER, William	23	E½NE	1830-02-05	FD	E2NE	R:MORGAN
3885	AYERS, Rescarrick	13	E½NW	1835-10-29	FD	E2NW	R:GREENE G:2
3803	BILLINGS, Abraham	26	SWSW	1836-02-08	FD	SWSW	
3817	BILLINGS, Arden Sen	35	NESW	1845-09-09	FD	NESW	
3916	BILLINGS, William	35	W½NE	1854-09-27	FD	W2NE	R:SCOTT
3915	" "	35	SE	1854-09-27	FD	SE	R:SCOTT
3824	BIRDSELL, Clark	25	SWSE	1836-02-01	FD	SWSE	R:MORGAN
3823	" "	24	NWSE	1836-11-21	FD	NWSE	R:MORGAN
3895	BIRDSELL, Rufus	36	NENW	1836-01-21	FD	NENW	R:MORGAN
3894	" "	1	SENE	1836-02-01	FD	SENE	R:MORGAN
3850	BLAIR, Joel P	1	NWNE	1836-12-08	FD	NWNE	R:MORGAN
3900	BLAIR, Solomon	11	SWNW	1838-03-15	FD	SWNW	R:MORGAN
3885	BLISH, Oaks Shaw	13	E½NW	1835-10-29	FD	E2NW	R:GREENE G:2
3873	CAINEY, Michael	2	W½SE	1854-09-27	FD	W2SE	R:GREENE
3825	CALDWELL, Dan P	1	SENW	1851-03-08	FD	SENW	R:SCOTT
3826	" "	2	E½NE	1852-03-08	FD	E2NE	R:MACOUPIN
3893	CALDWELL, Rollin C	11	NENE	1851-12-31	FD	NENE	R:MORGAN
3856	CARNEY, John	2	N½SW	1854-09-27	FD	N2SW	R:GREENE
3855	" "	2	E½NW	1854-09-27	FD	E2NW	R:GREENE
3842	CHILTON, James	26	SWNW	1853-05-31	FD	SWNW	
3875	COFFIN, Nathaniel	2	W½NE	1837-03-29	FD	W2NE	R:MORGAN
3881	" "	26	E½SW	1837-03-29	FD	E2SW	R:MORGAN
3880	" "	26	E½NW	1837-03-29	FD	E2NW	R:MORGAN
3879	" "	25	E½SE	1837-03-29	FD	E2SE	R:MORGAN
3878	" "	25	E½NW	1837-03-29	FD	E2NW	R:MORGAN
3876	" "	2	W½NW	1837-03-29	FD	W2NW	R:MORGAN
3882	" "	26	W½SE	1837-03-29	FD	W2SE	R:MORGAN
3874	" "	1	W½NW	1837-03-29	FD	W2NW	R:MORGAN
3877	" "	25	E½NE	1837-03-29	FD	E2NE	R:MORGAN
3902	COLE, Stephen	24	W½NW	1830-11-19	FD	W2NW	R:MORGAN
3819	COLLINS, Charles	24	E½SE	1837-01-18	FD	E2SE	R:ST. LOUIS
3820	" "	24	SWSE	1837-01-18	FD	SWSE	R:ST. LOUIS
3847	COONS, Jesse	1	E½SE	1830-11-29	FD	E2SE	R:MORGAN
3883	DEVOLT, Nicholas	24	SESW	1854-01-08	FD	SESW	R:MORGAN
3868	EDWARDS, Joseph B	25	SWNW	1837-02-16	FD	SWNW	R:MORGAN
3867	" "	23	NESE	1853-05-13	FD	NESE	
3887	FREEMAN, Richard	14	SENW	1835-12-28	FD	SENW	R:GREENE
3857	GALBRAITH, John	25	SWSW	1835-03-11	FD	SWSW	R:MORGAN
3917	GAMBLE, William	35	SESE	1836-02-22	FD	SESE	
3858	GRIGG, John	36	SW	1835-12-07	FD	SW	R:PHILADELPHIA
3859	" "	36	W½NE	1835-12-07	FD	W2NE	R:PHILADELPHIA
3836	HACKETT, George	35	NW	1835-12-24	FD	NW	R:MORGAN
3851	HAHN, Johanna P	36	SENW	1841-06-17	FD	SENW	S:F

ID	Individual in Patent	Sec.	Sec. Part	Purchase Date	Sale Type	IL Aliquot Part	For More Info . . .
3852	HAHN, Johanna P (Cont'd)	36	W½NW	1841-06-17	FD	W2NW	S:F
3830	HANES, Daniel	12	W½SE	1830-09-30	FD	W2SE	R:MORGAN
3828	" "	12	E½SW	1830-09-30	FD	E2SW	R:MORGAN
3831	" "	14	E½NW	1830-09-30	FD	E2NW	R:MORGAN
3827	" "	11	E½SW	1830-09-30	FD	E2SW	R:MORGAN
3829	" "	12	NE	1830-11-29	FD	NE	R:MORGAN
3918	HARP, William	12	E½NW	1831-05-05	FD	E2NW	R:MORGAN
3870	HEREN, Lewis	24	W½NE	1830-12-14	FD	W2NE	R:MORGAN
3871	HERRIN, Lewis	13	NWNW	1834-03-27	FD	NWNW	R:MORGAN G:74
3871	HERRIN, Simon	13	NWNW	1834-03-27	FD	NWNW	R:MORGAN G:74
3860	HERRING, John	13	W½NE	1831-07-22	FD	W2NEFS	R:MORGAN
3821	HOLLIDAY, Charles	13	E½NE	1829-10-23	FD	E2NE	R:OHIO
3888	HUSTON, Robert	26	NWSW	1837-04-06	FD	NWSW	R:MORGAN
3892	HUSTON, Robert Perry	35	SENE	1840-08-12	FD	SENE	
3891	" "	24	NWSW	1840-08-12	FD	NWSW	
3849	KENDALL, Jesse K	25	W½NE	1854-09-27	FD	W2NE	R:MADISON
3848	" "	25	NWSE	1854-09-27	FD	NWSE	R:MADISON
3838	LEMON, Hiram	35	SESW	1851-12-31	FD	SESW	
3839	LEMON, Jacob	23	W½NW	1830-10-18	FD	W2NW	R:MORGAN
3897	LOWRANCE, Samuel	14	W½NW	1834-04-15	FD	W2NW	R:MORGAN
3896	" "	11	E½NW	1836-03-15	FD	E2NW	R:MORGAN
3843	MASTERS, James M	12	SWNW	1835-12-14	FD	SWNW	R:MORGAN
3901	MASTERS, Squin Davis	36	NENE	1835-03-28	FD	NENE	R:MORGAN
3904	MASTERS, Thomas	11	SE	1830-09-14	FD	SE	R:MORGAN
3906	" "	14	W½NE	1830-09-14	FD	W2NE	R:MORGAN
3905	" "	14	E½NE	1830-11-13	FD	E2NE	R:MORGAN
3907	" "	36	SENE	1835-03-10	FD	SENE	R:MORGAN
3890	MCCRACKEN, Robert	2	S½SW	1853-11-24	FD	S2SW	R:MORGAN
3807	MCDONALD, Alexander	12	E½SE	1835-02-23	FD	E2SE	R:MORGAN
3810	" "	36	SWSE	1835-02-23	FD	SWSE	R:MORGAN
3808	" "	26	E½NE	1835-03-11	FD	E2NE	R:MORGAN
3809	" "	26	NESE	1835-03-11	FD	NESE	R:MORGAN
3861	MCDONALD, John	36	NWSE	1835-04-06	FD	NWSE	R:MORGAN
3845	MCFALLS, Jamus	1	SWSW	1851-02-07	FD	SWSW	R:MORGAN G:101
3804	MCPHEETERS, Addison	14	S½SW	1833-12-05	FD	S2SW	R:MISSOURI
3805	" "	23	E½NW	1833-12-05	FD	E2NW	R:MISSOURI
3806	" "	23	W½SE	1833-12-05	FD	W2SE	R:MISSOURI
3844	MCPHERSON, James	11	W½NE	1851-12-24	FD	W2NE	
3889	MCRACKIN, Robert Jr	11	NWNW	1853-12-15	FD	NWNW	R:MORGAN
3919	MCWILLIAM, William	35	NENE	1837-03-10	FD	NENE	R:GREENE
3845	MEISENHEIMER, Wilson	1	SWSW	1851-02-07	FD	SWSW	R:MORGAN G:101
3822	MILLS, Chester L	23	W½SW	1831-05-11	FD	W2SW	R:MORGAN
3920	MISENHEIMER, Wilson	12	NWNW	1843-11-28	FD	NWNW	
3864	MURRAY, John	1	SWNE	1851-02-04	FD	SWNE	R:MORGAN
3863	" "	1	NENE	1853-11-11	FD	NENEFR	R:MORGAN
3813	NEILL, Andrew	26	NWNW	1835-11-28	FD	NWNW	R:MORGAN
3814	NEILL, Andrew S	26	SWNE	1837-02-02	FD	SWNE	R:MORGAN
3872	ORR, Margaret G	36	NESE	1834-05-16	FD	NESE	R:MORGAN S:F
3862	PARKER, John Mclane	11	NWSW	1850-02-13	FD	NWSW	R:SANGAMON
3802	PENNOYER, A L	26	NWNE	1838-10-17	FD	NWNE	R:MORGAN S:I
3801	" "	14	W½SW	1838-10-17	FD	W2SW	R:MORGAN S:I
3812	PENNOYER, Andrew L	14	NWSE	1839-09-04	FD	NWSE	
3811	" "	14	E½SW	1839-09-04	FD	E2SW	
3815	PENNOYER, Andrew S	14	NESE	1840-07-29	FD	NESE	
3853	REID, John A	1	NWSW	1851-06-19	FD	NWSW	R:SCOTT
3899	REID, Samuel W	1	NENW	1851-02-07	FD	NENW	R:MORGAN
3898	ROBB, Samuel	35	W½SW	1837-02-06	FD	W2SW	R:MORGAN
3869	SCOTT, Levi	12	W½SW	1830-02-05	FD	W2SW	R:MORGAN
3816	SMITH, Anton	23	E½SW	1836-12-08	FD	E2SW	R:MORGAN
3818	SMITH, Bird	24	E½NW	1830-11-25	FD	E2NW	R:MORGAN
3846	STEWART, Jane	13	W½SW	1831-03-12	FD	W2SW	R:MORGAN S:F
3832	TUNNELL, David	13	E½SE	1830-11-15	FD	E2SE	R:MORGAN
3833	" "	13	E½SW	1830-11-15	FD	E2SW	R:MORGAN
3834	" "	25	E½SW	1831-11-17	FD	E2SW	R:MORGAN
3884	TUNNELL, Nicholas	24	E½NE	1831-11-17	FD	E2NE	R:MORGAN
3903	TUNNELL, Stephen	24	NESE	1839-08-31	FD	NESE	
3912	TUNNELL, Wesley	11	SWSW	1834-03-12	FD	SWSW	R:MORGAN
3865	WILSON, John	1	SWSE	1834-03-11	FD	SWSE	R:MORGAN
3886	WILSON, Richard B	1	NWSE	1836-10-14	FD	NWSE	R:MORGAN
3866	WRIGHT, John	36	SESE	1834-12-18	FD	SESE	R:MORGAN
3913	WRIGHT, Wiley	24	SWSW	1854-01-08	FD	SWSW	R:MORGAN
3835	WYATT, Edward	23	W½NE	1830-10-27	FD	W2NE	R:MORGAN
3909	WYATT, Thomas	13	W½SE	1830-10-27	FD	W2SE	R:MORGAN

ID	Individual in Patent	Sec.	Sec. Part	Purchase Date	Sale Type	IL Aliquot Part	For More Info . . .
3908	WYATT, Thomas (Cont'd)	13	SWNW	1835-11-12	FD	SWNW	R:MORGAN
3911	" "	25	NWSW	1836-03-05	FD	NWSW	
3910	" "	25	NWNW	1836-03-05	FD	NWNW	
3837	WYETH, George	23	SESE	1838-10-17	FD	SESE	R:MORGAN

Patent Map

T13-N R11-W
3rd PM Meridian

Map Group 16

Section 3

(no patents)

Section 2

COFFIN Nathaniel 1837
CARNEY John 1854
COFFIN Nathaniel 1837
CALDWELL Dan P 1852
CARNEY John 1854 — **2**
CAINEY Michael 1854
ASH James 1851
MCCRACKEN Robert 1853

Section 1

COFFIN Nathaniel 1837
REID Samuel W 1851
CALDWELL Dan P 1851
REID John A 1851
1
MCFALLS [101] Jamus 1851

Section (upper right)

BLAIR Joel P 1836
MURRAY John 1853
MURRAY John 1851
BIRDSELL Rufus 1836
WILSON Richard B 1836
WILSON John 1834
COONS Jesse 1830

Section 10

MCRACKIN Robert Jr 1853
BLAIR Solomon 1838
LOWRANCE Samuel 1836
PARKER John Mclane 1850 — **11**
TUNNELL Wesley 1834
HANES Daniel 1830
MCPHERSON James 1851
MASTERS Thomas 1830

Section 12

CALDWELL Rollin C 1851
ASH James 1851
MISENHEIMER Wilson 1843
MASTERS James M 1835
HARP William 1831
HANES Daniel 1830
12
SCOTT Levi 1830
HANES Daniel 1830
HANES Daniel 1830
MCDONALD Alexander 1835

Section 15

LOWRANCE Samuel 1834
HANES Daniel 1830
FREEMAN Richard 1835
MASTERS Thomas 1830
PENNOYER A L 1838 — **14**
PENNOYER Andrew L 1839
PENNOYER Andrew L 1839
PENNOYER Andrew S 1840
MCPHEETERS Addison 1833

Section 13

HERRIN [74] Lewis 1834
BLISH [2] Oaks Shaw 1835
WYATT Thomas 1835
HERRING John 1831
HOLLIDAY Charles 1829
13
TUNNELL David 1830
STEWART Jane 1831
WYATT Thomas 1830
TUNNELL David 1830

Section 22 — Scott / Morgan

(Scott, Morgan labels)

Section 23

LEMON Jacob 1830
MCPHEETERS Addison 1833
WYATT Edward 1830
ASHER William 1830
SMITH Anton 1836 — **23**
MCPHEETERS Addison 1833
EDWARDS Joseph B 1853
WYETH George 1838
MILLS Chester L 1831

Section 24

COLE Stephen 1830
SMITH Bird 1830
HEREN Lewis 1830
24
TUNNELL Nicholas 1831
HUSTON Robert Perry 1840
BIRDSELL Clark 1836
TUNNELL Stephen 1839
WRIGHT Wiley 1854
DEVOLT Nicholas 1854
COLLINS Charles 1837
COLLINS Charles 1837

Section 27

(no patents)

Section 26

NEILL Andrew 1835
COFFIN Nathaniel 1837
PENNOYER A L 1838
CHILTON James 1853 — **26**
NEILL Andrew S 1837
HUSTON Robert 1837
COFFIN Nathaniel 1837
COFFIN Nathaniel 1837
BILLINGS Abraham 1836
MCDONALD Alexander 1835
ABBOTT John 1855

Section 25

WYATT Thomas 1836
COFFIN Nathaniel 1837
KENDALL Jesse K 1854
EDWARDS Joseph B 1837 — **25**
COFFIN Nathaniel 1837
WYATT Thomas 1836
KENDALL Jesse K 1854
TUNNELL David 1831
GALBRAITH John 1835
BIRDSELL Clark 1836
COFFIN Nathaniel 1837

Section 34

(no patents)

Section 35

HACKETT George 1835
BILLINGS William 1854
MCWILLIAM William 1837
HUSTON Robert Perry 1840
35
ROBB Samuel 1837
BILLINGS Arden Sen 1845
BILLINGS William 1854
LEMON Hiram 1851
GAMBLE William 1836

Section 36

HAHN Johanna P 1841
BIRDSELL Rufus 1836
GRIGG John 1835
MASTERS Squin Davis 1835
HAHN Johanna P 1841
MASTERS Thomas 1835
36
GRIGG John 1835
MCDONALD John 1835
ORR Margaret G 1834
MCDONALD Alexander 1835
WRIGHT John 1834

Township Statistics

Parcels Mapped	:	120
Number of Patents	:	1
Number of Individuals	:	82
Patentees Identified	:	79
Number of Surnames	:	60
Multi-Patentee Parcels	:	3
Oldest Patent Date	:	10/23/1829
Most Recent Patent	:	11/1/1855
Block/Lot Parcels	:	0
Cities and Towns	:	0
Cemeteries	:	1

Note: the area contained in this map amounts to far less than a full Township. Therefore, its contents are completely on this single page (instead of a "normal" 2-page spread).

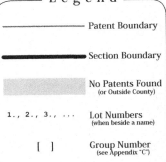

Legend

— Patent Boundary
— Section Boundary
No Patents Found (or Outside County)
1., 2., 3., ... Lot Numbers (when beside a name)
[ ] Group Number (see Appendix "C")

Scale: Section = 1 mile X 1 mile (generally, with some exceptions)

Road Map

T13-N R11-W
3rd PM Meridian

Map Group 16

Note: the area contained in this map amounts to far less than a full Township. Therefore, its contents are completely on this single page (instead of a "normal" 2-page spread).

Cities & Towns
None

Cemeteries
Bethel Cemetery

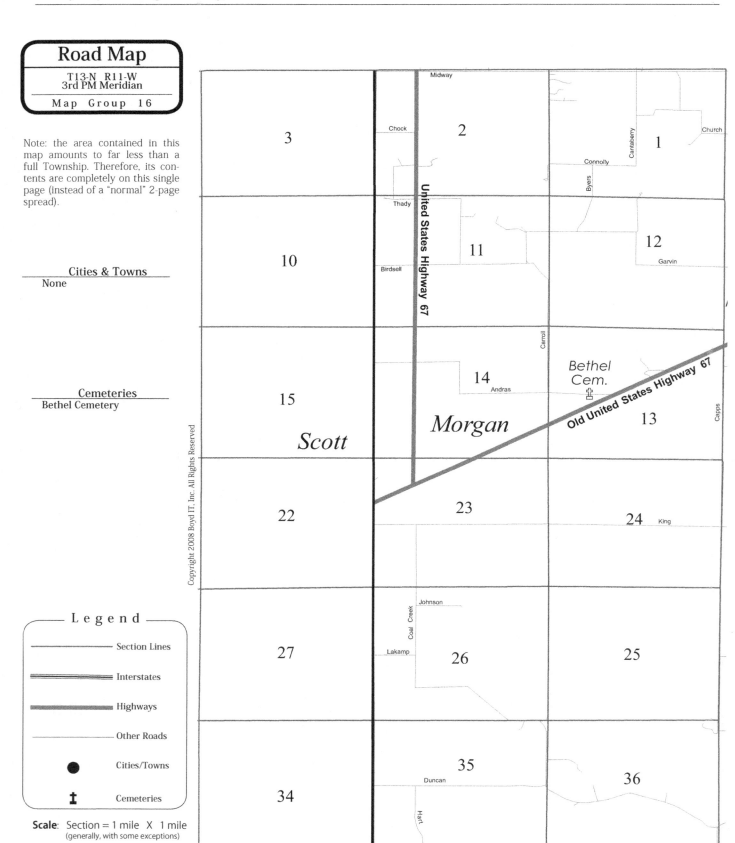

Legend

— Section Lines

═ Interstates

━ Highways

— Other Roads

● Cities/Towns

✝ Cemeteries

Scale: Section = 1 mile X 1 mile
(generally, with some exceptions)

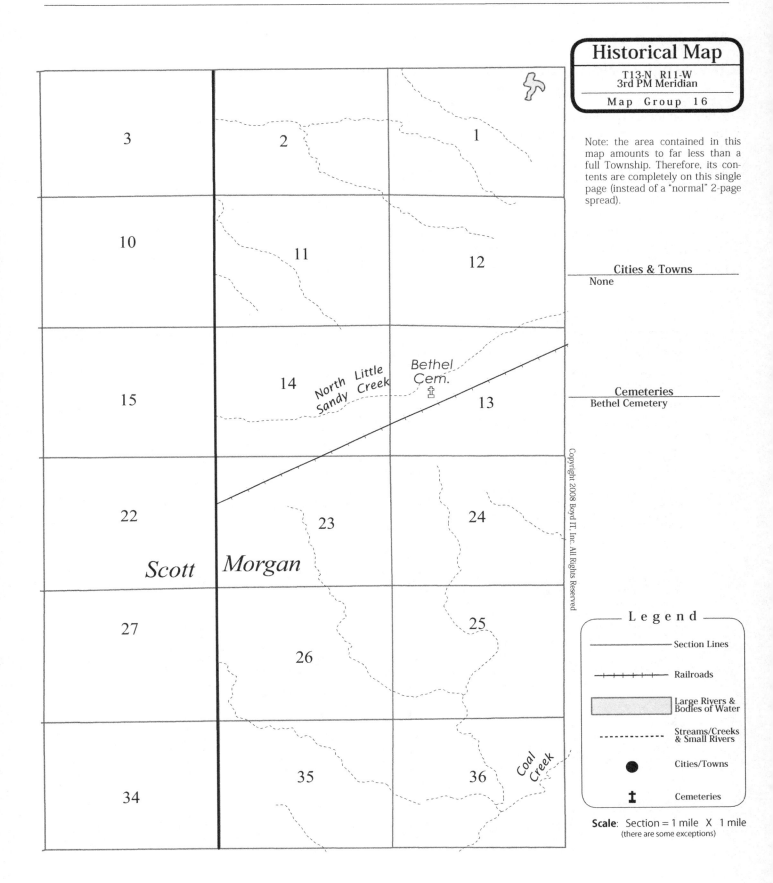

Historical Map

T13-N R11-W
3rd PM Meridian

Map Group 16

Note: the area contained in this map amounts to far less than a full Township. Therefore, its contents are completely on this single page (instead of a "normal" 2-page spread).

Cities & Towns
None

Cemeteries
Bethel Cemetery

Legend

———— Section Lines

++++++ Railroads

▭ Large Rivers & Bodies of Water

- - - - - Streams/Creeks & Small Rivers

● Cities/Towns

☨ Cemeteries

Scale: Section = 1 mile X 1 mile
(there are some exceptions)

Map Group 17: Index to Land Patents

Township 13-North Range 10-West (3rd PM)

After you locate an individual in this Index, take note of the Section and Section Part then proceed to the Land Patent map on the pages immediately following. You should have no difficulty locating the corresponding parcel of land.

The "For More Info" Column will lead you to more information about the underlying Patents. See the *Legend* at right, and the "How to Use this Book" chapter, for more information.

```
                    LEGEND
            "For More Info . . . " column
    G = Group  (Multi-Patentee Patent, see Appendix "C")
    R = Residence
    S = Social Status

    See Appendix A for list of abbreviations used by the
    Illinois State Archives in describing the place and
    nature of these land patents.

    Note: if the Abbreviations contain "L", "BL", "LOT",
    or "BLOCK", the exact whereabouts of the parcel within
    the section is not known.
```

ID	Individual in Patent	Sec.	Sec. Part	Purchase Date	Sale Type	IL Aliquot Part	For More Info . . .
4277	ADAMS, William	4	E2NE	1835-03-17	FD	E2NEPRE	R:MORGAN
4098	ANDERSON, James	13	E½NE	1831-11-01	FD	E2NE	R:MORGAN
4099	" "	2	E½SW	1831-11-01	FD	E2SW	R:MORGAN
4128	ANDERSON, James W	16	L6	1851-08-27	SC	LOT6SENW	
4152	ANDERSON, John	11	NWNE	1836-01-08	FD	NWNE	R:MORGAN
4061	" "	2	NESE	1836-02-05	FD	NESE	
4153	" "	2	NESE	1836-02-05	FD	NESE	
4154	" "	2	W½SE	1836-02-05	FD	W2SE	
4155	BAIRD, John	16	L4	1848-11-10	SC	LOT4NWNW	
4156	" "	16	L5	1848-11-10	SC	LOT5SWNW	
4158	" "	17	SENW	1851-10-08	FD	SENW	R:MORGAN
4157	" "	17	NESW	1854-09-25	FD	NESW	R:MORGAN
4159	BARD, John	21	NWSE	1846-01-09	FD	NWSE	
4007	BARNS, Daniel	35	SWSE	1854-09-25	FD	SWSE	R:GREENE
4223	BARNS, Ninian	35	SESW	1854-09-25	FD	SESW	R:MACOUPIN
4255	BARNS, Squire	29	SESW	1837-12-07	FD	SESW	R:MORGAN
4258	BARNS, Thomas J	32	NENW	1837-11-16	FD	NENW	R:MORGAN
4139	BARROW, Jesse T	25	SWSW	1854-02-21	FD	SWSW	R:MORGAN
4141	" "	36	NESW	1854-09-25	FD	NESW	R:MORGAN
4140	" "	36	E½NW	1854-09-25	FD	E2NW	R:MORGAN
4138	" "	25	SWSE	1854-11-20	FD	SWSE	R:MORGAN
4265	BARROW, Thornton L	25	NWSE	1854-05-02	FD	NWSE	R:MORGAN
4266	BARROW, Thornton S	36	NENE	1854-02-22	FD	NENE	R:MORGAN
4005	BELLOWS, Charles Smit	33	SWSW	1850-02-02	FD	SWSW	R:GREENE
4100	BELLOWS, James	35	SWNW	1839-06-18	FD	SWNW	
4000	BLACK, Charles Q	33	NWSW	1838-12-01	FD	NWSW	R:MORGAN
4146	BLAIR, Joel P	6	SWNW	1836-12-08	FD	SWNW	R:MORGAN
4076	BOYD, Hiram	24	SESE	1854-09-30	FD	SESE	R:MADISON
4077	" "	25	E½NE	1854-09-30	FD	E2NE	R:MADISON
4078	" "	25	NESE	1854-09-30	FD	NESE	R:MADISON
4048	BROWN, Franklin	14	E½SE	1830-12-04	FD	E2SE	R:MORGAN
4049	" "	16	L3	1850-02-18	SC	LOT3NENW	
4089	" "	16	L3	1850-02-18	SC	LOT3NENW	
4040	" "	29	NWNW	1851-10-08	FD	NWNW	R:MORGAN G:13
4052	" "	20	SESW	1854-01-18	FD	SESW	R:MORGAN
4050	" "	20	NESE	1854-01-18	FD	NESE	R:MORGAN
4051	" "	20	SENE	1854-01-18	FD	SENE	R:MORGAN
4053	" "	20	SWSE	1854-01-18	FD	SWSE	R:MORGAN
4131	BRUCE, Jeremiah	34	SWSW	1855-12-05	FD	SWSW	R:MORGAN
4242	BUGBY, Robert	35	NENW	1836-11-01	FD	NENW	R:MORGAN
4241	" "	34	SWSE	1836-11-01	FD	SWSE	R:MORGAN
4085	CAMPBELL, Hugh	1	NENE	1836-04-28	FD	NENE	R:MORGAN
3994	CASSEL, Benjamin	14	NWNE	1851-09-11	FD	NWNE	
4092	CHADWICK, Iram M	32	SENW	1836-06-06	FD	SENW	R:MORGAN
4091	" "	31	SWSW	1836-06-06	FD	SWSW	R:MORGAN
4093	" "	32	W½NW	1836-06-06	FD	W2NW	R:MORGAN

ID	Individual in Patent	Sec.	Sec. Part	Purchase Date	Sale Type	IL Aliquot Part	For More Info . . .
4199	CLARK, Matthew	31	W½NE	1831-05-02	FD	W2NEFS	R:MORGAN G:34
4200	CLARK, Matthew S	31	E½NE	1831-10-21	FD	E2NE	R:MORGAN G:33
4202	CLARKE, Matthew S	30	SE	1830-11-23	FD	SE	R:MORGAN G:38
4203	" "	31	E½NW	1832-08-20	FD	E2NW	R:MORGAN G:38
4201	" "	30	E½SW	1832-08-20	FD	E2SW	R:MORGAN G:38
4101	CRAIG, James	13	W½NE	1830-12-17	FD	W2NE	R:MORGAN
4218	CROUCH, Martin	36	SWSE	1849-09-20	FD	SWSE	
4163	DAVIDSON, John	31	NWSW	1835-12-03	FD	NWSW	R:MORGAN
4219	DEVOLT, Nicholas	19	E½NW	1854-01-08	FD	E2NWFR	R:MORGAN G:55
4006	DEWEESE, Cornelius H	14	SWSE	1855-02-22	FD	SWSE	R:MORGAN
4164	DICK, John	33	NENE	1849-09-22	FD	NENE	
4236	DICKERSON, Richard	34	S½NW	1854-09-25	FD	S2NW	R:MORGAN
4104	DICUS, James	28	SWNW	1839-06-12	FD	SWNW	
4103	" "	21	NWNE	1853-01-24	FD	NWNE	
4165	DIEUS, John	28	SESW	1836-01-01	FD	SESW	R:MADISON
4166	" "	33	NENW	1836-01-01	FD	NENW	R:MADISON
4106	DIKES, James	21	NENE	1845-12-27	FD	NENE	
4105	" "	16	L15	1851-03-12	SC	LOT15SWSE	
4168	DIKES, John	36	SENE	1854-09-25	FD	SENE	R:MORGAN
4167	" "	34	N½NW	1854-09-25	FD	N2NW	R:MORGAN
3975	DOWNS, Andrew	31	NESE	1836-06-15	FD	NESE	R:MORGAN
3974	DUFFIELD, Amos	12	NWNW	1852-07-19	FD	NWNW	
4202	DUNCAN, Joseph	30	SE	1830-11-23	FD	SE	R:MORGAN G:38
4199	" "	31	W½NE	1831-05-02	FD	W2NEFS	R:MORGAN G:34
4200	" "	31	E½NE	1831-10-21	FD	E2NE	R:MORGAN G:33
4203	" "	31	E½NW	1832-08-20	FD	E2NW	R:MORGAN G:38
4201	" "	30	E½SW	1832-08-20	FD	E2SW	R:MORGAN G:38
4198	" "	33	W½NW	1836-02-01	FD	W2NW	R:MORGAN
4197	" "	28	SWSW	1836-02-01	FD	SWSW	R:MORGAN
4150	EDWARDS, Joseph	18	E½NE	1835-07-30	FD	E2NE	R:MORGAN G:59
3936	FANNING, Abraham	25	W½NW	1830-11-13	FD	W2NW	R:MORGAN
3934	" "	24	E½SW	1831-03-17	FD	E2SW	R:MORGAN
3935	" "	24	W½SW	1836-02-04	FD	W2SW	
3933	" "	24	E½NE	1836-08-24	FD	E2NE	R:GREENE
3940	" "	26	SWNE	1840-12-01	FD	SWNE	
3932	" "	23	SWSE	1840-12-01	FD	SWSE	
3939	" "	26	NWSE	1850-02-07	FD	NWSE	R:MORGAN
3938	" "	26	NWNE	1850-02-07	FD	NWNE	R:MORGAN
3937	" "	26	NENE	1854-10-03	FD	NENE	R:MORGAN
4015	FANNING, Elias Ezra	14	NESW	1845-04-08	FD	NESW	
4039	FANNING, Ephraim	23	E½NW	1845-08-20	FD	E2NW	
4040	" "	29	NWNW	1851-10-08	FD	NWNW	R:MORGAN G:13
4040	FANNING, Henry	29	NWNW	1851-10-08	FD	NWNW	R:MORGAN G:13
4161	FANNING, John C	24	SWSE	1836-03-08	FD	SWSE	
4160	" "	23	NWSW	1836-03-18	FD	NWSW	
4173	FANNING, John K	23	E½SE	1854-10-03	FD	E2SE	R:MORGAN
4204	FANNING, Joseph	26	SENE	1851-11-28	FD	SENE	R:MORGAN
4207	FANNING, Levi	24	W½NE	1831-03-25	FD	W2NE	R:MORGAN
4206	" "	14	E½NW	1845-04-08	FD	E2NW	
4243	FANNING, Sampson	24	NESE	1835-08-17	FD	NESE	R:MORGAN
4040	FANNING, Samuel	29	NWNW	1851-10-08	FD	NWNW	R:MORGAN G:13
4055	FATHERKILE, George	5	NENE	1834-05-07	FD	NENE	R:MORGAN
4220	FATHERKILE, Nicholas	4	NWNW	1834-05-07	FD	NWNW	R:MORGAN
4056	FEATHERKILE, George	5	NWNE	1836-06-04	FD	NWNE	R:MORGAN
3943	FERNING, Abraham Jr	26	SWSE	1851-12-10	FD	SWSE	R:MORGAN
4280	FOLDEN, William	36	NWSW	1836-02-09	FD	NWSW	
3941	FULLER, Abraham	23	NWSE	1852-07-02	FD	NWSE	
3942	" "	23	W½NE	1854-09-26	FD	W2NE	R:MORGAN
4257	GILLILAND, Thomas	26	E½NW	1831-05-10	FD	E2NW	R:MORGAN
4294	GILLILAND, William P	24	E½NW	1830-12-17	FD	E2NW	R:MORGAN
4292	" "	13	SWNW	1835-08-12	FD	SWNW	R:MORGAN
4293	" "	2	NE	1836-02-22	FD	NEPRE	
4282	GREENUP, William	18	NESW	1836-06-02	FD	NESW	R:MORGAN
4170	GRIGG, John	31	E½SW	1835-12-07	FD	E2SW	R:PHILADELPHIA
4169	" "	29	W½SW	1836-05-12	FD	W2SW	R:PHILADELPHIA
4256	GRIGGS, Stephen	28	E½NW	1836-03-25	FD	E2NW	R:MADISON
4113	GUM, James	33	NWNE	1836-11-11	FD	NWNE	R:MADISON
4096	GUNN, Alexandeer S	20	SWNN	1853-11-24	FD	SWNE	
3963	" "	20	SWNE	1853-11-24	FD	SWNE	
3965	GUNN, Alexander	33	SENW	1835-06-02	FD	SENW	R:MORGAN
3964	" "	32	NESE	1851-12-17	FD	NESE	R:MORGAN
3999	GUNN, Bernard William	29	SESE	1845-04-15	FD	SESE	
4119	GUNN, James M	20	NENW	1852-01-12	FD	NENW	R:MORGAN

ID	Individual in Patent	Sec.	Sec. Part	Purchase Date	Sale Type	IL Aliquot Part	For More Info . . .
4132	GUNN, Jesse C	32	S½SE	1854-09-25	FD	S2SE	R:MORGAN
4133	GUNN, Jesse Carter	32	NENE	1845-05-05	FD	NENE	
4287	HAMILTON, William	13	E½SE	1831-11-02	FD	E2SE	R:VIRGINIA
4286	" "	1	NWNE	1833-05-07	FD	NWNE	R:MORGAN
3976	HARDIN, Andrew	17	SE	1850-09-27	FD	SE	
4289	" "	17	SE	1850-09-27	FD	SE	
4032	HENRY, Elijah	1	NESE	1848-04-10	FD	NESE	
4033	" "	12	N½NE	1851-01-29	FD	N2NE	
4060	HENRY, George	12	E½SE	1831-11-05	FD	E2SE	R:MORGAN
4058	" "	1	NW	1831-11-05	FD	NW	R:MORGAN
4059	" "	1	SWNE	1836-02-22	FD	SWNE	
4057	" "	1	NESW	1836-02-22	FD	NESW	
4068	HENRY, Greenup	1	SENE	1850-01-04	FD	SENE	R:MORGAN
4171	HENRY, John	1	SWSW	1839-05-11	FD	SWSW	
4172	HENRY, John Jr	1	NWSW	1836-10-10	FD	NWSW	R:MORGAN
4180	HENRY, John T	12	SWSE	1854-08-30	FD	SWSE	
4237	HENRY, Richard	1	W½SE	1836-12-13	FD	W2SE	R:MORGAN
4279	HENRY, William D	12	SWNE	1836-09-10	FD	SWNE	R:MORGAN
4278	" "	12	SENW	1836-09-10	FD	SENW	R:MORGAN
4208	HERRING, Lewis	32	W½SW	1836-01-11	FD	W2SW	R:MORGAN
4153	HEUY, George	2	NESE	1839-04-26	FD	NESE	
4061	" "	2	NESE	1839-04-26	FD	NESE	
4012	HICKMAN, David Mcclan	6	SW	1834-05-02	FD	SW	R:MISSOURI G:75
4054	HICKS, Franklin Z	17	NWNW	1835-08-15	FD	NWNW	R:MORGAN
4079	HOLLIDAY, Hiram	18	NWSW	1839-03-30	FD	NWSW	
4142	" "	18	NWSW	1839-03-30	FD	NWSW	
4229	HOLMES, Peris	13	E½SW	1831-04-16	FD	E2SW	R:MORGAN
4230	" "	24	W½NW	1831-04-16	FD	W2NW	R:MORGAN
4231	HOMES, Peris	23	E½SW	1831-05-10	FD	E2SW	R:MORGAN
4114	HOPPER, James	35	NESE	1836-06-11	FD	NESE	R:GREENE
4205	HOPPER, Joshua	36	SESE	1836-01-14	FD	SESE	R:GREENE
4147	HUGHES, John A	17	SWNW	1850-05-24	FD	SWNW	R:MORGAN
4148	HUGHES, John Allen	18	W½NE	1831-09-21	FD	W2NE	R:MORGAN
4149	" "	30	E½NE	1831-10-07	FD	E2NEFS	R:MORGAN
4150	" "	18	E½NE	1835-07-30	FD	E2NE	R:MORGAN G:59
4009	HULL, Daniel	36	NESE	1853-02-04	FD	NESE	
4031	HULL, Elijah Crouch	36	NWNW	1850-03-27	FD	NWNW	R:MORGAN
4144	KELLEY, Joan D	32	SESW	1851-08-08	FD	SESW	R:MORGAN S:F
4162	KELLEY, John D	32	NESW	1852-01-03	FD	NESW	R:MADISON
4288	KENNEDY, William	16	L9	1848-06-14	SC	LOT9NESE	
4228	KINGSTON, Paul	36	E½SE	1827-10-30	FD	E2SE	R:ST. CLAIR
4115	KIRKMAN, James	18	SESE	1836-06-02	FD	SESE	R:MORGAN
4012	LAMM, David Steele	6	SW	1834-05-02	FD	SW	R:MISSOURI G:75
4013	LAMME, David S	7	NW	1833-10-28	FD	NW	R:MISSOURI
4116	LEIGHTON, James	18	SWSE	1850-04-05	FD	SWSE	R:SCOTT
4117	" "	19	NENE	1851-07-22	FD	NENE	R:SCOTT
4014	LEONARD, Edward F	30	NWNE	1860-01-16	FD	NWNELS	
4145	LONG, Joel	9	E½NE	1831-11-28	FD	E2NE	R:MORGAN
4281	LUMSDEN, William G	17	SESW	1843-01-18	FD	SESW	
3929	MATHERS, John	24	NWSE	1857-04-08	FD	NWSE	G:96
3930	MATHUS, John	35	NWSE	1857-03-26	FD	NWSE	G:98
3931	" "	36	SWSW	1857-03-26	FD	SWSW	G:98
4289	MCAVOY, William	17	SE	1848-02-02	FD	SE	
3976	" "	17	SE	1848-02-02	FD	SE	
4044	MCCEARLY, Ezekiel	13	W½SE	1831-11-01	FD	W2SE	R:MORGAN
3968	MCDONALD, Alexander	7	NE	1835-02-23	FD	NE	R:MORGAN
3970	" "	7	SW	1835-02-23	FD	SW	R:MORGAN
3967	" "	6	SE	1835-02-23	FD	SE	R:MORGAN
3973	" "	8	W½NW	1835-02-23	FD	W2NW	R:MORGAN
3966	" "	5	W½SW	1835-02-23	FD	W2SW	R:MORGAN
3972	" "	8	SW	1835-03-11	FD	SW	R:MORGAN
3971	" "	8	E½NW	1835-03-11	FD	E2NW	R:MORGAN
3969	" "	7	SE	1835-04-06	FD	SE	R:MORGAN
4291	MCDONALD, William	5	NESW	1846-04-07	FD	NESW	
4290	" "	16	L7	1848-06-14	SC	LOT7SWNE	
4174	MCKEE, John	17	E½NE	1838-05-01	FD	E2NE	R:ST. LOUIS
4175	" "	17	W½NE	1838-05-01	FD	W2NE	R:ST. LOUIS
4073	MCLAUGHLIN, Henry	18	SESE	1849-08-02	FD	SESW	
4049	MILLION, Hugh	16	L3	1851-03-04	SC	LOT3SWSW	
4088	" "	16	L14	1851-03-04	SC	LOT14SESW	
4087	" "	16	L12	1851-03-04	SC	LOT12NWSW	
4089	" "	16	L3	1851-03-04	SC	LOT3SWSW	
4086	" "	16	L11	1851-03-04	SC	LOT11NESW	

ID	Individual in Patent	Sec.	Sec. Part	Purchase Date	Sale Type	IL Aliquot Part	For More Info . . .
4090	MILLION, Hugh (Cont'd)	21	NENW	1854-09-25	FD	NENW	R:MORGAN
3992	MORGAN, Ann J	35	NE	1854-09-29	FD	NE	R:MADISON S:F
3991	" "	26	E½SE	1854-09-29	FD	E2SE	R:MADISON S:F
3990	" "	25	W½SW	1854-09-29	FD	W2SW	R:MADISON S:F
4235	MORTON, Reuben	12	S½SW	1855-10-06	FD	S2SW	R:MORGAN
4194	MULLEN, Joseph B	12	NESW	1854-10-21	FD	NESW	R:MADISON
4195	" "	12	NWSE	1854-10-21	FD	NWSE	R:MADISON
4176	MURRY, John	6	NWNW	1852-01-07	FD	NWNW	R:MORGAN
4123	NELSON, James	5	W½SE	1835-09-21	FD	W2SE	R:MORGAN
4120	" "	5	SENE	1835-09-21	FD	SENE	R:MORGAN
4122	" "	5	SWNE	1837-04-28	FD	SWNE	R:MORGAN
4121	" "	5	SESW	1850-12-28	FD	SESW	R:MORGAN
3962	NICHOLLS, Agruppa	2	W½NE	1836-02-06	FD	W2NEVOID	G:104
3962	NICHOLS, Agrippa	2	W½NE	1836-02-06	FD	W2NEVOID	G:104
4111	NICHOLS, James F	22	NWSE	1852-07-02	FD	NWSE	
4109	" "	22	E½SW	1852-07-02	FD	E2SW	
4112	" "	22	SWSE	1854-09-26	FD	SWSE	R:MORGAN
4110	" "	22	NESE	1854-09-26	FD	NESE	R:MORGAN
4130	ORR, Jefferson	18	NESE	1834-04-21	FD	NESE	R:MORGAN
4216	ORR, Margaret G	18	NWSE	1834-04-23	FD	NWSE	R:MORGAN S:F
4070	PARKER, Grundy	29	SENW	1850-02-07	FD	SENW	R:MORGAN
4069	" "	29	NENW	1854-09-25	FD	NENW	R:MORGAN
4071	" "	29	SWNW	1854-09-25	FD	SWNW	R:MORGAN
4081	PARKER, Horace M	34	SESE	1854-09-29	FD	SESE	R:MADISON
4082	" "	34	W½SW	1854-09-29	FD	W2SW	R:MADISON
4083	" "	35	NESW	1854-09-29	FD	NESW	R:MADISON
4047	" "	34	W½SW	1854-09-29	FD	W2SW	R:MADISON
4084	PHILLIPS, Horace	29	NESE	1839-02-27	FD	NESE	
3993	POLAND, Azariah	20	SENW	1853-11-28	FD	SENW	R:MORGAN
4042	POLAND, Ezariah	20	NESW	1854-09-25	FD	NESW	R:MORGAN
4043	" "	20	NWSE	1854-09-25	FD	NWSE	R:MORGAN
4010	RANNELLS, David A	10	E½NE	1833-05-03	FD	E2NE	R:MORGAN
4011	" "	11	W½NW	1833-05-03	FD	W2NW	R:MORGAN
4004	REAUGH, Charles	35	SESE	1835-08-12	FD	SESE	R:MORGAN
4001	" "	11	SW	1836-02-22	FD	SW	
4002	" "	13	NWNW	1836-08-15	FD	NWNW	R:MORGAN
4003	" "	14	NENE	1836-08-15	FD	NENE	R:MORGAN
4102	REAUGH, James D	14	NWSE	1851-09-17	FD	NWSE	R:MORGAN
4151	REAUGH, John Allen	11	NWSE	1843-07-31	FD	NWSE	
4249	REAUGH, Samuel	13	W½SW	1830-12-17	FD	W2SW	R:MORGAN
4244	REAUGH, Samuel Q	11	SENW	1833-02-06	FD	SENW	R:MORGAN
4246	REAUGH, Samuel Querry	11	SWNE	1836-02-22	FD	SWNE	
4245	" "	11	E½NE	1836-02-22	FD	E2NE	
4248	REAUGH, Samuel Quincy	11	NENW	1834-03-05	FD	NENW	R:MORGAN
4247	" "	10	NESE	1834-03-05	FD	NESE	R:MORGAN
4285	REAUGH, William H	12	NENW	1848-07-17	FD	NENW	
4283	" "	1	SESW	1848-07-17	FD	SESW	
4284	" "	11	NESE	1854-08-29	FD	NESE	R:MORGAN
4217	REOUSEY, Margaret	29	NWSE	1839-02-27	FD	NWSE	S:F
4034	RIMBEY, Emanuel	21	NESW	1846-03-09	FD	NESW	
4036	" "	21	SWSE	1846-05-20	FD	SWSE	
4038	" "	28	E½NE	1854-09-25	FD	E2NE	R:MORGAN
4037	" "	22	W½SW	1854-09-25	FD	W2SW	R:MORGAN
4035	" "	21	SESE	1854-09-25	FD	SESE	R:MORGAN
4094	RIMBEY, Jacob	21	NWSW	1854-01-06	FD	NWSW	R:MORGAN
4268	RIMBEY, Uriah	28	NWNW	1845-08-14	FD	NWNW	
4267	RIMBEY, Uriah Jr	20	SESE	1852-08-05	FD	SESE	
4126	ROBINSON, James S	22	SESE	1836-11-05	FD	SESE	R:MORGAN
4127	" "	23	SWSW	1836-11-05	FD	SWSW	R:MORGAN
4134	RONSEY, Jesse P	21	SENE	1847-06-21	FD	SENE	
4295	ROSE, William	4	NENW	1835-10-29	FD	NENW	R:SCHUYLER
4137	ROUSEY, Jesse P	21	SWNE	1847-08-23	FD	SWNE	
4135	" "	20	N½NE	1854-09-25	FD	N2NE	R:MORGAN
4136	" "	21	S½NW	1854-09-25	FD	S2NW	R:MORGAN
4270	ROUSEY, Vincent	19	SENE	1854-01-30	FD	SENE	R:MORGAN
4271	" "	19	SWNW	1854-01-30	FD	SWNW	R:MORGAN
4272	" "	20	NWSW	1854-01-30	FD	NWSW	R:MORGAN
4269	" "	19	NESE	1854-01-30	FD	NESE	R:MORGAN
4296	ROUSEY, William	29	SWSE	1835-11-19	FD	SWSE	R:MORGAN
4177	RUCKER, John	18	NW	1830-11-15	FD	NWFR	R:MORGAN
3952	RUSSEL, Agnes	3	S½	1834-10-10	FD	S2	R:MORGAN S:F
3944	" "	10	N½	1834-10-10	FD	N2	R:MORGAN S:F
3946	" "	10	W½NE	1834-10-10	FD	W2NE	R:MORGAN S:F

ID	Individual in Patent	Sec.	Sec. Part	Purchase Date	Sale Type	IL Aliquot Part	For More Info . . .
3945	RUSSEL, Agnes (Cont'd)	10	SESE	1834-12-10	FD	SESE	R:MORGAN S:F
3947	" "	10	W½SE	1834-12-10	FD	W2SE	R:MORGAN S:F
3949	" "	2	W½NW	1834-12-10	FD	W2NW	R:MORGAN S:F
3951	" "	3	N½	1834-12-10	FD	N2	R:MORGAN S:F
3950	" "	2	W½SW	1834-12-10	FD	W2SW	R:MORGAN S:F
3954	" "	9	W½NE	1835-03-07	FD	W2NE	R:MORGAN S:F
3953	" "	4	W½NE	1835-03-17	FD	W2NE	R:MORGAN S:F
3948	" "	2	E½NW	1835-03-17	FD	E2NW	R:MORGAN S:F
3960	RUSSEL, Agnes Scott	4	S½NW	1835-10-31	FD	S2NW	R:MORGAN S:F
3981	RUSSEL, Andrew	14	NWNW	1834-12-10	FD	NWNW	R:MORGAN
3982	" "	15	NENE	1834-12-10	FD	NENE	R:MORGAN
3985	RUSSEL, Andrew Scott	15	E½SE	1835-10-31	FD	E2SE	R:MORGAN
3984	" "	14	W½SW	1835-10-31	FD	W2SW	R:MORGAN
3987	" "	23	E½NE	1836-02-17	FD	E2NE	
3986	" "	22	E½NE	1836-02-17	FD	E2NE	
4178	RUSSEL, John Scott	15	NENW	1835-03-07	FD	NENW	R:MORGAN
3955	RUSSELL, Agnes	15	W½NE	1835-05-20	FD	W2NE	R:MORGAN S:F
3956	" "	15	W½NW	1835-05-20	FD	W2NW	R:MORGAN S:F
3959	" "	23	W½NW	1845-04-08	FD	W2NW	S:F
3957	" "	15	W½SE	1845-04-08	FD	W2SE	S:F
3958	" "	22	W½NE	1845-04-24	FD	W2NE	S:F
3961	RUSSELL, Agnes Scott	15	SENW	1835-05-20	FD	SENW	R:MORGAN S:F
3983	RUSSELL, Andrew	16	L1	1848-06-14	SC	LOT1NENE	
3977	RUSSELL, Andrew J Jr	15	SW	1848-09-25	FD	SW	
3980	RUSSELL, Andrew Jr	22	NW	1848-09-25	FD	NW	
3988	RUSSELL, Andrew Scott	14	SWNW	1835-05-20	FD	SWNW	R:MORGAN
3989	" "	15	SENE	1835-05-20	FD	SENE	R:MORGAN
3995	SHEFLER, Benjamin	6	SENE	1840-06-06	FD	SENE	
3996	SHEPLER, Benjamin	6	SENW	1838-03-02	FD	SENW	R:MORGAN
4250	SHEUMAKER, Samuel	6	NENE	1853-03-11	FD	NENE	R:MORGAN
3997	SHIPLAR, Benjamin	6	NENW	1853-03-11	FD	NENW	R:MORGAN
3998	SHIPLER, Benjamin	6	W½NE	1836-05-27	FD	W2NE	R:MORGAN
4276	SIMS, Wesley	19	L2 (W½)	1852-08-16	FD	W2LOT2SW	R:MORGAN
4275	" "	19	L1 (N½)	1852-08-16	FD	N2LOT1SW	R:MORGAN
4080	SMADLEY, Hiram	30	SWSW	1836-01-16	FD	SWSW	R:MORGAN
3921	SMITH, Aaron	4	W½SE	1835-10-22	FD	W2SE	R:MACOUPIN
4252	SMITH, Samuel	4	E½SE	1835-10-22	FD	E2SE	R:MACOUPIN
4251	" "	29	NE	1836-11-24	FD	NE	R:MORGAN
4259	SOOY, Thomas	11	S½SE	1851-02-14	FD	S2SE	R:MORGAN
4125	SPENCER, James R	31	SESE	1844-03-20	FD	SESE	
4214	SPENCER, Major	31	NWSE	1848-10-29	FD	NWSE	
4215	" "	31	SWSE	1851-12-10	FD	SWSE	R:MORGAN
4179	SPIRES, John	5	SWSE	1836-03-18	FD	SWSE	
4096	STORY, James Allen	20	SWNE	1836-12-13	FD	SWNE	R:MORGAN
3963	" "	20	SWNE	1836-12-13	FD	SWNE	R:MORGAN
4124	STORY, James P	28	NESE	1851-10-07	FD	NESE	R:MORGAN
4181	STORY, John W	27	SESW	1854-09-25	FD	SESW	R:MORGAN
4183	" "	27	SWSE	1854-09-25	FD	SWSE	R:MORGAN
4184	" "	27	W½SW	1854-09-25	FD	W2SW	R:MORGAN
4185	" "	34	W½NE	1854-09-25	FD	W2NE	R:MORGAN
4182	" "	27	SWNW	1854-09-25	FD	SWNW	R:MORGAN
4186	STORY, John Williams	28	SESE	1847-06-30	FD	SESE	
4224	STORY, Paris	28	NESW	1835-06-06	FD	NESW	R:GREENE
4226	" "	28	W½SE	1839-09-26	FD	W2SE	
4225	" "	28	SWNE	1847-07-10	FD	SWNE	
4227	STORY, Parish	28	NWNE	1852-01-28	FD	NWNE	R:MORGAN
4232	STORY, Peter	32	SWNE	1836-11-24	FD	SWNE	R:MORGAN
4234	STORY, Porter	32	SENE	1847-08-23	FD	SENE	
4233	" "	32	NWSE	1851-12-16	FD	NWSE	R:MORGAN
4240	STORY, Riley	27	NWNW	1853-12-05	FD	NWNW	R:MORGAN
4273	STORY, Vincent	28	NWSW	1835-11-19	FD	NWSW	R:MORGAN
4274	" "	33	SWSE	1838-05-17	FD	SWSE	R:MORGAN
4095	STRONER, Jacob	21	S½SW	1845-04-19	FD	S2SW	
4062	TAYLOR, George	12	SENE	1836-01-12	FD	SENE	R:MORGAN
3978	THOMPSON, Andrew J	19	SESE	1854-10-07	FD	SESE	R:MONTGOMERY
3979	" "	20	SWSW	1854-10-07	FD	SWSW	R:MONTGOMERY
4107	TUCKER, James E	12	NWSW	1854-02-10	FD	NWSW	R:MORGAN
4108	" "	12	SWNW	1855-10-06	FD	SWNW	R:MORGAN
4143	TUNNELL, Jesse	31	W½NW	1831-11-17	FD	W2NW	R:MORGAN
4142	" "	18	NWSW	1834-09-04	FD	NWSW	R:MORGAN
4079	" "	18	NWSW	1834-09-04	FD	NWSW	R:MORGAN
4222	TUNNELL, Nicholas M	33	SESW	1836-11-15	FD	SESW	R:MORGAN
4221	" "	19	W½NW	1836-11-15	FD	W2NW	R:MORGAN

ID	Individual in Patent	Sec.	Sec. Part	Purchase Date	Sale Type	IL Aliquot Part	For More Info . . .
4008	VERTREES, Daniel H	21	NESE	1851-03-04	FD	NESE	R:MORGAN
3923	VOYLES, Aaron	36	SWNE	1854-10-02	FD	SWNE	R:MADISON
3922	"	36	NWSE	1854-10-02	FD	NWSE	R:MADISON
4129	VOYLES, Henry	14	SEN½	1854-10-03	FD	S2NE	R:MADISON
4074	"	14	SEN½	1854-10-03	FD	S2NE	R:MADISON
4297	WALKER, William	5	NW	1835-04-03	FD	NW	R:MORGAN
4074	WALSH, James	14	SEN½	1861-01-03	FD	S2NE	
4129	"	14	SEN½	1861-01-03	FD	S2NE	
4196	WASSON, Joseph D	14	SESW	1851-09-11	FD	SESW	R:MORGAN
4063	WEST, George W	33	NWSE	1836-01-06	FD	NWSE	R:MORGAN
4064	"	33	SESE	1836-02-09	FD	SESE	"
4118	WESTROPE, James Lewis	32	NWNE	1846-01-09	FD	NWNE	
4238	WESTROPE, Richard	29	NESW	1847-09-29	FD	NESW	
4075	WHEELER, Henry	36	SESW	1854-09-29	FD	SESW	R:GREENE
4254	WHITE, Sherwood	26	E½SW	1831-08-20	FD	E2SW	R:MORGAN
4253	"	25	E½SW	1831-11-26	FD	E2SW	R:MORGAN
4213	WHITLOCK, Luther	36	SWNW	1835-04-10	FD	SWNW	R:MORGAN
4211	"	35	NWNW	1837-02-01	FD	NWNW	R:MORGAN
4209	"	34	E½NE	1843-03-08	FD	E2NE	
4210	"	34	NESE	1851-12-05	FD	NESE	R:MORGAN
4212	"	35	SENW	1851-12-05	FD	SENW	R:MORGAN
4263	WHITLOCK, Thomas	34	SESW	1834-12-30	FD	SESW	R:MORGAN
4260	"	27	E½SE	1836-02-06	FD	E2SE	
4262	"	27	NWSE	1848-03-10	FD	NWSE	
4261	"	27	NESW	1852-01-28	FD	NESW	R:MORGAN
4298	WHITLOCK, William	26	W½SW	1831-11-26	FD	W2SW	R:MORGAN
4082	WILCOX, Francis M	34	W½SW	1854-09-23	FD	W2SW	R:GREENE
4046	"	34	NWSE	1854-09-23	FD	NWSE	R:GREENE
4045	"	34	NESW	1854-09-23	FD	NESW	R:GREENE
4047	"	34	W½SW	1854-09-23	FD	W2SW	R:GREENE
4239	WILKINSON, Richard	36	NWNE	1851-08-23	FD	NWNE	
4072	WILLIAMS, Hardin	4	E½SW	1836-05-07	FD	E2SW	R:MORGAN
4019	WOLCOTT, Elihu	25	W½NE	1831-03-17	FD	W2NE	R:MORGAN
4028	"	9	NW	1831-03-17	FD	NW	R:MORGAN
4018	"	25	E½NW	1831-03-17	FD	E2NW	R:MORGAN
4024	"	4	W½SW	1831-04-18	FD	W2SW	R:MORGAN
4016	"	10	E½SW	1831-04-18	FD	E2SW	R:MORGAN
4017	"	13	E½NW	1831-04-18	FD	E2NW	R:MORGAN
4021	"	27	E½NE	1831-09-23	FD	E2NE	R:ADAMS
4026	"	8	NE	1835-03-18	FD	NE	R:MORGAN
4023	"	27	W½NE	1835-03-18	FD	W2NE	R:MORGAN
4030	"	9	W½SE	1835-03-18	FD	W2SE	R:MORGAN
4020	"	26	W½NW	1835-03-18	FD	W2NW	R:MORGAN
4029	"	9	SW	1835-03-18	FD	SW	R:MORGAN
4027	"	8	SE	1835-03-21	FD	SE	R:MORGAN
4025	"	5	E½SE	1835-11-26	FD	E2SE	R:MORGAN
4022	"	27	E½NW	1837-09-08	FD	E2NW	R:MORGAN
4041	WRIGHT, Ester	33	SWNE	1837-02-27	FD	SWNE	R:MORGAN S:F
4066	WRIGHT, George	33	NESW	1835-04-13	FD	NESW	R:MORGAN
4067	"	33	SENE	1851-09-11	FD	SENE	R:MORGAN
4065	"	33	NESE	1854-09-25	FD	NESE	R:MORGAN
4097	WRIGHT, James Allen	21	NWNW	1836-06-16	FD	NWNW	R:MORGAN
4192	WRIGHT, John	9	NESE	1834-02-28	FD	NESE	R:MORGAN
4187	"	10	NWSW	1834-02-28	FD	NWSW	R:MORGAN
4188	"	10	SWSW	1835-10-23	FD	SWSW	R:MORGAN
4193	"	9	SESE	1836-06-02	FD	SESE	R:MORGAN
4189	"	16	L8	1848-06-14	SC	LOT8SENE	
4190	"	16	L16	1848-10-30	SC	LOT16SESE	
4191	"	16	L2	1851-03-12	SC	LOT2NWNE	
4219	WRIGHT, Wiley	19	E½NW	1854-01-08	FD	E2NWFR	R:MORGAN G:55
4264	WYATT, Thomas	17	SWSW	1836-03-05	FD	SWSW	
3928	YATES, Abner	19	L2 (S½)	1854-02-14	FD	S2LOT2SW	R:MORGAN
3927	"	19	L1 (S½)	1854-02-14	FD	S2LOT1SW	R:MORGAN
3924	"	19	NWNE	1854-02-17	FD	NWNE	R:MORGAN
3926	"	19	W½SE	1854-02-17	FD	W2SE	R:MORGAN
3925	"	19	SWNE	1854-02-28	FD	SWNE	R:MORGAN
3931	"	36	SWSW	1857-03-26	FD	SWSW	G:98
3930	"	35	NWSE	1857-03-26	FD	NWSE	G:98
3929	"	24	NWSE	1857-04-08	FD	NWSE	G:96

Patent Map

T13-N R10-W
3rd PM Meridian

Map Group 17

Township Statistics

Parcels Mapped	:	378
Number of Patents	:	1
Number of Individuals	:	214
Patentees Identified	:	210
Number of Surnames	:	131
Multi-Patentee Parcels	:	13
Oldest Patent Date	:	10/30/1827
Most Recent Patent	:	1/3/1861
Block/Lot Parcels	:	20
Cities and Towns	:	1
Cemeteries	:	8

Section 5 / 4 area (top row):

MURRY John 1852 | SHIPLAR Benjamin 1853 | SHIPLER Benjamin 1836 | SHEUMAKER Samuel 1853 | WALKER William 1835 **5** | | FEATHERKILE George 1836 | FATHERKILE George 1834 | FATHERKILE Nicholas 1834 | ROSE William 1835 | RUSSEL Agnes 1835 | ADAMS William 1835

BLAIR Joel P 1836 | SHEPLER Benjamin 1838 | | SHEFLER Benjamin 1840 | | NELSON James 1837 | NELSON James 1835 | RUSSEL Agnes Scott 1835 **4** | |

Section 6:
6 | HICKMAN [75] David Mcclan 1834 | MCDONALD Alexander 1835

MCDONALD William 1846 | MCDONALD Alexander 1835 | NELSON James 1835 | WOLCOTT Elihu 1835
NELSON James 1850 | SPIRES John 1836 | WOLCOTT Elihu 1831 | WILLIAMS Hardin 1836 | SMITH Aaron 1835 | SMITH Samuel 1835

Section 7 / 8 / 9:
LAMME David S 1833 | MCDONALD Alexander 1835 | MCDONALD Alexander 1835 | MCDONALD Alexander 1835 **8** | WOLCOTT Elihu 1835 | WOLCOTT Elihu 1831 **9** | RUSSEL Agnes 1835 | LONG Joel 1831

MCDONALD Alexander 1835 **7** | MCDONALD Alexander 1835 | MCDONALD Alexander 1835 | WOLCOTT Elihu 1835 | WOLCOTT Elihu 1835 | WOLCOTT Elihu 1835 | WRIGHT John 1834 / WRIGHT John 1836

Section 18 / 17 / 16:
RUCKER John 1830 **18** | HUGHES John Allen 1831 | HUGHES [59] John Allen 1835 | HICKS Franklin Z 1835 | | | |
HUGHES John A 1850 | BAIRD John 1851 | MCKEE John 1838 | MCKEE John 1838 **17**

HOLLIDAY Hiram / TUNNELL Jesse 1834 | GREENUP William 1836 | ORR Margaret G 1834 | ORR Jefferson 1834 | | BAIRD John 1854 | HARDIN Andrew 1850 | MCAVOY William 1848

MCLAUGHLIN Henry 1849 | LEIGHTON James 1850 | KIRKMAN James 1836 | WYATT Thomas 1836 | LUMSDEN William G 1843

Lots-Sec. 16:
L1 RUSSELL, Andrew 1848
L2 WRIGHT, John 1851
L3 MILLION, Hugh 1851
L3 BROWN, Franklin 1850
L4 BAIRD, John 1848
L5 BAIRD, John 1848
L6 ANDERSON, James W 1851
L7 MCDONALD, William 1848
L8 WRIGHT, John 1848
L9 KENNEDY, William 1848
L11 MILLION, Hugh 1851
L12 MILLION, Hugh 1851
L14 MILLION, Hugh 1851
L15 DIKES, James 1851
L16 WRIGHT, John 1848 **16**

Section 19 / 20 / 21:
TUNNELL Nicholas M 1836 | DEVOLT [55] Nicholas 1854 | YATES Abner 1854 | LEIGHTON James 1851 | GUNN James M 1852 | ROUSEY Jesse P 1854 | WRIGHT James Allen 1836 | MILLION Hugh 1854 | DICUS James 1853 | DIKES James 1845

ROUSEY Vincent 1854 **19** | YATES Abner 1854 | ROUSEY Vincent 1854 | POLAND Azariah 1853 **20** | STORY James Allen / GUNN 1836 / Alexandeer S 1853 | BROWN Franklin 1854 | ROUSEY Jesse P 1854 **21** | ROUSEY Jesse P 1847 | RONSEY Jesse P 1847

YATES Abner 1854 | ROUSEY Vincent 1854 | ROUSEY Vincent 1854 | POLAND Ezariah 1854 | POLAND Ezariah 1854 | BROWN Franklin 1854 | RIMBEY Jacob 1854 | RIMBEY Emanuel 1846 | BARD John 1846 | VERTREES Daniel H 1851

Lots-Sec. 19:
L1(N½) SIMS, Wesley 1852
L1(S½) YATES, Abner 1854
L2(S½) YATES, Abner 1854
L2(W½) SIMS, Wesley 1852

THOMPSON Andrew J 1854 | THOMPSON Andrew J 1854 | BROWN Franklin 1854 | BROWN Franklin 1854 | RIMBEY Uriah Jr 1852 | STRONER Jacob 1845 | RIMBEY Emanuel 1846 | RIMBEY Emanuel 1854

Section 30 / 29 / 28:
LEONARD Edward F 1860 | HUGHES John Allen 1831 | FANNING [13] Ephraim 1851 | PARKER Grundy 1854 | SMITH Samuel 1836 | RIMBEY Uriah 1845 | STORY Parish 1852 | RIMBEY Emanuel 1854

30 | PARKER Grundy 1854 | PARKER Grundy 1850 **29** | DICUS James 1839 | GRIGGS Stephen 1836 | STORY Paris 1847

SMADLEY Hiram 1836 | DUNCAN [38] Joseph 1832 | DUNCAN [38] Joseph 1830 | GRIGG John 1836 | WESTROPE Richard 1847 | REOUSEY Margaret 1839 | PHILLIPS Horace 1839 | STORY Vincent 1835 | STORY Paris 1835 **28** | STORY James P 1851

BARNS Squire 1837 | ROUSEY William 1835 | GUNN Bernard William 1845 | DUNCAN Joseph 1836 | DIEUS John 1836 | STORY Paris 1839 | STORY John Williams 1847

Section 31 / 32 / 33:
TUNNELL Jesse 1831 | DUNCAN [38] Joseph 1832 | DUNCAN [34] Joseph 1831 | DUNCAN [33] Joseph 1831 | BARNS Thomas J 1837 | WESTROPE James Lewis 1846 | GUNN Jesse Carter 1845 | | DIEUS John 1836 | GUM James 1836 | DICK John 1849

31 | CHADWICK Iram M 1836 | CHADWICK Iram M 1836 | STORY Peter 1836 **32** | STORY Porter 1847 | DUNCAN Joseph 1836 | GUNN Alexander 1835 **33** | WRIGHT Ester 1837 | WRIGHT George 1851

DAVIDSON John 1835 | SPENCER Major 1848 | DOWNS Andrew 1836 | HERRING Lewis 1836 | KELLEY John D 1852 | STORY Porter 1851 | GUNN Alexander 1851 | BLACK Charles Q 1838 | WRIGHT George 1835 | WEST George W 1836 | WRIGHT George 1854

CHADWICK Iram M 1836 | GRIGG John 1835 | SPENCER Major 1851 | SPENCER James R 1844 | KELLEY Joan D 1851 | GUNN Jesse C 1854 | BELLOWS Charles Smit 1850 | TUNNELL Nicholas M 1836 | STORY Vincent 1838 | WEST George W 1836

Section 3
RUSSEL Agnes 1834
RUSSEL Agnes 1834

Section 2
RUSSEL Agnes 1834
RUSSEL Agnes 1835
NICHOLS [104] Agrippa 1836
GILLILAND William P 1836
RUSSEL Agnes 1834
ANDERSON James 1831
ANDERSON John 1836
ANDERSON HEUY John George 1836 1839

Section 1
HENRY George 1831
HAMILTON William 1833
CAMPBELL Hugh 1836
HENRY George 1836
HENRY Greenup 1850
HENRY John Jr 1836
HENRY George 1836
HENRY Richard 1836
HENRY Elijah 1848
HENRY John 1839
REAUGH William H 1848

Section 10
RUSSEL Agnes 1834
RUSSEL Agnes 1834
RANNELLS David A 1833
WRIGHT John 1834
WOLCOTT Elihu 1831
RUSSEL Agnes 1834
REAUGH Samuel Quincy 1834
WRIGHT John 1835
RUSSEL Agnes 1834

Section 11
RANNELLS David A 1833
REAUGH Samuel Quincy 1834
REAUGH Samuel Q 1833
REAUGH Charles 1836
ANDERSON John 1836
REAUGH Samuel Querry 1836
REAUGH John Allen 1843
REAUGH Samuel Querry 1836

Section 12
DUFFIELD Amos 1852
REAUGH William H 1848
HENRY Elijah 1851
TUCKER James E 1855
HENRY William D 1836
HENRY William D 1836
HENRY William D 1836
HENRY George 1831
TAYLOR George 1836
TUCKER James E 1854
MULLEN Joseph B 1854
MULLEN Joseph B 1854
MORTON Reuben 1855
HENRY John T 1854
REAUGH William H 1854
SOOY Thomas 1851

Section 15
RUSSELL John Scott 1835
RUSSELL Agnes 1835
RUSSELL Agnes 1835
RUSSELL Agnes Scott 1835
RUSSELL Andrew J Jr 1848

Section 14
RUSSELL Andrew 1834
RUSSELL Andrew 1834
RUSSELL Andrew Scott 1835
RUSSELL Andrew Scott 1835
FANNING Levi 1845
VOYLES Henry 1854
FANNING Elias Ezra 1845
WASSON Joseph D 1851
RUSSELL Agnes 1845
RUSSELL Andrew Scott 1835
WALSH James 1861
CASSEL Benjamin 1851
REAUGH James D 1851
DEWEESE Cornelius H 1855

Section 13
REAUGH Charles 1836
GILLILAND William P 1835
WOLCOTT Elihu 1831
CRAIG James 1830
ANDERSON James 1831
BROWN Franklin 1830
REAUGH Samuel 1830
HOLMES Peris 1831
MCCEARLY Ezekiell 1831
HAMILTON William 1831
REAUGH Charles 1836

Section 22
RUSSELL Andrew Jr 1848
RUSSELL Agnes 1845
RUSSELL Andrew Scott 1836
RIMBEY Emanuel 1854
NICHOLS James F 1852
NICHOLS James F 1852
NICHOLS James F 1854

Section 23
RUSSELL Agnes 1845
FANNING Ephraim 1845
FANNING Agnes 1845
FULLER Abraham 1854
RUSSELL Andrew Scott 1836
NICHOLS James F 1854
ROBINSON James S 1836
FANNING John C 1836
HOMES Peris 1831
FULLER Abraham 1852
ROBINSON James S 1836
FANNING Abraham 1840

Section 24
GILLILAND William P 1830
HOLMES Peris 1831
FANNING Abraham 1831
FANNING Levi 1831
FANNING Abraham 1836
YATES [96] Abner 1857
FANNING Sampson 1835
FANNING John K 1854
FANNING John C 1836
BOYD Hiram 1854

Section 27
STORY Riley 1853
WOLCOTT Elihu 1837
STORY John W 1854
WOLCOTT Elihu 1835
WOLCOTT Elihu 1831
WHITLOCK Thomas 1852
STORY John W 1854
WHITLOCK Thomas 1848
STORY John W 1854
WHITLOCK Thomas 1836

Section 26
WOLCOTT Elihu 1835
GILLILAND Thomas 1831
WHITLOCK William 1831
FANNING Abraham 1850
FANNING Abraham 1840
FANNING Joseph 1851
WHITE Sherwood 1831
FANNING Abraham 1854
FANNING Abraham 1850
FERNING Abraham Jr 1851

Section 25
FANNING Abraham 1836
WOLCOTT Elihu 1831
BOYD Hiram 1854
MORGAN Ann J 1854
WOLCOTT Elihu 1831
BARROW Thornton L 1854
BOYD Hiram 1854
BARROW Jesse T 1854
MORGAN Ann J 1854
WHITE Sherwood 1831
BARROW Jesse T 1854

Section 34
DIKES John 1854
DICKERSON Richard 1854
STORY John W 1854
WHITLOCK Luther 1843
WHITLOCK Luther 1837
WILCOX Francis M 1854
PARKER Horace M 1854 BRUCE Jeremiah 1855
WILCOX Francis M 1854
WHITLOCK Thomas 1834
WILCOX Francis M 1854
BUGBY Robert 1836
WHITLOCK Luther 1851
PARKER Horace M 1854

Section 35
WHITLOCK Luther 1837
BUGBY Robert 1836
BELLOWS James 1839
WHITLOCK Luther 1851
MORGAN Ann J 1854
PARKER Horace M 1854
BARNS Ninian 1854
YATES [98] Abner 1857
BARNS Daniel 1854
HOPPER James 1836
REAUGH Charles 1835

Section 36
HULL Elijah Crouch 1850
BARROW Jesse T 1854
WILKINSON Richard 1851
BARROW Thornton S 1854
WHITLOCK Luther 1835
VOYLES Aaron 1854
DIKES John 1854
FOLDEN William 1836
BARROW Jesse T 1854
VOYLES Aaron 1854
KINGSTON Paul 1827 HULL Daniel 1853
YATES [98] Abner 1857
WHEELER Henry 1854
CROUCH Martin 1849
HOPPER Joshua 1836

Helpful Hints

1. This Map's INDEX can be found on the preceding pages.

2. Refer to Map "C" to see where this Township lies within Morgan County, Illinois.

3. Numbers within square brackets [ ] denote a multi-patentee land parcel (multi-owner). Refer to Appendix "C" for a full list of members in this group.

4. Areas that look to be crowded with Patentees usually indicate multiple sales of the same parcel (re-issues), cancellations or voided transactions (that we map, anyway) or overlapping parcels. We opt to show even these ambiguous parcels, which oftentimes lead to research avenues not yet taken.

Legend

— Patent Boundary

— Section Boundary

No Patents Found (or Outside County)

1., 2., 3., ... Lot Numbers (when beside a name)

[ ] Group Number (see Appendix "C")

Scale: Section = 1 mile X 1 mile (generally, with some exceptions)

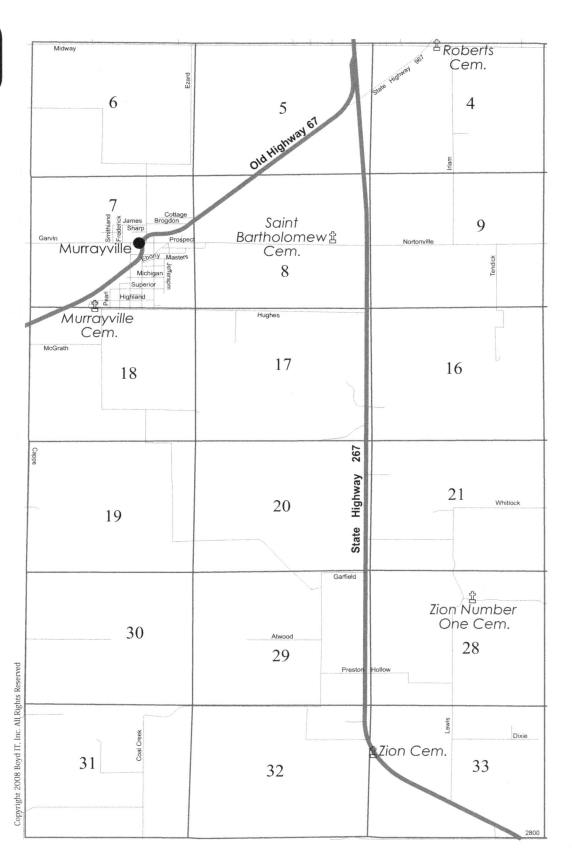

Road Map

T13-N R10-W
3rd PM Meridian

Map Group 17

Cities & Towns
Murrayville

Cemeteries
Henry Cemetery
Murrayville Cemetery
Roberts Cemetery
Saint Bartholomew Cemetery
Sooy Cemetery
Whitlock Cemetery
Zion Cemetery
Zion Number One Cemetery

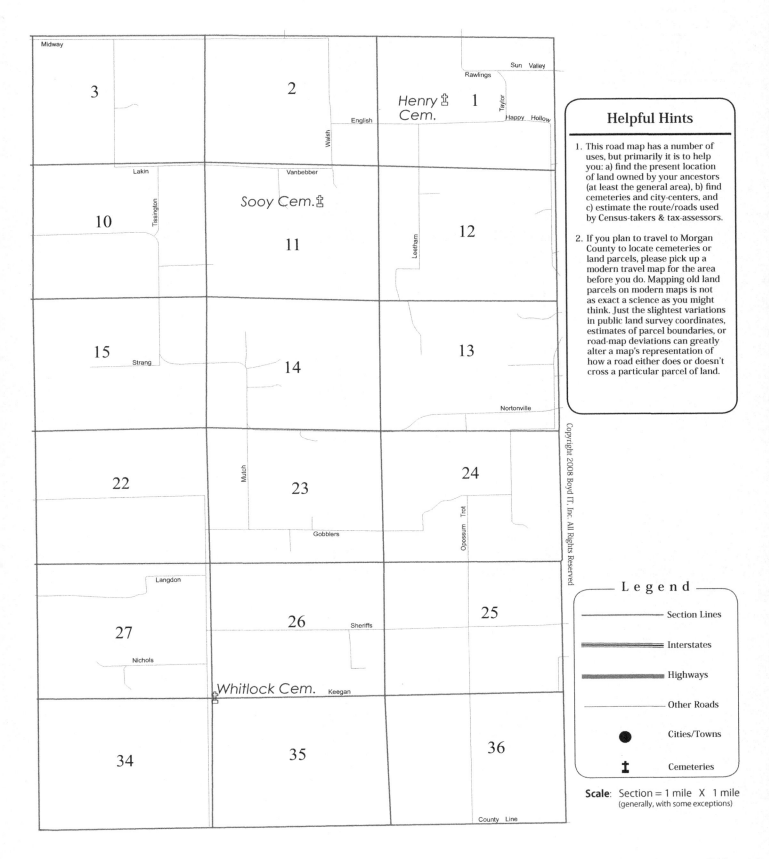

Historical Map

T13-N R10-W
3rd PM Meridian

Map Group 17

Cities & Towns
Murrayville

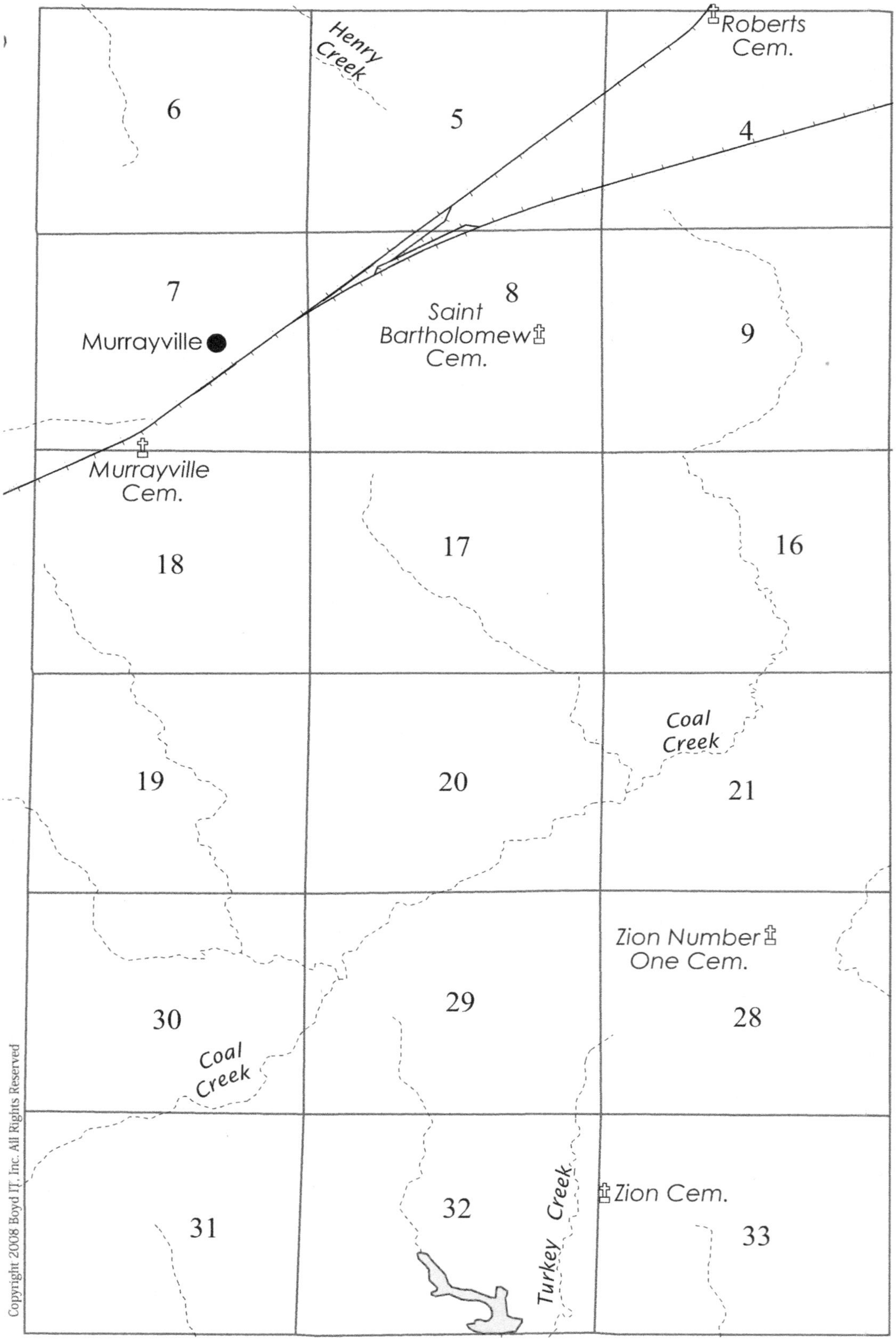

Cemeteries
Henry Cemetery
Murrayville Cemetery
Roberts Cemetery
Saint Bartholomew Cemetery
Sooy Cemetery
Whitlock Cemetery
Zion Cemetery
Zion Number One Cemetery

Henry
Creek

6

5

✞ Roberts
Cem.

4

7

Murrayville ●

8

Saint
Bartholomew ✞
Cem.

9

✞
Murrayville
Cem.

18

17

16

19

20

Coal
Creek

21

30

Coal
Creek

29

Zion Number ✞
One Cem.

28

31

32

Turkey Creek

✞ Zion Cem.

33

Copyright 2008 Boyd IT, Inc. All Rights Reserved

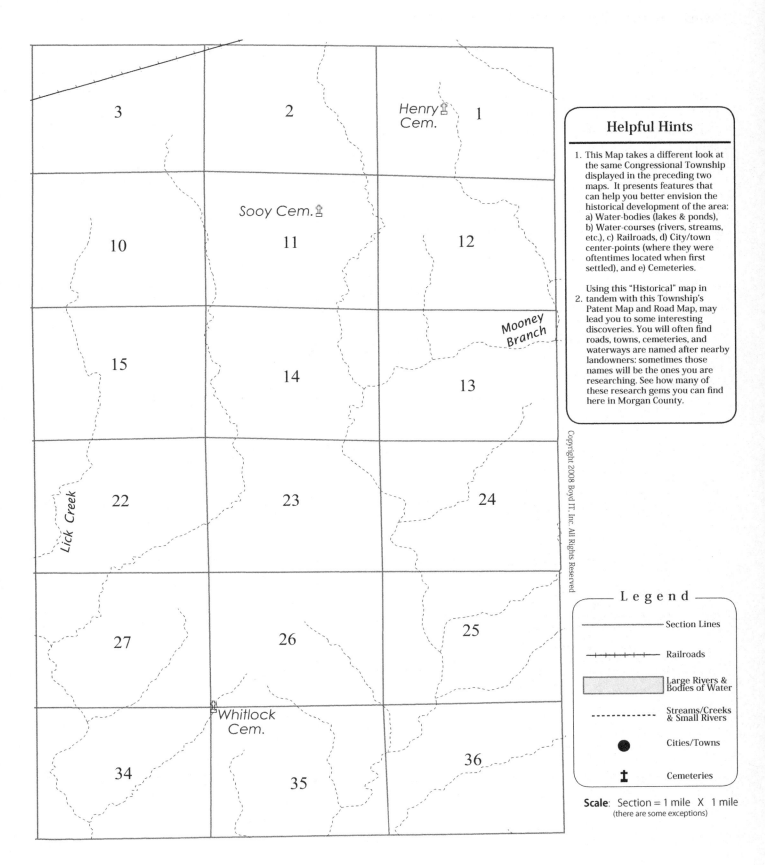

Helpful Hints

1. This Map takes a different look at the same Congressional Township displayed in the preceding two maps. It presents features that can help you better envision the historical development of the area: a) Water-bodies (lakes & ponds), b) Water-courses (rivers, streams, etc.), c) Railroads, d) City/town center-points (where they were oftentimes located when first settled), and e) Cemeteries.

2. Using this "Historical" map in tandem with this Township's Patent Map and Road Map, may lead you to some interesting discoveries. You will often find roads, towns, cemeteries, and waterways are named after nearby landowners: sometimes those names will be the ones you are researching. See how many of these research gems you can find here in Morgan County.

Legend

————————	Section Lines
‑+‑+‑+‑+‑	Railroads
▭	Large Rivers & Bodies of Water
- - - - - - -	Streams/Creeks & Small Rivers
●	Cities/Towns
✝	Cemeteries

Scale: Section = 1 mile X 1 mile
(there are some exceptions)

Map Group 18: Index to Land Patents

Township 13-North Range 9-West (3rd PM)

After you locate an individual in this Index, take note of the Section and Section Part then proceed to the Land Patent map on the pages immediately following. You should have no difficulty locating the corresponding parcel of land.

The "For More Info" Column will lead you to more information about the underlying Patents. See the *Legend* at right, and the "How to Use this Book" chapter, for more information.

```
                    LEGEND
           "For More Info . . . " column
 G = Group  (Multi-Patentee Patent, see Appendix "C")
 R = Residence
 S = Social Status


See Appendix A for list of abbreviations used by the
Illinois State Archives in describing the place and
nature of these land patents.

Note: if the Abbreviations contain "L", "BL", "LOT",
or "BLOCK", the exact whereabouts of the parcel within
the section is not known.
```

ID	Individual in Patent	Sec.	Sec. Part	Purchase Date	Sale Type	IL Aliquot Part	For More Info . . .
4362	ADAMS, Elijah	7	W½SW	1830-06-02	FD	W2SW	R:KENTUCKY
4412	ALLEN, Issac	25	SWSE	1854-09-27	FD	SWSE	R:MORGAN
4559	ATTEBERY, Melchisedec	33	SWSE	1836-05-26	FD	SWSE	R:MORGAN
4354	AUSTIN, Eli	14	W½SW	1835-03-06	FD	W2SW	R:MORGAN
4355	" "	22	SESE	1836-01-25	FD	SESE	R:MORGAN
4582	BALDWIN, Richard C	24	W½SW	1835-05-21	FD	W2SW	R:GEORGIA
4581	" "	23	E½SE	1835-05-21	FD	E2SE	R:GEORGIA
4452	BALL, Jesse Walker	23	W½SW	1835-10-21	FD	W2SW	R:MORGAN
4391	BARNETT, Harvey	26	NWNE	1849-11-26	FD	NWNE	R:MORGAN
4320	BARROWS, Barnabas	8	SENW	1852-11-17	FD	SENW	
4401	BARROWS, Isaac R	7	E½SW	1830-11-27	FD	E2SW	R:MORGAN
4400	" "	6	W½NW	1836-08-27	FD	W2NW	R:MORGAN
4423	BERDAN, James	9	SWNW	1855-11-29	FD	SWNW	R:MORGAN
4584	BOOKES, Richard M	27	SESW	1832-09-29	FD	SESWPRE	R:MORGAN
4650	BRIAN, William	27	W½NW	1829-10-27	FD	W2NW	R:MORGAN
4649	" "	27	SESE	1832-09-28	FD	SESE	R:MORGAN
4425	BRISTOW, James	36	SESW	1835-12-09	FD	SESW	R:MACOUPIN
4424	" "	35	NESE	1835-12-09	FD	NESE	R:MACOUPIN
4606	BROCKMAN, Samuel	7	W½NE	1831-11-09	FD	W2NE	R:MORGAN
4605	" "	6	E½SE	1831-11-09	FD	E2SE	R:MORGAN
4374	BROWN, George	4	E½SE	1830-01-29	FD	E2SE	R:MORGAN
4373	" "	21	W½NE	1831-03-24	FD	W2NE	R:MORGAN
4609	BROWN, Samuel	3	W½SW	1828-05-22	FD	W2SW	R:MORGAN
4608	" "	20	W½NW	1831-03-17	FD	W2NW	R:MORGAN
4607	" "	20	E½SE	1831-08-29	FD	E2SE	R:MORGAN
4568	BUCKMASTER, Nathaniel	32	NW	1848-03-10	FD	NWFR	
4453	BULL, Jesse Walker	22	NESE	1836-01-25	FD	NESE	R:MORGAN
4628	BULLARD, Theophilus	6	E½NE	1831-11-08	FD	E2NE	R:MORGAN
4471	CALDWELL, John Cook	26	E½SW	1835-05-30	FD	E2SW	R:MORGAN
4595	CALDWELL, Robert M	13	SENW	1834-11-22	FD	SENW	R:KENTUCKY
4651	CAMPBELL, William	26	E½NE	1836-02-23	FD	E2NE	
4345	CARLOCK, David	26	NWSE	1834-04-05	FD	NWSE	R:MORGAN
4454	CATLIN, Joel	24	E½NW	1835-05-21	FD	E2NW	R:HANCOCK G:30
4455	" "	24	E½SW	1835-05-21	FD	E2SW	R:HANCOCK G:30
4455	CATLIN, Willis	24	E½SW	1835-05-21	FD	E2SW	R:HANCOCK G:30
4454	" "	24	E½NW	1835-05-21	FD	E2NW	R:HANCOCK G:30
4469	CAUDEL, John	31	SESW	1853-11-26	FD	SESW	R:MORGAN
4470	" "	31	SWSE	1854-09-26	FD	SWSE	R:MORGAN
4367	CHANCE, Ezekiel	26	NESE	1839-03-02	FD	NESE	
4430	CHERRY, James H	36	E½NW	1835-12-14	FD	E2NW	R:MACOUPIN
4652	COOK, William	35	NWSW	1838-11-13	FD	NWSW	R:MORGAN
4472	COX, John	20	W½NE	1834-10-16	FD	W2NE	R:MORGAN
4473	" "	20	W½SW	1835-06-29	FD	W2SW	R:MORGAN
4396	CRAIG, Hugh Gilkerson	5	W½NE	1832-01-14	FD	W2NEFS	R:MORGAN
4375	CRISWELL, George	19	E½SE	1830-02-10	FD	E2SE	R:MORGAN
4376	" "	19	W½SE	1831-11-01	FD	W2SE	R:MORGAN

ID	Individual in Patent	Sec.	Sec. Part	Purchase Date	Sale Type	IL Aliquot Part	For More Info . . .
4377	CRISWELL, George (Cont'd)	29	W½SW	1831-11-07	FD	W2SW	R:MORGAN
4378	" "	30	E½NE	1835-10-06	FD	E2NE	R:MORGAN
4558	CYRUS, Matthew	1	NW	1831-04-07	FD	NW	R:MORGAN
4335	DALTON, Clayborn	22	NWNE	1854-10-06	FD	NWNE	R:MORGAN
4337	DALTON, Cluborn	15	E½SW	1835-08-20	FD	E2SW	R:MORGAN
4611	DALTON, Samuel	34	NWSE	1836-01-19	FD	NWSE	R:MORGAN
4610	" "	34	NWNE	1836-01-20	FD	NWNE	R:MORGAN
4474	DAUGHERTY, John	30	NESE	1835-03-06	FD	NESE	R:MORGAN
4475	" "	31	SENE	1836-08-24	FD	SENE	R:MORGAN
4476	" "	8	NENW	1851-10-29	FD	NENW	R:MORGAN
4629	DAVENPORT, Thomas	6	SWSW	1855-09-24	FD	SWSW	R:MORGAN
4623	DEATHERAGE, Stephen	24	E½SE	1835-10-31	FD	E2SE	R:MORGAN
4653	DELANEY, William	6	E½SW	1830-10-12	FD	E2SW	R:MORGAN
4352	DELPH, William H	18	NENW	1832-11-24	FD	NENW	R:MORGAN G:54
4627	DENNIS, Susannah	25	NESE	1836-06-02	FD	NESE	R:MORGAN S:F
4648	DENNIS, Wesley O	25	NESW	1854-01-31	FD	NESW	R:MORGAN
4477	DEVORE, John	31	NENE	1836-10-22	FD	NENE	R:MORGAN
4552	DEVORE, Martin Luther	30	SESE	1836-03-10	FD	SESE	R:MORGAN
4379	DICK, George	35	NENE	1833-04-02	FD	NENE	R:MORGAN
4667	DIKES, John	36	NWNW	1854-09-25	FD	NWNW	R:MORGAN
4478	" "	36	NWNW	1854-09-25	FD	NWNW	R:MORGAN
4366	DODSON, Elizabeth	31	SENW	1849-10-29	FD	SENW	R:MORGAN S:F
4630	DUDHOPE, Thomas	21	W½SW	1835-09-24	FD	W2SW	R:MORGAN
4398	DYE, Isaac	22	W½SE	1829-11-17	FD	W2SE	R:MORGAN
4626	EDGELL, Stephen M	36	SWNW	1836-02-01	FD	SWNW	R:MADISON
4632	EDWARDS, Thomas J	20	NESW	1854-09-30	FD	NESW	R:MADISON
4633	" "	20	NWSE	1854-09-30	FD	NWSE	R:MADISON
4631	ENGLAND, Thomas	25	NENE	1835-12-31	FD	NENE	R:MORGAN
4426	EVANS, James	16	L4	1833-01-24	SC	LOT4W2NW16	
4321	" "	16	L6	1833-11-22	SC	LOT6	
4427	" "	16	L6	1833-11-22	SC	LOT6	
4306	FANNING, Abraham	18	E½NE	1831-11-08	FD	E2NE	R:MORGAN
4432	" "	18	E½NE	1831-11-08	FD	E2NE	R:MORGAN
4381	FANNING, George	7	E½NW	1830-03-13	FD	E2NW	R:MORGAN
4380	" "	5	E½NW	1851-10-21	FD	E2NW	
4386	FANNING, George W	21	W½SE	1834-12-02	FD	W2SE	R:MORGAN
4385	" "	21	SESW	1836-12-09	FD	SESW	R:MORGAN
4413	FANNING, Jacob	17	E½NW	1831-03-09	FD	E2NW	R:MORGAN
4414	" "	17	SWNW	1835-08-17	FD	SWNW	R:MORGAN G:61
4415	" "	17	NWNW	1836-03-05	FD	NWNW	G:62
4480	FANNING, John	18	W½NW	1831-03-09	FD	W2NW	R:MORGAN
4481	" "	5	E½NE	1831-10-20	FD	E2NE	R:MORGAN
4530	FANNING, Joseph	19	E½NE	1830-01-25	FD	E2NE	R:MORGAN
4531	" "	4	NE	1831-08-25	FD	NE	R:MORGAN
4532	" "	4	NW	1836-02-01	FD	NW	R:MORGAN
4546	FANNING, Levi	18	W½SE	1831-08-20	FD	W2SE	R:MORGAN
4544	" "	10	E½SE	1835-08-18	FD	E2SE	R:MORGAN
4547	" "	27	NESE	1835-08-25	FD	NESE	R:MORGAN
4545	" "	16	L8	1835-08-28	SC	LOT8	
4593	FANNING, Robert	18	SENW	1854-10-02	FD	SENW	R:MORGAN
4603	FANNING, Sampson	19	NESW	1835-11-02	FD	NESW	R:MORGAN
4604	" "	19	W½SW	1835-12-30	FD	W2SW	R:MORGAN
4382	FARMING, George	8	W½NE	1831-11-15	FD	W2NE	R:MORGAN
4456	FINCH, Joel	33	SW	1836-06-17	FD	SW	R:MADISON
4482	FRASIN, John	2		1851-06-30	FD	W2L2NEWA	R:CLARK
4600	FRISBIE, Rufus K	29	SENW	1849-09-20	FD	SENW	
4560	FRY, Milton	8	W½SE	1835-11-12	FD	W2SE	R:MORGAN
4307	FULLER, Abraham	28	NWNE	1834-08-25	FD	NWNE	R:MORGAN
4308	" "	32	SENW	1835-12-22	FD	SENW	R:MORGAN
4654	GALLAHER, William G	14	NENE	1835-11-20	FD	NENE	R:MORGAN
4411	GIBSON, Isham	9	W½SE	1830-01-29	FD	W2SE	R:MORGAN
4409	" "	9	E½NE	1830-01-29	FD	E2NE	R:MORGAN
4408	" "	8	E½SW	1830-01-29	FD	E2SW	R:MORGAN
4404	" "	10	W½NW	1830-01-29	FD	W2NW	R:MORGAN
4405	" "	21	E½NE	1830-11-13	FD	E2NE	R:MORGAN
4407	" "	8	E½SE	1834-01-29	FD	E2SE	R:MORGAN
4410	" "	9	W½NE	1835-08-10	FD	W2NE	R:MORGAN
4406	" "	30	NWNE	1836-02-01	FD	NWNE	R:MORGAN
4429	GIBSON, James	18	SWNE	1835-08-17	FD	SWNE	R:MORGAN
4414	" "	17	SWNW	1835-08-17	FD	SWNW	R:MORGAN G:61
4428	" "	18	NWNE	1836-03-05	FD	NWNE	
4435	GIBSON, James Jr	8	W½SW	1830-01-29	FD	W2SW	R:MORGAN
4433	" "	18	E½SE	1830-01-29	FD	E2SE	R:MORGAN

ID	Individual in Patent	Sec.	Sec. Part	Purchase Date	Sale Type	IL Aliquot Part	For More Info . . .
4434	GIBSON, James Jr (Cont'd)	7	E½SE	1830-01-29	FD	E2SE	R:MORGAN
4432	" "	18	E½NE	1830-04-13	FD	E2NE	R:MORGAN
4306	" "	18	E½NE	1830-04-13	FD	E2NE	R:MORGAN
4415	GIDEON, James	17	NWNW	1836-03-05	FD	NWNW	G:62
4666	GIVENS, William T	7	E½NE	1835-07-02	FD	E2NE	R:MORGAN
4352	GREEN, James	18	NENW	1832-11-24	FD	NENW	R:MORGAN G:54
4488	GRIGG, John	36	SE	1835-12-07	FD	SE	R:PHILADELPHIA
4487	" "	32	W½NE	1835-12-07	FD	W2NE	R:PHILADELPHIA
4486	" "	32	E½SW	1835-12-07	FD	E2SW	R:PHILADELPHIA
4485	" "	29	W½SE	1835-12-07	FD	W2SE	R:PHILADELPHIA
4484	" "	29	W½NE	1835-12-07	FD	W2NE	R:PHILADELPHIA
4483	" "	29	E½SW	1835-12-07	FD	E2SW	R:PHILADELPHIA
4371	GRIMSLEY, Fielding	16	L1	1837-02-07	SC	L1E2NEMA	
4502	" "	16	L1	1837-02-07	SC	L1E2NEMA	
4342	GUNNELS, Daniel	25	SESE	1838-12-05	FD	SESE	R:MORGAN
4492	HALL, John	14	E½SW	1834-11-07	FD	E2SW	R:MORGAN
4668	HALL, William W	25	E2NW	1835-12-22	FD	E2NWPRE	R:MADISON
4489	HAM, John H	13	W½SE	1835-04-29	FD	W2SE	R:MORGAN
4463	HAMILTON, John C	26	W½NW	1835-10-27	FD	W2NW	R:MORGAN
4479	HAMILTON, John F	26	SENW	1835-10-27	FD	SENW	R:MORGAN
4464	HARLAN, John C	34	NWSW	1840-10-17	FD	NWSW	
4550	HARNEY, Margaret	6	W½SE	1830-02-10	FD	W2SE	R:MORGAN S:F
4339	HARP, Conrad	16	L5	1834-10-31	SC	LOT5	
4338	" "	16	L3	1834-10-31	SC	LOT3	
4543	HARRIS, Ledley C	36	SWSW	1835-02-23	FD	SWSW	R:MACOUPIN
4316	HART, Anderson	22	SESW	1833-05-28	FD	SESW	R:MORGAN
4317	" "	22	SWSW	1835-10-14	FD	SWSW	R:MORGAN
4332	HART, Charles	28	E½SE	1828-11-04	FD	E2SE	R:MORGAN
4331	" "	27	W½SW	1831-11-07	FD	W2SW	R:MORGAN
4330	" "	27	SWSE	1835-08-24	FD	SWSE	R:MORGAN
4333	" "	34	SENE	1835-08-24	FD	SENE	R:MORGAN
4346	HART, David	33	E½SE	1831-11-09	FD	E2SE	R:MORGAN
4349	" "	34	W½NW	1831-11-09	FD	W2NW	R:MORGAN
4347	" "	34	SESW	1834-04-14	FD	SESW	R:MORGAN
4348	" "	34	SWSW	1835-09-12	FD	SWSW	R:MORGAN
4539	HART, Joseph W	34	NENE	1835-10-14	FD	NENE	R:MORGAN
4565	HART, Nathan	33	E½NE	1831-11-07	FD	E2NE	R:MORGAN
4566	" "	33	NWSE	1834-12-27	FD	NWSE	R:MORGAN
4567	" "	33	W½NE	1835-10-14	FD	W2NE	R:MORGAN
4564	" "	31	SWSW	1852-05-11	FD	SWSW	
4618	HART, Solomon	28	W½SE	1828-11-04	FD	W2SE	R:MORGAN
4616	" "	28	E½SW	1829-12-05	FD	E2SW	R:MORGAN
4619	" "	32	W½NW	1832-01-14	FD	W2NW	R:MORGAN
4614	" "	26	W½SW	1834-12-27	FD	W2SW	R:MORGAN
4621	" "	34	SWSE	1835-09-03	FD	SWSE	R:MORGAN
4620	" "	34	E½SE	1835-09-03	FD	E2SE	R:MORGAN
4617	" "	28	SWNE	1835-09-03	FD	SWNE	R:MORGAN
4615	" "	28	E½NW	1835-10-14	FD	E2NW	R:MORGAN
4324	HAYNES, Bluford	15	SWSW	1834-12-22	FD	SWSW	R:MORGAN
4388	HAYNES, Green	14	SWNW	1854-10-18	FD	SWNW	R:MORGAN
4495	HAYNES, John	15	SWNE	1836-02-05	FD	SWNE	
4493	" "	15	E½NE	1836-02-05	FD	E2NE	
4494	" "	15	NWNE	1850-01-17	FD	NWNE	R:MORGAN
4457	HEADINGTON, Joel	11	NESW	1834-11-10	FD	NESW	R:MORGAN
4458	" "	11	W½NE	1835-09-14	FD	W2NE	R:MORGAN
4363	HENRY, Elijah	1	SESE	1851-01-29	FD	SESE	
4364	" "	7	NWNW	1851-01-29	FD	NWNW	
4397	HENRY, Hugh	6	NENW	1451-02-21	FD	NENW	R:MORGAN
4399	HINDES, Isaac	26	NENW	1854-03-08	FD	NENW	R:MORGAN
4352	HOWARD, Elakim	18	NENW	1832-11-24	FD	NENW	R:MORGAN G:54
4570	HOWARD, Palmer	6	NWSW	1852-03-04	FD	NWSW	R:MORGAN
4625	HOWARD, Stephen	19	W½NW	1831-03-08	FD	W2NW	R:GREENE
4624	" "	19	E½NW	1831-04-16	FD	E2NW	R:MORGAN
4343	HUEY, Daniel	15	SE	1835-10-22	FD	SE	R:MISSISSIPPI
4503	HURST, Jonathan	16	L11	1835-07-09	SC	LOT11	
4525	" "	16	L11	1835-07-09	SC	LOT11	
4526	HURTS, Jonathan	30	SWNE	1839-03-08	FD	SWNE	
4639	JANUARY, Thomas T	20	E½SE	1836-06-24	FD	E2SE	R:MORGAN
4353	JARMAN, Elford E	36	E½NE	1836-04-01	FD	E2NE	R:GREENE G:88
4392	JONES, Henry	24	W½NW	1835-05-21	FD	W2NW	R:MORGAN
4576	JONES, Reuben	24	E½NE	1835-03-12	FD	E2NE	R:MORGAN
4591	JONES, Robert A C	25	NWNW	1836-02-23	FD	NWNW	
4592	" "	25	SWNW	1836-09-29	FD	SWNW	R:MORGAN

ID	Individual in Patent	Sec.	Sec. Part	Purchase Date	Sale Type	IL Aliquot Part	For More Info . . .
4612	KIPLINGER, Samuel	14	W½NE	1834-12-19	FD	W2NE	R:MORGAN
4562	LESLIE, Miron	13	N½NW	1835-07-02	FD	N2NW	R:MORGAN
4561	" "	11	SE	1835-07-02	FD	SE	R:MORGAN
4563	" "	35	W½NW	1835-07-14	FD	W2NW	R:MORGAN
4395	LUTTRELL, Hiram	1	NE	1831-07-23	FD	NE	R:MORGAN
4549	LUTTRELL, Lott	32	SWSE	1838-06-25	FD	SWSE	R:MORGAN
4634	LUTTRELL, Thomas	1	E½SE	1826-12-23	FD	E2SE	R:MORGAN
4635	" "	1	W½SE	1829-11-09	FD	W2SE	R:MORGAN
4636	" "	1	W½SW	1831-06-08	FD	W2SW	R:MORGAN
4637	" "	13	E½SW	1835-09-28	FD	E2SW	R:MORGAN
4319	LUTTRILL, Armstrong	1	E½SW	1835-06-25	FD	E2SW	R:MORGAN
4310	MANSFIELD, Alfred	28	SWSW	1834-12-27	FD	SWSW	R:MORGAN
4311	" "	34	SWNE	1836-01-20	FD	SWNE	R:MORGAN
4438	MANSFIELD, James	33	NW	1829-12-07	FD	NW	R:MORGAN
4368	MCCEARLEY, Ezekiel	30	NENW	1836-02-01	FD	NENW	R:MORGAN
4369	" "	31	SESE	1836-02-01	FD	SESE	R:MORGAN
4370	MCCEARLY, Ezekiel	19	W½NE	1830-10-21	FD	W2NE	R:MORGAN
4536	MCCLEARLY, Joseph R	22	NENW	1836-01-30	FD	NENW	R:MORGAN
4496	MCCORMICK, John	14	SENE	1835-06-10	FD	SENE	R:MORGAN
4646	MCCORMICK, Walker	23	E½NE	1835-11-13	FD	E2NE	R:MORGAN
4647	MCCORMICK, Walter	5	W½NW	1852-04-13	FD	W2NW	
4497	MCCULLEY, John	26	SWNE	1836-03-08	FD	SWNE	
4439	MCFALL, James	8	NWNW	1854-03-27	FD	NWNW	
4440	" "	8	SWNW	1854-10-06	FD	SWNW	R:MORGAN
4441	MCNEELY, James	30	SWSW	1854-11-20	FD	SWSW	R:MORGAN
4459	MITCHELL, Joel	30	SESW	1851-12-24	FD	SESW	R:MORGAN
4460	" "	31	NENW	1851-12-24	FD	NENW	R:MORGAN
4431	MORLAN, James H	30	NESW	1854-11-20	FD	NESW	R:MACOUPIN
4533	MORTON, Joseph	16	L10	1833-01-15	SC	LOT10	
4322	" "	16	L7	1833-01-28	SC	LOT7	
4535	" "	16	L9	1833-01-28	SC	LOT9	
4534	" "	16	L7	1833-01-28	SC	LOT7	
4569	MURPHY, Nimrod C	17	W½NE	1830-11-27	FD	W2NE	R:GREENE
4498	NALL, John	27	NENE	1852-11-19	FD	NENE	
4602	NALL, Russel	22	SWNW	1836-01-21	FD	SWNW	R:MORGAN
4601	" "	14	NWNW	1836-02-04	FD	NWNW	R:MORGAN
4554	NELSON, Martin	31	NESW	1836-01-12	FD	NESW	R:MORGAN
4553	" "	31	NESE	1836-01-12	FD	NESE	R:MORGAN
4583	NELSON, Richard H	13	W½SW	1835-12-12	FD	W2SW	R:MACOUPIN
4383	NICHOLLS, George	19	SESW	1835-10-27	FD	SESW	R:MORGAN
4384	" "	32	NWSW	1835-11-02	FD	NWSW	R:MORGAN
4387	NICHOLLS, George W	30	NWNW	1836-02-04	FD	NWNW	
4462	NICHOLS, John B	30	NWSW	1854-02-18	FD	NWFRSW	R:MONTGOMERY
4309	NICKOL, Agrippa	30	SENW	1839-04-03	FD	SENW	
4499	NOLL, John	11	W½SW	1829-08-11	FD	W2SW	R:MORGAN G:105
4499	NOLL, Russell	11	W½SW	1829-08-11	FD	W2SW	R:MORGAN G:105
4499	NOLL, William T	11	W½SW	1829-08-11	FD	W2SW	R:MORGAN G:105
4542	PACK, Julius Benjamin	36	NESW	1837-04-06	FD	NESW	R:MORGAN
4443	PARKINSON, James	13	NE	1833-10-15	FD	NE	R:MORGAN
4655	PATTERSON, William	32	NENE	1834-05-22	FD	NENE	R:MORGAN
4656	" "	32	NENW	1835-09-03	FD	NENW	R:MORGAN
4323	PEARSON, Benjamin	21	NESW	1835-09-24	FD	NESW	R:MORGAN
4416	PETTYJOHN, Jacob	31	NWSW	1836-03-08	FD	NWSW	
4393	PEXTON, Henry	21	NENW	1835-02-17	FD	NENW	R:MORGAN
4503	PIPER, John	16	L11	1833-05-27	SC	LOT11	
4525	" "	16	L11	1833-05-27	SC	LOT11	
4502	" "	16	L1	1833-05-27	SC	LOT1	
4371	" "	16	L1	1833-05-27	SC	LOT1	
4573	RANSDELL, Presley	29	E½NE	1835-10-23	FD	E2NE	R:MORGAN
4640	RANSDELL, Thomas T	20	SWSE	1836-11-15	FD	SWSE	R:MORGAN
4541	REED, Julius A	26	SESE	1836-02-01	FD	SESE	R:MORGAN
4555	REED, Martin	9	NESW	1835-08-10	FD	NESW	R:MORGAN
4556	" "	9	SESW	1836-01-11	FD	SESW	R:MORGAN
4490	REES, John H	10	SESW	1835-12-31	FD	SESW	R:MORGAN
4491	" "	15	NWNW	1835-12-31	FD	NWNW	R:MORGAN
4507	REYNOLDS, John	28	E½NE	1829-12-05	FD	E2NE	R:MORGAN
4506	" "	21	E½SE	1831-11-12	FD	E2SEFS	R:MORGAN
4537	REYNOLDS, Joseph	2	NE	1828-03-29	FD	NE	R:MORGAN
4509	RHODES, John	34	E2NW	1835-12-24	FD	E2NWPRE	R:MORGAN
4508	" "	29	SESE	1837-02-03	FD	SESE	R:MORGAN
4643	RICHARDSON, Vincent S	21	W½NW	1835-01-05	FD	W2NW	R:MORGAN
4645	" "	9	NWNW	1835-01-05	FD	NWNW	R:MORGAN
4642	" "	21	SENW	1835-01-05	FD	SENW	R:MORGAN

ID	Individual in Patent	Sec.	Sec. Part	Purchase Date	Sale Type	IL Aliquot Part	For More Info . . .
4644	RICHARDSON, Vincent S (Cont'd)	5	E½SE	1836-02-19	FD	E2SE	
4418	ROBERTS, James A	23	NESW	1850-11-30	FD	NESW	R:MORGAN
4419	" "	23	W½SE	1854-09-21	FD	W2SE	R:MORGAN
4538	ROBERTS, Joseph V	5	NWSW	1854-03-21	FD	NWSW	R:MORGAN
4658	ROBERTS, William	22	NWNW	1834-11-08	FD	NWNW	R:MORGAN
4657	"	15	NWSW	1837-02-06	FD	NWSW	R:MORGAN
4466	ROBINSON, John C	30	W½SE	1854-09-26	FD	W2SE	R:MADISON
4467	" "	31	NWSE	1854-09-26	FD	NWSE	R:MADISON
4468	" "	31	W½NE	1854-09-26	FD	W2NE	R:MADISON
4465	" "	30	W½SE	1854-09-26	FD	W2SE	R:MADISON
4466	"	30	W½SE	1856-11-17	FD	W2SE	
4465	"	30	W½SE	1856-11-17	FD	W2SE	
4334	ROLAND, Christian L	25	SESW	1836-09-06	FD	SESW	R:MORGAN S:F
4372	ROLAND, Gasper	25	NWSE	1836-08-25	FD	NWSE	R:MORGAN
4336	SALTER, Cleveland J	24	W½NE	1835-05-21	FD	W2NE	R:CONNECTICUT
4353	SALTER, James D B	36	E½NE	1836-04-01	FD	E2NE	R:GREENE G:88
4596	SCARTH, Robert	12	W½NW	1835-06-26	FD	W2NW	R:MORGAN
4444	SCOTT, James	10	SWSE	1852-02-20	FD	SWSE	
4350	SEAMORE, Edward	27	SWNE	1851-11-21	FD	SWNE	
4511	SEAMORE, John	2	E½SE	1830-01-25	FD	E2SE	R:MORGAN
4590	SEAMORE, Richardson	27	NWNE	1851-11-21	FD	NWNE	
4512	SEMOORE, John	3	NW	1829-05-27	FD	NW	R:MORGAN
4326	SEYMORE, Burges	11	SESW	1833-02-20	FD	SESW	R:MORGAN
4351	SEYMORE, Edward	23	W½NW	1833-02-20	FD	W2NW	R:MORGAN
4442	SEYMORE, James P	4	SESW	1836-01-25	FD	SESW	R:MORGAN
4514	SEYMORE, John	4	NWSE	1836-03-05	FD	NWSE	
4513	" "	4	NESW	1837-01-12	FD	NESW	R:MORGAN
4515	" "	4	W½SW	1837-01-12	FD	W2SW	R:MORGAN
4571	SEYMORE, Peter	27	NENW	1836-12-03	FD	NENW	R:MORGAN
4572	" "	27	SENW	1837-02-22	FD	SENW	R:MORGAN
4597	SEYMORE, Robert	4	SWSE	1836-01-25	FD	SWSE	R:MORGAN
4598	" "	9	NENW	1837-01-12	FD	NENW	R:MORGAN
4659	SEYMORE, William	22	E½NE	1836-01-25	FD	E2NE	R:MORGAN
4661	" "	27	SENE	1836-04-11	FD	SENE	R:MORGAN
4660	" "	22	SWNE	1837-01-12	FD	SWNE	R:MORGAN
4327	SEYMOUR, Burgess	14	NENW	1834-12-22	FD	NENW	R:MORGAN
4548	SHEPHERD, Lewis J	17	E½SW	1829-10-26	FD	E2SW	R:MORGAN
4500	SHEPPARD, John O	16	L12	1833-02-04	SC	LOT12	
4501	SHEPPARD, John Oaks	17	NWSE	1834-11-21	FD	NWSE	R:MORGAN G:110
4501	SHEPPARD, Lewis J	17	NWSE	1834-11-21	FD	NWSE	R:MORGAN G:110
4528	SHORES, Jonathan	28	NWSW	1852-08-27	FD	NWSW	
4527	" "	20	SESW	1854-09-26	FD	SESW	R:MORGAN
4529	" "	29	NENW	1854-09-26	FD	NENW	R:MORGAN
4586	SHORES, Richard	29	NESE	1854-09-30	FD	NESE	R:MORGAN
4585	" "	28	W½NW	1854-09-30	FD	W2NW	R:MORGAN
4365	" "	29	NESE	1854-09-30	FD	NESE	R:MORGAN
4329	SNOW, Charles G	27	NWSE	1854-09-21	FD	NWSE	R:MORGAN
4328	" "	27	NESW	1854-09-21	FD	NESW	R:MORGAN
4599	SOWRY, Robert	15	SWNW	1852-02-20	FD	SWNW	
4557	SPARKS, Matthew B	35	SWSE	1836-01-21	FD	SWSE	R:MORGAN
4357	SPERRY, Eli	36	NWSW	1841-02-04	FD	NWSW	
4662	SPIRES, William	17	E½SE	1831-04-21	FD	E2SE	R:MORGAN
4664	" "	17	W½SW	1831-08-06	FD	W2SW	R:MORGAN
4663	" "	17	SWSE	1835-12-31	FD	SWSE	R:MORGAN
4665	" "	20	NWNE	1836-01-11	FD	NWNE	R:MORGAN
4322	STEWART, Benjamin F	16	L7	1837-06-20	SC	L7W2SWMA	G:123
4321	" "	16	L6	1837-06-20	SC	L6E2SWMA	G:123
4534	" "	16	L7	1837-06-20	SC	L7W2SWMA	G:123
4427	" "	16	L6	1837-06-20	SC	L6E2SWMA	G:123
4325	STEWART, Brice	24	W½SE	1836-02-02	FD	W2SE	R:MORGAN
4534	STEWART, Robert	16	L7	1837-06-20	SC	L7W2SWMA	G:123
4321	" "	16	L6	1837-06-20	SC	L6E2SWMA	G:123
4322	" "	16	L7	1837-06-20	SC	L7W2SWMA	G:123
4427	" "	16	L6	1837-06-20	SC	L6E2SWMA	G:123
4594	STICE, Robert Lee	26	SWSE	1835-10-31	FD	SWSE	R:MORGAN
4344	STURGIS, Daniel	11	E½NW	1829-11-10	FD	E2NW	R:BOND
4340	STURGIS, Daniel B	10	W½SW	1831-03-14	FD	W2SW	R:MORGAN
4341	" "	9	E½SE	1831-11-01	FD	E2SE	R:MORGAN
4421	STURGIS, James B	2	W½SW	1828-02-28		W2SW	R:MORGAN
4420	" "	2	E½SW	1830-02-08	FD	E2SW	R:MORGAN
4422	" "	3	E½SE	1833-10-19	FD	E2SE	R:MORGAN
4504	STURGIS, John R	22	NWSW	1853-02-02	FD	NWSW	
4505	" "	22	SENW	1854-09-21	FD	SENW	R:MORGAN

ID	Individual in Patent	Sec.	Sec. Part	Purchase Date	Sale Type	IL Aliquot Part	For More Info . . .
4638	STURGIS, Thomas S	22	NESW	1839-12-16	FD	NESW	
4394	SUMMERS, Henry	25	SWNE	1836-04-06	FD	SWNE	R:MORGAN
4461	SWEET, Joel	7	W½SE	1831-03-08	FD	W2SEFS	R:MORGAN
4478	TALKINGTON, William	36	NWNW	1835-10-14	FD	NWNW	R:MORGAN
4667	" "	36	NWNW	1835-10-14	FD	NWNW	R:MORGAN
4312	TANNEHILL, Alfred	34	NESW	1836-08-12	FD	NESW	R:MORGAN
4313	TAUMHILL, Alfred	3	NWSE	1833-01-05	FD	NWSE	R:MORGAN
4365	TAYLOR, Eliza H	29	NESE	1869-09-17	FD	NESE	S:F
4586	" "	29	NESE	1869-09-17	FD	NESE	S:F
4578	TENNISON, Reuben	25	SENE	1835-11-27	FD	SENE	R:MORGAN
4577	" "	25	NWNE	1835-12-31	FD	NWNE	R:MORGAN
4318	THOMPSON, Andrew	36	W2NE	1835-12-30	FD	W2NEPRE	R:MORGAN
4517	THOMPSON, John	35	SENW	1854-09-27	FD	SENW	R:MORGAN
4516	" "	35	NWSE	1854-09-27	FD	NWSE	R:MORGAN
4524	THOMPSON, Jonas	35	SESE	1832-06-26	FD	SESE	R:MACOUPIN
4613	THOMPSON, Samuel	35	SENE	1836-02-04	FD	SENE	
4445	TODD, James	20	E½NW	1834-02-28	FD	E2NW	R:MORGAN
4518	TOLKINTON, John	13	NESE	1833-11-28	FD	NESE	R:MORGAN
4450	TUCKER, Jesse	6	SENW	1852-02-05	FD	SENW	
4451	" "	6	SWNE	1852-02-05	FD	SWNE	
4403	VANCIL, Isaac	35	W½NE	1836-03-08	FD	W2NE	
4402	" "	35	NENW	1836-03-21	FD	NENW	R:MORGAN
4417	VANOATE, Jacob	14	SENW	1837-07-25	FD	SENW	R:MORGAN
4574	VANWINKLE, Ransom	2	NW	1830-02-02	FD	NW	R:MORGAN
4575	VANWINKLE, Ranson	3	NE	1829-10-31	FD	NE	R:MORGAN
4540	WATERS, Joseph	35	E½SW	1835-10-29	FD	E2SW	R:MORGAN
4669	WATSON, William	35	SWSW	1834-04-05	FD	SWSW	R:MACOUPIN
4390	WEATHERFORD, Hardin	11	W½NW	1829-08-14	FD	W2NW	R:MORGAN
4389	" "	10	E½NE	1829-08-14	FD	E2NE	R:MORGAN
4446	WEATHERFORD, James	15	SENW	1835-08-20	FD	SENW	R:MORGAN
4449	WEATHERFORD, Jefferso	2	W½SE	1828-03-10	FD	W2SE	R:MORGAN
4670	WEATHERFORD, William	10	E½NW	1829-04-18	FD	E2NW	R:MORGAN
4672	" "	11	E½NE	1830-01-25	FD	E2NE	R:MORGAN
4673	" "	3	E½SW	1831-08-15	FD	E2SW	R:MORGAN
4671	" "	10	NESW	1833-10-23	FD	NESW	R:MORGAN
4674	" "	3	SWSE	1833-10-23	FD	SWSE	R:MORGAN
4522	WEST, John	5	NWSE	1854-10-02	FD	NWSE	R:MADISON
4520	" "	5	E½SW	1854-10-02	FD	E2SW	R:MADISON
4519	" "	5	E½SW	1854-10-02	FD	E2SW	R:MADISON
4521	" "	5	NWSE	1854-10-02	FD	NWSE	R:MADISON
4522	" "	5	NWSE	1856-11-19	FD	NWSE	
4521	" "	5	NWSE	1856-11-19	FD	NWSE	
4519	" "	5	E½SW	1856-11-19	FD	E2SW	
4520	" "	5	E½SW	1856-11-19	FD	E2SW	
4447	WHEELER, James	31	SWNW	1850-01-08	FD	SWNW	R:GREENE
4675	WHITE, William	25	W½SW	1854-09-27	FD	W2SW	R:MORGAN
4551	WHITWORTH, Margaret	5	SESE	1851-02-07	FD	SESE	R:MACOUPIN S:F
4510	WILKINSON, John S	32	NWSE	1854-09-30	FD	NWSE	R:MORGAN
4587	WILKINSON, Richard	32	E½SE	1835-09-03	FD	E2SE	R:MORGAN
4589	" "	32	SWSW	1835-10-14	FD	SWSW	R:MORGAN
4588	" "	32	SENE	1836-02-06	FD	SENE	
4361	WOLCOTT, Elihu	29	W½NW	1831-05-25	FD	W2NW	R:MORGAN
4359	" "	18	E½SW	1831-10-06	FD	E2SW	R:MORGAN
4358	" "	10	W½NE	1832-01-21	FD	W2NE	R:MORGAN
4360	" "	18	W½SW	1835-11-26	FD	W2SW	R:MORGAN
4622	WOODS, Starting	13	SWNW	1835-05-26	FD	SWNW	R:MORGAN
4302	WRIGHT, Abner	23	W½NE	1829-11-09	FD	W2NE	R:MORGAN
4301	" "	23	E½NW	1829-11-09	FD	E2NW	R:MORGAN
4300	" "	14	SE	1829-11-09	FD	SE	R:MORGAN
4299	" "	12	E½NE	1829-11-09	FD	E2NE	R:MORGAN
4448	WRIGHT, James	12	SE	1829-11-09	FD	SE	R:MORGAN
4437	WRIGHT, James Jr	12	SENW	1833-01-05	FD	SENW	R:MORGAN
4436	" "	12	NENW	1834-03-17	FD	NENW	R:MORGAN
4579	WRIGHT, Reuben	12	SW	1829-11-09	FD	SW	
4580	" "	23	SESW	1852-03-04	FD	SESW	
4641	WRIGHT, Thomas	13	SESE	1835-07-06	FD	SESE	R:MORGAN
4356	WYATT, Eli Martin	20	NWNW	1847-07-16	FD	NWNW	
4523	WYATT, John	12	W½NE	1829-10-31	FD	W2NE	R:MORGAN
4305	YATES, Abner	7	SWNW	1855-11-29	FD	SWNW	R:MORGAN
4304	" "	6	NWNE	1855-11-29	FD	NWNE	R:MORGAN
4303	" "	15	NENW	1857-03-24	FD	NENW	
4314	YOUNGBLOOD, Ambrose	17	E½NE	1829-09-08	FD	E2NE	R:MORGAN
4315	" "	9	W½SW	1832-01-21	FD	W2SW	R:MORGAN

Patent Map

T13-N R9-W
3rd PM Meridian

Map Group 18

Township Statistics

Parcels Mapped	:	377
Number of Patents	:	1
Number of Individuals	:	243
Patentees Identified	:	236
Number of Surnames	:	164
Multi-Patentee Parcels	:	10
Oldest Patent Date	:	2/21/1451
Most Recent Patent	:	9/17/1869
Block/Lot Parcels	:	18
Cities and Towns	:	1
Cemeteries	:	9

Section 5
BARROWS Isaac R 1836
HENRY Hugh 1451
TUCKER Jesse 1852
YATES Abner 1855
TUCKER Jesse 1852
BULLARD Theophilus 1831
MCCORMICK Walter 1852
FANNING George 1851
CRAIG Hugh Gilkerson 1832
FANNING John 1831

Section 4
FANNING Joseph 1836
FANNING Joseph 1831

Section 6
HOWARD Palmer 1852
DELANEY William 1830
DAVENPORT Thomas 1855
HARNEY Margaret 1830
BROCKMAN Samuel 1831
ROBERTS Joseph V 1854
WEST John 1854
WEST John 1854
WEST John 1856
RICHARDSON Vincent S 1836
WHITWORTH Margaret 1851
SEYMORE John 1837
SEYMORE John 1837
SEYMORE James P 1836
SEYMORE John 1836
SEYMORE Robert 1836
BROWN George 1830

Section 7
HENRY Elijah 1851
FANNING George 1830
BROCKMAN Samuel 1831
YATES Abner 1855
ADAMS Elijah 1830
BARROWS Isaac R 1830
GIVENS William T 1835
SWEET Joel 1831
GIBSON James Jr 1830
MCFALL James 1854
MCFALL James 1854
DAUGHERTY John 1851
BARROWS Barnabas 1852
FARMING George 1831
RICHARDSON Vincent S 1835
BERDAN James 1855
SEYMORE Robert 1837
GIBSON Isham 1835
GIBSON Isham 1830

Section 8
GIBSON James Jr 1830
GIBSON Isham 1830
FRY Milton 1835
GIBSON Isham 1834
YOUNGBLOOD Ambrose 1832
REED Martin 1835
REED Martin 1836
GIBSON Isham 1830
STURGIS Daniel B 1831

Section 18
FANNING John 1831
HOWARD Elakim [54] 1832
FANNING Robert 1854
GIBSON James 1836
GIBSON James 1835
GIBSON James Jr 1830
FANNING Abraham 1831
FANNING [62] Jacob 1836
FANNING [61] Jacob 1835
FANNING Jacob 1831
WOLCOTT Elihu 1835
WOLCOTT Elihu 1831
FANNING Levi 1831
GIBSON James Jr 1830
SPIRES William 1831

Section 17
MURPHY Nimrod C 1830
YOUNGBLOOD Ambrose 1829
SHEPPARD [110] John Oaks 1834
SHEPHERD Lewis J 1829
SPIRES William 1831
SPIRES William 1835

Lots-Sec. 16
L1	PIPER, John	1833
L1	GRIMSLEY, Fielding	1837
L3	HARP, Conrad	1834
L4	EVANS, James	1833
L5	HARP, Conrad	1834
L6	EVANS, James	1833
L6	STEWART, Benjam[123]	1837
L7	STEWART, Benjam[123]	1837
L7	MORTON, Joseph	1833
L8	FANNING, Levi	1835
L9	MORTON, Joseph	1833
L10	MORTON, Joseph	1833
L11	HURST, Jonathan	1835
L11	PIPER, John	1833
L12	SHEPPARD, John O	1833

Section 16

Section 19
HOWARD Stephen 1831
HOWARD Stephen 1831
MCCEARLY Ezekiel 1830
FANNING Joseph 1830
WYATT Eli Martin 1847
BROWN Samuel 1831
TODD James 1834
SPIRES William 1836
COX John 1834
JANUARY Thomas T 1836
RICHARDSON Vincent S 1835
PEXTON Henry 1835
RICHARDSON Vincent S 1835
BROWN George 1831
GIBSON Isham 1830

Section 20

Section 21
FANNING Sampson 1835
FANNING Sampson 1835
NICHOLLS George 1835
CRISWELL George 1831
CRISWELL George 1830
COX John 1835
EDWARDS Thomas J 1854
SHORES Jonathan 1854
EDWARDS Thomas J 1854
RANSDELL Thomas T 1836
BROWN Samuel 1831
DUDHOPE Thomas 1835
PEARSON Benjamin 1835
FANNING George W 1836
FANNING George W 1834
REYNOLDS John 1831

Section 30
NICHOLLS George W 1836
MCCEARLEY Ezekiel 1836
NICKOL Agrippa 1839
GIBSON Isham 1836
HURTS Jonathan 1839
CRISWELL George 1835
WOLCOTT Elihu 1831
SHORES Jonathan 1854
FRISBIE Rufus K 1849
GRIGG John 1835
RANSDELL Presley 1835
SHORES Richard 1854
HART Solomon 1835
FULLER Abraham 1834
HART Solomon 1835
REYNOLDS John 1829

Section 29
NICHOLS John B 1854
MORLAN James H 1854
ROBINSON John C 1854
ROBINSON John C 1856
DAUGHERTY John 1835
DEVORE Martin Luther 1836
MCNEELY James 1854
MITCHELL Joel 1851
CRISWELL George 1831
GRIGG John 1835
GRIGG John 1835
TAYLOR Eliza H 1869
SHORES Richard 1854
SHORES Jonathan 1852
RHODES John 1837
MANSFIELD Alfred 1834
SHORES Solomon 1829
HART Solomon 1835

Section 28
HART Charles 1828
HART Solomon 1828

Section 31
WHEELER James 1850
MITCHELL Joel 1851
DODSON Elizabeth 1849
ROBINSON John C 1854
DEVORE John 1836
DAUGHERTY John 1836
HART Solomon 1832
BUCKMASTER Nathaniel 1848
PATTERSON William 1835
FULLER Abraham 1835
GRIGG John 1835
PATTERSON William 1834
WILKINSON Richard 1836
MANSFIELD James 1829
HART Nathan 1835
HART Nathan 1831

Section 32
PETTYJOHN Jacob 1836
HART Nathan 1852
NELSON Martin 1836
CAUDEL John 1853
ROBINSON John C 1854
CAUDEL John 1854
NELSON Martin 1836
MCCEARLEY Ezekiel 1836
NICHOLLS George 1835
WILKINSON Richard 1835
GRIGG John 1835
WILKINSON John S 1854
LUTTRELL Lott 1838
WILKINSON Richard 1835

Section 33
FINCH Joel 1836
HART Nathan 1834
ATTEBERY Melchisedec 1836
HART Nathan 1835
HART David 1831

SEMOORE John 1829 **3**	VANWINKLE Ranson 1829		VANWINKLE Ransom 1830		REYNOLDS Joseph 1828 **2**		CYRUS Matthew 1831 **1**		LUTTRELL Hiram 1831

Helpful Hints

1. This Map's INDEX can be found on the preceding pages.

2. Refer to Map "C" to see where this Township lies within Morgan County, Illinois.

3. Numbers within square brackets [ ] denote a multi-patentee land parcel (multi-owner). Refer to Appendix "C" for a full list of members in this group.

4. Areas that look to be crowded with Patentees usually indicate multiple sales of the same parcel (re-issues), cancellations or voided transactions (that we map, anyway) or overlapping parcels. We opt to show even these ambiguous parcels, which oftentimes lead to research avenues not yet taken.

Section 3
BROWN Samuel 1828 — WEATHERFORD William 1831 — TAUMHILL Alfred 1833 — STURGIS James B 1833 — WEATHERFORD William 1833

Section 2
STURGIS James B 1830 — STURGIS James B 1828 — WEATHERFORD Jefferso 1828 — SEAMORE John 1830

Section 1
LUTTRELL Thomas 1831 — LUTTRILL Armstrong 1835 — LUTTRELL Thomas 1829 — LUTTRELL Thomas 1826 — HENRY Elijah 1851

GIBSON Isham 1830 — WEATHERFORD William 1829 — WOLCOTT Elihu 1832 — WEATHERFORD Hardin 1829

WEATHERFORD Hardin 1829 — STURGIS Daniel 1829 — HEADINGTON Joel 1835 — WEATHERFORD William 1830

SCARTH Robert 1835 — WRIGHT James Jr 1834 — WRIGHT James Jr 1833 — WYATT John 1829 — WRIGHT Abner 1829

STURGIS Daniel B 1831 — WEATHERFORD William 1833 **10** — REES John H 1835 — SCOTT James 1852 — FANNING Levi 1835

NOLL [105] John 1829 — HEADINGTON Joel 1834 **11** — SEYMORE Burges 1833 — LESLIE Miron 1835

WRIGHT Reuben 1829 **12** — WRIGHT James 1829

REES John H 1835 — SOWRY Robert 1852 — YATES Abner 1857 — HAYNES John 1850 — WEATHERFORD James 1835 — HAYNES John 1836 — HAYNES John 1836

NALL Russel 1836 — SEYMOUR Burgess 1834 — KIPLINGER Samuel 1834 — HAYNES Green 1854 — VANOATE Jacob 1837

GALLAHER William G 1835 — MCCORMICK John 1835

LESLIE Miron 1835 — WOODS Starling 1835 — CALDWELL Robert M 1834 **13** — PARKINSON James 1833

ROBERTS William 1837 — HAYNES Bluford 1834 — DALTON Cluborn 1835 **15** — HUEY Daniel 1835

AUSTIN Eli 1835 — HALL John 1834 **14** — WRIGHT Abner 1829

NELSON Richard H 1835 — LUTTRELL Thomas 1835 — HAM John H 1835 — TOLKINTON John 1833 — WRIGHT Thomas 1835

ROBERTS William 1834 — NALL Russel 1836 — MCCLEARLY Joseph R 1836 — STURGIS John R 1854 — DALTON Clayborn 1854 — SEYMORE William 1837 — SEYMORE William 1836

SEYMORE Edward 1833 — WRIGHT Abner 1829 — WRIGHT Abner 1829 **23** — MCCORMICK Walker 1835

JONES Henry 1835 — CATLIN [30] Joel 1835 **24** — SALTER Cleveland J 1835 — JONES Reuben 1835

STURGIS John R 1853 — HART Anderson 1835 — STURGIS Thomas S 1839 — HART Anderson 1833 **22** — DYE Isaac 1829 — BULL Jesse Walker 1836 — BALL Jesse Walker 1835 — AUSTIN Eli 1836

ROBERTS James A 1850 — WRIGHT Reuben 1852 — ROBERTS James A 1854 — BALDWIN Richard C 1835

BALDWIN Richard C 1835 — CATLIN [30] Joel 1835 — STEWART Brice 1836 — DEATHERAGE Stephen 1835

BRIAN William 1829 — SEYMORE Peter 1836 — SEYMORE Peter 1837 **27** — SEAMORE Richardson 1851 — SEAMORE Edward 1851 — NALL John 1852 — SEYMORE William 1836

HAMILTON John C 1835 — HAMILTON John F 1835 — HINDES Isaac 1854 — MCCULLEY John 1836 — BARNETT Harvey 1849 — CAMPBELL William 1836

JONES Robert A C 1836 — JONES Robert A C 1836 **25** — HALL William W 1835 — TENNISON Reuben 1835 — SUMMERS Henry 1836 — ENGLAND Thomas 1835 — TENNISON Reuben 1835

HART Charles 1831 — SNOW Charles G 1854 — BOOKES Richard M 1832 — SNOW Charles G 1854 — HART Charles 1835 — FANNING Levi 1835 — BRIAN William 1832

HART Solomon 1834 **26** — CARLOCK David 1834 — CALDWELL John Cook 1835 — CHANCE Ezekiel 1839 — STICE Robert Lee 1835 — REED Julius A 1836

WHITE William 1854 — DENNIS Wesley O 1854 — ROLAND Christian L 1836 — ROLAND Gasper 1836 — ALLEN Issac 1854 — DENNIS Susannah 1836 — GUNNELS Daniel 1838

HART David 1831 — HARLAN John C 1840 **34** — RHODES John 1835 — MANSFIELD Alfred 1836 — TANNEHILL Alfred 1836 — DALTON Samuel 1836 — HART Joseph W 1835 — HART Charles 1835 — DALTON Samuel 1836 — HART Solomon 1835

LESLIE Miron 1835 — VANCIL Isaac 1836 — THOMPSON John 1854 **35** — VANCIL Isaac 1836 — COOK William 1838 — WATSON William 1834 — WATERS Joseph 1835

DICK George 1833 — THOMPSON Samuel 1836 — THOMPSON John 1854 — BRISTOW James 1835 — SPARKS Matthew B 1836 — THOMPSON Jonas 1832

TALKINGTON William 1835 — DIKES John 1854 — EDGELL Stephen M 1836 — SPERRY Eli 1841 — HARRIS Ledley C 1835 — CHERRY James H 1835 — PACK Julius Benjamin 1837 — BRISTOW James 1835 **36** — THOMPSON Andrew 1835 — JARMAN [88] Elford E 1836 — GRIGG John 1835

Legend

Patent Boundary

Section Boundary

No Patents Found (or Outside County)

1., 2., 3., ... Lot Numbers (when beside a name)

[ ] Group Number (see Appendix "C")

Scale: Section = 1 mile X 1 mile (generally, with some exceptions)

Road Map

T13-N R9-W
3rd PM Meridian

Map Group 18

Cities & Towns
Nortonville

Cemeteries
Bull Cemetery
Criswell George Cemetery
Fanning Ollie Cemetery
Harts Prairie Cemetery
Providence Cemetery
Reed Cemetery
Robert Cemetery
Seymour Bird Cemetery
Youngblood Cemetery

Durbin

Sun Valley

6

5

Crow

Providence Cem.

Mooney

4

Highway 14

Sierra

County

Reed Cem.

7

8

9

Ryan

Carpenter

18

17

16

Gerbending

Youngblood Cem.

Nortonville

Oak

Carpenter

McCurly

19

Fair

20

21

Jackson

Sheriffs

30

Frog Hill

28

29

Clayton

Nortonville

Campbell

Claussen

31

32

Elliot

33

County Highway 9

County Line

252

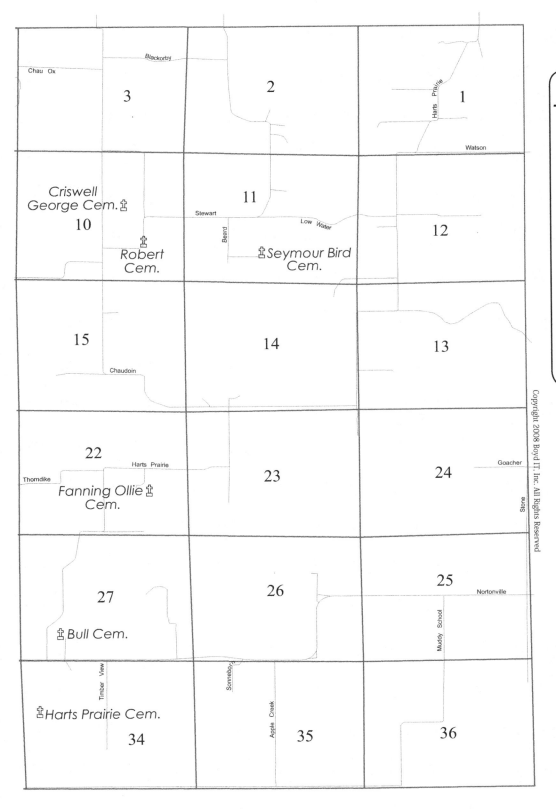

Helpful Hints

1. This road map has a number of uses, but primarily it is to help you: a) find the present location of land owned by your ancestors (at least the general area), b) find cemeteries and city-centers, and c) estimate the route/roads used by Census-takers & tax-assessors.

2. If you plan to travel to Morgan County to locate cemeteries or land parcels, please pick up a modern travel map for the area before you do. Mapping old land parcels on modern maps is not as exact a science as you might think. Just the slightest variations in public land survey coordinates, estimates of parcel boundaries, or road-map deviations can greatly alter a map's representation of how a road either does or doesn't cross a particular parcel of land.

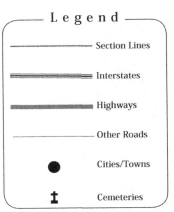

L e g e n d

————————	Section Lines
════════════	Interstates
════════════	Highways
————————	Other Roads
⬤	Cities/Towns
✝	Cemeteries

Scale: Section = 1 mile X 1 mile
(generally, with some exceptions)

Historical Map

T13-N R9-W
3rd PM Meridian

Map Group 18

Cities & Towns
Nortonville

Cemeteries
Bull Cemetery
Criswell George Cemetery
Fanning Ollie Cemetery
Harts Prairie Cemetery
Providence Cemetery
Reed Cemetery
Robert Cemetery
Seymour Bird Cemetery
Youngblood Cemetery

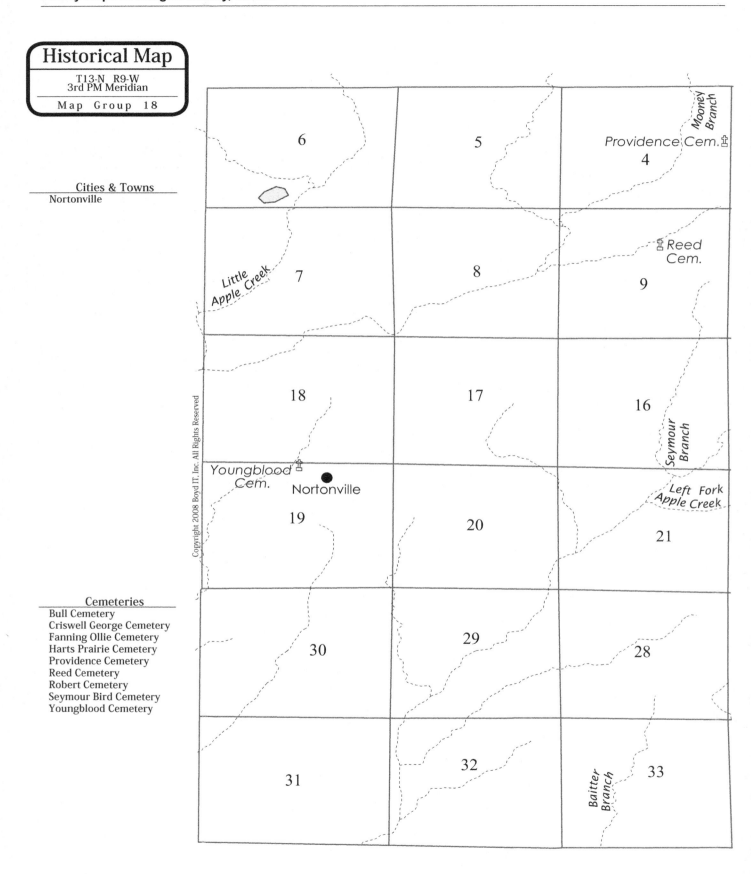

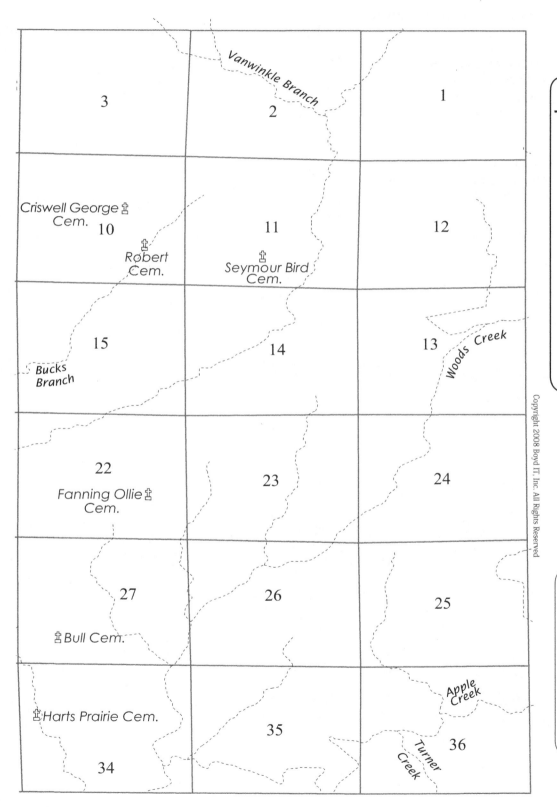

Vanwinkle Branch

3

2

1

Criswell George ‡
Cem.   10

‡
Robert
Cem.

11

‡
Seymour Bird
Cem.

12

15

14

Woods Creek

13

Bucks
Branch

22

23

24

Fanning Ollie ‡
Cem.

27

26

25

‡ Bull Cem.

‡ Harts Prairie Cem.

35

Apple
Creek

Turner
Creek

36

34

Copyright 2008 Boyd IT, Inc. All Rights Reserved

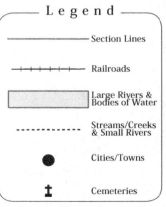

L e g e n d

———————— Section Lines

+++++++ Railroads

Large Rivers &
Bodies of Water

- - - - - - Streams/Creeks
& Small Rivers

● Cities/Towns

‡ Cemeteries

Scale: Section = 1 mile X 1 mile
(there are some exceptions)

Map Group 19: Index to Land Patents

Township 13-North Range 8-West (3rd PM)

After you locate an individual in this Index, take note of the Section and Section Part then proceed to the Land Patent map on the pages immediately following. You should have no difficulty locating the corresponding parcel of land.

The "For More Info" Column will lead you to more information about the underlying Patents. See the *Legend* at right, and the "How to Use this Book" chapter, for more information.

```
┌─────────────────────────────────────────────────────────────┐
│                         LEGEND                               │
│            "For More Info . . . " column                     │
│ ──────────────────────────────────────────────────────────  │
│ G = Group  (Multi-Patentee Patent, see Appendix "C")         │
│ R = Residence                                                │
│ S = Social Status                                            │
│                                                              │
│                                                              │
│ See Appendix A for list of abbreviations used by the         │
│ Illinois State Archives in describing the place and          │
│ nature of these land patents.                                │
│                                                              │
│ Note: if the Abbreviations contain "L", "BL", "LOT",         │
│ or "BLOCK", the exact whereabouts of the parcel within       │
│ the section is not known.                                    │
└─────────────────────────────────────────────────────────────┘
```

ID	Individual in Patent	Sec.	Sec. Part	Purchase Date	Sale Type	IL Aliquot Part	For More Info . . .
4969	ALLIS, Stephen G	27	NESE	1838-11-30	FD	NESE	R:MORGAN
4790	ARMSTRONG, Hugh M	23	SENW	1833-02-07	FD	SENW	R:SANGAMON
4789	" "	23	NWNE	1833-02-07	FD	NWNE	R:SANGAMON
4973	ARMSTRONG, Thomas	22	E½NW	1830-01-29	FD	E2NW	R:MADISON
4847	ARNETT, John	19	NENE	1833-10-17	FD	NENE	R:MORGAN
4848	" "	19	SENE	1835-12-30	FD	SENE	R:MORGAN
4723	ASHBAUGH, Christopher	8	E½SE	1830-02-16	FD	E2SE	R:MORGAN
4724	" "	8	W½SE	1835-10-14	FD	W2SE	R:MORGAN
4722	ASHBRAUGH, Christophe	16	L11	1835-11-21	SC	LOT11	
4843	AUSTIN, Jauvier J	32	NESE	1853-10-08	FD	NESE	
4947	BALDWIN, Richard C	25	E½NW	1835-05-14	FD	E2NW	R:GEORGIA
4946	" "	24	W½	1835-05-14	FD	W2	R:GEORGIA
4945	" "	13	E½SW	1835-05-14	FD	E2SW	R:GEORGIA
4774	BARKER, George White	28	SWNE	1837-11-29	FD	SWNE	R:MADISON
4807	BEASLEY, James	20	NWNE	1835-11-07	FD	NWNE	R:MORGAN
4808	" "	20	SWNE	1836-08-22	FD	SWNE	R:MORGAN
4775	BEFON, Henry	27	SENW	00/30/1836	FD	SENW	R:MORGAN
4793	BENNETT, Isham	5	N½NW	1830-10-28	FD	N2NW	R:MORGAN
4849	BLANEY, John	35	E½NE	1828-01-17	FD	E2NE	R:MORGAN
4850	" "	36	W½SW	1836-02-11	FD	W2SW	
4953	BLANEY, Roling G	28	NESW	1852-04-08	FD	NESW	R:MORGAN
4954	" "	33	NWNW	1854-01-18	FD	NWNW	
4812	BLEVINS, James C	28	NWNE	1836-06-10	FD	NWNE	R:MORGAN
4940	BOULWARE, Philip	5	SESW	1834-06-07	FD	SESW	R:MORGAN
4994	BOWYER, William	4	W½SW	1831-09-30	FD	W2SW	R:MORGAN
4993	" "	3	W½NW	1831-09-30	FD	W2NW	R:MORGAN
4809	BRIAN, James	28	SWSE	1835-10-05	FD	SWSE	R:MORGAN
4811	" "	33	SWNW	1836-02-10	FD	SWNW	
4810	" "	33	NENE	1851-11-11	FD	NENE	
4827	BRIAN, James Lafayet	36	SESE	1848-11-24	FD	SESE	
4978	BRIAN, Thomas Jeffers	36	NWSE	1849-04-24	FD	NWSE	
5021	BRIAN, William W	36	NESE	1848-11-24	FD	NESE	
4683	BROKENBOUGH, A	16	L7	1835-11-21	SC	LOT7	S:I
4676	" "	16	L13	1835-11-21	SC	LOT13	S:I
4677	" "	16	L14	1835-11-21	SC	LOT14	S:I
4678	" "	16	L15	1835-11-21	SC	LOT15	S:I
4679	" "	16	L16	1835-11-21	SC	LOT16	S:I
4680	" "	16	L4	1835-11-21	SC	LOT4	S:I
4682	" "	16	L6	1835-11-21	SC	LOT06	S:I
4681	" "	16	L5	1835-11-21	SC	LOT5	S:I
4684	BROKENBROUGH, A	16	L2	1835-11-21	SC	LOT02	S:I
4685	" "	16	L3	1835-11-21	SC	LOT3	S:I
4905	BROWN, Joseph	34	E½SW	1821-12-28	FD	E2SWFS	R:MORGAN
4960	BROWN, Samuel Jr	34	SWSE	1832-10-22	FD	SWSE	R:SANGAMON
4959	" "	34	NWSE	1835-09-29	FD	NWSE	R:MORGAN
4987	BURCH, Walter	6	N½NW	1828-08-08	FD	N2NW	R:MORGAN

ID	Individual in Patent	Sec.	Sec. Part	Purchase Date	Sale Type	IL Aliquot Part	For More Info . . .
4906	BURNS, Joseph	21	W2SE	1836-02-10	FD	W2SEPRE	
4854	CALDWELL, John	6	W½SE	1828-12-03	FD	W2SE	R:MORGAN G:23
4853	CALDWELL, John C	6	E½SW	1831-07-18	FD	E2SW	R:MORGAN G:21
4852	" "	6	E½SE	1831-11-09	FD	E2SE	R:MORGAN G:21
4851	" "	5	L1	1853-11-19	FD	W2LOT01NW	R:MORGAN
4855	CALDWELL, John Cook	6	W½NE	1831-10-08	FD	W2NE	R:MORGAN G:22
4950	CALDWELL, Robert M	7	E½SE	1834-11-21	FD	E2SE	R:KENTUCKY
4854	CALDWELL, William	6	W½SE	1828-12-03	FD	W2SE	R:MORGAN G:23
4853	" "	6	E½SW	1831-07-18	FD	E2SW	R:MORGAN G:21
4855	" "	6	W½NE	1831-10-08	FD	W2NE	R:MORGAN G:22
4852	" "	6	E½SE	1831-11-09	FD	E2SE	R:MORGAN G:21
4997	" "	7	NWNE	1853-11-19	FD	NWNE	R:MORGAN
4999	CAMPBELL, William	24	SENE	1833-06-03	FD	SENE	R:MORGAN
4998	" "	23	E½NE	1833-06-03	FD	E2NE	R:MORGAN
4955	CARRATHER, Samuel	21	NESE	1836-02-06	FD	NESE	
4956	CARRUTHERS, Samuel	21	SESE	1837-11-03	FD	SESE	R:MADISON
4814	CARUTHERS, James	14	W½SE	1827-12-10	FD	W2SE	R:MORGAN
4813	" "	14	E½SE	1831-08-23	FD	E2SE	R:MORGAN
4957	CARUTHERS, Samuel	13	W½SW	1834-12-15	FD	W2SW	R:MORGAN
4974	CARY, Thomas	21	E½NW	1833-03-18	FD	E2NW	R:MADISON
4975	" "	21	NWNW	1833-05-18	FD	NWNW	R:MORGAN
4846	CATLIN, Joel	13	N½	1835-05-14	FD	N2	R:HANCOCK G:30
4846	CATLIN, Willis	13	N½	1835-05-14	FD	N2	R:HANCOCK G:30
4845	CAWOOD, Jeremiah	28	NWSW	1833-05-30	FD	NWSW	R:MORGAN
4844	CAWOOD, Jeremiah B	28	NENW	1837-02-27	FD	NENW	R:MORGAN
4912	CAWOOD, Joshua Brown	32	SWSW	1839-03-01	FD	SWSW	
4791	CHAPMAN, Isaac	22	W½SW	1837-11-27	FD	W2SW	R:MORGAN
4749	CHASTAIN, Elijah	7	SWNW	1833-09-16	FD	SWNW	R:MORGAN
4815	CHESNUTT, James	20	SW	1836-08-25	FD	SW	R:MORGAN
4816	CLACK, James	31	NESE	1835-11-10	FD	NESE	R:MORGAN
4817	" "	32	SENW	1835-11-10	FD	SENW	R:MORGAN
5000	CLACKE, William	17	NW	1835-10-01	FD	NW	R:MORGAN
4753	CLARK, Norman	18	W½NW	1827-11-07	FD	W2NW	R:MORGAN G:35
4939	CLOUD, Newton	4	W½SE	1831-04-14	FD	W2SE	R:MORGAN
4938	" "	4	SESE	1833-07-10	FD	SESE	R:MORGAN
4937	" "	16	L12	1835-11-21	SC	LOT12	
4792	CONLEE, Isaac	36	NESW	1849-10-29	FD	NESW	R:MORGAN
4771	COOKE, George W	14	E½NW	1831-08-23	FD	E2NW	R:MORGAN
4768	" "	11	E½SW	1831-08-23	FD	E2SW	R:MORGAN
4770	" "	14	E½NE	1831-08-23	FD	E2NE	R:MORGAN
4769	" "	11	NE	1831-08-23	FD	NE	R:MORGAN
4772	" "	8	W½NW	1832-01-27	FD	W2NW	R:MORGAN
4914	COULEE, Josiah	36	NENE	1847-08-19	FD	NENE	
4742	COWAN, David	7	SWSE	1833-12-17	FD	SWSE	R:MORGAN G:47
4742	COWAN, John Henry	7	SWSE	1833-12-17	FD	SWSE	R:MORGAN G:47
4958	CUMMING, Samuel	32	SESE	1839-03-18	FD	SESE	
4856	CUMMINGS, John	31	E½NE	1834-11-13	FD	E2NE	R:MACOUPIN
5001	CUMMINGS, William	31	NWNE	1835-03-21	FD	NWNE	R:MACOUPIN
4976	CURTIS, Thomas E	21	SESW	1836-06-02	FD	SESW	R:MORGAN
4696	DEATHERAGE, Achelas	10	W½NE	1829-03-23	FD	W2NE	R:MORGAN
4698	DEATHERAGE, Achilles	3	SWSE	1833-07-24	FD	SWSE	R:MORGAN G:52
4697	" "	19	E½SW	1836-02-06	FD	E2SW	G:52
4700	DEATHERAGE, Alfred	18	E½SE	1828-12-04	FD	E2SE	R:MORGAN
4942	DEATHERAGE, Coleman	9	W½SE	1826-11-20	FD	W2SE	R:MORGAN
4737	" "	9	W½SE	1826-11-20	FD	W2SE	R:MORGAN
4736	" "	9	E½SE	1827-11-03	FD	E2SE	R:MORGAN
4735	" "	15	W½NW	1831-04-14	FD	W2NW	R:MORGAN
4762	DEATHERAGE, George	10	SE	1826-11-20	FD	SE	R:MORGAN G:53
4763	" "	3	E½SW	1831-09-02	FD	E2SWFS	R:MORGAN G:53
4698	" "	3	SWSE	1833-07-24	FD	SWSE	R:MORGAN G:52
4697	" "	19	E½SW	1836-02-06	FD	E2SW	G:52
4773	DEATHERAGE, George W	30	SWNW	1839-04-08	FD	SWNW	R:MORGAN
4788	DEATHERAGE, Holman	20	NWSE	1837-03-23	FD	NWSE	R:MORGAN
4820	DEATHERAGE, James	20	SWSE	1835-07-02	FD	SWSE	R:MASON
4821	" "	29	SWNW	1835-07-02	FD	SWNW	R:MASON
4819	" "	20	E½SE	1836-08-22	FD	E2SE	R:MORGAN
4941	DEATHERAGE, Philip	9	E½NW	1827-12-10	FD	E2NW	R:MORGAN
4737	" "	9	W½SE	1829-03-23	FD	W2SE	R:MORGAN
4942	" "	9	W½SE	1829-03-23	FD	W2SE	R:MORGAN
4971	DEATHERAGE, Stevens	9	NWNW	1835-01-09	FD	NWNW	R:MORGAN
4762	DEATHERAGE, William	10	SE	1826-11-20	FD	SE	R:MORGAN G:53
4763	" "	3	E½SW	1831-09-02	FD	E2SWFS	R:MORGAN G:53
4698	" "	3	SWSE	1833-07-24	FD	SWSE	R:MORGAN G:52

ID	Individual in Patent	Sec.	Sec. Part	Purchase Date	Sale Type	IL Aliquot Part	For More Info . . .
5002	DEATHERAGE, William (Cont'd)	19	W½SW	1836-02-06	FD	W2SW	
4697	" "	19	E½SW	1836-02-06	FD	E2SW	G:52
5003	" "	30	NWNE	1855-10-03	FD	NWNE	R:MORGAN
5014	DEATHERAGE, William R	30	NWSW	1855-09-27	FD	NWSW	R:MORGAN
5006	DENNIS, William G	32	SESW	1854-09-27	FD	SESW	R:MORGAN
4750	DODD, Elijah	19	E½NW	1834-04-12	FD	E2NW	R:MADISON
4751	" "	19	SWNW	1834-04-12	FD	SWNW	R:MORGAN
4885	DOSGOOD, Jonathan W	5	NESE	1836-04-25	FD	NESE	R:MORGAN G:56
4755	DOUGHTY, Felix	27	SWNW	1851-01-08	FD	SWNW	
4756	" "	27	W½SW	1851-01-08	FD	W2SW	
4757	" "	28	SENE	1851-01-08	FD	SENE	
4963	DUNN, Shadrack	17	NWSW	1835-10-26	FD	NWSW	R:MORGAN
4870	DURYEE, John Richard	27	NWSE	1839-01-04	FD	NWSE	R:SANGAMON
5004	DYER, William	34	W½SW	1827-11-12	FD	W2SW	R:MORGAN
4766	EASTMAN, George	3	NWSE	1835-06-04	FD	NWSE	R:MORGAN
4767	" "	8	E½SW	1835-06-04	FD	E2SW	R:MORGAN
4765	" "	21	W½NE	1835-09-04	FD	W2NE	R:MORGAN
4764	" "	20	NW	1836-02-05	FD	NW	
4970	EDGELL, Stephen M	7	E½NE	1836-01-16	FD	E2NE	R:MADISON
4776	EDWARDS, Henry	5	W½SE	1831-10-06	FD	W2SEFS	R:MORGAN
4718	ENGLAND, Caswell	30	NWNW	1836-01-15	FD	NWNW	R:MORGAN
5005	ENGLAND, William	35	W½SW	1827-08-28	FD	W2SW	R:MORGAN
4746	FANCIL, Edmund C	31	SWNE	1834-12-09	FD	SWNE	R:MACOUPIN
5019	GIVENS, William T	8	E½NW	1833-12-02	FD	E2NW	R:MORGAN
4778	GLESENER, Henry	29	SWSE	1854-10-05	FD	SWSE	R:MADISON
4777	" "	29	E½SW	1854-10-05	FD	E2SW	R:MADISON
4686	GOFF, Aaron	34	NWNE	1835-06-01	FD	NWNE	R:MORGAN
4687	" "	36	SENW	1835-12-14	FD	SENW	R:MORGAN
4920	GOFF, Lindsey	30	SENW	1836-08-23	FD	SENW	R:MORGAN
4860	GRIGG, John	31	W½SE	1835-12-07	FD	W2SE	R:PHILADELPHIA
4858	" "	29	W½SW	1835-12-07	FD	W2SW	R:PHILADELPHIA
4857	" "	19	W½SE	1835-12-07	FD	W2SE	R:PHILADELPHIA
4859	" "	31	E½SW	1835-12-07	FD	E2SW	R:PHILADELPHIA
4861	" "	32	W½NW	1835-12-07	FD	W2NW	R:PHILADELPHIA
4799	GROVES, Jacob	17	SWSW	1833-03-06	FD	SWSW	R:MORGAN
4824	GROVES, James	30	SWSE	1836-09-29	FD	SWSE	R:MORGAN
4823	" "	30	NWSE	1839-03-09	FD	NWSE	
5020	GWENS, William T	8	SENE	1835-12-30	FD	SENE	R:MORGAN
4748	HAGGARD, Edmund	4	E½NW	1831-11-14	FD	E2NW	R:MORGAN
4779	HAMMER, Henry	27	S½SE	1835-11-21	FD	S2SE	R:MORGAN
4977	HAMPTON, Thomas	6	S½NW	1829-11-02	FD	S2NW	R:MORGAN
4982	HARRIS, Thomas Rander	33	SENE	1835-09-14	FD	SENE	R:MORGAN
4981	HARRISS, Thomas R	33	E½SW	1835-11-10	FD	E2SW	R:MORGAN
4702	HART, Anderson	28	SESW	1852-05-06	FD	SESW	
4780	HART, Henry	34		1835-11-10	FD	NWPREAC	R:MORGAN
4785	HART, Henry Philip	34	E½SE	1821-12-28	FD	E2SE	R:MORGAN
4884	HART, John Wesley	32	SWSE	1848-02-22	FD	SWSE	
4741	HUEY, Daniel	31	W½NW	1835-10-22	FD	W2NW	R:MISSISSIPPI
4739	" "	19	E½SE	1835-10-22	FD	E2SE	R:MISSISSIPPI
4740	" "	31	SENW	1835-10-22	FD	SENW	R:MISSISSIPPI
5009	HUNTLY, William	18	NWNE	1837-01-31	FD	NWNE	R:MORGAN
4826	HUTCHESON, James	27	NWNE	1833-09-03	FD	NWNE	R:MORGAN
4825	" "	27	NENW	1833-09-03	FD	NENW	R:MORGAN
4717	JACKSON, Brice B	4	W½NW	1835-11-30	FD	W2NW	R:MORGAN
4918	JACKSON, Levi L	4	W2NE	1835-10-14	FD	W2NEPRE	R:MORGAN
4695	" "	4	NENE	1835-10-14	FD	NENE	R:MORGAN G:85
4781	JONES, Henry	18	NWNW	1835-05-12	FD	NWNW	R:MORGAN
4944	JONES, Reuben	19	NWNW	1835-03-12	FD	NWNW	R:MORGAN
4990	JONES, Watemon	18		1833-12-11	FD	S2WSUBDSW	R:MORGAN
4991	" "	18		1833-12-11	FD	S2WSUBDSW	R:MORGAN
4990	" "	18		1834-10-28	FD	N2WSUBSW	R:MORGAN
4991	" "	18		1834-10-28	FD	N2WSUBSW	R:MORGAN
4992	JONES, Waterman	18	E½SW	1829-05-20	FD	E2SW	R:MORGAN
4862	KER, John	7	E½NW	1835-08-12	FD	E2NW	R:MORGAN
4863	KIBLINGER, John	18	SWNW	1833-04-25	FD	SWNW	R:MORGAN
4752	KILPATRICK, Ephraim	10	E½NE	1829-02-04	FD	E2NE	R:MORGAN
4886	LANDRETH, Jonathan	31	SESE	1838-03-03	FD	SESE	R:MACOUPIN
4972	LANHAM, Sylvester	6	W½SW	1829-01-21	FD	W2SW	R:MORGAN
4933	LESLIE, Miron	5	W½SW	1835-06-25	FD	W2SW	R:MORGAN
4934	" "	8	W½SW	1835-06-25	FD	W2SW	R:MORGAN
4932	" "	30	E½NE	1835-07-14	FD	E2NE	R:MORGAN
4930	" "	16	L10	1835-11-21	SC	LOT10	
4931	" "	16	L8	1835-11-21	SC	LOT8	

ID	Individual in Patent	Sec.	Sec. Part	Purchase Date	Sale Type	IL Aliquot Part	For More Info . . .
5010	LEWIS, William	28	E½SE	1854-09-27	FD	E2SE	R:JERSEY
5011	" "	28	NWSE	1854-09-27	FD	NWSE	R:JERSEY
4979	LEWIS, William H	32	NENW	1856-05-30	FD	NENW	R:JACKSON
5018	" "	32	NWNE	1856-05-30	FD	NWNE	R:MADISON
5007	" "	32	NENW	1856-05-30	FD	NENW	R:JACKSON
5017	" "	32	NENW	1856-05-30	FD	NENW	R:JACKSON
5008	" "	32	NWNE	1856-05-30	FD	NWNE	R:MADISON
4907	LOGSDON, Joseph	35	E½SW	1828-11-04	FD	E2SW	R:MADISON
5012	LOLLARS, William	28	W½NW	1832-02-21	FD	W2NW	R:SANGAMON
4829	LONDON, James	26	E½SW	1827-11-10	FD	E2SW	R:MORGAN
4828	" "	26	E½NW	1832-03-15	FD	E2NWFS	R:MORGAN
4868	LOVE, John	15	NE	1825-04-04	FD	NE	R:GREENE
4867	" "	15	E½SE	1826-08-29	FD	E2SE	R:GREENE
4866	" "	14	W½SW	1826-12-04	FD	W2SW	R:GREENE
4865	" "	14	W½NW	1827-11-26	FD	W2NW	R:GREENE
4864	" "	14	W½NE	1831-08-22	FD	W2NE	R:MORGAN
4758	MAUPIN, Fleming Cobbs	26	W½NW	1831-08-03	FD	W2NW	R:MORGAN
4759	" "	27	E½NE	1831-08-03	FD	E2NE	R:MORGAN
4760	MAUPIN, Flemming C	26	NWSW	1836-11-07	FD	NWSW	R:MORGAN
4798	MCCAULEY, Jackson	32	NWSE	1839-03-18	FD	NWSE	
4949	MCCAULEY, Richard T	32	SWNE	1839-03-18	FD	SWNE	
4961	MCLAIN, Samuel	21	SWSW	1836-06-13	FD	SWSW	R:MORGAN
5013	MCLAIN, William	21	SWNW	1836-01-30	FD	SWNW	R:MORGAN
4761	MEADOWS, Francis J	23	SWNE	1833-12-03	FD	SWNE	R:MORGAN
4699	MONTGOMERY, Alexander	33	W½SW	1834-12-03	FD	W2SW	R:MACOUPIN
4712	NEVINS, Austin Sims	31	NWSW	1836-01-16	FD	NWSW	R:MACOUPIN
4830	NOWLAN, James	16	L1	1835-11-21	SC	LOT1	
4831	NOWLIN, James	9	SWNW	1835-11-10	FD	SWNW	R:MORGAN
4745	NOYES, Ebernezer	33		1852-08-11	FD	SECTION	R:MOULTRIE
4784	PEARCY, Henry	24	E½SE	1828-01-12	FD	E2SE	R:MADISON
4915	REED, Julius A	17	W½SE	1836-02-01	FD	W2SE	R:MORGAN
4916	" "	29	W½NE	1836-02-01	FD	W2NE	R:MORGAN
4917	" "	5	SESE	1836-02-01	FD	SESE	R:MORGAN
4921	REED, Marc M L	29	NWNW	1836-01-25	FD	NWNW	R:MORGAN
4922	" "	29	NWSE	1836-01-25	FD	NWSE	R:MORGAN
4923	REED, Maro	29		1837-09-04	FD	F2NW	R:MORGAN S:F
4924	REED, Mary Eliza	18	NENE	1836-01-25	FD	NENE	R:MORGAN S:F
4908	REYNOLDS, Joseph	36	SWNE	1852-08-17	FD	SWNE	
4833	RHEA, James	28	SENW	1836-01-30	FD	SENW	R:MORGAN
4832	" "	21	NESW	1841-05-24	FD	NESW	
4887	RHORER, Jonathan	26	SWSW	1837-09-25	FD	SWSW	R:MORGAN
4988	RICE, Walter W	17	E½SE	1831-06-29	FD	E2SE	R:MORGAN
4989	RICE, Walter Wesley	20	E½NE	1835-07-14	FD	E2NE	R:MORGAN
4966	RICHARDSON, Solomon	30	SWNE	1836-01-15	FD	SWNE	R:MORGAN
4753	ROBERTS, Ephraim	18	W½NW	1827-11-07	FD	W2NW	R:MORGAN G:35
4909	ROGERS, Joseph	17	SESW	1834-12-11	FD	SESW	R:MORGAN
5016	ROGERS, William	10	E½SW	1826-11-20	FD	E2SW	R:MORGAN
5015	" "	10	E½NW	1830-03-05	FD	E2NW	R:MORGAN
4888	ROHER, Jonathan	26	NE	1832-04-19	FD	NE	R:MORGAN
4800	ROHRER, Jacob	9	E½SW	1826-11-20	FD	E2SW	R:MORGAN
4801	" "	9	W½NE	1826-11-20	FD	W2NE	R:MORGAN
4891	ROHRER, Jonathan	25	W½SW	1827-11-03	FD	W2SW	R:MORGAN
4892	" "	26	SE	1827-11-03	FD	SE	R:MORGAN
4893	" "	33	E½SE	1828-10-21	FD	E2SE	R:MORGAN
4897	" "	36	W½NW	1829-12-16	FD	W2NW	R:MORGAN
4895	" "	35	W½SE	1831-06-29	FD	W2SE	R:MORGAN
4890	" "	25	W½NW	1831-09-09	FD	W2NW	R:MORGAN
4894	" "	34	NENE	1833-01-05	FD	NENE	R:MORGAN
4889	" "	25	E½SW	1835-05-26	FD	E2SW	R:MORGAN
4896	" "	36	NWNE	1849-10-09	FD	NWNE	
4898	ROHRER, Jonathon	25	W½SE	1836-02-02	FD	W2SE	R:MORGAN
4900	" "	36	NENW	1836-02-02	FD	NENW	R:MORGAN
4899	" "	34	SEN½	1836-02-02	FD	S2NE	R:MORGAN
4871	ROSS, John	33	W½NE	1835-11-16	FD	W2NE	R:MORGAN
4980	ROSS, Thomas Pierson	33	NENW	1833-05-30	FD	NENW	R:MORGAN
4979	" "	32	NENW	1836-02-10	FD	NENW	
5017	" "	32	NENW	1836-02-10	FD	NENW	
5007	" "	32	NENW	1836-02-10	FD	NENW	
4948	ROSSON, Richard	32	N½SW	1854-09-23	FD	N2SW	R:MORGAN
4968	ROSSON, Staunton	29	SESE	1854-03-17	FD	SESE	R:MORGAN
4967	" "	28	SWSW	1854-03-17	FD	SWSW	R:MORGAN
4787	RUSSELL, Hezekiah	22	E½SW	1836-02-08	FD	E2SW	
4703	RYNDERS, Andrew	18	E½NE	1836-02-17	FD	E2NE	

ID	Individual in Patent	Sec.	Sec. Part	Purchase Date	Sale Type	IL Aliquot Part	For More Info . . .
4731	SALTER, Cleveland J	24	W½SE	1835-05-14	FD	W2SE	R:CONNECTICUT
4734	" "	25	W½NE	1835-05-14	FD	W2NE	R:CONNECTICUT
4733	" "	25	SENE	1835-05-14	FD	SENE	R:CONNECTICUT
4730	" "	2	N½	1835-05-14	FD	N2	R:CONNECTICUT
4729	" "	13	W½SE	1835-05-14	FD	W2SE	R:CONNECTICUT
4728	" "	12	E½	1835-05-14	FD	E2	R:CONNECTICUT
4727	" "	1	SE	1835-05-14	FD	SE	R:CONNECTICUT
4726	" "	1	N½	1835-05-14	FD	N2	R:CONNECTICUT
4725	" "	1	E½SW	1835-05-14	FD	E2SW	R:CONNECTICUT
4732	" "	25	E½SE	1838-01-16	FD	E2SE	R:MORGAN
4818	SALTER, James D B	25	NENE	1835-02-14	FD	NENE	R:NEW YORK CITY
4837	SALTER, Jane	11	E½SE	1835-02-14	FD	E2SE	R:NEW YORK CITY
4842	" "	3	E½SE	1835-02-14	FD	E2SE	R:NEW YORK CITY
4836	" "	1	W½SW	1835-02-14	FD	W2SW	R:NEW YORK CITY
4838	" "	12	W½	1835-02-14	FD	W2	R:NEW YORK CITY
4839	" "	2	E½SW	1835-02-14	FD	E2SW	R:NEW YORK CITY
4840	" "	2	NWSW	1835-02-14	FD	NWSW	R:NEW YORK CITY
4841	" "	2	SE	1835-02-14	FD	SE	R:NEW YORK CITY
4689	SAMPLE, Aaron	3	W½SW	1831-09-17	FD	W2SW	R:MORGAN
4688	" "	17	NWNW	1835-07-20	FD	NWNW	R:MORGAN
4705	SAMPLE, Andrew	9	E½NE	1831-08-31	FD	E2NE	R:MORGAN
4704	" "	17	NESW	1833-08-31	FD	NESW	R:MORGAN
4876	SAMPLE, Jacob	4	SESW	1835-10-12	FD	SESW	R:MORGAN
4803	" "	4	SESW	1835-10-12	FD	SESW	R:MORGAN
4802	" "	4	NWNE	1835-10-12	FD	NWNE	R:MORGAN
4919	SAMPLE, Light	29	NESE	1835-08-18	FD	NESE	R:MORGAN
4786	SANNDERSON, Henry	18	E½NW	1835-03-11	FD	E2NW	R:MORGAN
4782	SANNDERSON, Henry Jr	7	NWSE	1835-03-11	FD	NWSE	R:MORGAN
4783	" "	7	SWNE	1835-03-11	FD	SWNE	R:MORGAN
4719	SCOTT, Charles G	31	NENW	1835-07-14	FD	NENW	R:MORGAN
4943	SCOTT, Ranson B	17	W½NE	1836-02-17	FD	W2NE	
4983	SCOTT, Thomas	5	E½SW	1834-10-03	FD	E2SWBDNW	R:MORGAN
4986	SEVIDE, Valentine S	30	SWSW	1837-12-02	FD	SWSW	R:MORGAN
4714	SHURTLEFF, Benjamin	11	E½NW	1829-06-17	FD	E2NW	R:MORGAN G:112
4715	" "	11	W½SE	1830-02-12	FD	W2SE	R:MORGAN G:112
4714	SHURTLEFF, Lot	11	E½NW	1829-06-17	FD	E2NW	R:MORGAN G:112
4715	" "	11	W½SE	1830-02-12	FD	W2SE	R:MORGAN G:112
4925	SHURTLEFF, Milton	11	W½SW	1826-11-23	FD	W2SW	R:MORGAN
4926	" "	15	E½NW	1827-02-09	FD	E2NW	R:MORGAN
4927	SHURTLIFF, Milton	11	W½NW	1825-01-22	FD	W2NW	R:MORGAN
4707	SIMS, Austin	15	W½SE	1827-09-17	FD	W2SE	R:MADISON
4711	" "	23	W½SW	1827-11-09	FD	W2SW	R:MADISON
4708	" "	22	W½SE	1828-01-22	FD	W2SE	R:MORGAN
4710	" "	23	SESW	1833-07-29	FD	SESW	R:MORGAN
4709	" "	23	S½SE	1835-12-07	FD	S2SE	R:MORGAN
4834	SIMS, James	35	W½NW	1827-11-12	FD	W2NW	R:MORGAN
4964	SIMS, Silas	23	NENW	1832-10-06	FD	NENW	R:MORGAN
4754	SMITH, Evin	22	W½NE	1827-12-10	FD	W2NE	R:MORGAN
4804	SMITH, Jacob	3	E½NW	1832-12-17	FD	E2NW	R:MORGAN
4805	" "	4	NESW	1833-02-05	FD	NESW	R:MORGAN
4872	SMITH, John	14	E½SW	1831-05-16	FD	E2SW	R:MORGAN
4744	SPRINGER, Dennis	36	SENE	1849-09-19	FD	SENE	
4979	ST LEWIS, WILLIAM	32	NENW	1854-10-23	FD	NENW	R:MADISON
5018	" "	32	NWNE	1854-10-23	FD	NWNE	R:MADISON
5007	" "	32	NENW	1854-10-23	FD	NENW	R:MADISON
5008	" "	32	NWNE	1854-10-23	FD	NWNE	R:MADISON
5017	" "	32	NENW	1854-10-23	FD	NENW	R:MADISON
4883	STEEL, John Walker	27	SWNE	1837-12-25	FD	SWNE	R:MORGAN
4806	STEELE, James A	21	NWSW	1839-01-24	FD	NWSW	
4965	STODDARD, Solomon Cur	27	E½SW	1849-12-08	FD	E2SW	R:MORGAN
4876	STULL, John Truman	4	SESW	1836-06-16	FD	SESW	R:MORGAN
4803	" "	4	SESW	1836-06-16	FD	SESW	R:MORGAN
4738	TANNER, Cyrus	8	W½NE	1835-10-15	FD	W2NE	R:MORGAN
4902	TANNER, Joseph A	24	NENE	1835-05-14	FD	NENE	R:MORGAN
4901	" "	13	E½SE	1835-05-14	FD	E2SE	R:MORGAN
4903	" "	24	W½NE	1835-05-14	FD	W2NE	R:MORGAN
4904	TANNER, Joseph Allen	23	NESE	1835-08-08	FD	NESE	R:MORGAN
4962	TAYLOR, Samuel	30	SESW	1855-11-13	FD	SESW	R:MORGAN
4822	THOMAS, James F	35	SESE	1846-01-22	FD	SESE	
4910	THOMAS, Joseph	22	SWNW	1833-03-26	FD	SWNW	R:MORGAN
4873	THOMPSON, John	31		1833-03-05	FD	SWSWFS	R:MACOUPIN
4874	TOLKINTON, John	10	W½NW	1830-11-20	FD	W2NW	R:KENTUCKY
4875	" "	10	W½SW	1830-11-20	FD	W2SW	R:KENTUCKY

ID	Individual in Patent	Sec.	Sec. Part	Purchase Date	Sale Type	IL Aliquot Part	For More Info . . .
4706	TURNER, Andrew	22	E½SE	1827-11-09	FD	E2SE	R:MADISON
4713	TURNER, Avery	3	NE	1835-05-21	FD	NE	R:MORGAN G:128
4721	TURNER, Charles	28	NENE	1837-11-27	FD	NENE	R:MORGAN
4795	TURNER, Israel	23	W½NW	1827-11-03	FD	W2NW	R:MORGAN
4797	" "	29	E½NE	1830-12-24	FD	E2NE	R:MORGAN
4794	" "	23	NESW	1833-02-11	FD	NESW	R:MORGAN
4796	" "	27	NWNW	1835-12-07	FD	NWNW	R:MORGAN
4881	TURNER, John	33	W½SE	1828-10-22	FD	W2SE	R:MORGAN
4878	" "	21	E½NE	1828-11-05	FD	E2NE	R:MORGAN
4877	" "	15	W½SW	1828-11-05	FD	W2SW	R:MORGAN
4879	" "	22	NWNW	1833-09-17	FD	NWNW	R:MORGAN
4880	" "	30	NESW	1852-02-07	FD	NESW	
4713	TURNER, Jonathan B	3	NE	1835-05-21	FD	NE	R:MORGAN G:128
4885	" "	5	NESE	1836-04-25	FD	NESE	R:MORGAN G:56
4913	TURNER, Milton	36	SWSE	1848-02-03	FD	SWSE	
4928	" "	36	SESW	1848-02-03	FD	SESW	
4929	" "	36	SWSW	1848-02-03	FD	SWSW	
4935	TURNER, Nathan	15	E½SW	1827-11-27	FD	E2SW	R:MORGAN
4936	" "	22	E½NE	1827-11-27	FD	E2NE	R:MORGAN
4747	VANCIL, Edmund G	30	E½SE	1835-03-18	FD	E2SE	R:MACOUPIN
4882	VANWINKLE, John	5	NE	1831-08-20	FD	NE	R:MORGAN
4913	VEACH, Joshua	36	SWSE	1836-12-09	FD	SWSE	R:COLES
4929	" "	36	SWSE	1836-12-09	FD	SWSE	R:COLES
4743	WATKINS, David	17	E½NE	1830-02-23	FD	E2NE	R:MORGAN
4911	WESSON, Joseph	30	NENW	1836-02-27	FD	NENW	
4869	WHITE, John Rendell	2	SWSW	1834-05-23	FD	SWSW	R:MORGAN
4951	WHITEAKER, Robert	35	E½NW	1825-10-13	FD	E2NW	R:GREENE
4952	" "	35	W½NE	1825-10-13	FD	W2NE	R:GREENE
4693	WHITEHEAD, Abraham	14	SENE	1834-05-30	FD	SENE	R:MORGAN
4695	" "	4	NENE	1835-10-14	FD	NENE	R:MORGAN G:85
4694	" "	4	W½NE	1835-10-14	FD	W2NE	R:MORGAN
4720	WINSLOW, Charles P	5	NESW	1837-07-28	FD	NESW	R:MORGAN
4716	WOOD, Blatchley C	16	L9	1835-11-21	SC	LOT9	
4835	WOOD, James	35	NESE	1846-01-22	FD	NESE	
4995	WOOD, William C	4	NESE	1833-09-23	FD	NESE	R:MORGAN
4996	WOODS, William C	6	E½NE	1835-10-09	FD	E2NE	R:MORGAN
4691	WRIGHT, Abner	7	NWNW	1833-11-12	FD	NWNW	R:MORGAN
4692	" "	7	SW	1835-09-28	FD	SW	R:MORGAN
4690	" "	19	W½NE	1835-11-12	FD	W2NE	R:MORGAN
4985	WRIGHT, Thomas	18	W½SE	1830-02-01	FD	W2SE	R:MORGAN
4984	" "	18	SWNE	1835-07-06	FD	SWNE	R:MORGAN
4701	YORK, Alfred	32	E½NE	1835-10-05	FD	E2NE	R:MORGAN

Patent Map

T13-N R8-W
3rd PM Meridian

Map Group 19

Township Statistics

Parcels Mapped	:	346
Number of Patents	:	1
Number of Individuals	:	219
Patentees Identified	:	216
Number of Surnames	:	142
Multi-Patentee Parcels	:	16
Oldest Patent Date	:	12/28/1821
Most Recent Patent	:	5/30/1856
Block/Lot Parcels	:	20
Cities and Towns	:	4
Cemeteries	:	8

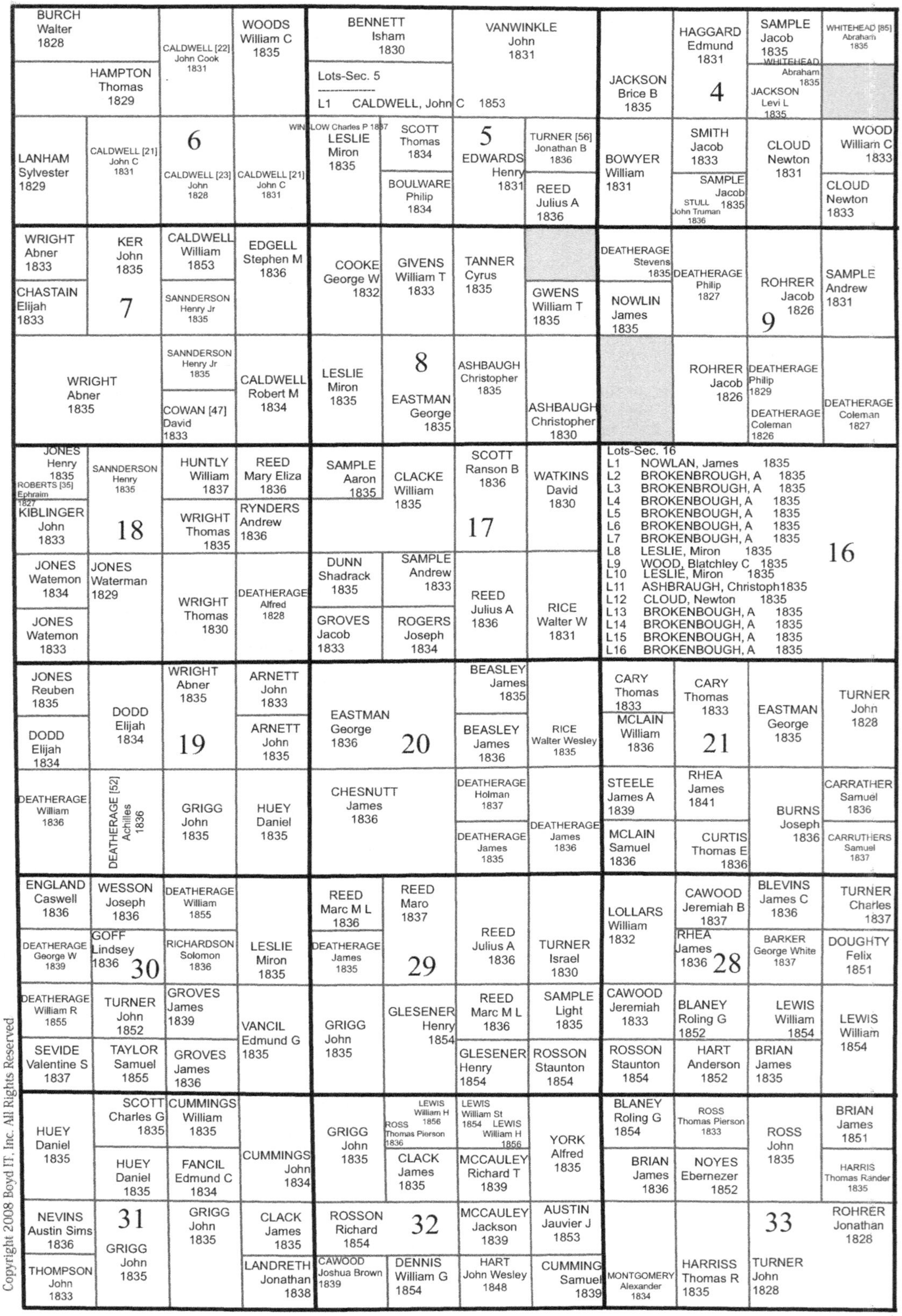

BOWYER William 1831	SMITH Jacob 1832	TURNER [128] Avery 1835 **3**	SALTER Cleveland J 1835 **2**		**1**	SALTER Cleveland J 1835
SAMPLE Aaron 1831	DEATHERAGE [53] George 1831	EASTMAN George 1835 / DEATHERAGE [52] Achelas 1833 / SALTER Jane 1835	SALTER Jane 1835 / WHITE John Rendell 1834	SALTER Jane 1835	SALTER Jane 1835	SALTER Jane 1835 / SALTER Cleveland J 1835

Sangamon

Morgan

SALTER Cleveland J 1835

Section 10 / 11 / 12 / 15 / 14 / 13

TOLKINTON John 1830 · ROGERS William 1830 · DEATHERAGE Achelas 1829 · KILPATRICK Ephraim 1829 · SHURTLIFF Milton 1825 · SHURTLEFF [112] Benjamin 1829 · COOKE George W 1831 · **11**

TOLKINTON John 1830 · ROGERS William 1826 · **10** · DEATHERAGE [53] George 1826 · SHURTLEFF Milton 1826 · COOKE George W 1831 · SHURTLEFF [112] Benjamin 1830 · SALTER Jane 1835

SALTER Jane 1835 **12**

DEATHERAGE Coleman 1831 · SHURTLEFF Milton 1827 · LOVE John 1825 **15** · LOVE John 1827 · COOKE George W 1831 · LOVE John 1831 · COOKE George W 1831 / WHITEHEAD Abraham 1834 · CATLIN [30] Joel 1835 **13**

TURNER Nathan 1827 · SIMS Austin 1827 · LOVE John 1826 · LOVE John 1826 · SMITH John 1831 · CARUTHERS James 1827 · CARUTHERS James 1831 · CARUTHERS Samuel 1834 · BALDWIN Richard C 1835 · SALTER Cleveland J 1835 · TANNER Joseph 1835

TURNER John 1828 **14**

Section 22 / 23 / 24 / 27 / 26 / 25

TURNER John 1833 / THOMAS Joseph 1833 · ARMSTRONG Thomas 1830 · SMITH Evin 1827 · TURNER Nathan 1827 · TURNER Israel 1827 · SIMS Silas 1832 · ARMSTRONG Hugh M 1833 · CAMPBELL William 1833 · TANNER Joseph A 1835 · TANNER Joseph A 1835 / CAMPBELL William 1833

ARMSTRONG Hugh M 1833 · MEADOWS Francis J 1833

24

CHAPMAN Isaac 1837 · RUSSELL Hezekiah 1836 **22** · SIMS Austin 1828 · TURNER Andrew 1827 · SIMS Austin 1827 · TURNER Israel 1833 · **23** (No Patents Found) · TANNER Joseph Allen 1835 · SIMS Austin 1833 · SIMS Austin 1835 · BALDWIN Richard C 1835 · SALTER Cleveland J 1835 · PEARCY Henry 1828

TURNER Israel 1835 · HUTCHESON James 1833 · HUTCHESON James 1833 · MAUPIN Fleming Cobbs 1831 · LONDON James 1832 · ROHER Jonathan 1832 · ROHRER Jonathan 1831 · SALTER Cleveland J 1835 · SALTER James D B 1835

DOUGHTY Felix 1851 · BEFON Henry 00/3 · STEEL John Walker 1837 · MAUPIN Fleming Cobbs 1831 **27** · **26** · BALDWIN Richard C 1835 **25** · SALTER Cleveland J 1835

DOUGHTY Felix 1851 · DURYEE John Richard 1839 · ALLIS Stephen G 1838 · MAUPIN Flemming C 1836 · LONDON James 1827 · ROHRER Jonathan 1827 · ROHRER Jonathan 1827 · ROHRER Jonathan 1836 · SALTER Cleveland J 1838

STODDARD Solomon Cur 1849 · HAMMER Henry 1835 · RHORER Jonathan 1837 · ROHRER Jonathan 1835

Section 34 / 35 / 36

HART Henry 1835 **34** · GOFF Aaron 1835 · ROHRER Jonathan 1833 · ROHRER Jonathan 1836 · SIMS James 1827 · WHITEAKER Robert 1825 · WHITEAKER Robert 1825 · BLANEY John 1828 · ROHRER Jonathan 1829 · ROHRER Jonathan 1836 · ROHRER Jonathan 1849 · COULEE Josiah 1847

GOFF Aaron 1835 · REYNOLDS Joseph 1852 · SPRINGER Dennis 1849 **36**

35

DYER William 1827 · BROWN Samuel Jr 1835 · BROWN Joseph 1821 · BROWN Samuel Jr 1832 · HART Henry Philip 1821 · ENGLAND William 1827 · LOGSDON Joseph 1828 · ROHRER Jonathan 1831 · WOOD James 1846 · THOMAS James F 1846 · BLANEY John 1836 · CONLEE Isaac 1849 · BRIAN Thomas Jeffers 1849 · BRIAN William W 1848 · TURNER Milton 1848 / VEACH Joshua 1836 · BRIAN James Lafayet 1848

Helpful Hints

1. This Map's INDEX can be found on the preceding pages.

2. Refer to Map "C" to see where this Township lies within Morgan County, Illinois.

3. Numbers within square brackets [ ] denote a multi-patentee land parcel (multi-owner). Refer to Appendix "C" for a full list of members in this group.

4. Areas that look to be crowded with Patentees usually indicate multiple sales of the same parcel (re-issues), cancellations or voided transactions (that we map, anyway) or overlapping parcels. We opt to show even these ambiguous parcels, which oftentimes lead to research avenues not yet taken.

Legend

— Patent Boundary

— Section Boundary

▨ No Patents Found (or Outside County)

1., 2., 3., ... Lot Numbers (when beside a name)

[ ] Group Number (see Appendix "C")

Scale: Section = 1 mile X 1 mile (generally, with some exceptions)

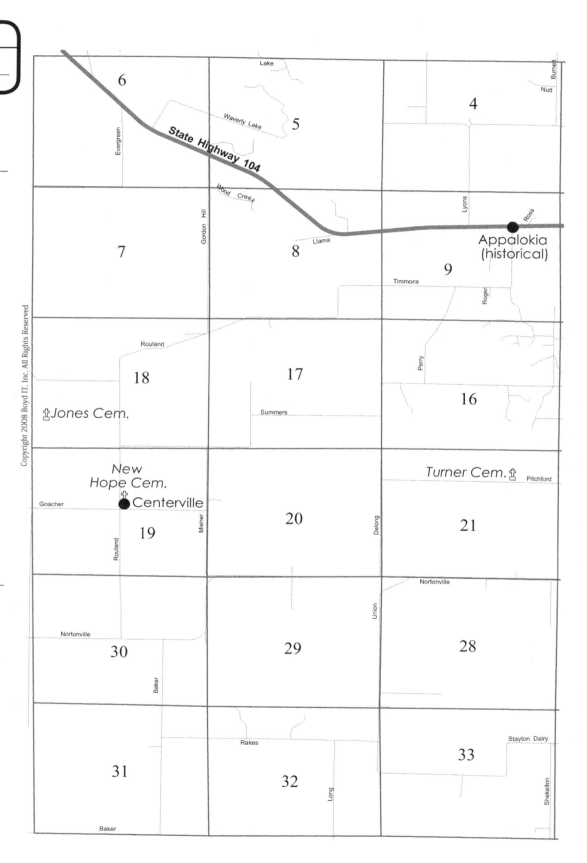

Road Map

T13-N R8-W
3rd PM Meridian

Map Group 19

Cities & Towns
Appalokia (historical)
Centerville
Rohrer
Waverly

Cemeteries
Allis Cemetery
Conlee Cemetery
East Cemetery
Jones Cemetery
New Hope Cemetery
Rogers Cemetery
Saint Sebastians Cemetery
Turner Cemetery

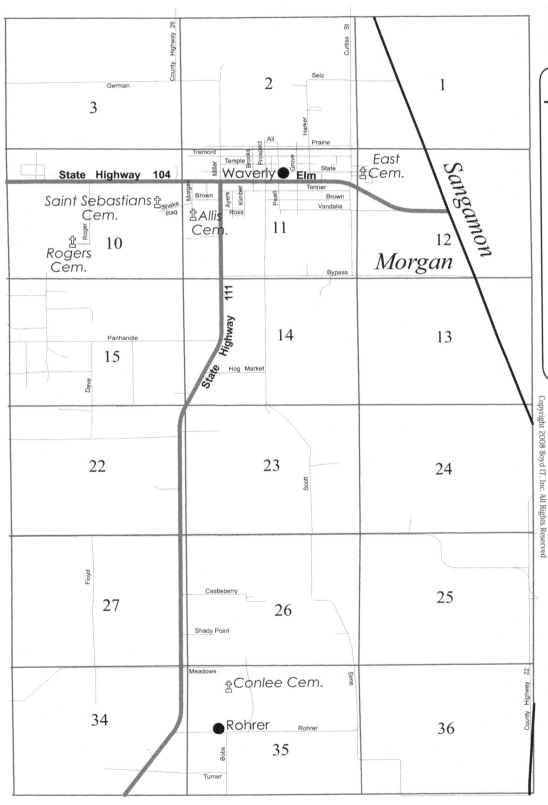

County Highway 26

German

3

2

Seiz

1

Curtiss St

All

Prairie

Harker

Tremont

Temple

Prospect

Miller

Brooks

State Highway 104

Waverly ● Elm

East
✝ Cem.

Saint Sebastians ✝
Cem.   ✝ Shake
              Rag

Morgan

Brown

Kimber

Ayers

Ross

Pearl

Grove

State

Tanner

Brown

Vandalia

✝ Allis
Cem.

Roger

10

11

12

Rogers
Cem.

Bypass

Morgan

State Highway 111

Panhandle

15

14

13

Dave

Hog Market

22

23

24

Scott

Floyd

Castleberry

27

26

25

Shady Point

Meadows

✝ *Conlee Cem.*

Sims

34

● Rohrer

Rohrer

36

Bobs

35

Turner

Sangamon

County Highway 22

Copyright 2008 Boyd IT. Inc. All Rights Reserved

Helpful Hints

1. This road map has a number of uses, but primarily it is to help you: a) find the present location of land owned by your ancestors (at least the general area), b) find cemeteries and city-centers, and c) estimate the route/roads used by Census-takers & tax-assessors.

2. If you plan to travel to Morgan County to locate cemeteries or land parcels, please pick up a modern travel map for the area before you do. Mapping old land parcels on modern maps is not as exact a science as you might think. Just the slightest variations in public land survey coordinates, estimates of parcel boundaries, or road-map deviations can greatly alter a map's representation of how a road either does or doesn't cross a particular parcel of land.

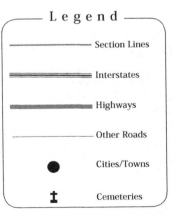

Legend

—————— Section Lines

══════ Interstates

—————— Highways

—————— Other Roads

● Cities/Towns

✝ Cemeteries

Scale: Section = 1 mile X 1 mile
(generally, with some exceptions)

Historical Map

T13-N R8-W
3rd PM Meridian

Map Group 19

Cities & Towns
Appalokia (historical)
Centerville
Rohrer
Waverly

Cemeteries
Allis Cemetery
Conlee Cemetery
East Cemetery
Jones Cemetery
Rogers Cemetery
Saint Sebastians Cemetery
Turner Cemetery
New Hope Cemetery

6	5 Waverly Lake	4
7	8	Appalokia (historical) ● 9
18 Jones Cem.	17	16
New Hope Cem. ● Centerville 19	20	Turner Cem. 21
30	29	28
Apple Creek 31	32	33

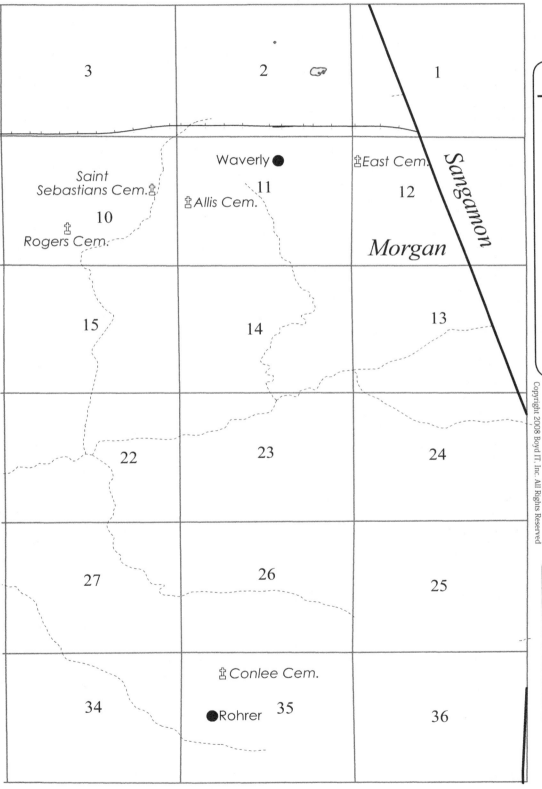

Helpful Hints

1. This Map takes a different look at the same Congressional Township displayed in the preceding two maps. It presents features that can help you better envision the historical development of the area: a) Water-bodies (lakes & ponds), b) Water-courses (rivers, streams, etc.), c) Railroads, d) City/town center-points (where they were oftentimes located when first settled), and e) Cemeteries.

2. Using this "Historical" map in tandem with this Township's Patent Map and Road Map, may lead you to some interesting discoveries. You will often find roads, towns, cemeteries, and waterways are named after nearby landowners: sometimes those names will be the ones you are researching. See how many of these research gems you can find here in Morgan County.

Legend

————	Section Lines
＋＋＋＋＋	Railroads
▭	Large Rivers & Bodies of Water
- - - - -	Streams/Creeks & Small Rivers
●	Cities/Towns
✝	Cemeteries

Scale: Section = 1 mile X 1 mile
(there are some exceptions)

267

Appendices

Appendix A - Illinois Archives Abbreviations

The following abbreviations are used by the Illinois State Archives in describing the nature and locations of the land-patents in their "Tract Indexes" at www.cyberdriveillinois.com. Most line-items in the Patent Indexes in this volume will contain one or more of these abbreviations. When multiple abbreviations are used, no space will be found between each (and that can sometimes be confusing). Many of these are fairly easy to decipher, but many ambiguities exist. Only after reviewing a copy of the original land-patent can one be certain of the meaning of any given abbreviations.

Abbrev.	Description	Abbrev.	Description
A	assumed	COM	Commission(er)(s)
AA	acres assumed	COR	corner
AB	Alton & Shelbyville Railroad	CP	captive
AC	act	CPE	cape
AD	addition	CR	corner
AG	Agricultural College	CT	cattle
AI	alias	CY	city
AL	others	D	deceased veteran of War of 1812
AM	Alton & Mt. Carmel Railroad	DANE CNTY	Dane County
AN	Administrator	DD	date-of-deed
APR	Apple River	DE	date
AR	Army	DESR	Des Plaines River
ART	artillery	DG	DuPage
AS	assignee	DH	detached
ASC	associate	DI	description
ASM	assemble	DIIO	description incomplete
ASS	association	DINT	description notation
AT	attorney (lawyer)	DIV	division
AW	Alton & Shawneetown Railroad	DO	donation
B	block, outblock, inblock, bank	DP	date-of-purchase
BAP	Baptist	DPT	detached part
BET	between	DQ	DuQuoin
BL	block, outblock, inblock, boundary line	DR	doctor
BMR	Big Muddy River	DS	discount
BNK	bank	DT	district
BO	board	DU	Dutch
BR	British	E	East
BRO	brothers	E2	East half
BT	Baptist	EC	excess
BUXTON ISL	Buxton Island	EDGE	Edgewood
C	claim	EL	Eldena
CA	Catholic	EMP	emporium
CALR	Calumet River	END	end
CARB	carbon	EP	Episcopal
CE	center	ES	estate
CEM	cemetery	ET	and
CEN	central	ET AL	and others
CENT	Centralia	ETG	unknown symbol meaning
CFT	counterfeit	EV	Evangelical
CG	Congregation(al)	EX	executor
CH	Church	EXCPT	except
CHI	Chicago	F	feet
CHR	Christian	FD	federal
CI	Centralia	FEED	feeder
CK	creek	FEL	Fellons
CL	college	FFR	forfeited land redeemed
CM	Commerce Street, County Microfilm	FK	Franklin Street
CN	canal	FL	float
CNTY	county	FNB	First National Bank
CO	company	FO	forgery

Abbrev.	Description	Abbrev.	Description
FOR	Forrestor	MA	money assumed
FR	fractional	MAIN	main
FS	forfeited land stock	MANT	Manteno
FT	first	MANUF	manufacture(r)(s)(ing)
FUL	Fulton	MARS	Marshal(l)
FV	Fox River	MATT	Matthiessen
FX	Fox River	ME	Methodist
GAL	Galena	MID	middle
GD	guard	MIN	mining
GEN	General	MISSR	Mississippi River
GER	German	MLK	Milwaukee
GIR	Girardeau	MNLD	mainland
GLD	gold	MO	Missouri
GN	guardian	MT	military tract
GR	grand	MU	Minuscule
GT	Gratiot Street	N	North
H	heir of deceased veteran of War of 1812	N2	North half
HEG	Hegeler	NAT	national
HO	house	NE	Northeast
HR	heir or heirs	NEG	Negro
HS	Homestead	NM	name
I	initials	NMA	name assumed
IBL	Indian boundary line	NO	number
IC	included	NR	Nora
IL	inlot	NT	note
ILL	Illinois	NW	Northwest
ILLR	Illinois River	OA	Ottawa
IM	improvement	OD	Odin
IN	Indian	OF	office
INST	institute	OL	outlot
IO	incomplete	OT	original town
IR	Iroquois River	P	[unknown currency]
ISL	island	PA	paper
JL	Joliet	PE	Presbyterian
JOHNS ISL	Johns Island	PECK	Pecatonica River
JR	Junior	PEN	Pennsylvannia
KA	Kankakee	PET	petroleum
KANKR	Kankakee River	PLK	plank
KNOX CNTY	Knox County	PM	[unknown currency]
KP	Kappa	PNT	patent
KSRR	Kaskaskia River	PR	Plum River
L	lot, outlot, inlot, line	PRA	prairie
LA	Loda	PRE	pre-emption
LD	land	PRES	president
LG	lodge	PT	part
LI	listed	PY	payment
LIB	liberal	R	river
LK	Lake	RAILRD	railroad
LL	little	RC	recorded
LNT	Lieutenant	RD	railroad
LO	lot, outlot, inlot	RE	reservation
LOC	locust	REL	real
LOCK	lock	REV	ecclesiastical title, Reverend, Bishop, etc.
LP	Lockport	RI	reinstated
LS	(military) land scrip or LaSalle	RIC	Richview
LT	left	RIP	ripple
LU	Lutheran	RL	release
LUT	Lutheran	RM	redeemed
M	money		

Abbrev.	Description
RO	Roman
RP	receipt
RQ	relinquished
RR	Rock River or railroad
RS	residence
RT	right
RTW	right of way
RV	reserved
S	South
S2	South half
SA	saline
SAND	Sandoval
SANGR	Sangamon River
SC	section or school
SD	side
SE	Southeast
SECT	section (640 acres)
SEN	senior
SH	Shawneetown
SIDE	side
SIL	silver
SK	stock
SL	saline, slough or sublot
SM	seminary
SN	senior
SOC	society
SPR	Spoon River
SR	Sugar River
ST	state
STC	St. Charles
STCK	Stillman Creek
STIS	St. Isadore (Church)
STP	St. Paul
STPET	St. Peter
SUBD	subdivision
SUP	Superintendent
SURV	survey
SW	Southwest or swamp
SX	settlement
SY	sale
TAB	tabernacle
TB	timber
TE	treaty
TF	transferred
TIMLT	timberlot
TN	town
TOL	Tolono
TOW	tower
TR	trustees
TRA	transportation
TS	township
TT	tract
TX	tax
TY	treasury
UN	Unitarian
UNKWN	Unknown
V	void, canceled, etc.
VC	Vincennes
VI	village

Abbrev.	Description
VO	void, canceled, etc.
VOID	void, canceled, etc.
W	West
W2	West half
WA	warrant
WAR	CNTY Warren County
WB	Wabash
WP	Wapella
WT	Water Street
X	exclusive

Appendix B - Section Parts (Aliquot Parts)

The following represent the various abbreviations we have found thus far in describing the parts of a Public Land Section. Some of these are very obscure and rarely used, but we wanted to list them for just that reason. A full section is 1 square mile or 640 acres.

Section Part	Description	Acres
<none>	Full Acre (if no Section Part is listed, presumed a full Section)	640
<1-??>	A number represents a Lot Number and can be of various sizes	?
E½	East Half-Section	320
E½E½	East Half of East Half-Section	160
E½E½SE	East Half of East Half of Southeast Quarter-Section	40
E½N½	East Half of North Half-Section	160
E½NE	East Half of Northeast Quarter-Section	80
E½NENE	East Half of Northeast Quarter of Northeast Quarter-Section	20
E½NENW	East Half of Northeast Quarter of Northwest Quarter-Section	20
E½NESE	East Half of Northeast Quarter of Southeast Quarter-Section	20
E½NESW	East Half of Northeast Quarter of Southwest Quarter-Section	20
E½NW	East Half of Northwest Quarter-Section	80
E½NWNE	East Half of Northwest Quarter of Northeast Quarter-Section	20
E½NWNW	East Half of Northwest Quarter of Northwest Quarter-Section	20
E½NWSE	East Half of Northwest Quarter of Southeast Quarter-Section	20
E½NWSW	East Half of Northwest Quarter of Southwest Quarter-Section	20
E½S½	East Half of South Half-Section	160
E½SE	East Half of Southeast Quarter-Section	80
E½SENE	East Half of Southeast Quarter of Northeast Quarter-Section	20
E½SENW	East Half of Southeast Quarter of Northwest Quarter-Section	20
E½SESE	East Half of Southeast Quarter of Southeast Quarter-Section	20
E½SESW	East Half of Southeast Quarter of Southwest Quarter-Section	20
E½SW	East Half of Southwest Quarter-Section	80
E½SWNE	East Half of Southwest Quarter of Northeast Quarter-Section	20
E½SWNW	East Half of Southwest Quarter of Northwest Quarter-Section	20
E½SWSE	East Half of Southwest Quarter of Southeast Quarter-Section	20
E½SWSW	East Half of Southwest Quarter of Southwest Quarter-Section	20
E½W½	East Half of West Half-Section	160
N½	North Half-Section	320
N½E½NE	North Half of East Half of Northeast Quarter-Section	40
N½E½NW	North Half of East Half of Northwest Quarter-Section	40
N½E½SE	North Half of East Half of Southeast Quarter-Section	40
N½E½SW	North Half of East Half of Southwest Quarter-Section	40
N½N½	North Half of North Half-Section	160
N½NE	North Half of Northeast Quarter-Section	80
N½NENE	North Half of Northeast Quarter of Northeast Quarter-Section	20
N½NENW	North Half of Northeast Quarter of Northwest Quarter-Section	20
N½NESE	North Half of Northeast Quarter of Southeast Quarter-Section	20
N½NESW	North Half of Northeast Quarter of Southwest Quarter-Section	20
N½NW	North Half of Northwest Quarter-Section	80
N½NWNE	North Half of Northwest Quarter of Northeast Quarter-Section	20
N½NWNW	North Half of Northwest Quarter of Northwest Quarter-Section	20
N½NWSE	North Half of Northwest Quarter of Southeast Quarter-Section	20
N½NWSW	North Half of Northwest Quarter of Southwest Quarter-Section	20
N½S½	North Half of South Half-Section	160
N½SE	North Half of Southeast Quarter-Section	80
N½SENE	North Half of Southeast Quarter of Northeast Quarter-Section	20
N½SENW	North Half of Southeast Quarter of Northwest Quarter-Section	20
N½SESE	North Half of Southeast Quarter of Southeast Quarter-Section	20

Section Part	Description	Acres
N½SESW	North Half of Southeast Quarter of Southwest Quarter-Section	20
N½SESW	North Half of Southeast Quarter of Southwest Quarter-Section	20
N½SW	North Half of Southwest Quarter-Section	80
N½SWNE	North Half of Southwest Quarter of Northeast Quarter-Section	20
N½SWNW	North Half of Southwest Quarter of Northwest Quarter-Section	20
N½SWSE	North Half of Southwest Quarter of Southeast Quarter-Section	20
N½SWSE	North Half of Southwest Quarter of Southeast Quarter-Section	20
N½SWSW	North Half of Southwest Quarter of Southwest Quarter-Section	20
N½W½NW	North Half of West Half of Northwest Quarter-Section	40
N½W½SE	North Half of West Half of Southeast Quarter-Section	40
N½W½SW	North Half of West Half of Southwest Quarter-Section	40
NE	Northeast Quarter-Section	160
NEN½	Northeast Quarter of North Half-Section	80
NENE	Northeast Quarter of Northeast Quarter-Section	40
NENENE	Northeast Quarter of Northeast Quarter of Northeast Quarter	10
NENENW	Northeast Quarter of Northeast Quarter of Northwest Quarter	10
NENESE	Northeast Quarter of Northeast Quarter of Southeast Quarter	10
NENESW	Northeast Quarter of Northeast Quarter of Southwest Quarter	10
NENW	Northeast Quarter of Northwest Quarter-Section	40
NENWNE	Northeast Quarter of Northwest Quarter of Northeast Quarter	10
NENWNW	Northeast Quarter of Northwest Quarter of Northwest Quarter	10
NENWSE	Northeast Quarter of Northwest Quarter of Southeast Quarter	10
NENWSW	Northeast Quarter of Northwest Quarter of Southwest Quarter	10
NESE	Northeast Quarter of Southeast Quarter-Section	40
NESENE	Northeast Quarter of Southeast Quarter of Northeast Quarter	10
NESENW	Northeast Quarter of Southeast Quarter of Northwest Quarter	10
NESESE	Northeast Quarter of Southeast Quarter of Southeast Quarter	10
NESESW	Northeast Quarter of Southeast Quarter of Southwest Quarter	10
NESW	Northeast Quarter of Southwest Quarter-Section	40
NESWNE	Northeast Quarter of Southwest Quarter of Northeast Quarter	10
NESWNW	Northeast Quarter of Southwest Quarter of Northwest Quarter	10
NESWSE	Northeast Quarter of Southwest Quarter of Southeast Quarter	10
NESWSW	Northeast Quarter of Southwest Quarter of Southwest Quarter	10
NW	Northwest Quarter-Section	160
NWE½	Northwest Quarter of Eastern Half-Section	80
NWN½	Northwest Quarter of North Half-Section	80
NWNE	Northwest Quarter of Northeast Quarter-Section	40
NWNENE	Northwest Quarter of Northeast Quarter of Northeast Quarter	10
NWNENW	Northwest Quarter of Northeast Quarter of Northwest Quarter	10
NWNESE	Northwest Quarter of Northeast Quarter of Southeast Quarter	10
NWNESW	Northwest Quarter of Northeast Quarter of Southwest Quarter	10
NWNW	Northwest Quarter of Northwest Quarter-Section	40
NWNWNE	Northwest Quarter of Northwest Quarter of Northeast Quarter	10
NWNWNW	Northwest Quarter of Northwest Quarter of Northwest Quarter	10
NWNWSE	Northwest Quarter of Northwest Quarter of Southeast Quarter	10
NWNWSW	Northwest Quarter of Northwest Quarter of Southwest Quarter	10
NWSE	Northwest Quarter of Southeast Quarter-Section	40
NWSENE	Northwest Quarter of Southeast Quarter of Northeast Quarter	10
NWSENW	Northwest Quarter of Southeast Quarter of Northwest Quarter	10
NWSESE	Northwest Quarter of Southeast Quarter of Southeast Quarter	10
NWSESW	Northwest Quarter of Southeast Quarter of Southwest Quarter	10
NWSW	Northwest Quarter of Southwest Quarter-Section	40
NWSWNE	Northwest Quarter of Southwest Quarter of Northeast Quarter	10
NWSWNW	Northwest Quarter of Southwest Quarter of Northwest Quarter	10
NWSWSE	Northwest Quarter of Southwest Quarter of Southeast Quarter	10
NWSWSW	Northwest Quarter of Southwest Quarter of Southwest Quarter	10
S½	South Half-Section	320
S½E½NE	South Half of East Half of Northeast Quarter-Section	40
S½E½NW	South Half of East Half of Northwest Quarter-Section	40
S½E½SE	South Half of East Half of Southeast Quarter-Section	40

Section Part	Description	Acres
S½E½SW	South Half of East Half of Southwest Quarter-Section	40
S½N½	South Half of North Half-Section	160
S½NE	South Half of Northeast Quarter-Section	80
S½NENE	South Half of Northeast Quarter of Northeast Quarter-Section	20
S½NENW	South Half of Northeast Quarter of Northwest Quarter-Section	20
S½NESE	South Half of Northeast Quarter of Southeast Quarter-Section	20
S½NESW	South Half of Northeast Quarter of Southwest Quarter-Section	20
S½NW	South Half of Northwest Quarter-Section	80
S½NWNE	South Half of Northwest Quarter of Northeast Quarter-Section	20
S½NWNW	South Half of Northwest Quarter of Northwest Quarter-Section	20
S½NWSE	South Half of Northwest Quarter of Southeast Quarter-Section	20
S½NWSW	South Half of Northwest Quarter of Southwest Quarter-Section	20
S½S½	South Half of South Half-Section	160
S½SE	South Half of Southeast Quarter-Section	80
S½SENE	South Half of Southeast Quarter of Northeast Quarter-Section	20
S½SENW	South Half of Southeast Quarter of Northwest Quarter-Section	20
S½SESE	South Half of Southeast Quarter of Southeast Quarter-Section	20
S½SESW	South Half of Southeast Quarter of Southwest Quarter-Section	20
S½SESW	South Half of Southeast Quarter of Southwest Quarter-Section	20
S½SW	South Half of Southwest Quarter-Section	80
S½SWNE	South Half of Southwest Quarter of Northeast Quarter-Section	20
S½SWNW	South Half of Southwest Quarter of Northwest Quarter-Section	20
S½SWSE	South Half of Southwest Quarter of Southeast Quarter-Section	20
S½SWSE	South Half of Southwest Quarter of Southeast Quarter-Section	20
S½SWSW	South Half of Southwest Quarter of Southwest Quarter-Section	20
S½W½NE	South Half of West Half of Northeast Quarter-Section	40
S½W½NW	South Half of West Half of Northwest Quarter-Section	40
S½W½SE	South Half of West Half of Southeast Quarter-Section	40
S½W½SW	South Half of West Half of Southwest Quarter-Section	40
SE	Southeast Quarter Section	160
SEN½	Southeast Quarter of North Half-Section	80
SENE	Southeast Quarter of Northeast Quarter-Section	40
SENENE	Southeast Quarter of Northeast Quarter of Northeast Quarter	10
SENENW	Southeast Quarter of Northeast Quarter of Northwest Quarter	10
SENESE	Southeast Quarter of Northeast Quarter of Southeast Quarter	10
SENESW	Southeast Quarter of Northeast Quarter of Southwest Quarter	10
SENW	Southeast Quarter of Northwest Quarter-Section	40
SENWNE	Southeast Quarter of Northwest Quarter of Northeast Quarter	10
SENWNW	Southeast Quarter of Northwest Quarter of Northwest Quarter	10
SENWSE	Souteast Quarter of Northwest Quarter of Southeast Quarter	10
SENWSW	Southeast Quarter of Northwest Quarter of Southwest Quarter	10
SESE	Southeast Quarter of Southeast Quarter-Section	40
SESENE	SoutheastQuarter of Southeast Quarter of Northeast Quarter	10
SESENW	Southeast Quarter of Southeast Quarter of Northwest Quarter	10
SESESE	Southeast Quarter of Southeast Quarter of Southeast Quarter	10
SESESW	Southeast Quarter of Southeast Quarter of Southwest Quarter	10
SESW	Southeast Quarter of Southwest Quarter-Section	40
SESWNE	Southeast Quarter of Southwest Quarter of Northeast Quarter	10
SESWNW	Southeast Quarter of Southwest Quarter of Northwest Quarter	10
SESWSE	Southeast Quarter of Southwest Quarter of Southeast Quarter	10
SESWSW	Southeast Quarter of Southwest Quarter of Southwest Quarter	10
SW	Southwest Quarter-Section	160
SWNE	Southwest Quarter of Northeast Quarter-Section	40
SWNENE	Southwest Quarter of Northeast Quarter of Northeast Quarter	10
SWNENW	Southwest Quarter of Northeast Quarter of Northwest Quarter	10
SWNESE	Southwest Quarter of Northeast Quarter of Southeast Quarter	10
SWNESW	Southwest Quarter of Northeast Quarter of Southwest Quarter	10
SWNW	Southwest Quarter of Northwest Quarter-Section	40
SWNWNE	Southwest Quarter of Northwest Quarter of Northeast Quarter	10
SWNWNW	Southwest Quarter of Northwest Quarter of Northwest Quarter	10

Section Part	Description	Acres
SWNWSE	Southwest Quarter of Northwest Quarter of Southeast Quarter	10
SWNWSW	Southwest Quarter of Northwest Quarter of Southwest Quarter	10
SWSE	Southwest Quarter of Southeast Quarter-Section	40
SWSENE	Southwest Quarter of Southeast Quarter of Northeast Quarter	10
SWSENW	Southwest Quarter of Southeast Quarter of Northwest Quarter	10
SWSESE	Southwest Quarter of Southeast Quarter of Southeast Quarter	10
SWSESW	Southwest Quarter of Southeast Quarter of Southwest Quarter	10
SWSW	Southwest Quarter of Southwest Quarter-Section	40
SWSWNE	Southwest Quarter of Southwest Quarter of Northeast Quarter	10
SWSWNW	Southwest Quarter of Southwest Quarter of Northwest Quarter	10
SWSWSE	Southwest Quarter of Southwest Quarter of Southeast Quarter	10
SWSWSW	Southwest Quarter of Southwest Quarter of Southwest Quarter	10
W½	West Half-Section	320
W½E½	West Half of East Half-Section	160
W½N½	West Half of North Half-Section (same as NW)	160
W½NE	West Half of Northeast Quarter	80
W½NENE	West Half of Northeast Quarter of Northeast Quarter-Section	20
W½NENW	West Half of Northeast Quarter of Northwest Quarter-Section	20
W½NESE	West Half of Northeast Quarter of Southeast Quarter-Section	20
W½NESW	West Half of Northeast Quarter of Southwest Quarter-Section	20
W½NW	West Half of Northwest Quarter-Section	80
W½NWNE	West Half of Northwest Quarter of Northeast Quarter-Section	20
W½NWNW	West Half of Northwest Quarter of Northwest Quarter-Section	20
W½NWSE	West Half of Northwest Quarter of Southeast Quarter-Section	20
W½NWSW	West Half of Northwest Quarter of Southwest Quarter-Section	20
W½S½	West Half of South Half-Section	160
W½SE	West Half of Southeast Quarter-Section	80
W½SENE	West Half of Southeast Quarter of Northeast Quarter-Section	20
W½SENW	West Half of Southeast Quarter of Northwest Quarter-Section	20
W½SESE	West Half of Southeast Quarter of Southeast Quarter-Section	20
W½SESW	West Half of Southeast Quarter of Southwest Quarter-Section	20
W½SW	West Half of Southwest Quarter-Section	80
W½SWNE	West Half of Southwest Quarter of Northeast Quarter-Section	20
W½SWNW	West Half of Southwest Quarter of Northwest Quarter-Section	20
W½SWSE	West Half of Southwest Quarter of Southeast Quarter-Section	20
W½SWSW	West Half of Southwest Quarter of Southwest Quarter-Section	20
W½W½	West Half of West Half-Section	160

Appendix C - Multi-Patentee Groups

The following index presents groups of people who jointly received patents in Morgan County, Illinois. The Group Numbers are used in the Patent Maps and their Indexes so that you may then turn to this Appendix in order to identify all the members of the each buying group.

Group Number 1
AUSEMNS, F; SHARTZER, Ben

Group Number 2
AYERS, Rescarrick; BLISH, Oaks Shaw

Group Number 3
AYLESWORTH, Philip; COBB, Jonathon

Group Number 4
BANNING, David; BANNING, Jeremiah W

Group Number 5
BARNETT, Vina; BARNETT, William

Group Number 6
BARROWS, Barnabas; BARROWS, Isaac R

Group Number 7
BARTLETT, Milton; GRAVES, William

Group Number 8
BARTLETT, Milton; GRAVES, William H

Group Number 9
BERRY, Samuel; ROACH, Nedom

Group Number 10
BERRY, Samuel; VANNEST, Peter

Group Number 11
BRACKENRIDGE, Caleb; BRACKENRIDGE, John B

Group Number 12
BRACKENRIDGE, Marcus; BRACKENRIDGE, Robert

Group Number 13
BROWN, Franklin; FANNING, Ephraim; FANNING, Henry; FANNING, Samuel

Group Number 14
BROWN, James N; BROWN, William

Group Number 15
BROWN, Loyd W; BROWN, William

Group Number 16
BROWN, Preston M; TILTON, James J

Group Number 17
BRYAMT, John; BRYANT, John; REEVIS, Lazarus

Group Number 18
BRYANT, Arthur; BRYANT, John H

Group Number 19
BRYANT, John; REEVES, Lazarus

Group Number 20
BRYANT, John; REEVIS, Lazarus

Group Number 21
CALDWELL, John C; CALDWELL, William

Group Number 22
CALDWELL, John Cook; CALDWELL, William

Group Number 23
CALDWELL, John; CALDWELL, William

Group Number 24
CARTER, John; HOUSTON, Nicholas

Group Number 25
CARTER, William B; SMITH, John

Group Number 26
CARTER, Zadock; MEEK, Allen

Group Number 27
CARTER, Zadock; MEEKS, Allen

Group Number 28
CASSELL, John T; TILTON, James J

Group Number 29
CASTLEBERRY, Elizabet; COX, Beverly

Group Number 30
CATLIN, Joel; CATLIN, Willis

Group Number 31
CAUBY, Merit; MANDAIN, Arnold; TATNALL, Edward

Group Number 32
CHAMBERLIN, Griffin; CHAMBERLIN, James

Group Number 33
CLARK, Matthew S; DUNCAN, Joseph

Group Number 34
CLARK, Matthew; DUNCAN, Joseph

Group Number 35
CLARK, Norman; ROBERTS, Ephraim

Group Number 36
CLARKE, Mathew S; DUNCAN, Joseph

Group Number 37
CLARKE, Mathew; DUNCAN, Joseph

Group Number 38
CLARKE, Matthew S; DUNCAN, Joseph

Group Number 39
CLAYTON, William; CLAYTON, William R

Group Number 40
COBB, Orson P; LUDWICK, Kennedy; MANCHESTER, John; MCKEE, Jesse; SMITH, Isaac R

Group Number 41
CODDINGTON, Joseph; GILLETT, Bazateil

Group Number 42
COFFIN, Charles; WEEKS, W

Group Number 43
COFFMAN, Philip; LINDSEY, William

Group Number 44
COFFMAN, Philip; LINDSEY, William K

Group Number 45
COLLINS, Charles; DUNCAN, Thomas O

Group Number 46
CONN, William A; PLANTE, George P

Group Number 47
COWAN, David; COWAN, John Henry

Group Number 48
COX, Abel; COX, John

Group Number 49
COX, James; COX, Warren

Group Number 50
COX, William; GREEN, Reynolds

Group Number 51
CROW, Joshua; MILLER, William

Group Number 52
DEATHERAGE, Achilles; DEATHERAGE, George; DEATHERAGE, William

Group Number 53
DEATHERAGE, George; DEATHERAGE, William

Group Number 54
DELPH, William H; GREEN, James; HOWARD, Elakim

Group Number 55
DEVOLT, Nicholas; WRIGHT, Wiley

Group Number 56
DOSGOOD, Jonathan W; TURNER, Jonathan B

Group Number 57
DOWLING, John; MCCOY, William

Group Number 58
EASTHAM, Marvillous; HAWN, Frederick; LOOSE, Joseph B; REED, James F

Group Number 59
EDWARDS, Joseph; HUGHES, John Allen

Group Number 60
FAIRFIELD, Joseph M; HACKETT, George

Group Number 61
FANNING, Jacob; GIBSON, James

Group Number 62
FANNING, Jacob; GIDEON, James

Group Number 63
FRENCH, William; MORGAN, William B

Group Number 64
FRENCH, William; WARREN, William B

Group Number 65
FUNK, Martin; TODD, Coleman

Group Number 66
GREEN, Stephen; GREEN, William

Group Number 67
GREEN, William B; SLATTEN, James

Group Number 68
HAMILTON, William L; VARY, William

Group Number 69
HAMILTON, William S; SPENCER, Stephen W

Group Number 70
HANEY, Alldon; SMITH, George

Group Number 71
HARTMORE, Thomas J; LARIMORE, Thomas J

Group Number 72
HARVY, J; SAVAGE, P

Group Number 73
HAYES, William; MONDON, Frederick

Group Number 74
HERRIN, Lewis; HERRIN, Simon

Group Number 75
HICKMAN, David Mcclan; LAMM, David Steele

Group Number 76
HILL, John; HILL, John Jr; HILL, Luther

Group Number 77
HOAGLAND, George W; HOAGLAND, John

Group Number 78
HOSKINS, Barnet; HOSKINS, John

Group Number 79
HOUGHAN, Thomas; MOBLEY, Mordecai; RIDGLEY, Nicholas

Group Number 80
HOUSTON, Starett B; HOUSTON, William T

Group Number 81
HOWARD, Reubin; TODD, Henry

Group Number 82
HURST, James; HURST, John

Group Number 83
HUSTON, Jonas; HUSTON, Squire

Group Number 84
ISRAEL, Isaac G; TAGGART, Joseph J

Group Number 85
JACKSON, Levi L; WHITEHEAD, Abraham

Group Number 86
JANUARY, Thomas T; STITINIUS, Joseph

Group Number 87
JANUARY, Thomas; STETTINIUS, Joseph

Group Number 88
JARMAN, Elford E; SALTER, James D B

Group Number 89
JOHNSON, Jane; MOORE, Samuel

Group Number 90
KEYES, James W; REED, James F

Group Number 91
LANDRUM, Francis A; TUCKER, James

Group Number 92
LONG, George; PURVINE, John

sGroup Number 93
LONG, John; LONG, William

Group Number 94
LOOSE, Jacob G; LOOSE, Joseph B

Group Number 95
LUCAS, George; LUCAS, Hanah

Group Number 96
MATHERS, John; YATES, Abner

Group Number 97
MATHEWS, Samuel T; SCOTT, John

Group Number 98
MATHUS, John; YATES, Abner

Group Number 99
MATTHEWS, John; MATTHEWS, Richard

Group Number 100
MAYFIELD, Enness; MAYFIELD, Manning

Group Number 101
MCFALLS, Jamus; MEISENHEIMER, Wilson

Group Number 102
MCFILLON, James; ROBERTSON, Kirker

Group Number 103
NASH, Moses; SPENCER, Stephen W

Group Number 104
NICHOLLS, Agruppa; NICHOLS, Agrippa

Group Number 105
NOLL, John; NOLL, Russell; NOLL, William T

Group Number 106
POINTER, James; POINTER, William

Group Number 107
REED, Andrew; STRODE, Mahlon

Group Number 108
ROUNDS, James; ROUNDS, William

Group Number 109
SHEPHERD, Peter; SMITH, Thomas

Group Number 110
SHEPPARD, John Oaks; SHEPPARD, Lewis J

Group Number 111
SHREWBURY, Michael; WOOSTER, Sheldon

Group Number 112
SHURTLEFF, Benjamin; SHURTLEFF, Lot

Group Number 113
SMITH, Absalom; SMITH, James

Group Number 114
SMITH, Anderson; SMITH, Pleasant

Group Number 115
SMITH, Arnton; SMITH, Samuel

Group Number 116
SMITH, Clarke; SMITH, Isaac; SMITH, John

Group Number 117
SMITH, David; SMITH, Michael

Group Number 118
SMITH, Hannah; SMITH, Ruth

Group Number 119
SMITH, Isaac; SMITH, William

Group Number 120
SMITH, James; SMITH, Pleasant

Group Number 121
SMITH, Westly; SMITH, William Jr

Group Number 122
STARR, Isaac W; VANDEGRIFT, Thomas

Group Number 123
STEWART, Benjamin F; STEWART, Robert

Group Number 124
STEWART, Peter; STEWART, William

Group Number 125
THOMPSON, John B; THOMPSON, Richard D

Group Number 126
THOMPSON, John; THOMPSON, Phillip

Group Number 127
THOMPSON, Joseph C; THOMPSON, Samuel P

Group Number 128
TURNER, Avery; TURNER, Jonathan B

Group Number 129
TURNER, Lydia; TURNER, Walter

Group Number 130
VERRY, William C; WISWALL, Thomas

Group Number 131
WALDO, Daniel; WALDO, James E

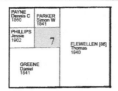

Extra! Extra! (about our Indexes)

We purposefully do not have an all-name index in the back of this volume so that our readers do not miss one of the best uses of this book: finding misspelled names among more specialized indexes.

Without repeating the text of our "How-to" chapter, we have nonetheless tried to assist our more anxious researchers by delivering a short-cut to the two county-wide Surname Indexes, the second of which will lead you to all-name indexes for each Congressional Township mapped in this volume :

For your convenience, the "How To Use this Book" Chart on page 2 is repeated on the reverse of this page.

We should be releasing new titles every week for the foreseeable future. We urge you to write, fax, call, or email us any time for a current list of titles. Of course, our web-page will always have the most current information about current and upcoming books.

Arphax Publishing Co.
2210 Research Park Blvd.
Norman, Oklahoma 73069
(800) 681-5298 toll-free
(405) 366-6181 local
(405) 366-8184 fax
info@arphax.com

www.arphax.com

How to Use This Book - A Graphical Summary

Part I
"The Big Picture"

Map A ▸ *Counties in the State*

Map B ▸ *Surrounding Counties*

Map C ▸ *Congressional Townships (Map Groups) in the County*

Map D ▸ *Cities & Towns in the County*

Map E ▸ *Cemeteries in the County*

Surnames in the County ▸ *Number of Land-Parcels for Each Surname*

Surname/Township Index ▸ Directs you to Township Map Groups in Part II

The <u>Surname/Township Index</u> can direct you to any number of **Township Map Groups**

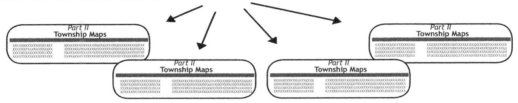

Part II
Township Map Groups
(1 for each Township in the County)

Each Township Map Group contains all four of of the following tools . . .

Land Patent Index ▸ *Every-name Index of Patents Mapped in this Township*

Land Patent Map ▸ *Map of Patents as listed in above Index*

Road Map ▸ *Map of Roads, City-centers, and Cemeteries in the Township*

Historical Map ▸ *Map of Railroads, Lakes, Rivers, Creeks, City-Centers, and Cemeteries*

Appendices

Appendix A ▸ *Illinois State Archives Abbreviations*

Appendix B ▸ *Section-Parts / Aliquot Parts (a comprehensive list)*

Appendix C ▸ *Multi-patentee Groups (Individuals within Buying Groups)*

Made in the USA
Coppell, TX
16 April 2022